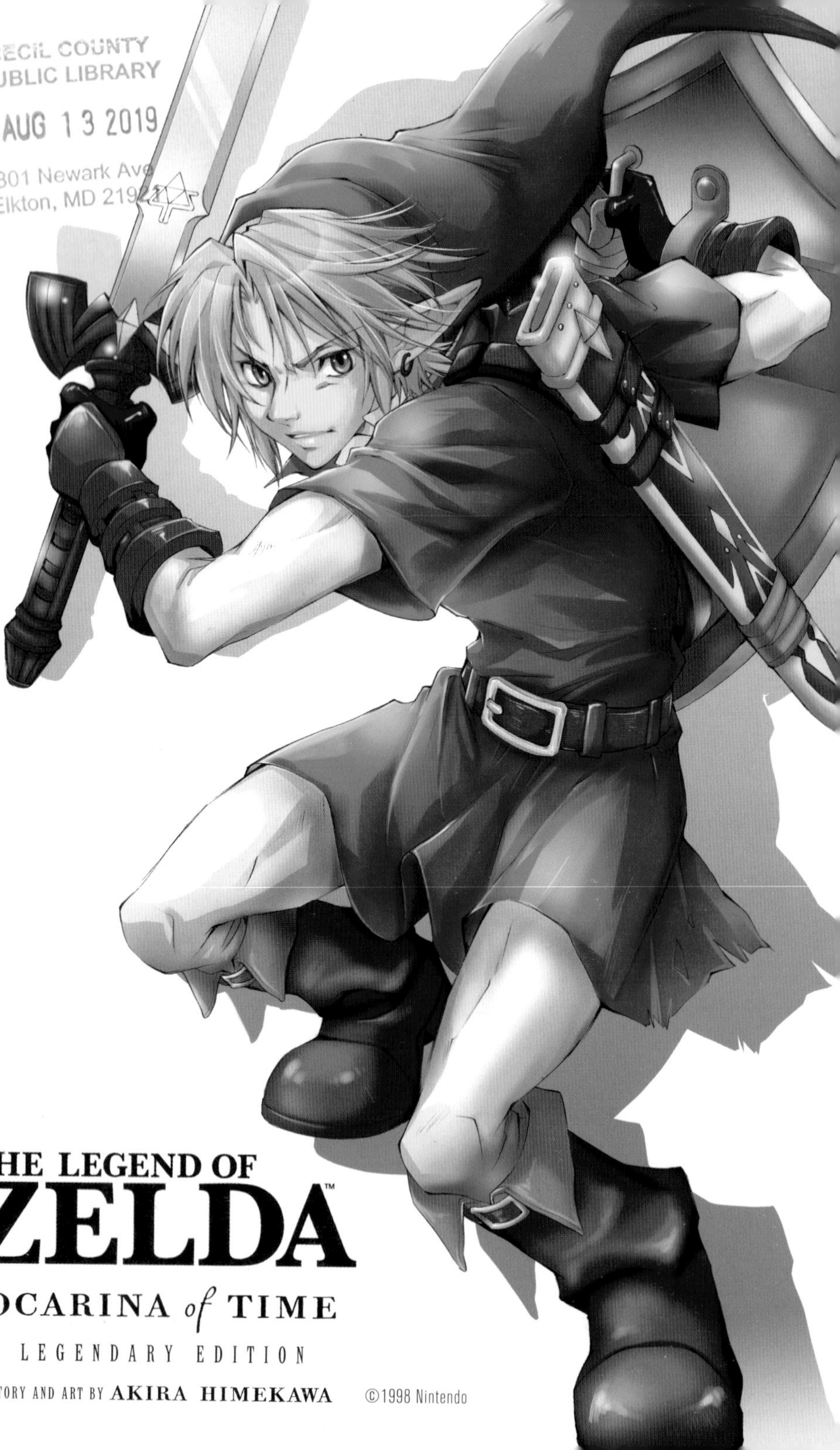

THE LEGEND OF ZELDA™

OCARINA of TIME

LEGENDARY EDITION

STORY AND ART BY AKIRA HIMEKAWA

THE LEGEND OF ZELDA™

OCARINA *of* TIME

LEGENDARY EDITION

HERO OF TIME

HERO OF TIME—BONUS STORY

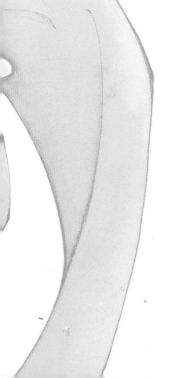

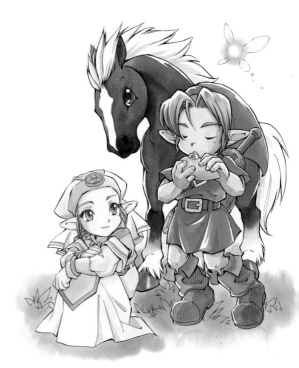

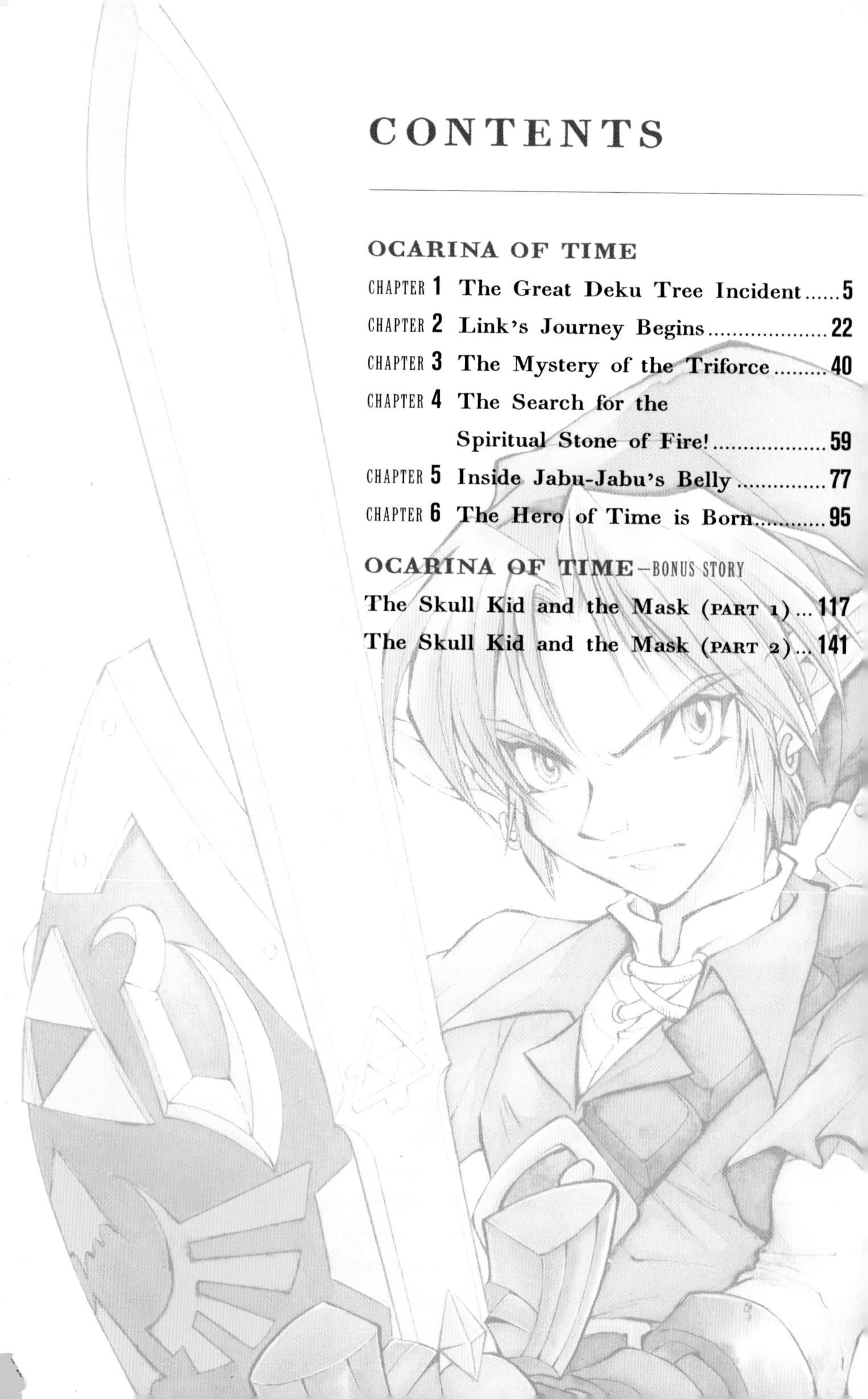

CONTENTS

OCARINA OF TIME

OCARINA OF TIME—BONUS STORY

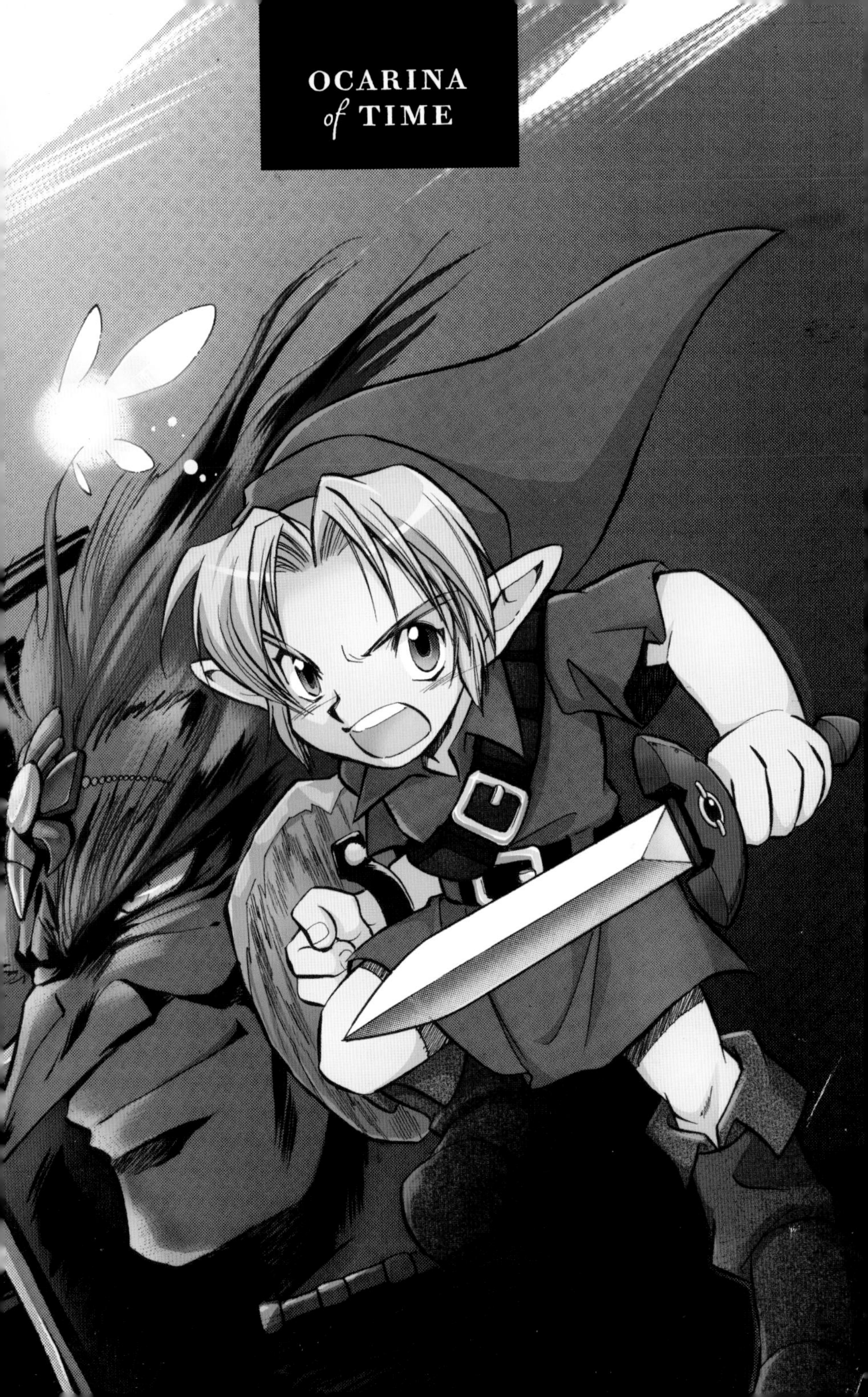
OCARINA
of TIME

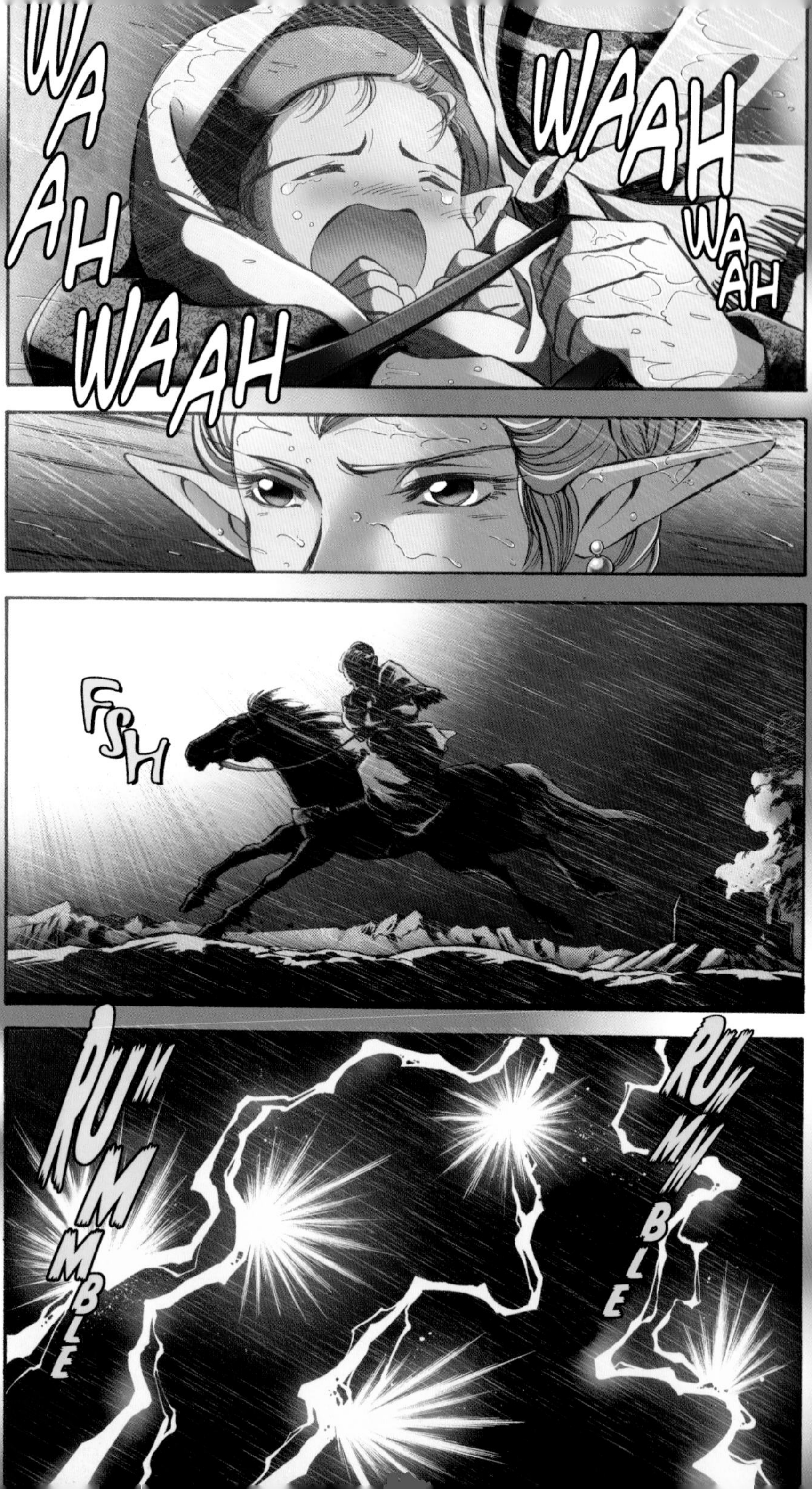

WAAH
WAAH
WAAH
WAAH
FSH
RUMMMBLE
RUMMMBLE

CHAPTER 1
THE GREAT DEKU TREE INCIDENT

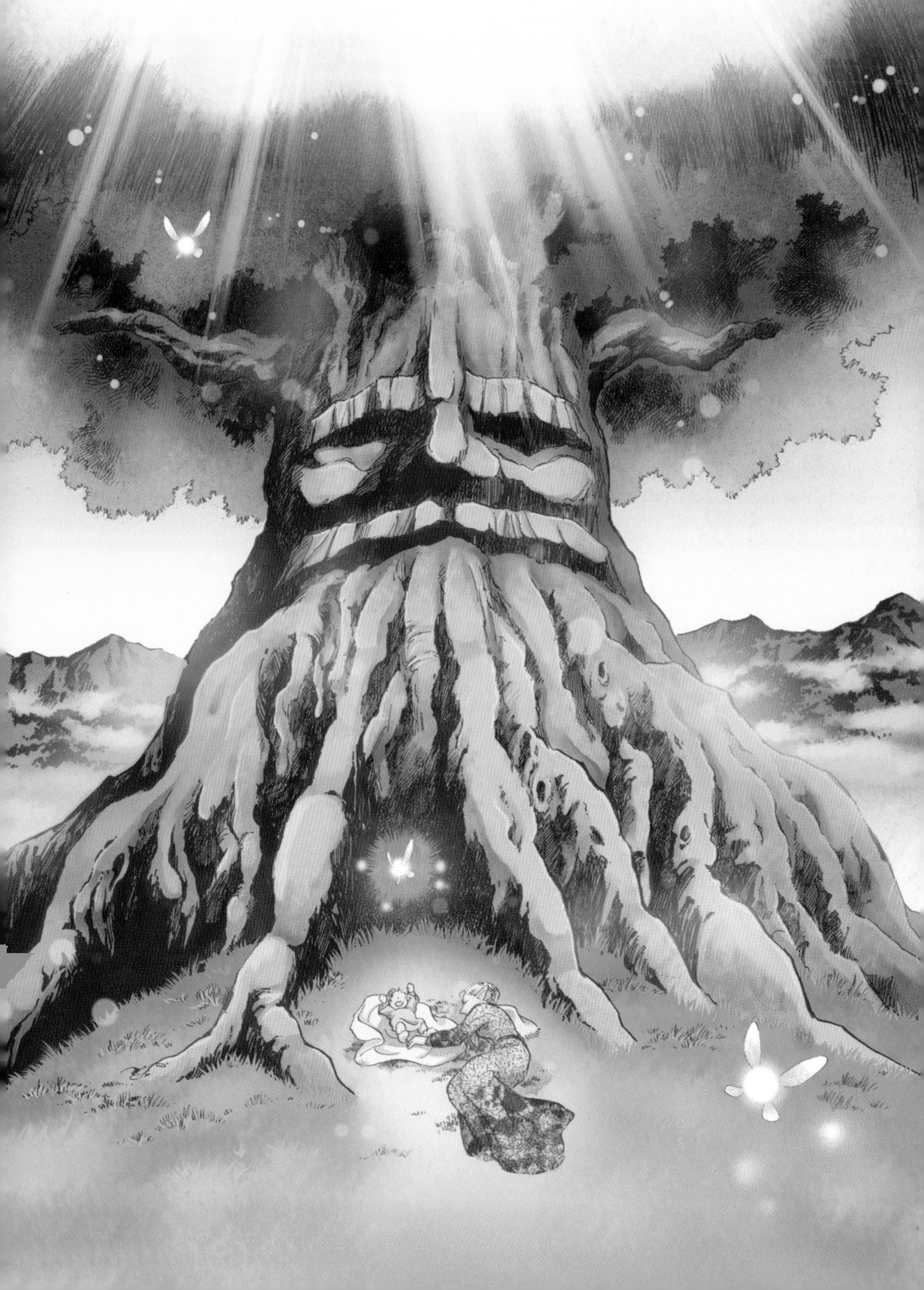

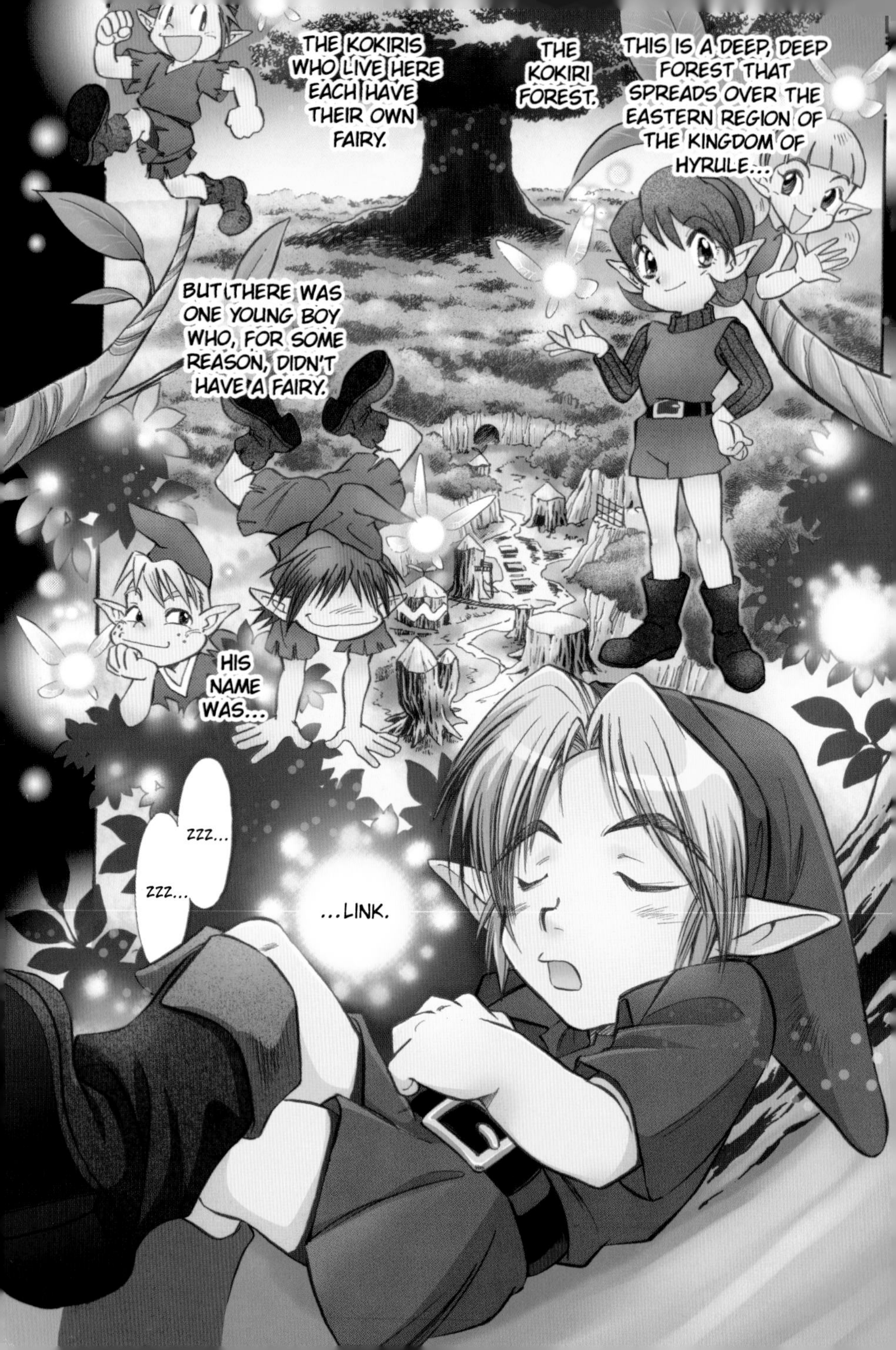
THIS IS A DEEP, DEEP FOREST THAT SPREADS OVER THE EASTERN REGION OF THE KINGDOM OF HYRULE...
THE KOKIRI FOREST.
THE KOKIRIS WHO LIVE HERE EACH HAVE THEIR OWN FAIRY.
BUT THERE WAS ONE YOUNG BOY WHO, FOR SOME REASON, DIDN'T HAVE A FAIRY.
HIS NAME WAS...
...LINK.
ZZZ...
ZZZ...

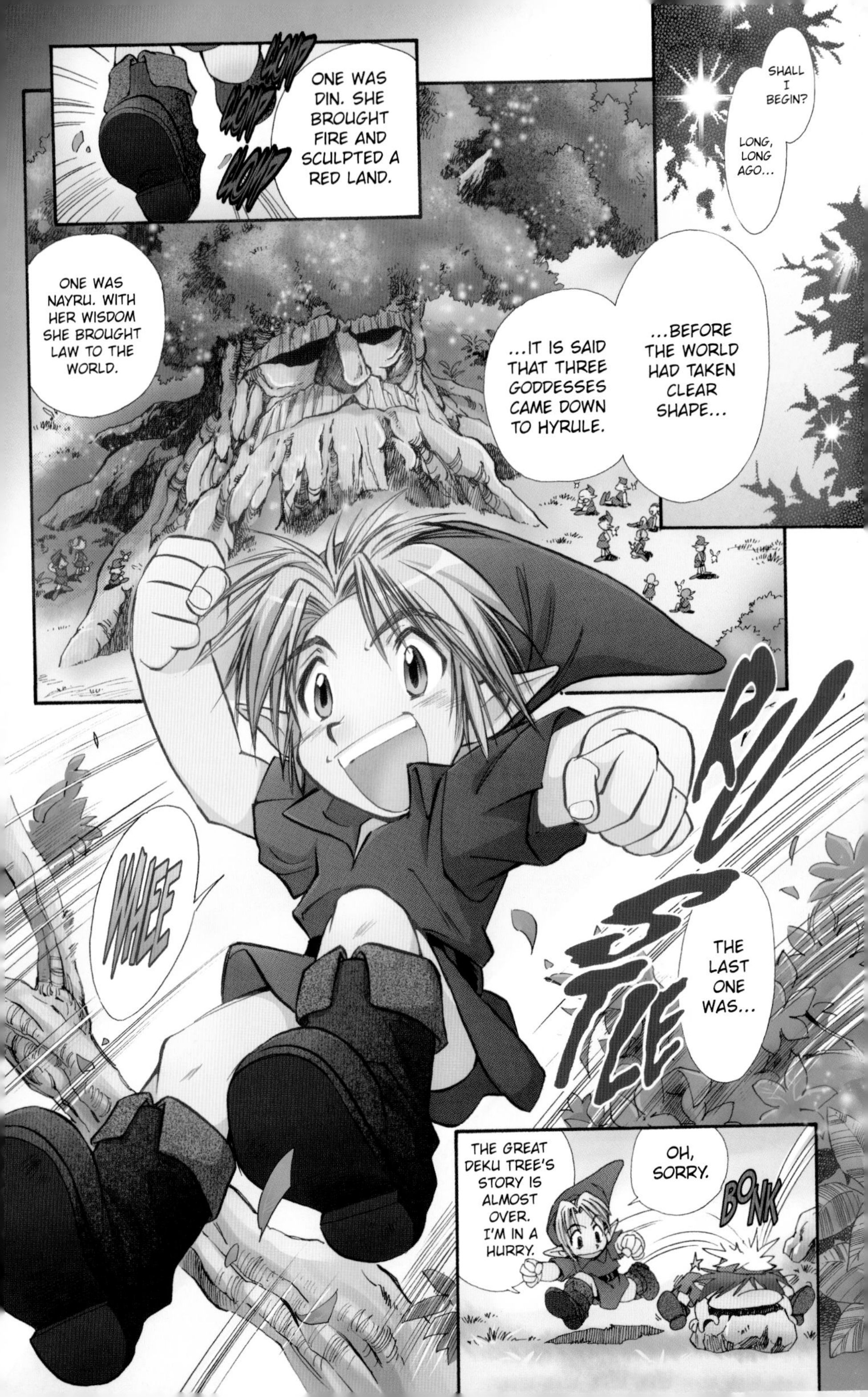
SHALL I BEGIN?
LONG, LONG AGO...
...BEFORE THE WORLD HAD TAKEN CLEAR SHAPE...
...IT IS SAID THAT THREE GODDESSES CAME DOWN TO HYRULE.
WOMP WOMP WOMP
ONE WAS DIN. SHE BROUGHT FIRE AND SCULPTED A RED LAND.
ONE WAS NAYRU. WITH HER WISDOM SHE BROUGHT LAW TO THE WORLD.
RUSTLE
THE LAST ONE WAS...
WHEE
OH, SORRY.
BONK
THE GREAT DEKU TREE'S STORY IS ALMOST OVER. I'M IN A HURRY.

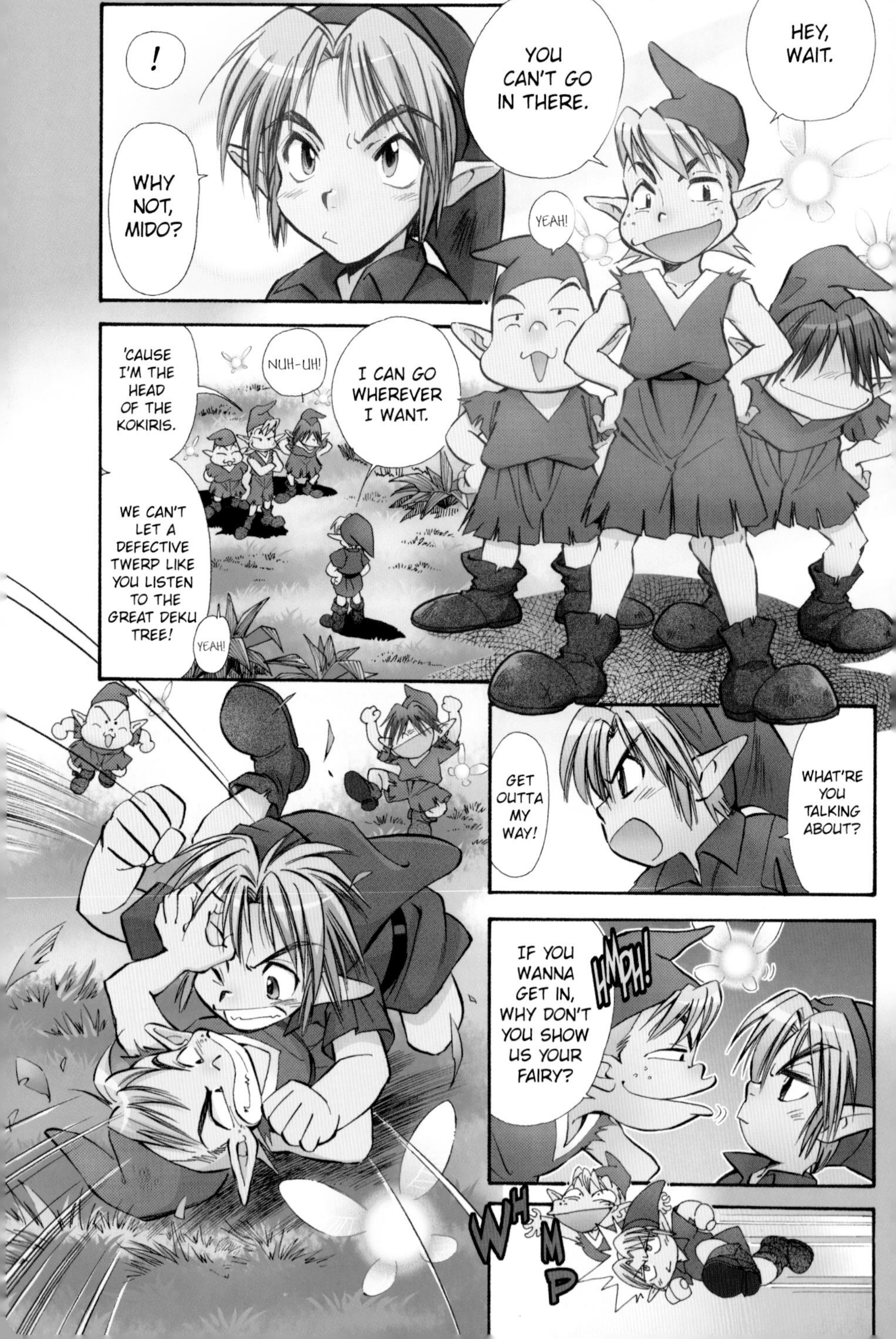
HEY, WAIT.
YOU CAN'T GO IN THERE.
YEAH!
!
WHY NOT, MIDO?
I CAN GO WHEREVER I WANT.
NUH-UH!
'CAUSE I'M THE HEAD OF THE KOKIRIS.
WE CAN'T LET A DEFECTIVE TWERP LIKE YOU LISTEN TO THE GREAT DEKU TREE!
YEAH!
WHAT'RE YOU TALKING ABOUT?
GET OUTTA MY WAY!
HMPH!
IF YOU WANNA GET IN, WHY DON'T YOU SHOW US YOUR FAIRY?
WHMP

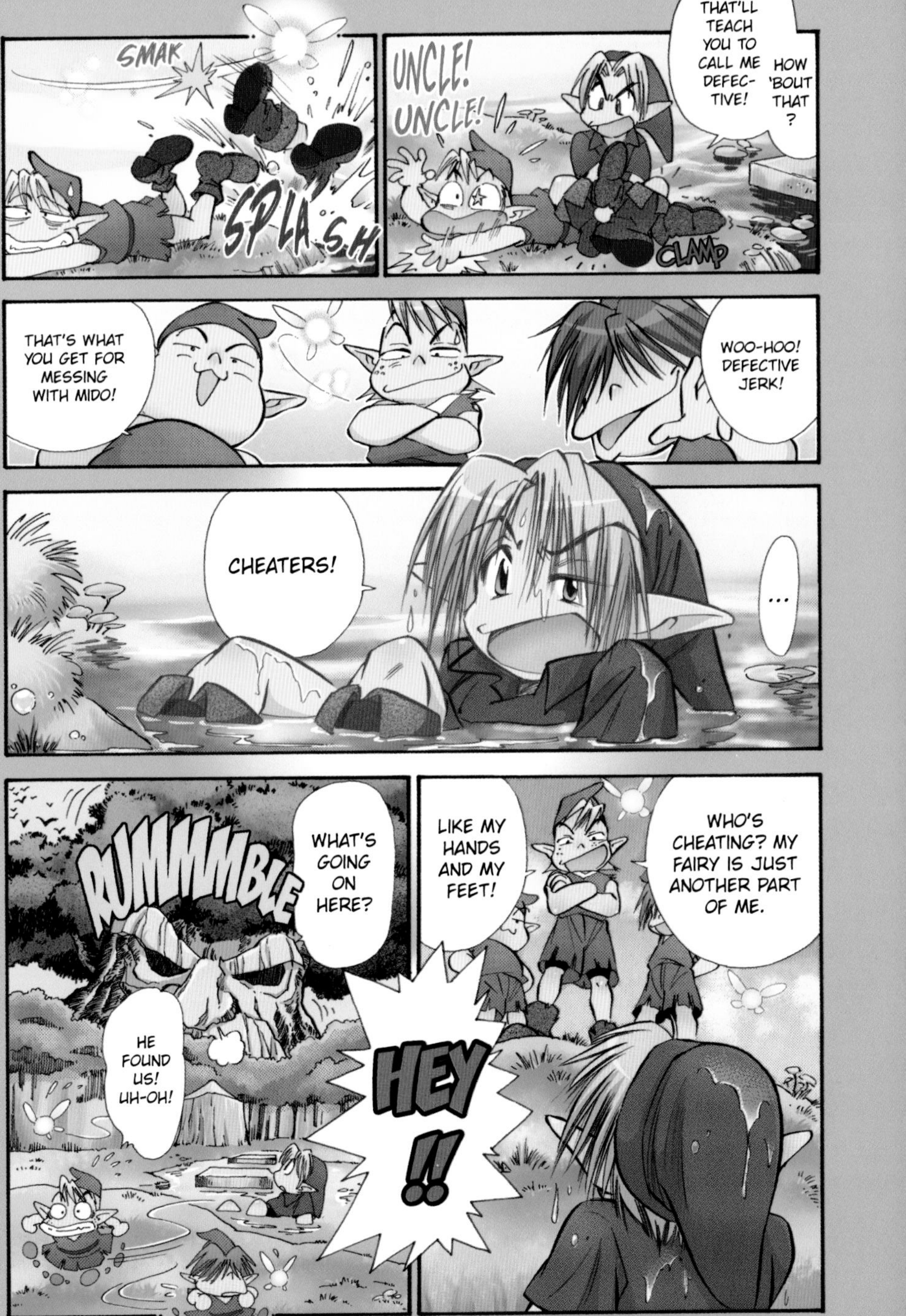
THAT'LL TEACH YOU TO CALL ME DEFEC-TIVE!
HOW 'BOUT THAT?
UNCLE! UNCLE!
CLAMP
SMAK
SPLASH
WOO-HOO! DEFECTIVE JERK!
THAT'S WHAT YOU GET FOR MESSING WITH MIDO!
...
CHEATERS!
WHO'S CHEATING? MY FAIRY IS JUST ANOTHER PART OF ME.
LIKE MY HANDS AND MY FEET!
HEY!!
WHAT'S GOING ON HERE?
RUMMMMBLE
HE FOUND US! UH-OH!

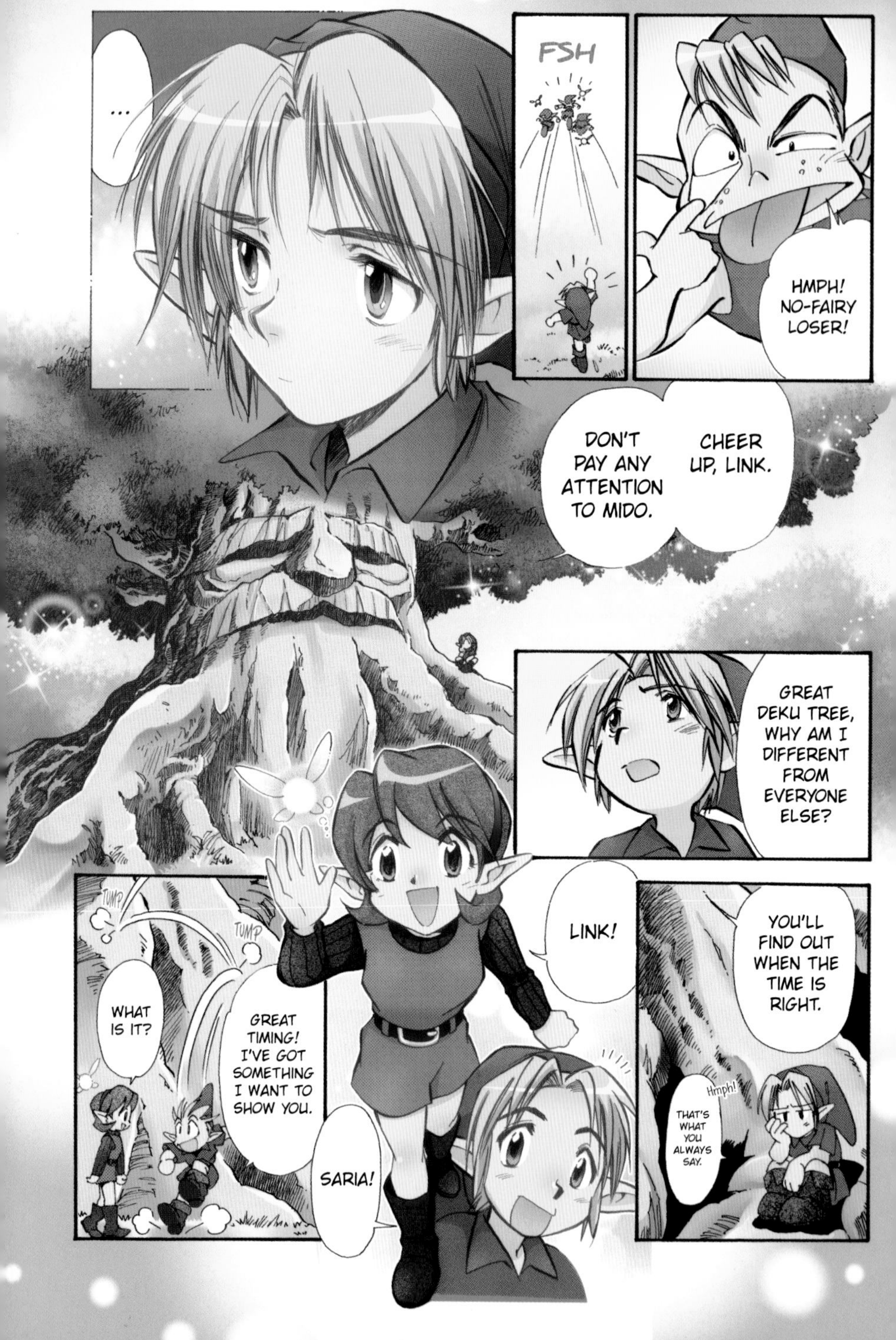
HMPH! NO-FAIRY LOSER!
FSH
...
CHEER UP, LINK.
DON'T PAY ANY ATTENTION TO MIDO.
GREAT DEKU TREE, WHY AM I DIFFERENT FROM EVERYONE ELSE?
YOU'LL FIND OUT WHEN THE TIME IS RIGHT.
Hmph!
THAT'S WHAT YOU ALWAYS SAY.
LINK!
SARIA!
TUMP
TUMP
GREAT TIMING! I'VE GOT SOMETHING I WANT TO SHOW YOU.
WHAT IS IT?

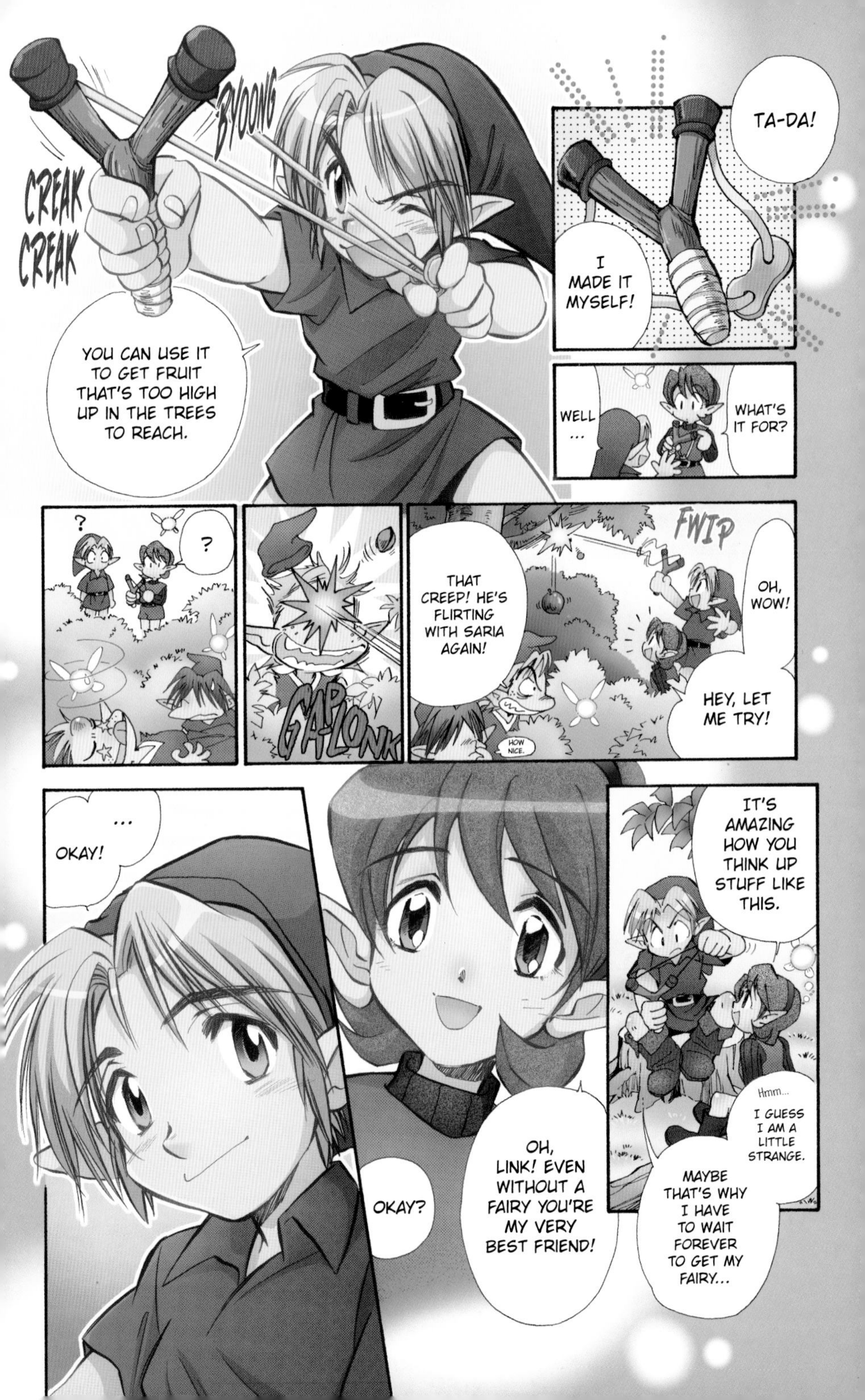
TA-DA!
I MADE IT MYSELF!
WHAT'S IT FOR?
WELL...
BYOONG
CREAK CREAK
YOU CAN USE IT TO GET FRUIT THAT'S TOO HIGH UP IN THE TREES TO REACH.
FWIP
OH, WOW!
HEY, LET ME TRY!
THAT CREEP! HE'S FLIRTING WITH SARIA AGAIN!
HOW NICE.
GA-LONK
?
?
IT'S AMAZING HOW YOU THINK UP STUFF LIKE THIS.
Hmm...
I GUESS I AM A LITTLE STRANGE.
MAYBE THAT'S WHY I HAVE TO WAIT FOREVER TO GET MY FAIRY...
OH, LINK! EVEN WITHOUT A FAIRY YOU'RE MY VERY BEST FRIEND!
OKAY?
...
OKAY!

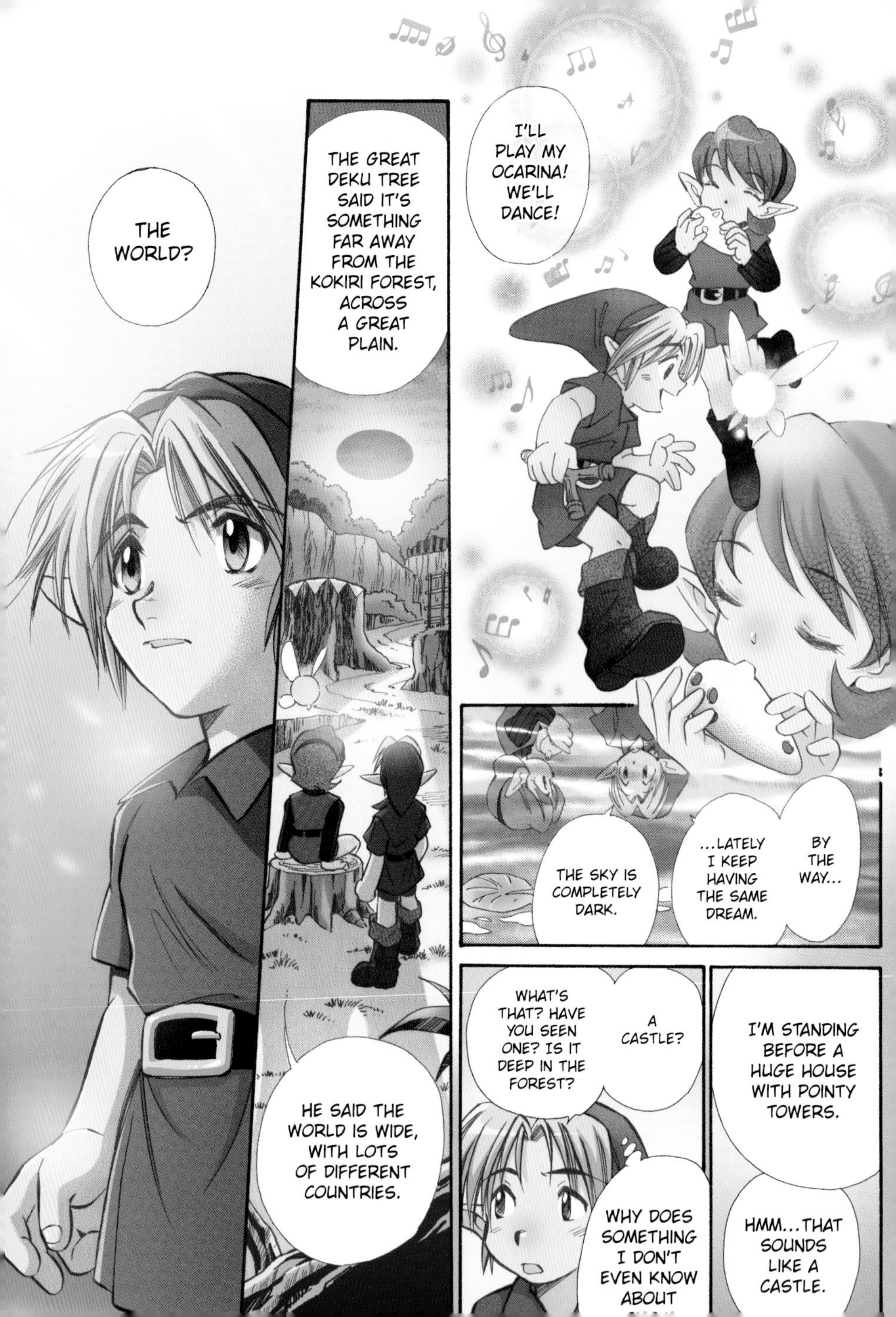
THE WORLD?
THE GREAT DEKU TREE SAID IT'S SOMETHING FAR AWAY FROM THE KOKIRI FOREST, ACROSS A GREAT PLAIN.
HE SAID THE WORLD IS WIDE, WITH LOTS OF DIFFERENT COUNTRIES.
I'LL PLAY MY OCARINA! WE'LL DANCE!
BY THE WAY...
...LATELY I KEEP HAVING THE SAME DREAM.
THE SKY IS COMPLETELY DARK.
I'M STANDING BEFORE A HUGE HOUSE WITH POINTY TOWERS.
HMM...THAT SOUNDS LIKE A CASTLE.
A CASTLE?
WHAT'S THAT? HAVE YOU SEEN ONE? IS IT DEEP IN THE FOREST?
WHY DOES SOMETHING I DON'T EVEN KNOW ABOUT

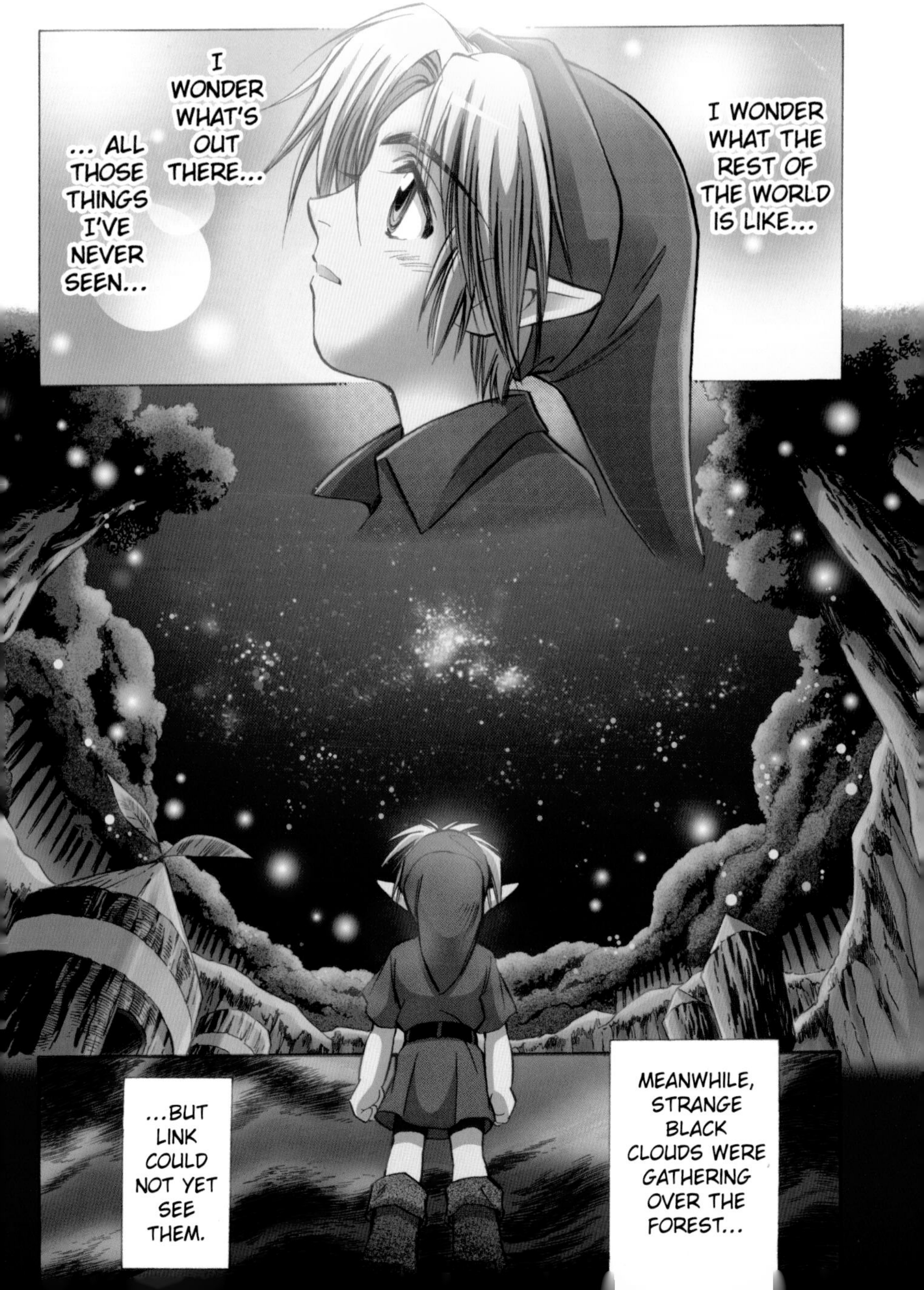
I WONDER WHAT THE REST OF THE WORLD IS LIKE...
I WONDER WHAT'S OUT THERE...
... ALL THOSE THINGS I'VE NEVER SEEN...
MEANWHILE, STRANGE BLACK CLOUDS WERE GATHERING OVER THE FOREST...
...BUT LINK COULD NOT YET SEE THEM.

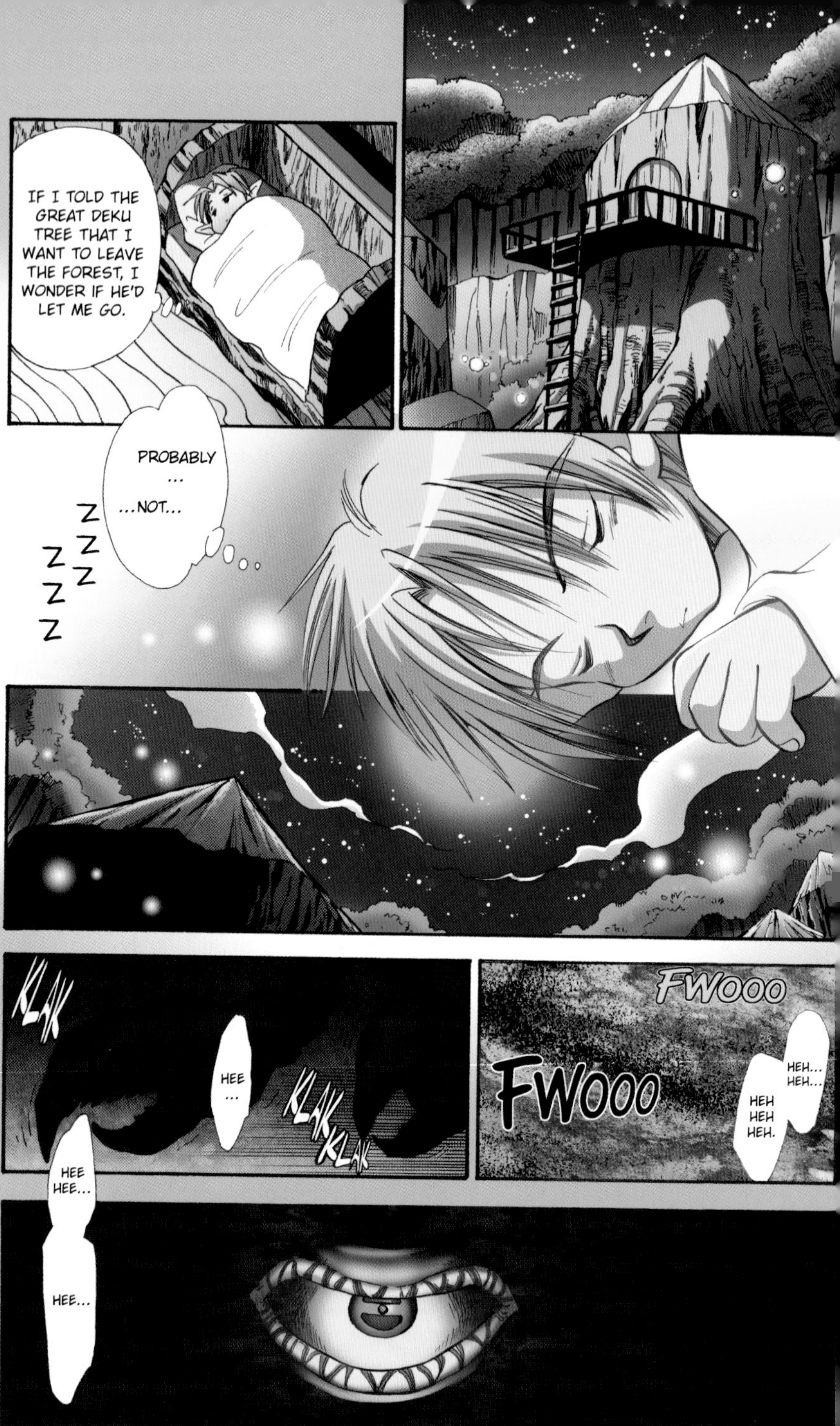
IF I TOLD THE GREAT DEKU TREE THAT I WANT TO LEAVE THE FOREST, I WONDER IF HE'D LET ME GO.
PROBABLY ... ...NOT...
Z Z Z Z Z Z
FWOOO
FWOOO
HEH... HEH...
HEH HEH HEH.
KLAK
HEE ...
KLAK KLAK
HEE HEE...
HEE...

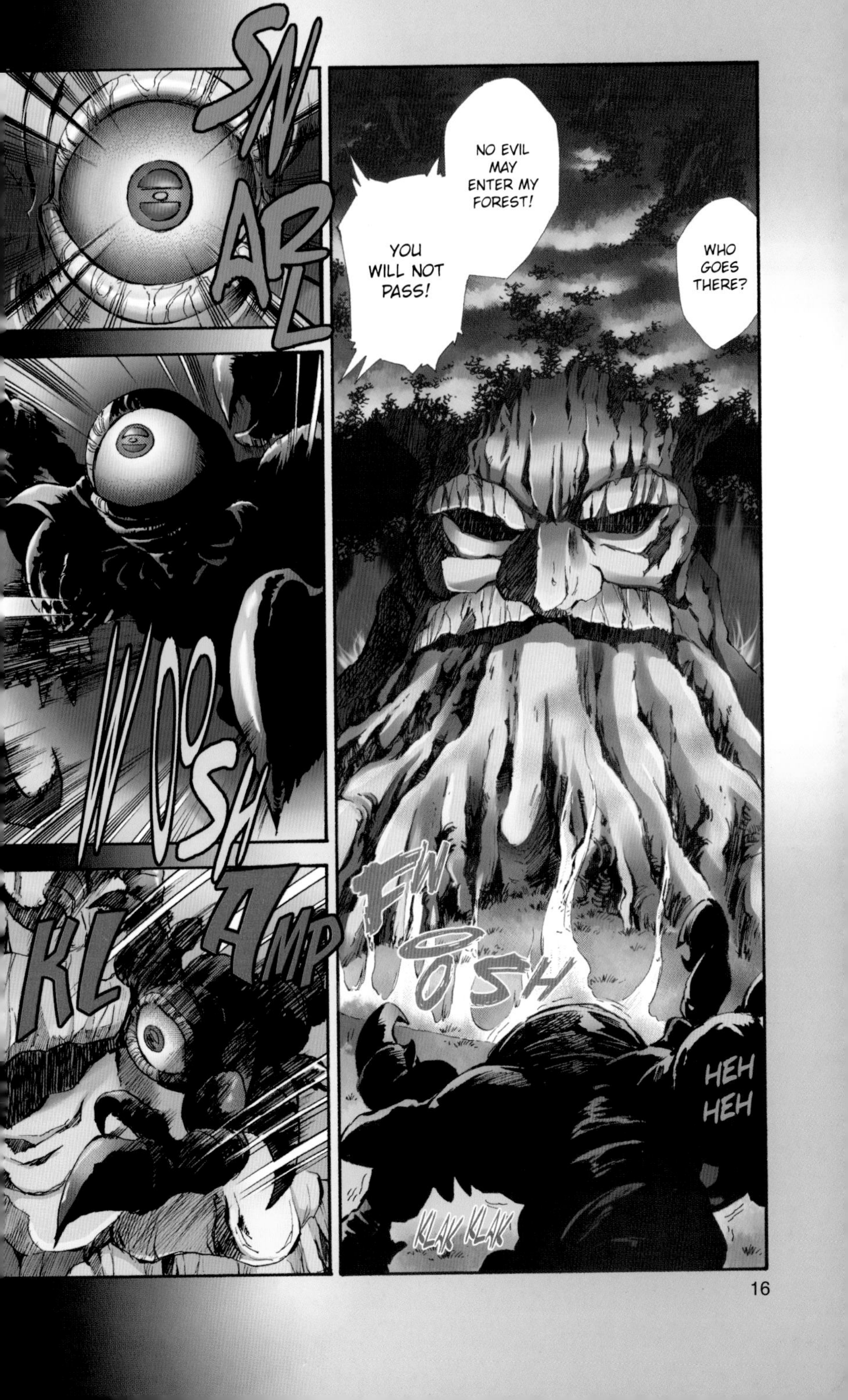
WHO GOES THERE?
NO EVIL MAY ENTER MY FOREST!
YOU WILL NOT PASS!
FWOOSH
HEH HEH
KLAK KLAK
SNARL
WOOSH
KLAMP

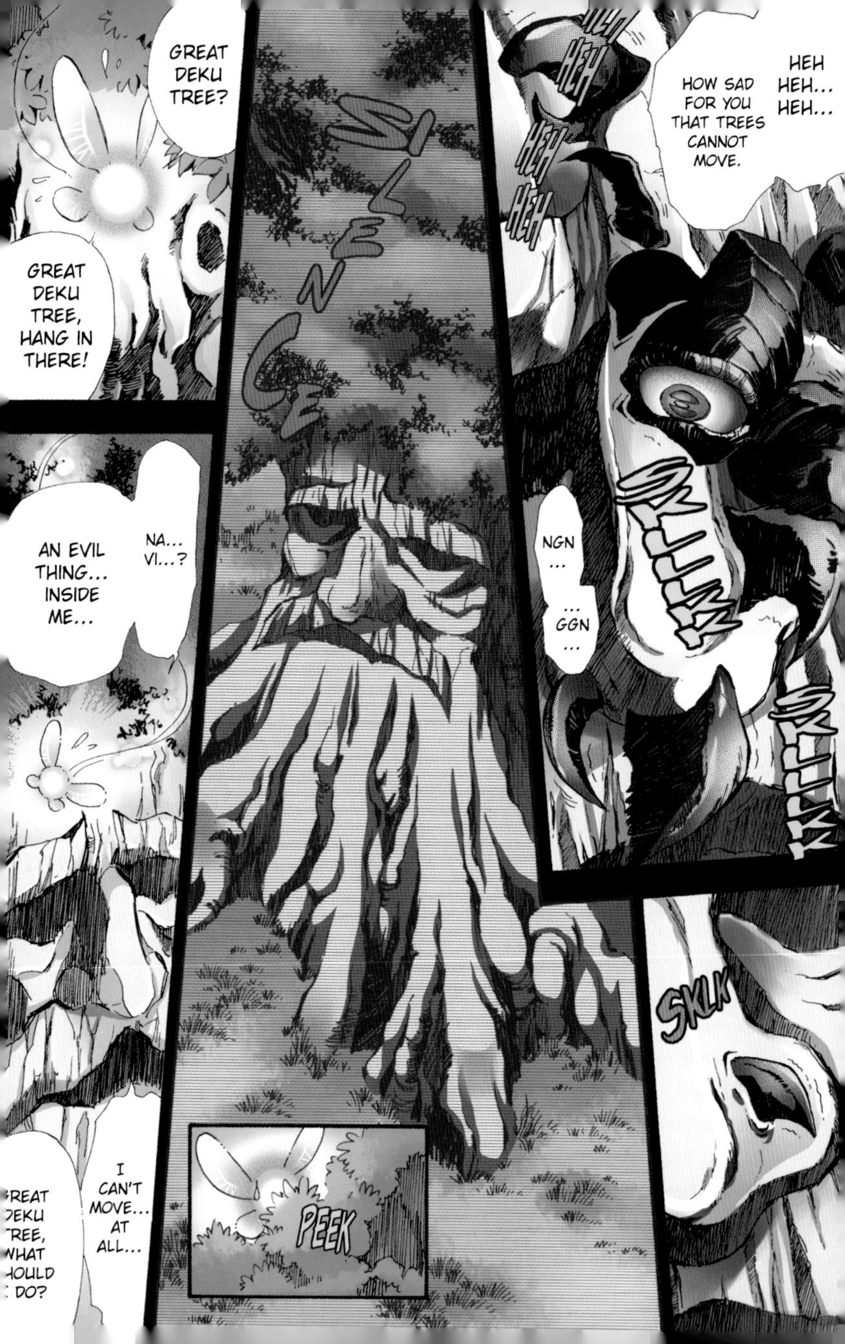
HEH HEH... HEH...
HOW SAD FOR YOU THAT TREES CANNOT MOVE.
HEH HEH HEH HEH
NGN... ...GGN...
SKLK
SILENCE
PEEK
GREAT DEKU TREE?
GREAT DEKU TREE, HANG IN THERE!
NA... VI...?
AN EVIL THING... INSIDE ME...
I CAN'T MOVE... AT ALL...
REAT EKU REE, WHAT HOULD DO?

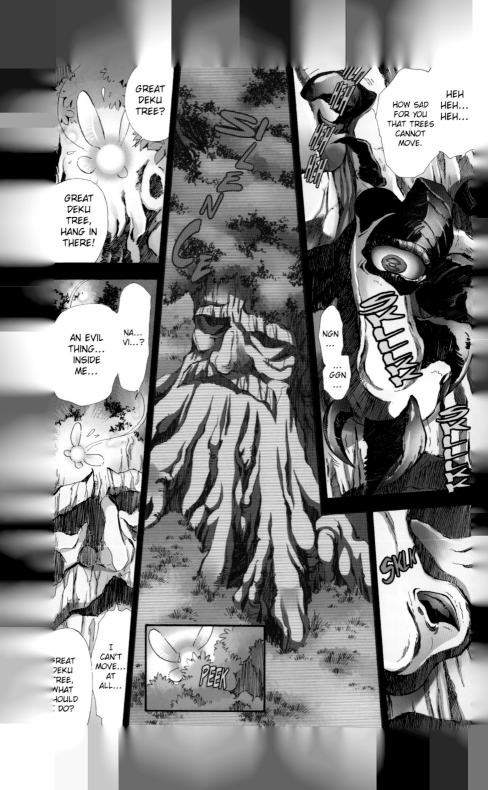

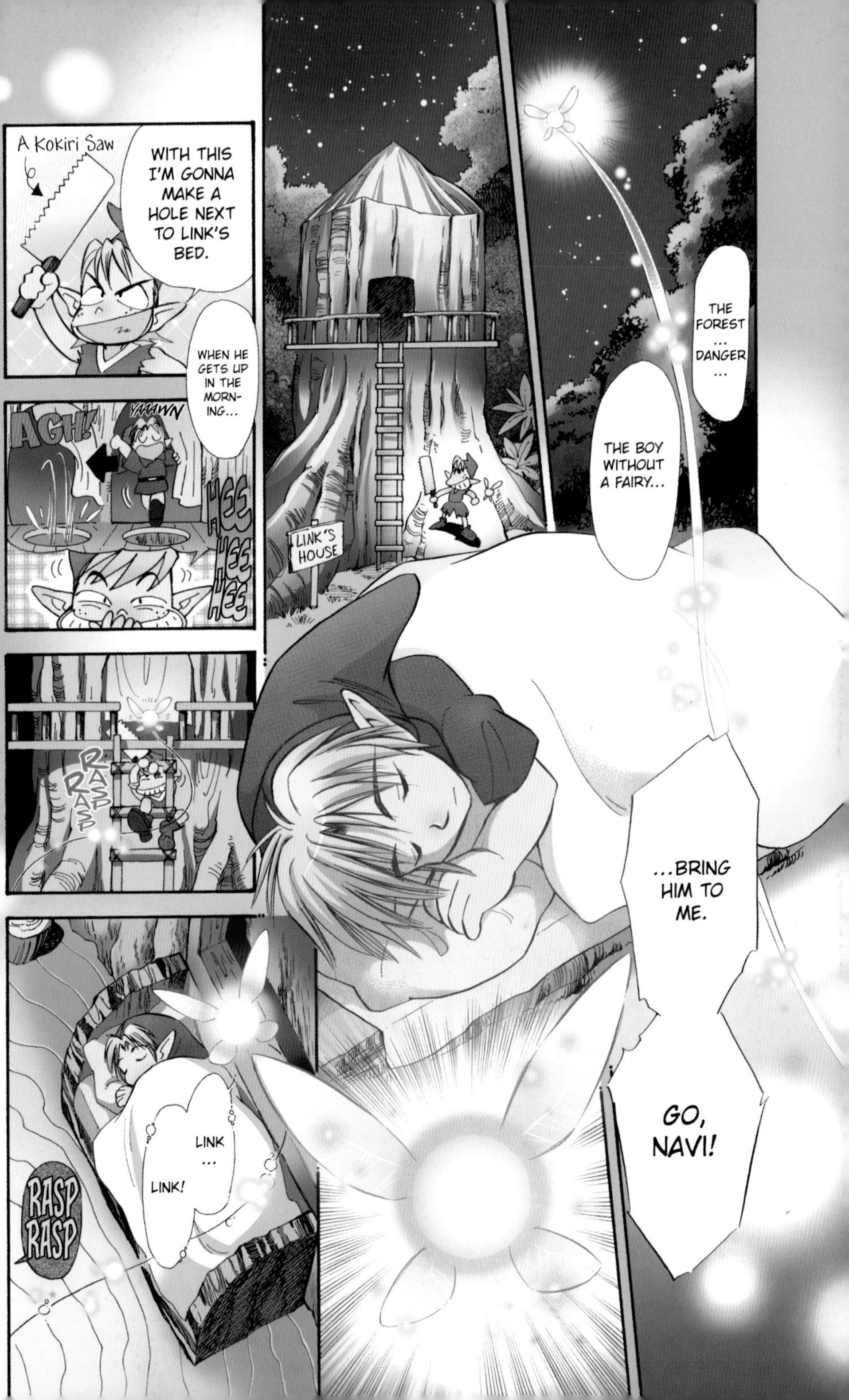
THE FOREST ... DANGER ...
THE BOY WITHOUT A FAIRY...
LINK'S HOUSE
...BRING HIM TO ME.
GO, NAVI!
A Kokiri Saw
WITH THIS I'M GONNA MAKE A HOLE NEXT TO LINK'S BED.
WHEN HE GETS UP IN THE MORNING...
YAAAWN
AGH!
HEE HEE HEE
RASP RASP
LINK ...
LINK!
RASP RASP

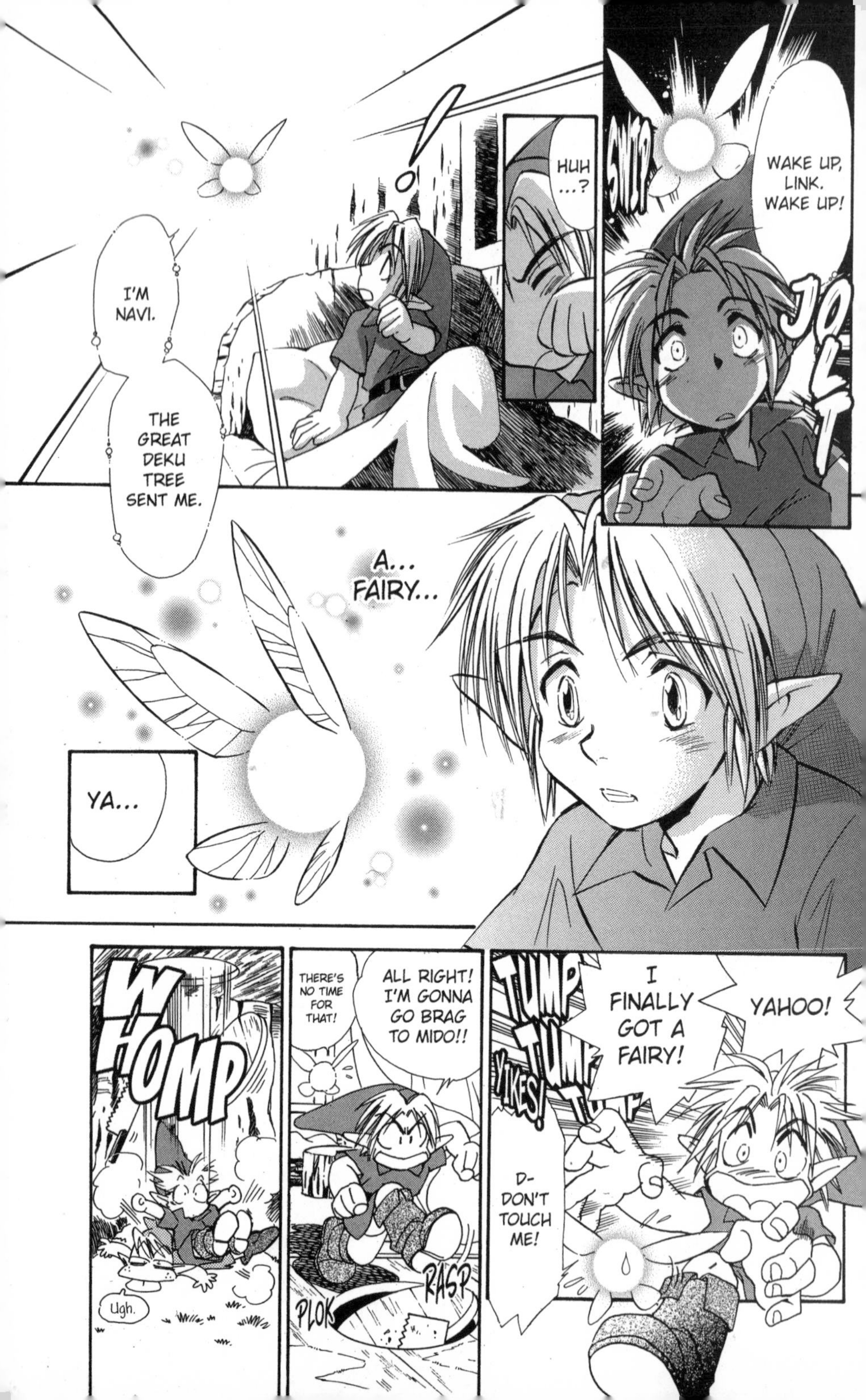
WAKE UP, LINK. WAKE UP!
JOLT
HUH ...?
!
I'M NAVI.
THE GREAT DEKU TREE SENT ME.
A... FAIRY...
YA...
YAHOO!
I FINALLY GOT A FAIRY!
TUMP TUMP
YIKES!
D-DON'T TOUCH ME!
ALL RIGHT! I'M GONNA GO BRAG TO MIDO!!
THERE'S NO TIME FOR THAT!
RASP
PLOK
WHOMP
Ugh.

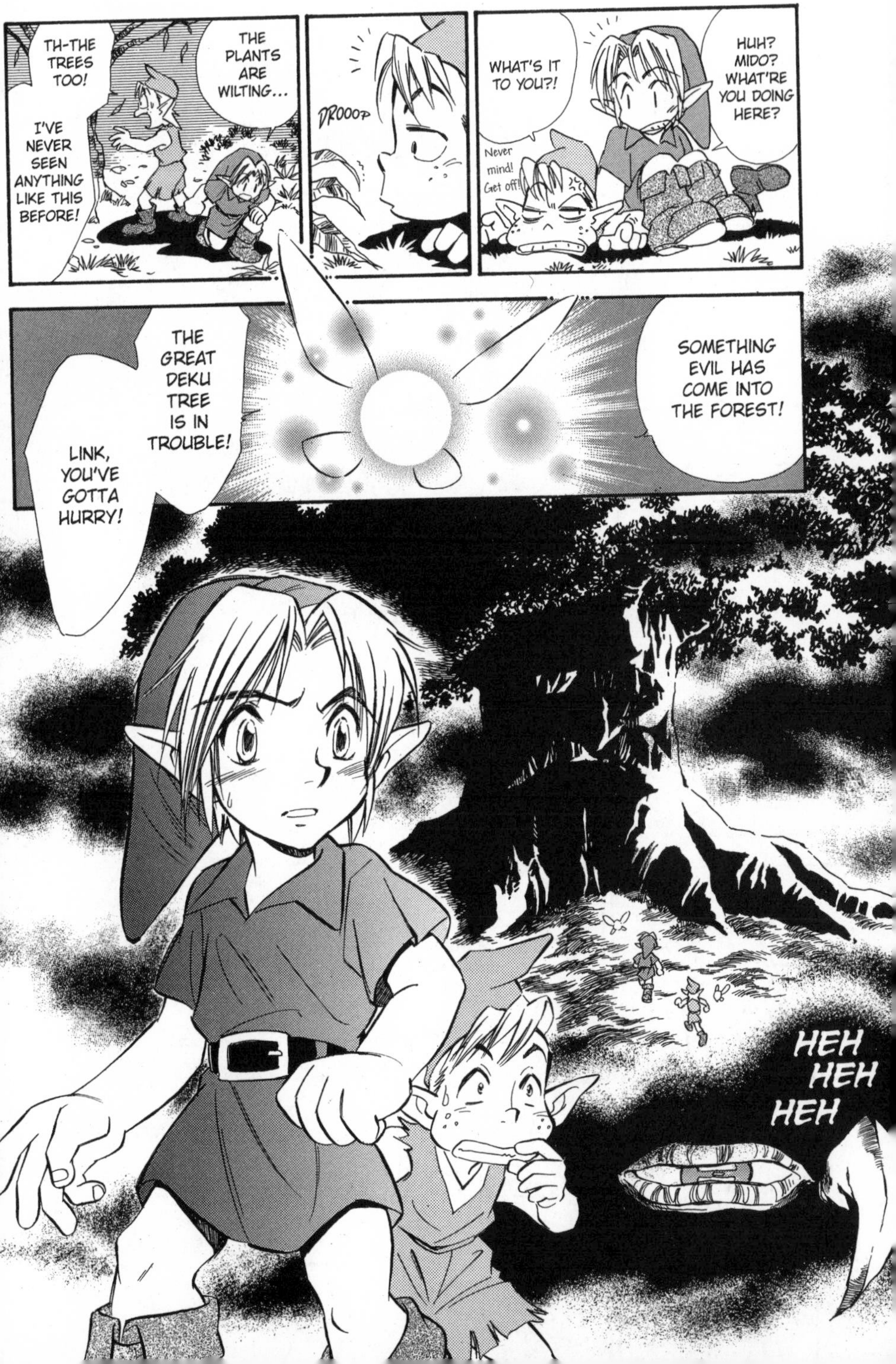
HUH? MIDO? WHAT'RE YOU DOING HERE?
WHAT'S IT TO YOU?!
Never mind! Get off!
DROOOP
THE PLANTS ARE WILTING...
TH-THE TREES TOO!
I'VE NEVER SEEN ANYTHING LIKE THIS BEFORE!
SOMETHING EVIL HAS COME INTO THE FOREST!
THE GREAT DEKU TREE IS IN TROUBLE!
LINK, YOU'VE GOTTA HURRY!
HEH HEH HEH

BONUS ILLUSTRATION 1
ROUGH SKETCHES HIMEKAWA SENSEI DREW BEFORE THE SERIES

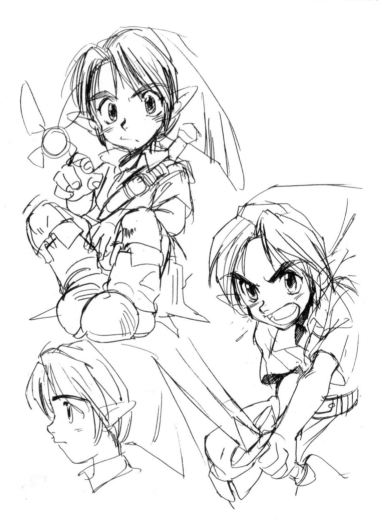

HAPTER 2
INK'S JOURNEY BEGINS

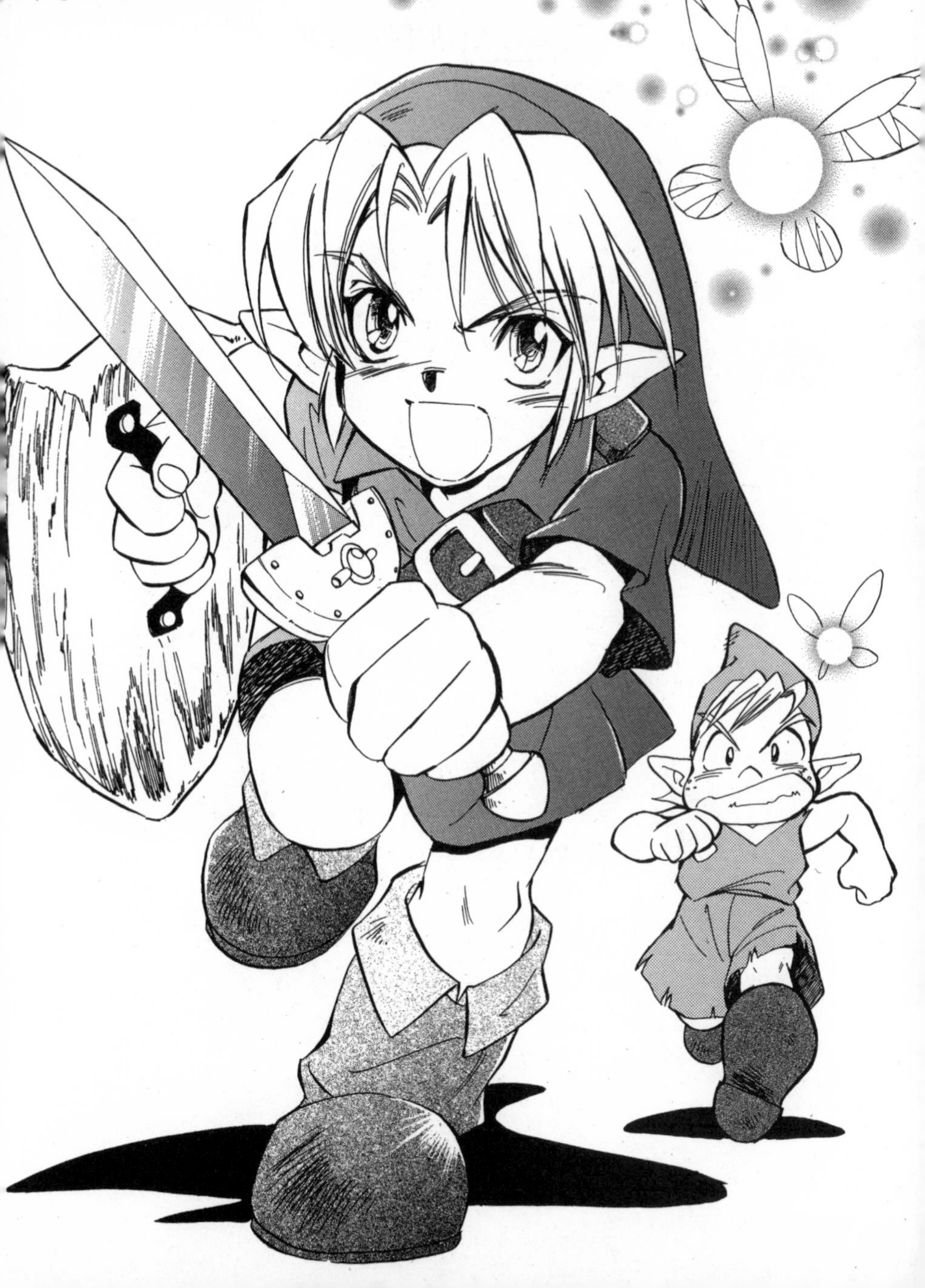

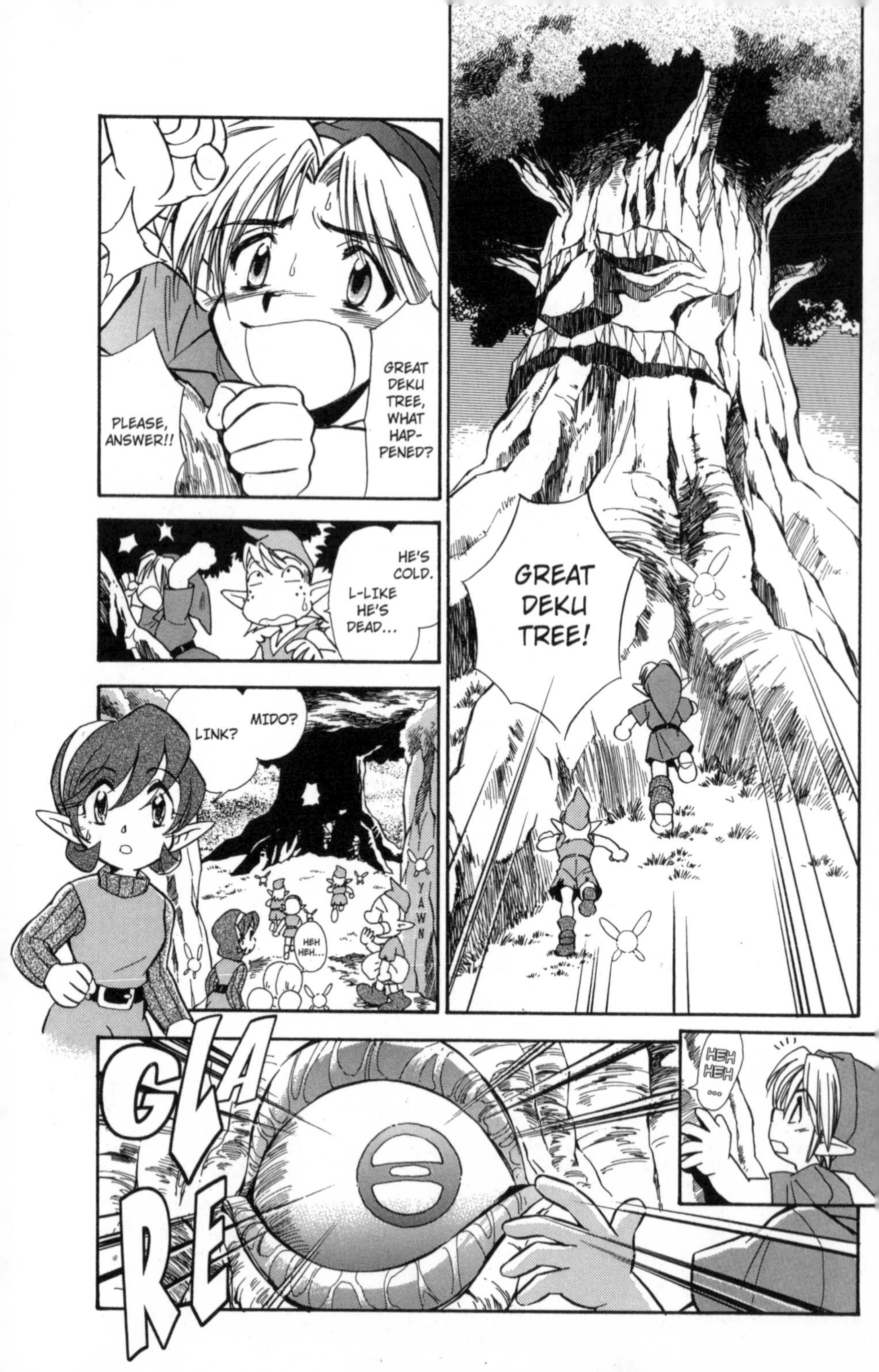
GREAT DEKU TREE!
GREAT DEKU TREE, WHAT HAP-PENED?
PLEASE, ANSWER!!
HE'S COLD.
L-LIKE HE'S DEAD...
MIDO?
LINK?
YAWN
HEH HEH...
HEH HEH...
GLARE

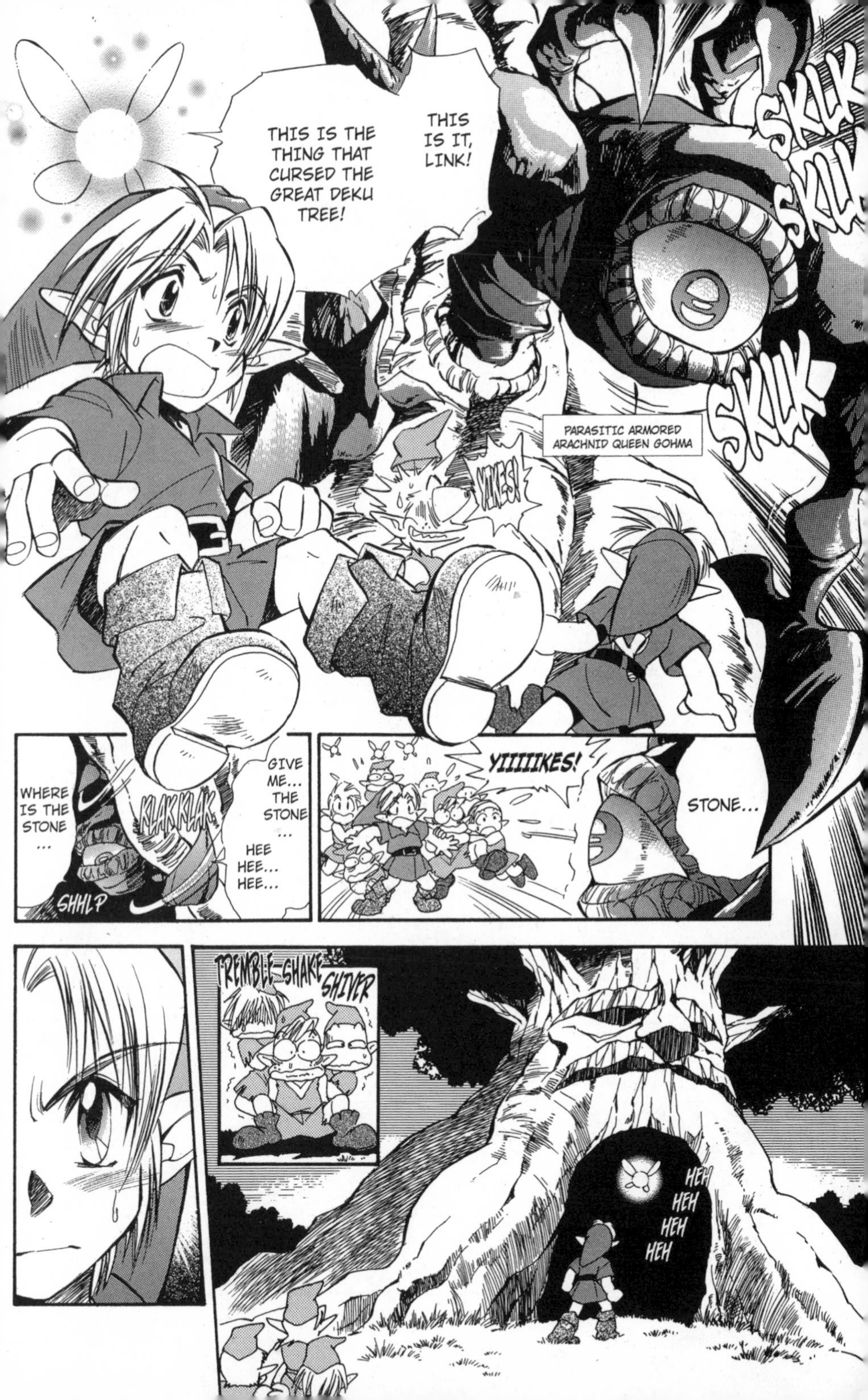
THIS IS IT, LINK!
THIS IS THE THING THAT CURSED THE GREAT DEKU TREE!
SKLK
SKLK
SKLK
PARASITIC ARMORED ARACHNID QUEEN GOHMA
YIKES!
STONE...
YIIIIIKES!
GIVE ME... THE STONE...
HEE HEE... HEE...
WHERE IS THE STONE...
KLAK KLAK
SHHLP
HEH HEH HEH HEH
TREMBLE-SHAKE
SHIVER

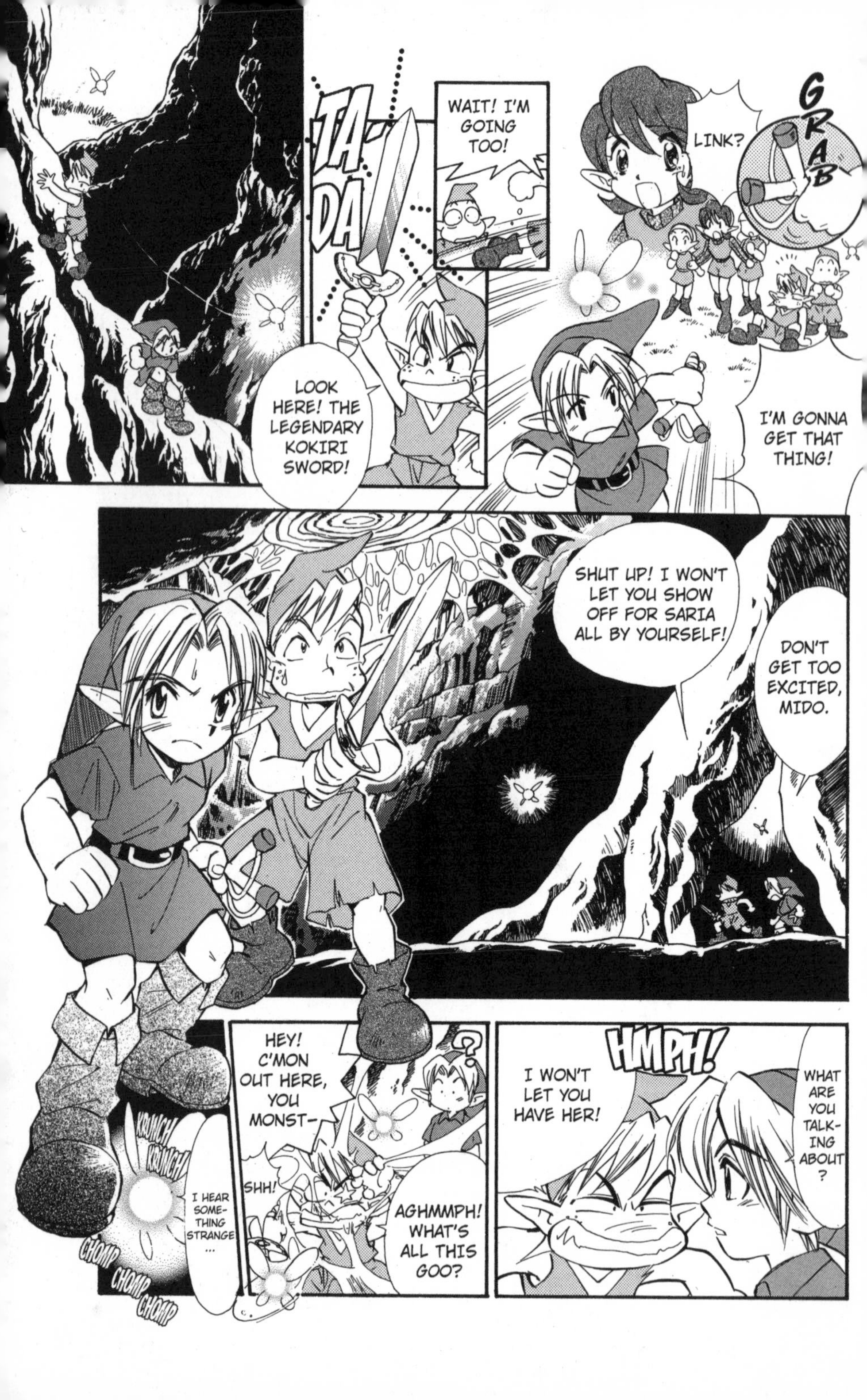

LINK?
GRAB
I'M GONNA GET THAT THING!
WAIT! I'M GOING TOO!
TA-DA
LOOK HERE! THE LEGENDARY KOKIRI SWORD!
DON'T GET TOO EXCITED, MIDO.
SHUT UP! I WON'T LET YOU SHOW OFF FOR SARIA ALL BY YOURSELF!
WHAT ARE YOU TALKING ABOUT?
HMPH!
I WON'T LET YOU HAVE HER!
HEY! C'MON OUT HERE, YOU MONST-
SHH!
AGHMMPH! WHAT'S ALL THIS GOO?
KRUNCH KRUNCH
I HEAR SOMETHING STRANGE...
CHOMP CHOMP CHOMP

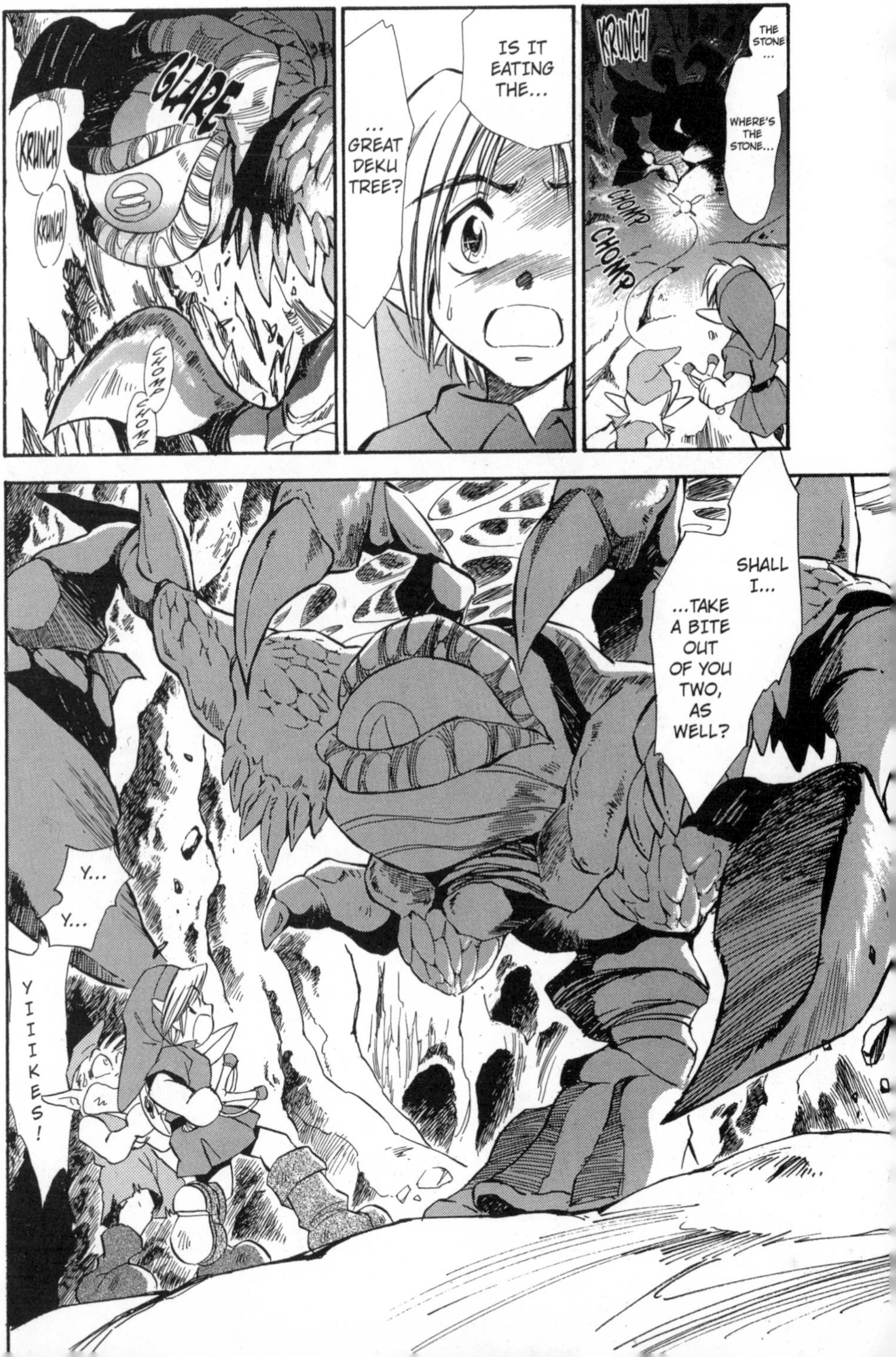
KRUNCH
THE STONE...
WHERE'S THE STONE...
CHOMP
CHOMP
IS IT EATING THE...
... GREAT DEKU TREE?
GLARE
KRUNCH
KRUNCH
CHOMP CHOMP CHOMP
SHALL I...
...TAKE A BITE OUT OF YOU TWO, AS WELL?
Y...
Y...
YIIIKES!

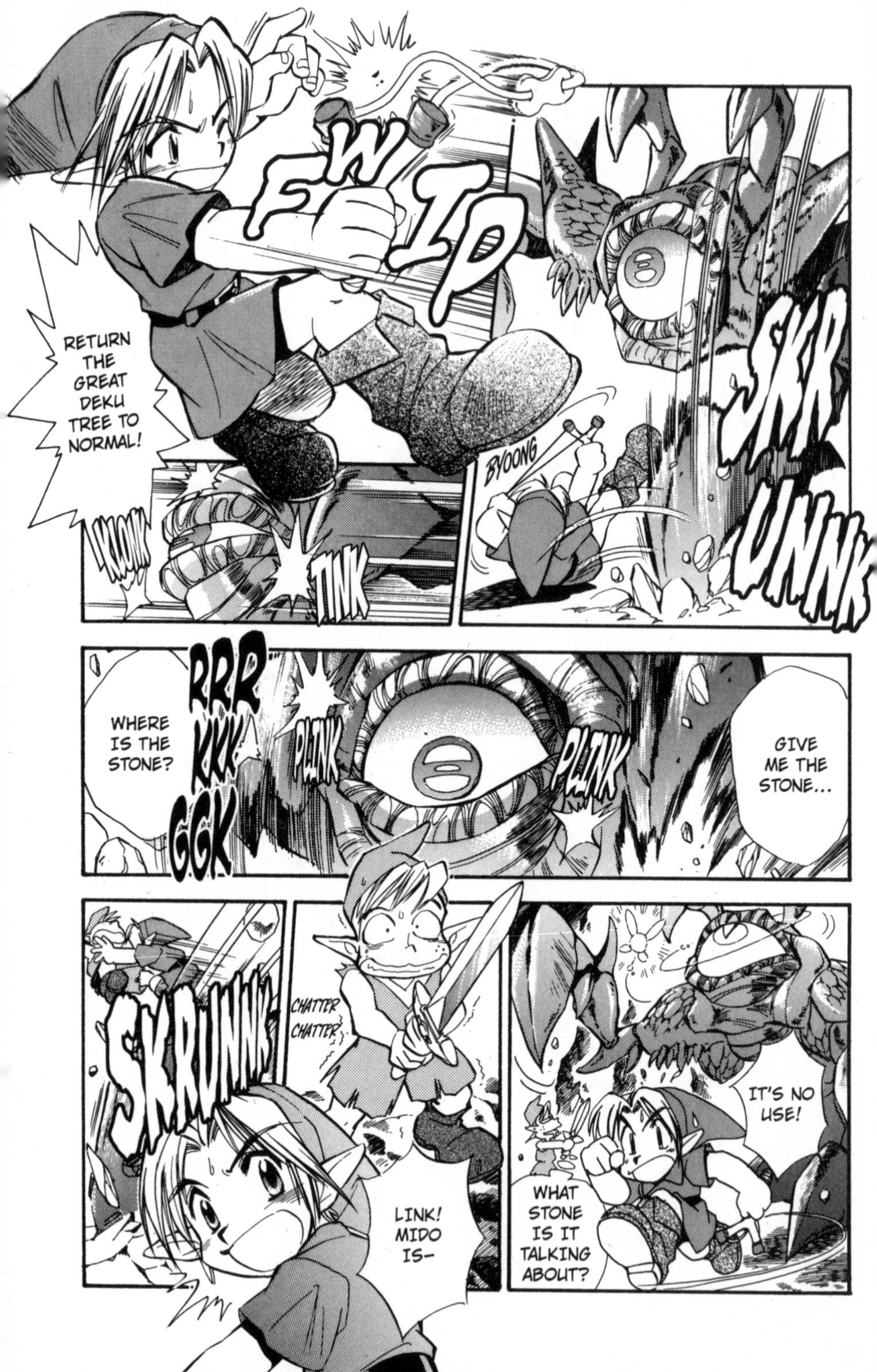
SKR UNNK
BYOONG
FWIP
RETURN THE GREAT DEKU TREE TO NORMAL!
KLONK
TINK
GIVE ME THE STONE...
PLINK
PLINK
RRR KKK GGK
WHERE IS THE STONE?
IT'S NO USE!
WHAT STONE IS IT TALKING ABOUT?
CHATTER CHATTER
SKRUNNK
LINK! MIDO IS-

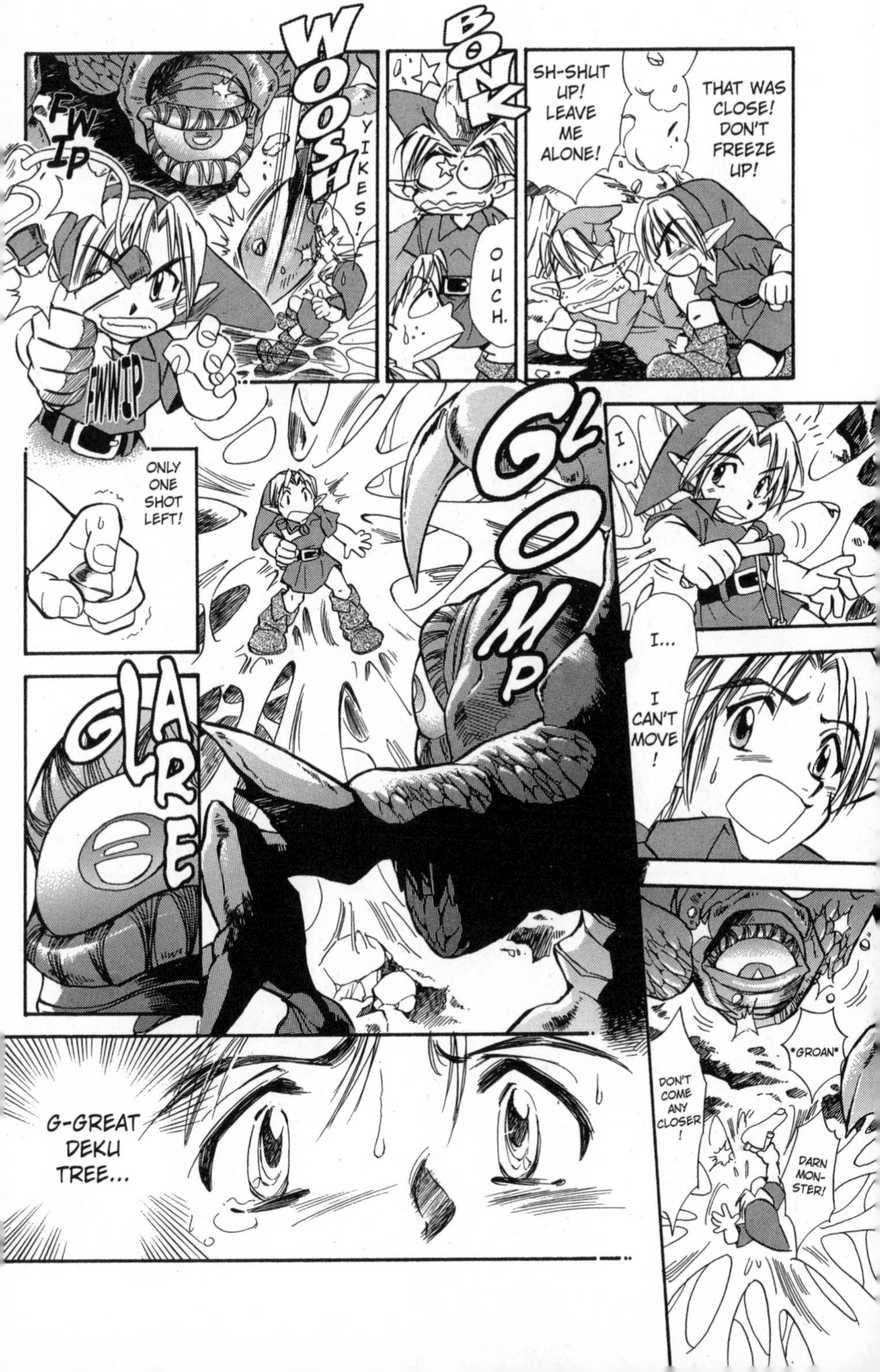
THAT WAS CLOSE! DON'T FREEZE UP!
SH-SHUT UP! LEAVE ME ALONE!
BONK
OUCH.
WOOSH
YIKES!
FWIP
FWWIP
I...
I...
I CAN'T MOVE!
GLOMP
ONLY ONE SHOT LEFT!
GLARE
GROAN
DARN MON-STER!
DON'T COME ANY CLOSER!
G-GREAT DEKU TREE...

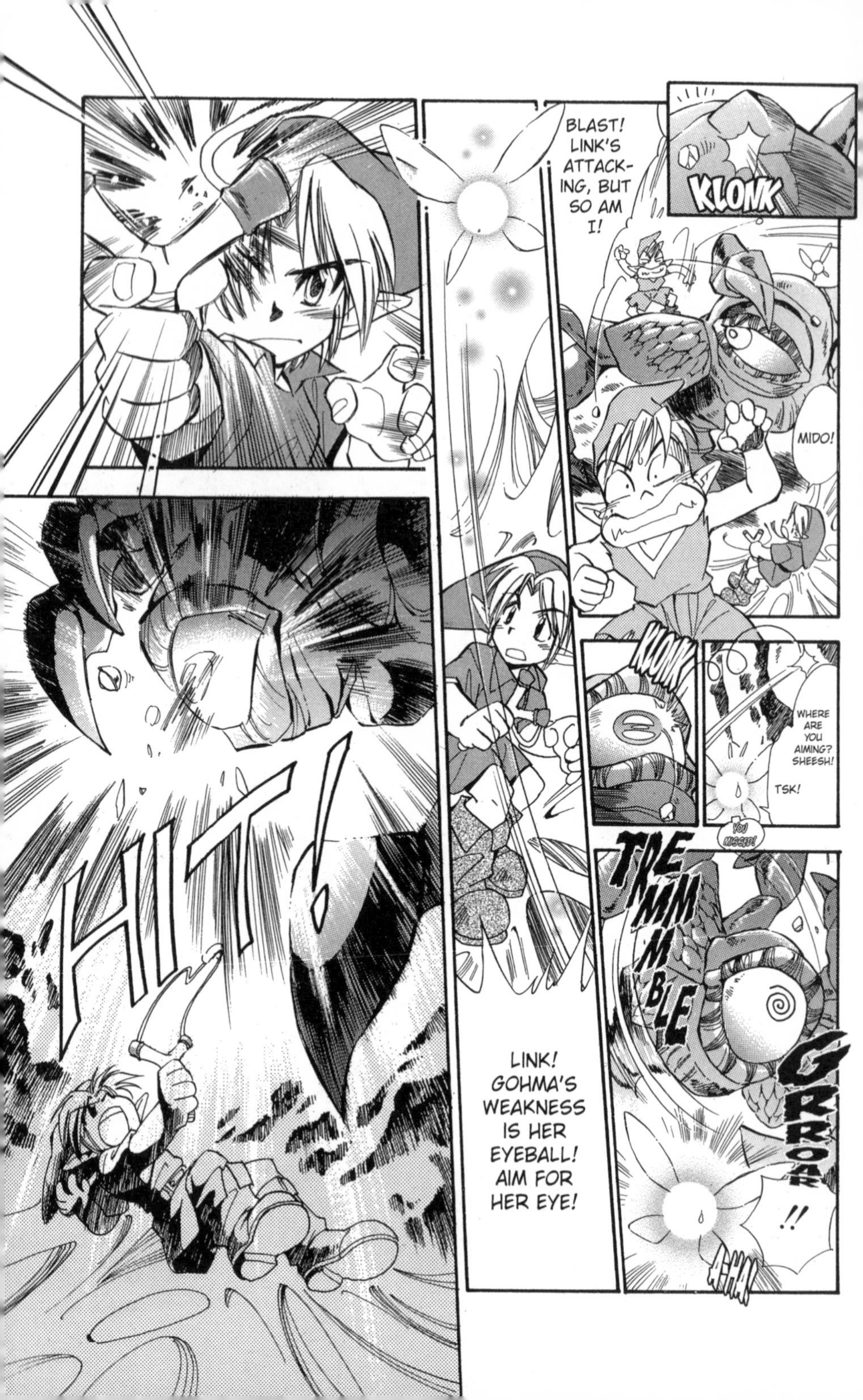
KLONK
BLAST! LINK'S ATTACKING, BUT SO AM I!
MIDO!
KLONK
WHERE ARE YOU AIMING? SHEESH!
TSK!
YOU MISSED!
TREMMMMBLE
GRROAR!!
LINK! GOHMA'S WEAKNESS IS HER EYEBALL! AIM FOR HER EYE!
HIT!

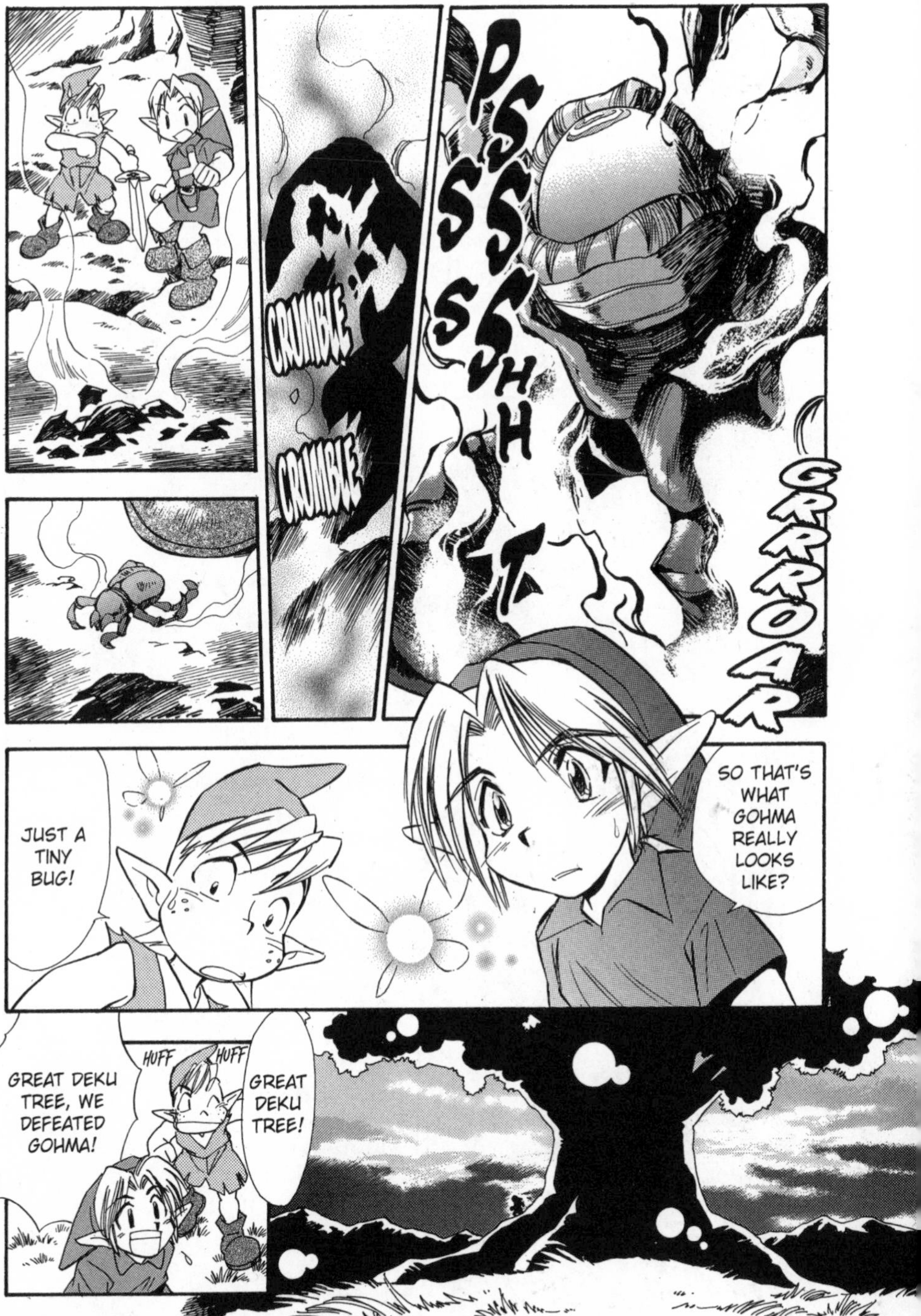
PSSSSHHT
GRRROAR
CRUMBLE
CRUMBLE
SO THAT'S WHAT GOHMA REALLY LOOKS LIKE?
JUST A TINY BUG!
GREAT DEKU TREE!
HUFF
HUFF
GREAT DEKU TREE, WE DEFEATED GOHMA!

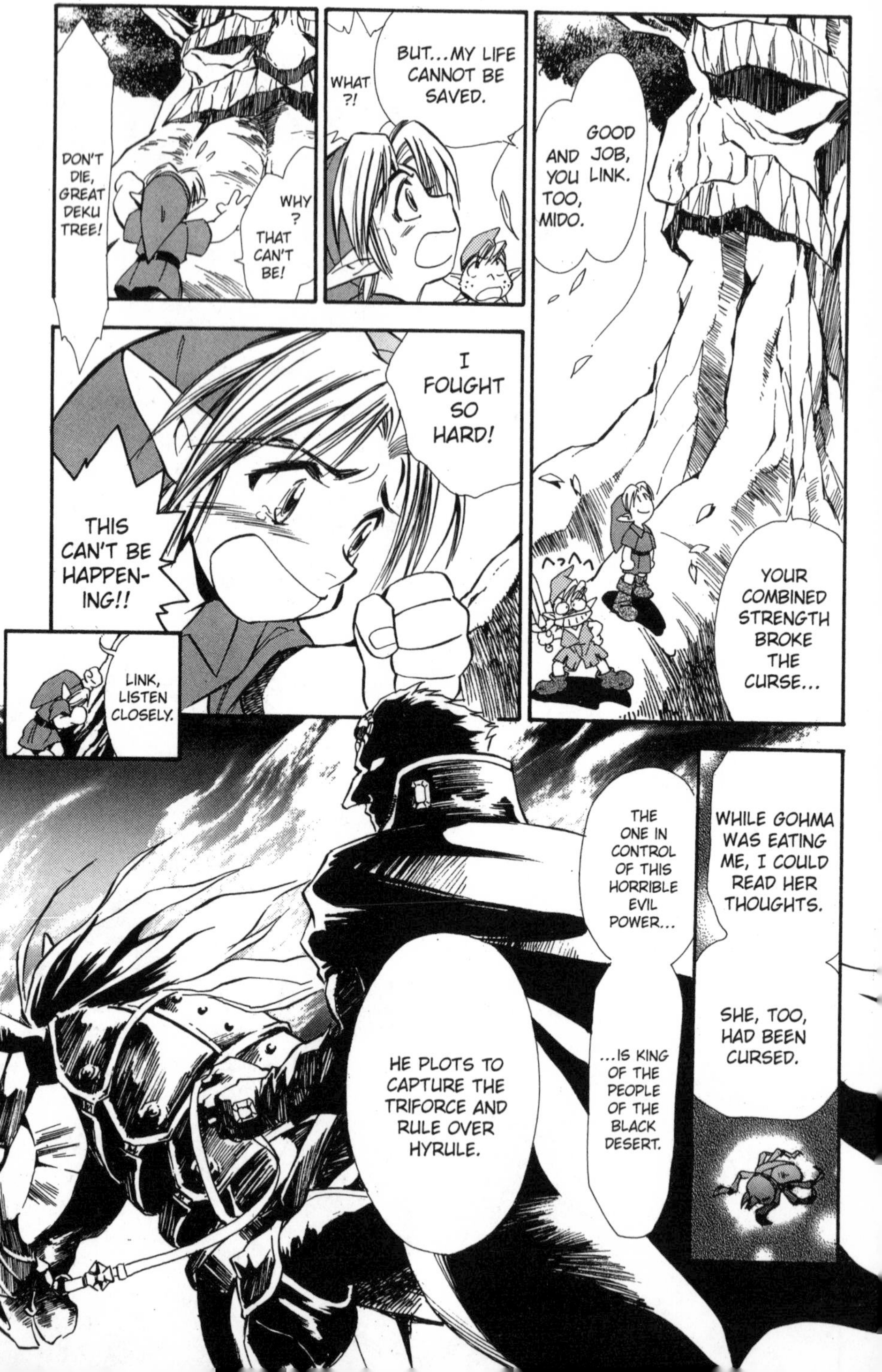
GOOD JOB, LINK.
AND YOU TOO, MIDO.
YOUR COMBINED STRENGTH BROKE THE CURSE...
BUT...MY LIFE CANNOT BE SAVED.
WHAT?!
WHY? THAT CAN'T BE!
DON'T DIE, GREAT DEKU TREE!
I FOUGHT SO HARD!
THIS CAN'T BE HAPPENING!!
LINK, LISTEN CLOSELY.
WHILE GOHMA WAS EATING ME, I COULD READ HER THOUGHTS.
SHE, TOO, HAD BEEN CURSED.
THE ONE IN CONTROL OF THIS HORRIBLE EVIL POWER...
...IS KING OF THE PEOPLE OF THE BLACK DESERT.
HE PLOTS TO CAPTURE THE TRIFORCE AND RULE OVER HYRULE.

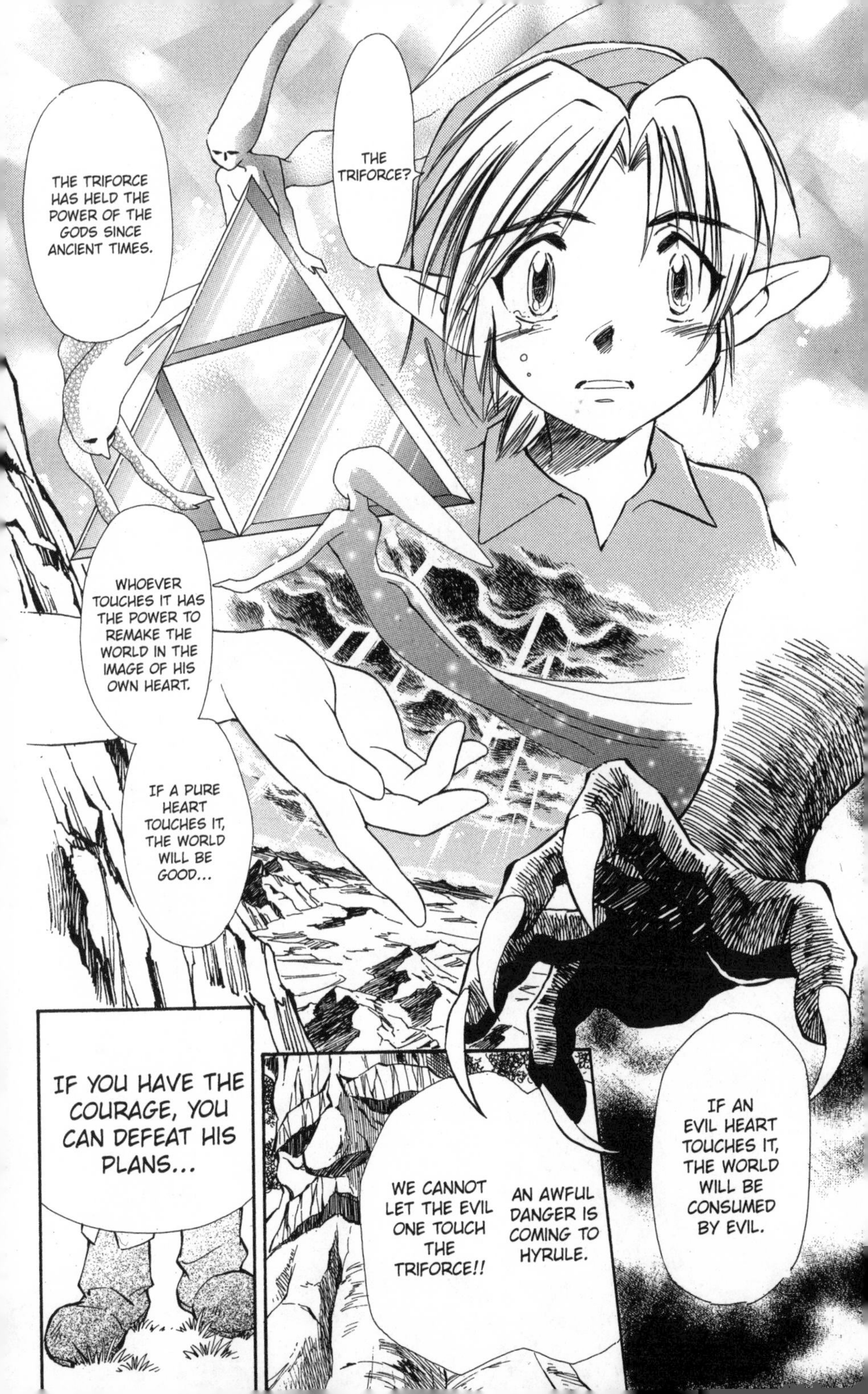
THE TRIFORCE?
THE TRIFORCE HAS HELD THE POWER OF THE GODS SINCE ANCIENT TIMES.
WHOEVER TOUCHES IT HAS THE POWER TO REMAKE THE WORLD IN THE IMAGE OF HIS OWN HEART.
IF A PURE HEART TOUCHES IT, THE WORLD WILL BE GOOD...
IF AN EVIL HEART TOUCHES IT, THE WORLD WILL BE CONSUMED BY EVIL.
AN AWFUL DANGER IS COMING TO HYRULE.
WE CANNOT LET THE EVIL ONE TOUCH THE TRIFORCE!!
IF YOU HAVE THE COURAGE, YOU CAN DEFEAT HIS PLANS...

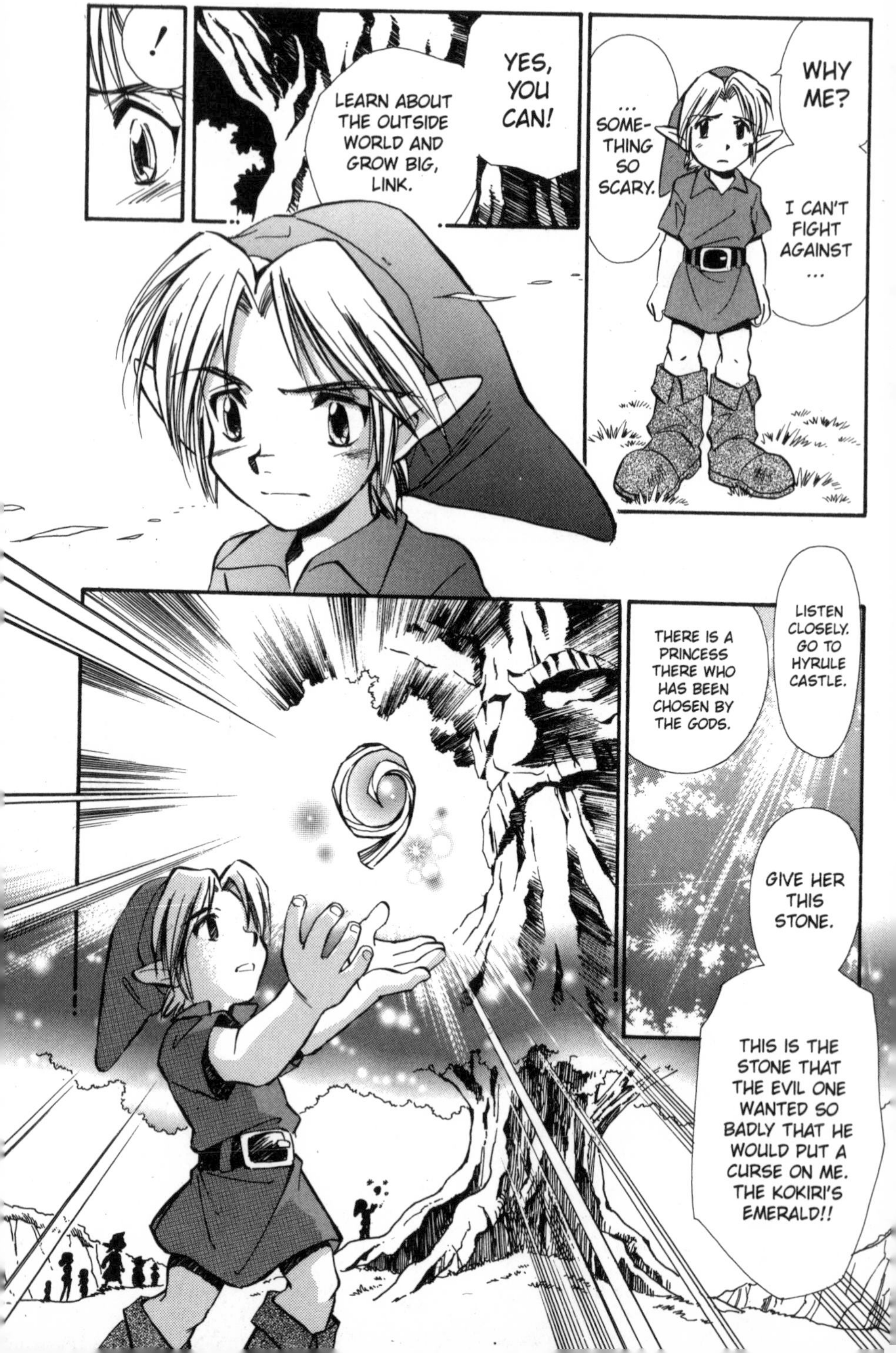
WHY ME?
I CAN'T FIGHT AGAINST ...
... SOMETHING SO SCARY.
YES, YOU CAN!
LEARN ABOUT THE OUTSIDE WORLD AND GROW BIG, LINK.
!
LISTEN CLOSELY. GO TO HYRULE CASTLE.
THERE IS A PRINCESS THERE WHO HAS BEEN CHOSEN BY THE GODS.
GIVE HER THIS STONE.
THIS IS THE STONE THAT THE EVIL ONE WANTED SO BADLY THAT HE WOULD PUT A CURSE ON ME. THE KOKIRI'S EMERALD!!

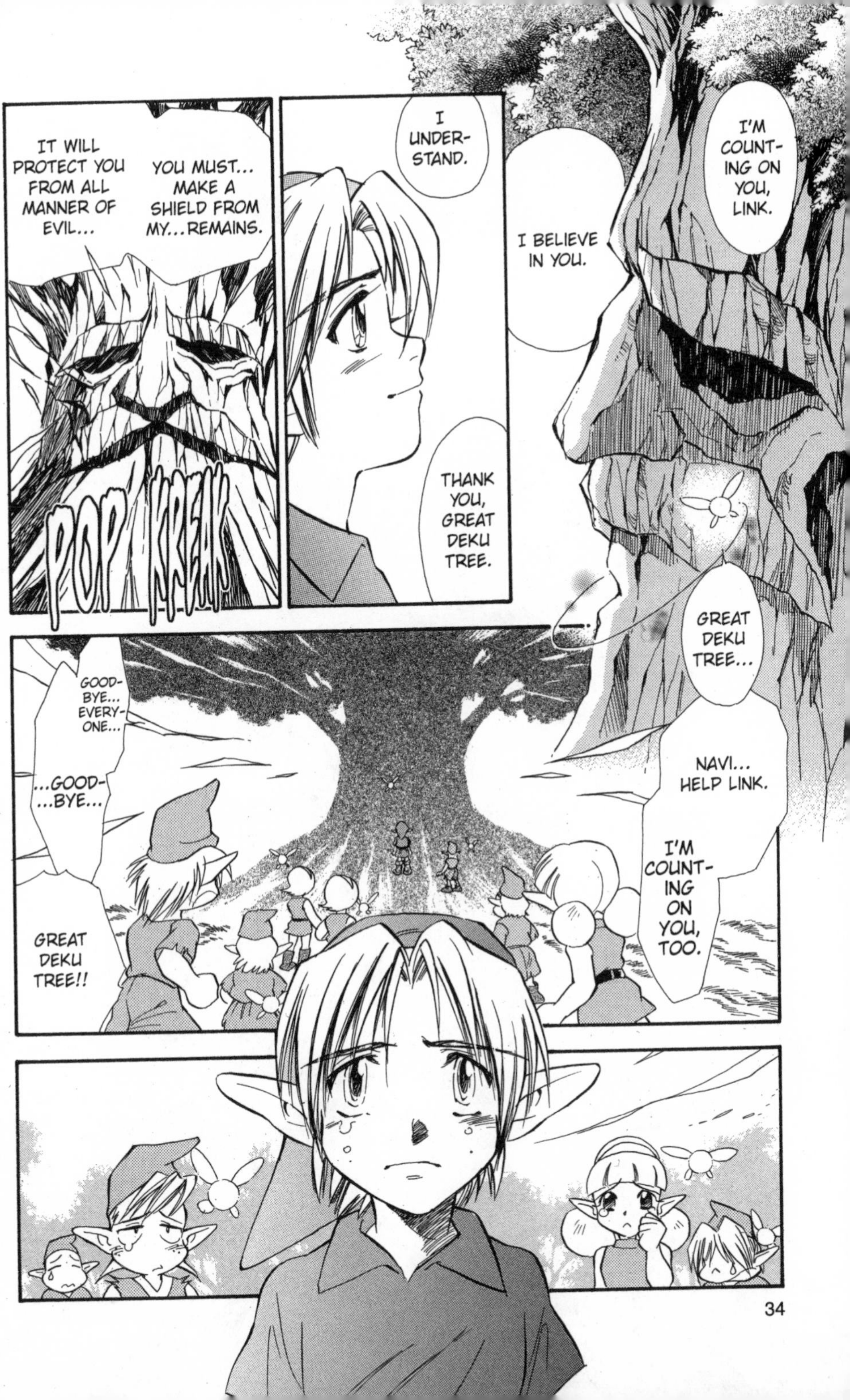
I'M COUNTING ON YOU, LINK.
I BELIEVE IN YOU.
GREAT DEKU TREE...
NAVI... HELP LINK.
I'M COUNTING ON YOU, TOO.
I UNDERSTAND.
THANK YOU, GREAT DEKU TREE.
YOU MUST... MAKE A SHIELD FROM MY... REMAINS.
IT WILL PROTECT YOU FROM ALL MANNER OF EVIL...
POP
KREAK
GOOD-BYE... EVERYONE...
...GOOD- ...BYE...
GREAT DEKU TREE!!

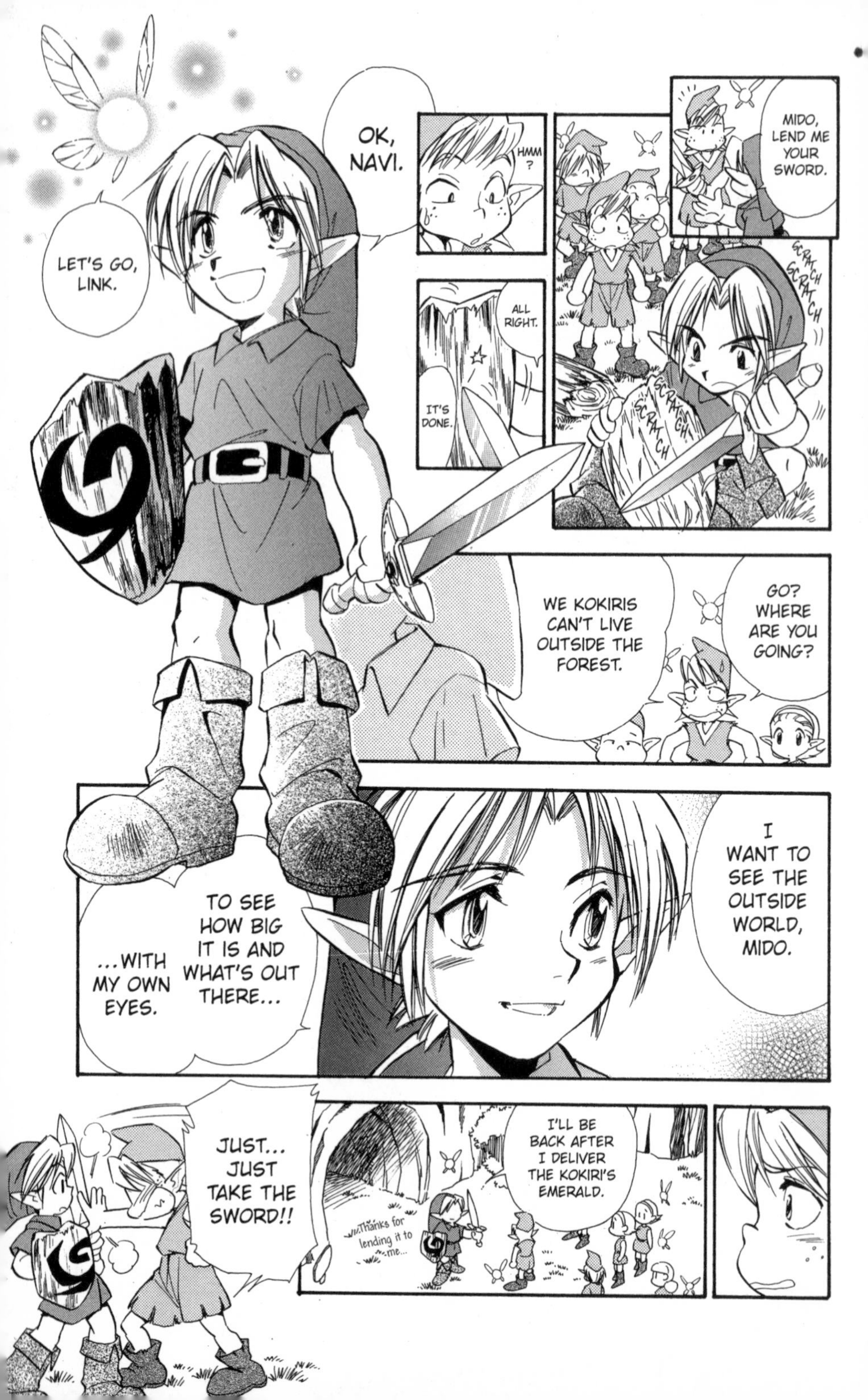

MIDO, LEND ME YOUR SWORD.
SCRATCH SCRATCH
SCRATCH SCRATCH
HMM?
ALL RIGHT.
IT'S DONE.
LET'S GO, LINK.
OK, NAVI.
GO? WHERE ARE YOU GOING?
WE KOKIRIS CAN'T LIVE OUTSIDE THE FOREST.
I WANT TO SEE THE OUTSIDE WORLD, MIDO.
TO SEE HOW BIG IT IS AND WHAT'S OUT THERE...
...WITH MY OWN EYES.
I'LL BE BACK AFTER I DELIVER THE KOKIRI'S EMERALD.
Thanks for lending it to me...
JUST... JUST TAKE THE SWORD!!

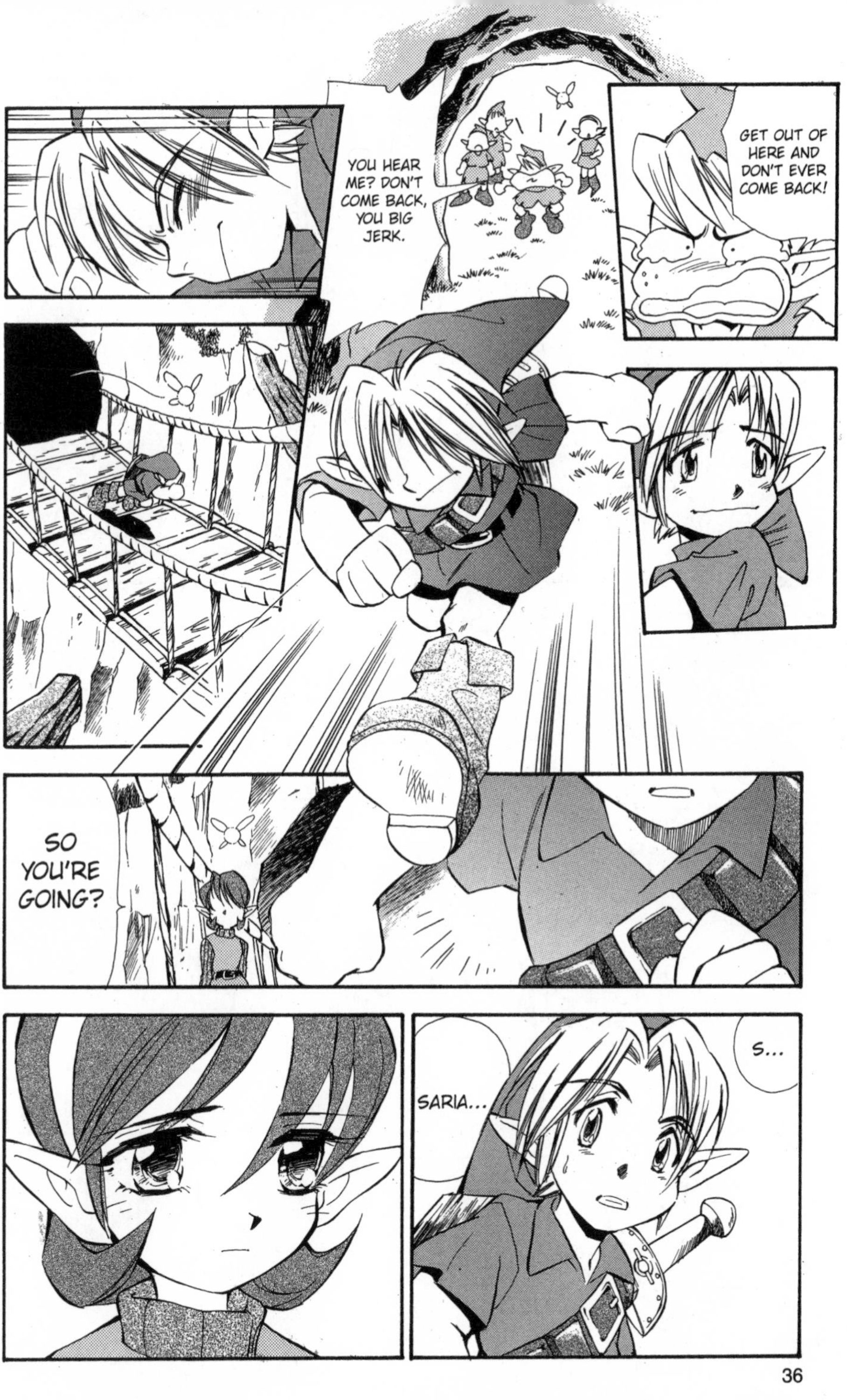
GET OUT OF HERE AND DON'T EVER COME BACK!
YOU HEAR ME? DON'T COME BACK, YOU BIG JERK.
SO YOU'RE GOING?
S...
SARIA...

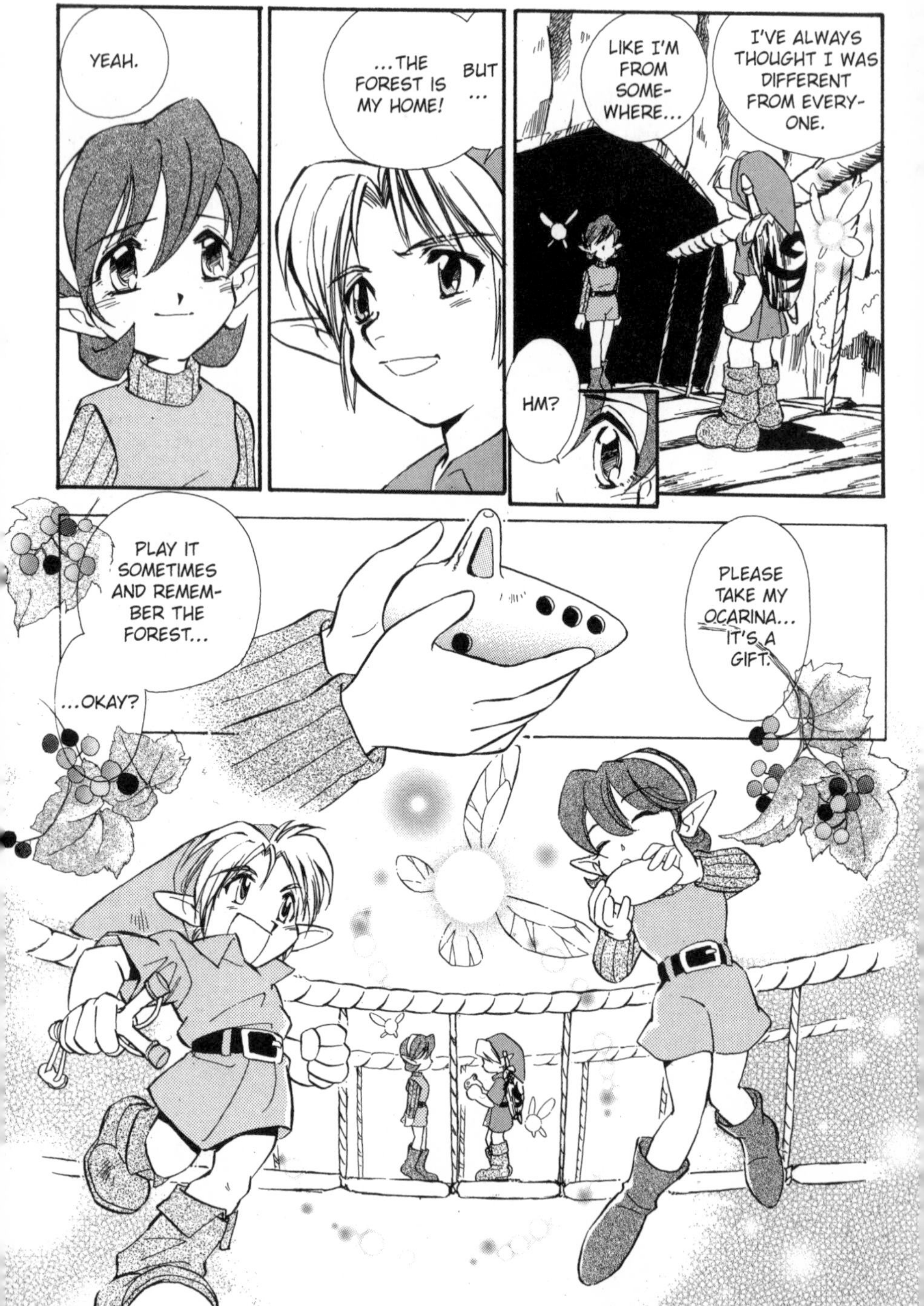
I'VE ALWAYS THOUGHT I WAS DIFFERENT FROM EVERYONE.
LIKE I'M FROM SOMEWHERE...
HM?
BUT...
...THE FOREST IS MY HOME!
YEAH.
PLEASE TAKE MY OCARINA... IT'S A GIFT.
PLAY IT SOMETIMES AND REMEMBER THE FOREST...
...OKAY?

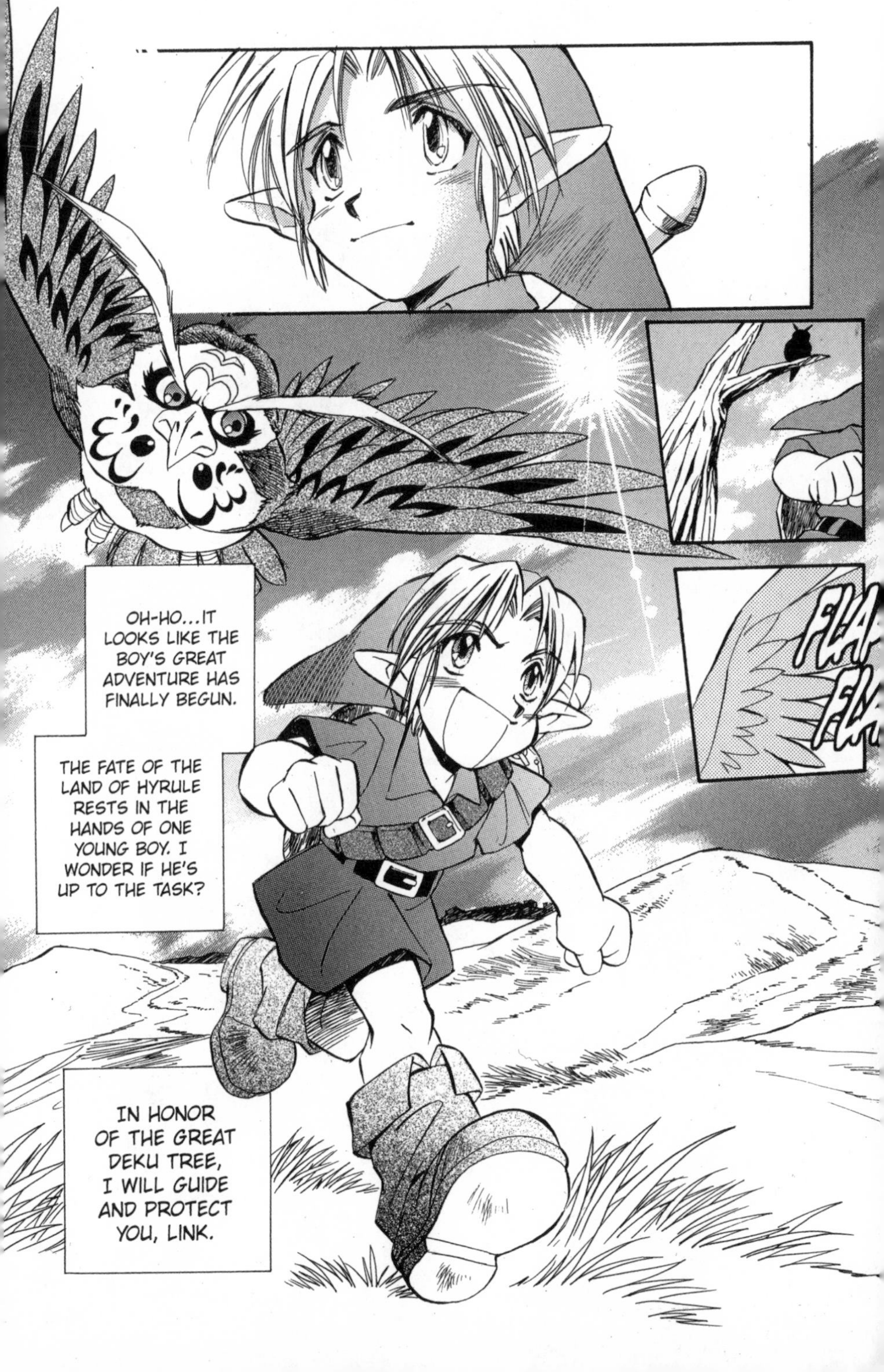
OH-HO...IT LOOKS LIKE THE BOY'S GREAT ADVENTURE HAS FINALLY BEGUN.
THE FATE OF THE LAND OF HYRULE RESTS IN THE HANDS OF ONE YOUNG BOY. I WONDER IF HE'S UP TO THE TASK?
IN HONOR OF THE GREAT DEKU TREE, I WILL GUIDE AND PROTECT YOU, LINK.

BONUS ILLUSTRATION 2

THIS ROUGH SKETCH WAS DRAWN BEFORE THE SERIES BEGAN.

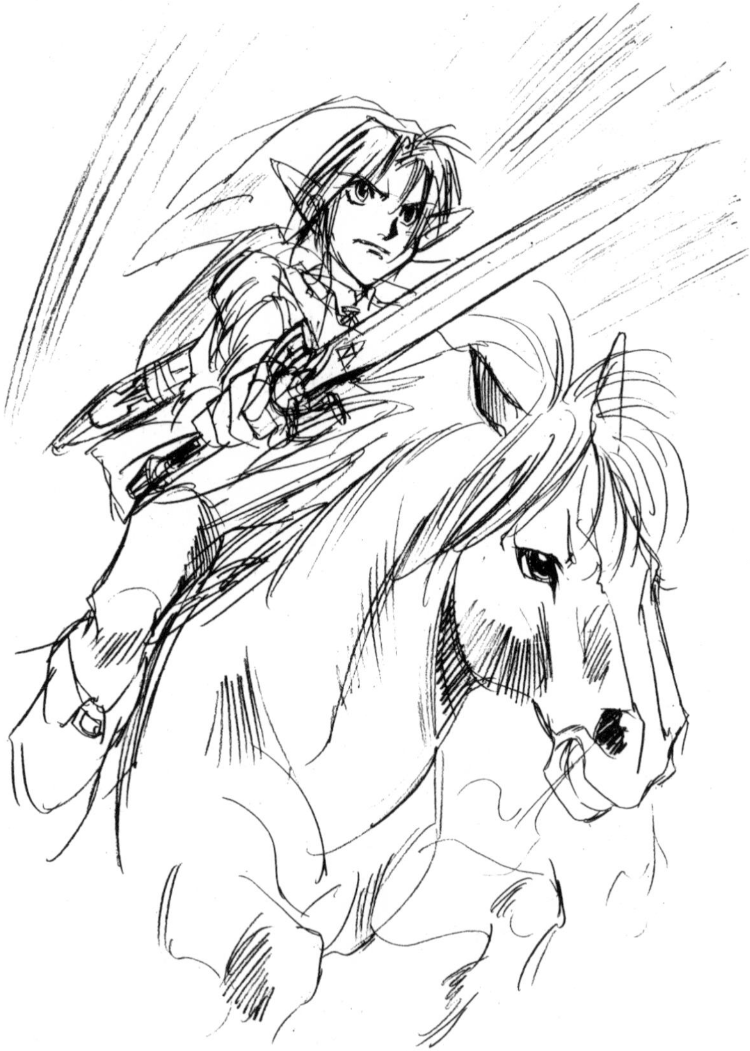

CHAPTER 3
THE MYSTERY OF THE TRIFORCE

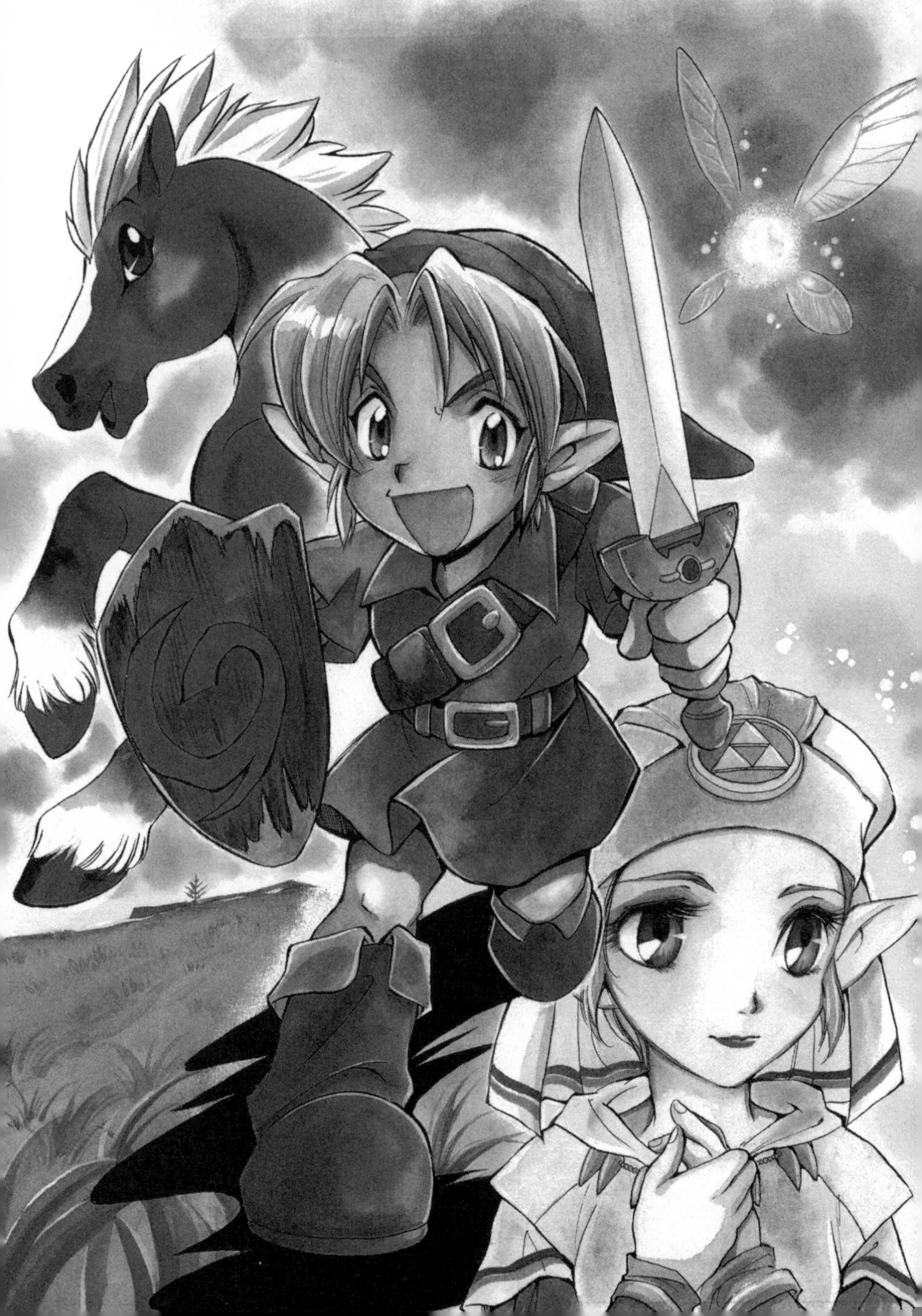

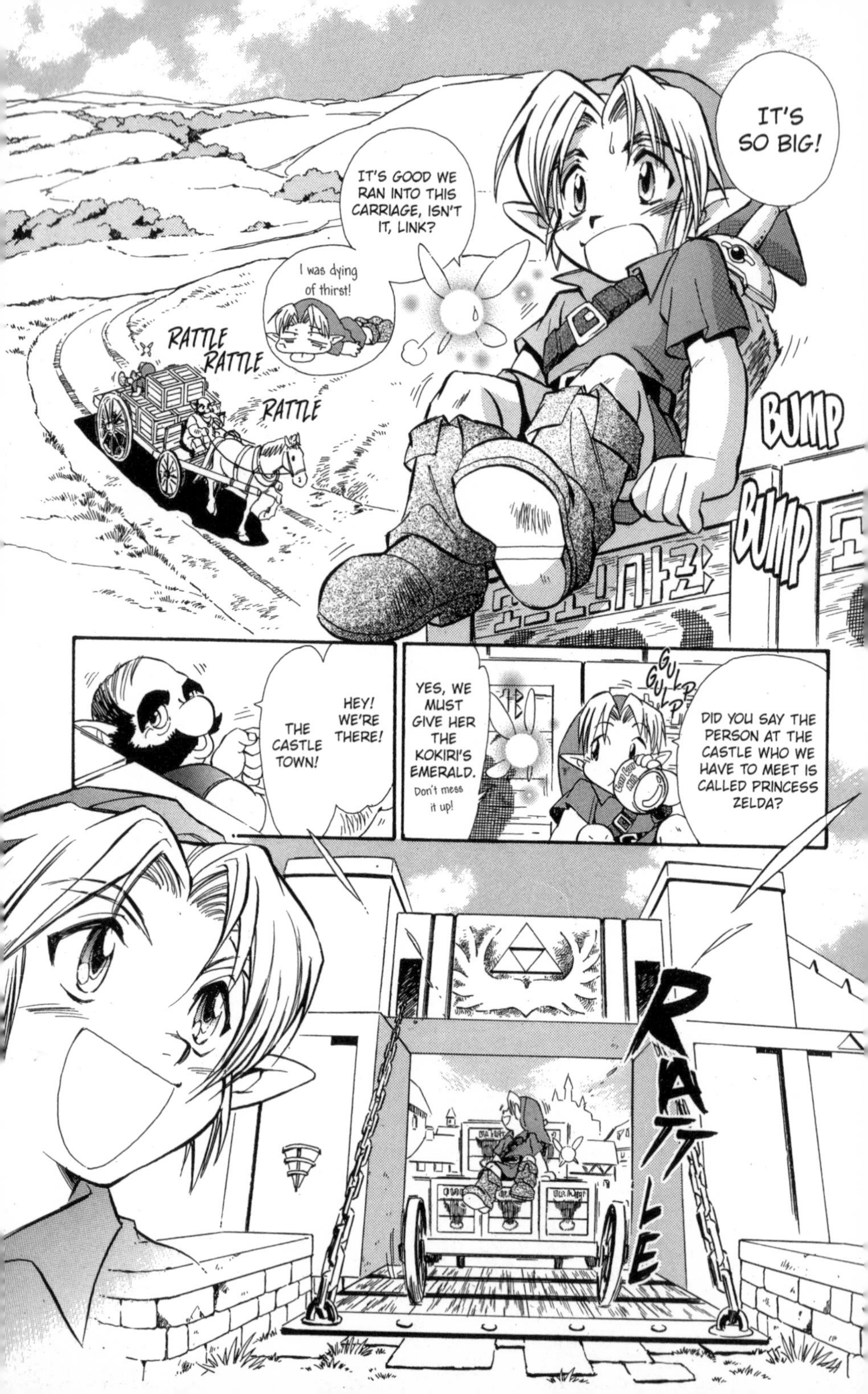
IT'S SO BIG!
IT'S GOOD WE RAN INTO THIS CARRIAGE, ISN'T IT, LINK?
I was dying of thirst!
BUMP
BUMP
RATTLE RATTLE
RATTLE
DID YOU SAY THE PERSON AT THE CASTLE WHO WE HAVE TO MEET IS CALLED PRINCESS ZELDA?
GULP GULP
YES, WE MUST GIVE HER THE KOKIRI'S EMERALD.
Don't mess it up!
HEY! WE'RE THERE!
THE CASTLE TOWN!
RATTLE

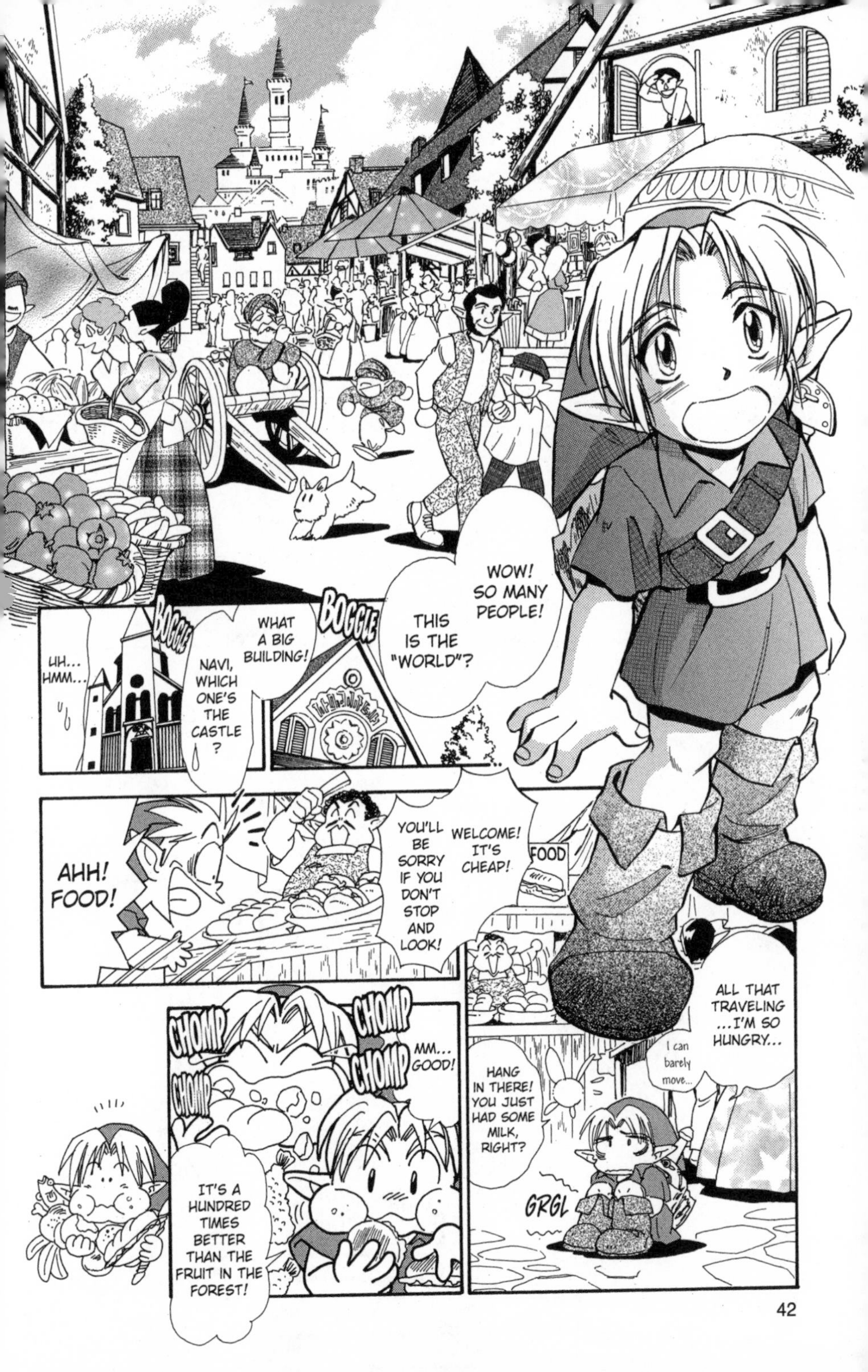
WOW! SO MANY PEOPLE!
THIS IS THE "WORLD"?
BOGGLE
WHAT A BIG BUILDING!
BOGGLE
UH... HMM...
NAVI, WHICH ONE'S THE CASTLE?
WELCOME! IT'S CHEAP!
YOU'LL BE SORRY IF YOU DON'T STOP AND LOOK!
FOOD
AHH! FOOD!
ALL THAT TRAVELING ...I'M SO HUNGRY...
I can barely move...
HANG IN THERE! YOU JUST HAD SOME MILK, RIGHT?
GRGL
CHOMP
CHOMP
MM... GOOD!
CHOMP
CHOMP
IT'S A HUNDRED TIMES BETTER THAN THE FRUIT IN THE FOREST!

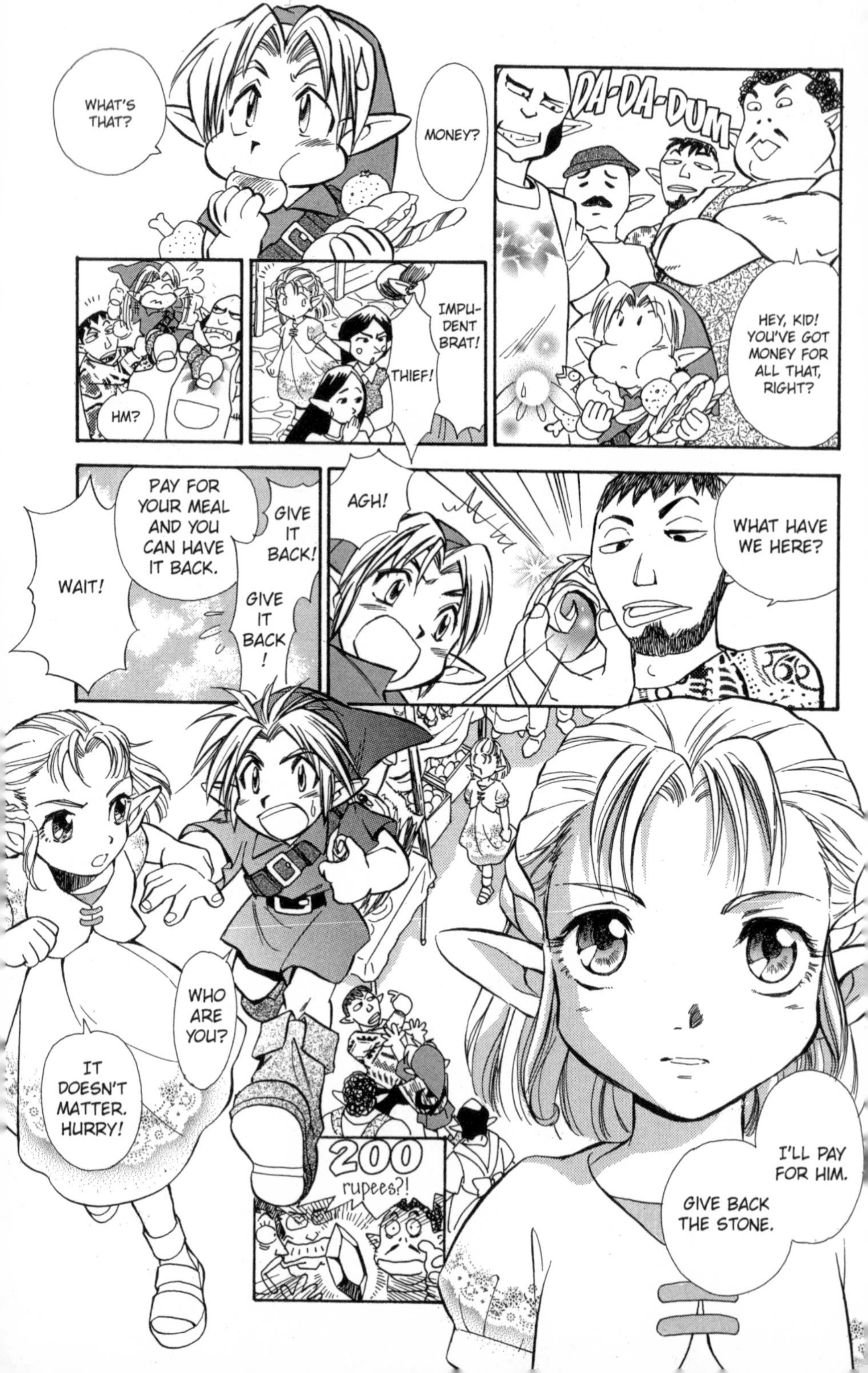
DA-DA-DUM
HEY, KID! YOU'VE GOT MONEY FOR ALL THAT, RIGHT?
MONEY?
WHAT'S THAT?
IMPU-DENT BRAT!
THIEF!
HM?
WHAT HAVE WE HERE?
AGH!
GIVE IT BACK!
GIVE IT BACK!
PAY FOR YOUR MEAL AND YOU CAN HAVE IT BACK.
WAIT!
I'LL PAY FOR HIM.
GIVE BACK THE STONE.
200 rupees?!
WHO ARE YOU?
IT DOESN'T MATTER. HURRY!

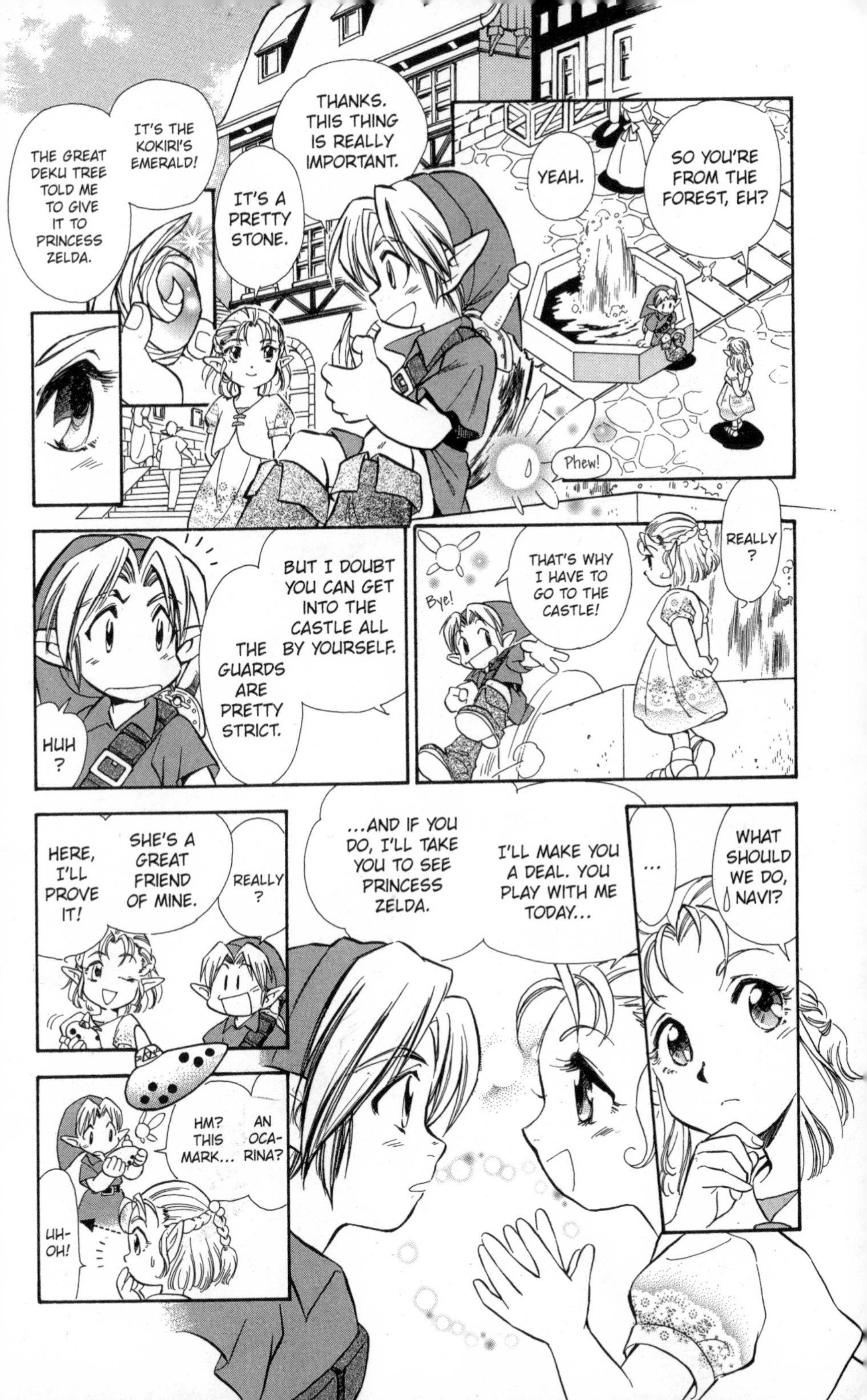
SO YOU'RE FROM THE FOREST, EH?
YEAH.
THANKS. THIS THING IS REALLY IMPORTANT.
IT'S A PRETTY STONE.
IT'S THE KOKIRI'S EMERALD!
THE GREAT DEKU TREE TOLD ME TO GIVE IT TO PRINCESS ZELDA.
Phew!
REALLY?
THAT'S WHY I HAVE TO GO TO THE CASTLE!
Bye!
BUT I DOUBT YOU CAN GET INTO THE CASTLE ALL BY YOURSELF.
THE GUARDS ARE PRETTY STRICT.
HUH?
WHAT SHOULD WE DO, NAVI?
...
I'LL MAKE YOU A DEAL. YOU PLAY WITH ME TODAY...
...AND IF YOU DO, I'LL TAKE YOU TO SEE PRINCESS ZELDA.
SHE'S A GREAT FRIEND OF MINE.
REALLY?
HERE, I'LL PROVE IT!
AN OCA-RINA?
HM? THIS MARK...
UH-OH!

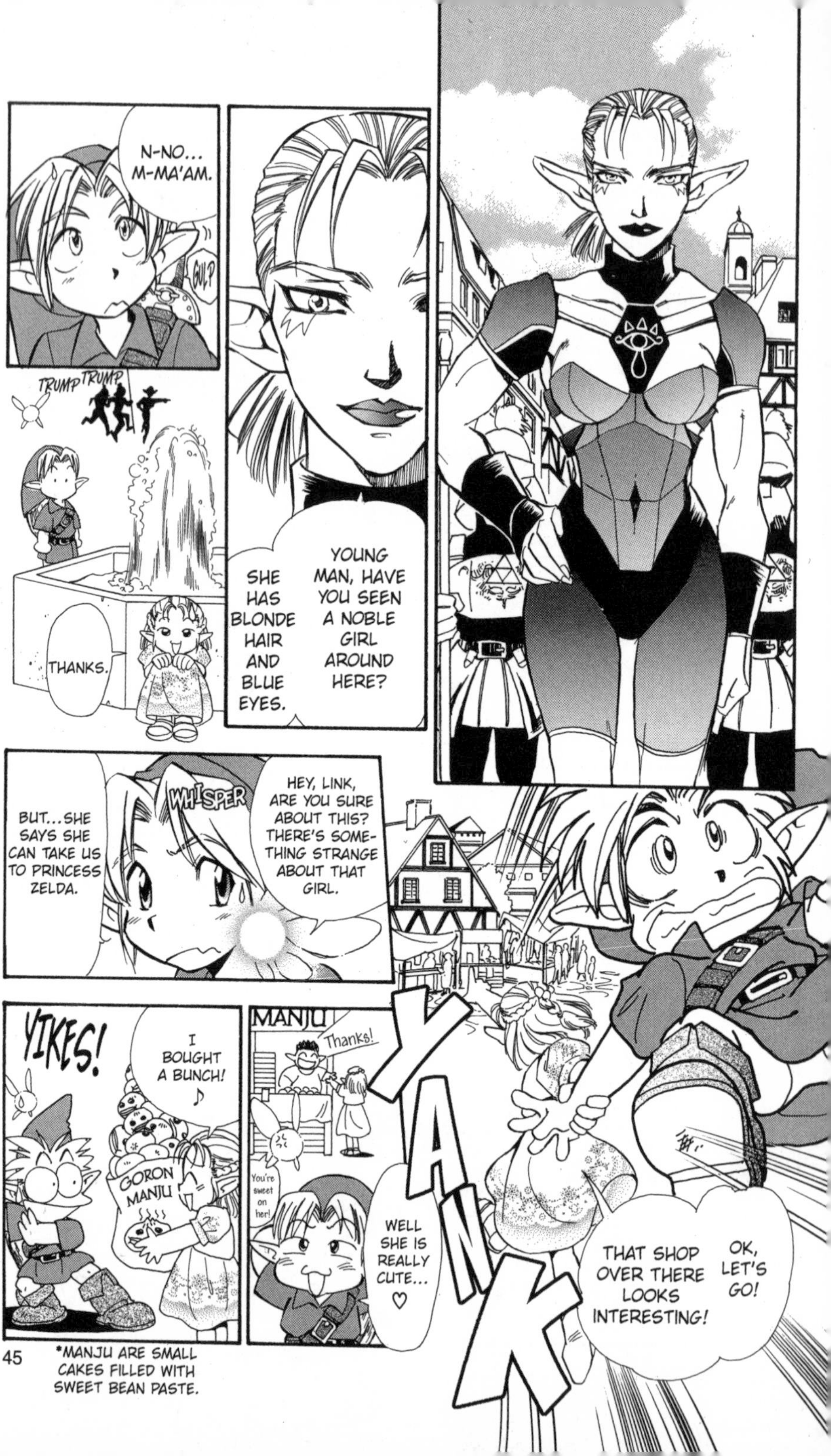
YOUNG MAN, HAVE YOU SEEN A NOBLE GIRL AROUND HERE?
SHE HAS BLONDE HAIR AND BLUE EYES.
N-NO... M-MA'AM.
GULP
TRUMP TRUMP
THANKS.
YANK
OK, LET'S GO!
THAT SHOP OVER THERE LOOKS INTERESTING!
HEY, LINK, ARE YOU SURE ABOUT THIS? THERE'S SOMETHING STRANGE ABOUT THAT GIRL.
WHISPER
BUT...SHE SAYS SHE CAN TAKE US TO PRINCESS ZELDA.
MANJU
Thanks!
You're sweet on her!
WELL SHE IS REALLY CUTE... ♡
I BOUGHT A BUNCH! ♪
YIKES!
GORON MANJU

*MANJU ARE SMALL CAKES FILLED WITH SWEET BEAN PASTE.

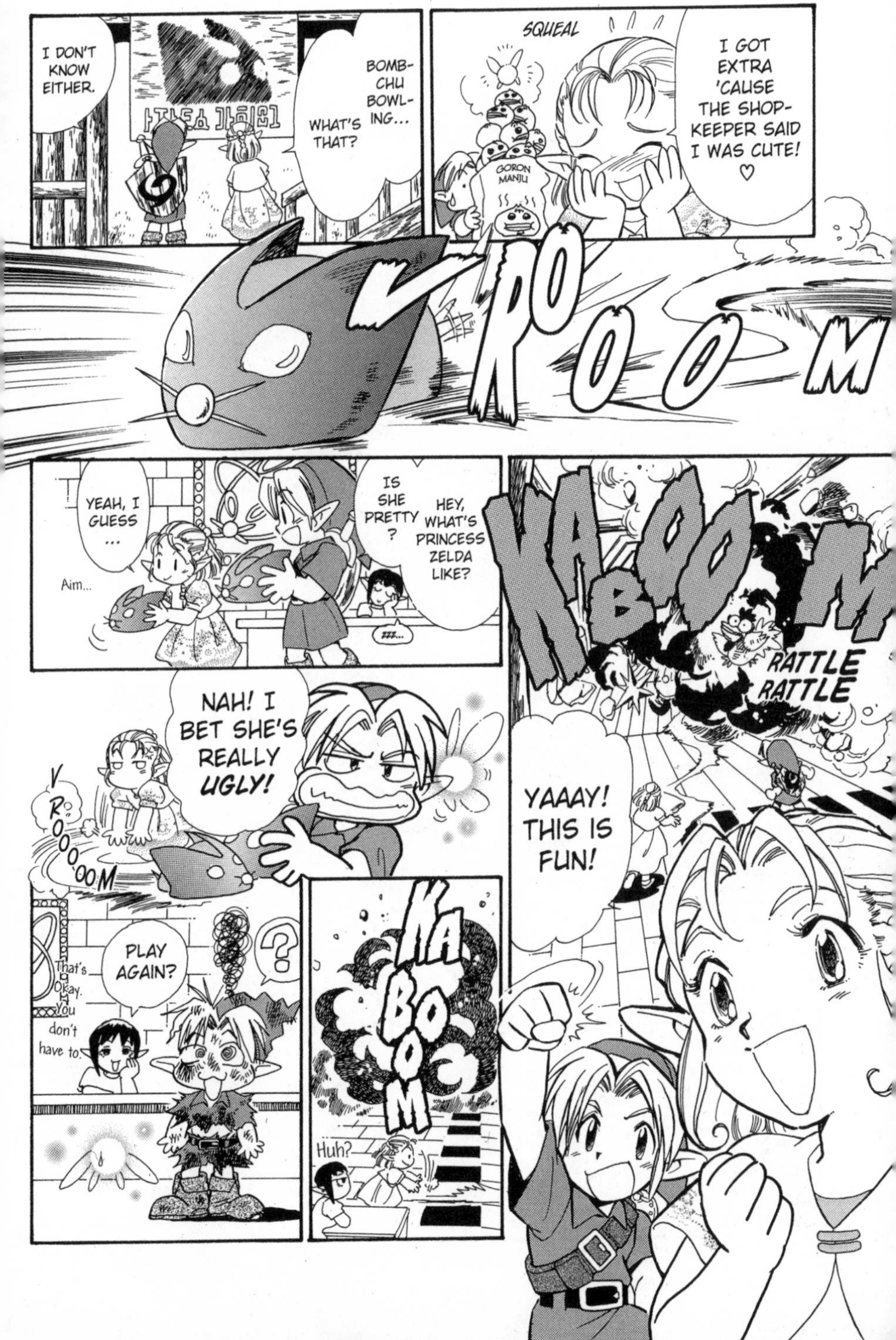
SQUEAL
I GOT EXTRA 'CAUSE THE SHOPKEEPER SAID I WAS CUTE! ♡
GORON MANJU
BOMB-CHU BOWLING...
WHAT'S THAT?
I DON'T KNOW EITHER.
VROOOM
KABOOM
RATTLE RATTLE
YAAAY! THIS IS FUN!
HEY, WHAT'S PRINCESS ZELDA LIKE?
IS SHE PRETTY?
YEAH, I GUESS...
Aim...
zzz...
NAH! I BET SHE'S REALLY UGLY!
VROOOOOM
KABOOM
Huh?
?
PLAY AGAIN?
That's okay. You don't have to.

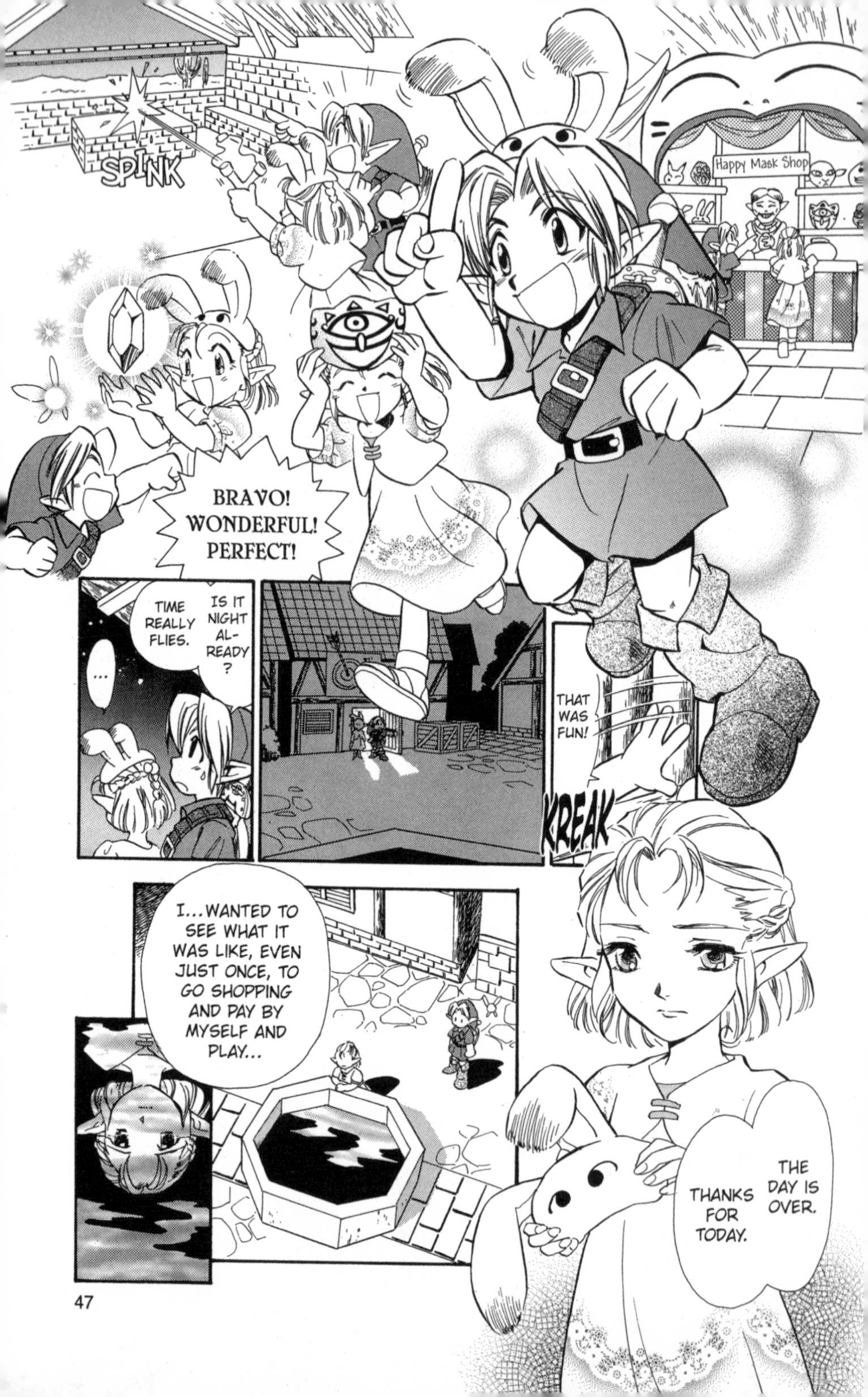
SPINK
BRAVO! WONDERFUL! PERFECT!
THAT WAS FUN!
KREAK
IS IT NIGHT AL-READY?
TIME REALLY FLIES.
...
THE DAY IS OVER.
THANKS FOR TODAY.
I...WANTED TO SEE WHAT IT WAS LIKE, EVEN JUST ONCE, TO GO SHOPPING AND PAY BY MYSELF AND PLAY...

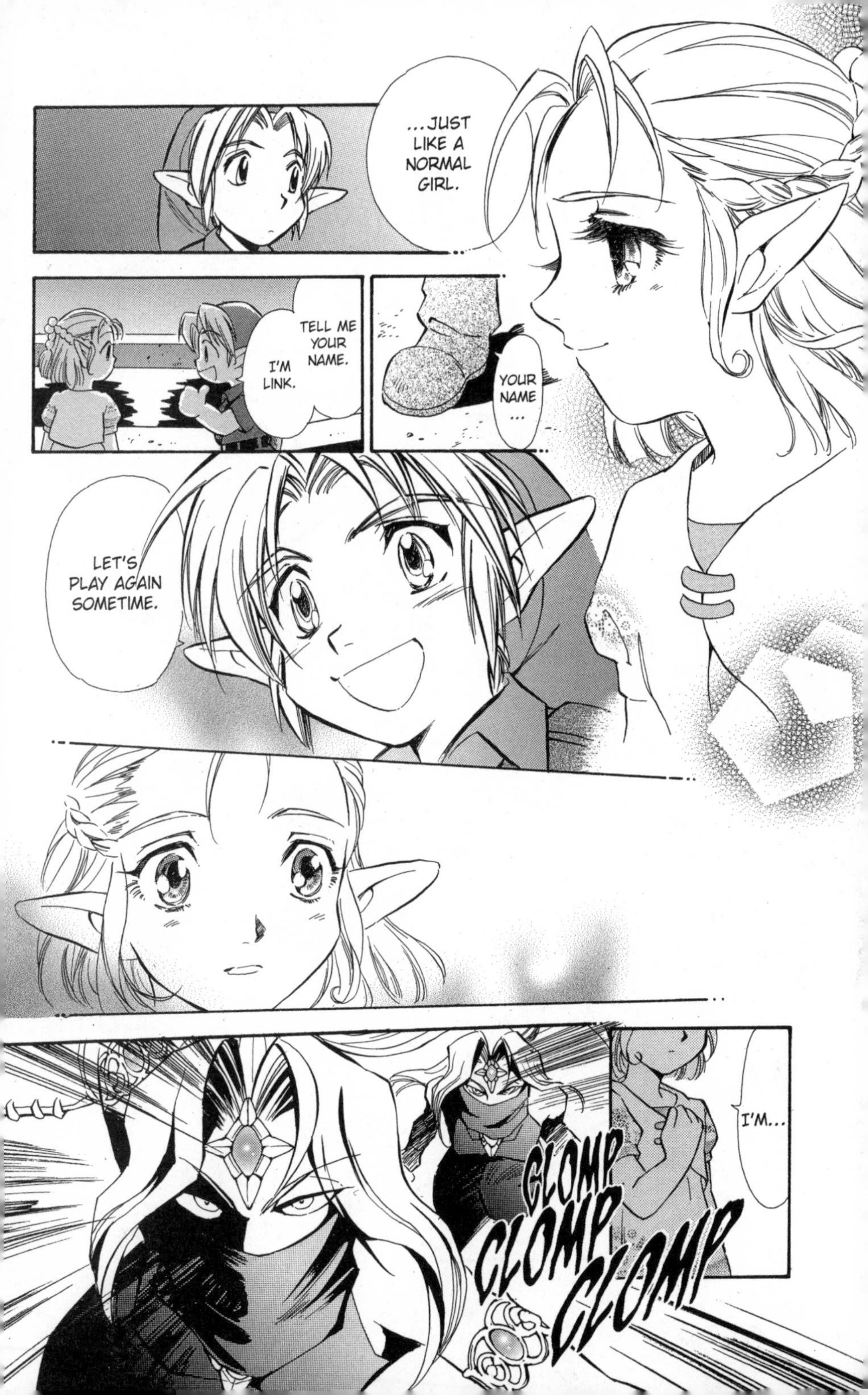
...JUST LIKE A NORMAL GIRL.
YOUR NAME ...
TELL ME YOUR NAME.
I'M LINK.
LET'S PLAY AGAIN SOMETIME.
I'M...
CLOMP CLOMP CLOMP

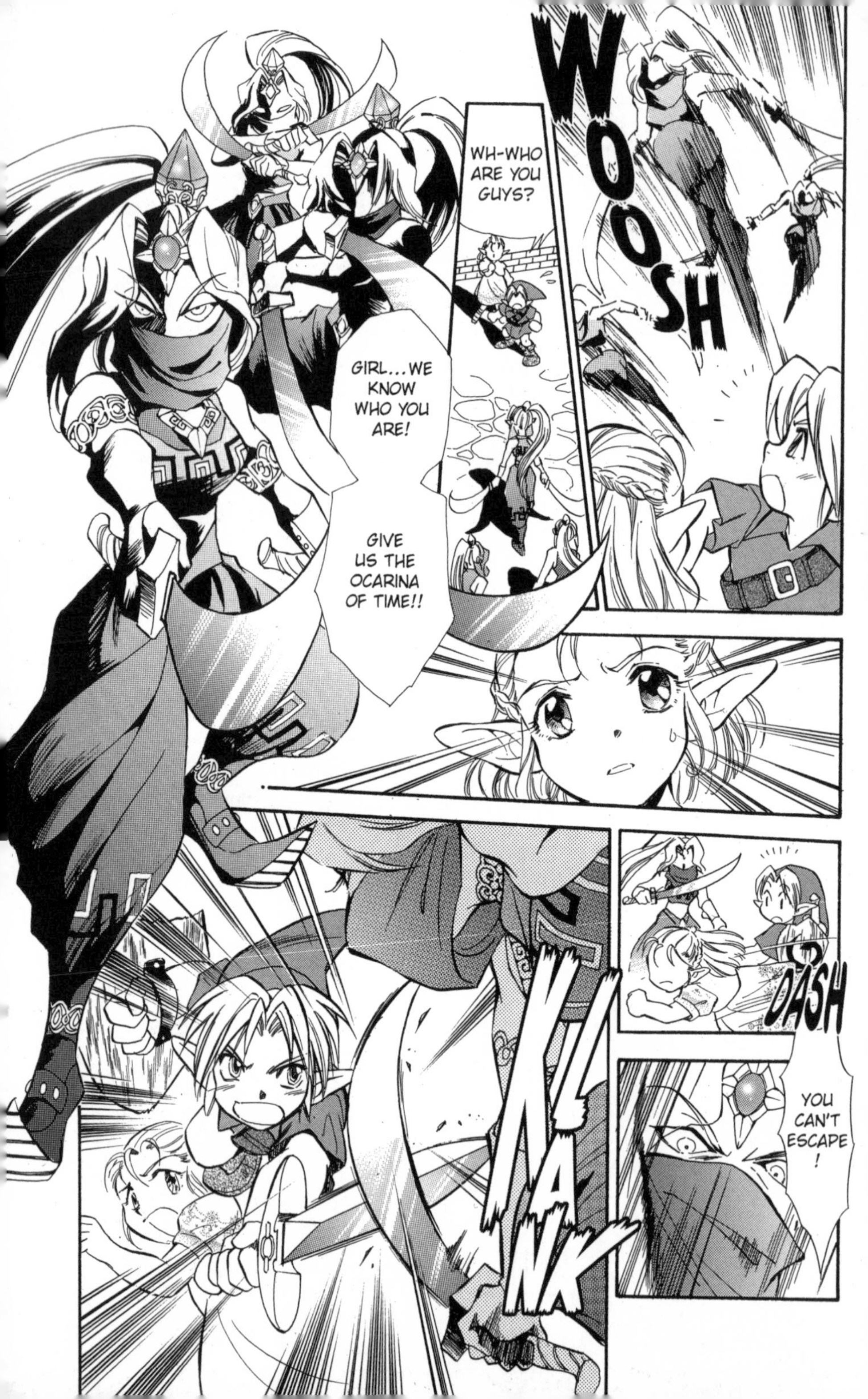
WOOSH
WH-WHO ARE YOU GUYS?
GIRL...WE KNOW WHO YOU ARE!
GIVE US THE OCARINA OF TIME!!
DASH
YOU CAN'T ESCAPE!
KLANK

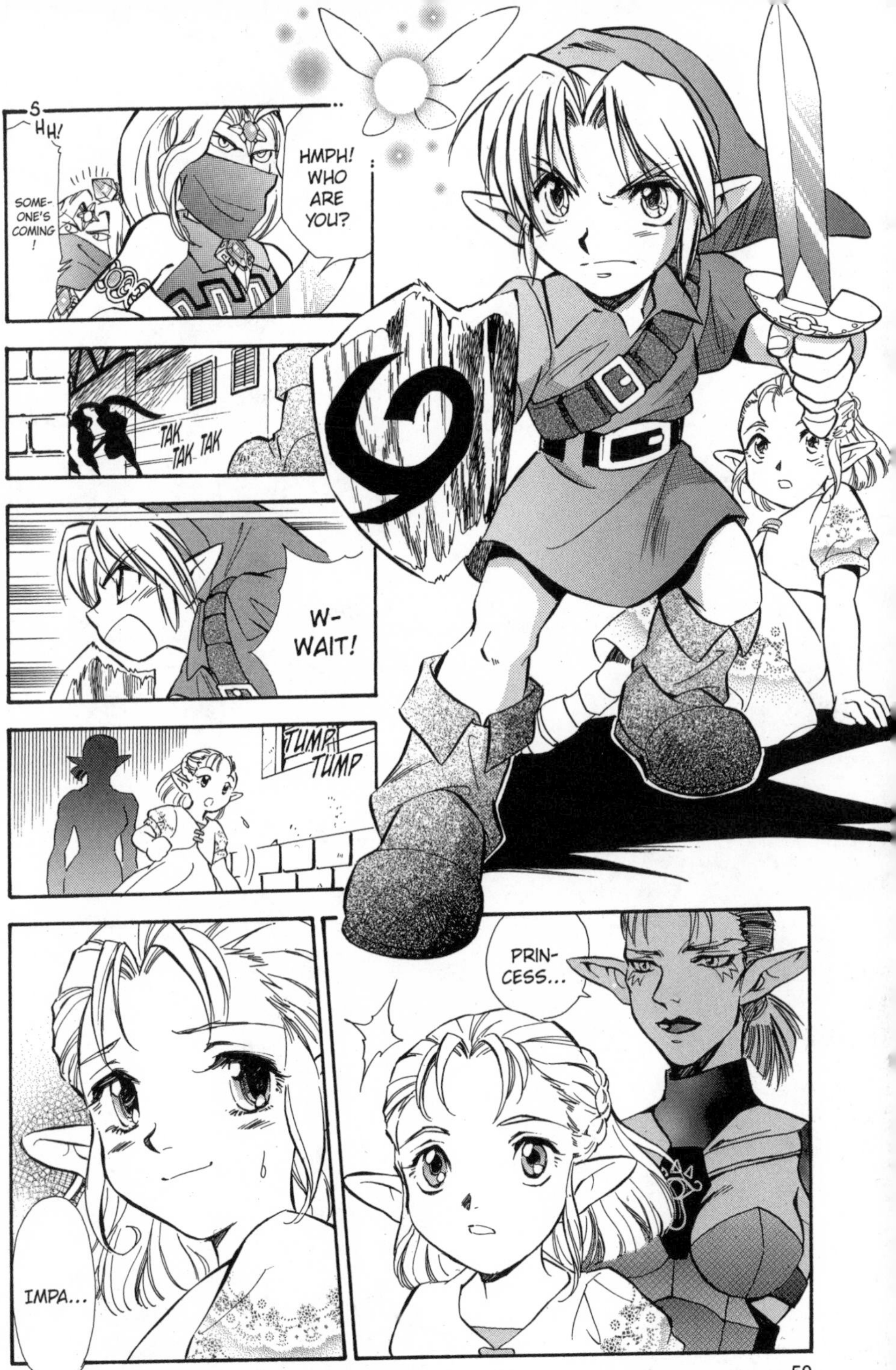
HMPH! WHO ARE YOU?
S HH!
SOME-ONE'S COMING!
TAK TAK TAK
W-WAIT!
TUMP TUMP
PRIN-CESS...
IMPA...

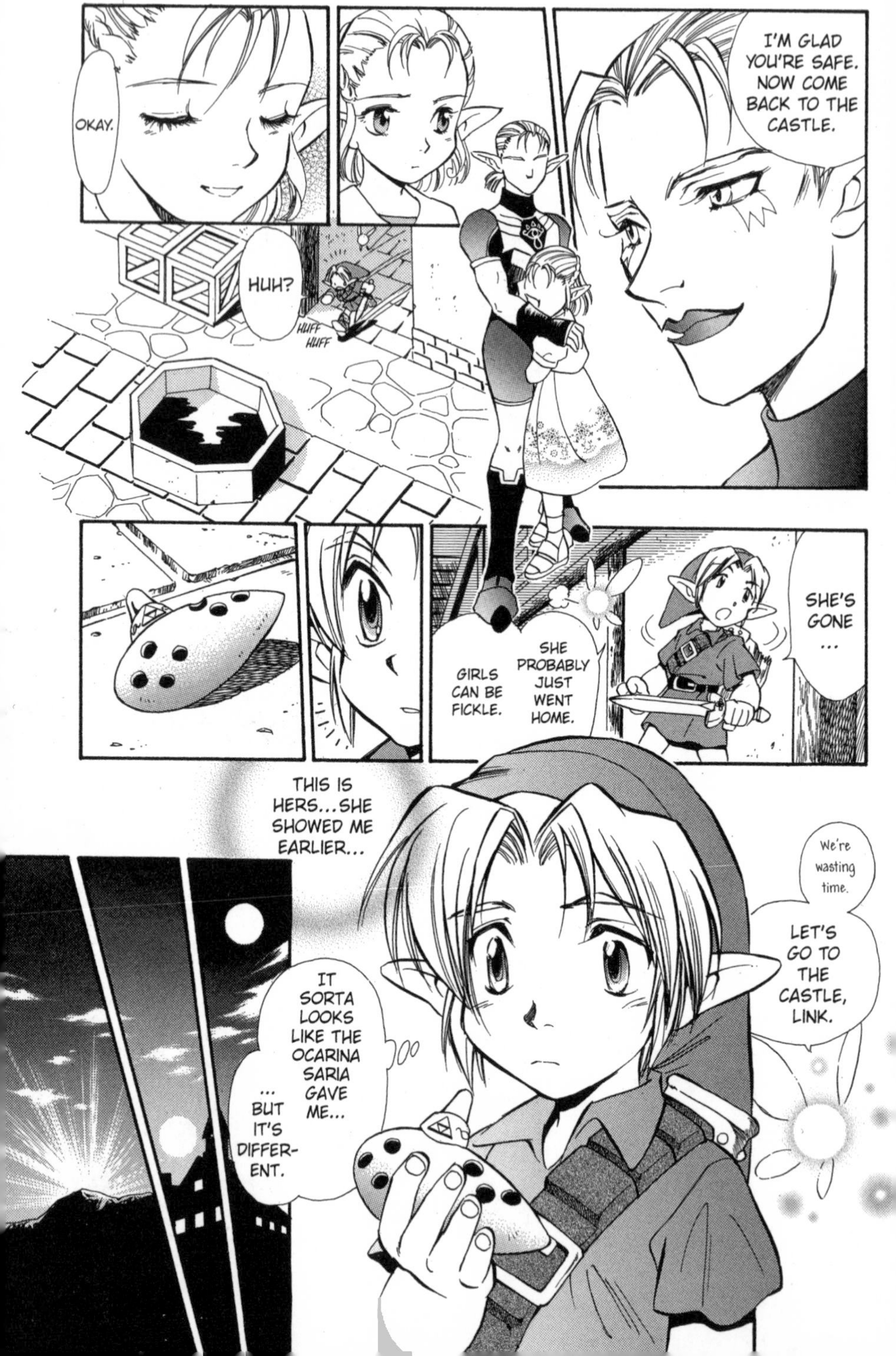
I'M GLAD YOU'RE SAFE. NOW COME BACK TO THE CASTLE.
OKAY.
HUH?
HUFF HUFF
SHE'S GONE ...
SHE PROBABLY JUST WENT HOME.
GIRLS CAN BE FICKLE.
THIS IS HERS...SHE SHOWED ME EARLIER...
We're wasting time.
LET'S GO TO THE CASTLE, LINK.
IT SORTA LOOKS LIKE THE OCARINA SARIA GAVE ME...
...BUT IT'S DIFFERENT.

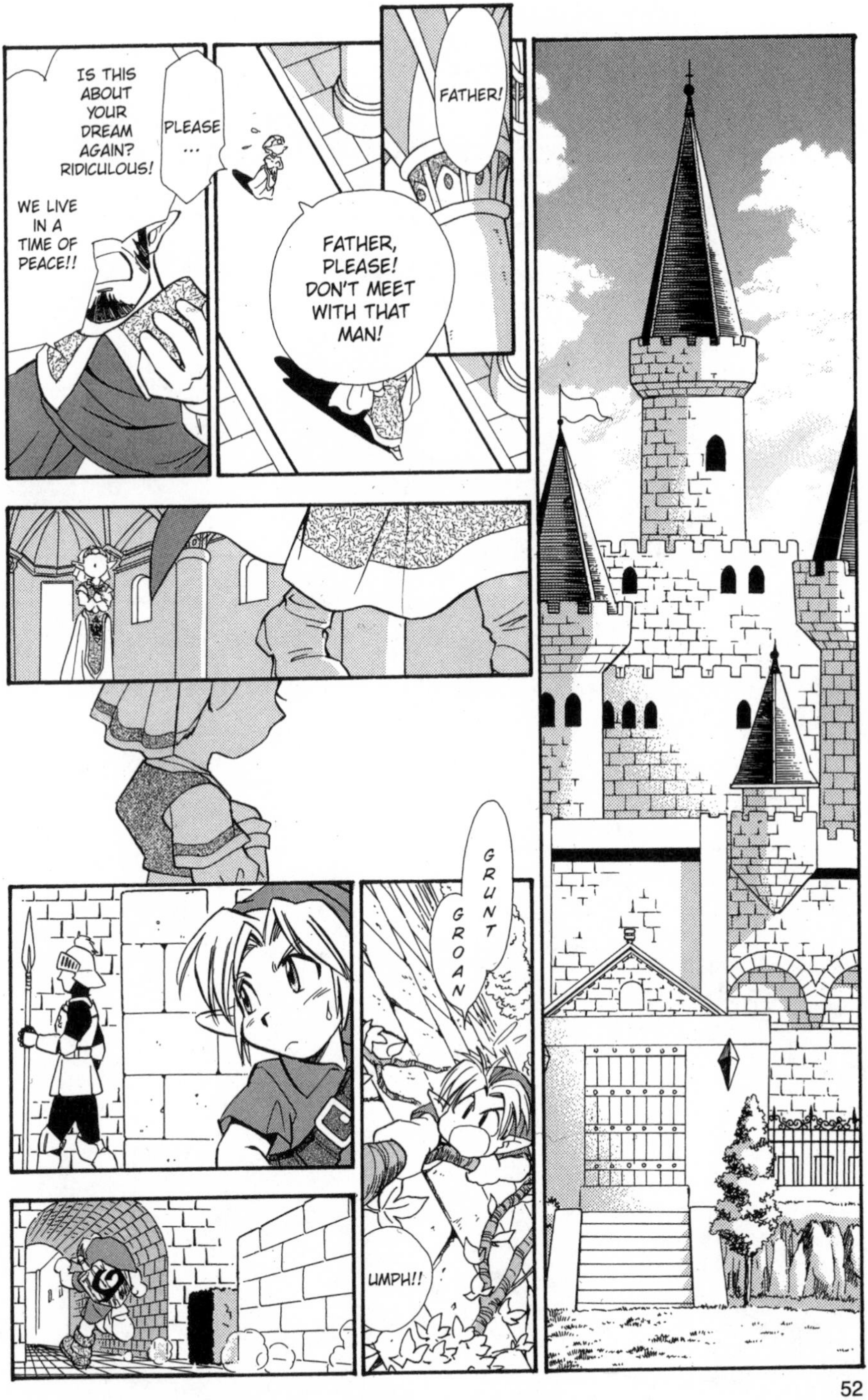
FATHER!
FATHER, PLEASE! DON'T MEET WITH THAT MAN!
PLEASE...
IS THIS ABOUT YOUR DREAM AGAIN? RIDICULOUS!
WE LIVE IN A TIME OF PEACE!!
GRUNT
GROAN
UMPH!!

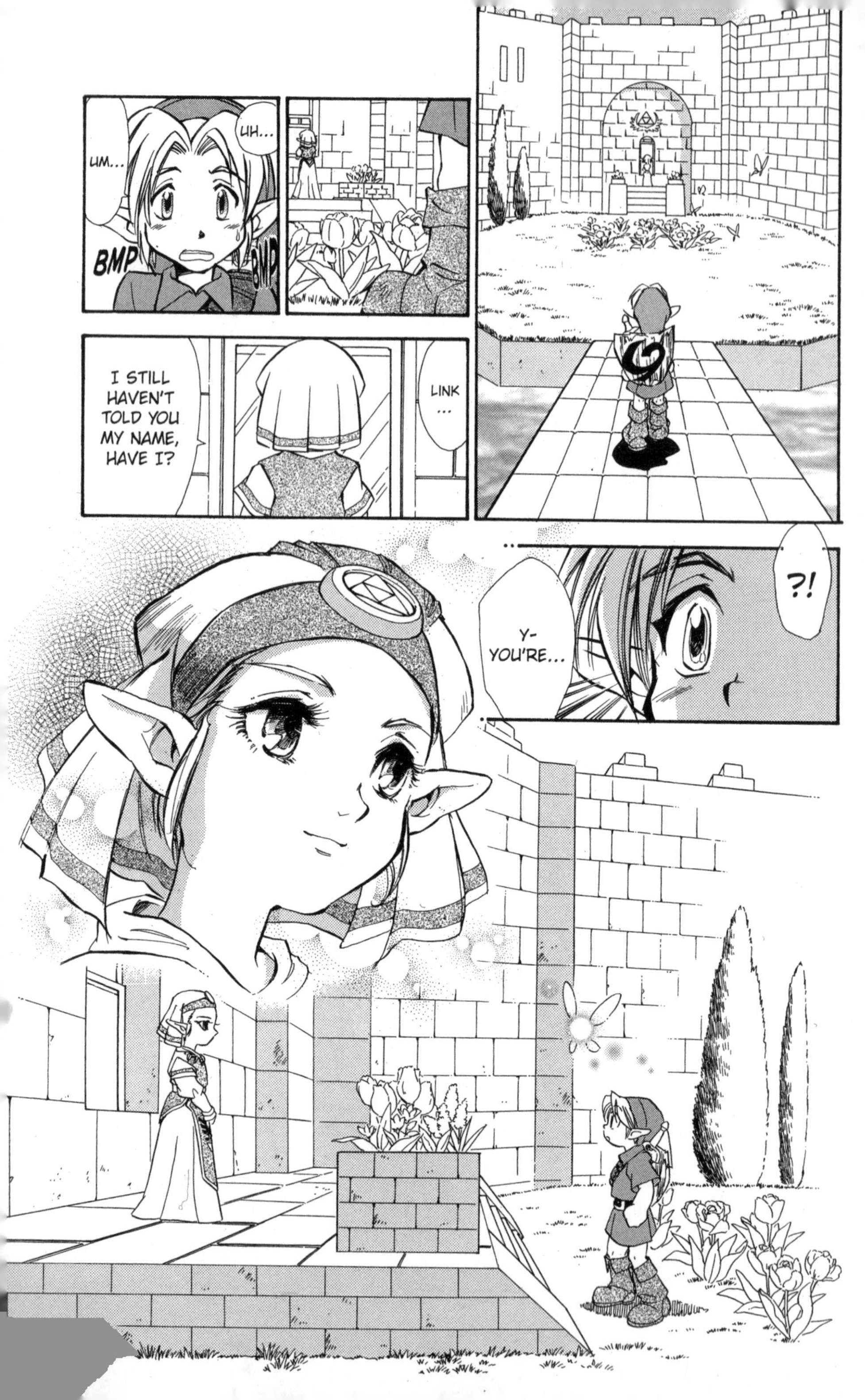
UH...
UM...
BMP
BMP
LINK...
I STILL HAVEN'T TOLD YOU MY NAME, HAVE I?
?!
Y- YOU'RE...

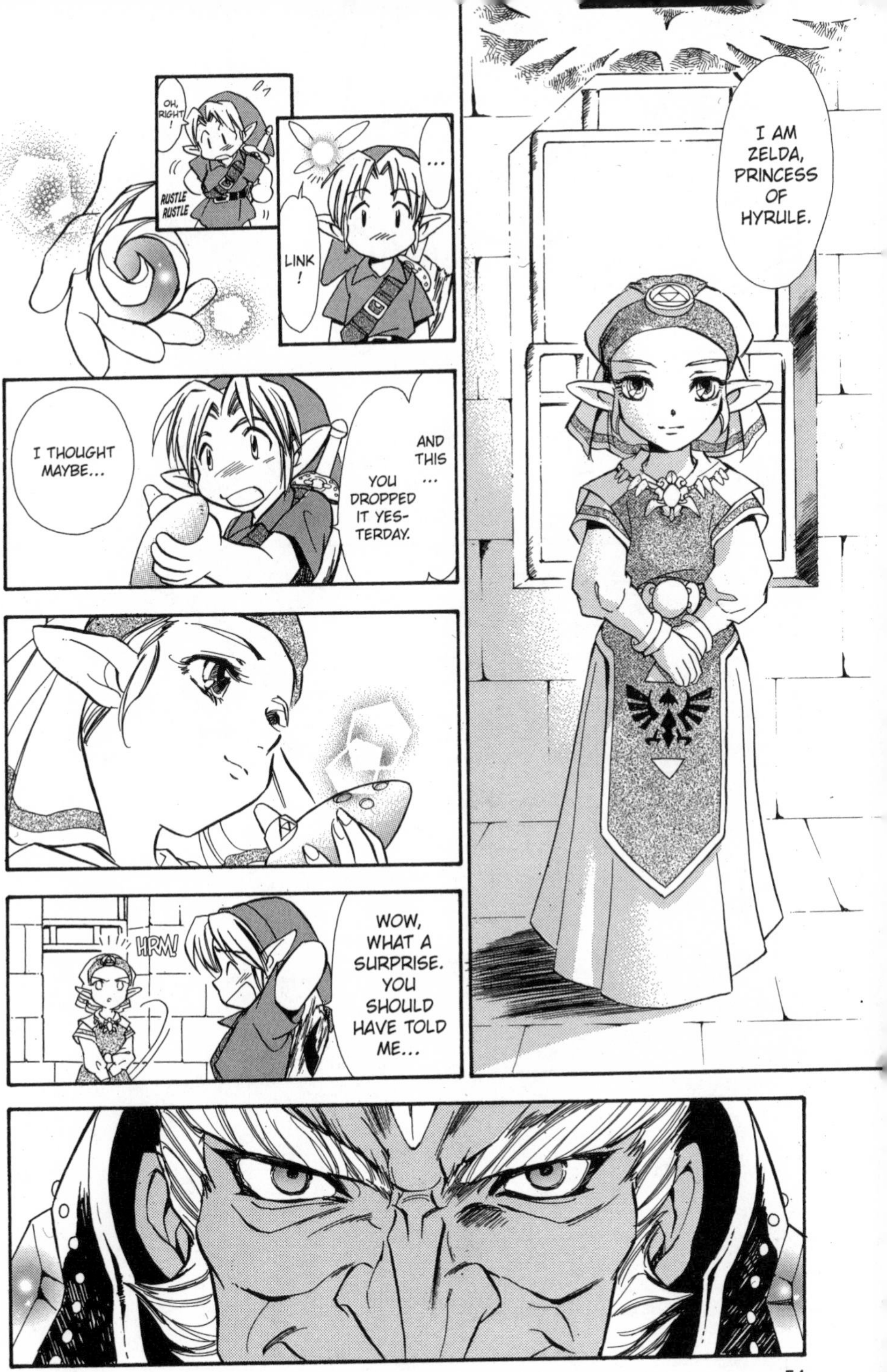
I AM ZELDA, PRINCESS OF HYRULE.
...
LINK!
OH, RIGHT!
RUSTLE RUSTLE
AND THIS...
YOU DROPPED IT YES-TERDAY.
I THOUGHT MAYBE...
WOW, WHAT A SURPRISE. YOU SHOULD HAVE TOLD ME...
HRM!

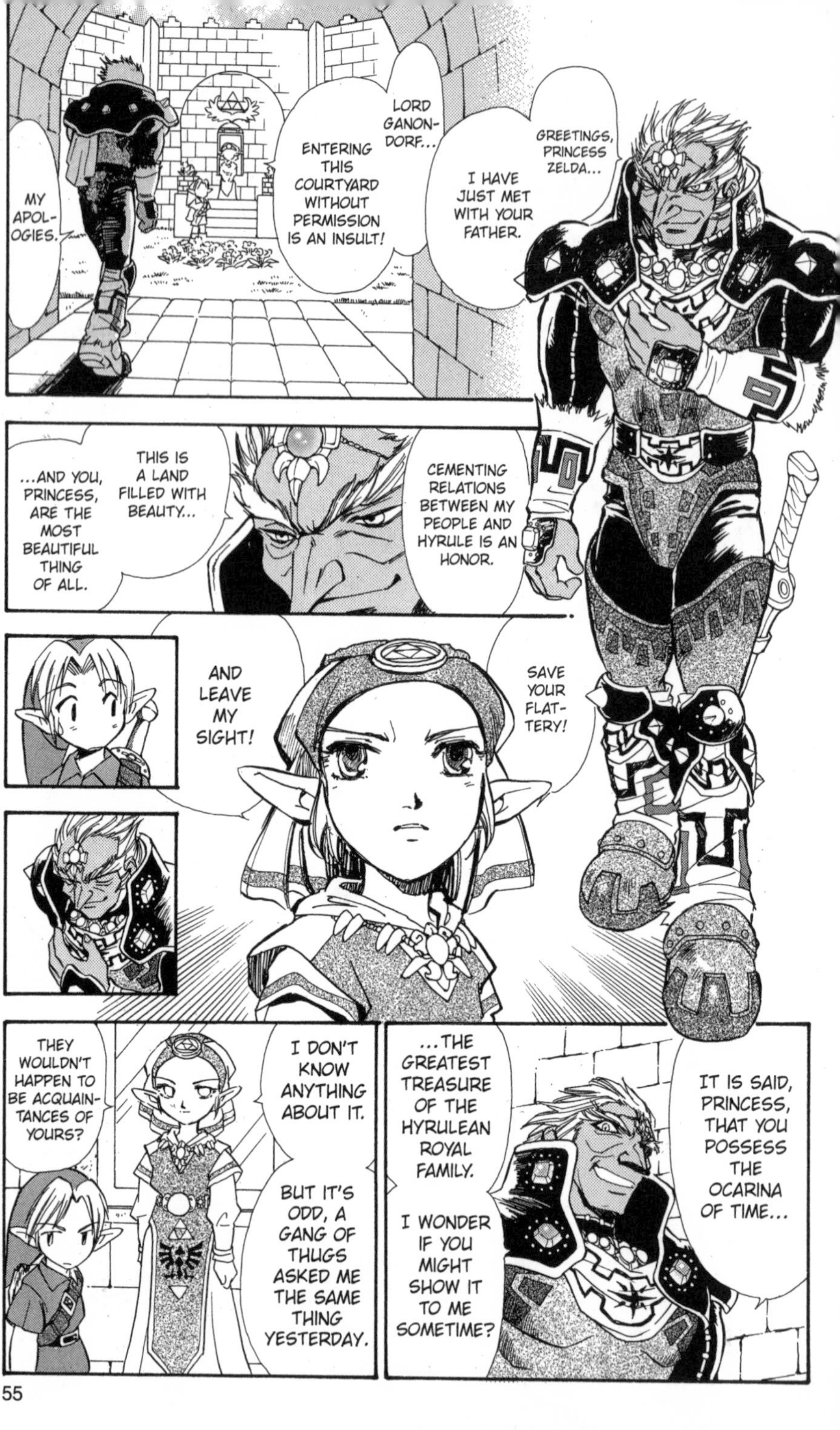
GREETINGS, PRINCESS ZELDA...
I HAVE JUST MET WITH YOUR FATHER.
LORD GANONDORF...
ENTERING THIS COURTYARD WITHOUT PERMISSION IS AN INSULT!
MY APOLOGIES.
CEMENTING RELATIONS BETWEEN MY PEOPLE AND HYRULE IS AN HONOR.
THIS IS A LAND FILLED WITH BEAUTY...
...AND YOU, PRINCESS, ARE THE MOST BEAUTIFUL THING OF ALL.
SAVE YOUR FLATTERY!
AND LEAVE MY SIGHT!
IT IS SAID, PRINCESS, THAT YOU POSSESS THE OCARINA OF TIME...
...THE GREATEST TREASURE OF THE HYRULEAN ROYAL FAMILY.
I WONDER IF YOU MIGHT SHOW IT TO ME SOMETIME?
I DON'T KNOW ANYTHING ABOUT IT.
BUT IT'S ODD, A GANG OF THUGS ASKED ME THE SAME THING YESTERDAY.
THEY WOULDN'T HAPPEN TO BE ACQUAINTANCES OF YOURS?

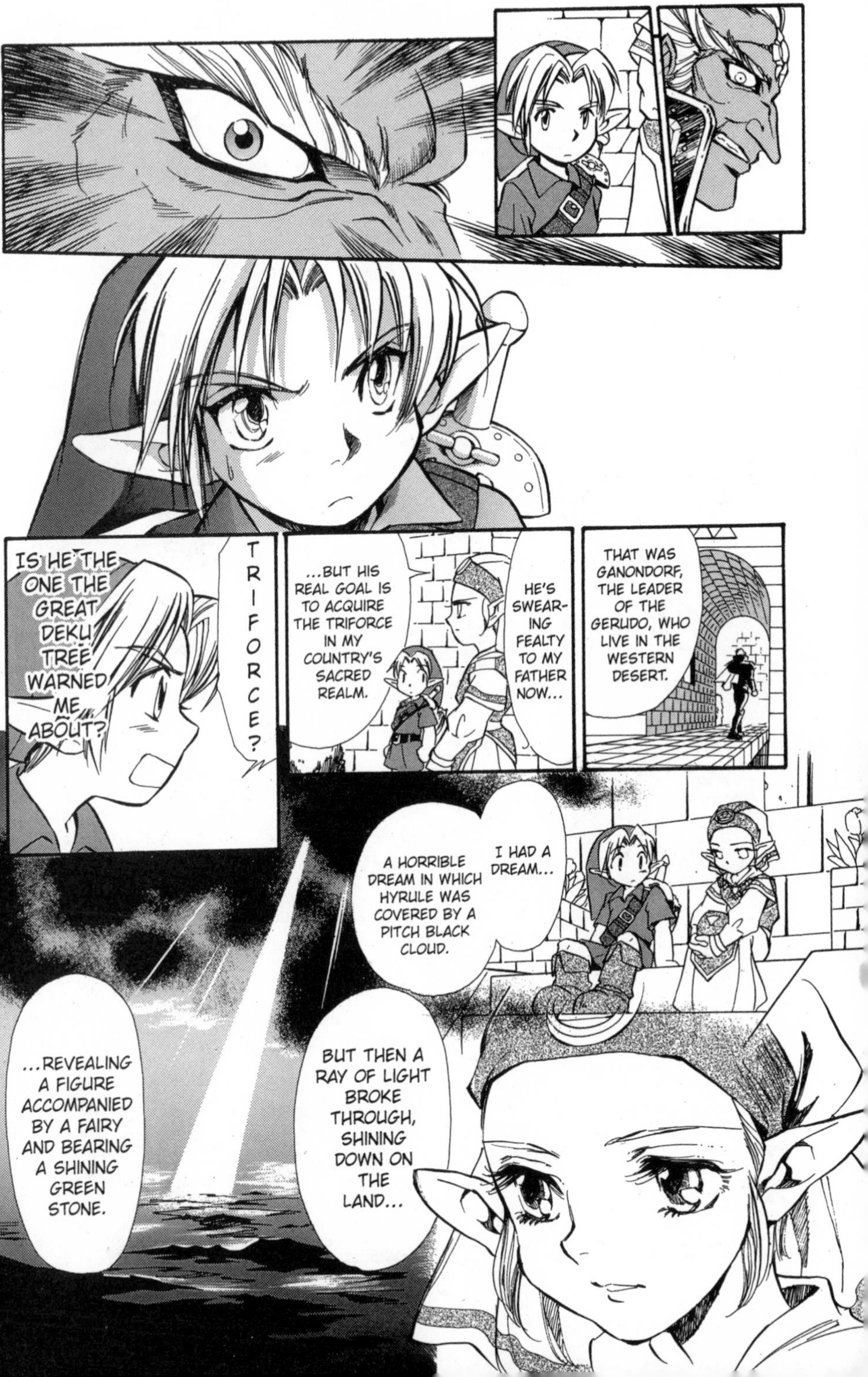
THAT WAS GANONDORF, THE LEADER OF THE GERUDO, WHO LIVE IN THE WESTERN DESERT.
HE'S SWEAR-ING FEALTY TO MY FATHER NOW...
...BUT HIS REAL GOAL IS TO ACQUIRE THE TRIFORCE IN MY COUNTRY'S SACRED REALM.
TRIFORCE?
IS HE THE ONE THE GREAT DEKU TREE WARNED ME ABOUT?
I HAD A DREAM...
A HORRIBLE DREAM IN WHICH HYRULE WAS COVERED BY A PITCH BLACK CLOUD.
BUT THEN A RAY OF LIGHT BROKE THROUGH, SHINING DOWN ON THE LAND...
...REVEALING A FIGURE ACCOMPANIED BY A FAIRY AND BEARING A SHINING GREEN STONE.

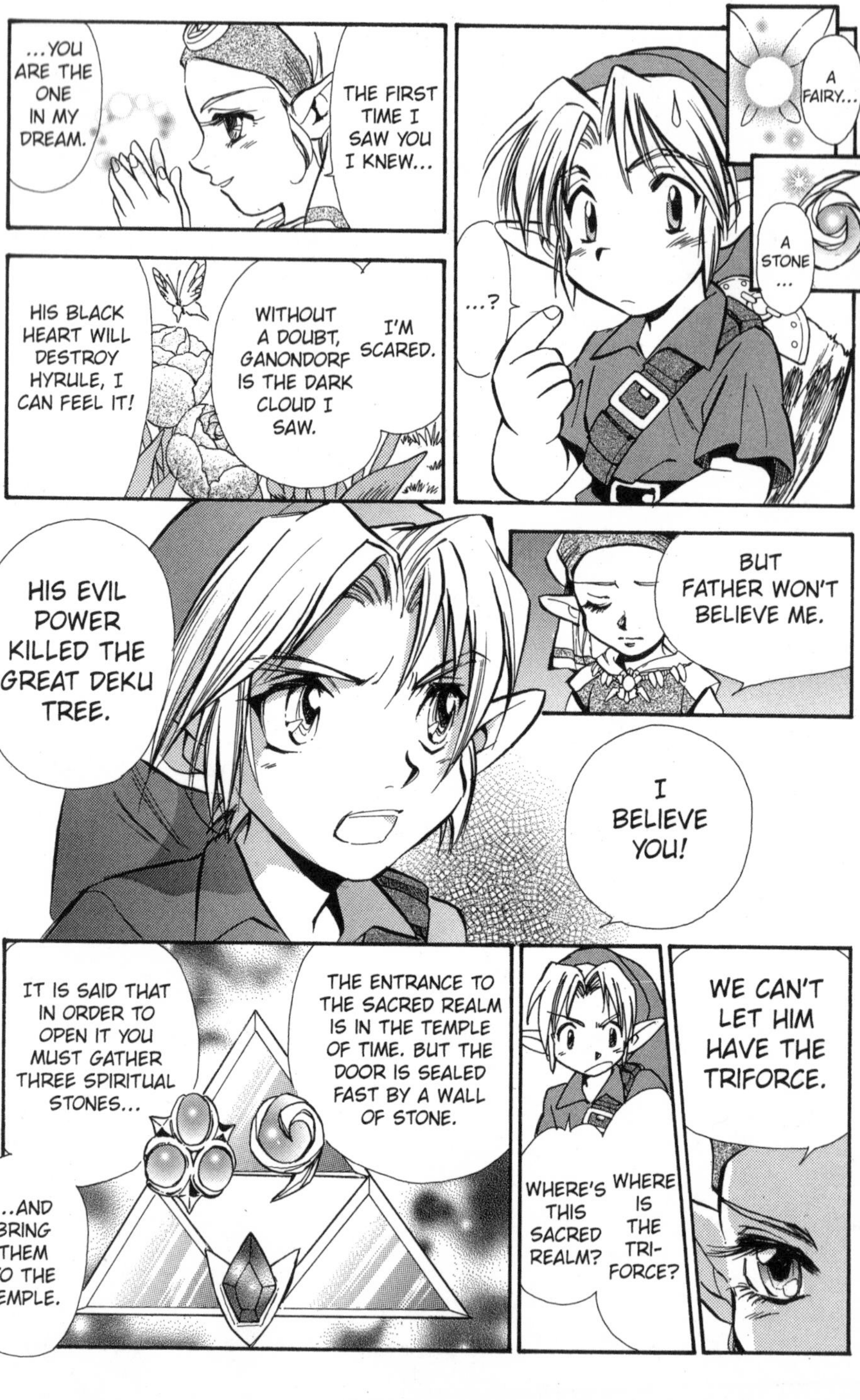
A FAIRY...
A STONE...
...?
THE FIRST TIME I SAW YOU I KNEW...
...YOU ARE THE ONE IN MY DREAM.
I'M SCARED.
WITHOUT A DOUBT, GANONDORF IS THE DARK CLOUD I SAW.
HIS BLACK HEART WILL DESTROY HYRULE, I CAN FEEL IT!
BUT FATHER WON'T BELIEVE ME.
I BELIEVE YOU!
HIS EVIL POWER KILLED THE GREAT DEKU TREE.
WE CAN'T LET HIM HAVE THE TRIFORCE.
WHERE IS THE TRI-FORCE?
WHERE'S THIS SACRED REALM?
THE ENTRANCE TO THE SACRED REALM IS IN THE TEMPLE OF TIME. BUT THE DOOR IS SEALED FAST BY A WALL OF STONE.
IT IS SAID THAT IN ORDER TO OPEN IT YOU MUST GATHER THREE SPIRITUAL STONES...
...AND BRING THEM TO THE TEMPLE.

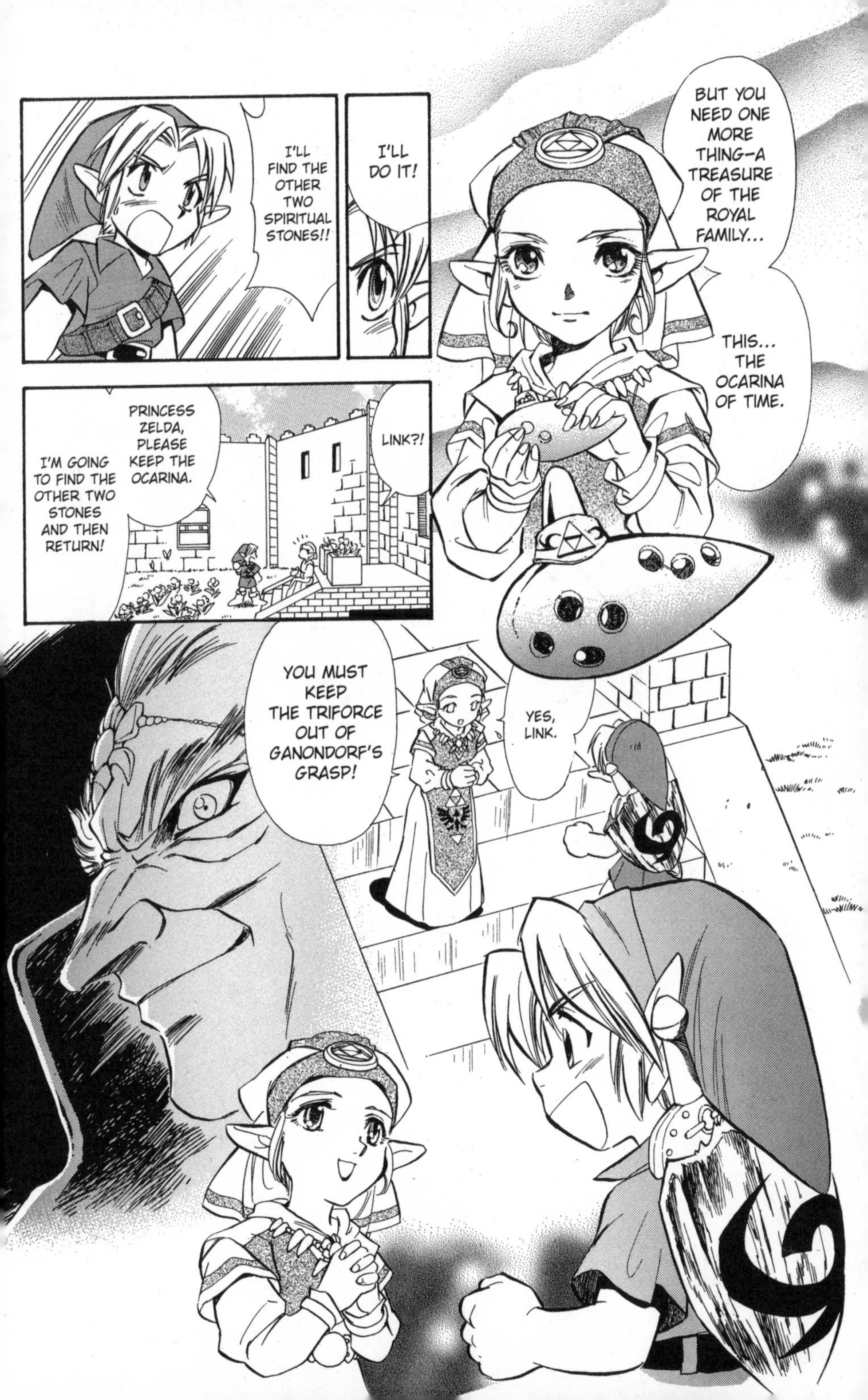
BUT YOU NEED ONE MORE THING—A TREASURE OF THE ROYAL FAMILY...
THIS... THE OCARINA OF TIME.
I'LL DO IT!
I'LL FIND THE OTHER TWO SPIRITUAL STONES!!
LINK?!
PRINCESS ZELDA, PLEASE KEEP THE OCARINA.
I'M GOING TO FIND THE OTHER TWO STONES AND THEN RETURN!
YOU MUST KEEP THE TRIFORCE OUT OF GANONDORF'S GRASP!
YES, LINK.

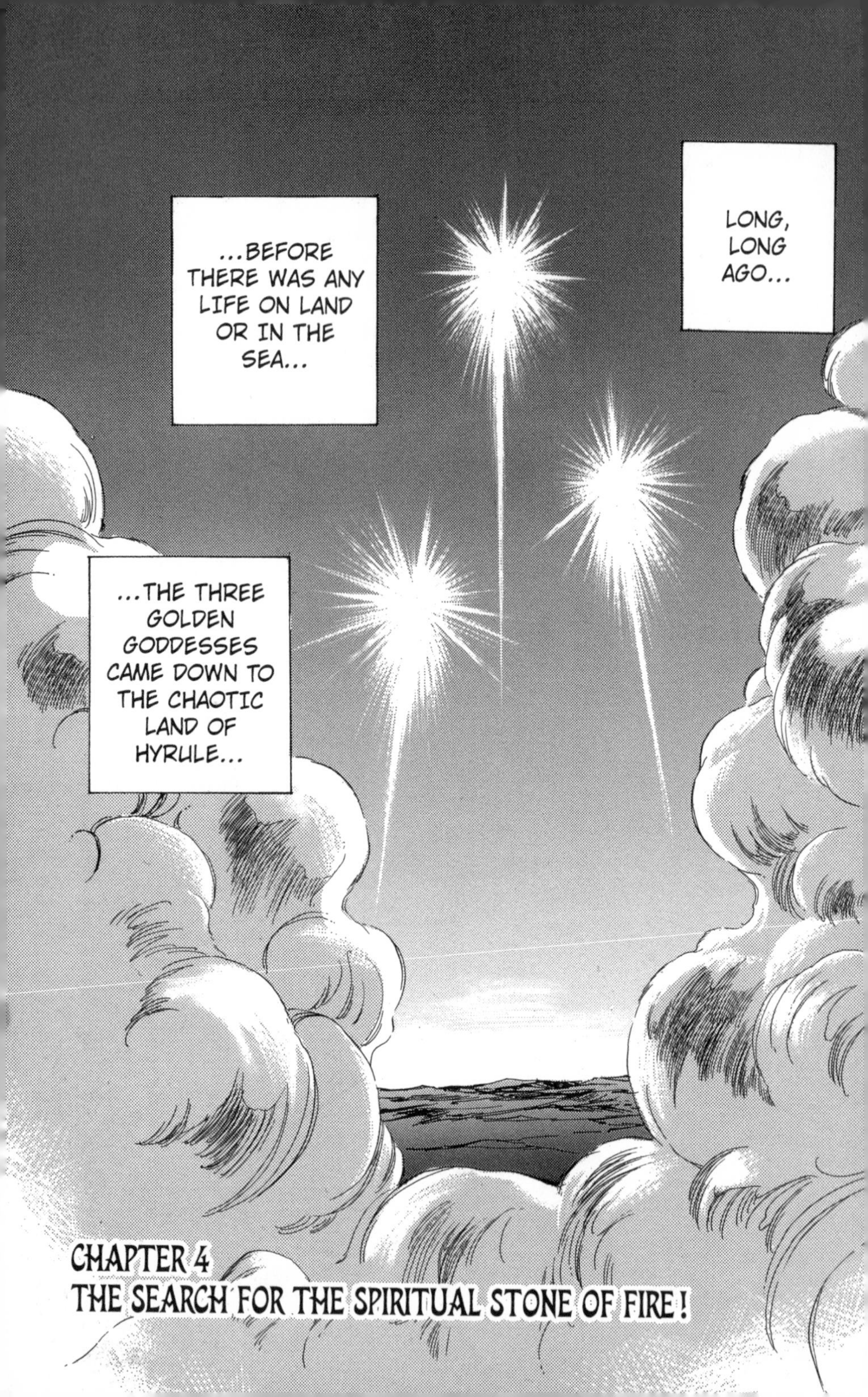
LONG, LONG AGO...
...BEFORE THERE WAS ANY LIFE ON LAND OR IN THE SEA...
...THE THREE GOLDEN GODDESSES CAME DOWN TO THE CHAOTIC LAND OF HYRULE...
CHAPTER 4
THE SEARCH FOR THE SPIRITUAL STONE OF FIRE!

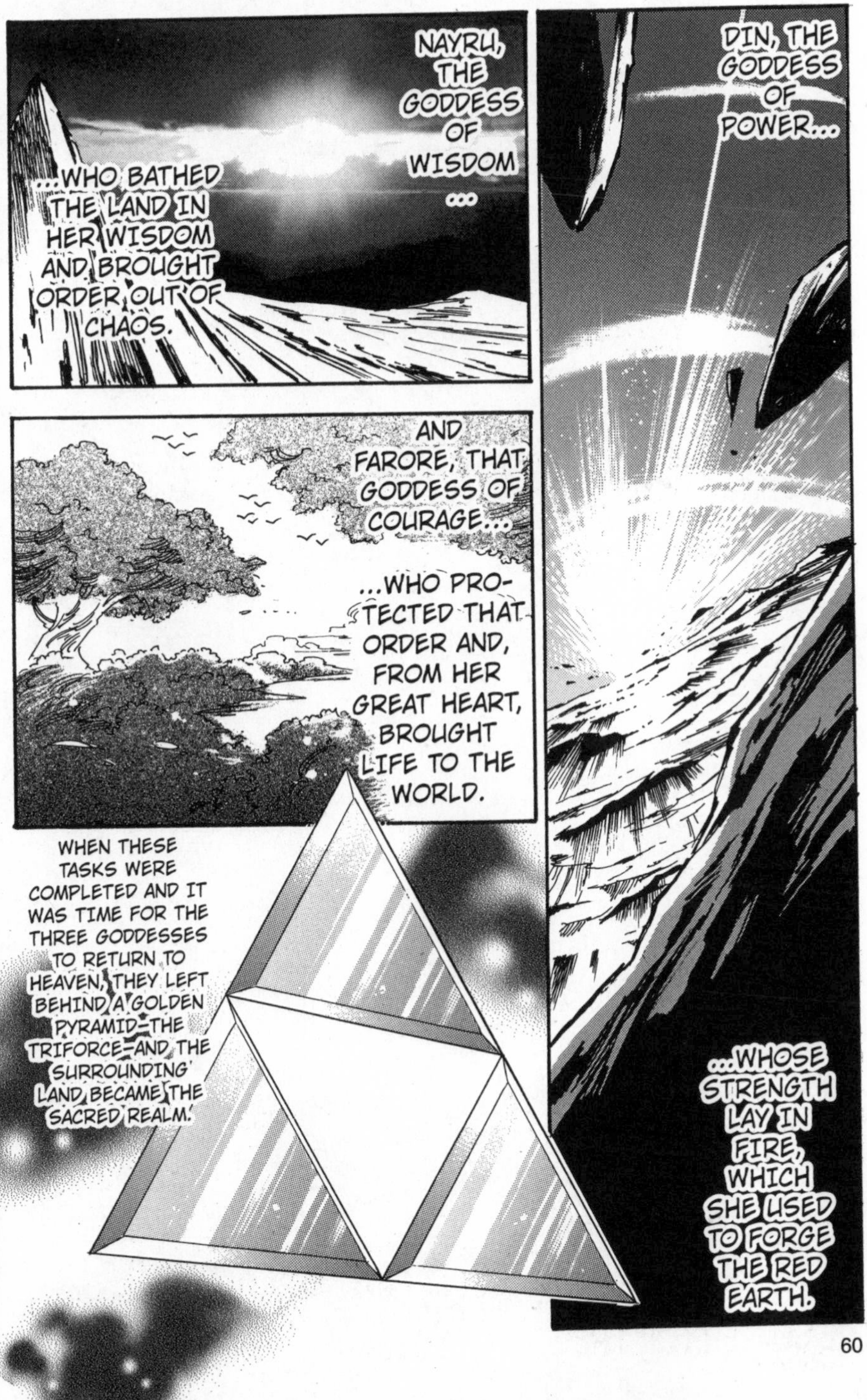
DIN, THE GODDESS OF POWER...
...WHOSE STRENGTH LAY IN FIRE, WHICH SHE USED TO FORGE THE RED EARTH.
NAYRU, THE GODDESS OF WISDOM...
...WHO BATHED THE LAND IN HER WISDOM AND BROUGHT ORDER OUT OF CHAOS.
AND FARORE, THAT GODDESS OF COURAGE...
...WHO PROTECTED THAT ORDER AND, FROM HER GREAT HEART, BROUGHT LIFE TO THE WORLD.
WHEN THESE TASKS WERE COMPLETED AND IT WAS TIME FOR THE THREE GODDESSES TO RETURN TO HEAVEN, THEY LEFT BEHIND A GOLDEN PYRAMID—THE TRIFORCE—AND THE SURROUNDING LAND BECAME THE SACRED REALM.

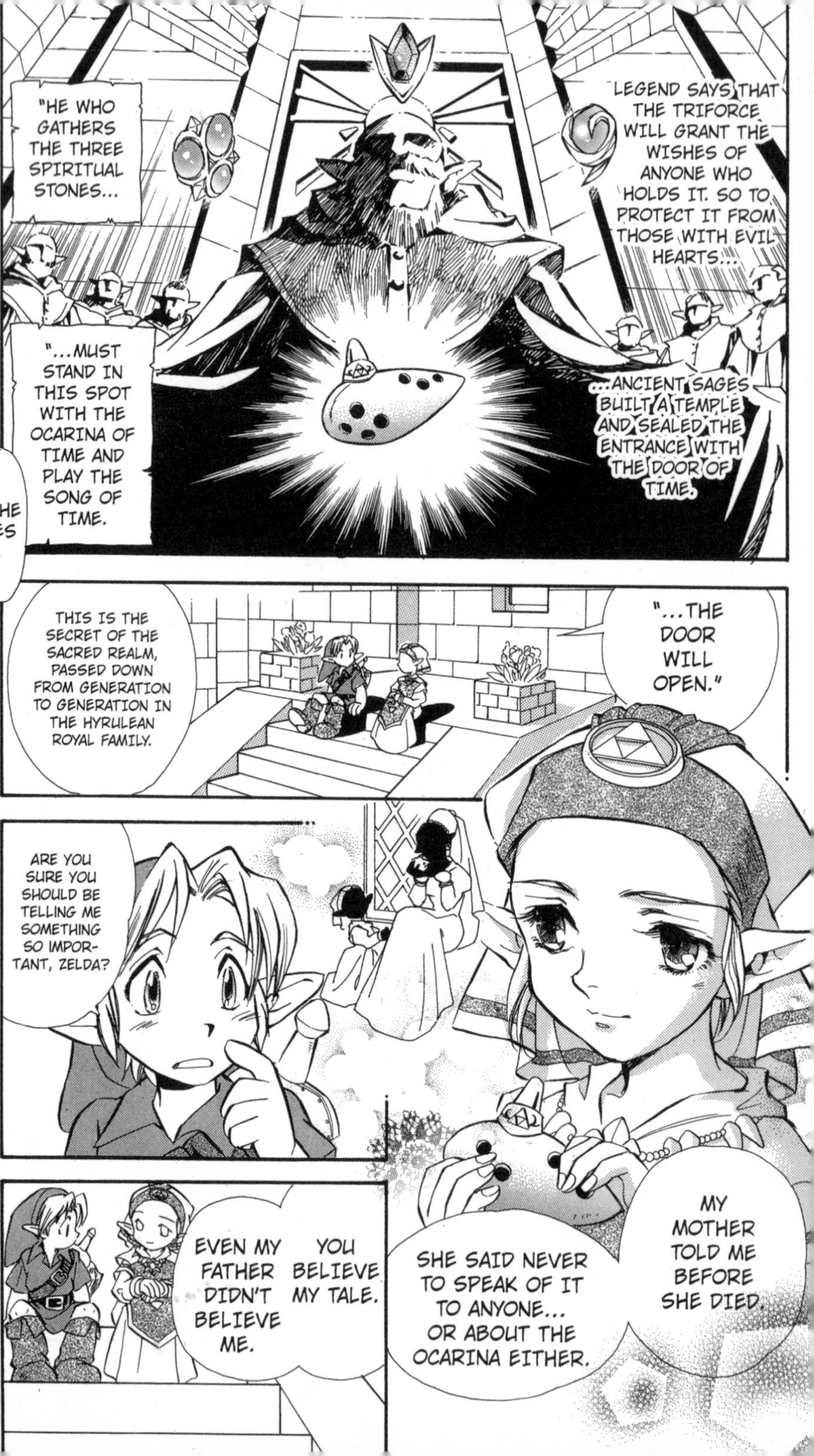
LEGEND SAYS THAT THE TRIFORCE WILL GRANT THE WISHES OF ANYONE WHO HOLDS IT. SO TO PROTECT IT FROM THOSE WITH EVIL HEARTS...
...ANCIENT SAGES BUILT A TEMPLE AND SEALED THE ENTRANCE WITH THE DOOR OF TIME.
"HE WHO GATHERS THE THREE SPIRITUAL STONES...
"...MUST STAND IN THIS SPOT WITH THE OCARINA OF TIME AND PLAY THE SONG OF TIME.
"IF HE DOES...
"...THE DOOR WILL OPEN."
THIS IS THE SECRET OF THE SACRED REALM, PASSED DOWN FROM GENERATION TO GENERATION IN THE HYRULEAN ROYAL FAMILY.
ARE YOU SURE YOU SHOULD BE TELLING ME SOMETHING SO IMPORTANT, ZELDA?
MY MOTHER TOLD ME BEFORE SHE DIED.
SHE SAID NEVER TO SPEAK OF IT TO ANYONE... OR ABOUT THE OCARINA EITHER.
YOU BELIEVE MY TALE.
EVEN MY FATHER DIDN'T BELIEVE ME.

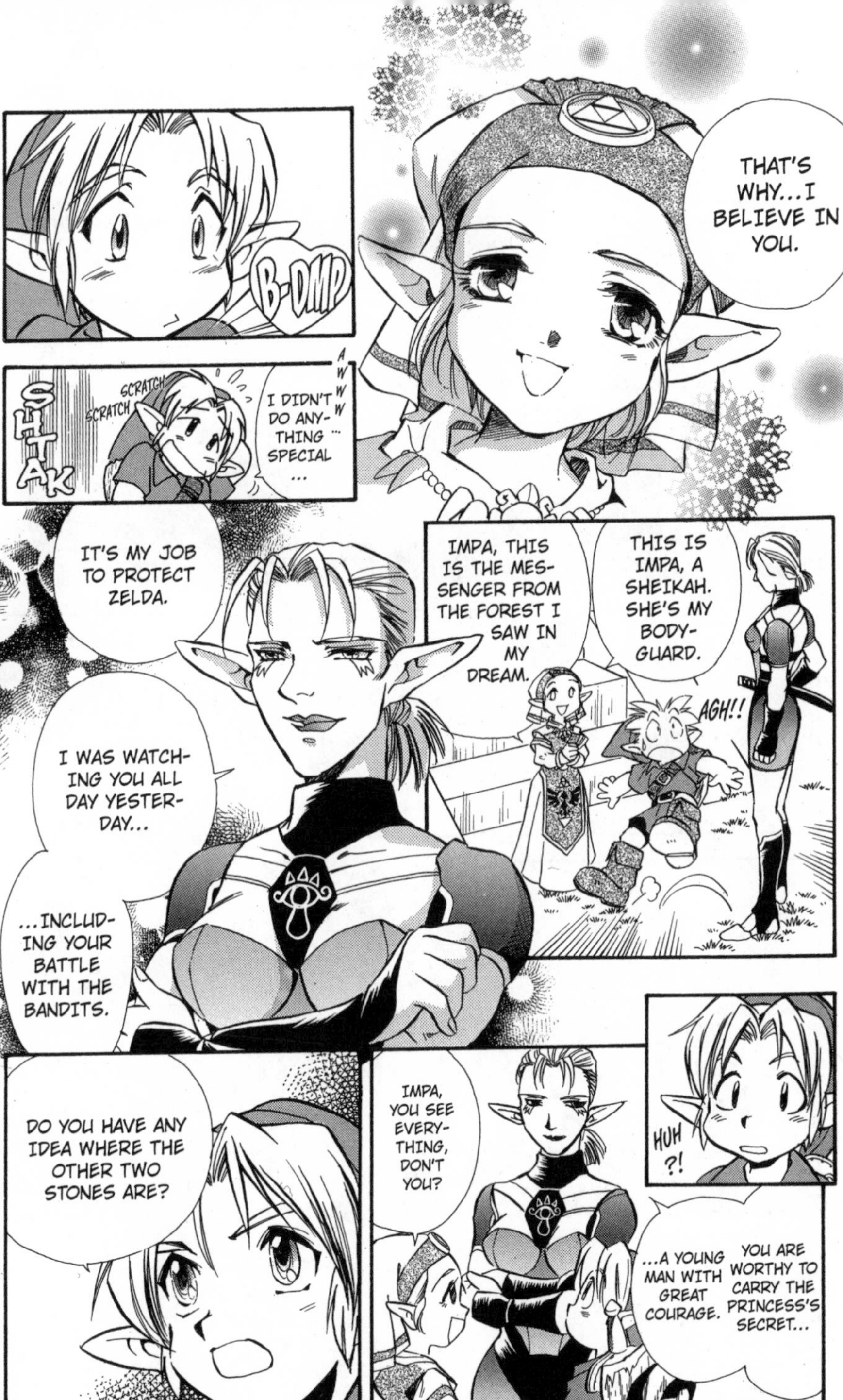
THAT'S WHY...I BELIEVE IN YOU.
B-DMP
SHTAK
SCRATCH SCRATCH
I DIDN'T DO ANYTHING SPECIAL...
AWWW...
THIS IS IMPA, A SHEIKAH. SHE'S MY BODYGUARD.
IMPA, THIS IS THE MESSENGER FROM THE FOREST I SAW IN MY DREAM.
AGH!!
IT'S MY JOB TO PROTECT ZELDA.
I WAS WATCHING YOU ALL DAY YESTERDAY...
...INCLUDING YOUR BATTLE WITH THE BANDITS.
HUH ?!
YOU ARE WORTHY TO CARRY THE PRINCESS'S SECRET...
...A YOUNG MAN WITH GREAT COURAGE.
IMPA, YOU SEE EVERYTHING, DON'T YOU?
DO YOU HAVE ANY IDEA WHERE THE OTHER TWO STONES ARE?

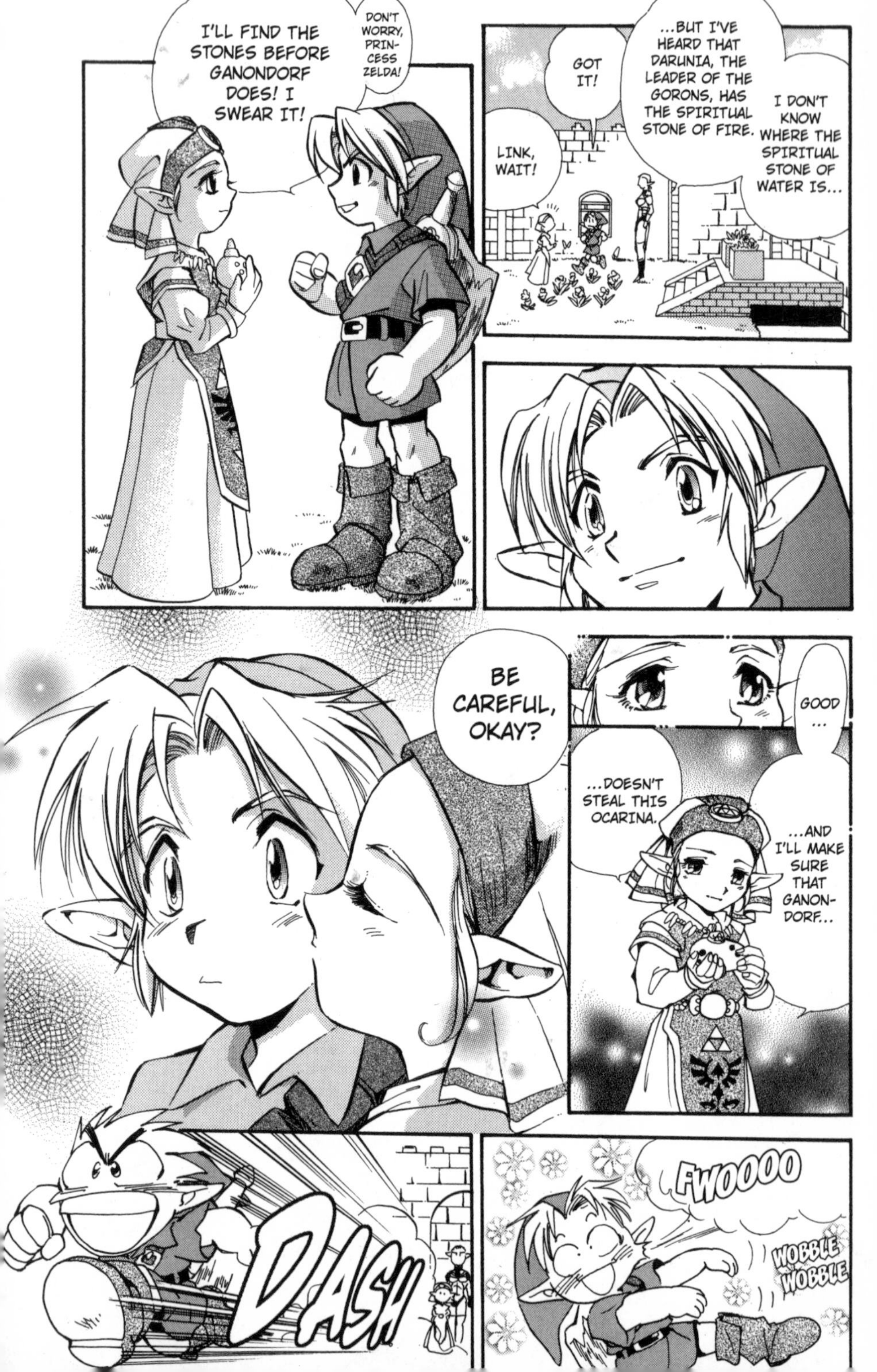
I DON'T KNOW WHERE THE SPIRITUAL STONE OF WATER IS...
...BUT I'VE HEARD THAT DARUNIA, THE LEADER OF THE GORONS, HAS THE SPIRITUAL STONE OF FIRE.
GOT IT!
LINK, WAIT!
DON'T WORRY, PRINCESS ZELDA!
I'LL FIND THE STONES BEFORE GANONDORF DOES! I SWEAR IT!
GOOD...
...AND I'LL MAKE SURE THAT GANONDORF...
...DOESN'T STEAL THIS OCARINA.
BE CAREFUL, OKAY?
FWOOOO
WOBBLE WOBBLE
DASH

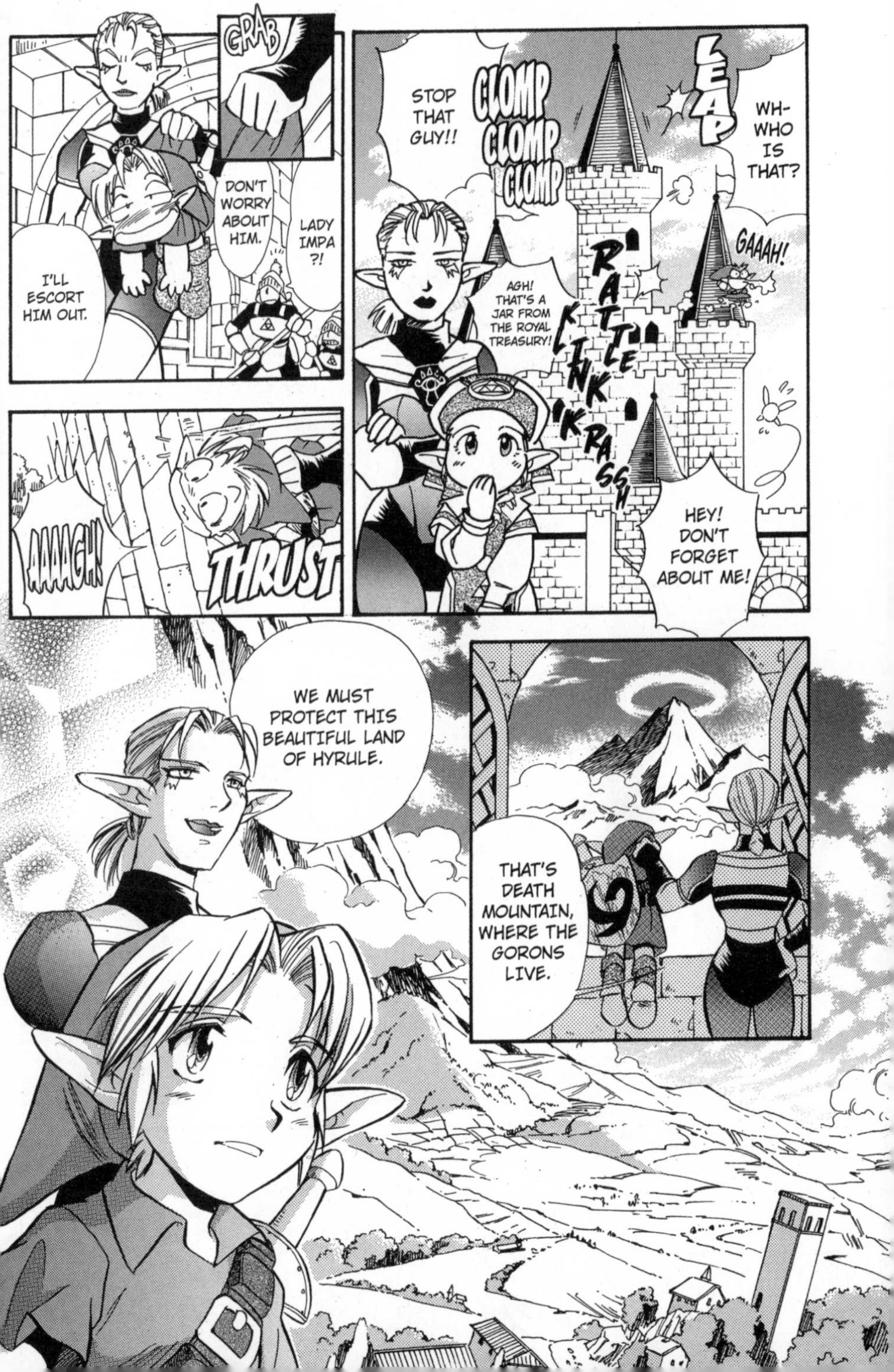
LEAP
WH-WHO IS THAT?
CLOMP CLOMP CLOMP
STOP THAT GUY!!
GAAAH!
RATTLE
KLINK
KRASSH
AGH! THAT'S A JAR FROM THE ROYAL TREASURY!
HEY! DON'T FORGET ABOUT ME!
GRAB
LADY IMPA?!
DON'T WORRY ABOUT HIM.
I'LL ESCORT HIM OUT.
THRUST
AAAAGH!
THAT'S DEATH MOUNTAIN, WHERE THE GORONS LIVE.
WE MUST PROTECT THIS BEAUTIFUL LAND OF HYRULE.

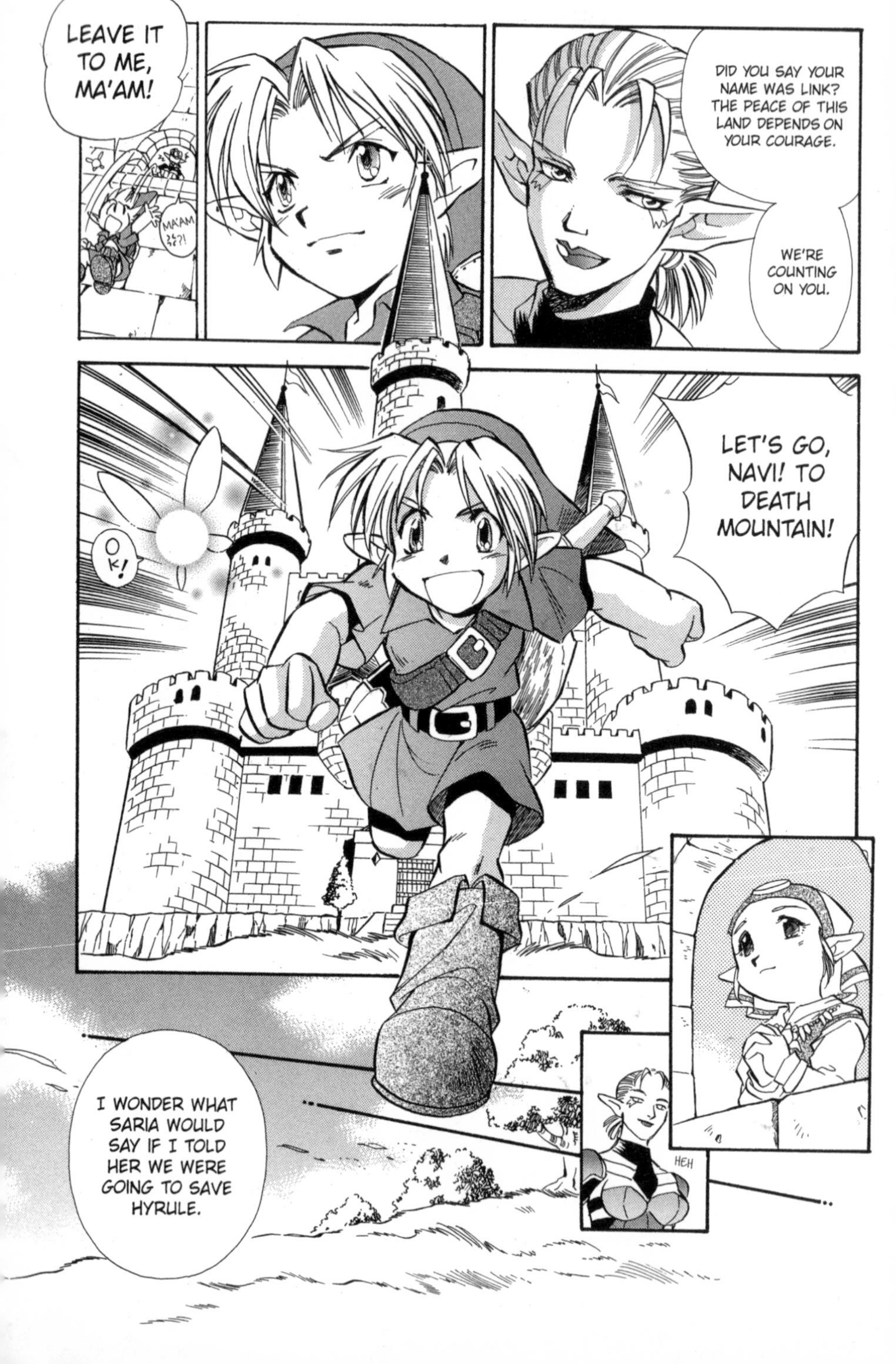
DID YOU SAY YOUR NAME WAS LINK? THE PEACE OF THIS LAND DEPENDS ON YOUR COURAGE.
WE'RE COUNTING ON YOU.
LEAVE IT TO ME, MA'AM!
MA'AM ??!
LET'S GO, NAVI! TO DEATH MOUNTAIN!
OK!
HEH
I WONDER WHAT SARIA WOULD SAY IF I TOLD HER WE WERE GOING TO SAVE HYRULE.

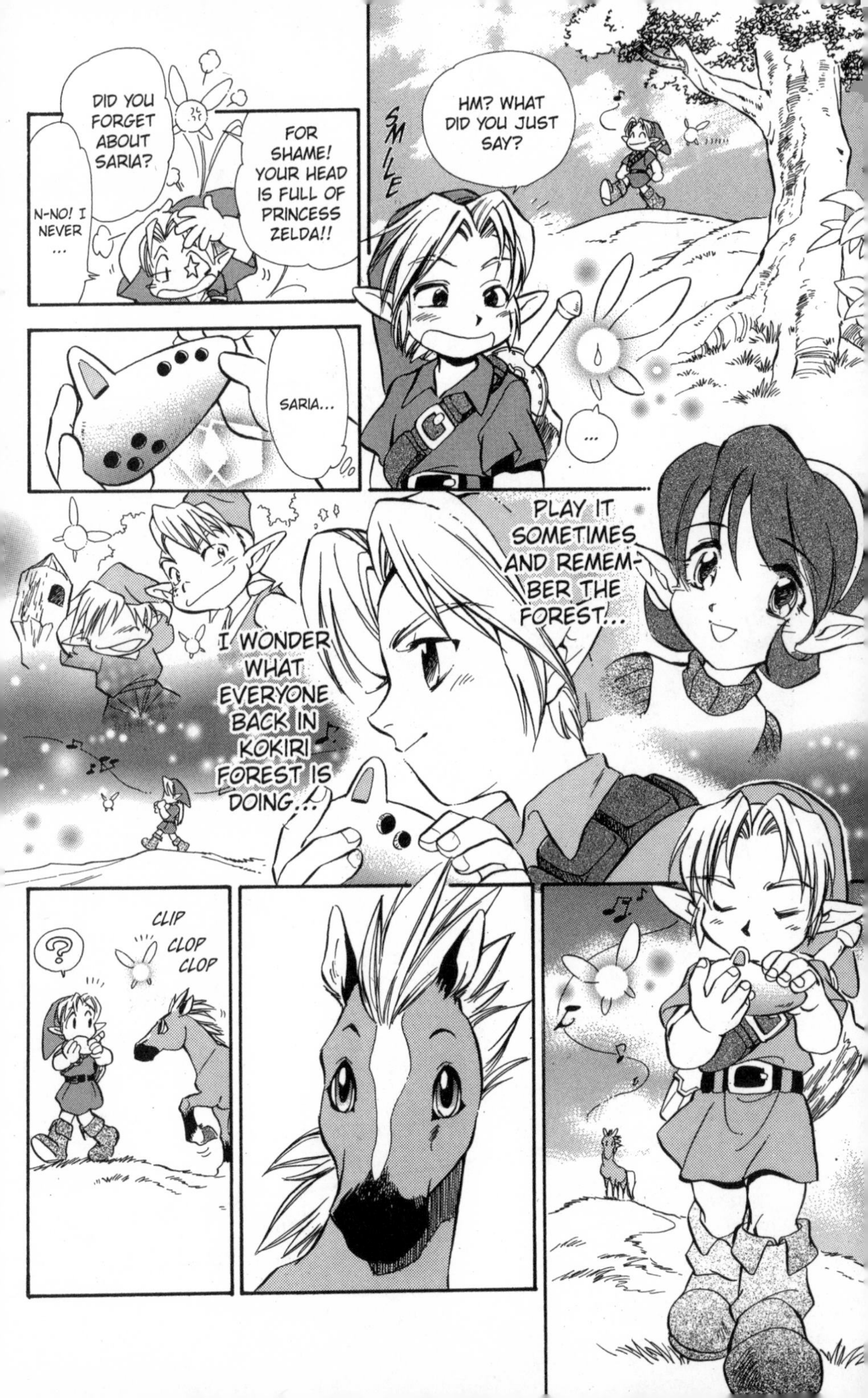
SMILE
HM? WHAT DID YOU JUST SAY?
FOR SHAME! YOUR HEAD IS FULL OF PRINCESS ZELDA!!
DID YOU FORGET ABOUT SARIA?
N-NO! I NEVER ...
...
SARIA...
PLAY IT SOMETIMES AND REMEMBER THE FOREST...
I WONDER WHAT EVERYONE BACK IN KOKIRI FOREST IS DOING...
CLIP
CLOP
CLOP
?

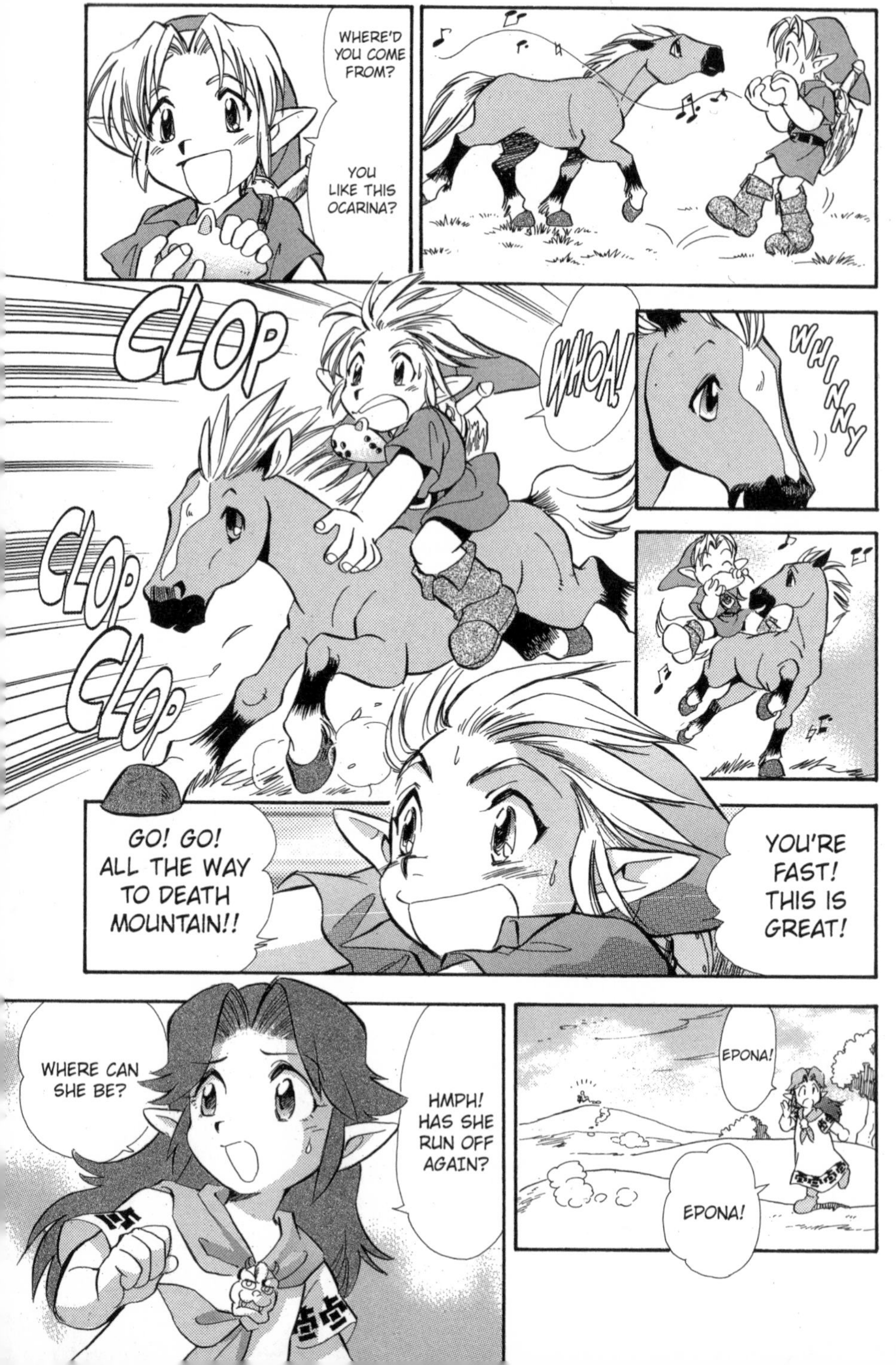
WHERE'D YOU COME FROM?
YOU LIKE THIS OCARINA?
WHINNY
WHOA!
CLOP
CLOP
CLOP
YOU'RE FAST! THIS IS GREAT!
GO! GO! ALL THE WAY TO DEATH MOUNTAIN!!
EPONA!
EPONA!
HMPH! HAS SHE RUN OFF AGAIN?
WHERE CAN SHE BE?

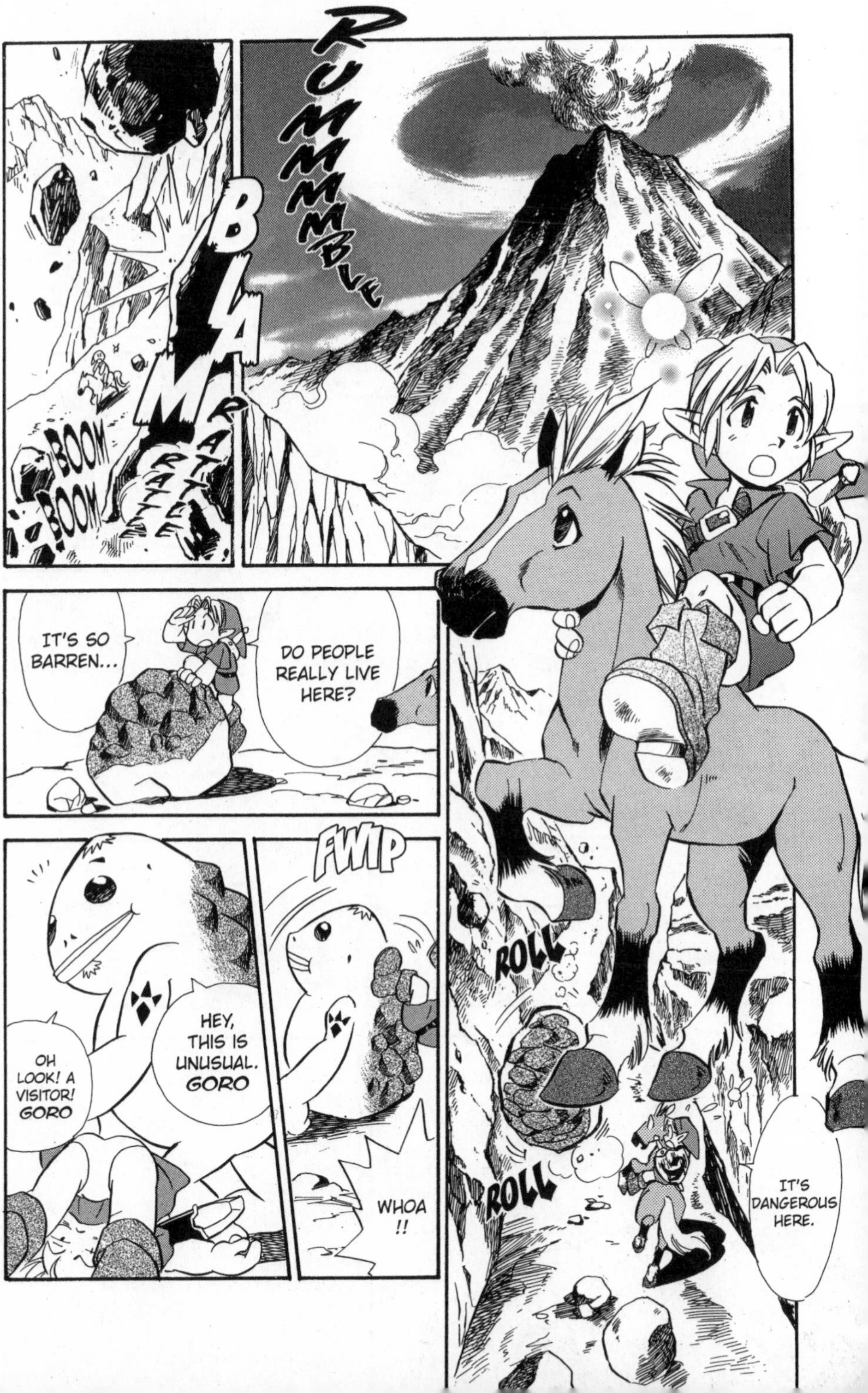

RUMMMMBLE
BLAM
RATTATTLE
BOOM BOOM
ROLL
ROLL
IT'S DANGEROUS HERE.
IT'S SO BARREN...
DO PEOPLE REALLY LIVE HERE?
FWIP
WHOA !!
HEY, THIS IS UNUSUAL. GORO
OH LOOK! A VISITOR! GORO

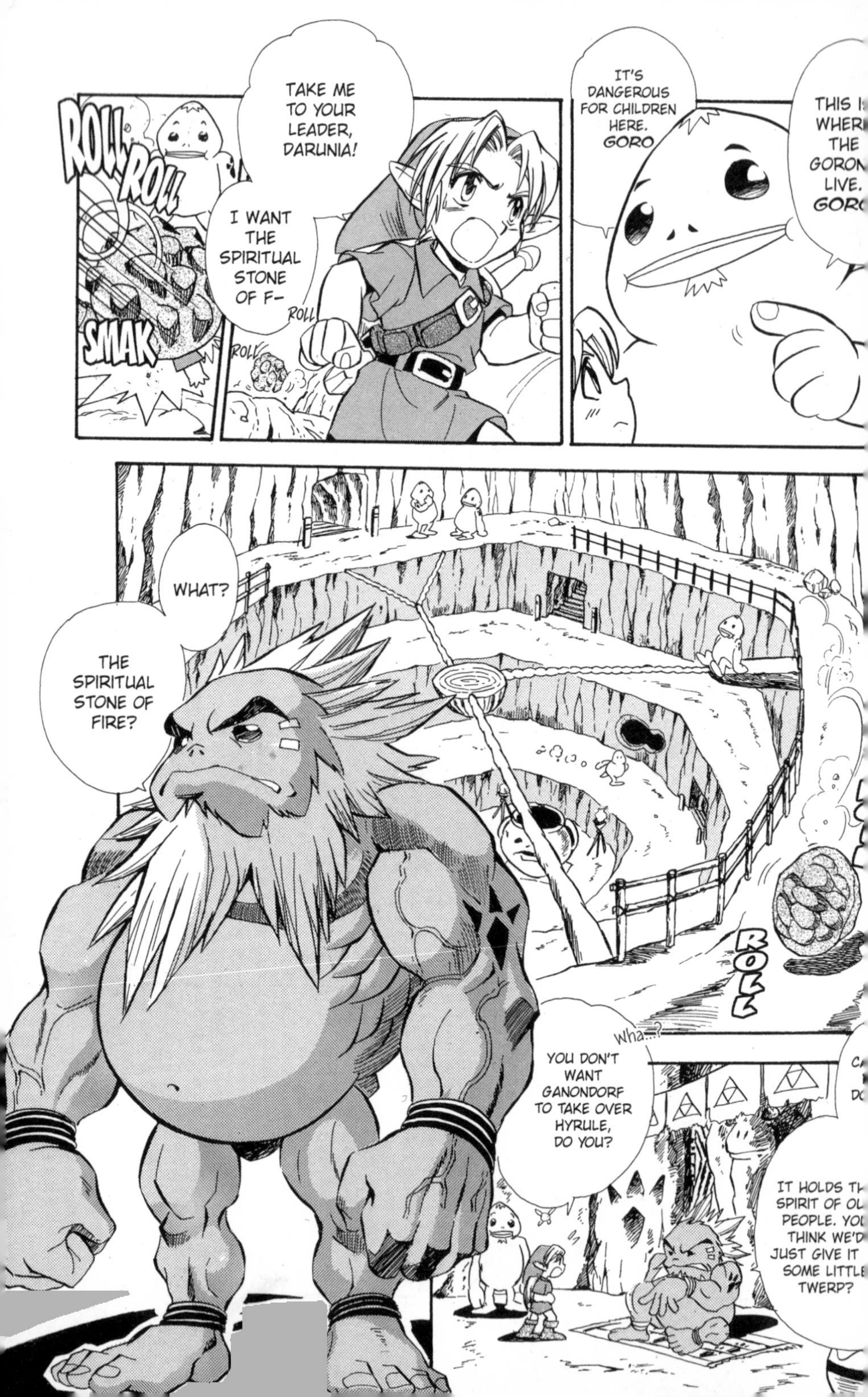
THIS I WHER THE GORON LIVE. GORO
IT'S DANGEROUS FOR CHILDREN HERE. GORO
TAKE ME TO YOUR LEADER, DARUNIA!
I WANT THE SPIRITUAL STONE OF F—
ROLL
ROLL
ROLL ROLL
SMAK
WHAT?
THE SPIRITUAL STONE OF FIRE?
ROLL
YOU DON'T WANT GANONDORF TO TAKE OVER HYRULE, DO YOU?
Wha...?
IT HOLDS TH SPIRIT OF OL PEOPLE. YO THINK WE'D JUST GIVE IT SOME LITTL TWERP?

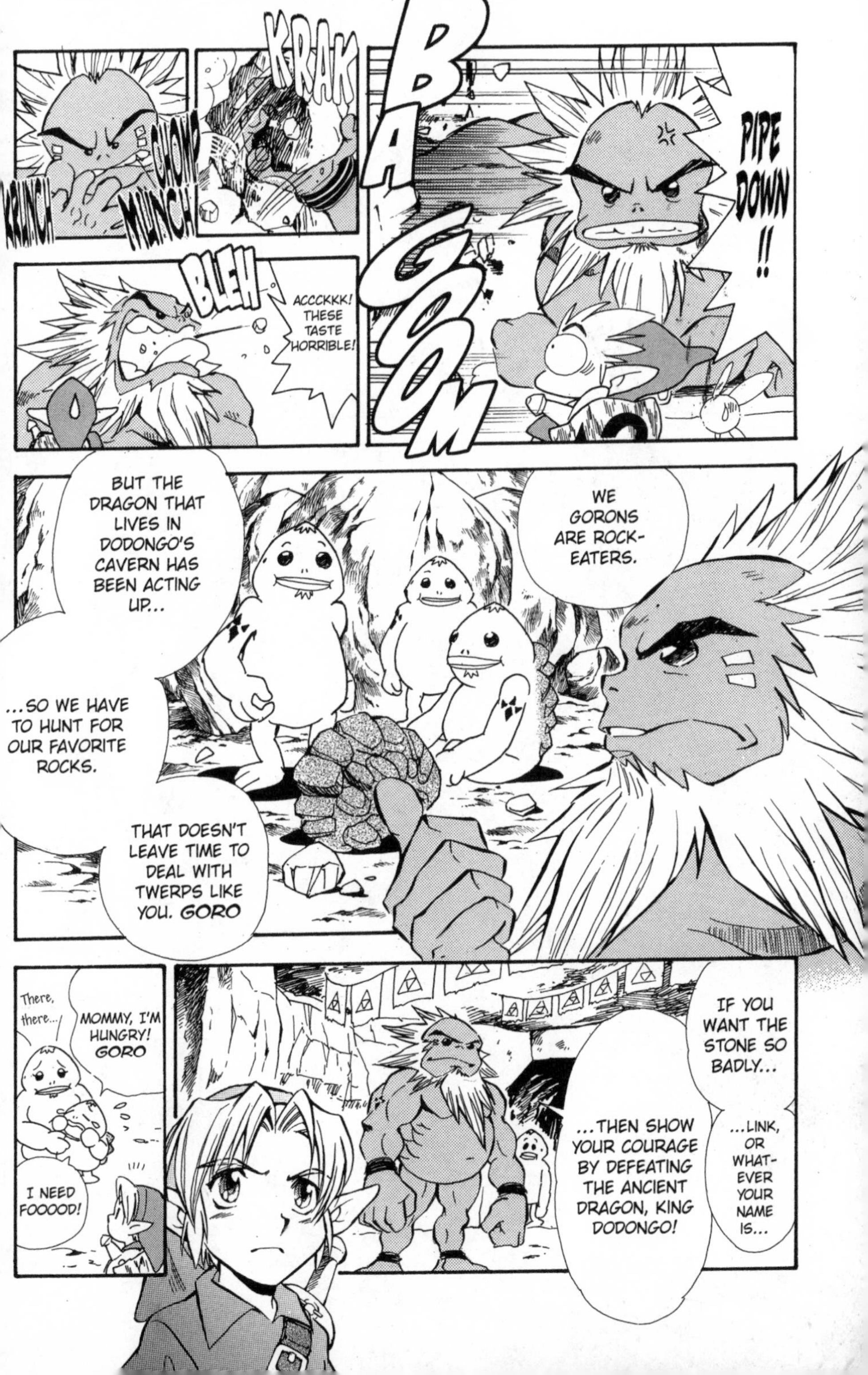
BAGOOM
PIPE DOWN!!
KRAK
CHOMP
MUNCH
KRUNCH
BLEH
ACCCKKK! THESE TASTE HORRIBLE!
WE GORONS ARE ROCK-EATERS.
BUT THE DRAGON THAT LIVES IN DODONGO'S CAVERN HAS BEEN ACTING UP...
...SO WE HAVE TO HUNT FOR OUR FAVORITE ROCKS.
THAT DOESN'T LEAVE TIME TO DEAL WITH TWERPS LIKE YOU. GORO
IF YOU WANT THE STONE SO BADLY...
...LINK, OR WHATEVER YOUR NAME IS...
...THEN SHOW YOUR COURAGE BY DEFEATING THE ANCIENT DRAGON, KING DODONGO!
MOMMY, I'M HUNGRY! GORO
There, there...
I NEED FOOOOD!

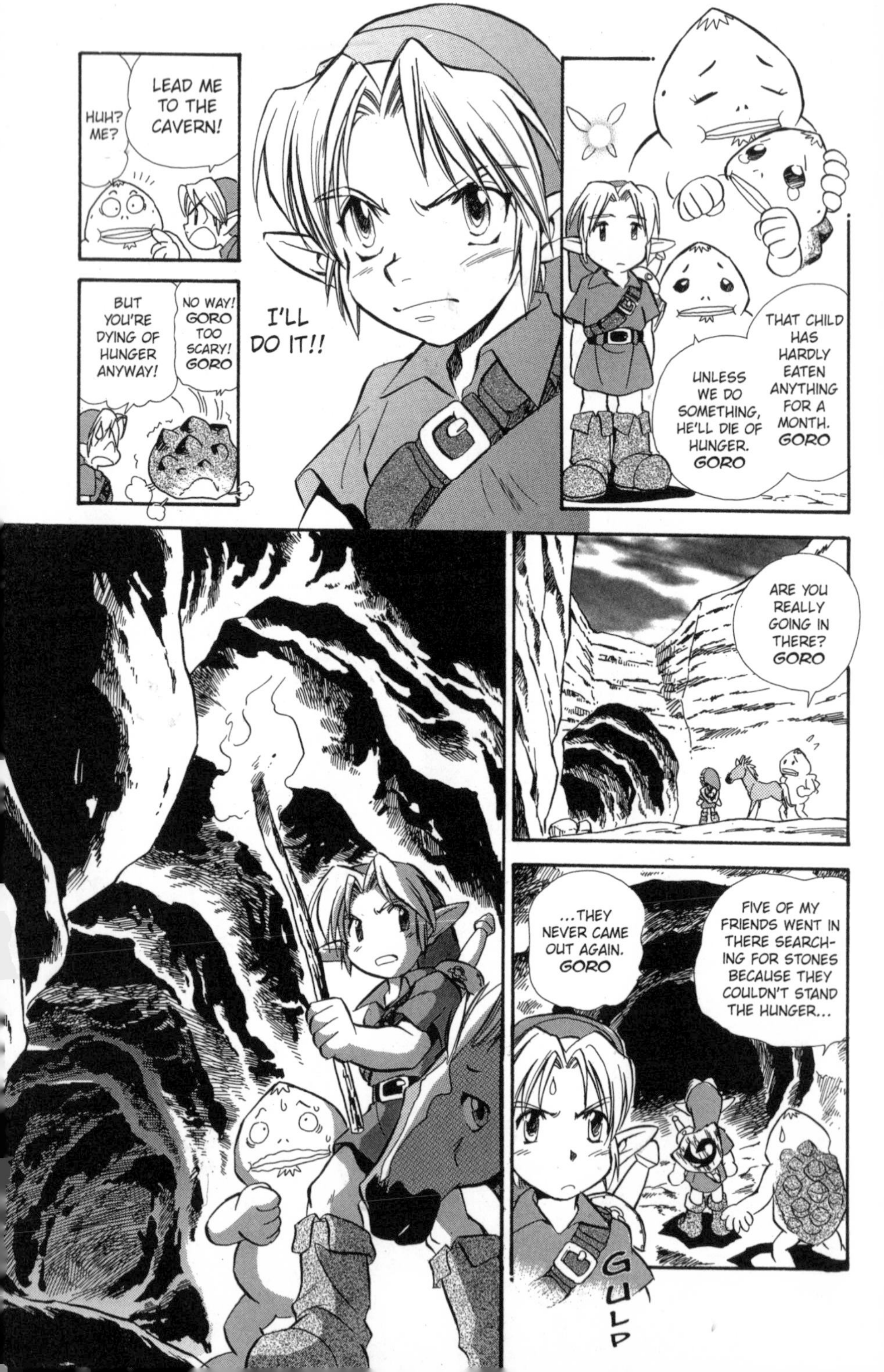
THAT CHILD HAS HARDLY EATEN ANYTHING FOR A MONTH. GORO
UNLESS WE DO SOMETHING, HE'LL DIE OF HUNGER. GORO
I'LL DO IT!!
LEAD ME TO THE CAVERN!
HUH? ME?
NO WAY! GORO TOO SCARY! GORO
BUT YOU'RE DYING OF HUNGER ANYWAY!
ARE YOU REALLY GOING IN THERE? GORO
FIVE OF MY FRIENDS WENT IN THERE SEARCHING FOR STONES BECAUSE THEY COULDN'T STAND THE HUNGER...
...THEY NEVER CAME OUT AGAIN. GORO
GULP

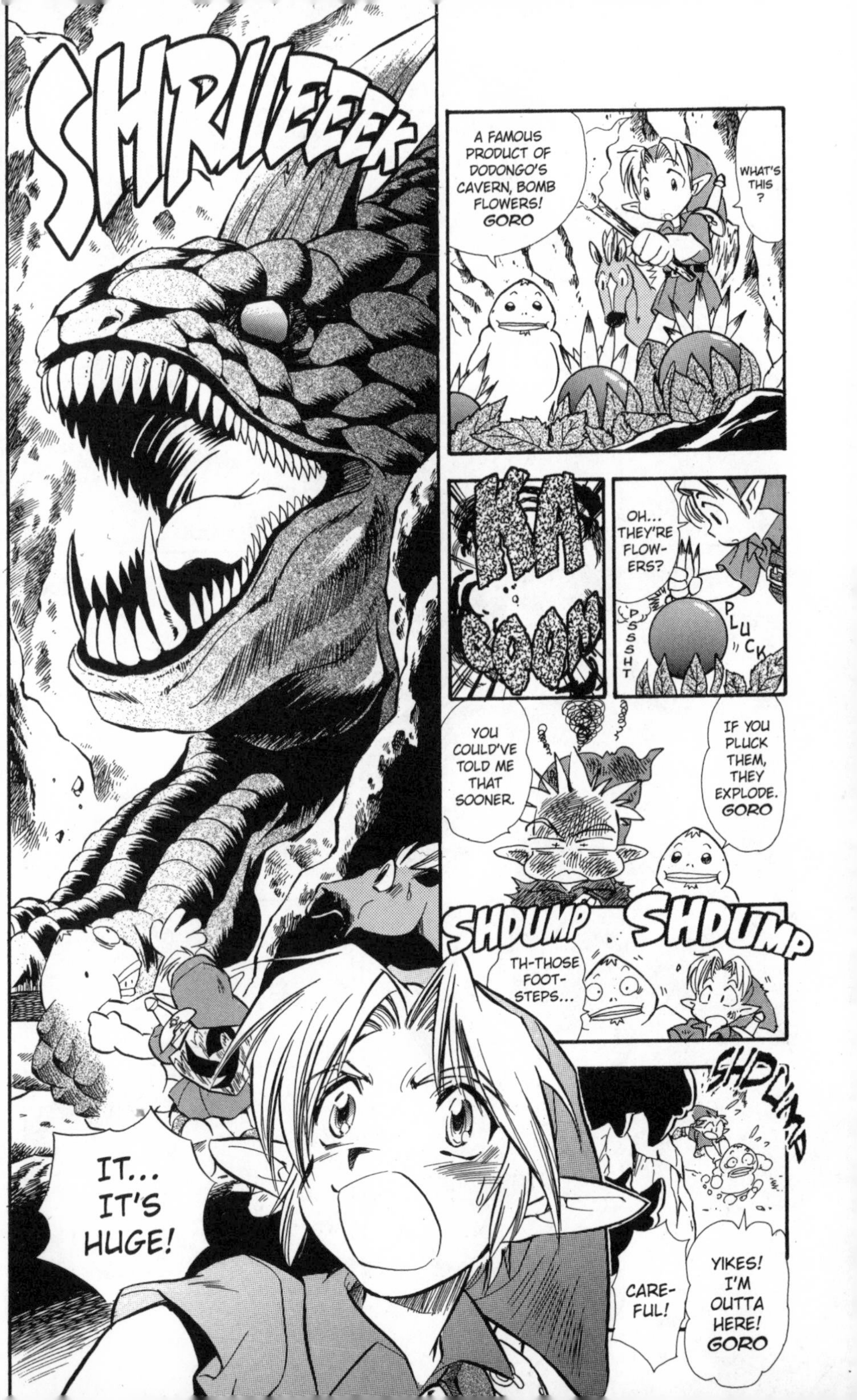
WHAT'S THIS ?
A FAMOUS PRODUCT OF DODONGO'S CAVERN, BOMB FLOWERS! GORO
OH... THEY'RE FLOW-ERS?
PSSSHT
PLUCK
KA BOOM
IF YOU PLUCK THEM, THEY EXPLODE. GORO
YOU COULD'VE TOLD ME THAT SOONER.
SHDUMP
SHDUMP
TH-THOSE FOOT-STEPS...
SHDUMP
YIKES! I'M OUTTA HERE! GORO
CARE-FUL!
SHRIEEEK
IT... IT'S HUGE!

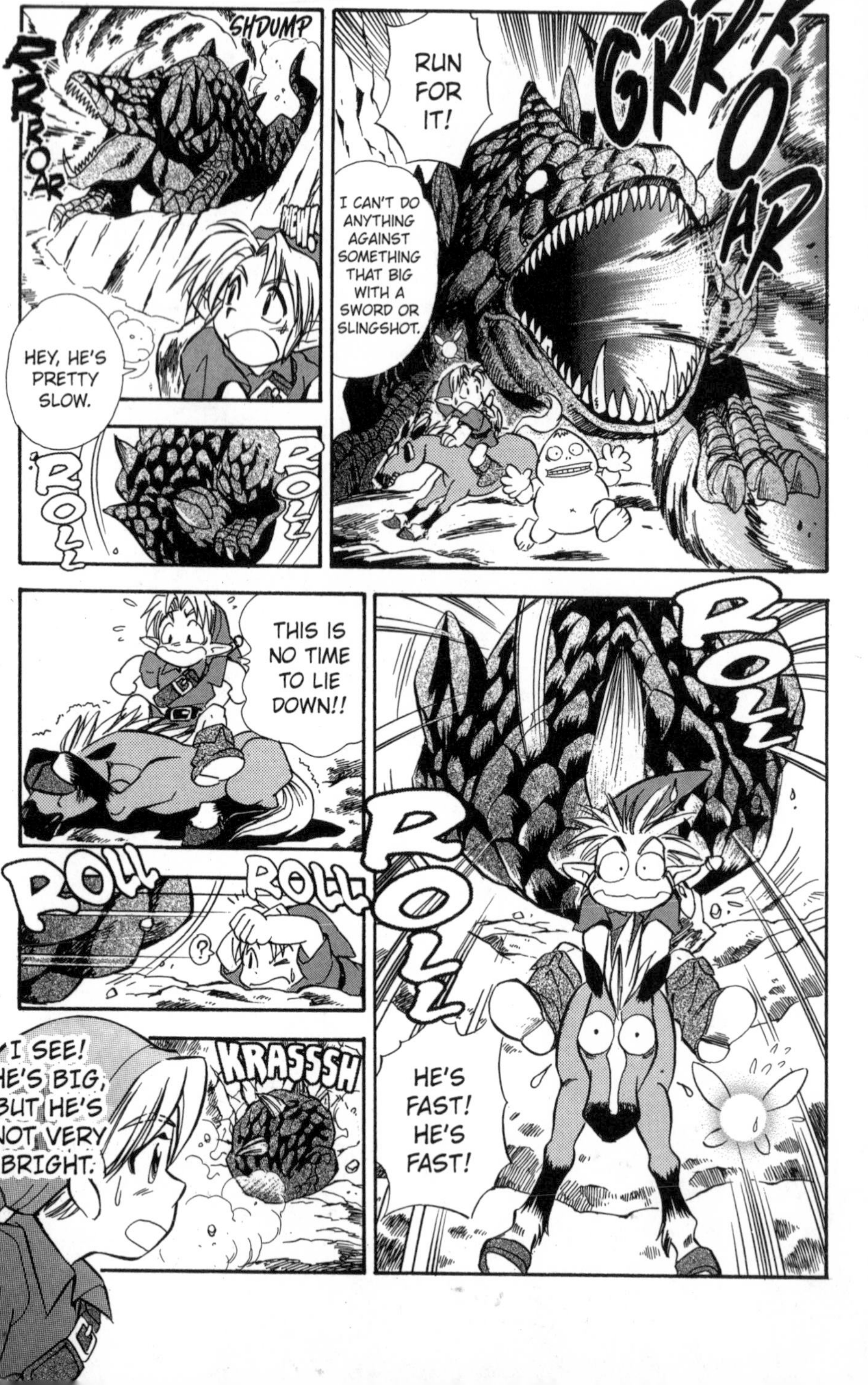
GRRROAR
RUN FOR IT!
I CAN'T DO ANYTHING AGAINST SOMETHING THAT BIG WITH A SWORD OR SLINGSHOT.
SHDUMP
RRROAR
PHEW!
HEY, HE'S PRETTY SLOW.
ROLL
ROLL
ROLL
ROLL
HE'S FAST! HE'S FAST!
THIS IS NO TIME TO LIE DOWN!!
ROLL
ROLL
?
KRASSSH
I SEE! HE'S BIG, BUT HE'S NOT VERY BRIGHT.

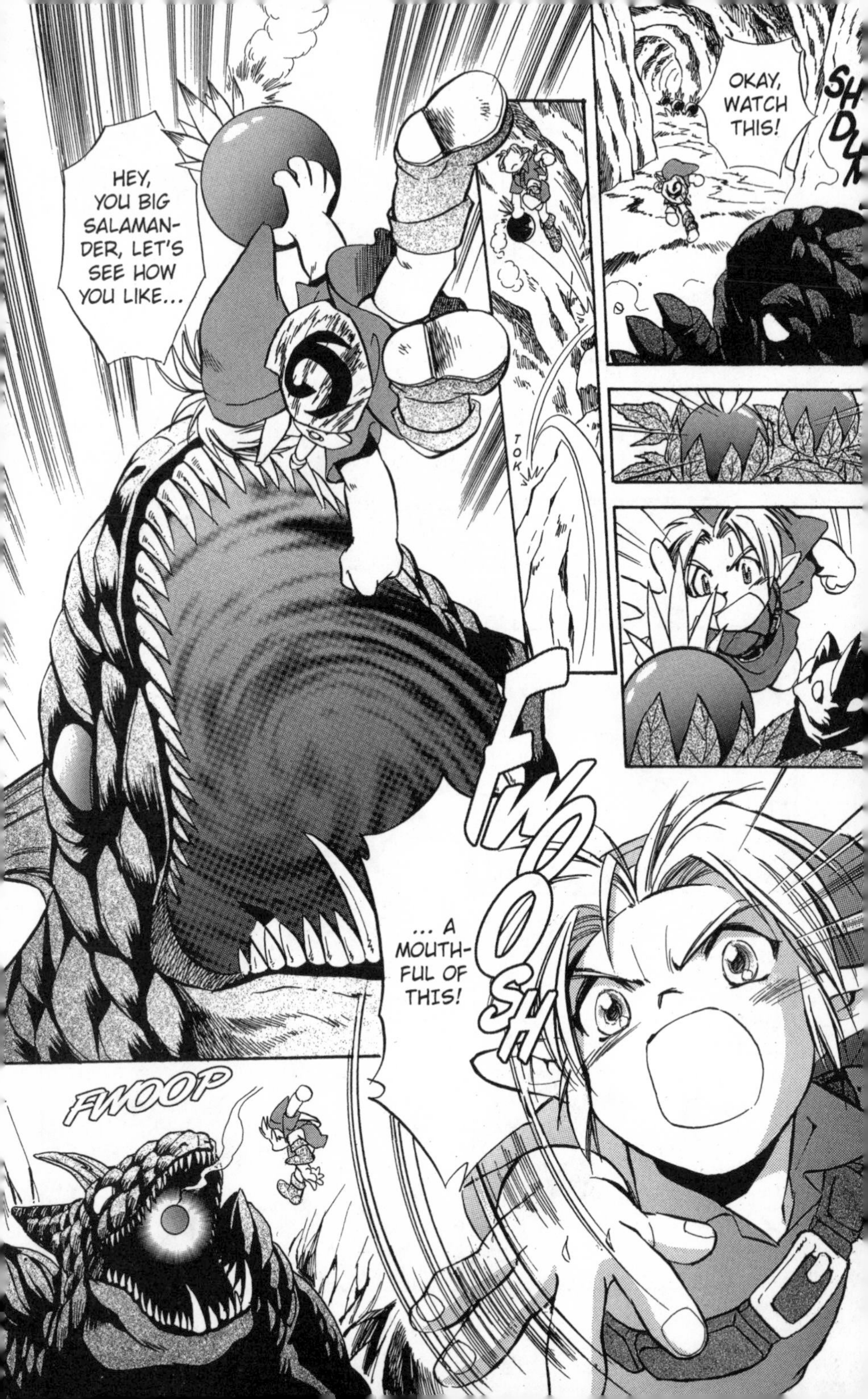
OKAY, WATCH THIS!
SHDUN
TOK
HEY, YOU BIG SALAMANDER, LET'S SEE HOW YOU LIKE...
... A MOUTHFUL OF THIS!
FWOOSH
FWOOP

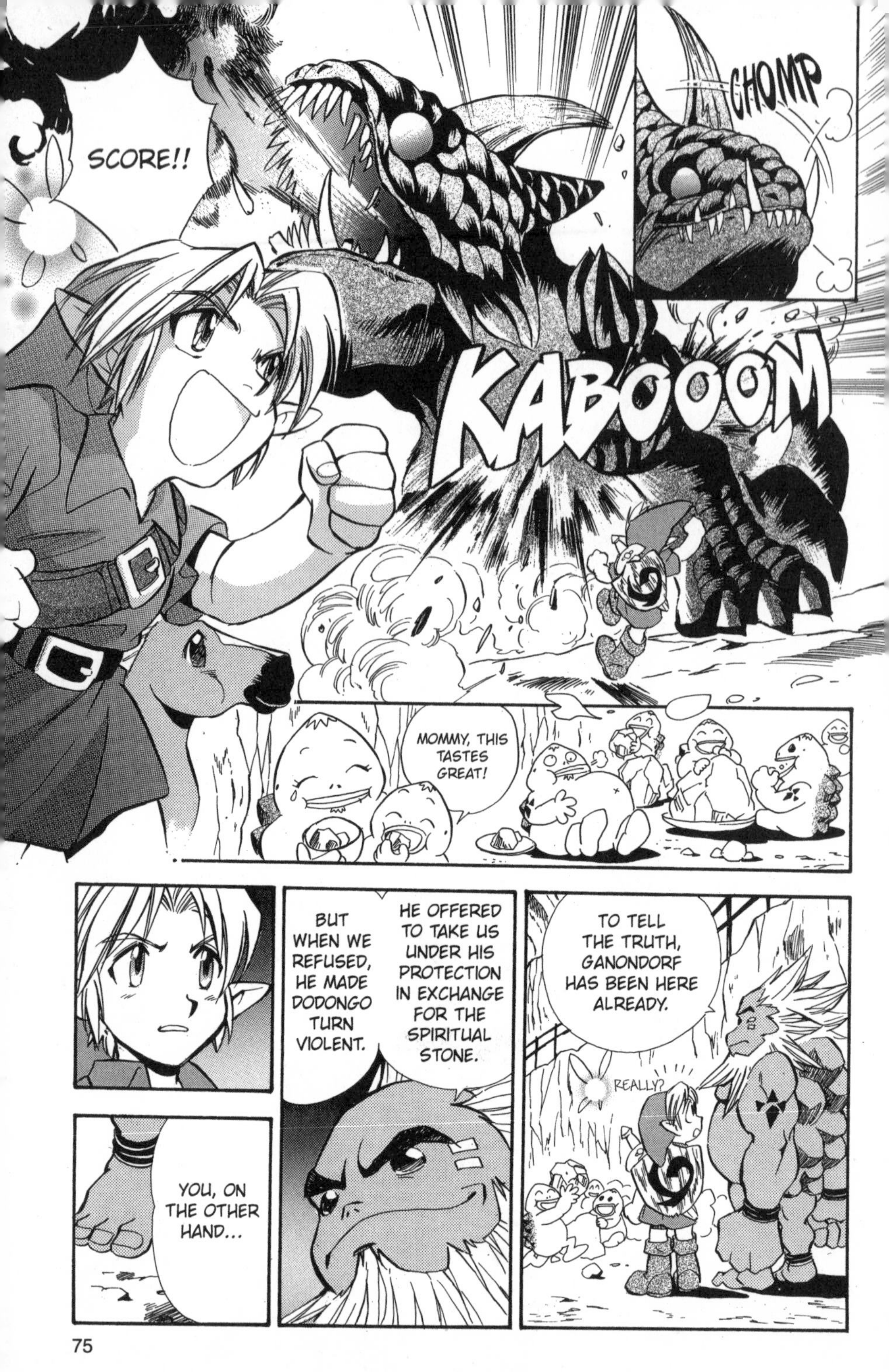
CHOMP
SCORE!!
KABOOOM
MOMMY, THIS TASTES GREAT!
TO TELL THE TRUTH, GANONDORF HAS BEEN HERE ALREADY.
REALLY?
HE OFFERED TO TAKE US UNDER HIS PROTECTION IN EXCHANGE FOR THE SPIRITUAL STONE.
BUT WHEN WE REFUSED, HE MADE DODONGO TURN VIOLENT.
YOU, ON THE OTHER HAND...

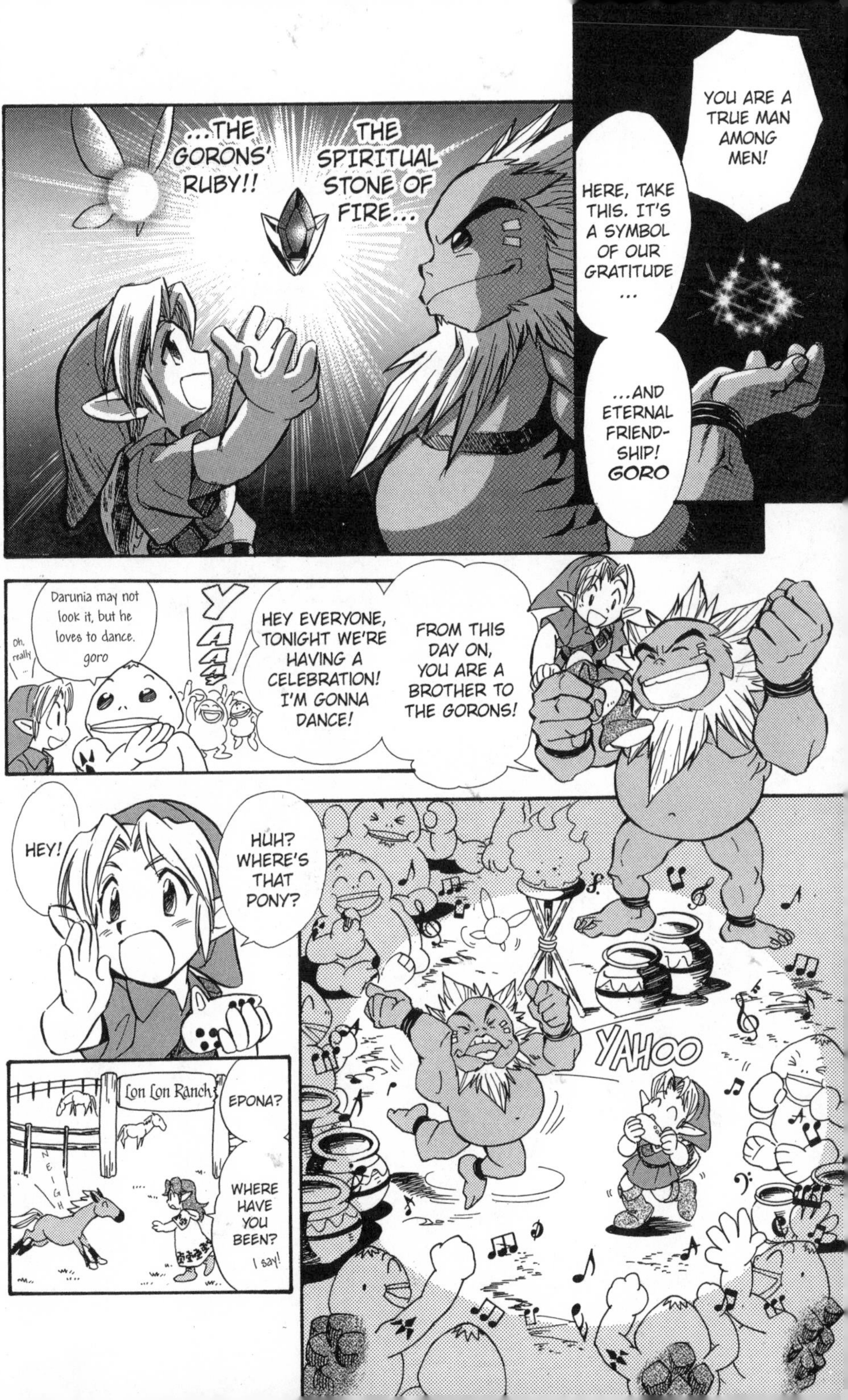
YOU ARE A TRUE MAN AMONG MEN!
HERE, TAKE THIS. IT'S A SYMBOL OF OUR GRATITUDE ...
...AND ETERNAL FRIEND-SHIP! GORO
THE SPIRITUAL STONE OF FIRE...
...THE GORONS' RUBY!!
FROM THIS DAY ON, YOU ARE A BROTHER TO THE GORONS!
HEY EVERYONE, TONIGHT WE'RE HAVING A CELEBRATION! I'M GONNA DANCE!
YAAAA
Darunia may not look it, but he loves to dance. goro
Oh, really ...
YAHOO
HUH? WHERE'S THAT PONY?
HEY!
EPONA?
Lon Lon Ranch
WHERE HAVE YOU BEEN?
I say!
NEIGH

CHAPTER 5
INSIDE JABU-JABU'S BELLY

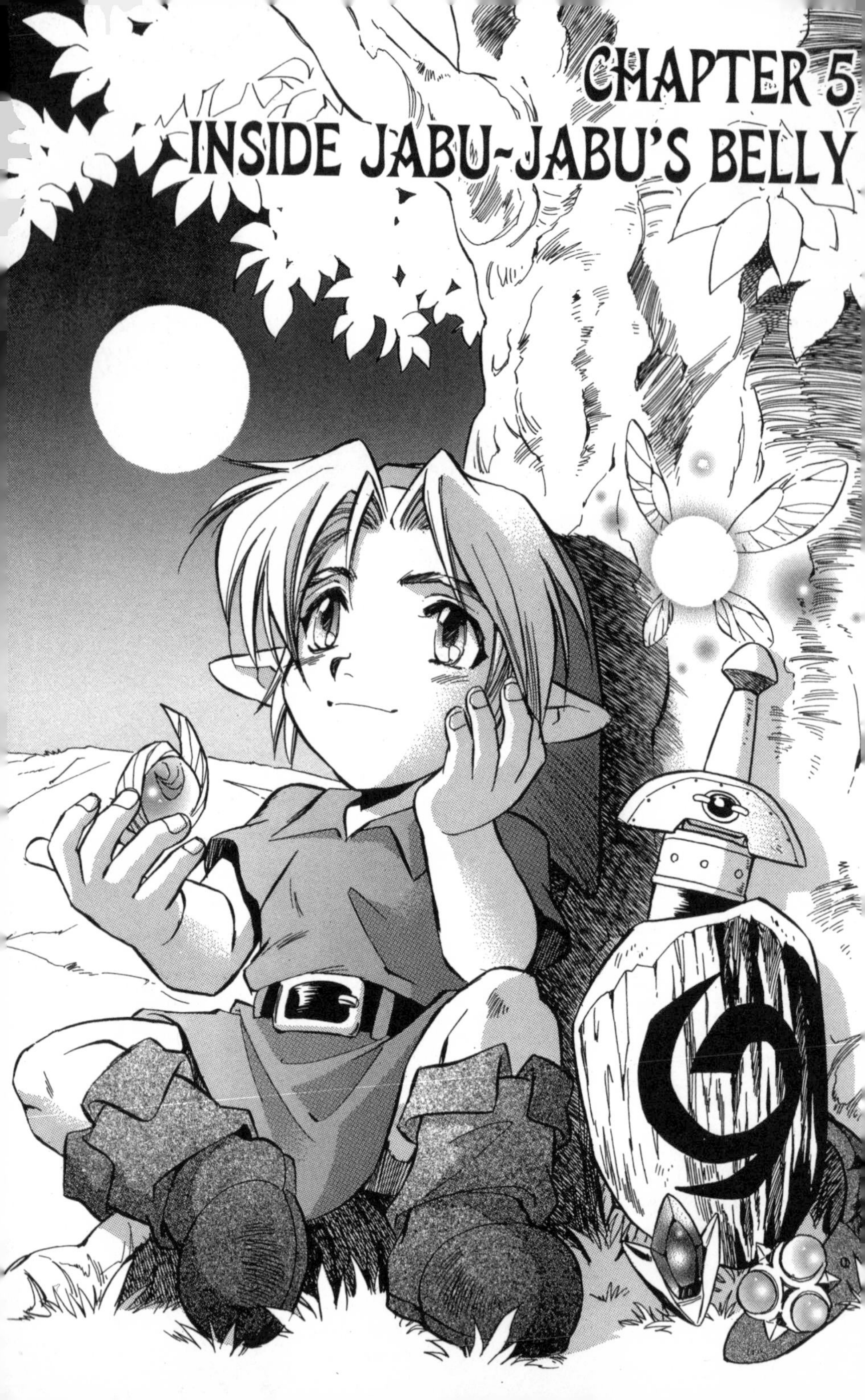

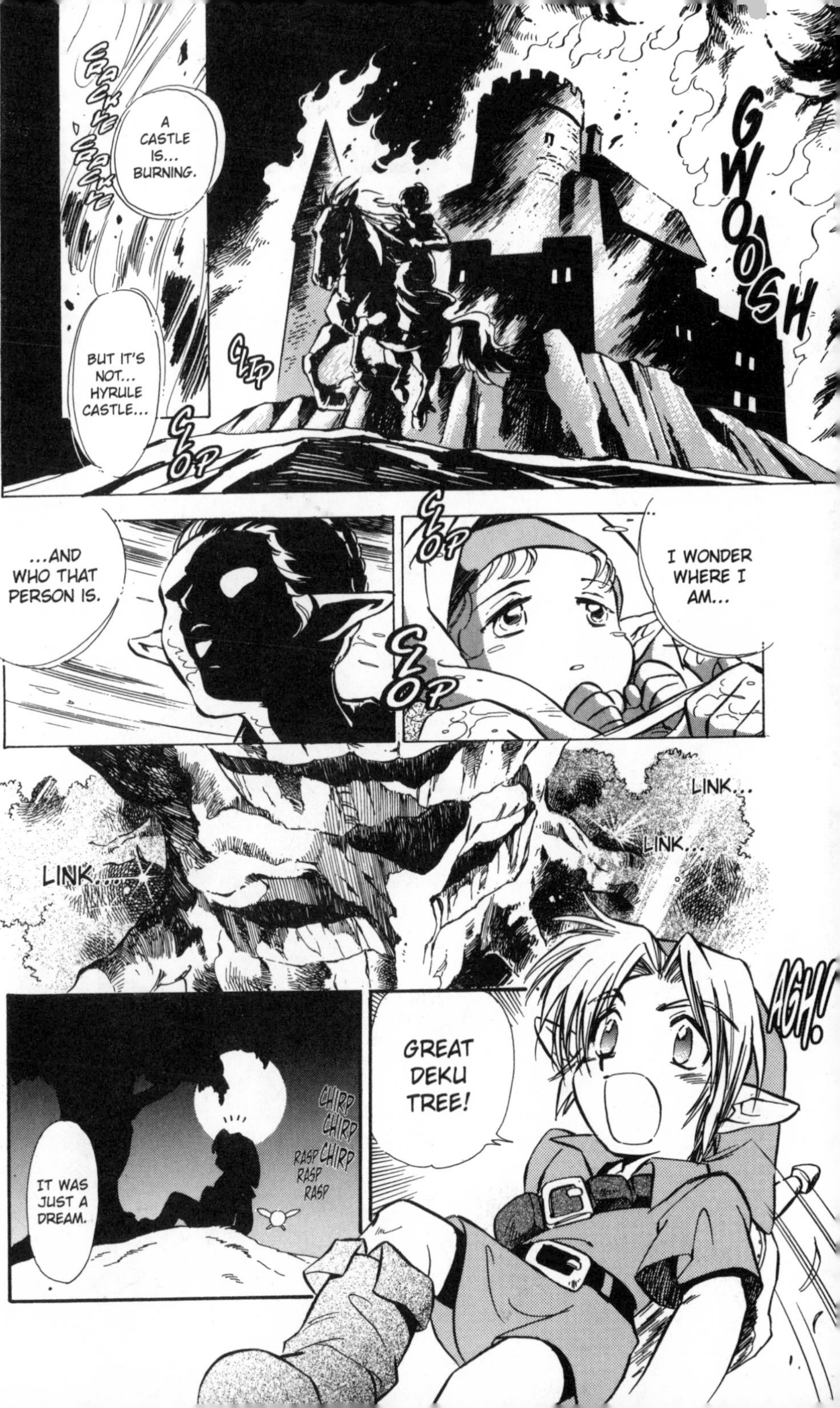
GWOOSH
A CASTLE IS... BURNING.
CLIP
CLOP
BUT IT'S NOT... HYRULE CASTLE...
I WONDER WHERE I AM...
CLOP
CLOP
...AND WHO THAT PERSON IS.
LINK...
LINK...
LINK...
AGH!
GREAT DEKU TREE!
CHIRP CHIRP CHIRP
RASP RASP RASP
IT WAS JUST A DREAM.

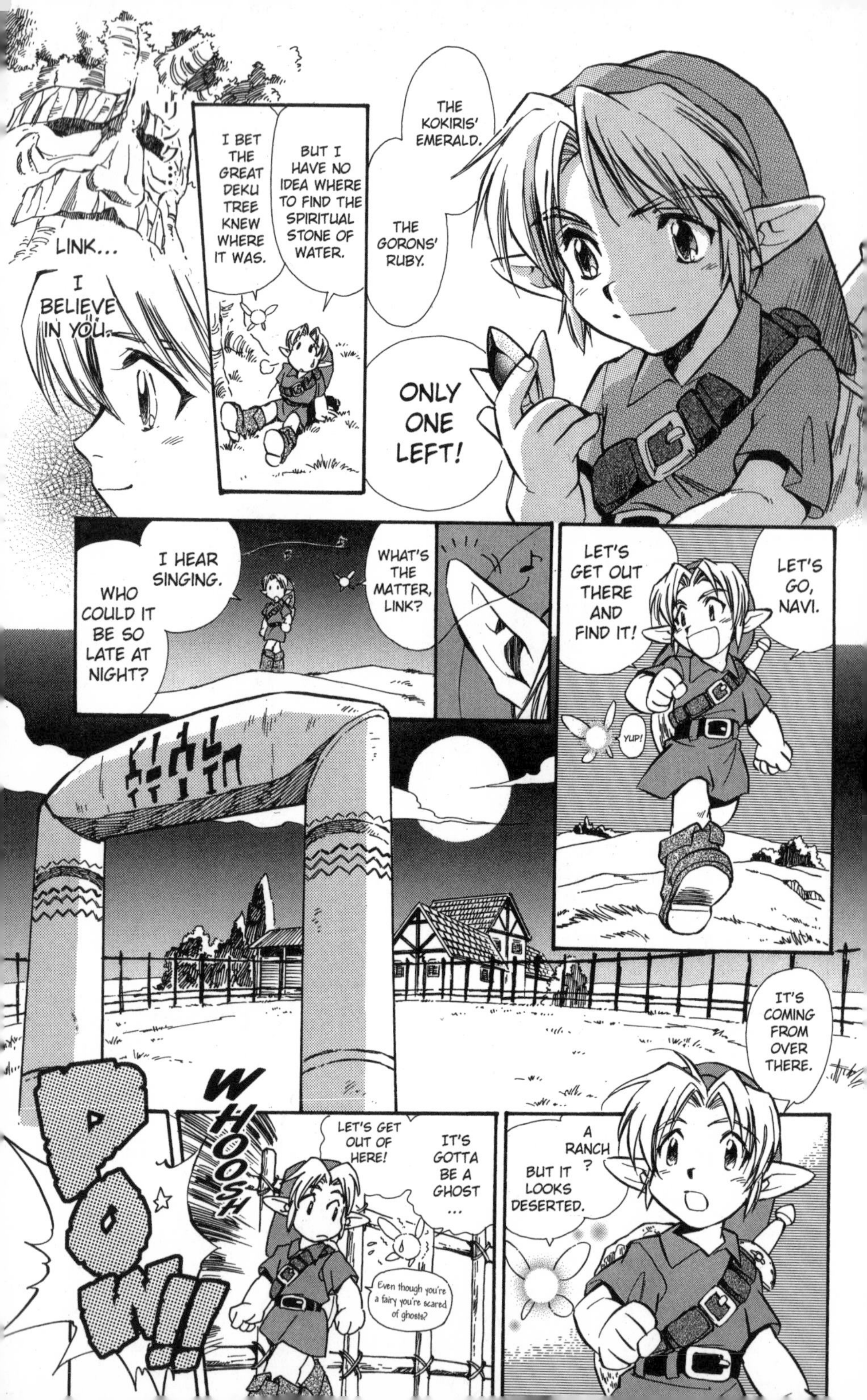
THE KOKIRIS' EMERALD.
THE GORONS' RUBY.
ONLY ONE LEFT!
BUT I HAVE NO IDEA WHERE TO FIND THE SPIRITUAL STONE OF WATER.
I BET THE GREAT DEKU TREE KNEW WHERE IT WAS.
LINK...
I BELIEVE IN YOU.
LET'S GO, NAVI.
LET'S GET OUT THERE AND FIND IT!
YUP!
WHAT'S THE MATTER, LINK?
I HEAR SINGING.
WHO COULD IT BE SO LATE AT NIGHT?
IT'S COMING FROM OVER THERE.
A RANCH?
BUT IT LOOKS DESERTED.
IT'S GOTTA BE A GHOST...
LET'S GET OUT OF HERE!
Even though you're a fairy you're scared of ghosts?
WHOOSH
POW!!

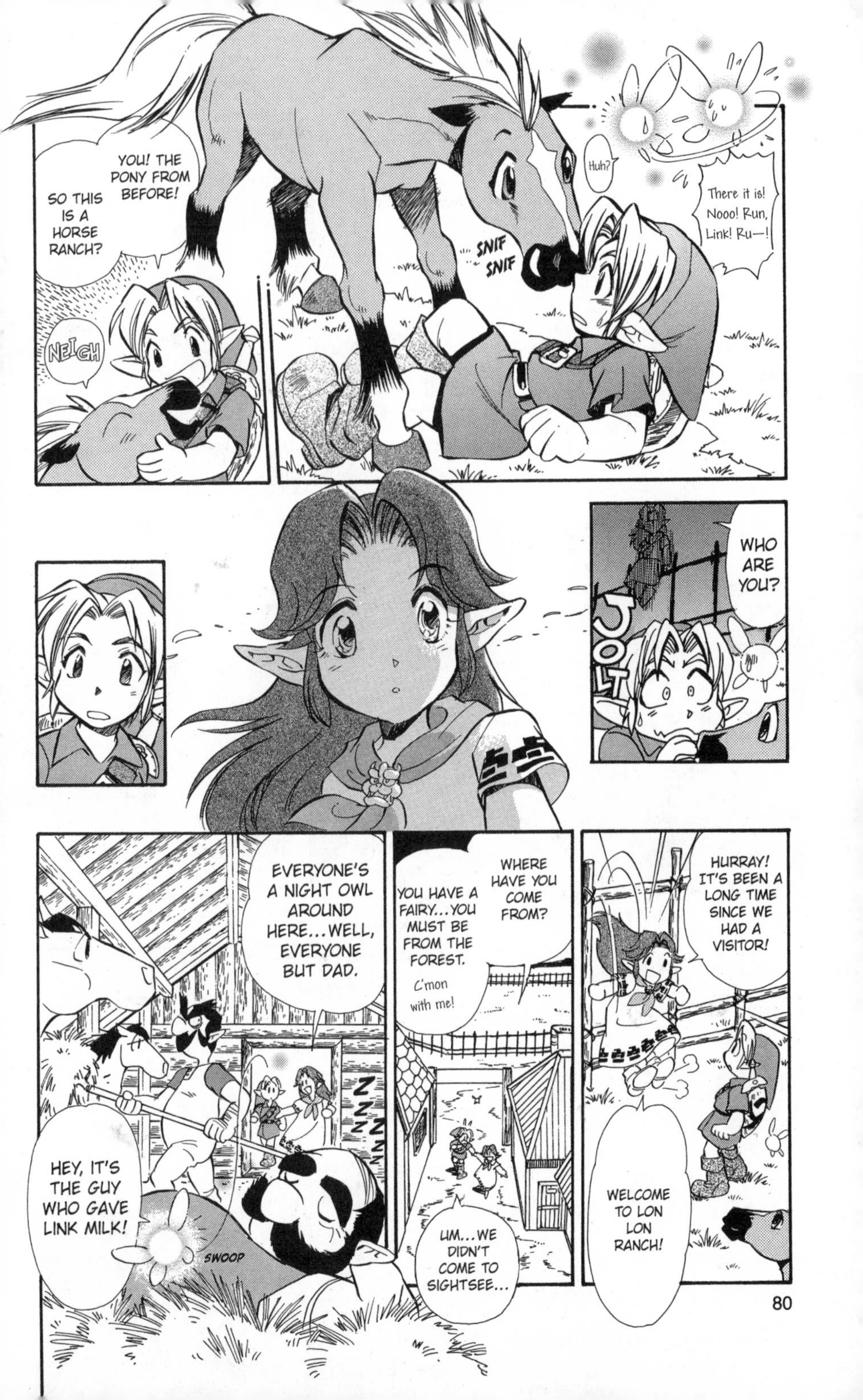
There it is! Nooo! Run, Link! Ru—!
Huh?
SNIF SNIF
YOU! THE PONY FROM BEFORE!
SO THIS IS A HORSE RANCH?
NEIGH
WHO ARE YOU?
JOLT
HURRAY! IT'S BEEN A LONG TIME SINCE WE HAD A VISITOR!
WELCOME TO LON LON RANCH!
WHERE HAVE YOU COME FROM?
YOU HAVE A FAIRY...YOU MUST BE FROM THE FOREST.
C'mon with me!
UM...WE DIDN'T COME TO SIGHTSEE...
EVERYONE'S A NIGHT OWL AROUND HERE...WELL, EVERYONE BUT DAD.
ZZZZ
HEY, IT'S THE GUY WHO GAVE LINK MILK!
SWOOP

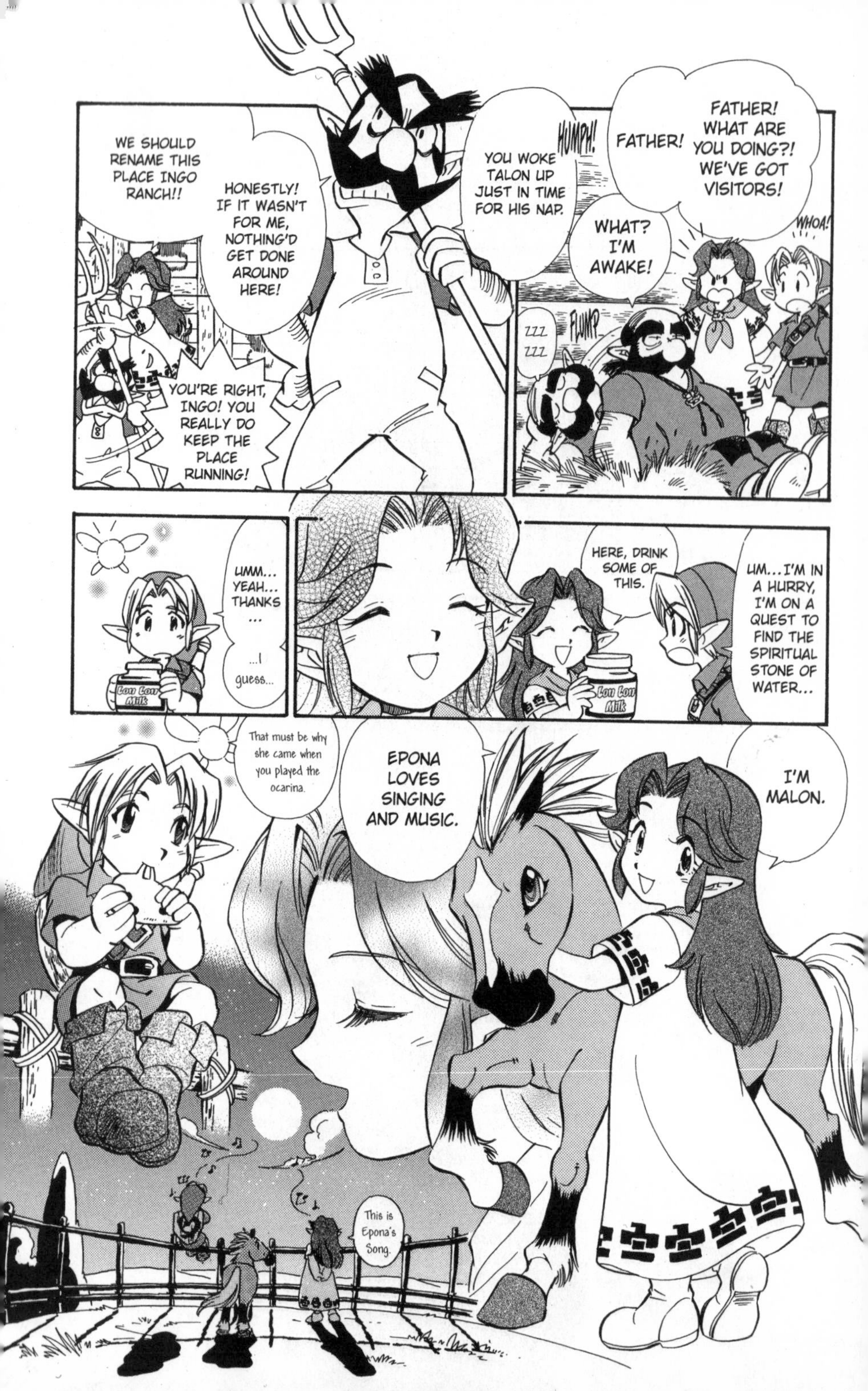
FATHER! WHAT ARE YOU DOING?! WE'VE GOT VISITORS!
FATHER!
WHOA!
WHAT? I'M AWAKE!
ZZZ ZZZ
FLUMP
HUMPH!
YOU WOKE TALON UP JUST IN TIME FOR HIS NAP.
HONESTLY! IF IT WASN'T FOR ME, NOTHING'D GET DONE AROUND HERE!
WE SHOULD RENAME THIS PLACE INGO RANCH!!
YOU'RE RIGHT, INGO! YOU REALLY DO KEEP THE PLACE RUNNING!
UM...I'M IN A HURRY, I'M ON A QUEST TO FIND THE SPIRITUAL STONE OF WATER...
HERE, DRINK SOME OF THIS.
Lon Lon Milk
UMM... YEAH... THANKS ...
...I guess...
Lon Lon Milk
I'M MALON.
EPONA LOVES SINGING AND MUSIC.
That must be why she came when you played the ocarina.
This is Epona's Song.

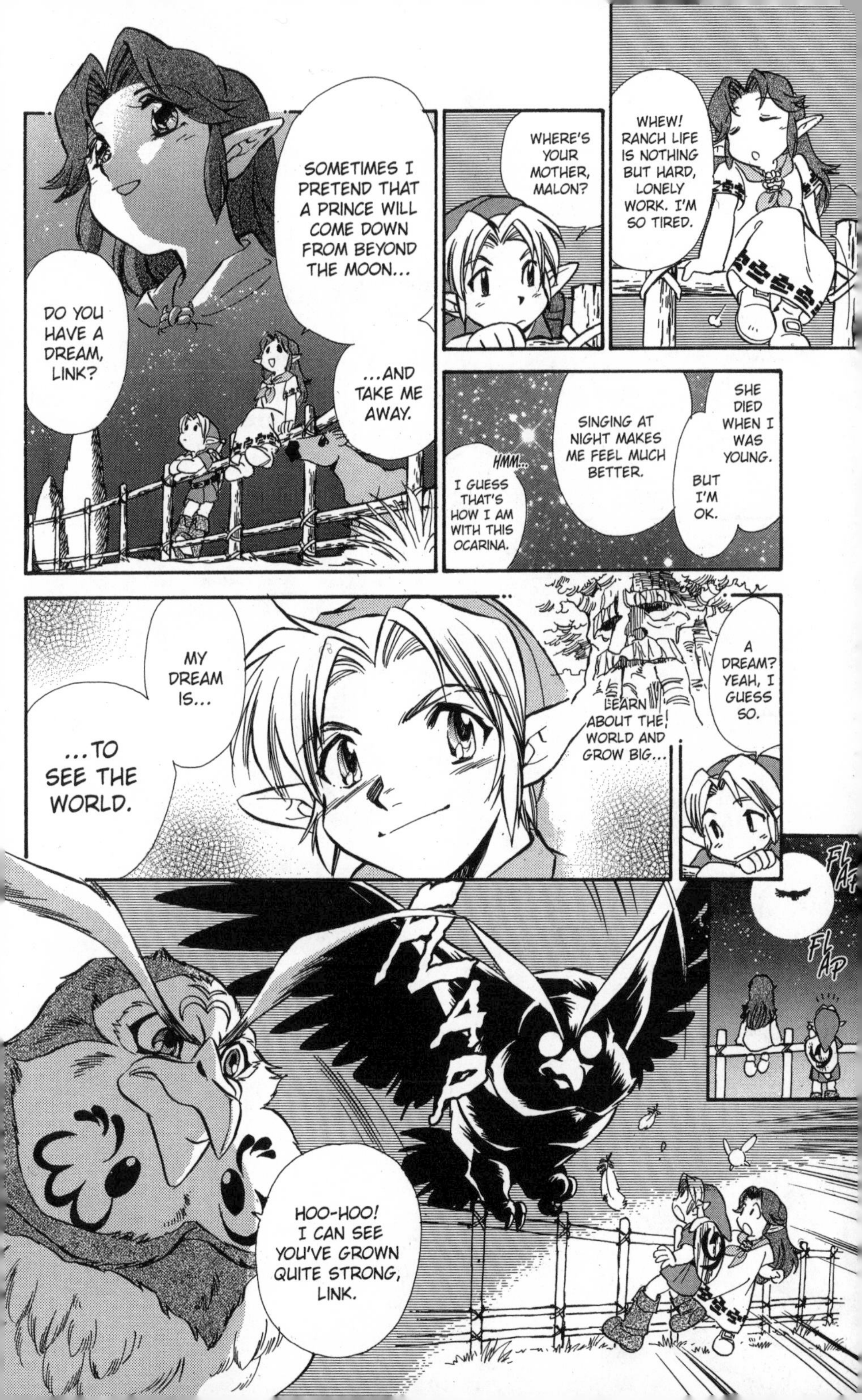
WHEW! RANCH LIFE IS NOTHING BUT HARD, LONELY WORK. I'M SO TIRED.
WHERE'S YOUR MOTHER, MALON?
SHE DIED WHEN I WAS YOUNG.
BUT I'M OK.
SINGING AT NIGHT MAKES ME FEEL MUCH BETTER.
HMM...
I GUESS THAT'S HOW I AM WITH THIS OCARINA.
SOMETIMES I PRETEND THAT A PRINCE WILL COME DOWN FROM BEYOND THE MOON...
...AND TAKE ME AWAY.
DO YOU HAVE A DREAM, LINK?
A DREAM? YEAH, I GUESS SO.
LEARN ABOUT THE WORLD AND GROW BIG...
MY DREAM IS...
...TO SEE THE WORLD.
FLAP
FLAP
FLAP
HOO-HOO! I CAN SEE YOU'VE GROWN QUITE STRONG, LINK.

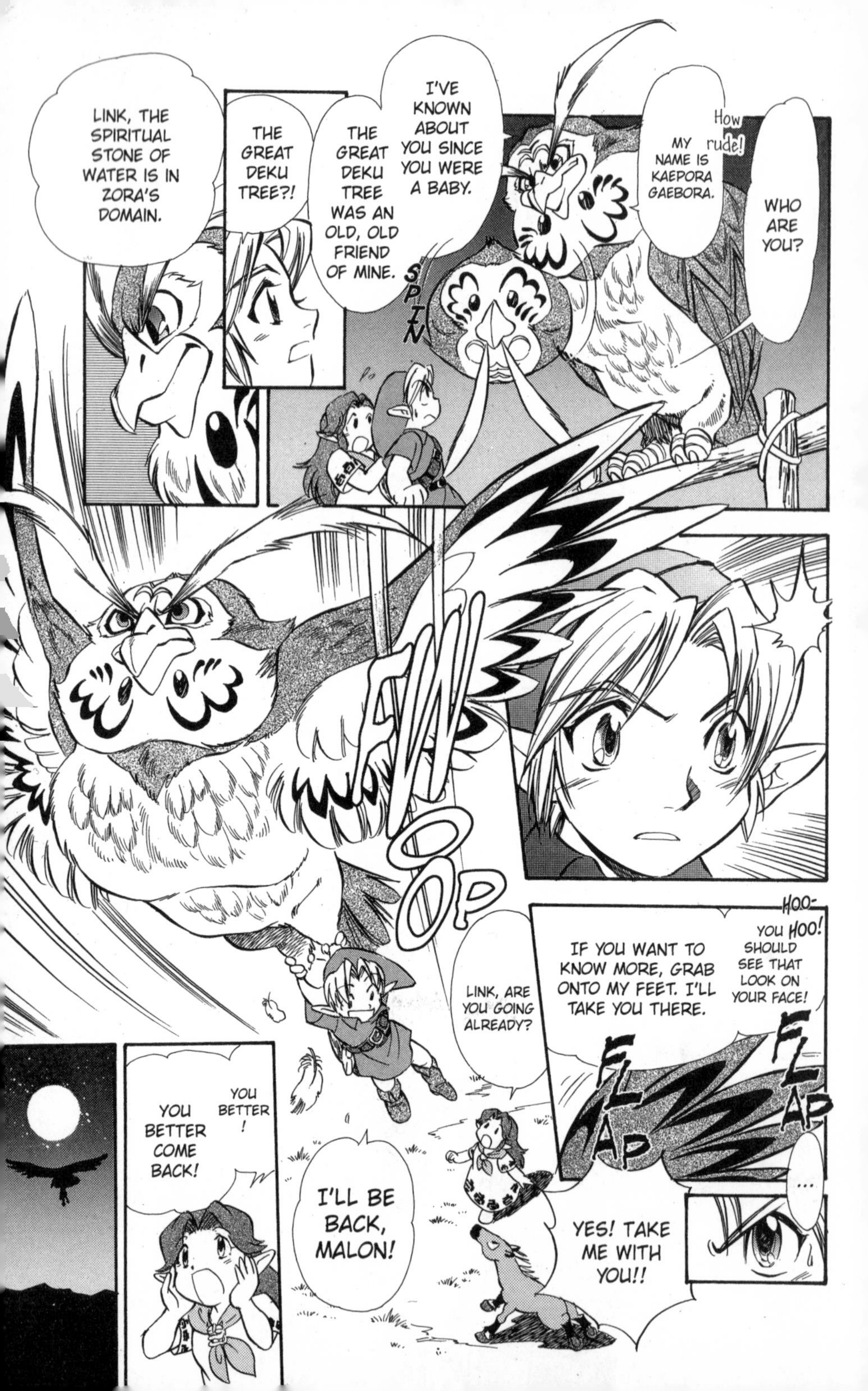
WHO ARE YOU?
How rude!
MY NAME IS KAEPORA GAEBORA.
I'VE KNOWN ABOUT YOU SINCE YOU WERE A BABY.
THE GREAT DEKU TREE WAS AN OLD, OLD FRIEND OF MINE.
SPIN
THE GREAT DEKU TREE?!
LINK, THE SPIRITUAL STONE OF WATER IS IN ZORA'S DOMAIN.
FWOOP
HOO-HOO! YOU SHOULD SEE THAT LOOK ON YOUR FACE!
IF YOU WANT TO KNOW MORE, GRAB ONTO MY FEET. I'LL TAKE YOU THERE.
FLAP FLAP
LINK, ARE YOU GOING ALREADY?
...
YES! TAKE ME WITH YOU!!
I'LL BE BACK, MALON!
YOU BETTER COME BACK!
YOU BETTER!

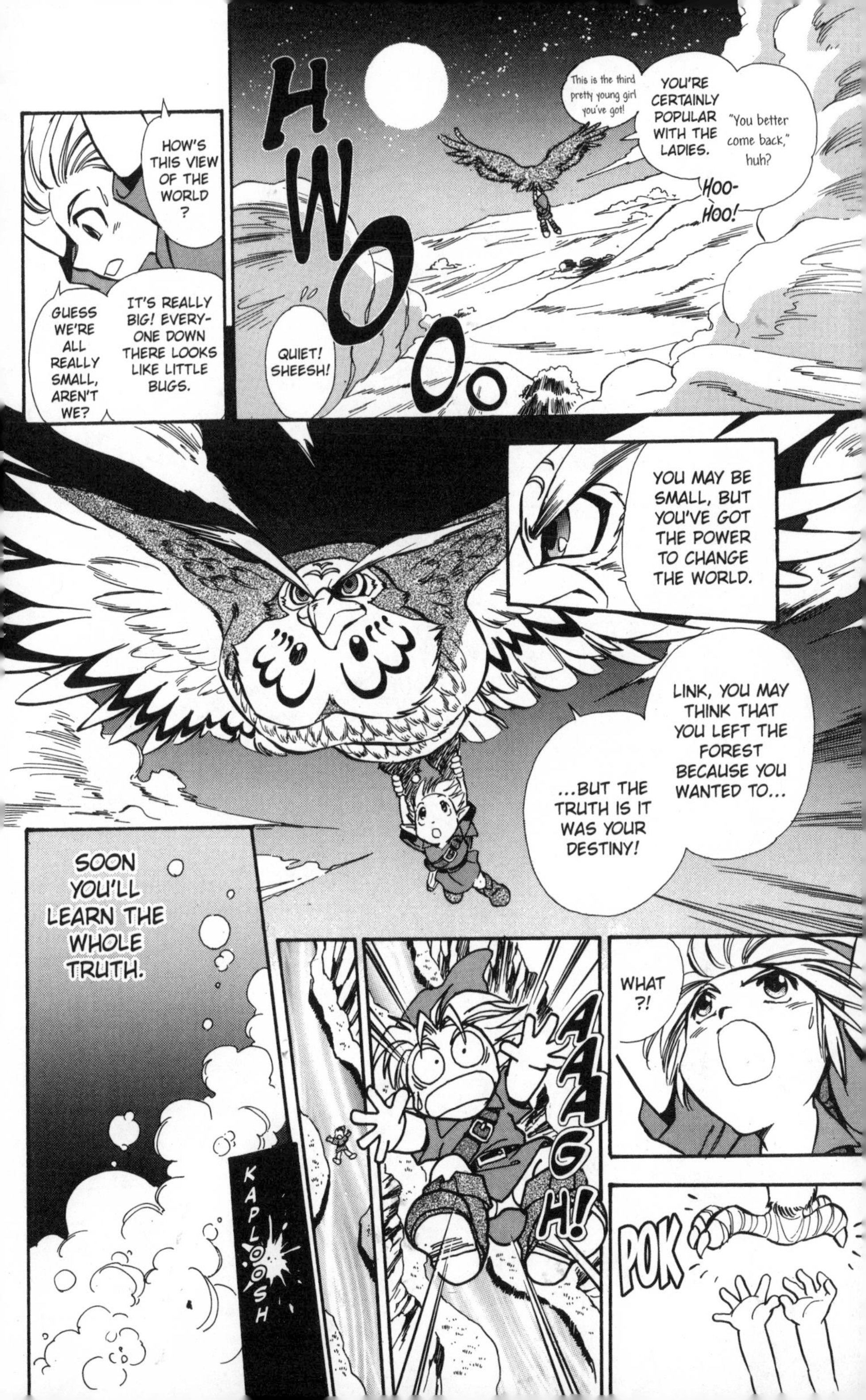
"You better come back," huh?
HOO-HOO!
YOU'RE CERTAINLY POPULAR WITH THE LADIES.
This is the third pretty young girl you've got!
HWOOoo
QUIET! SHEESH!
HOW'S THIS VIEW OF THE WORLD?
IT'S REALLY BIG! EVERYONE DOWN THERE LOOKS LIKE LITTLE BUGS.
GUESS WE'RE ALL REALLY SMALL, AREN'T WE?
YOU MAY BE SMALL, BUT YOU'VE GOT THE POWER TO CHANGE THE WORLD.
LINK, YOU MAY THINK THAT YOU LEFT THE FOREST BECAUSE YOU WANTED TO...
...BUT THE TRUTH IS IT WAS YOUR DESTINY!
WHAT?!
POK
AAAAGH!
SOON YOU'LL LEARN THE WHOLE TRUTH.
KAPLOOSH

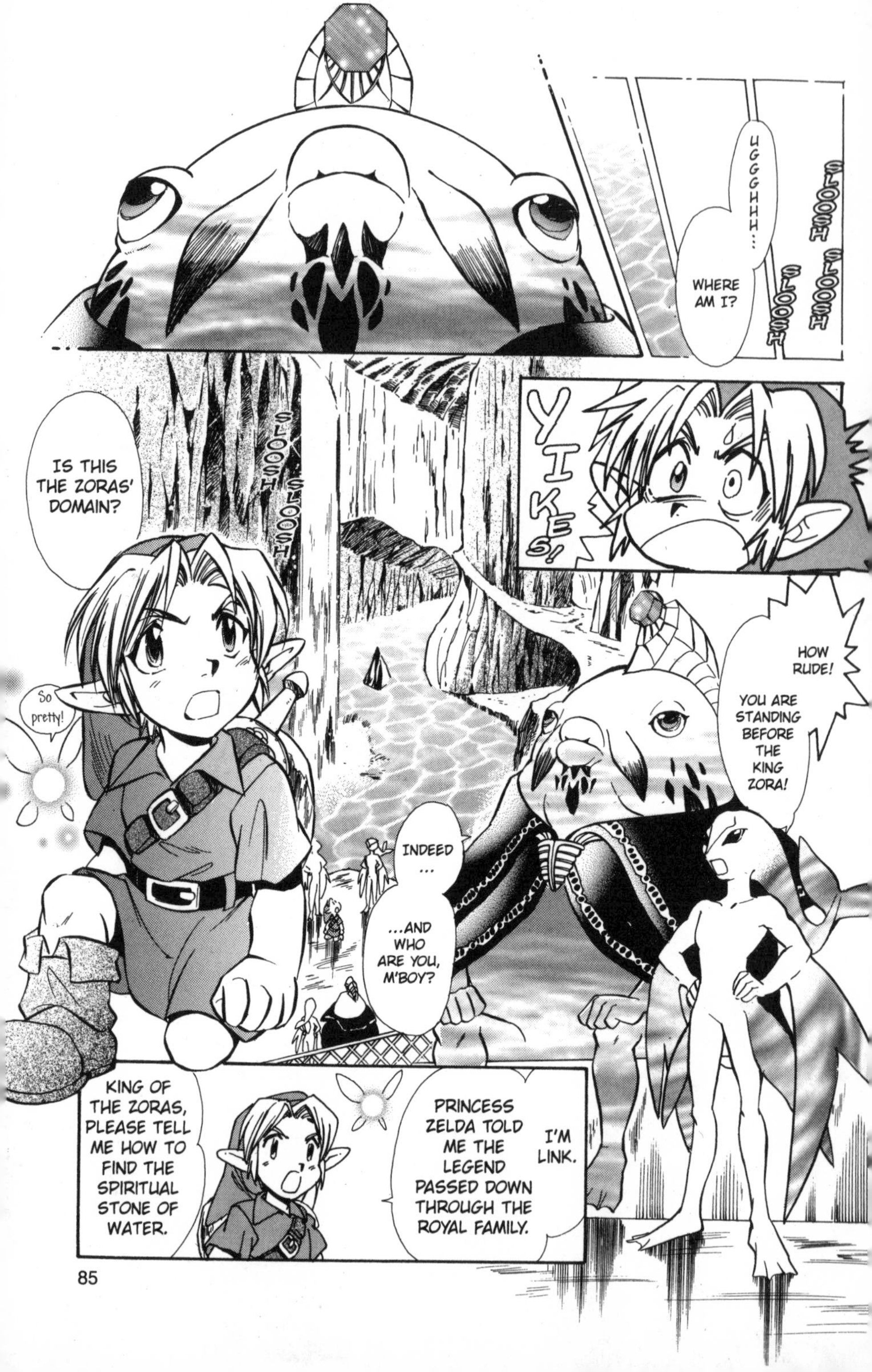

SLOOSH SLOOSH
SLOOSH
UGGGHHH...
WHERE AM I?
YIKES!
IS THIS THE ZORAS' DOMAIN?
SLOOSH SLOOSH
HOW RUDE!
YOU ARE STANDING BEFORE THE KING ZORA!
So pretty!
INDEED...
...AND WHO ARE YOU, M'BOY?
I'M LINK.
PRINCESS ZELDA TOLD ME THE LEGEND PASSED DOWN THROUGH THE ROYAL FAMILY.
KING OF THE ZORAS, PLEASE TELL ME HOW TO FIND THE SPIRITUAL STONE OF WATER.

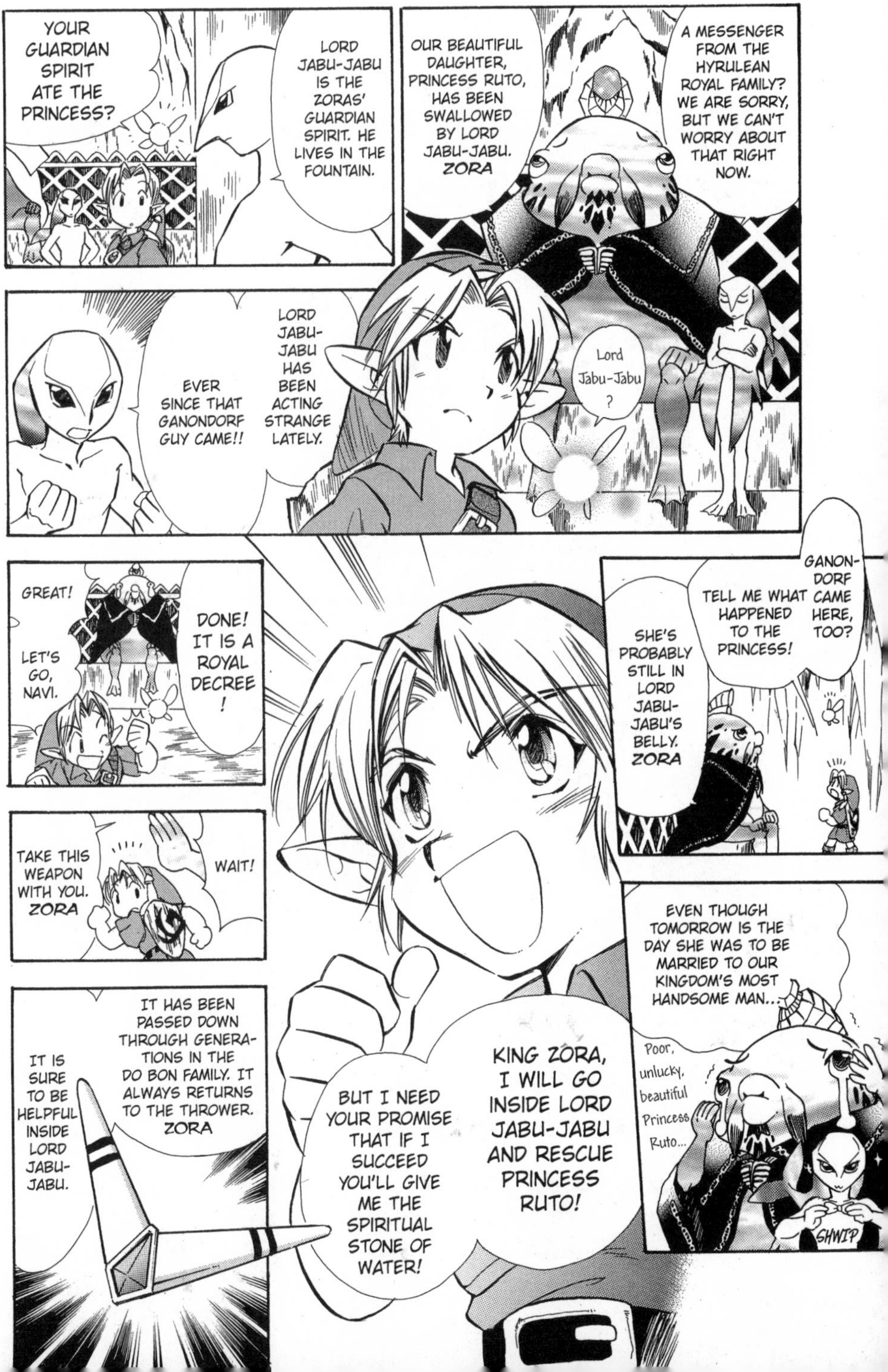
A MESSENGER FROM THE HYRULEAN ROYAL FAMILY? WE ARE SORRY, BUT WE CAN'T WORRY ABOUT THAT RIGHT NOW.
OUR BEAUTIFUL DAUGHTER, PRINCESS RUTO, HAS BEEN SWALLOWED BY LORD JABU-JABU. ZORA
Lord Jabu-Jabu?
LORD JABU-JABU IS THE ZORAS' GUARDIAN SPIRIT. HE LIVES IN THE FOUNTAIN.
YOUR GUARDIAN SPIRIT ATE THE PRINCESS?
LORD JABU-JABU HAS BEEN ACTING STRANGE LATELY.
EVER SINCE THAT GANONDORF GUY CAME!!
GANONDORF CAME HERE, TOO?
TELL ME WHAT HAPPENED TO THE PRINCESS!
SHE'S PROBABLY STILL IN LORD JABU-JABU'S BELLY. ZORA
EVEN THOUGH TOMORROW IS THE DAY SHE WAS TO BE MARRIED TO OUR KINGDOM'S MOST HANDSOME MAN...
Poor, unlucky, beautiful Princess Ruto...
SHWIP
KING ZORA, I WILL GO INSIDE LORD JABU-JABU AND RESCUE PRINCESS RUTO!
BUT I NEED YOUR PROMISE THAT IF I SUCCEED YOU'LL GIVE ME THE SPIRITUAL STONE OF WATER!
DONE! IT IS A ROYAL DECREE!
GREAT!
LET'S GO, NAVI.
WAIT!
TAKE THIS WEAPON WITH YOU. ZORA
IT HAS BEEN PASSED DOWN THROUGH GENERATIONS IN THE DO BON FAMILY. IT ALWAYS RETURNS TO THE THROWER. ZORA
IT IS SURE TO BE HELPFUL INSIDE LORD JABU-JABU.

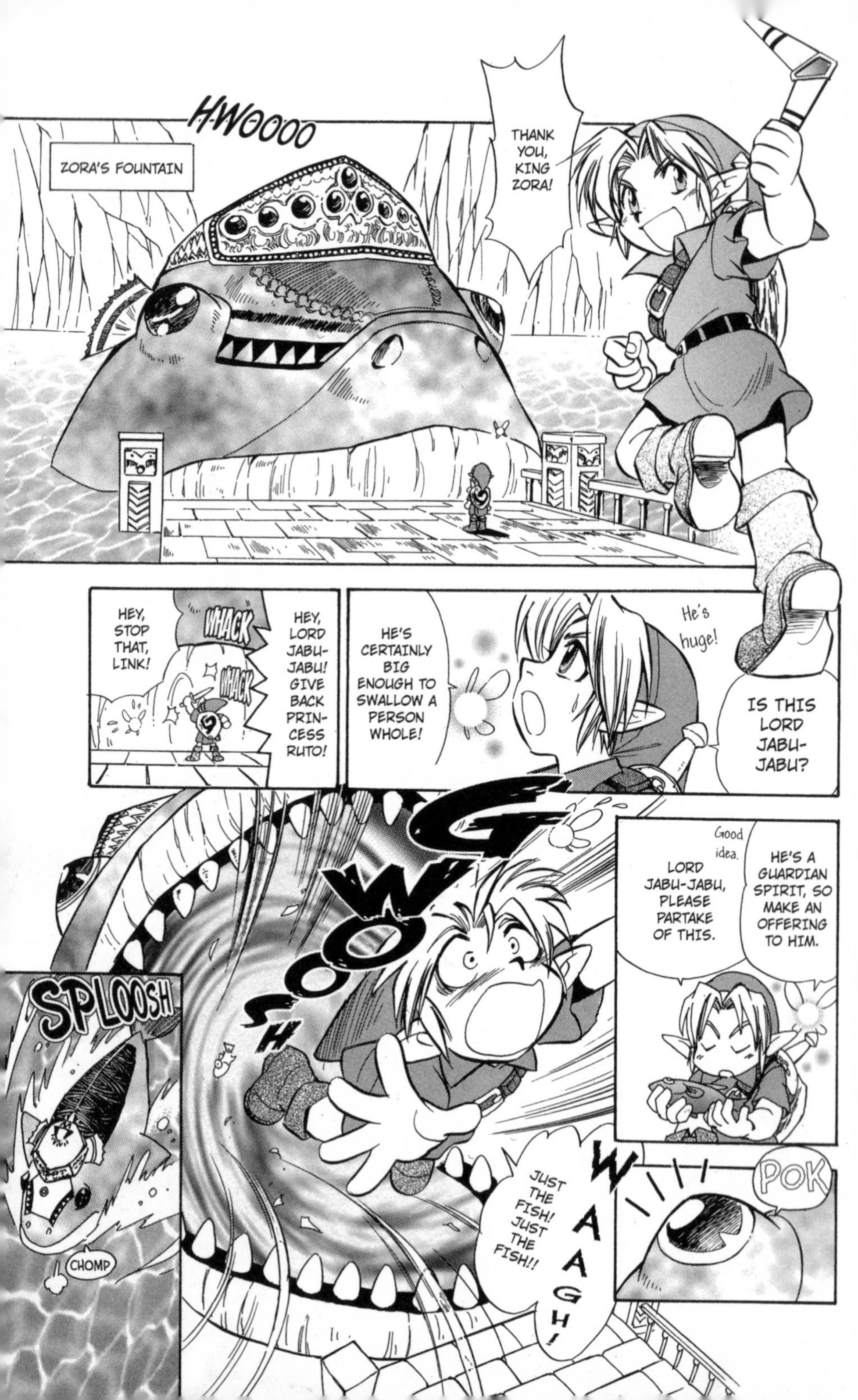
THANK YOU, KING ZORA!
HWOOOO
ZORA'S FOUNTAIN
He's huge!
IS THIS LORD JABU-JABU?
HE'S CERTAINLY BIG ENOUGH TO SWALLOW A PERSON WHOLE!
HEY, LORD JABU-JABU! GIVE BACK PRINCESS RUTO!
WHACK
WHACK
HEY, STOP THAT, LINK!
HE'S A GUARDIAN SPIRIT, SO MAKE AN OFFERING TO HIM.
Good idea.
LORD JABU-JABU, PLEASE PARTAKE OF THIS.
POK
GWOOOSH
WAAGH!
JUST THE FISH! JUST THE FISH!!
SPLOOSH
CHOMP

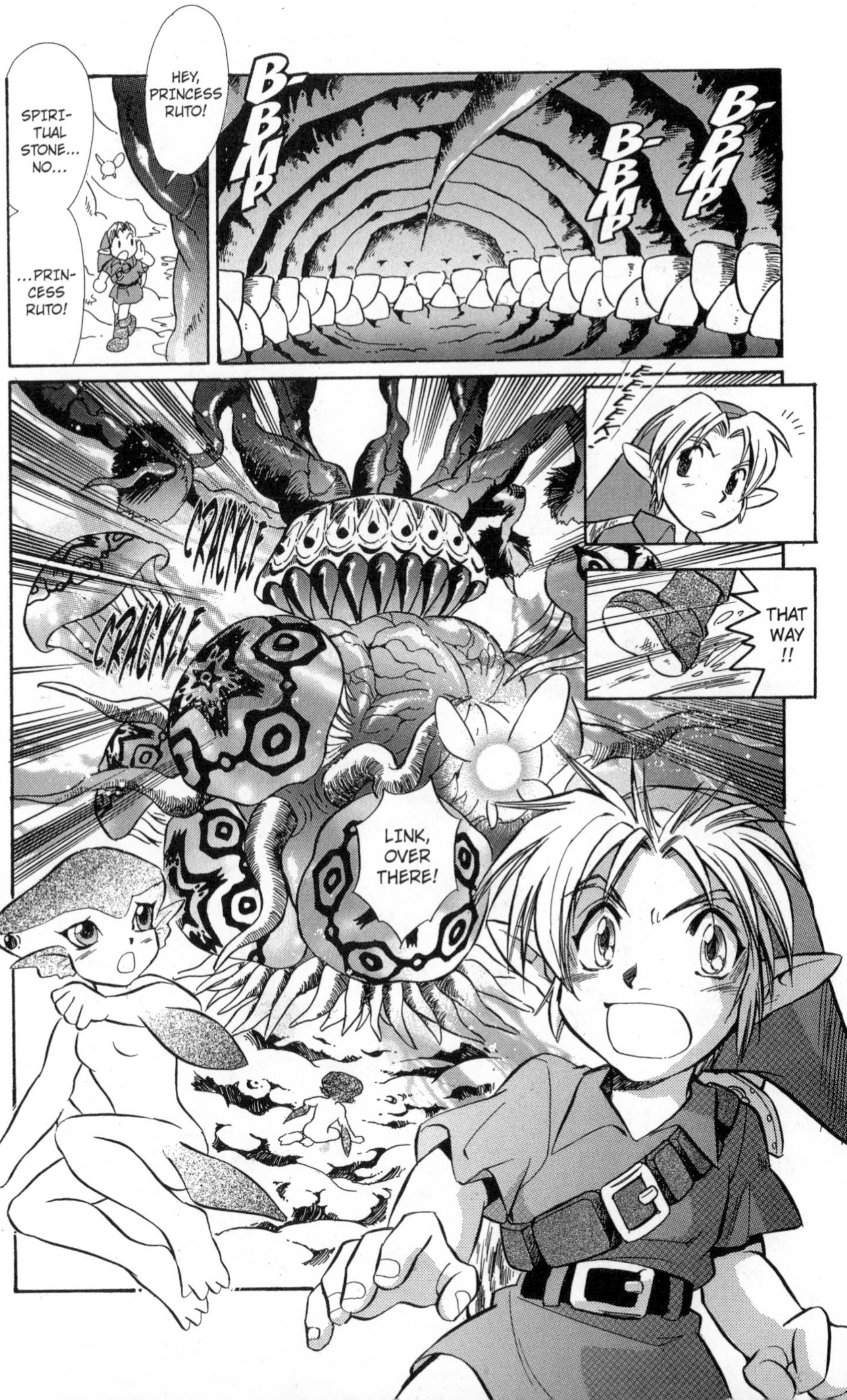
B-BBMP
B-BBMP
B-BBMP
HEY, PRINCESS RUTO!
SPIRI-TUAL STONE... NO...
...PRIN-CESS RUTO!
EEEEEK!
THAT WAY !!
CRACKLE
CRACKLE
LINK, OVER THERE!

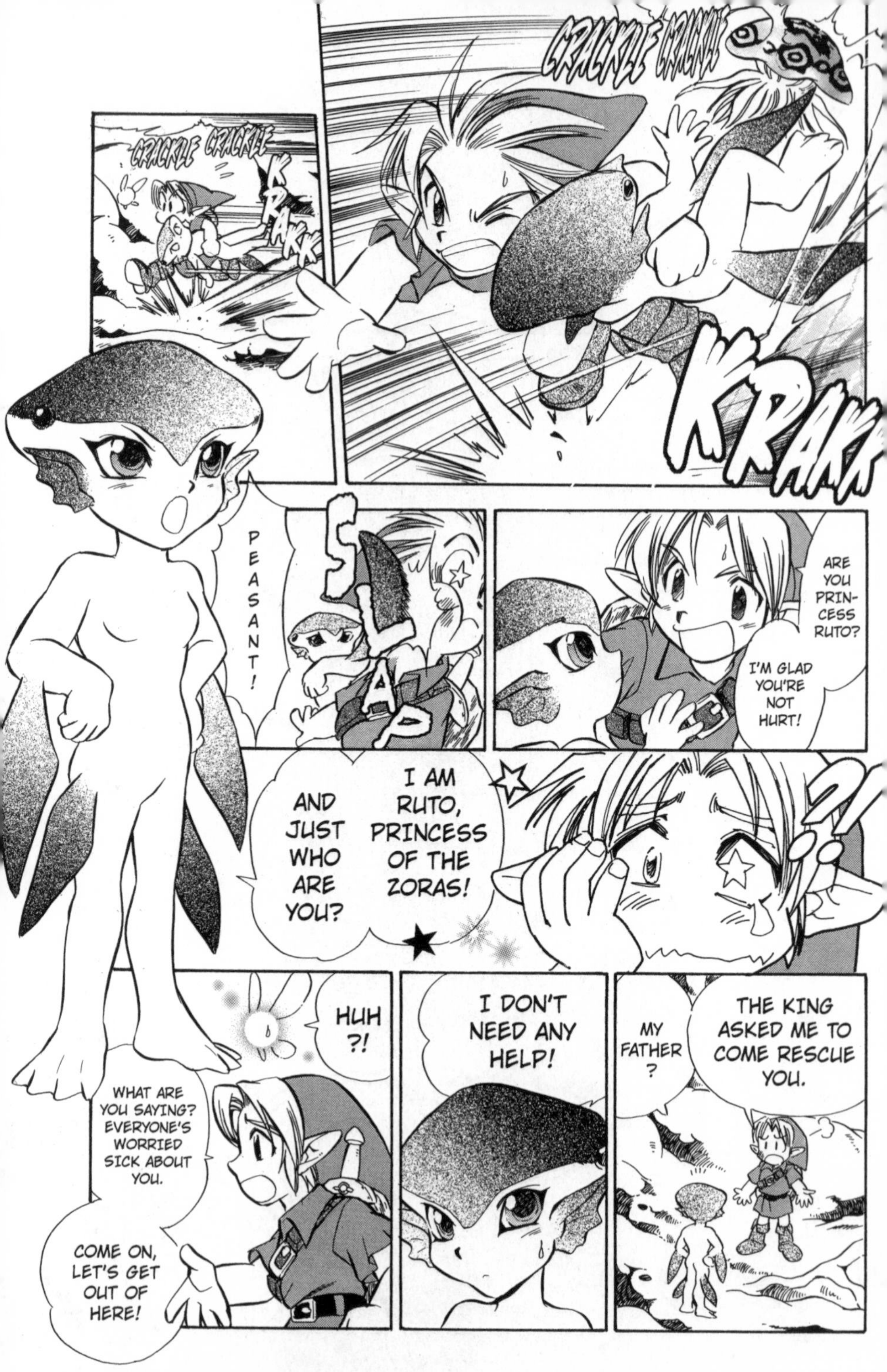
CRACKLE CRACK!!
KRAK
CRACKLE CRACKLE
KRAKK
ARE YOU PRINCESS RUTO?
I'M GLAD YOU'RE NOT HURT!
SLAP
PEASANT!
?!
I AM RUTO, PRINCESS OF THE ZORAS!
AND JUST WHO ARE YOU?
THE KING ASKED ME TO COME RESCUE YOU.
MY FATHER?
I DON'T NEED ANY HELP!
HUH?!
WHAT ARE YOU SAYING? EVERYONE'S WORRIED SICK ABOUT YOU.
COME ON, LET'S GET OUT OF HERE!

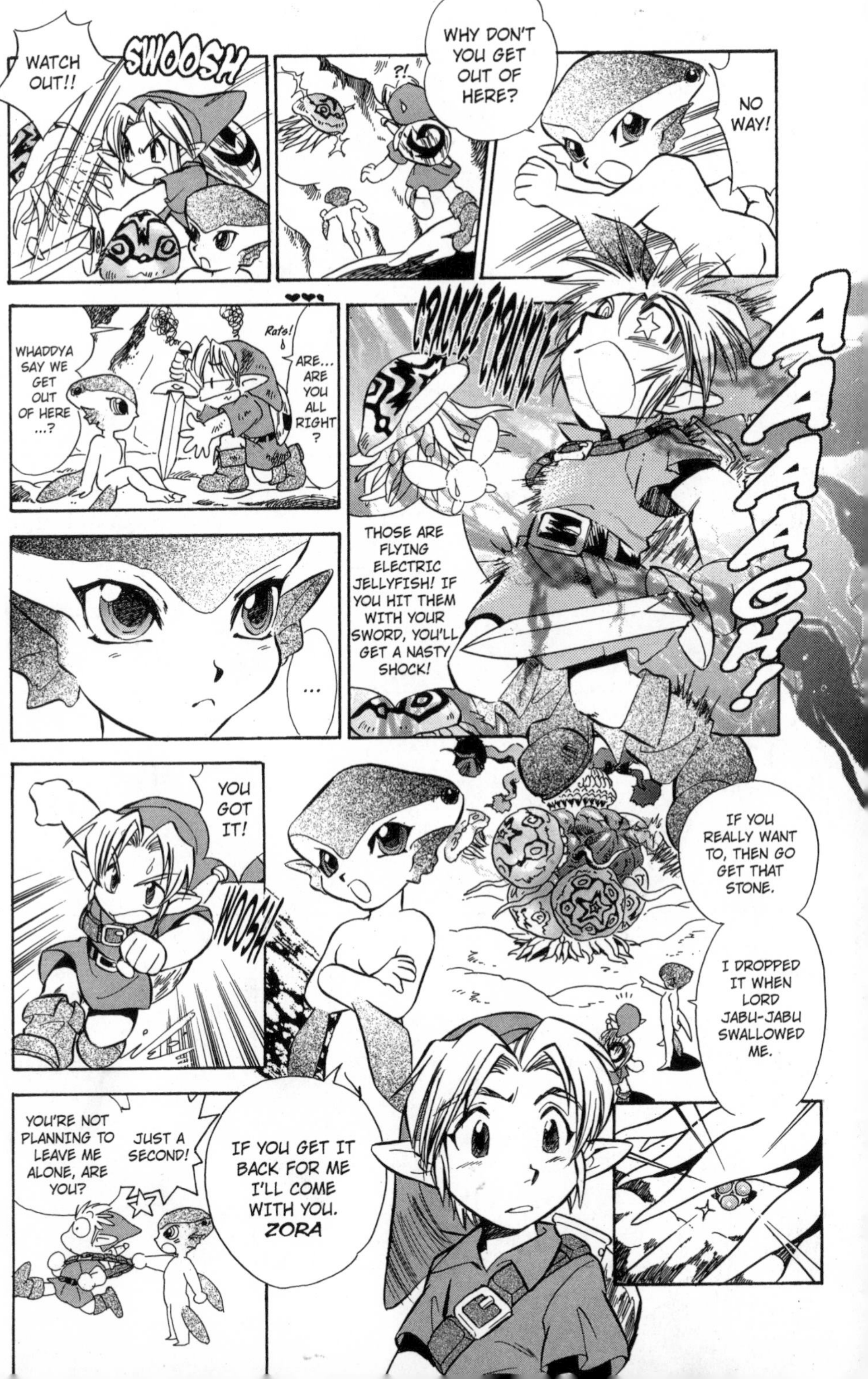
WHY DON'T YOU GET OUT OF HERE?
NO WAY!
?!
WATCH OUT!!
SWOOSH
CRACKLE CRACKLE
AAAAAGH!
THOSE ARE FLYING ELECTRIC JELLYFISH! IF YOU HIT THEM WITH YOUR SWORD, YOU'LL GET A NASTY SHOCK!
ARE... ARE YOU ALL RIGHT?
Rats!
WHADDYA SAY WE GET OUT OF HERE ...?
...
IF YOU REALLY WANT TO, THEN GO GET THAT STONE.
I DROPPED IT WHEN LORD JABU-JABU SWALLOWED ME.
YOU GOT IT!
WOOSH
IF YOU GET IT BACK FOR ME I'LL COME WITH YOU.
ZORA
JUST A SECOND!
YOU'RE NOT PLANNING TO LEAVE ME ALONE, ARE YOU?

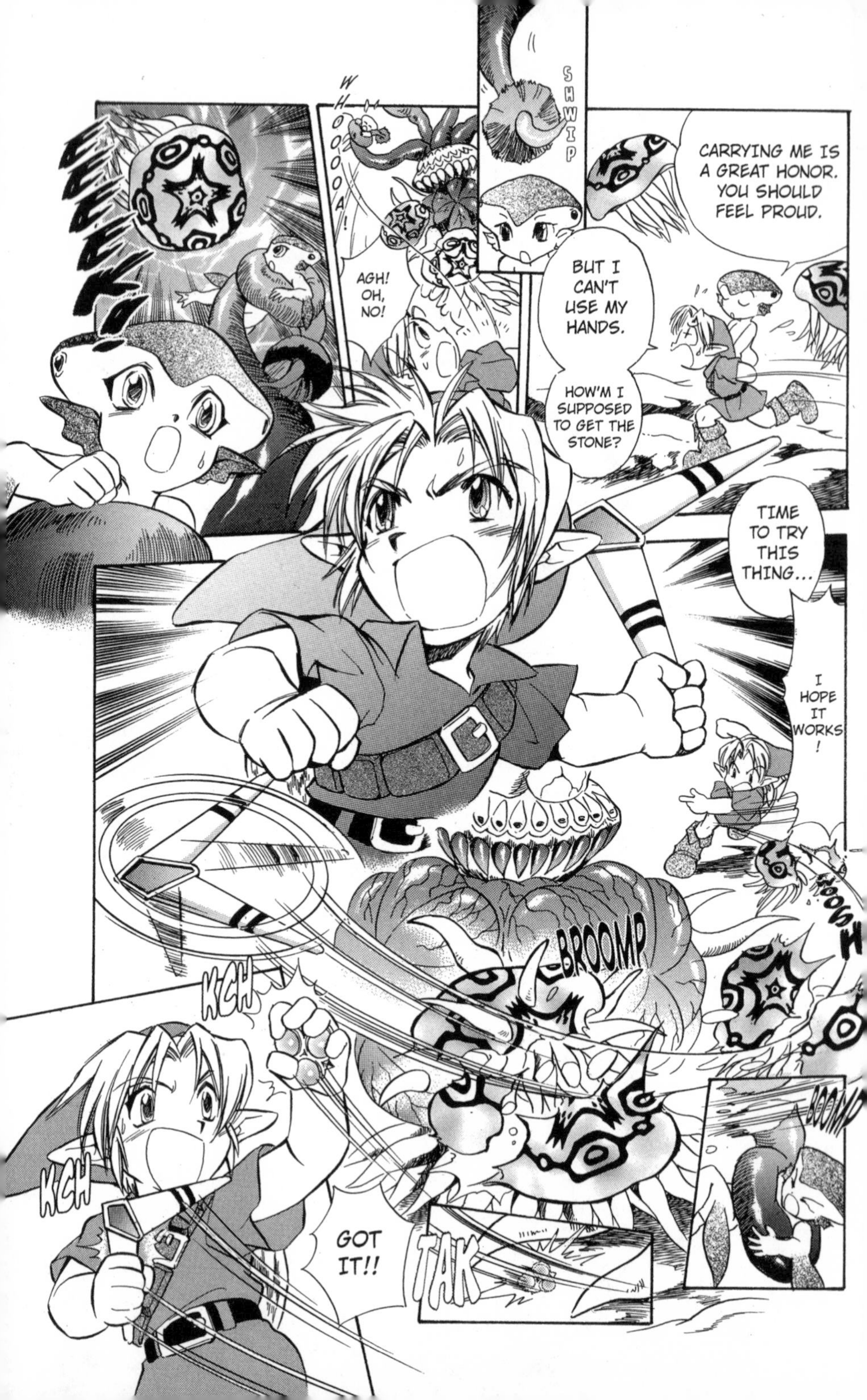
CARRYING ME IS A GREAT HONOR. YOU SHOULD FEEL PROUD.
BUT I CAN'T USE MY HANDS.
HOW'M I SUPPOSED TO GET THE STONE?
SHWIP
WHOOOOOA!
AGH! OH, NO!
TIME TO TRY THIS THING...
I HOPE IT WORKS!
WHOOSH
BROOMP
KCH
BOOMP
TAK
GOT IT!!
KCH

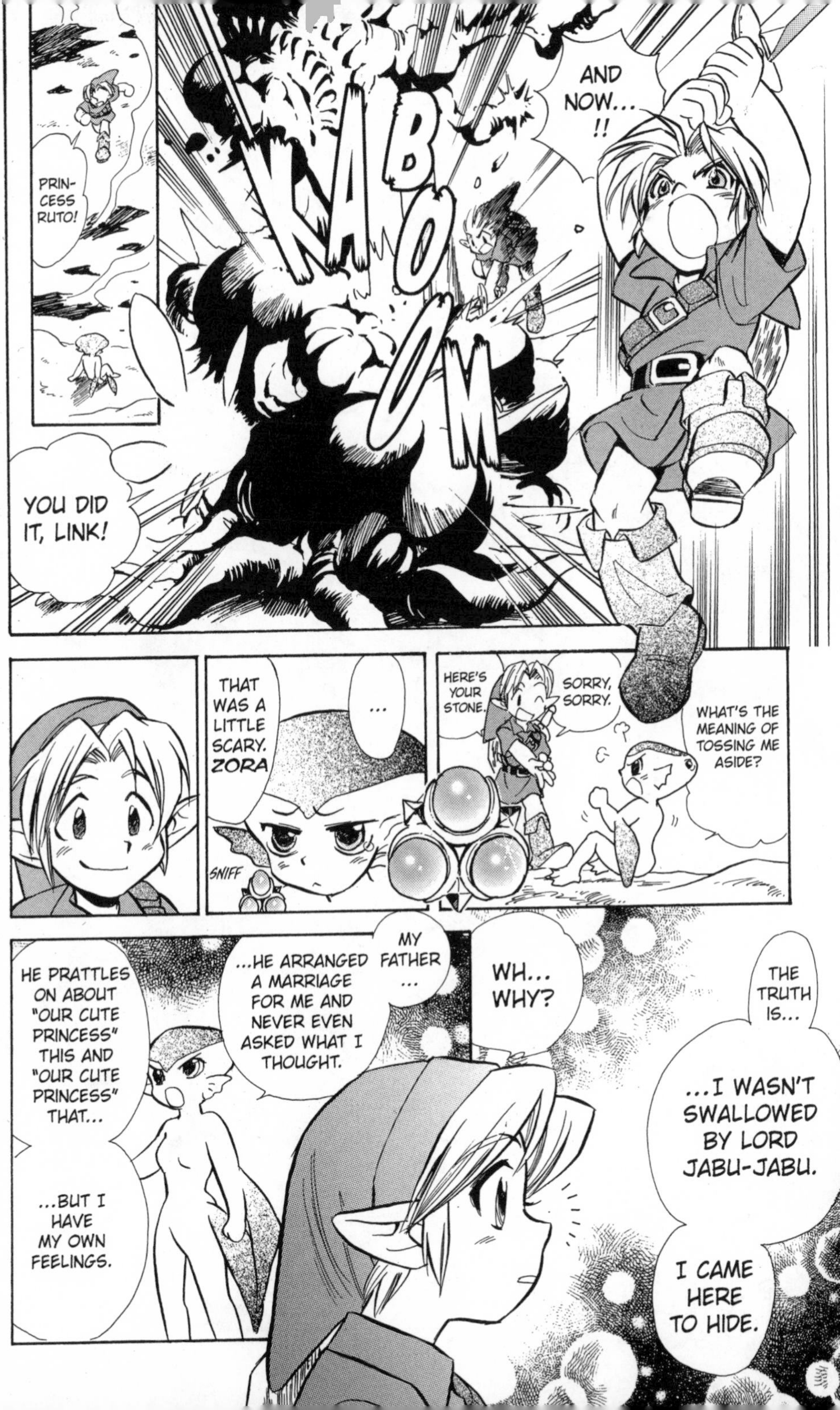
AND NOW... !!
KABOOM
YOU DID IT, LINK!
PRINCESS RUTO!
WHAT'S THE MEANING OF TOSSING ME ASIDE?
SORRY, SORRY.
HERE'S YOUR STONE.
...
THAT WAS A LITTLE SCARY.
ZORA
SNIFF
THE TRUTH IS...
...I WASN'T SWALLOWED BY LORD JABU-JABU.
I CAME HERE TO HIDE.
WH... WHY?
MY FATHER...
...HE ARRANGED A MARRIAGE FOR ME AND NEVER EVEN ASKED WHAT I THOUGHT.
HE PRATTLES ON ABOUT "OUR CUTE PRINCESS" THIS AND "OUR CUTE PRINCESS" THAT...
...BUT I HAVE MY OWN FEELINGS.

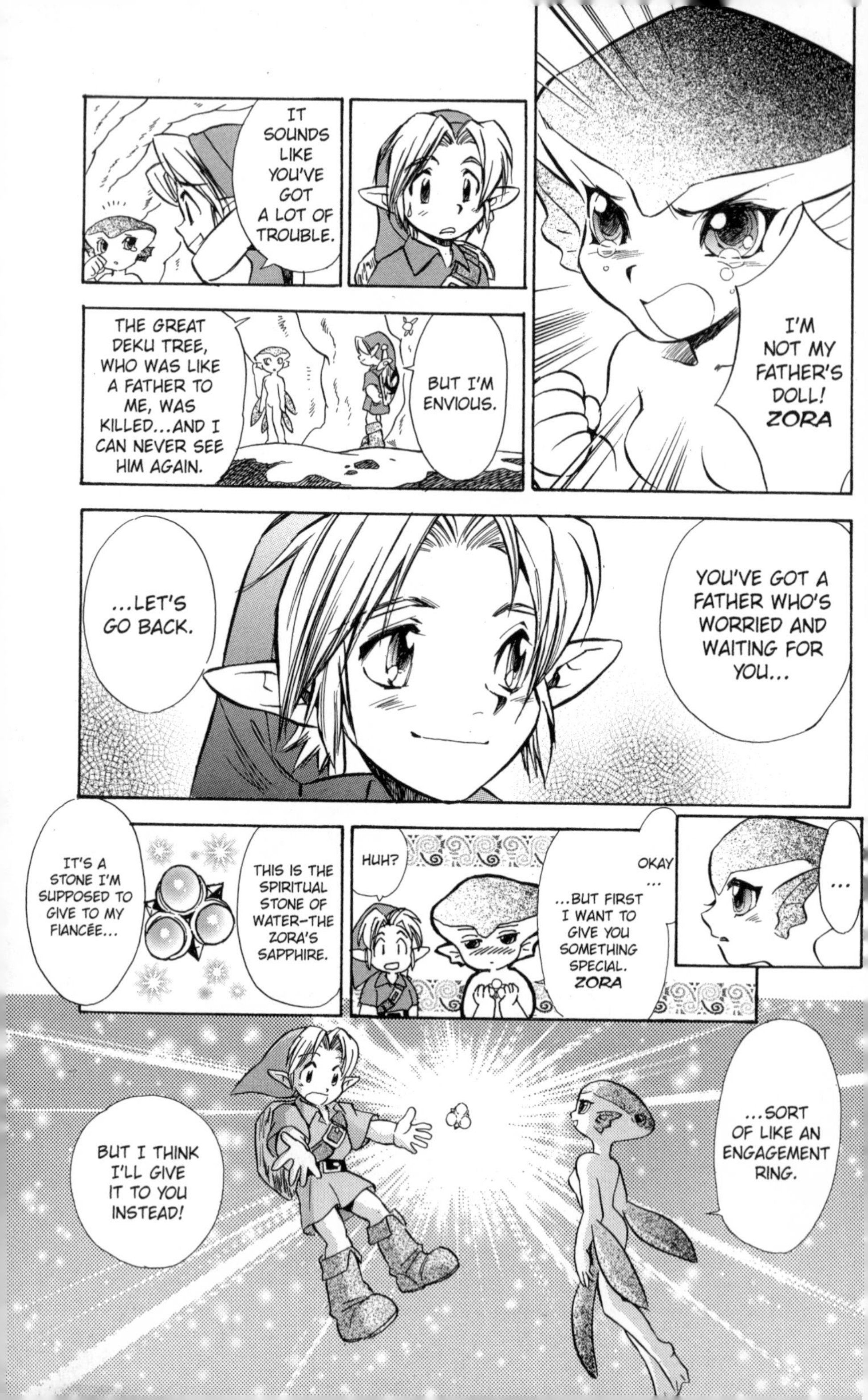

I'M NOT MY FATHER'S DOLL! ZORA
IT SOUNDS LIKE YOU'VE GOT A LOT OF TROUBLE.
BUT I'M ENVIOUS.
THE GREAT DEKU TREE, WHO WAS LIKE A FATHER TO ME, WAS KILLED...AND I CAN NEVER SEE HIM AGAIN.
YOU'VE GOT A FATHER WHO'S WORRIED AND WAITING FOR YOU...
...LET'S GO BACK.
...
OKAY ...
...BUT FIRST I WANT TO GIVE YOU SOMETHING SPECIAL. ZORA
HUH?
THIS IS THE SPIRITUAL STONE OF WATER—THE ZORA'S SAPPHIRE.
IT'S A STONE I'M SUPPOSED TO GIVE TO MY FIANCÉE...
...SORT OF LIKE AN ENGAGEMENT RING.
BUT I THINK I'LL GIVE IT TO YOU INSTEAD!

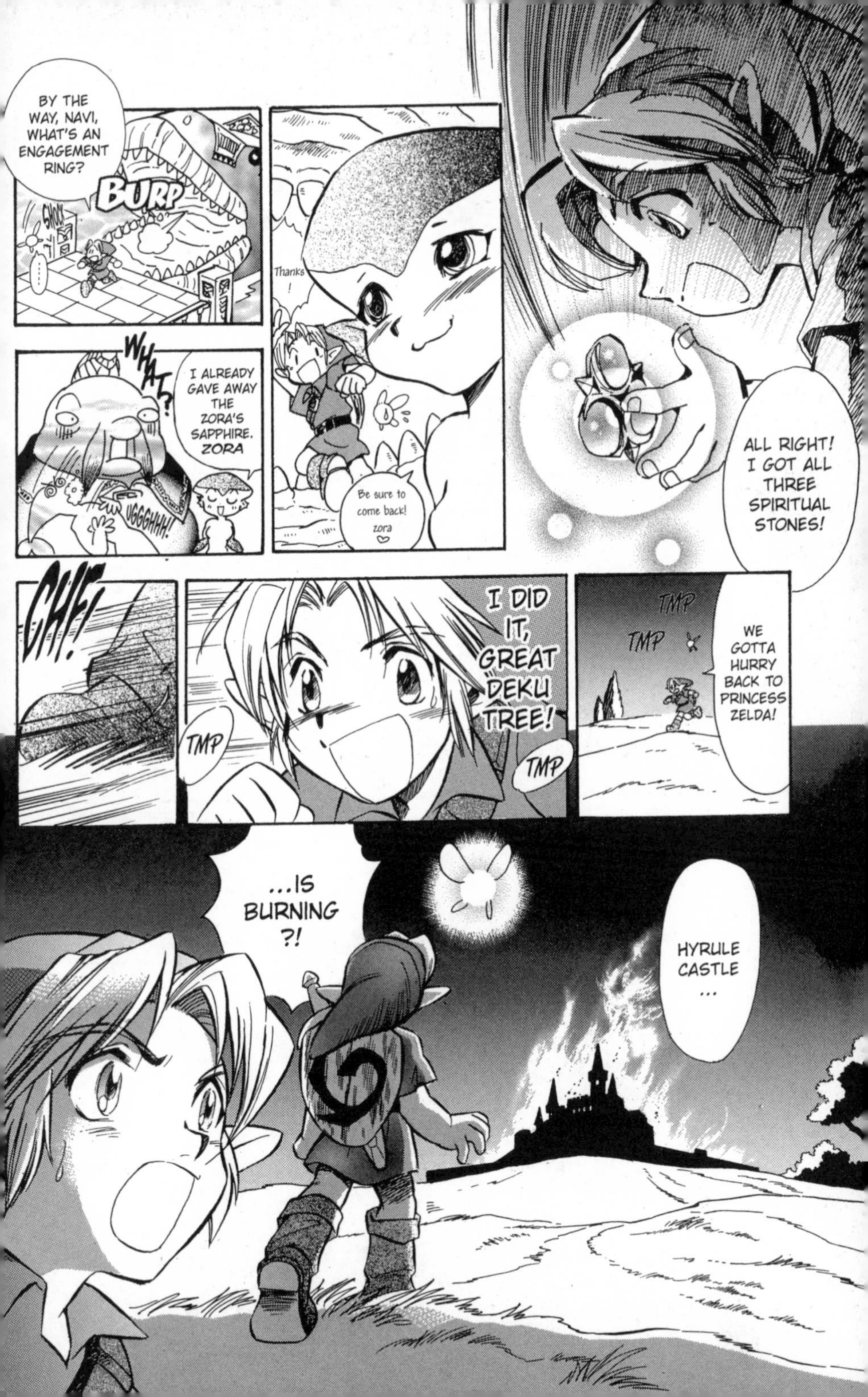
ALL RIGHT! I GOT ALL THREE SPIRITUAL STONES!
Thanks!
Be sure to come back! zora
BY THE WAY, NAVI, WHAT'S AN ENGAGEMENT RING?
BURP
SHOCK
...
WHAT?!
I ALREADY GAVE AWAY THE ZORA'S SAPPHIRE. ZORA
UGGGHHH!
TMP
TMP
WE GOTTA HURRY BACK TO PRINCESS ZELDA!
I DID IT, GREAT DEKU TREE!
TMP
TMP
CHF!
HYRULE CASTLE ...
...IS BURNING ?!

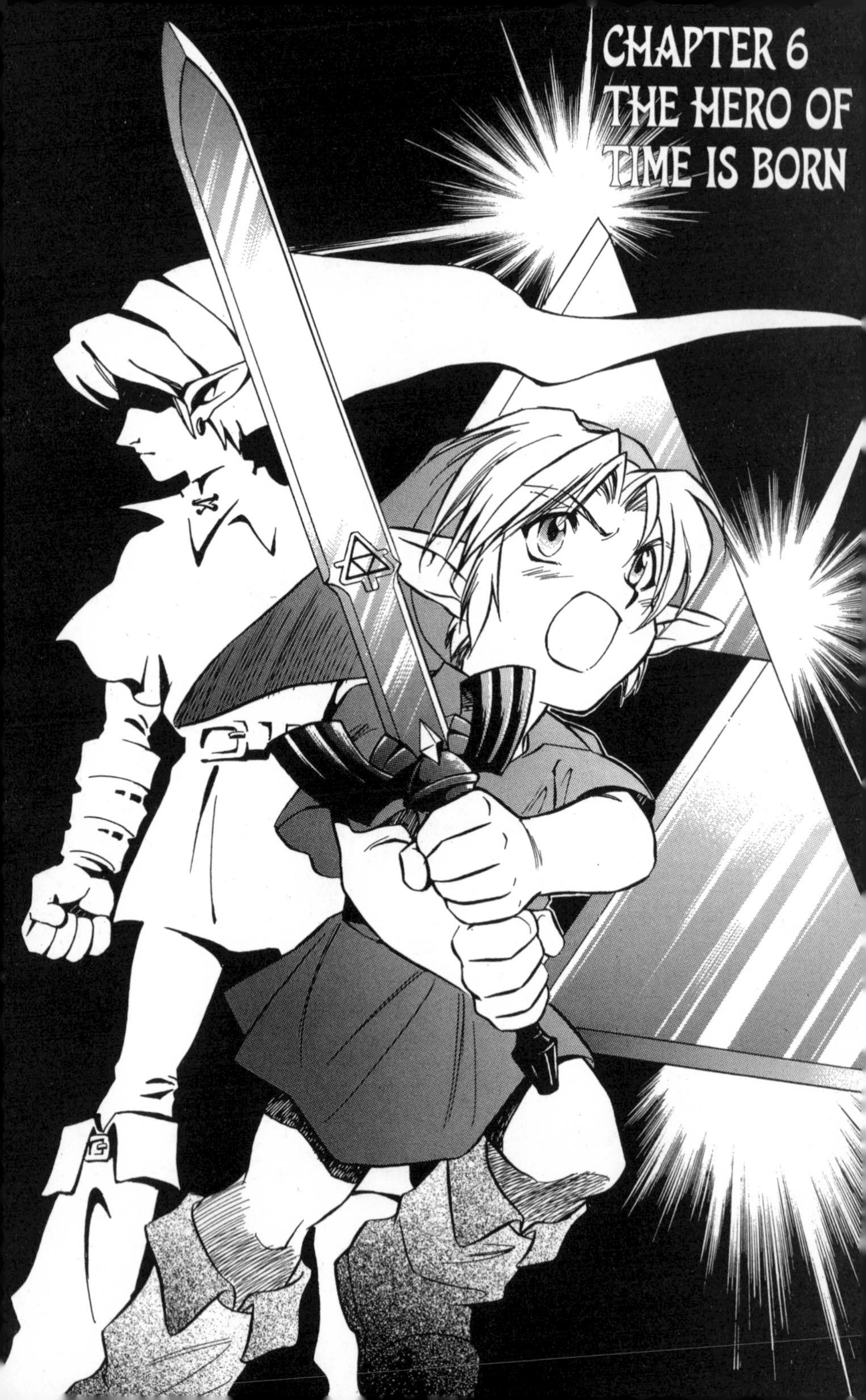
CHAPTER 6
THE HERO OF
TIME IS BORN

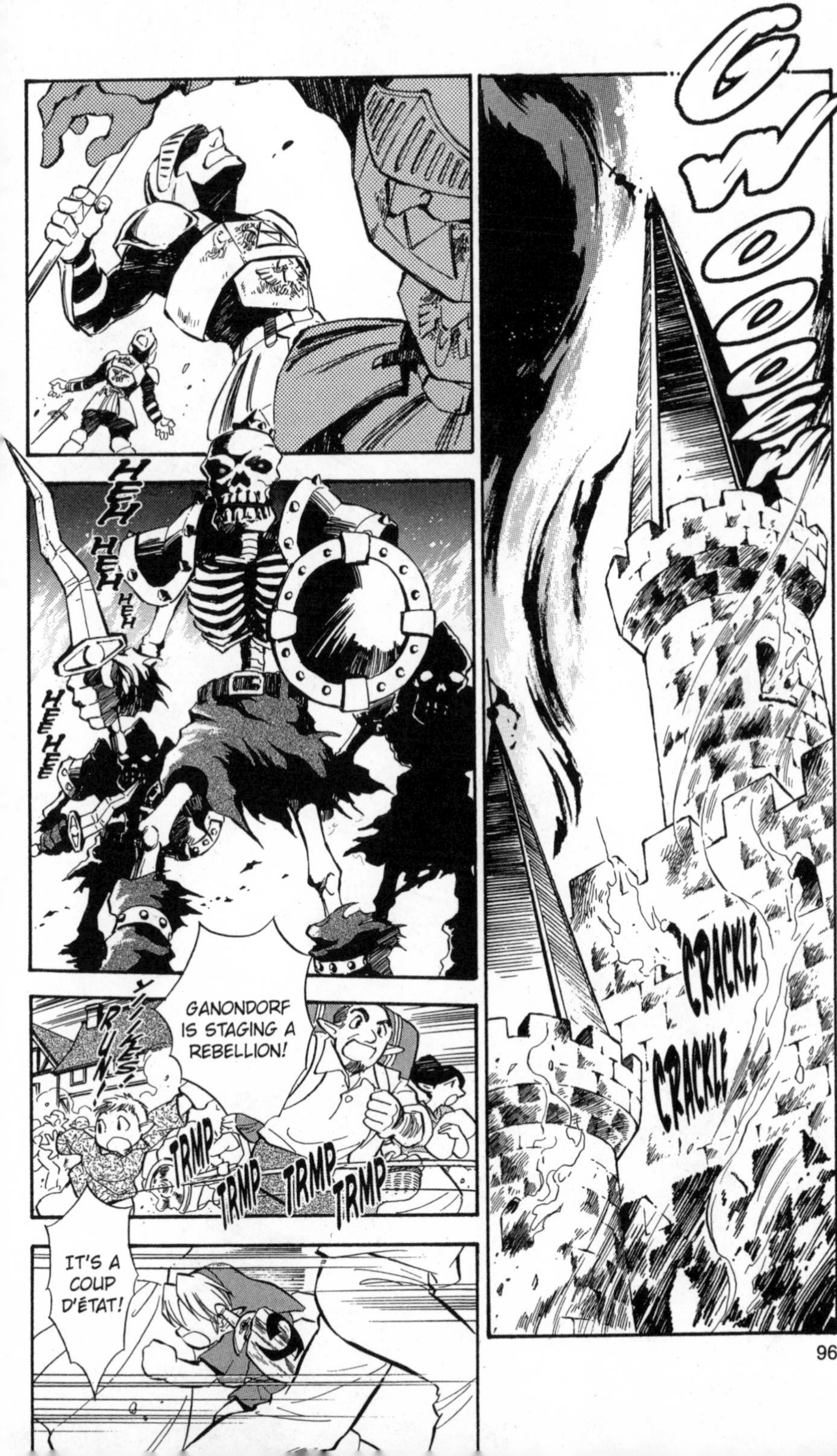
GWOOOOOM
CRACKLE
CRACKLE
HEH HEH HEH HEH
HEHEE
GANONDORF IS STAGING A REBELLION!
YIKES!
RUN!
TRMP TRMP TRMP TRMP
IT'S A COUP D'ÉTAT!

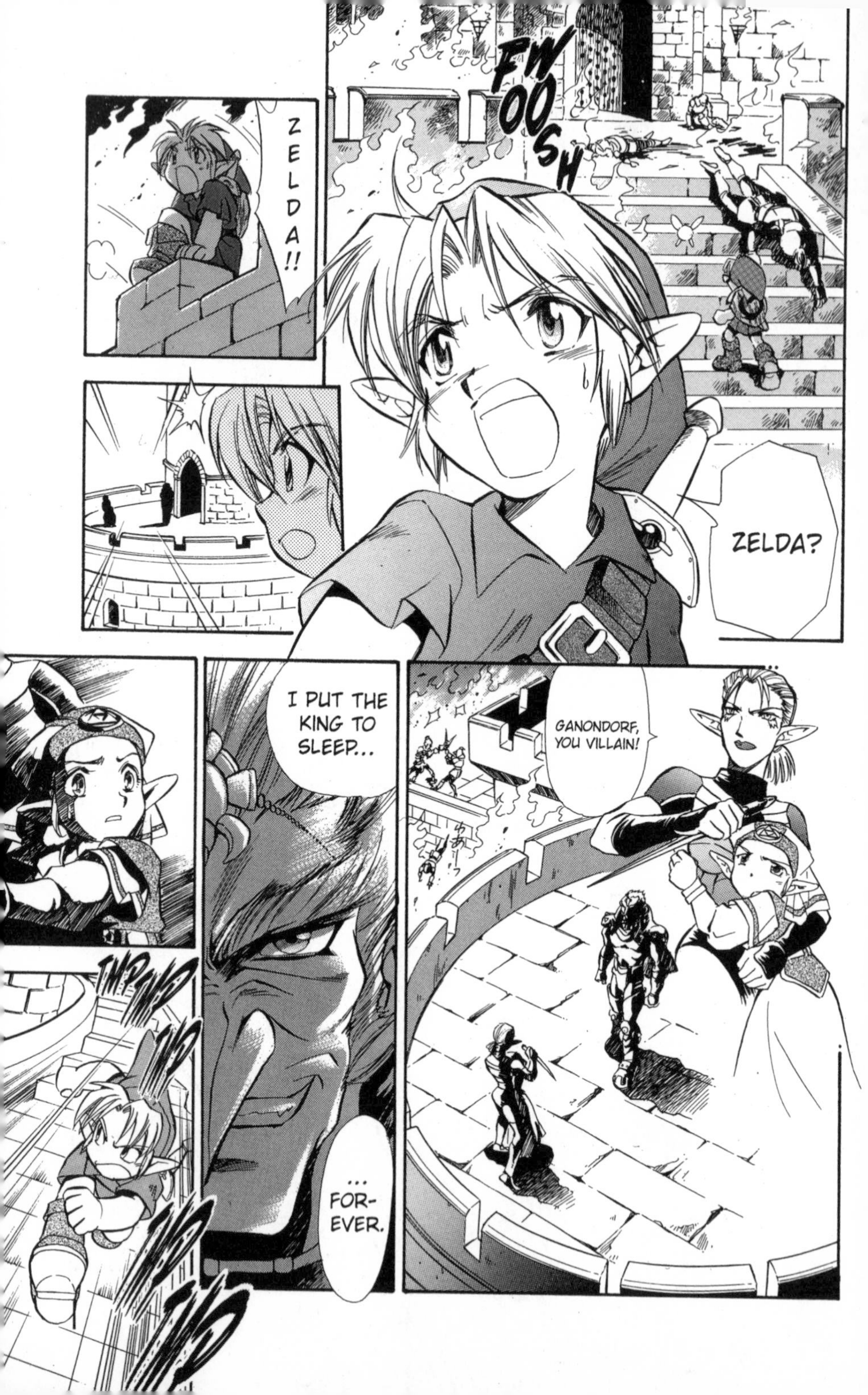
FWOOSH
ZELDA?
ZELDA!!
GANONDORF, YOU VILLAIN!
I PUT THE KING TO SLEEP...
...FOR-EVER.
TMP TMP

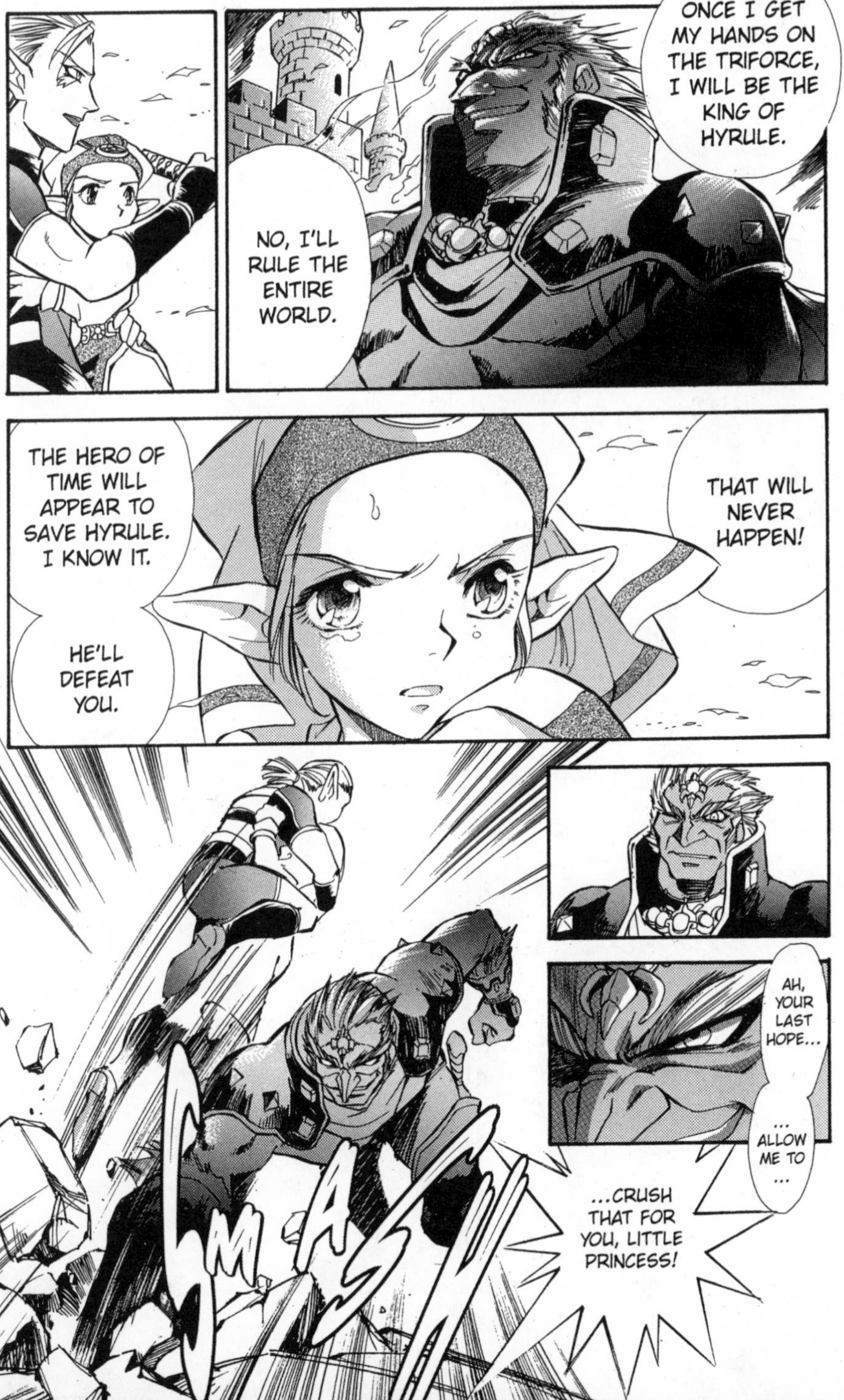
ONCE I GET MY HANDS ON THE TRIFORCE, I WILL BE THE KING OF HYRULE.
NO, I'LL RULE THE ENTIRE WORLD.
THAT WILL NEVER HAPPEN!
THE HERO OF TIME WILL APPEAR TO SAVE HYRULE. I KNOW IT.
HE'LL DEFEAT YOU.
AH, YOUR LAST HOPE...
...ALLOW ME TO...
...CRUSH THAT FOR YOU, LITTLE PRINCESS!
SMASH

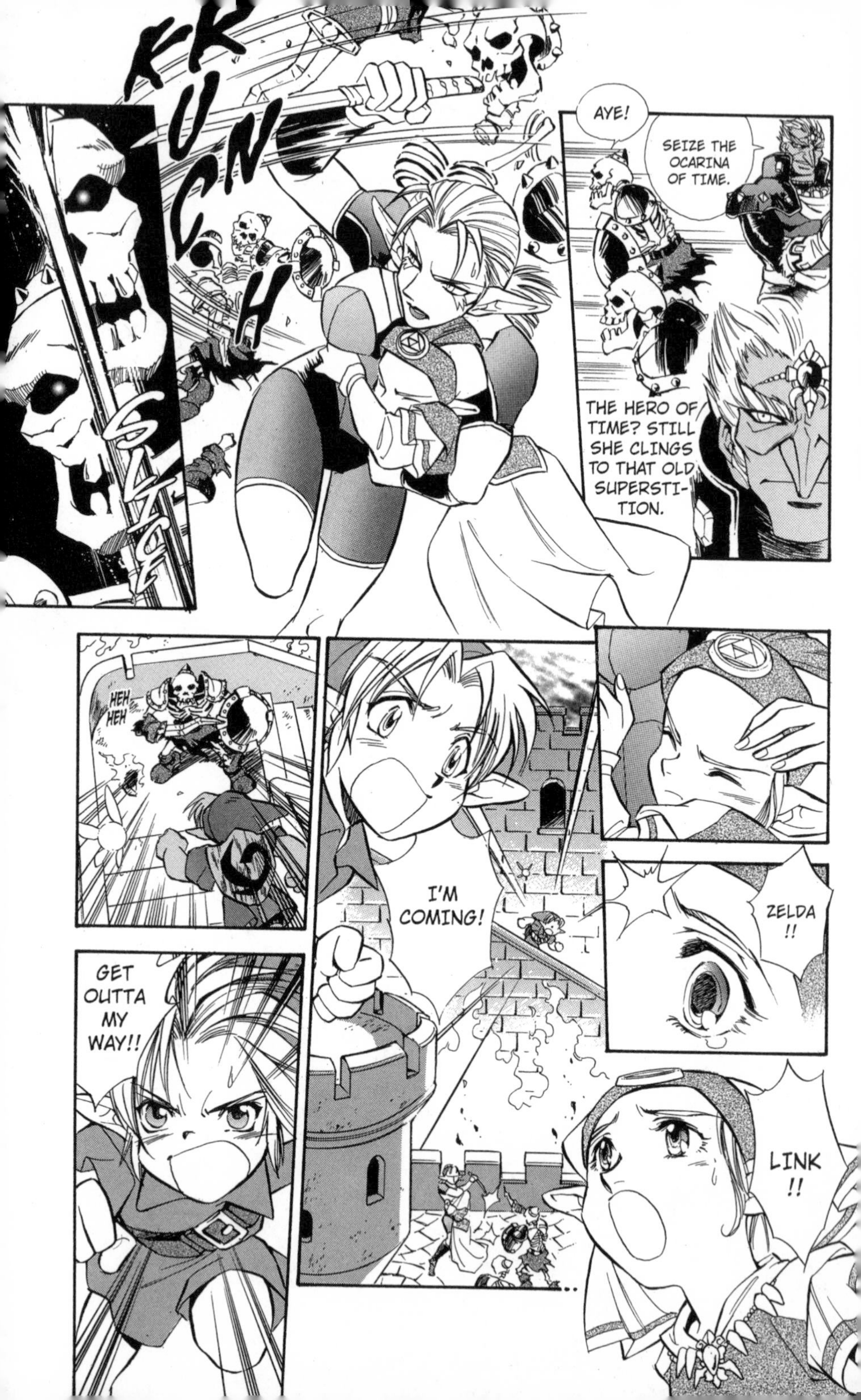
SEIZE THE OCARINA OF TIME.
AYE!
THE HERO OF TIME? STILL SHE CLINGS TO THAT OLD SUPERSTITION.
KRUNCH
SLICE
ZELDA !!
LINK !!
I'M COMING!
HEH HEH
GET OUTTA MY WAY!!

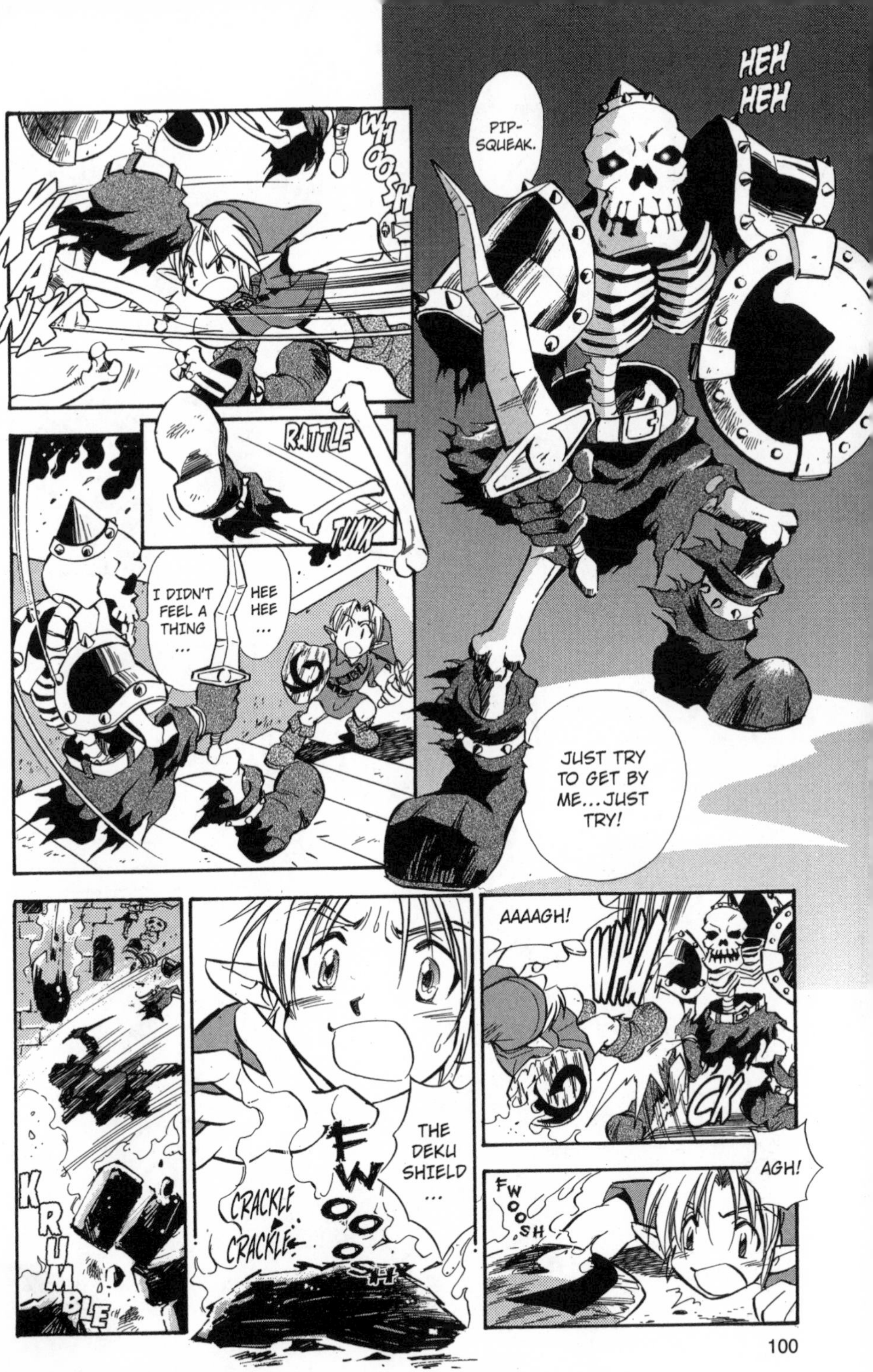
HEH HEH
PIP-SQUEAK.
JUST TRY TO GET BY ME...JUST TRY!
WHOOSH
KLANK
RATTLE
TUNK
HEE HEE ...
I DIDN'T FEEL A THING ...
AAAAGH!
AGH!
FWOOSH
THE DEKU SHIELD ...
FWOOOOSH
CRACKLE CRACKLE
KRUMBLE

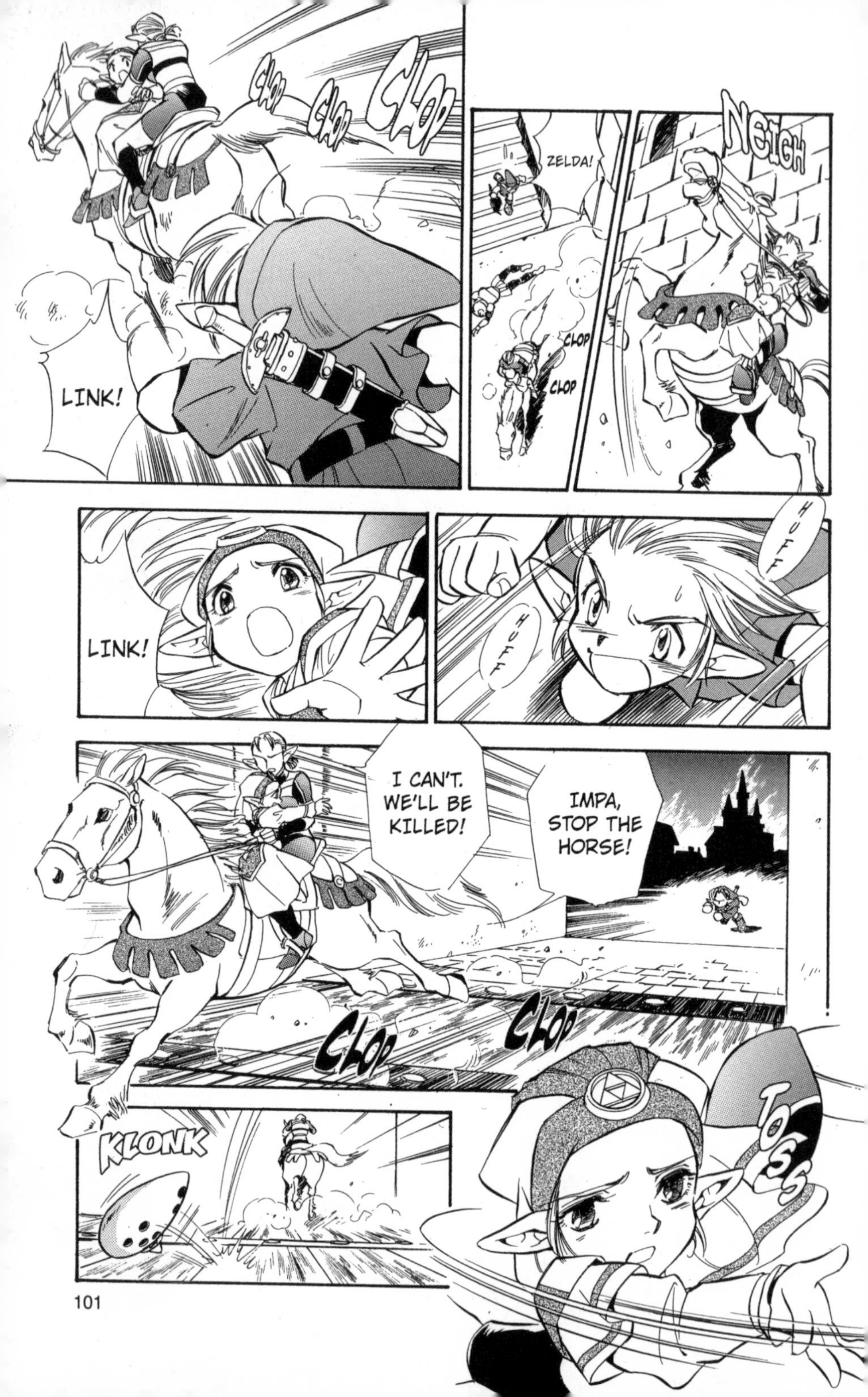
NEIGH
ZELDA!
CLOP
CLOP
CLOP
CLOP
CLOP
LINK!
HUFF
HUFF
LINK!
IMPA, STOP THE HORSE!
I CAN'T. WE'LL BE KILLED!
CLOP
CLOP
TOSS
KLONK

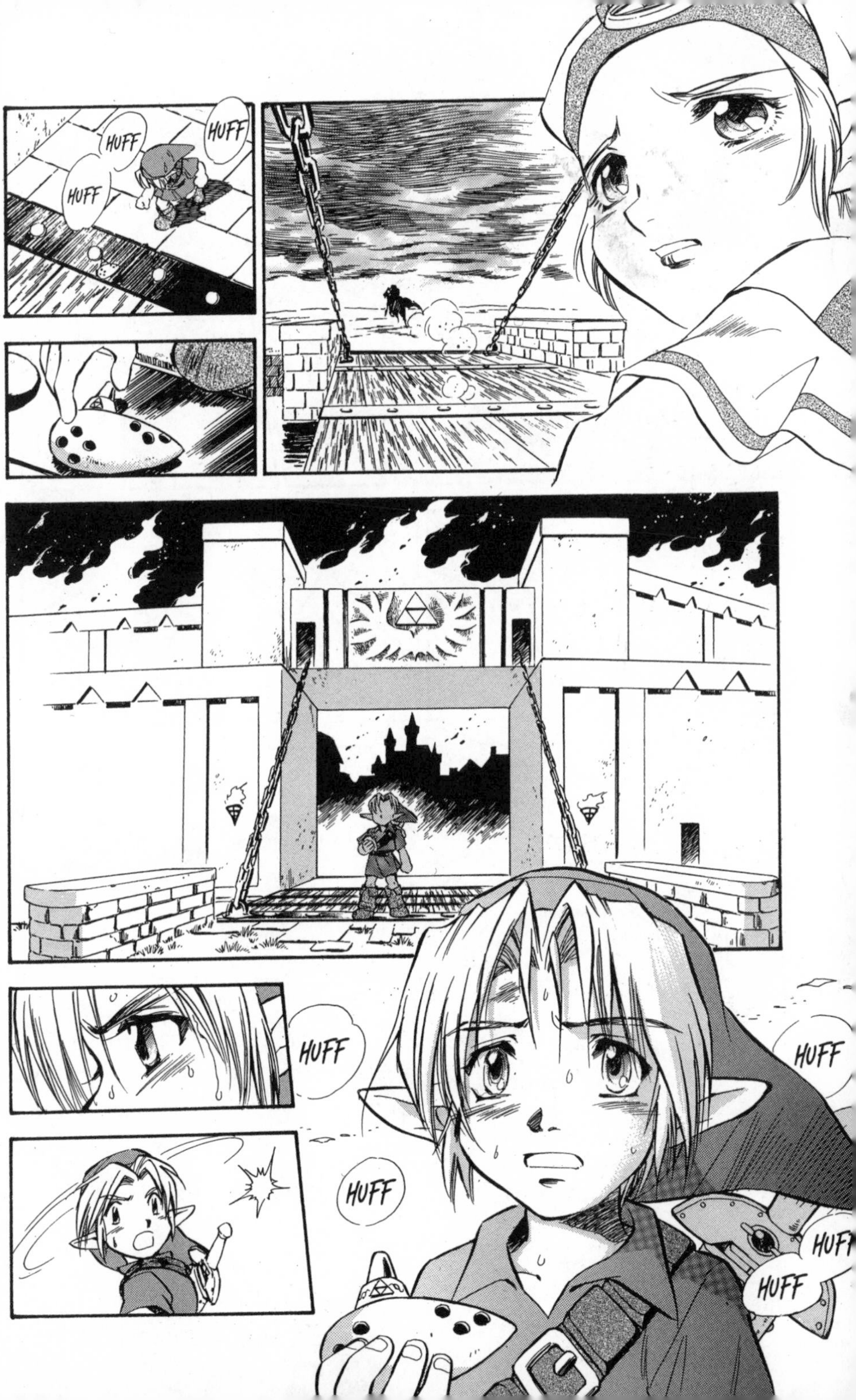
HUFF
HUFF
HUFF
HUFF
HUFF
HUFF
HUFF
HUFF

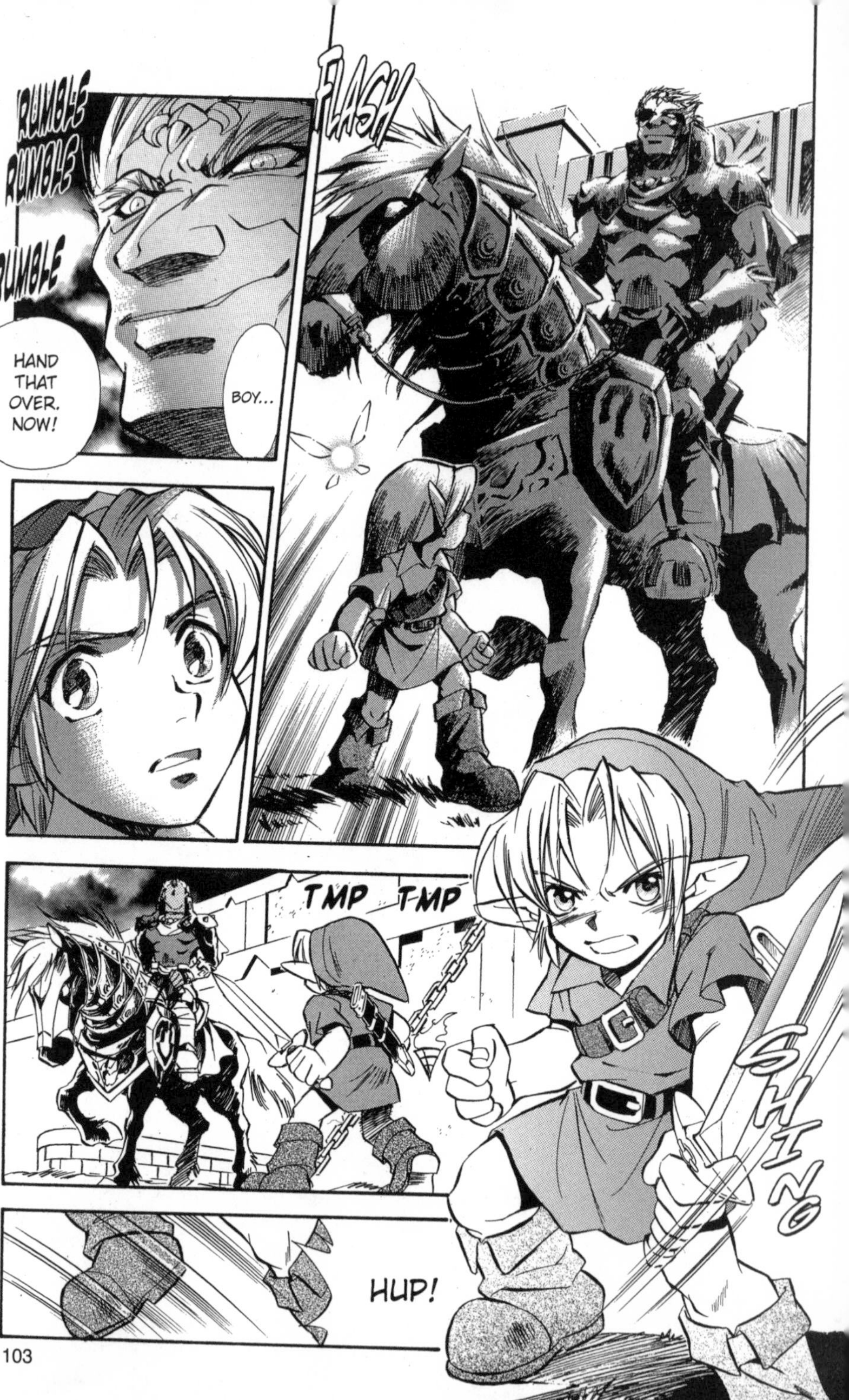
FLASH
RUMBLE RUMBLE
RUMBLE
BOY...
HAND THAT OVER. NOW!
SHING
TMP TMP
HUP!

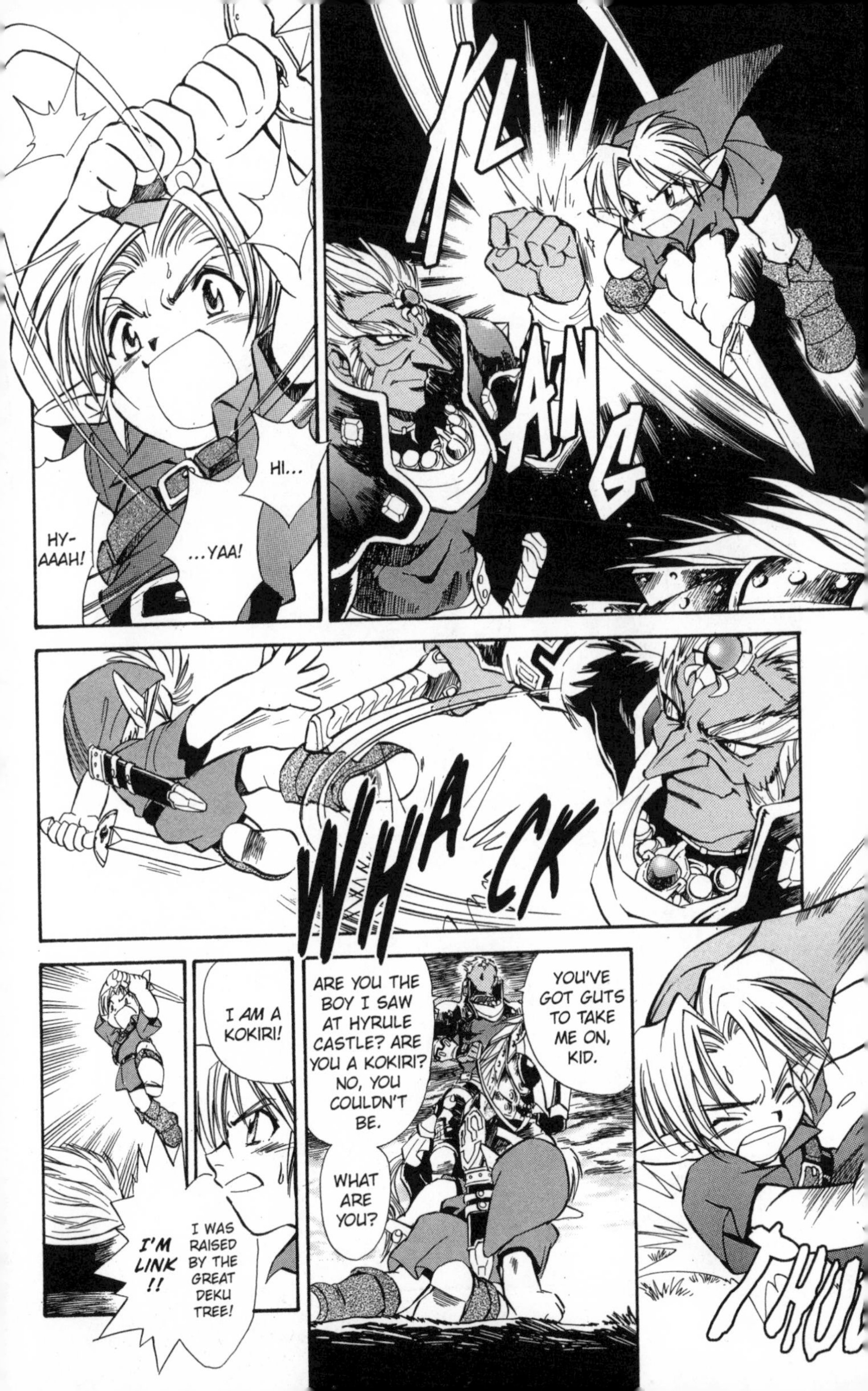

KLANG
HI...
...YAA!
HY-AAAH!
WHACK
THU
YOU'VE GOT GUTS TO TAKE ME ON, KID.
ARE YOU THE BOY I SAW AT HYRULE CASTLE? ARE YOU A KOKIRI? NO, YOU COULDN'T BE.
WHAT ARE YOU?
I AM A KOKIRI!
I WAS RAISED BY THE GREAT DEKU TREE!
I'M LINK!!

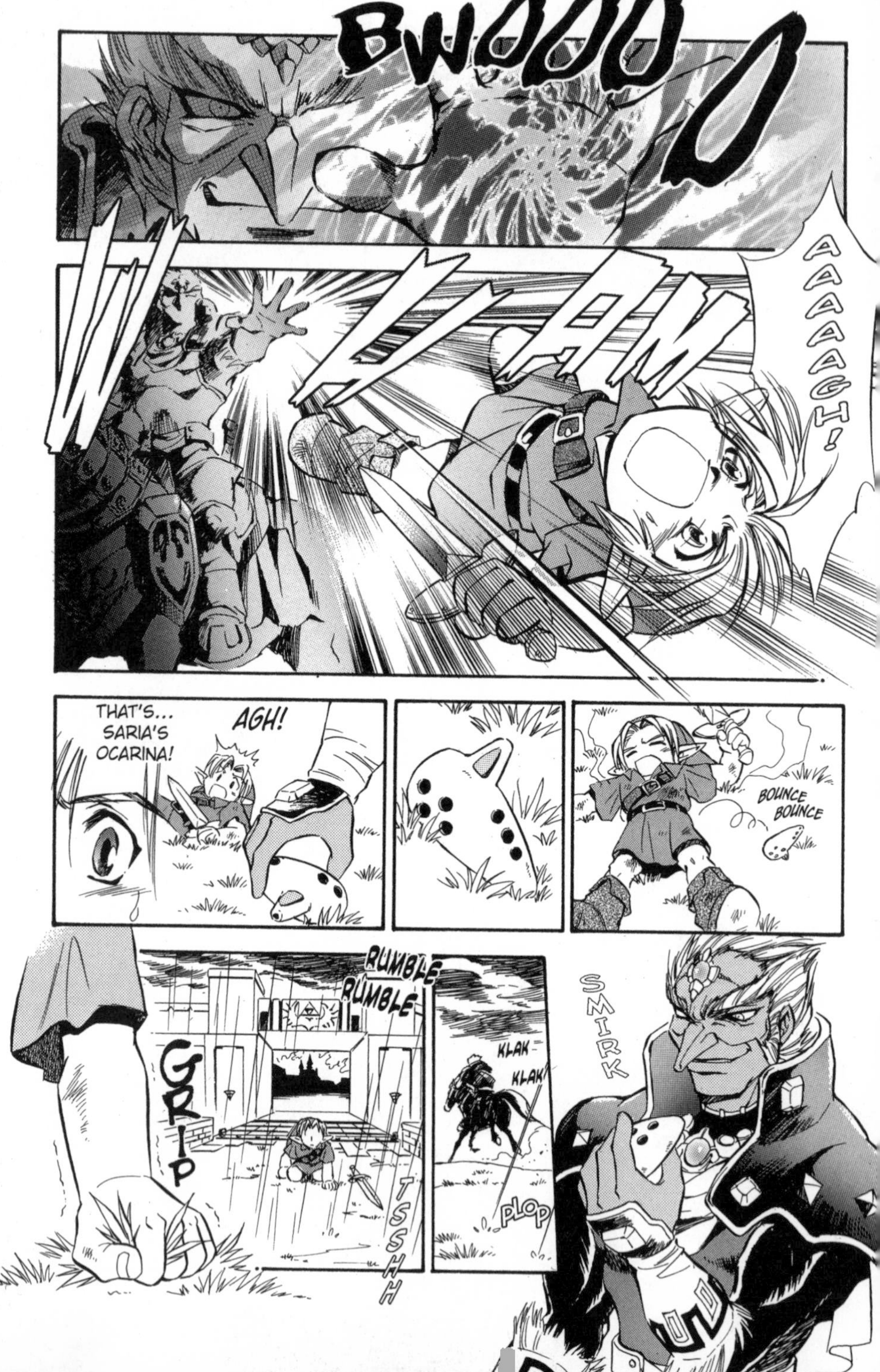
BWOOOO
AAAAAAGH!
WHAM
BOUNCE BOUNCE
AGH!
THAT'S... SARIA'S OCARINA!
SMIRK
KLAK
KLAK
PLOP
RUMBLE RUMBLE
GRIP
TSSHH

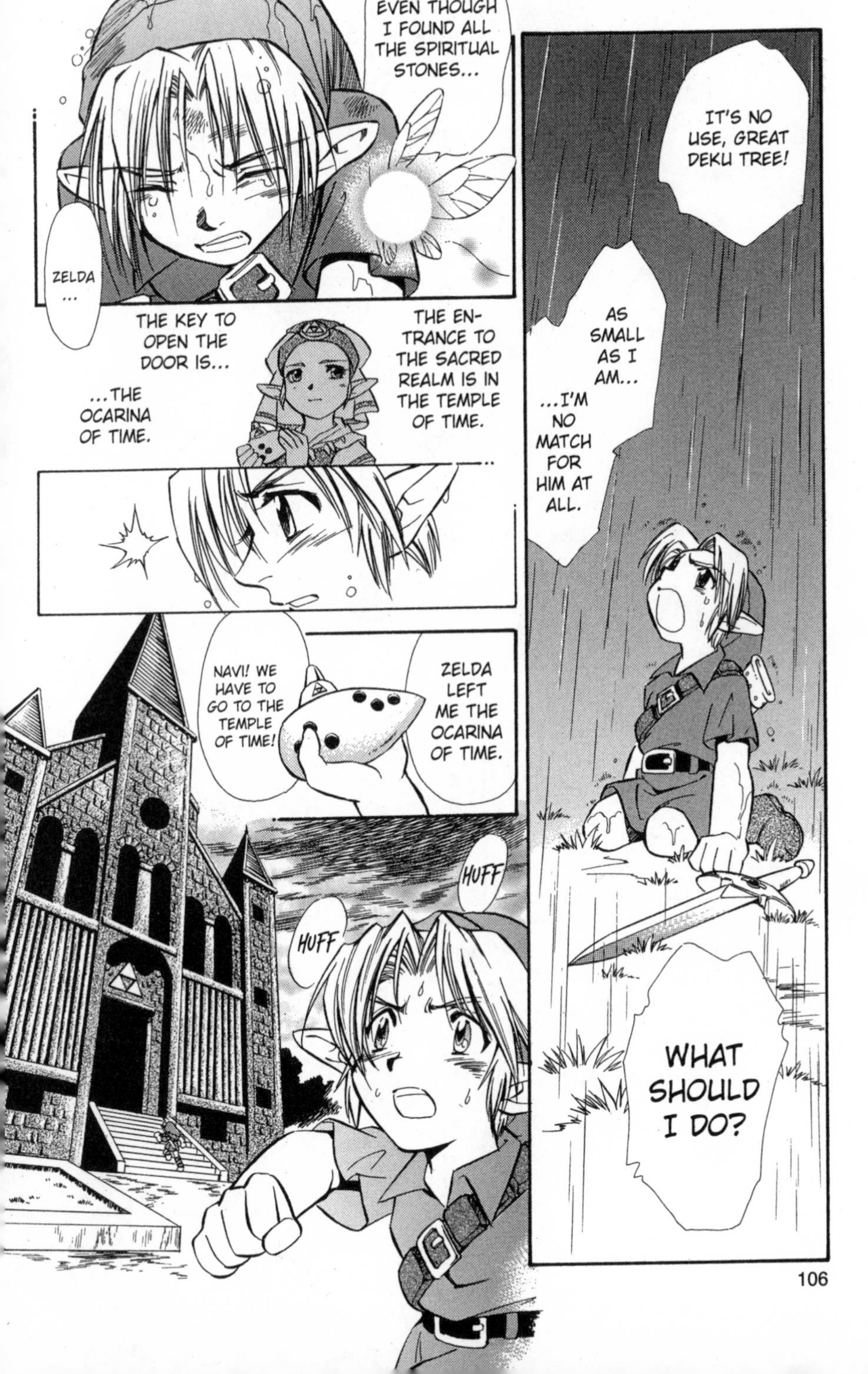
IT'S NO USE, GREAT DEKU TREE!
AS SMALL AS I AM...
...I'M NO MATCH FOR HIM AT ALL.
WHAT SHOULD I DO?
EVEN THOUGH I FOUND ALL THE SPIRITUAL STONES...
ZELDA ...
THE ENTRANCE TO THE SACRED REALM IS IN THE TEMPLE OF TIME.
THE KEY TO OPEN THE DOOR IS...
...THE OCARINA OF TIME.
ZELDA LEFT ME THE OCARINA OF TIME.
NAVI! WE HAVE TO GO TO THE TEMPLE OF TIME!
HUFF
HUFF

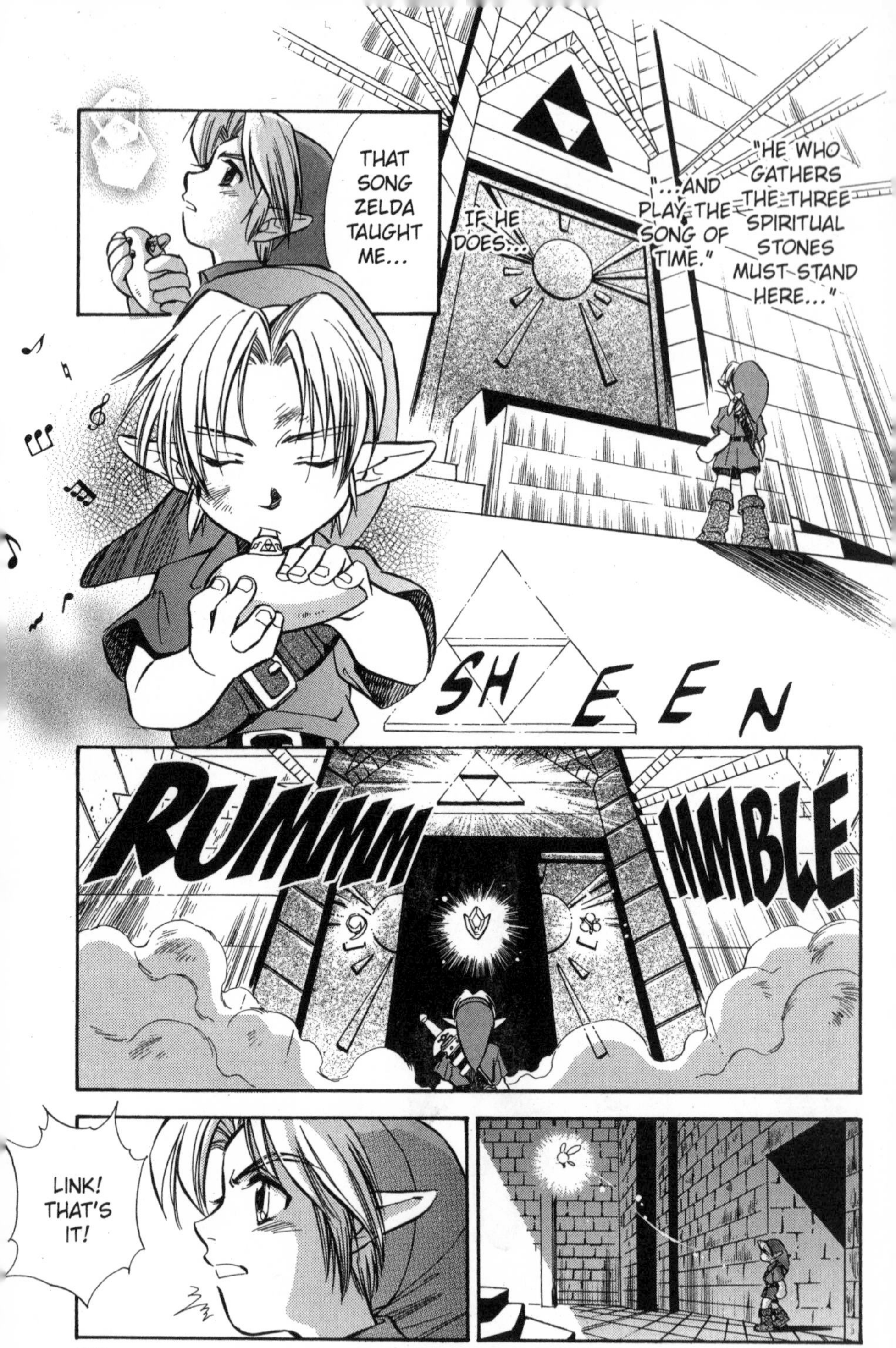
"HE WHO GATHERS THE THREE SPIRITUAL STONES MUST STAND HERE..."
"...AND PLAY THE SONG OF TIME."
IF HE DOES...
THAT SONG ZELDA TAUGHT ME...
SHEEN
RUMMMMMMBLE
LINK! THAT'S IT!

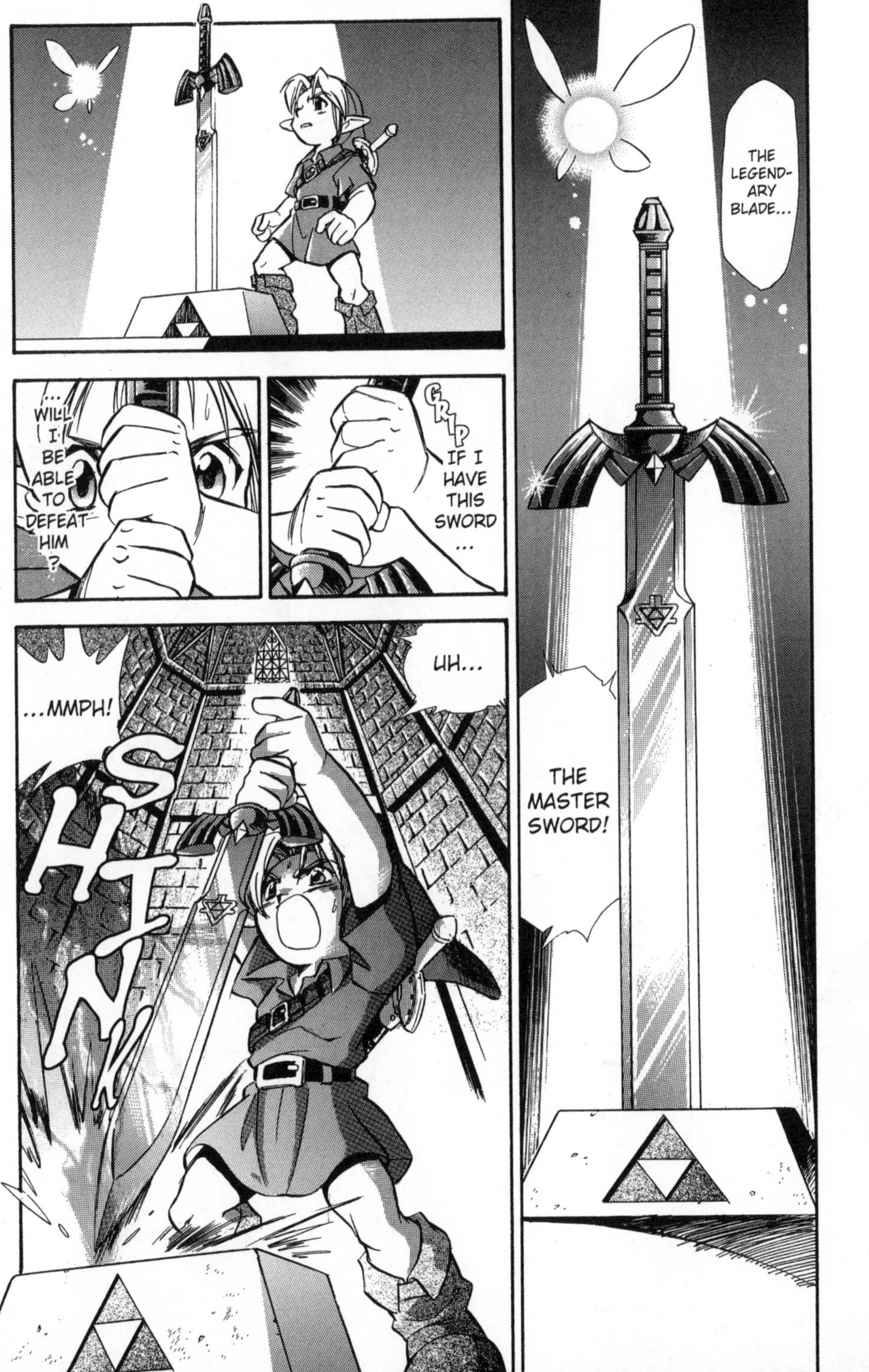
THE LEGENDARY BLADE...
THE MASTER SWORD!
GRIP
IF I HAVE THIS SWORD...
...WILL I BE ABLE TO DEFEAT HIM?
UH...
...MMPH!
SHIN

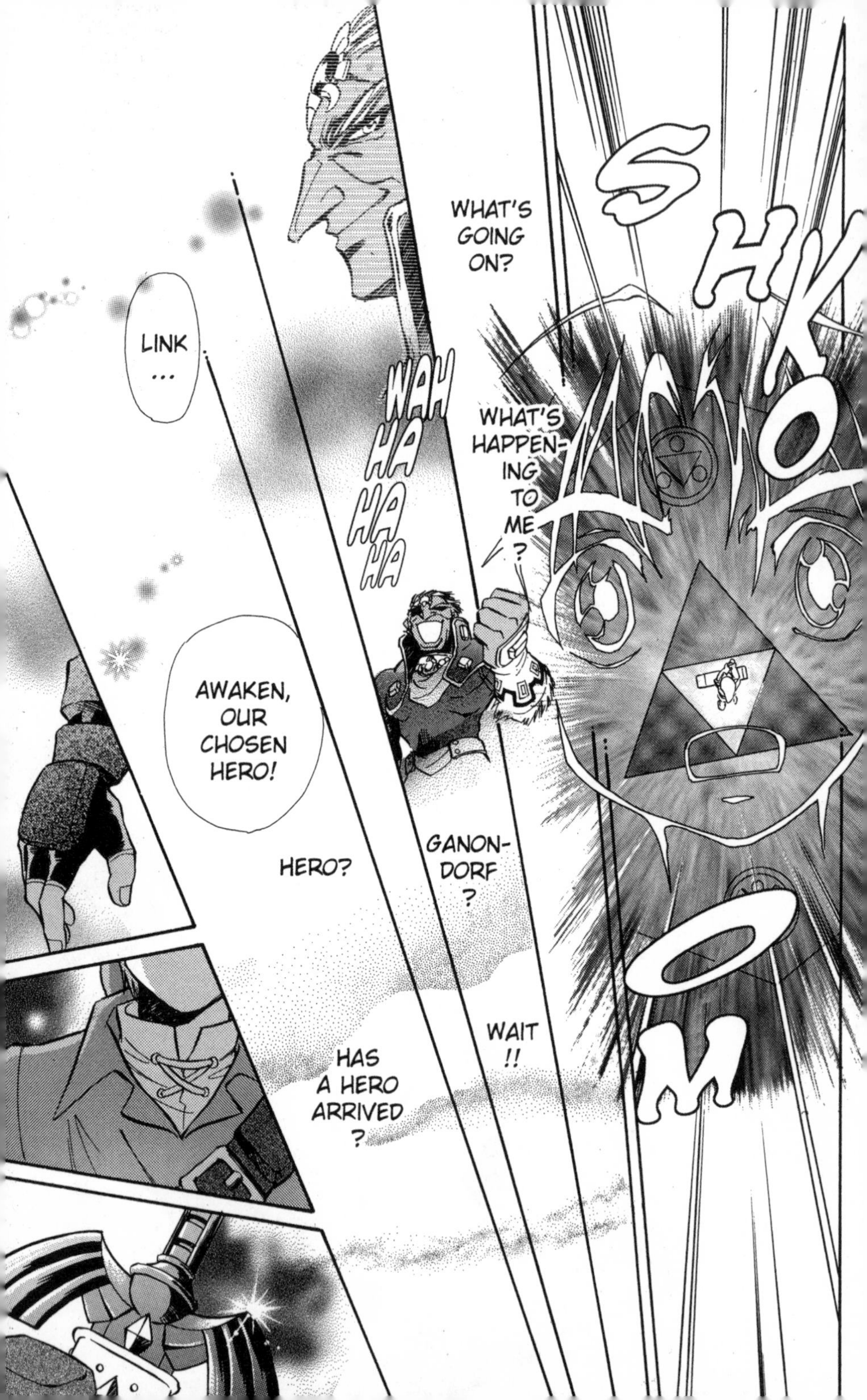
SHKOOM
WHAT'S GOING ON?
WHAT'S HAPPENING TO ME?
GANONDORF?
WAIT!!
WAH HA HA HA HA
HERO?
HAS A HERO ARRIVED?
LINK...
AWAKEN, OUR CHOSEN HERO!

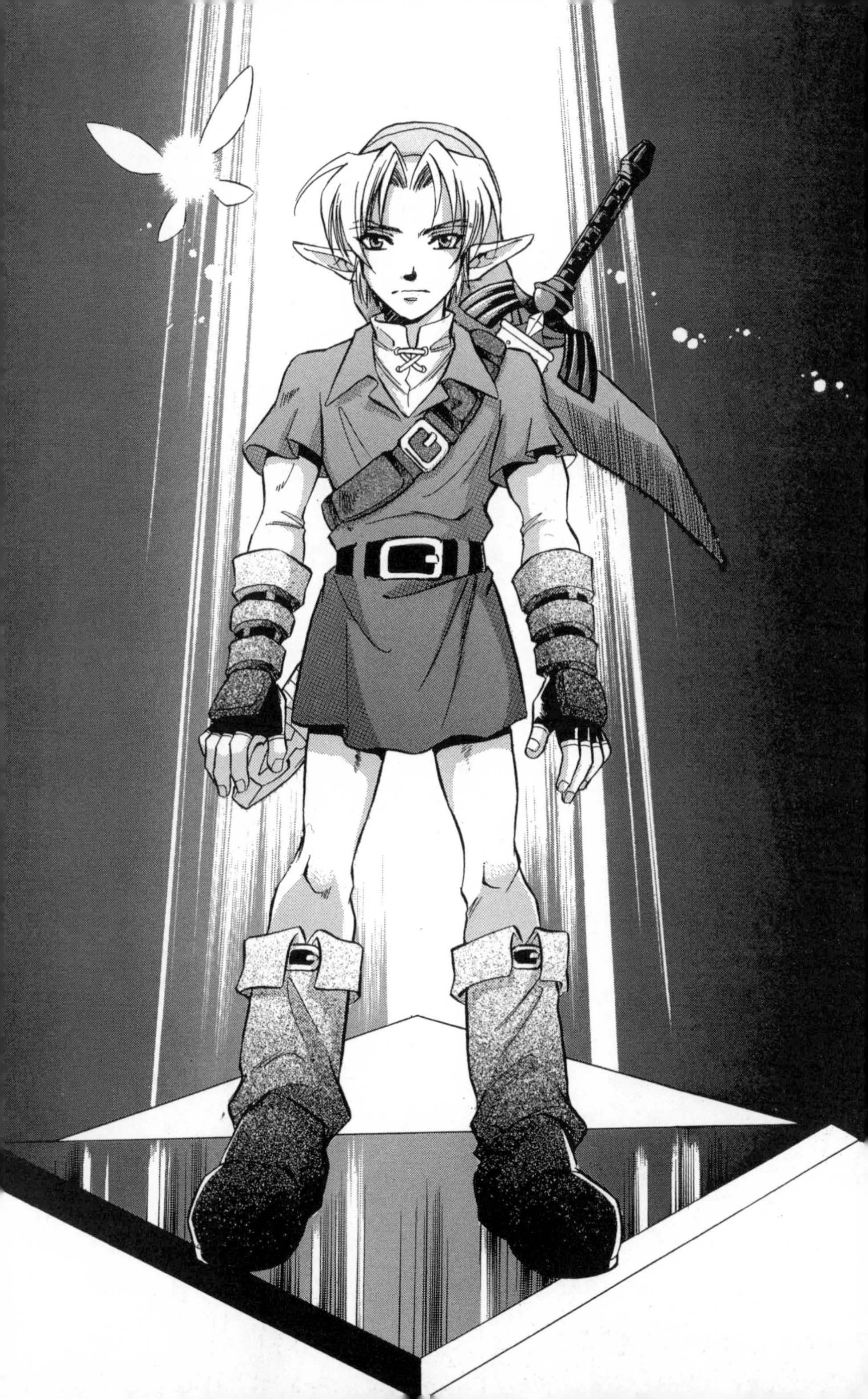

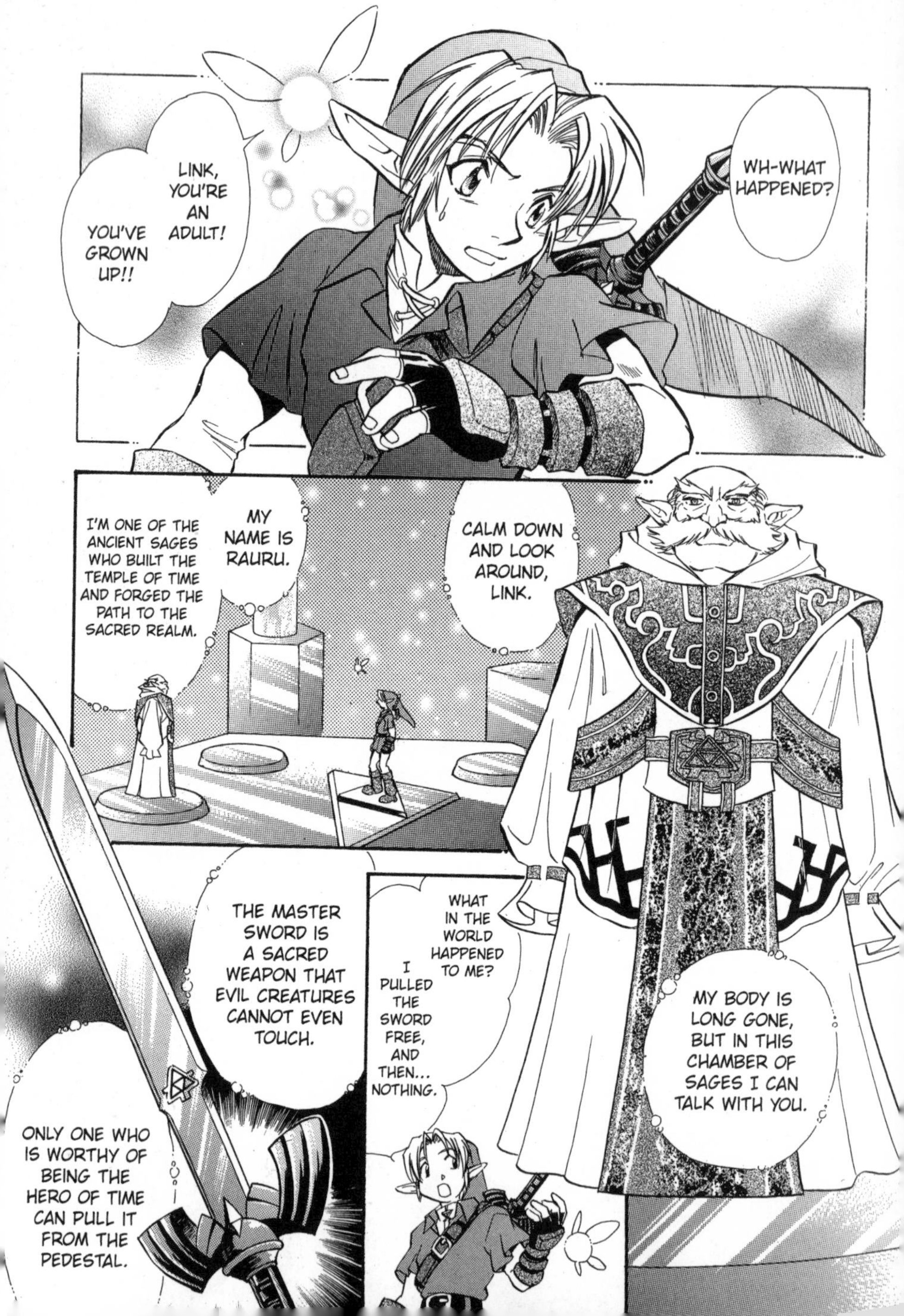
WH-WHAT HAPPENED?
LINK, YOU'RE AN ADULT!
YOU'VE GROWN UP!!
CALM DOWN AND LOOK AROUND, LINK.
MY NAME IS RAURU.
I'M ONE OF THE ANCIENT SAGES WHO BUILT THE TEMPLE OF TIME AND FORGED THE PATH TO THE SACRED REALM.
MY BODY IS LONG GONE, BUT IN THIS CHAMBER OF SAGES I CAN TALK WITH YOU.
WHAT IN THE WORLD HAPPENED TO ME?
I PULLED THE SWORD FREE, AND THEN... NOTHING.
THE MASTER SWORD IS A SACRED WEAPON THAT EVIL CREATURES CANNOT EVEN TOUCH.
ONLY ONE WHO IS WORTHY OF BEING THE HERO OF TIME CAN PULL IT FROM THE PEDESTAL.

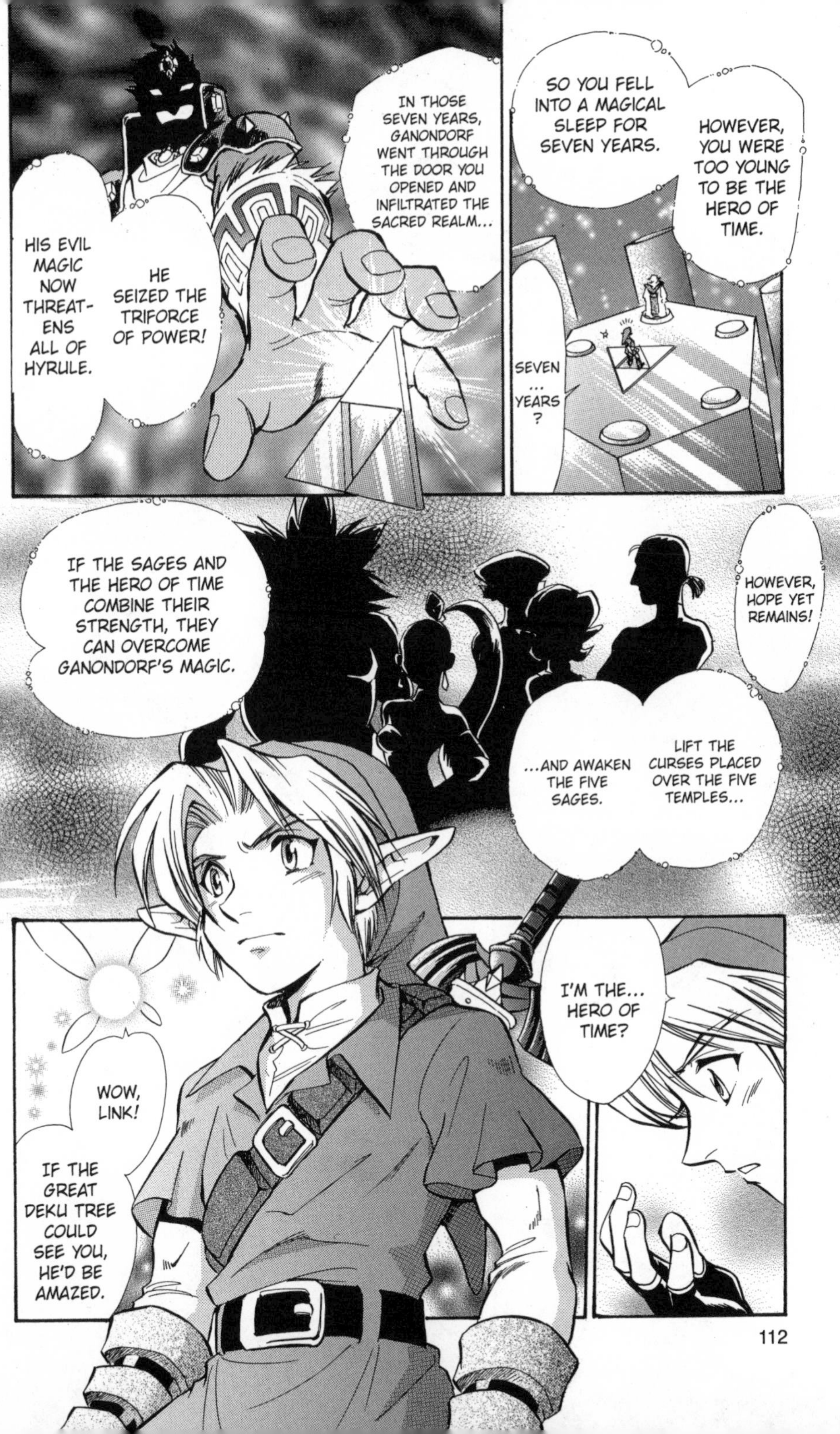
SO YOU FELL INTO A MAGICAL SLEEP FOR SEVEN YEARS.
HOWEVER, YOU WERE TOO YOUNG TO BE THE HERO OF TIME.
SEVEN ... YEARS ?
IN THOSE SEVEN YEARS, GANONDORF WENT THROUGH THE DOOR YOU OPENED AND INFILTRATED THE SACRED REALM...
HE SEIZED THE TRIFORCE OF POWER!
HIS EVIL MAGIC NOW THREAT- ENS ALL OF HYRULE.
HOWEVER, HOPE YET REMAINS!
LIFT THE CURSES PLACED OVER THE FIVE TEMPLES...
...AND AWAKEN THE FIVE SAGES.
IF THE SAGES AND THE HERO OF TIME COMBINE THEIR STRENGTH, THEY CAN OVERCOME GANONDORF'S MAGIC.
I'M THE... HERO OF TIME?
WOW, LINK!
IF THE GREAT DEKU TREE COULD SEE YOU, HE'D BE AMAZED.

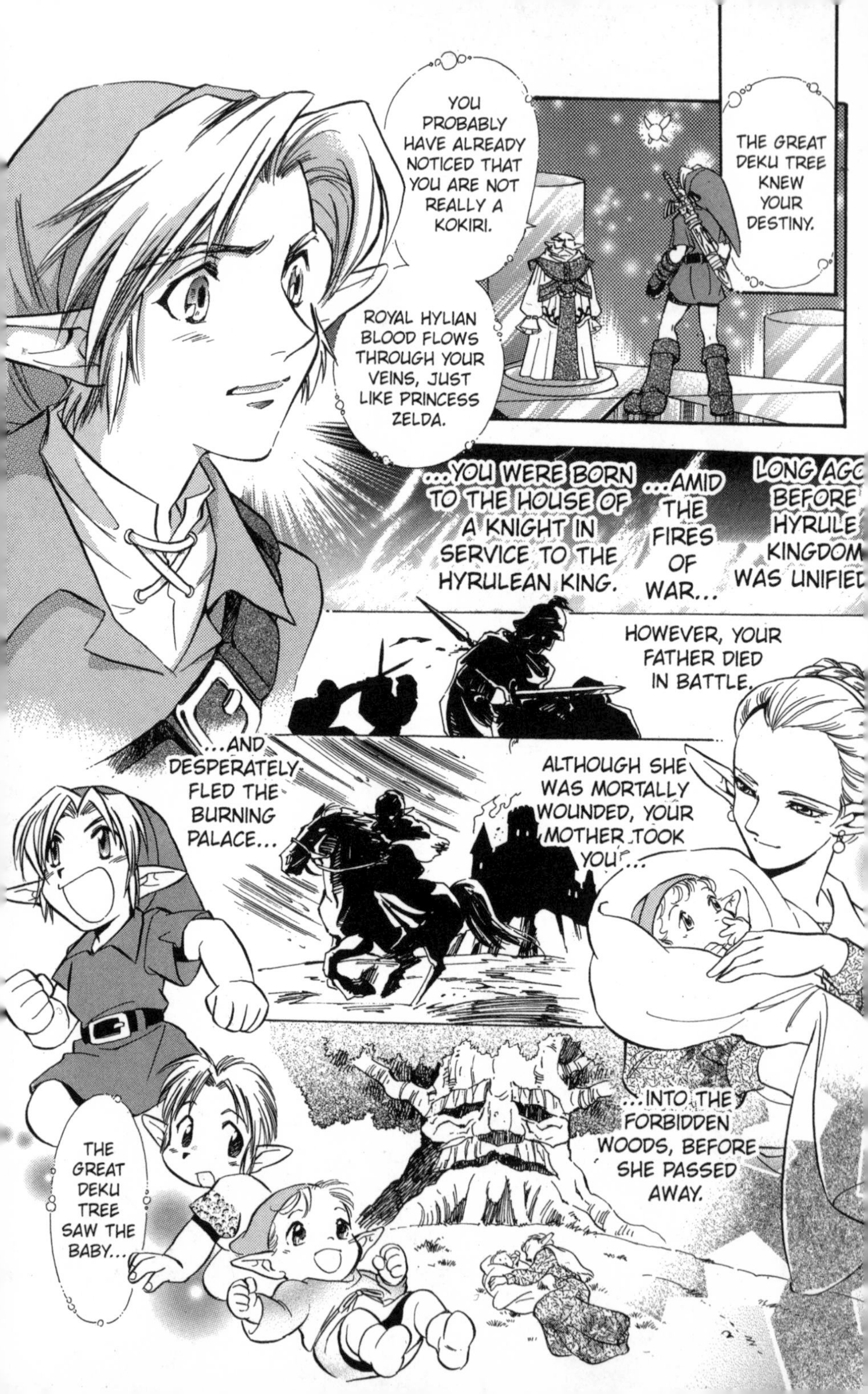
THE GREAT DEKU TREE KNEW YOUR DESTINY.
YOU PROBABLY HAVE ALREADY NOTICED THAT YOU ARE NOT REALLY A KOKIRI.
ROYAL HYLIAN BLOOD FLOWS THROUGH YOUR VEINS, JUST LIKE PRINCESS ZELDA.
LONG AGO BEFORE HYRULE KINGDOM WAS UNIFIED
...AMID THE FIRES OF WAR...
...YOU WERE BORN TO THE HOUSE OF A KNIGHT IN SERVICE TO THE HYRULEAN KING.
HOWEVER, YOUR FATHER DIED IN BATTLE.
ALTHOUGH SHE WAS MORTALLY WOUNDED, YOUR MOTHER TOOK YOU...
...AND DESPERATELY FLED THE BURNING PALACE...
...INTO THE FORBIDDEN WOODS, BEFORE SHE PASSED AWAY.
THE GREAT DEKU TREE SAW THE BABY...

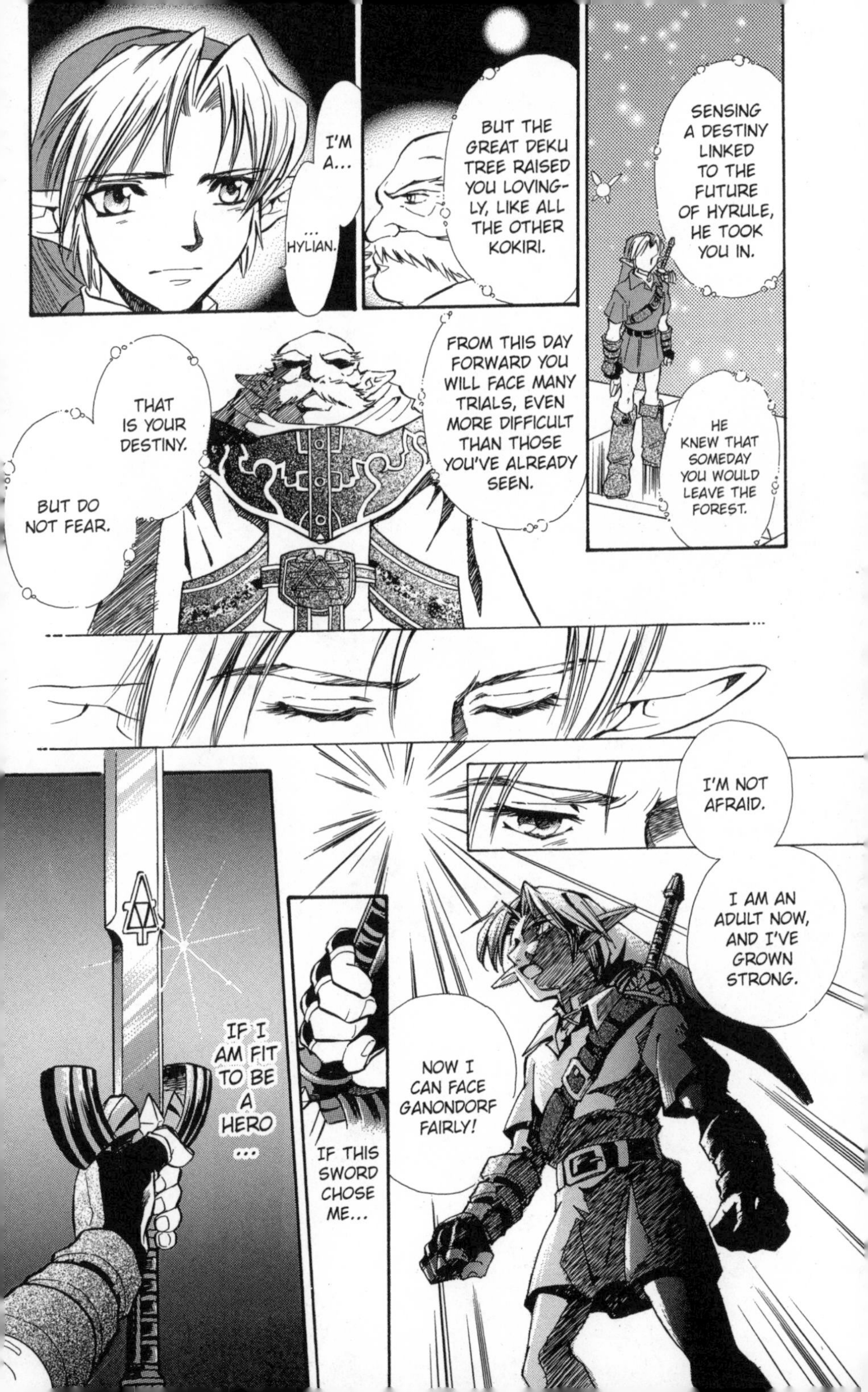
I'M A...
...HYLIAN.
BUT THE GREAT DEKU TREE RAISED YOU LOVING-LY, LIKE ALL THE OTHER KOKIRI.
SENSING A DESTINY LINKED TO THE FUTURE OF HYRULE, HE TOOK YOU IN.
HE KNEW THAT SOMEDAY YOU WOULD LEAVE THE FOREST.
FROM THIS DAY FORWARD YOU WILL FACE MANY TRIALS, EVEN MORE DIFFICULT THAN THOSE YOU'VE ALREADY SEEN.
THAT IS YOUR DESTINY.
BUT DO NOT FEAR.
IF I AM FIT TO BE A HERO...
IF THIS SWORD CHOSE ME...
I'M NOT AFRAID.
I AM AN ADULT NOW, AND I'VE GROWN STRONG.
NOW I CAN FACE GANONDORF FAIRLY!

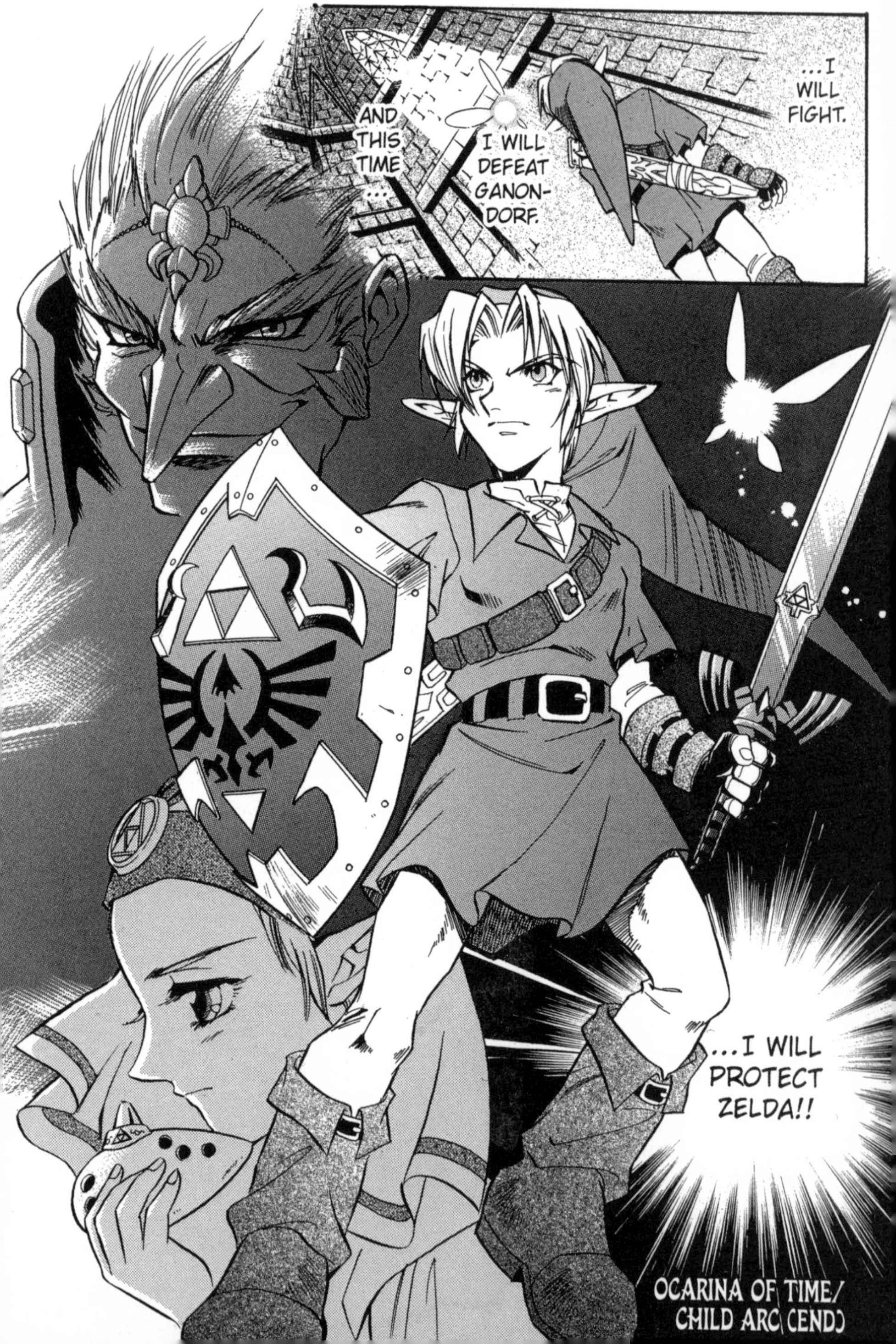
...I WILL FIGHT.
I WILL DEFEAT GANON-DORF.
AND THIS TIME ...
...I WILL PROTECT ZELDA!!
OCARINA OF TIME/ CHILD ARC (END)

OCARINA OF TIME ~ BONUS STORY
THE SKULL KID AND THE MASK ~ PART 1

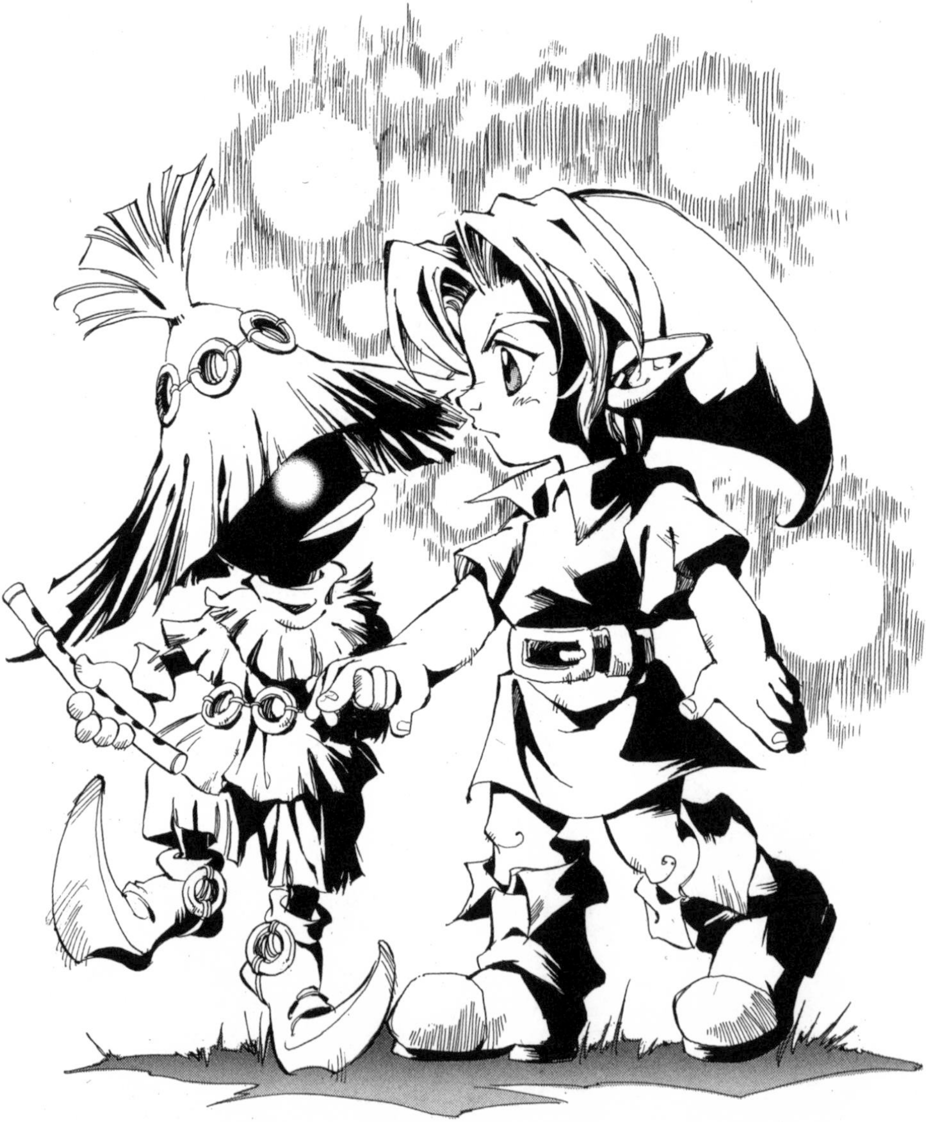

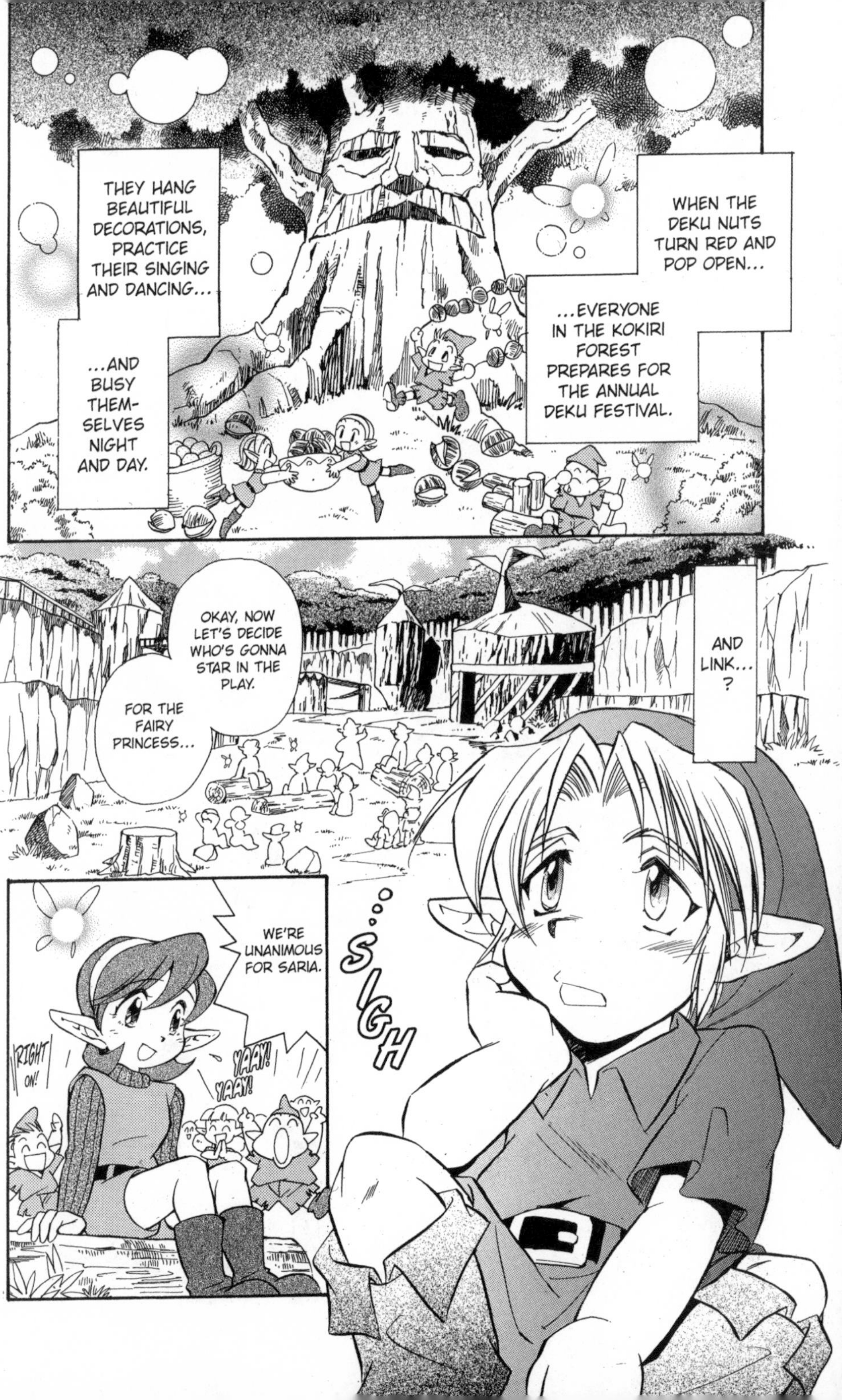
WHEN THE DEKU NUTS TURN RED AND POP OPEN...
...EVERYONE IN THE KOKIRI FOREST PREPARES FOR THE ANNUAL DEKU FESTIVAL.
THEY HANG BEAUTIFUL DECORATIONS, PRACTICE THEIR SINGING AND DANCING...
...AND BUSY THEM-SELVES NIGHT AND DAY.
OKAY, NOW LET'S DECIDE WHO'S GONNA STAR IN THE PLAY.
FOR THE FAIRY PRINCESS...
AND LINK...?
SIGH
WE'RE UNANIMOUS FOR SARIA.
YAAY! YAAY!
RIGHT ON!

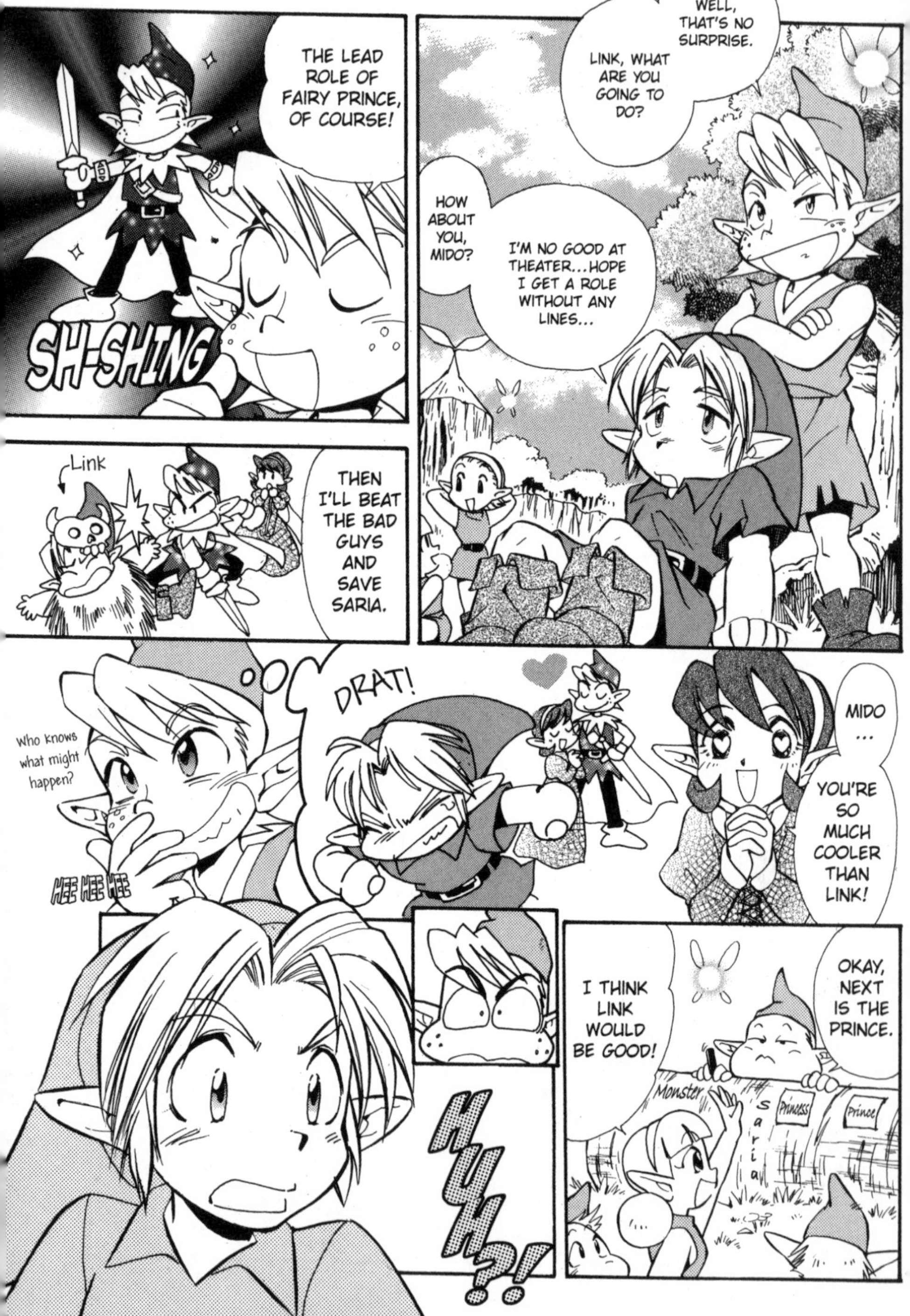
WELL, THAT'S NO SURPRISE.
LINK, WHAT ARE YOU GOING TO DO?
I'M NO GOOD AT THEATER...HOPE I GET A ROLE WITHOUT ANY LINES...
HOW ABOUT YOU, MIDO?
THE LEAD ROLE OF FAIRY PRINCE, OF COURSE!
SH-SHING
THEN I'LL BEAT THE BAD GUYS AND SAVE SARIA.
Link
MIDO ... YOU'RE SO MUCH COOLER THAN LINK!
DRAT!
Who knows what might happen?
HEE HEE HEE
OKAY, NEXT IS THE PRINCE.
I THINK LINK WOULD BE GOOD!
Prince
Princess
Saria
Monster
HUH?!

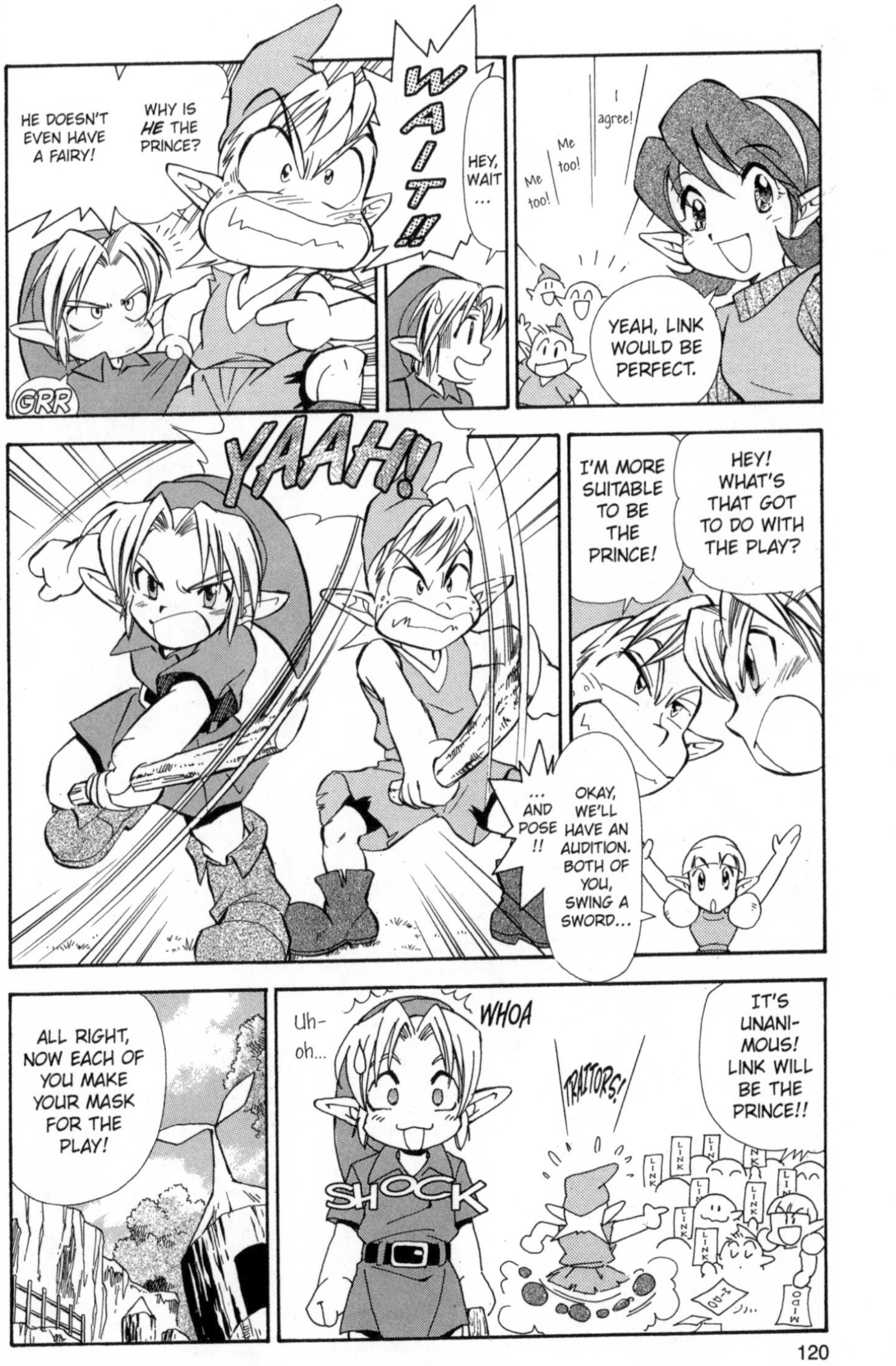
I agree!
Me too!
Me too!
YEAH, LINK WOULD BE PERFECT.
HEY, WAIT ...
WAIT!!
WHY IS *HE* THE PRINCE?
HE DOESN'T EVEN HAVE A FAIRY!
GRR
HEY! WHAT'S THAT GOT TO DO WITH THE PLAY?
I'M MORE SUITABLE TO BE THE PRINCE!
OKAY, WE'LL HAVE AN AUDITION. BOTH OF YOU, SWING A SWORD...
... AND POSE !!
YAAH!
IT'S UNANIMOUS! LINK WILL BE THE PRINCE!!
TRAITORS!
WHOA
Uh-oh...
SHOCK
ALL RIGHT, NOW EACH OF YOU MAKE YOUR MASK FOR THE PLAY!

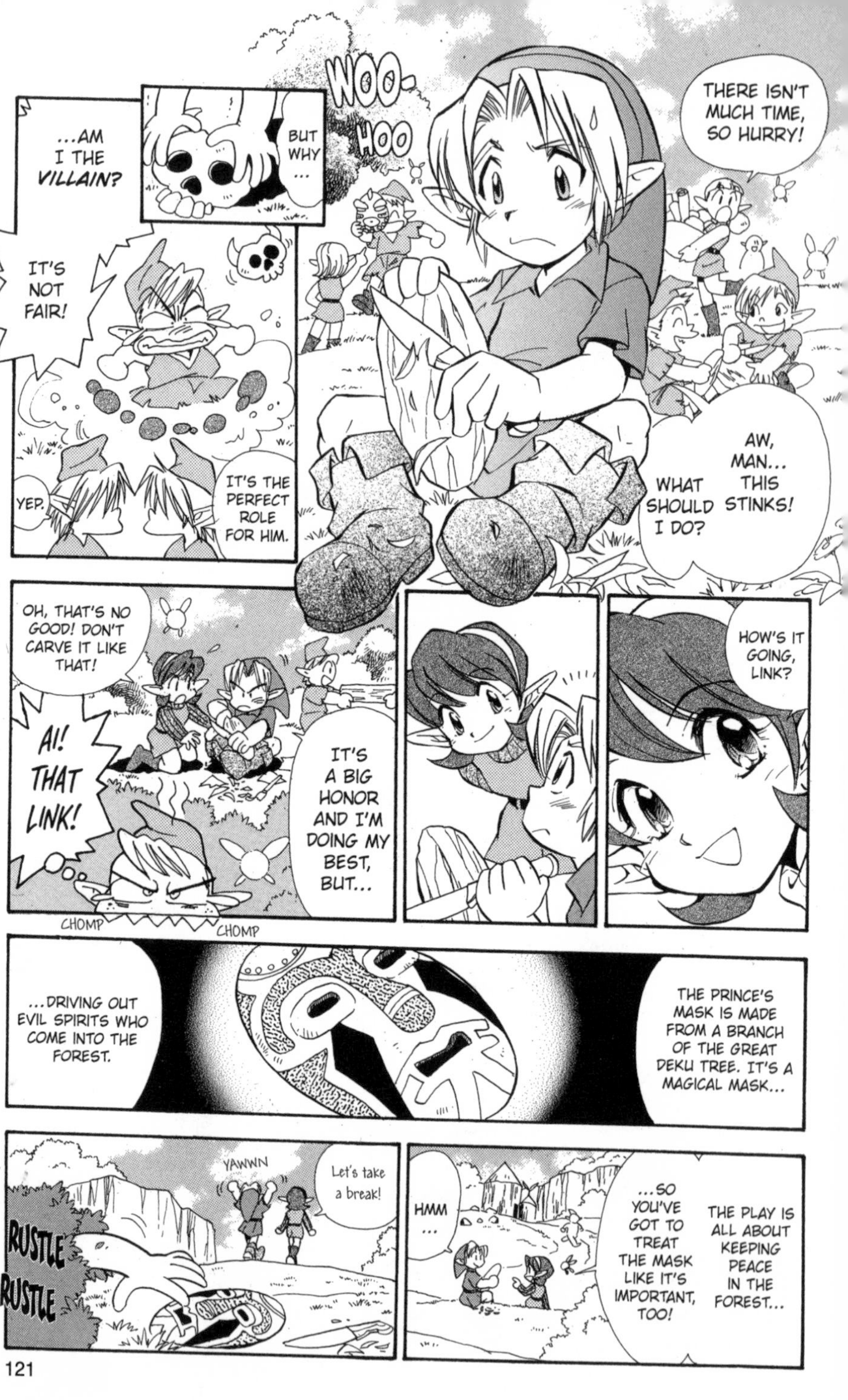
THERE ISN'T MUCH TIME, SO HURRY!
WOO-HOO
AW, MAN... THIS STINKS!
WHAT SHOULD I DO?
BUT WHY...
...AM I THE *VILLAIN?*
IT'S NOT FAIR!
IT'S THE PERFECT ROLE FOR HIM.
YEP.
HOW'S IT GOING, LINK?
IT'S A BIG HONOR AND I'M DOING MY BEST, BUT...
OH, THAT'S NO GOOD! DON'T CARVE IT LIKE THAT!
AI! THAT LINK!
CHOMP
CHOMP
THE PRINCE'S MASK IS MADE FROM A BRANCH OF THE GREAT DEKU TREE. IT'S A MAGICAL MASK...
...DRIVING OUT EVIL SPIRITS WHO COME INTO THE FOREST.
THE PLAY IS ALL ABOUT KEEPING PEACE IN THE FOREST...
...SO YOU'VE GOT TO TREAT THE MASK LIKE IT'S IMPORTANT, TOO!
HMM...
Let's take a break!
YAWWN
RUSTLE
RUSTLE

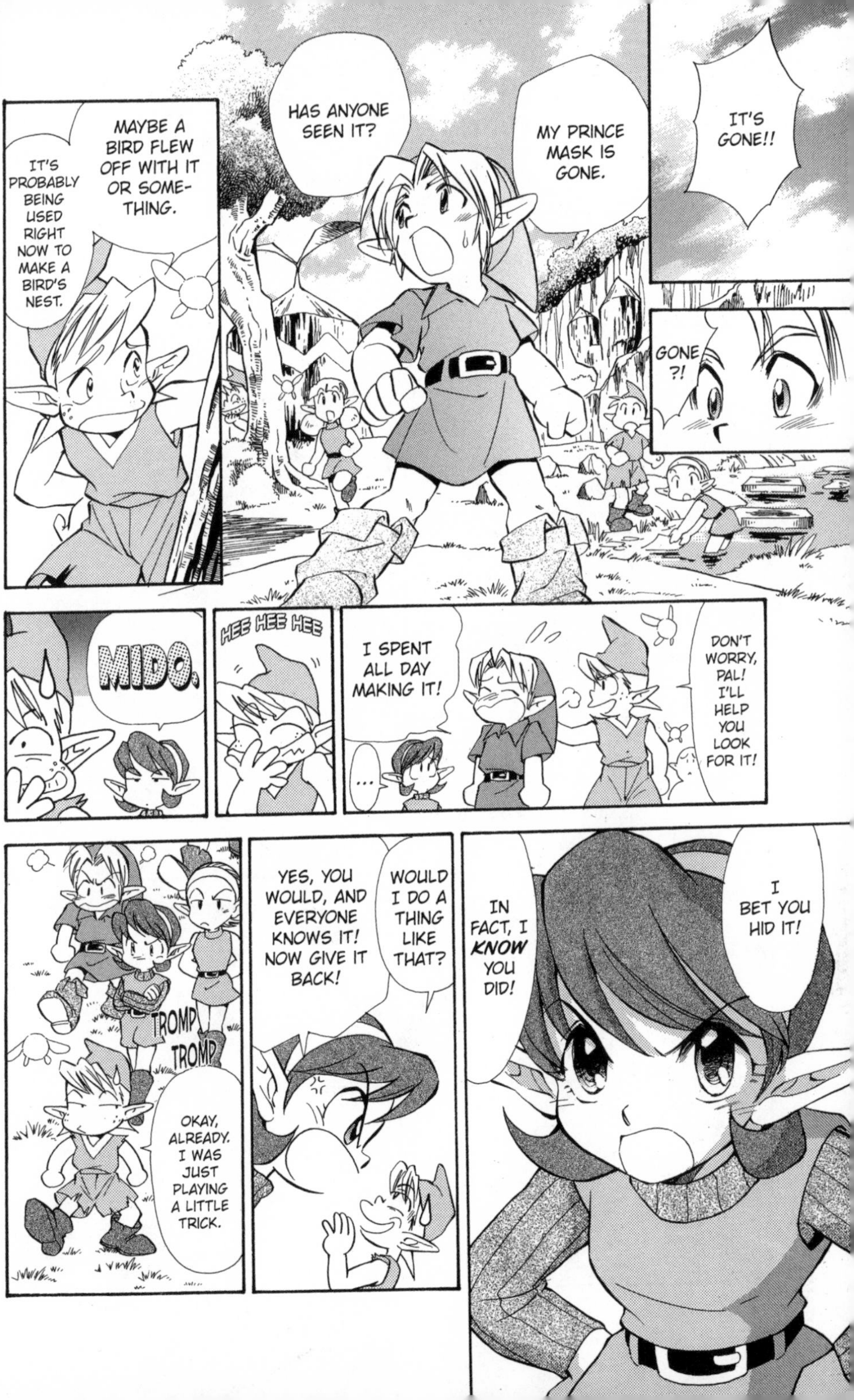
IT'S GONE!!
GONE?!
MY PRINCE MASK IS GONE.
HAS ANYONE SEEN IT?
MAYBE A BIRD FLEW OFF WITH IT OR SOME-THING.
IT'S PROBABLY BEING USED RIGHT NOW TO MAKE A BIRD'S NEST.
DON'T WORRY, PAL! I'LL HELP YOU LOOK FOR IT!
I SPENT ALL DAY MAKING IT!
...
HEE HEE HEE
MIDO.
I BET YOU HID IT!
IN FACT, I *KNOW* YOU DID!
WOULD I DO A THING LIKE THAT?
YES, YOU WOULD, AND EVERYONE KNOWS IT! NOW GIVE IT BACK!
TROMP TROMP
OKAY, ALREADY. I WAS JUST PLAYING A LITTLE TRICK.

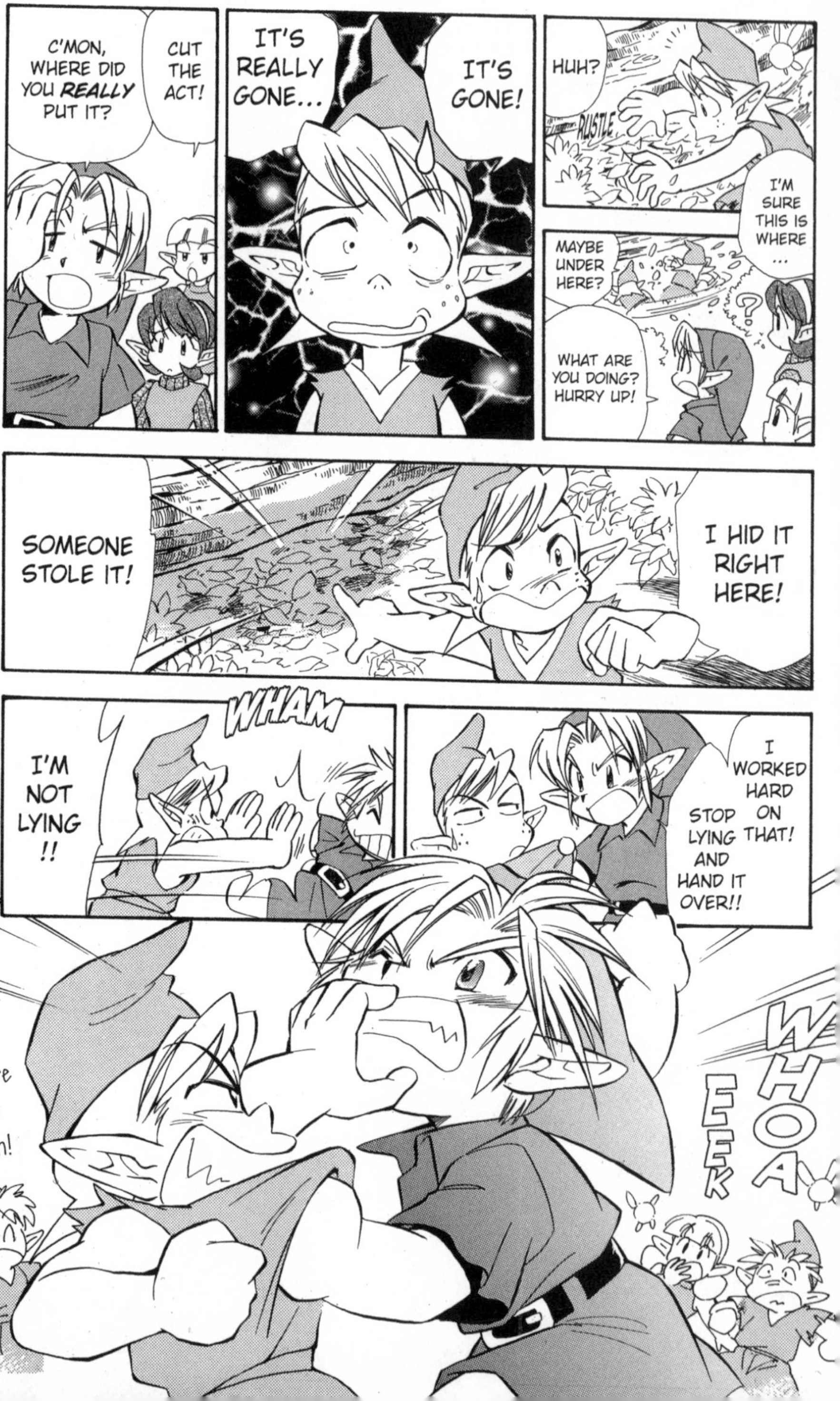
HUH?
RUSTLE
I'M SURE THIS IS WHERE ...
MAYBE UNDER HERE?
WHAT ARE YOU DOING? HURRY UP!
IT'S GONE!
IT'S REALLY GONE...
CUT THE ACT!
C'MON, WHERE DID YOU REALLY PUT IT?
I HID IT RIGHT HERE!
SOMEONE STOLE IT!
I WORKED HARD ON THAT!
STOP LYING AND HAND IT OVER!!
WHAM
I'M NOT LYING !!
WHOA
EEK
They're at it again!

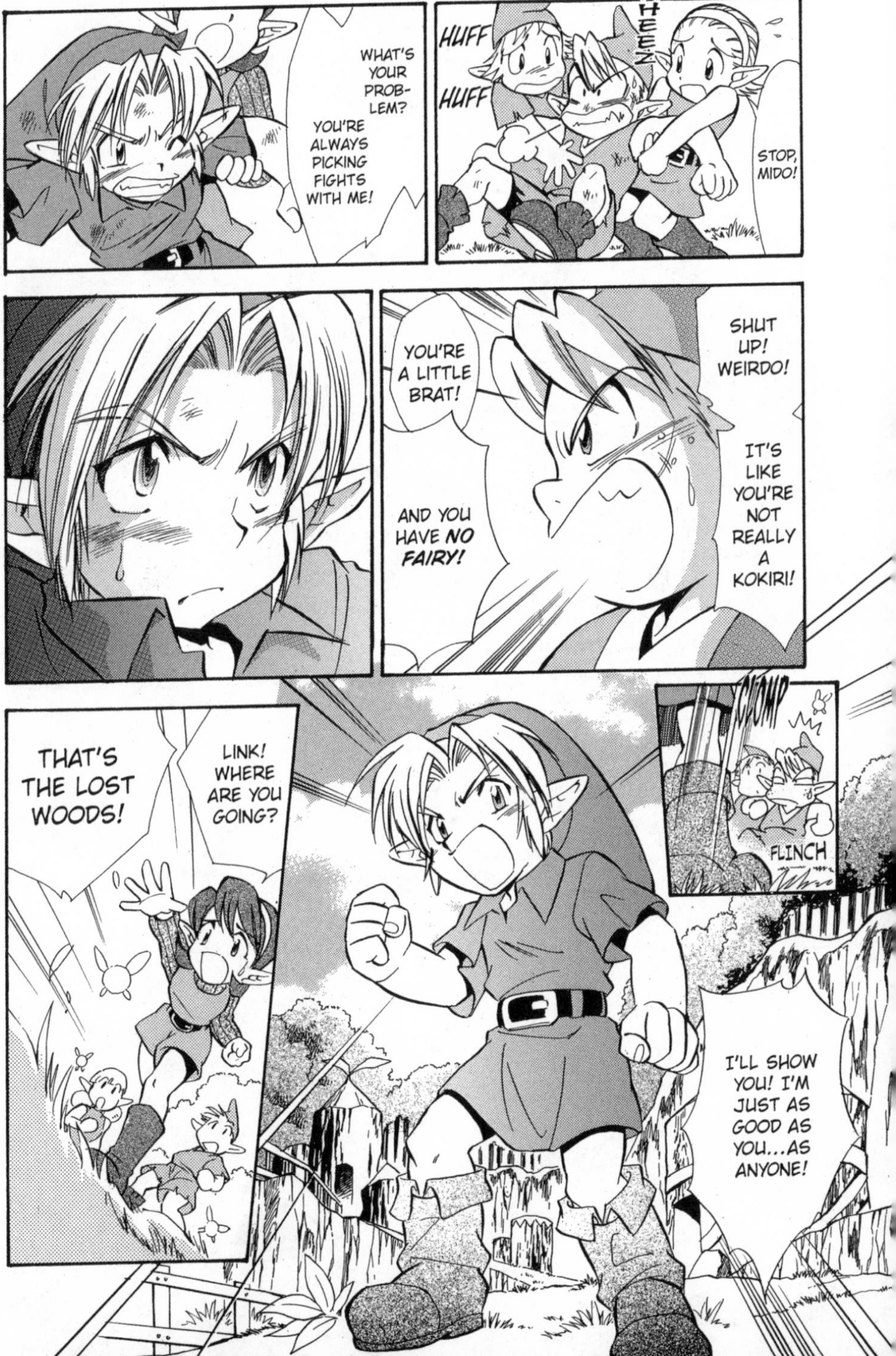
WHEEZE
STOP, MIDO!
HUFF
HUFF
WHAT'S YOUR PROBLEM?
YOU'RE ALWAYS PICKING FIGHTS WITH ME!
SHUT UP! WEIRDO!
IT'S LIKE YOU'RE NOT REALLY A KOKIRI!
YOU'RE A LITTLE BRAT!
AND YOU HAVE *NO FAIRY!*
CLOMP
FLINCH
I'LL SHOW YOU! I'M JUST AS GOOD AS YOU...AS ANYONE!
LINK! WHERE ARE YOU GOING?
THAT'S THE LOST WOODS!

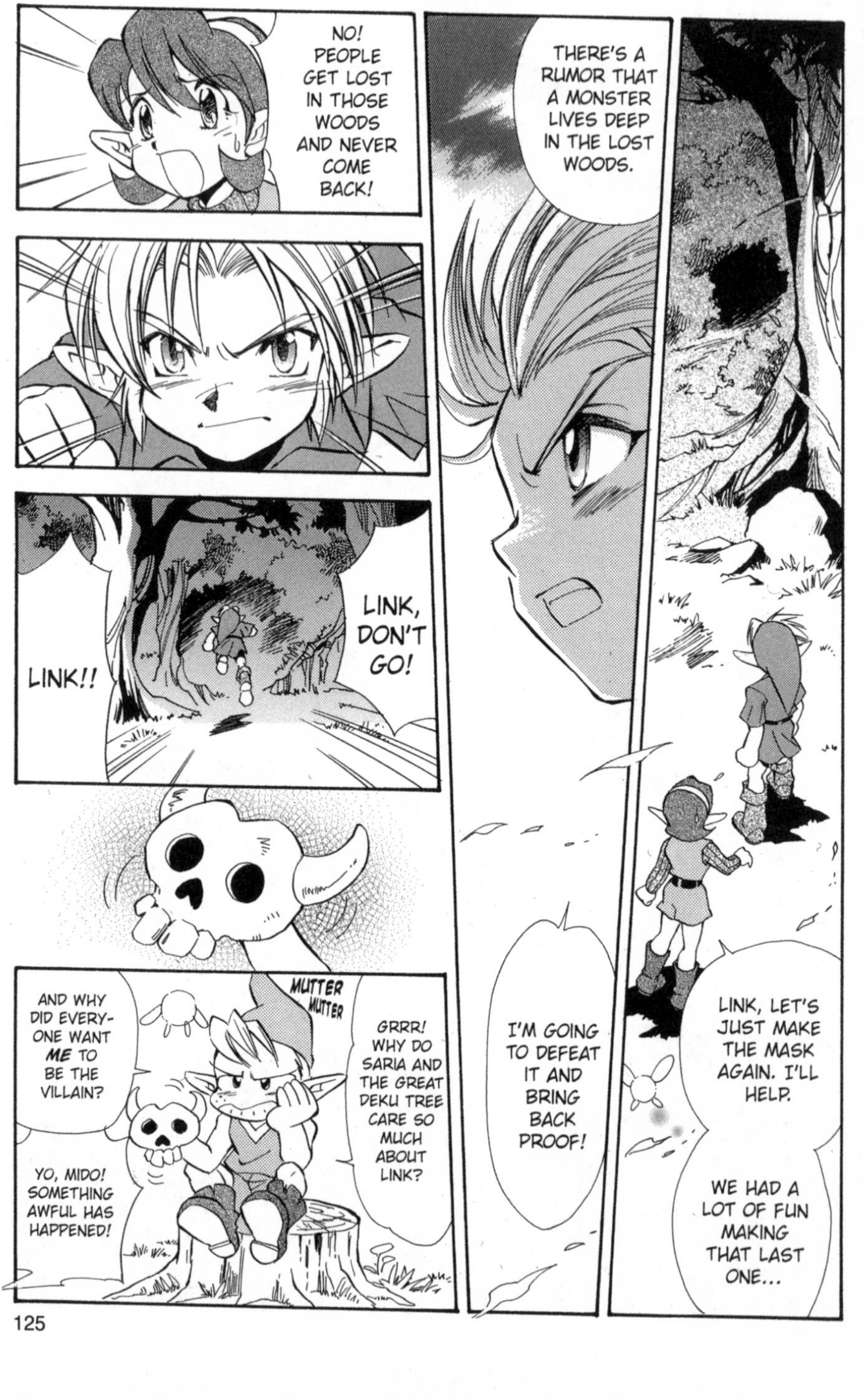
LINK, LET'S JUST MAKE THE MASK AGAIN. I'LL HELP.
WE HAD A LOT OF FUN MAKING THAT LAST ONE...
THERE'S A RUMOR THAT A MONSTER LIVES DEEP IN THE LOST WOODS.
I'M GOING TO DEFEAT IT AND BRING BACK PROOF!
NO! PEOPLE GET LOST IN THOSE WOODS AND NEVER COME BACK!
LINK, DON'T GO!
LINK!!
MUTTER MUTTER
GRRR! WHY DO SARIA AND THE GREAT DEKU TREE CARE SO MUCH ABOUT LINK?
AND WHY DID EVERY-ONE WANT ***ME*** TO BE THE VILLAIN?
YO, MIDO! SOMETHING AWFUL HAS HAPPENED!

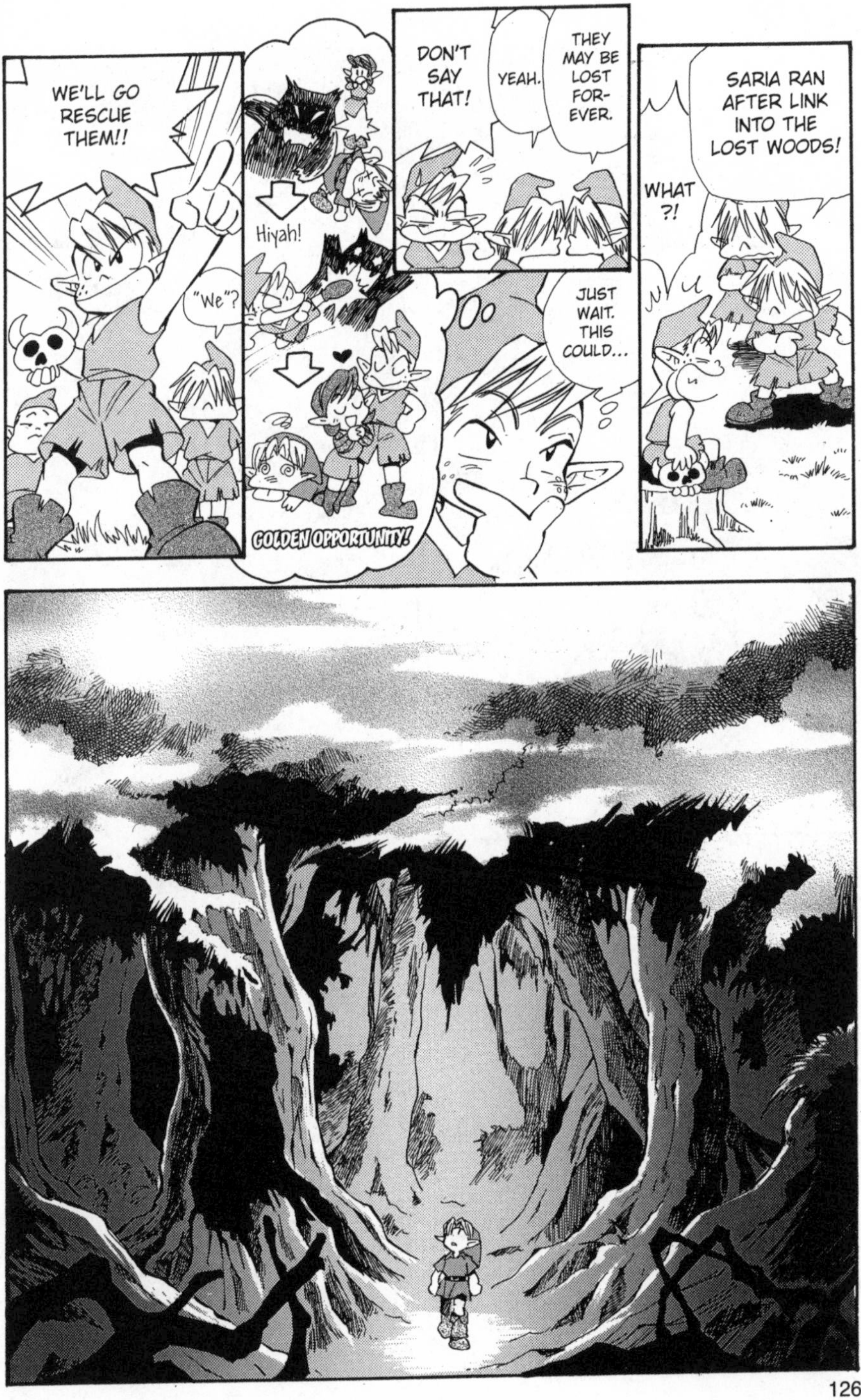
SARIA RAN AFTER LINK INTO THE LOST WOODS!
WHAT?!
THEY MAY BE LOST FOR-EVER.
YEAH.
DON'T SAY THAT!
JUST WAIT. THIS COULD...
Hiyah!
GOLDEN OPPORTUNITY!
WE'LL GO RESCUE THEM!!
"We"?

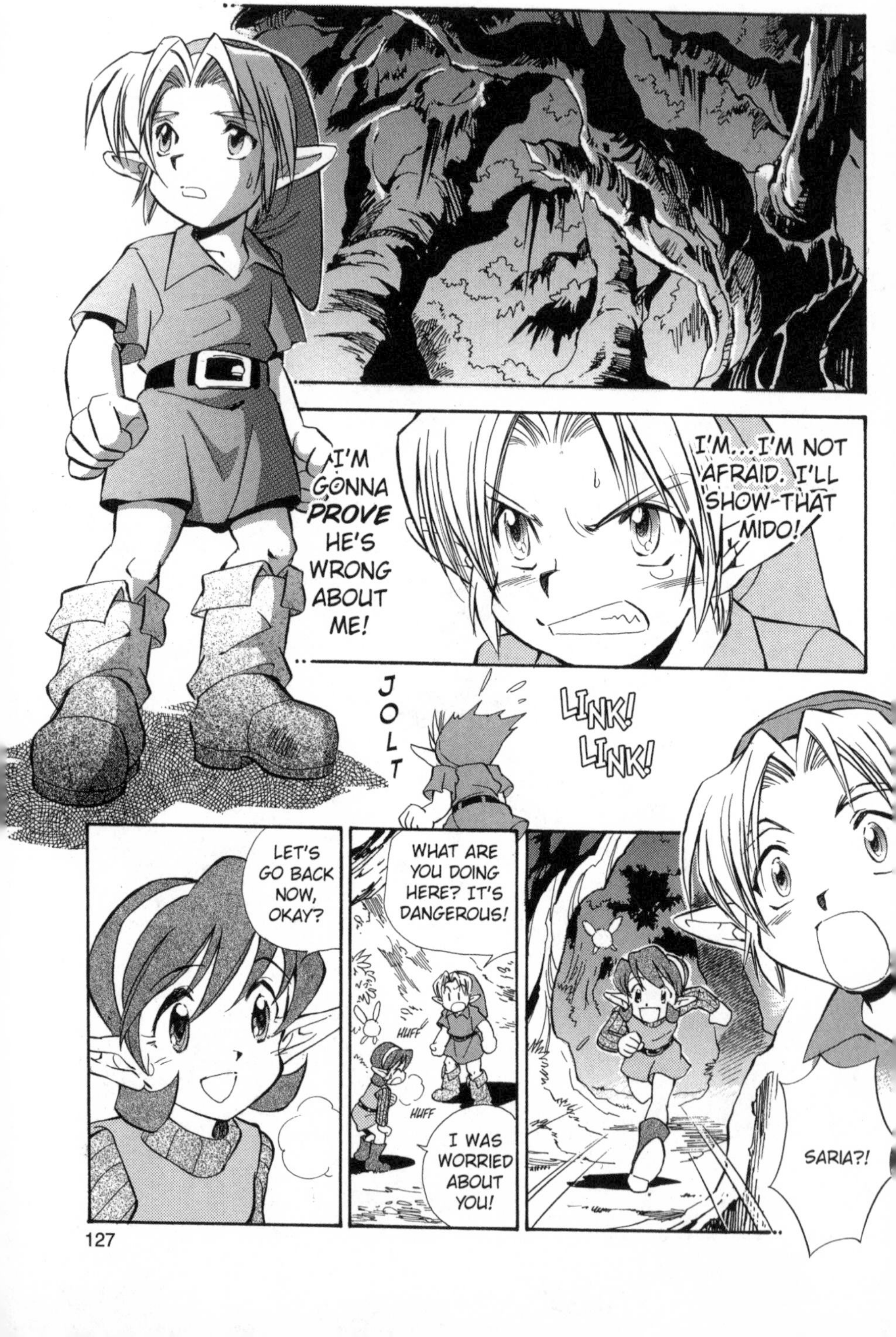
I'M... I'M NOT AFRAID. I'LL SHOW-THAT MIDO!
I'M GONNA **PROVE** HE'S WRONG ABOUT ME!
LINK! LINK!
JOLT
SARIA?!
WHAT ARE YOU DOING HERE? IT'S DANGEROUS!
HUFF
HUFF
I WAS WORRIED ABOUT YOU!
LET'S GO BACK NOW, OKAY?

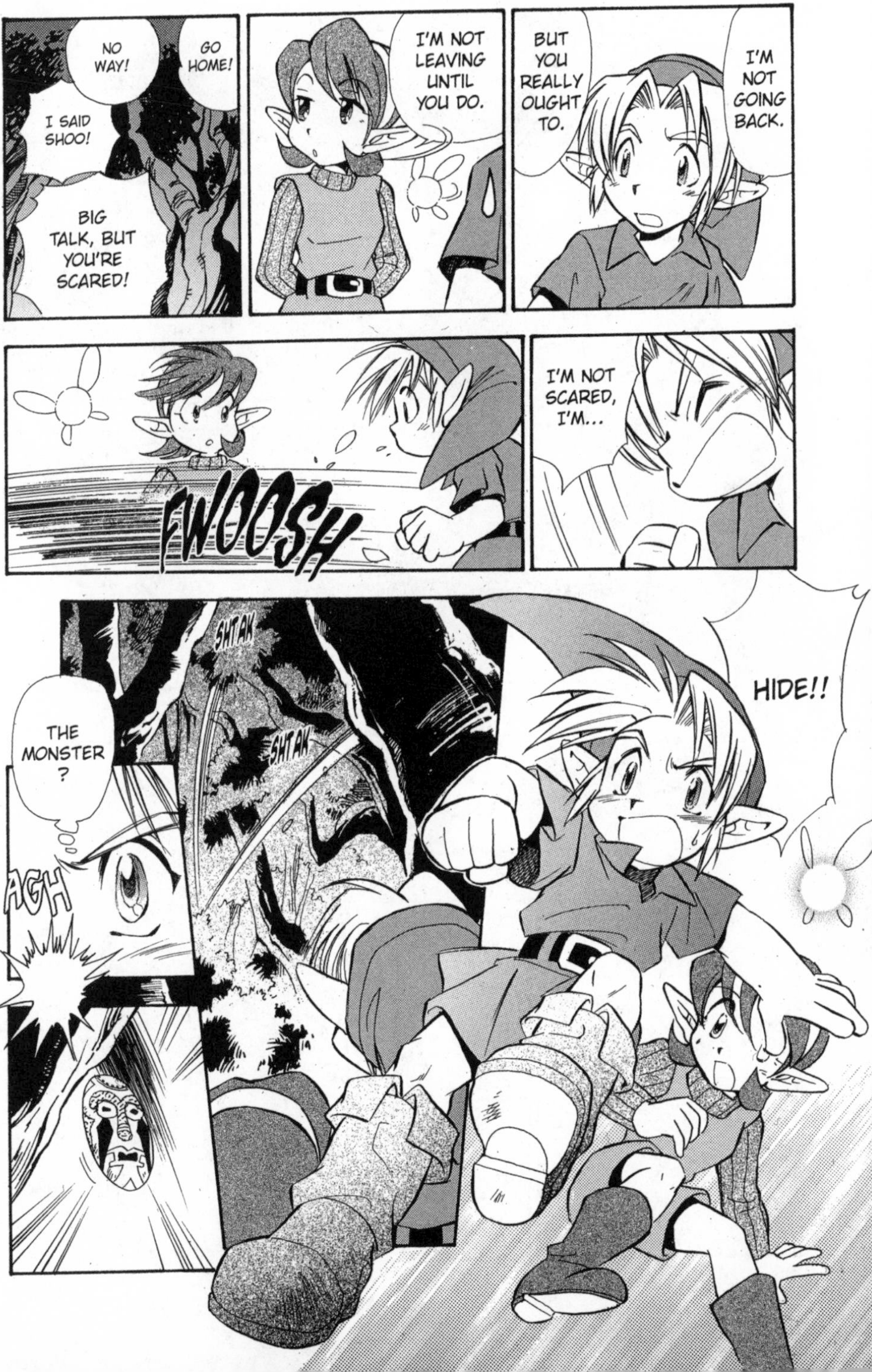
I'M NOT GOING BACK.
BUT YOU REALLY OUGHT TO.
I'M NOT LEAVING UNTIL YOU DO.
GO HOME!
NO WAY!
I SAID SHOO!
BIG TALK, BUT YOU'RE SCARED!
I'M NOT SCARED, I'M...
FWOOSH
HIDE!!
SHTAK
SHTAK
THE MONSTER ?
AGH

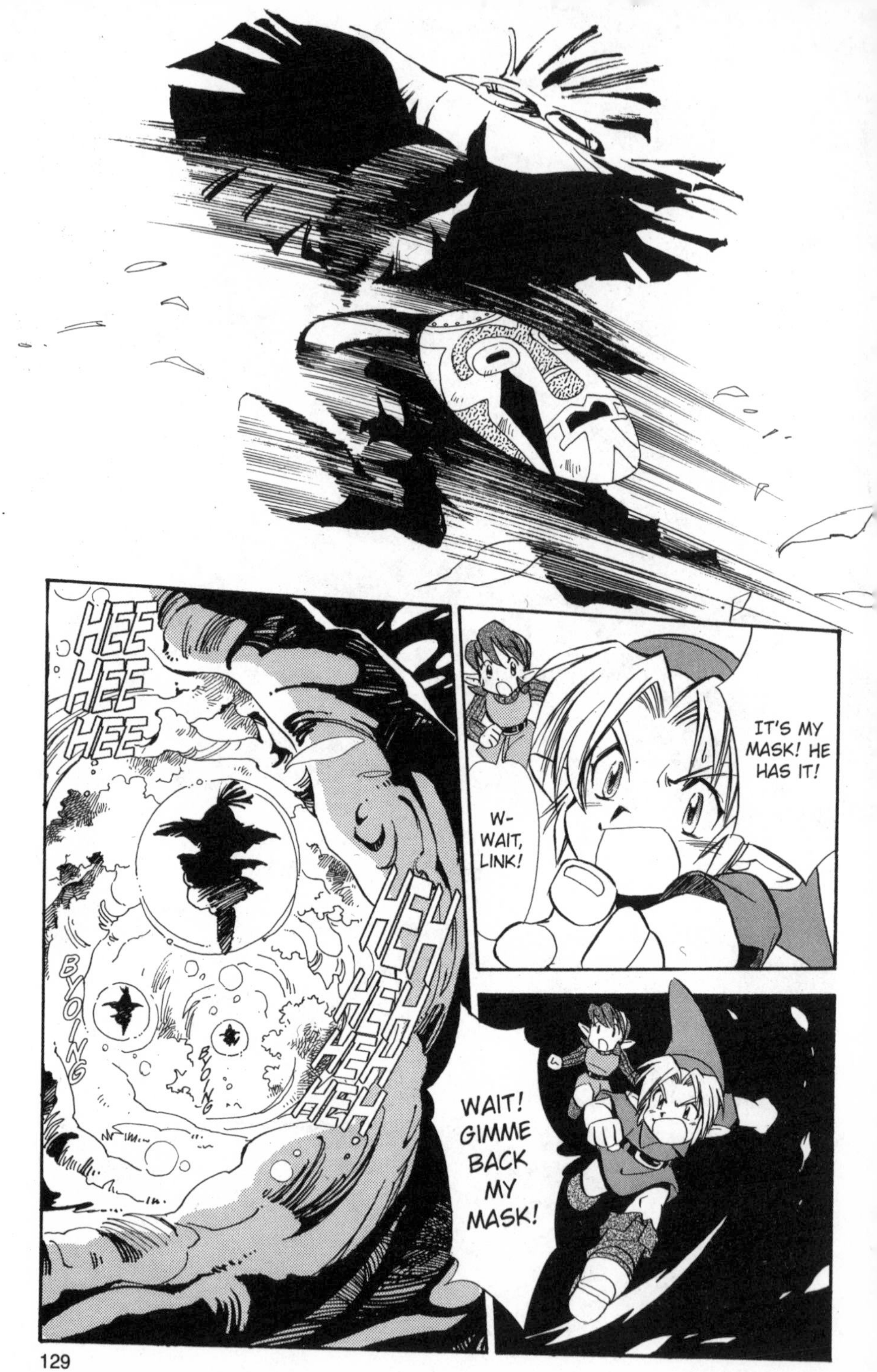
IT'S MY MASK! HE HAS IT!
W-WAIT, LINK!
WAIT! GIMME BACK MY MASK!
HEE HEE HEE
HEH HEH HEH HEH
BYOING
BYOING

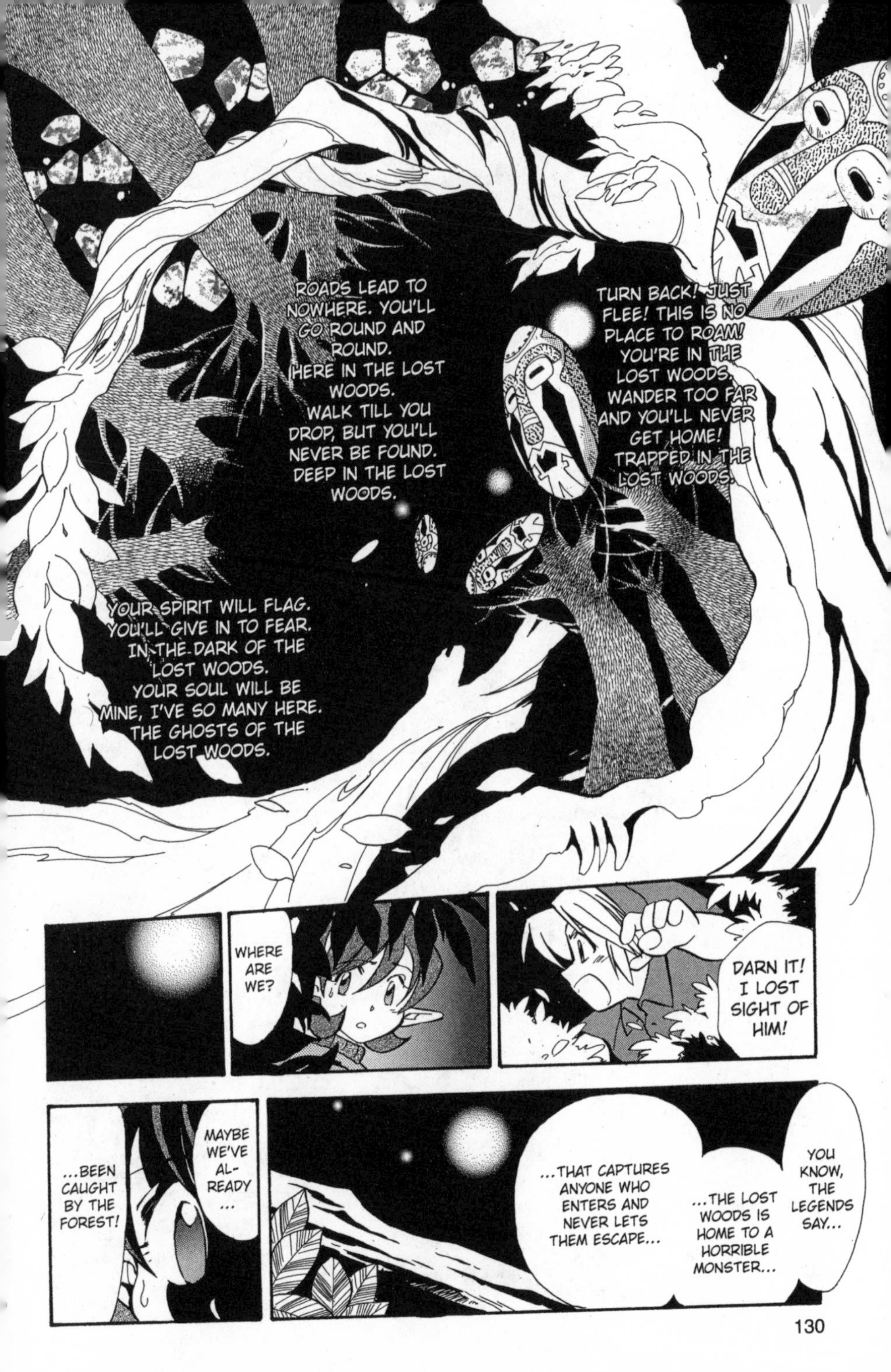
TURN BACK! JUST FLEE! THIS IS NO PLACE TO ROAM! YOU'RE IN THE LOST WOODS. WANDER TOO FAR AND YOU'LL NEVER GET HOME! TRAPPED IN THE LOST WOODS.
ROADS LEAD TO NOWHERE. YOU'LL GO ROUND AND ROUND. HERE IN THE LOST WOODS. WALK TILL YOU DROP, BUT YOU'LL NEVER BE FOUND. DEEP IN THE LOST WOODS.
YOUR SPIRIT WILL FLAG. YOU'LL GIVE IN TO FEAR. IN THE DARK OF THE LOST WOODS. YOUR SOUL WILL BE MINE, I'VE SO MANY HERE. THE GHOSTS OF THE LOST WOODS.
DARN IT! I LOST SIGHT OF HIM!
WHERE ARE WE?
YOU KNOW, THE LEGENDS SAY...
...THE LOST WOODS IS HOME TO A HORRIBLE MONSTER...
...THAT CAPTURES ANYONE WHO ENTERS AND NEVER LETS THEM ESCAPE...
MAYBE WE'VE AL-READY...
...BEEN CAUGHT BY THE FOREST!

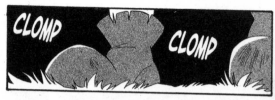

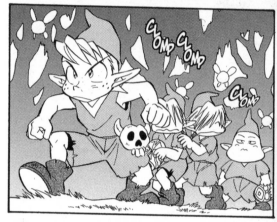

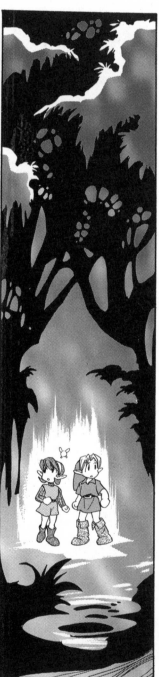

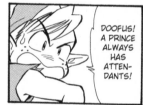

CLOMP
CLOMP
CLOMP CLOMP
CLOMP
WHY DO WE HAVE TO GO, TOO?
PICK PICK
DOOFUS! A PRINCE ALWAYS HAS ATTEN-DANTS!
IT'S ACTUALLY 'CAUSE HE'S SCARED.
HURRY UP, YOU TWO!!
RUSTLE
GYAAH!
IT'S A GIANT MON-STER!

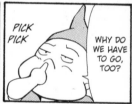

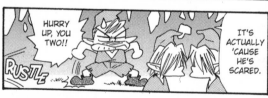

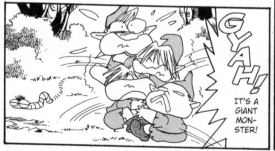

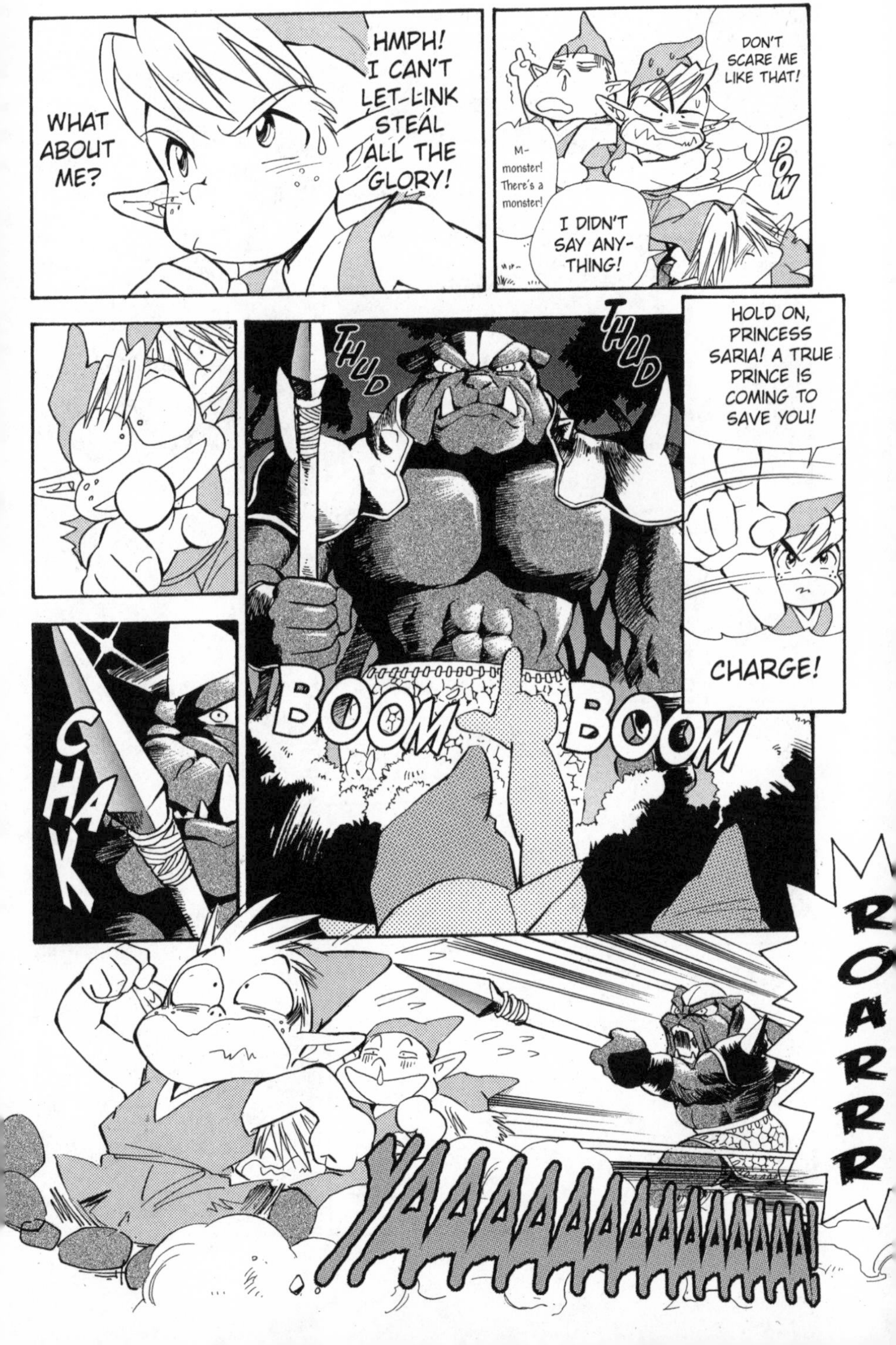
DON'T SCARE ME LIKE THAT!
POW
M-monster! There's a monster!
I DIDN'T SAY ANY-THING!
HMPH! I CAN'T LET LINK STEAL ALL THE GLORY!
WHAT ABOUT ME?
HOLD ON, PRINCESS SARIA! A TRUE PRINCE IS COMING TO SAVE YOU!
CHARGE!
THUD
THUD
BOOM
BOOM
CHAK
ROARRR
YAAAAAAAAAAAAAAA!

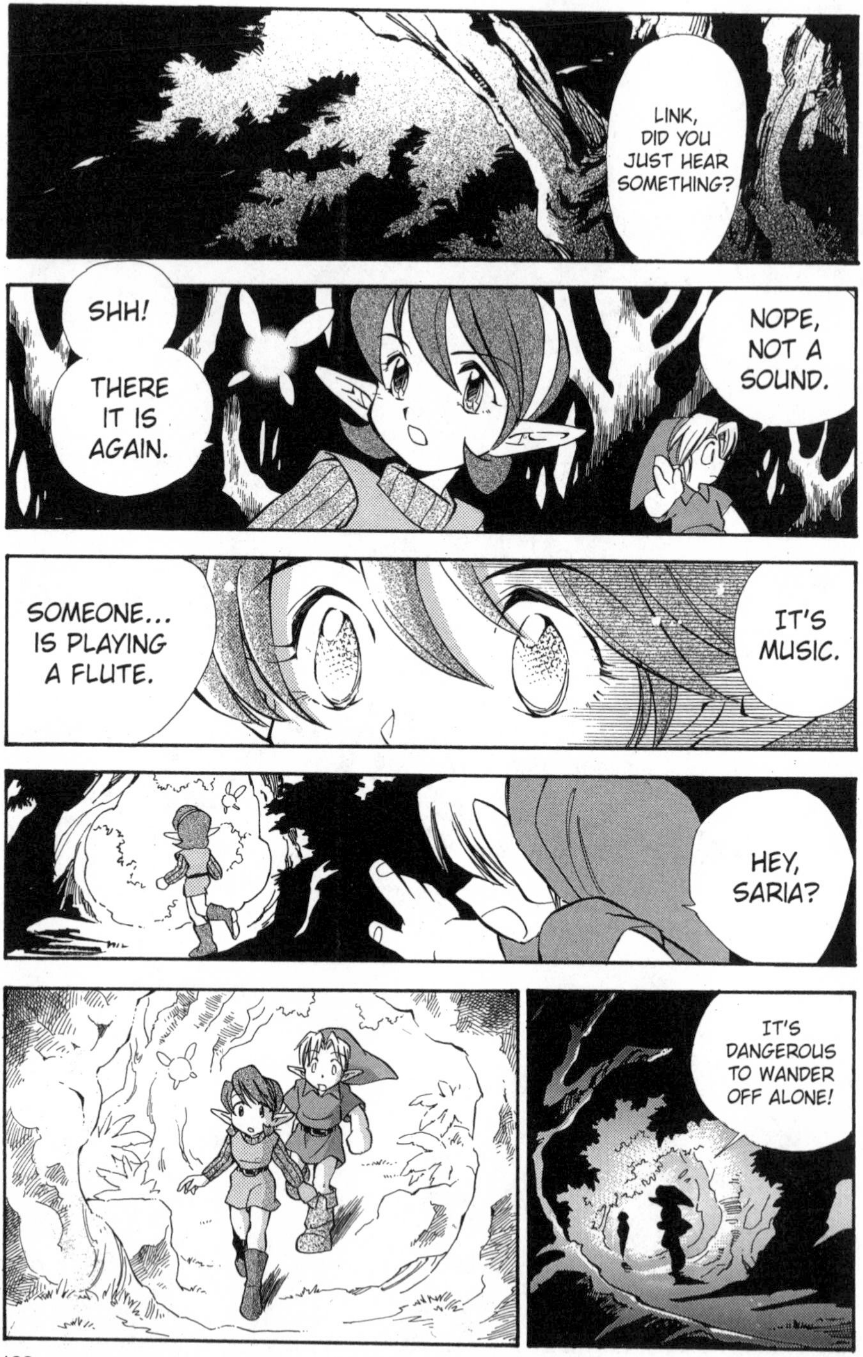
LINK, DID YOU JUST HEAR SOMETHING?
NOPE, NOT A SOUND.
SHH!
THERE IT IS AGAIN.
IT'S MUSIC.
SOMEONE... IS PLAYING A FLUTE.
HEY, SARIA?
IT'S DANGEROUS TO WANDER OFF ALONE!

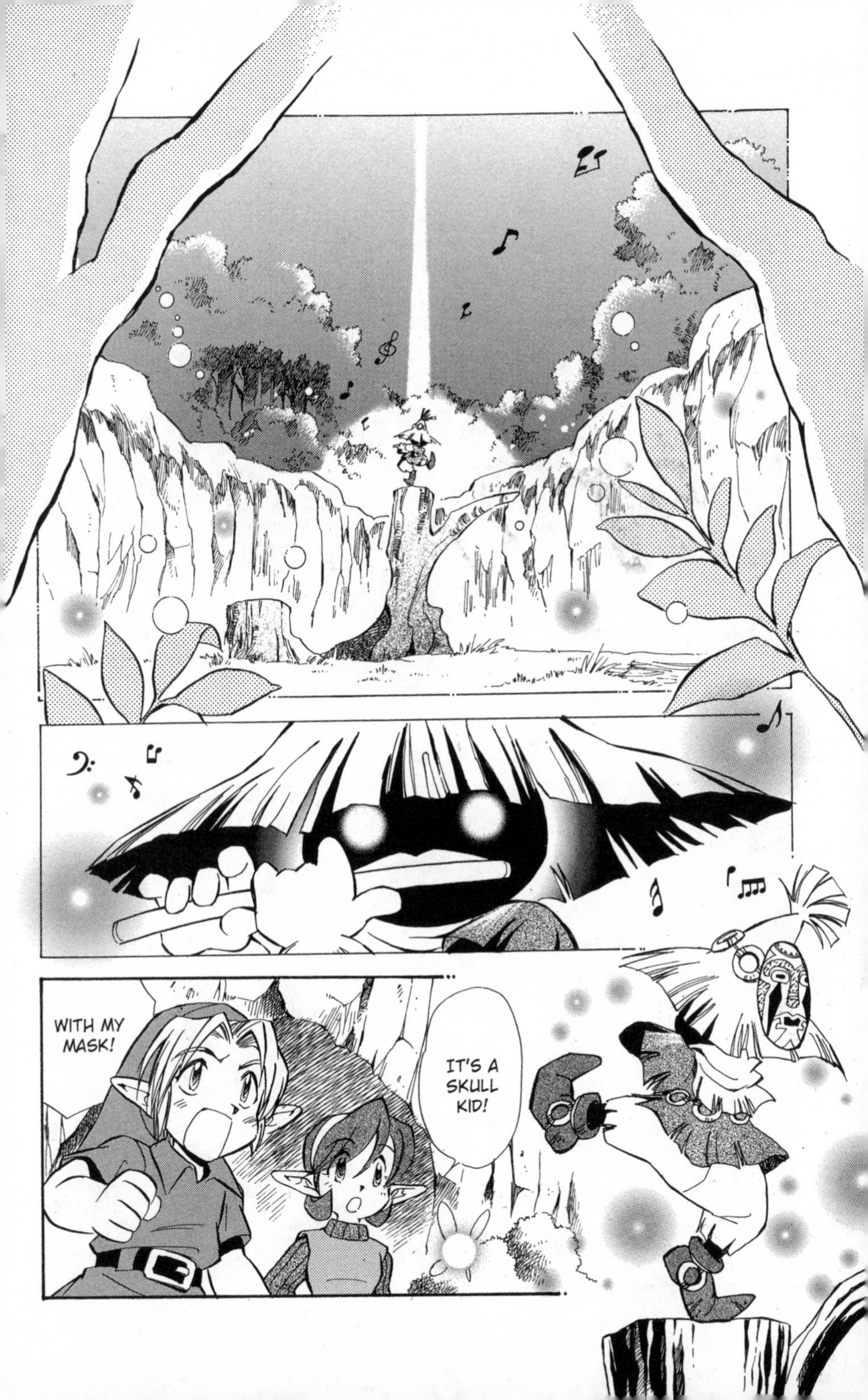
IT'S A SKULL KID!
WITH MY MASK!

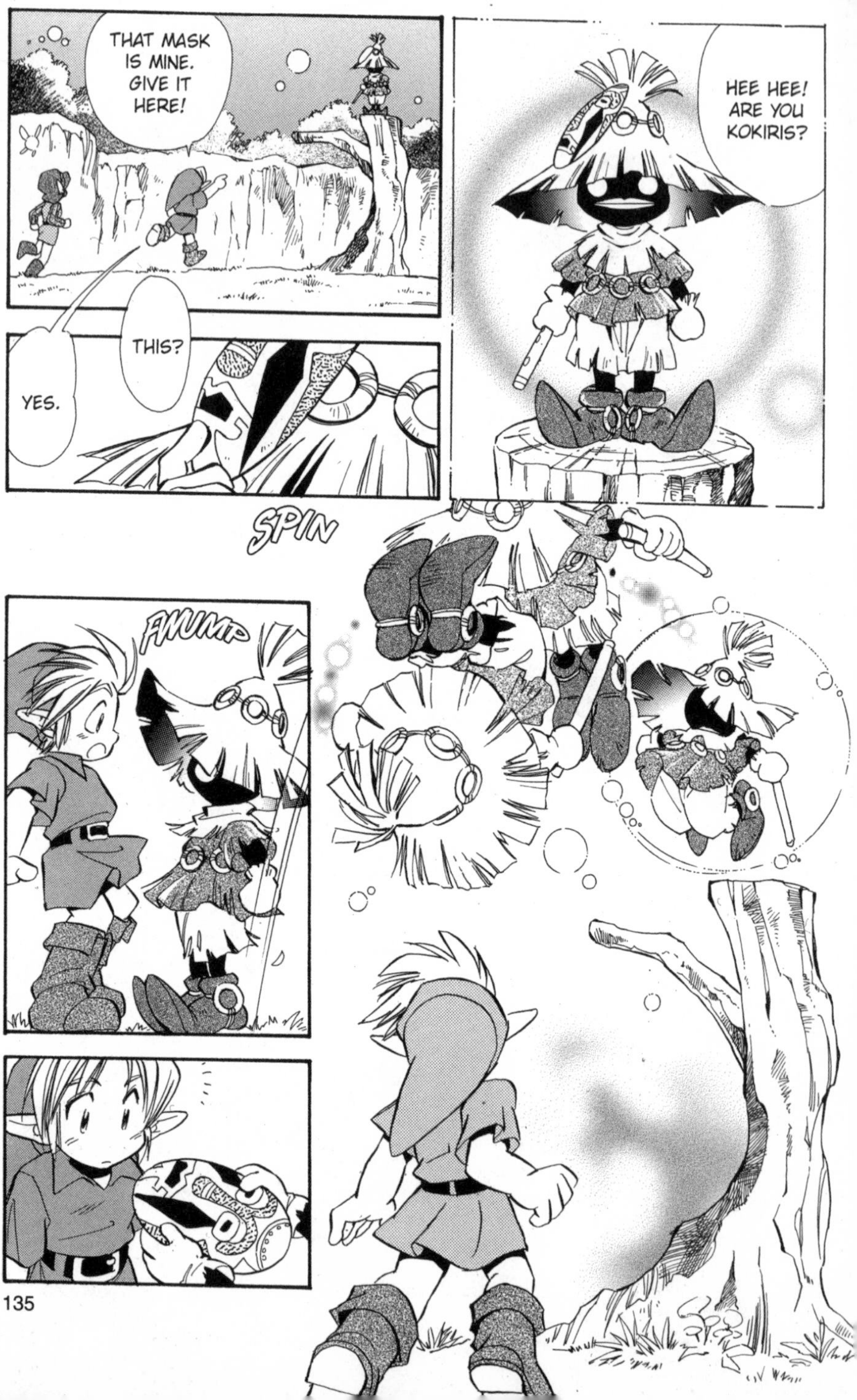
HEE HEE! ARE YOU KOKIRIS?
THAT MASK IS MINE. GIVE IT HERE!
THIS?
YES.
SPIN
FWUMP

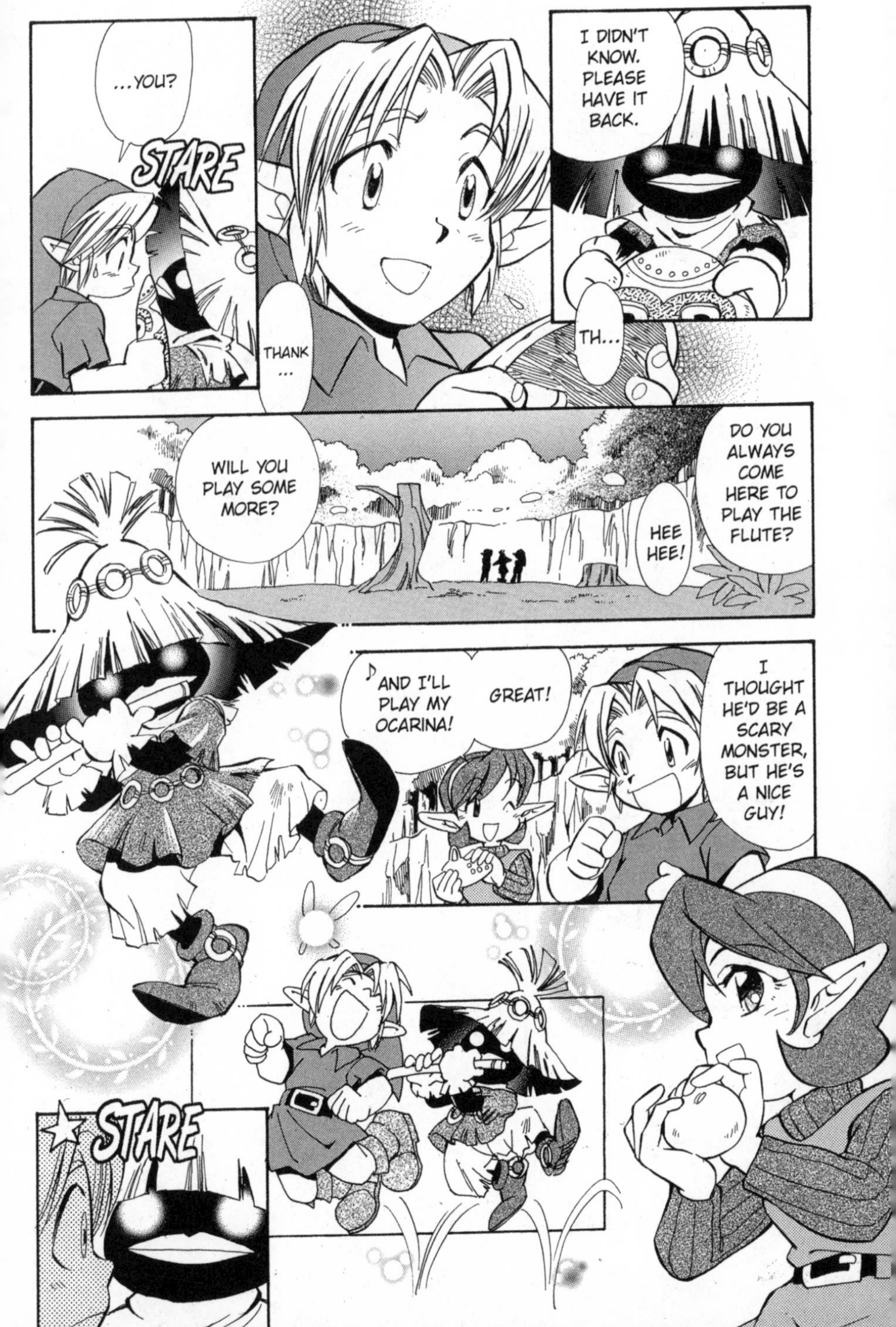
I DIDN'T KNOW. PLEASE HAVE IT BACK.
TH...
THANK ...
...YOU?
STARE
DO YOU ALWAYS COME HERE TO PLAY THE FLUTE?
HEE HEE!
WILL YOU PLAY SOME MORE?
I THOUGHT HE'D BE A SCARY MONSTER, BUT HE'S A NICE GUY!
GREAT!
♪ AND I'LL PLAY MY OCARINA!
STARE

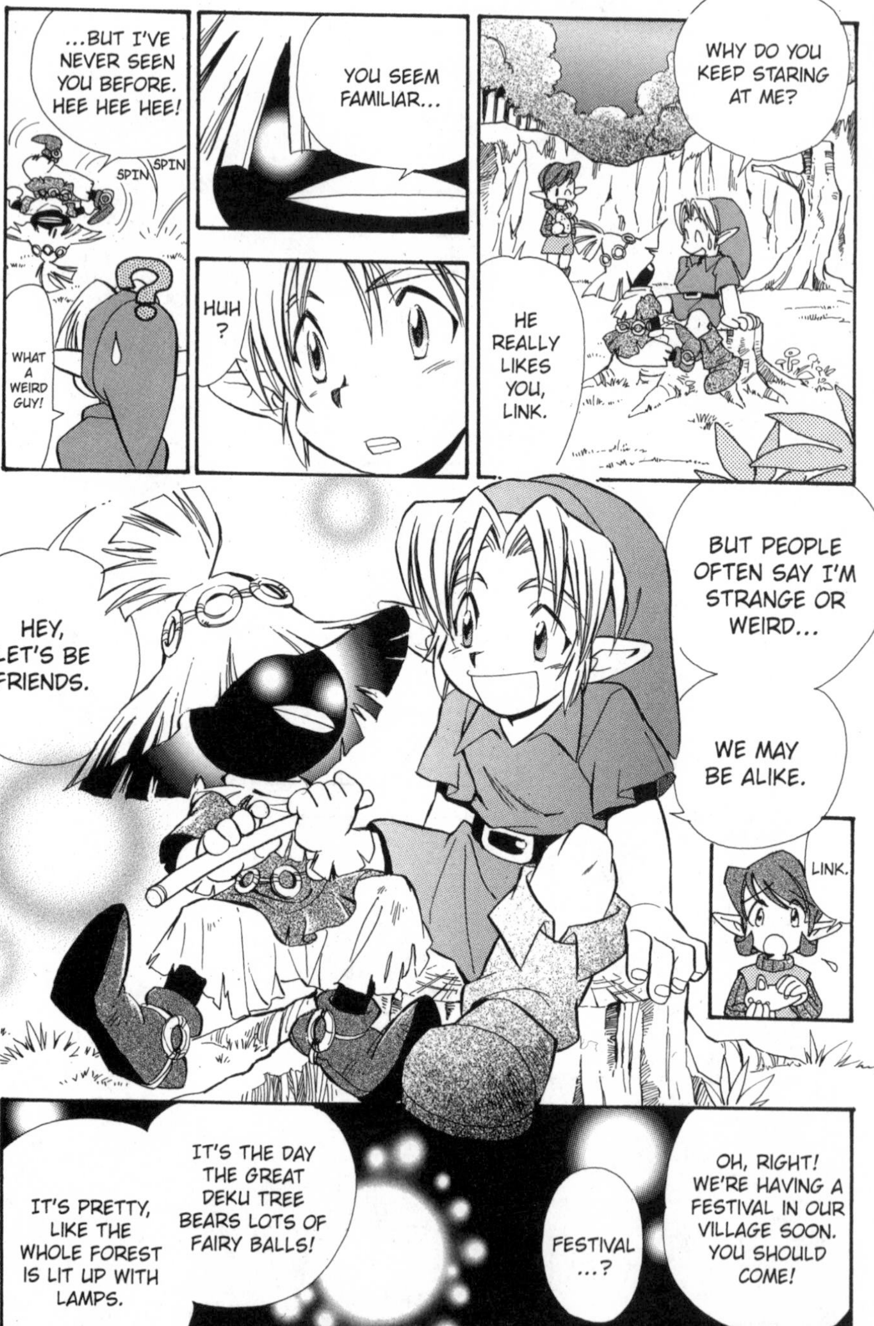
WHY DO YOU KEEP STARING AT ME?
HE REALLY LIKES YOU, LINK.
YOU SEEM FAMILIAR...
HUH ?
...BUT I'VE NEVER SEEN YOU BEFORE. HEE HEE HEE!
SPIN
SPIN
WHAT A WEIRD GUY!
BUT PEOPLE OFTEN SAY I'M STRANGE OR WEIRD...
WE MAY BE ALIKE.
HEY, LET'S BE FRIENDS.
LINK.
OH, RIGHT! WE'RE HAVING A FESTIVAL IN OUR VILLAGE SOON. YOU SHOULD COME!
FESTIVAL ...?
IT'S THE DAY THE GREAT DEKU TREE BEARS LOTS OF FAIRY BALLS!
IT'S PRETTY, LIKE THE WHOLE FOREST IS LIT UP WITH LAMPS.

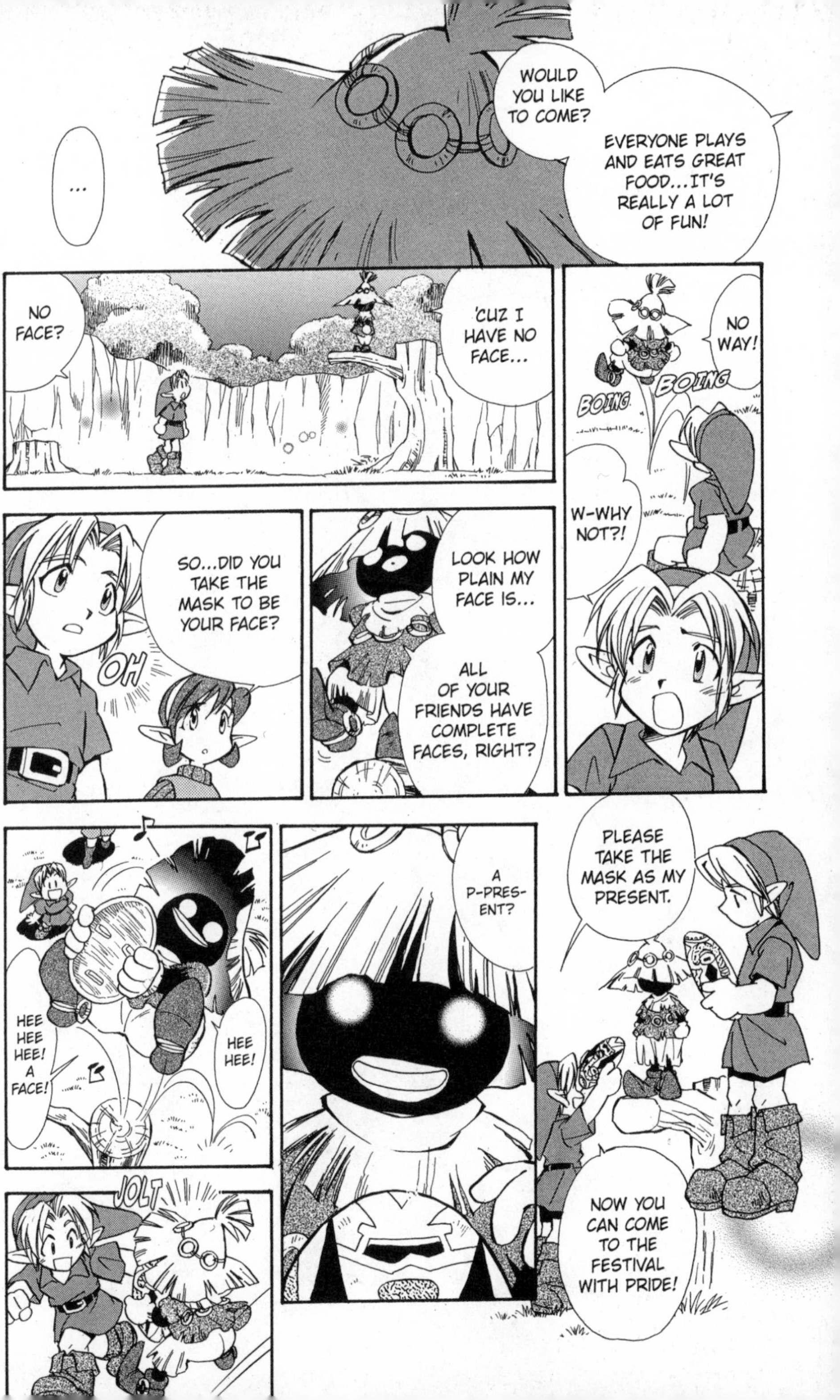
WOULD YOU LIKE TO COME?
EVERYONE PLAYS AND EATS GREAT FOOD...IT'S REALLY A LOT OF FUN!
...
NO WAY!
BOING
BOING
W-WHY NOT?!
'CUZ I HAVE NO FACE...
NO FACE?
LOOK HOW PLAIN MY FACE IS...
ALL OF YOUR FRIENDS HAVE COMPLETE FACES, RIGHT?
SO...DID YOU TAKE THE MASK TO BE YOUR FACE?
OH
PLEASE TAKE THE MASK AS MY PRESENT.
NOW YOU CAN COME TO THE FESTIVAL WITH PRIDE!
A P-PRES-ENT?
HEE HEE!
HEE HEE HEE! A FACE!
JOLT

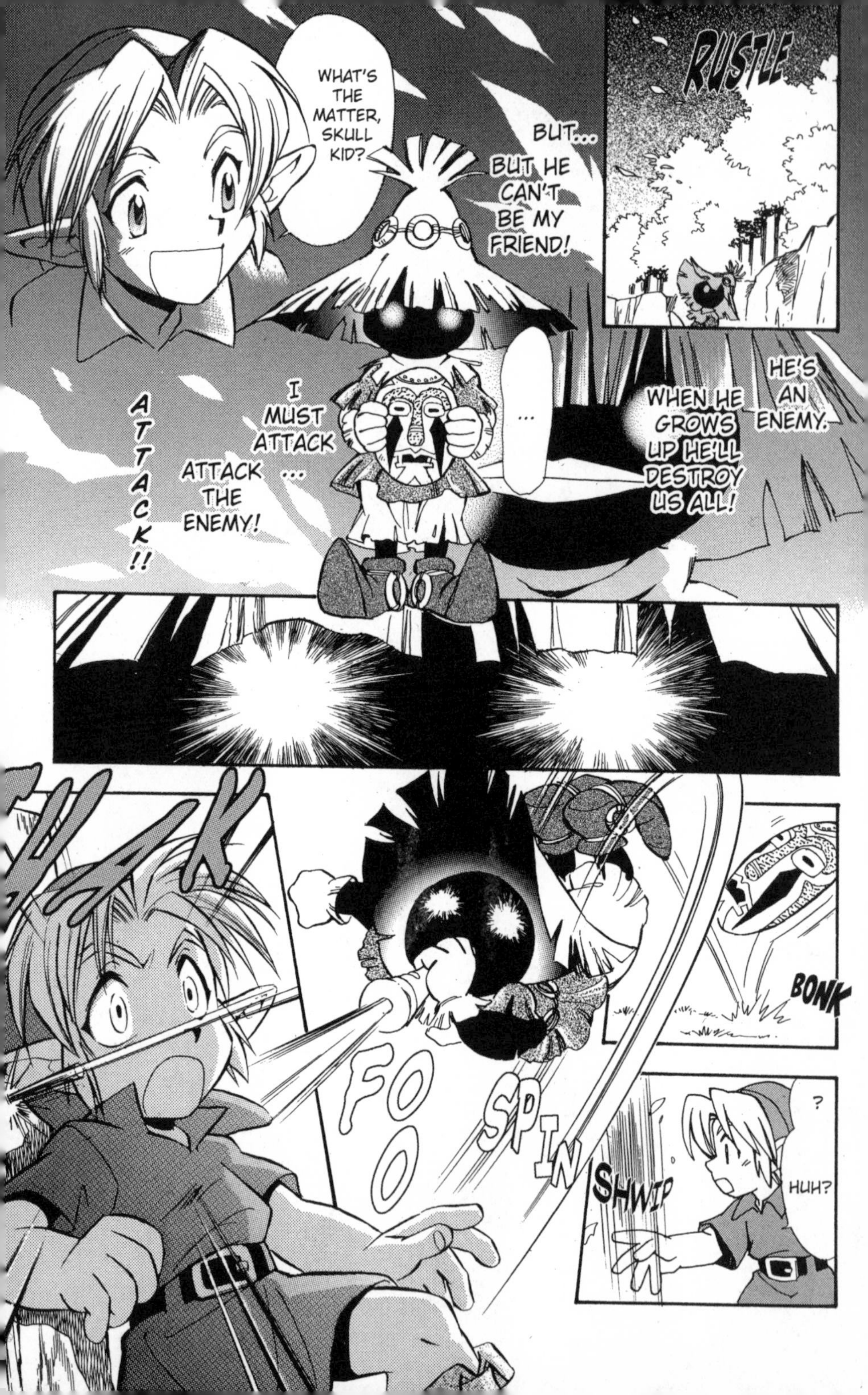
RUSTLE
WHAT'S THE MATTER, SKULL KID?
BUT...
BUT HE CAN'T BE MY FRIEND!
...
HE'S AN ENEMY.
WHEN HE GROWS UP HE'LL DESTROY US ALL!
I MUST ATTACK ...
ATTACK THE ENEMY!
ATTACK!!
BONK
?
HUH?
SHWIP
SPIN
FOO

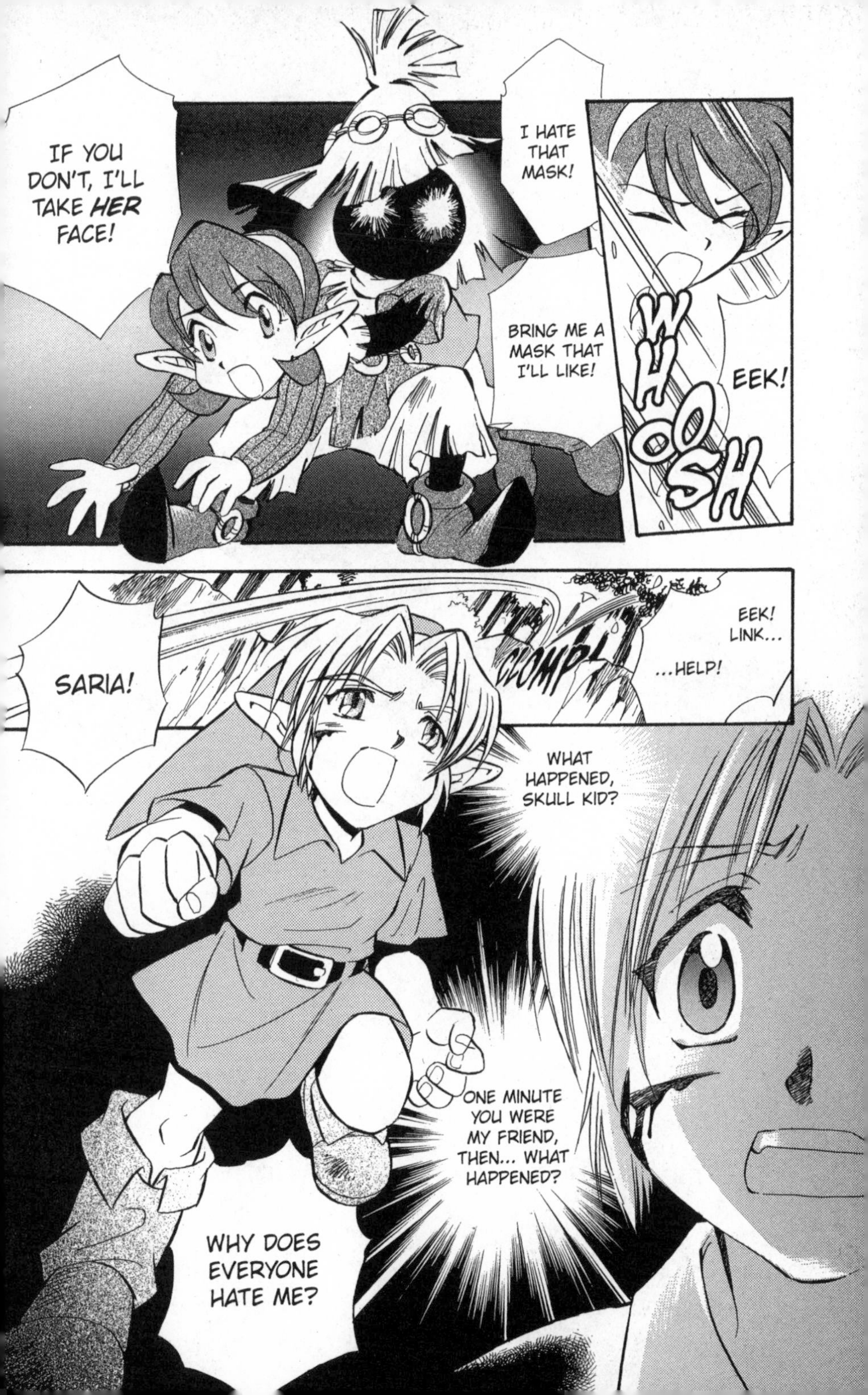
EEK!
WHOOSH
I HATE THAT MASK!
BRING ME A MASK THAT I'LL LIKE!
IF YOU DON'T, I'LL TAKE *HER* FACE!
EEK! LINK...
...HELP!
CLOMP!
SARIA!
WHAT HAPPENED, SKULL KID?
ONE MINUTE YOU WERE MY FRIEND, THEN... WHAT HAPPENED?
WHY DOES EVERYONE HATE ME?

OCARINA OF TIME ~ BONUS STORY
THE SKULL KID AND THE MASK ~ PART 2

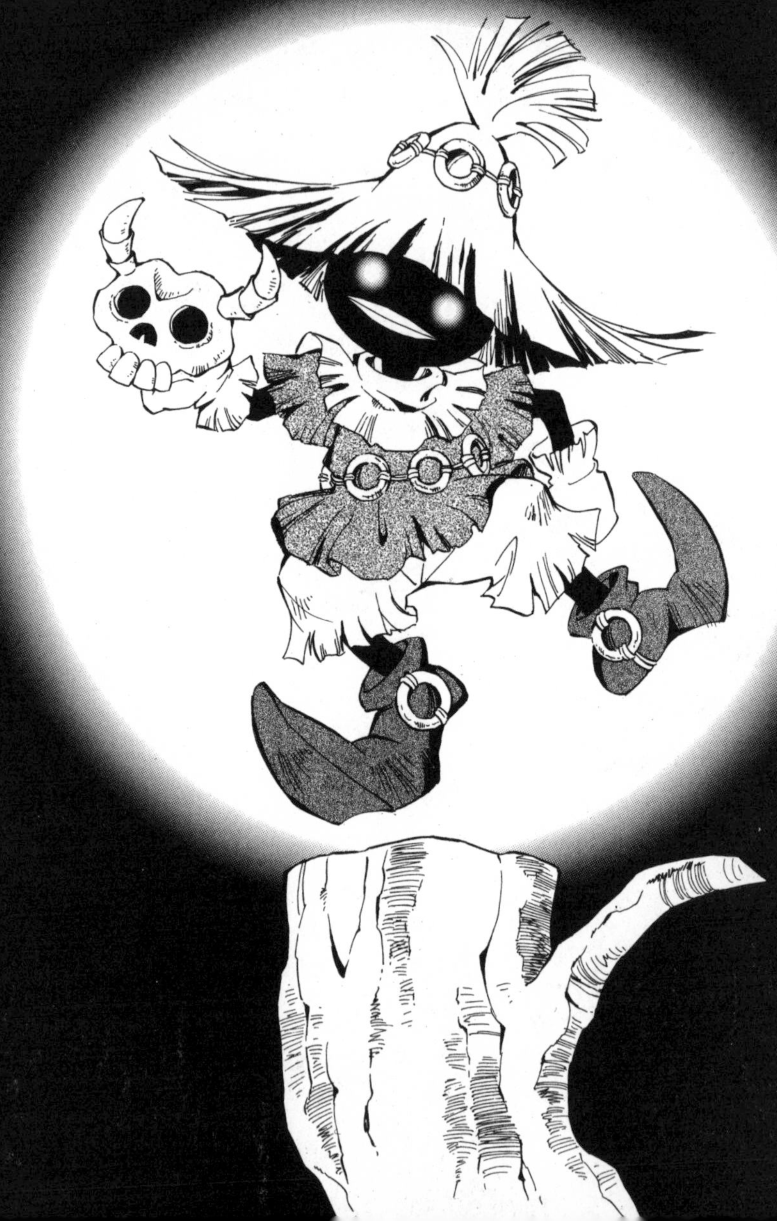

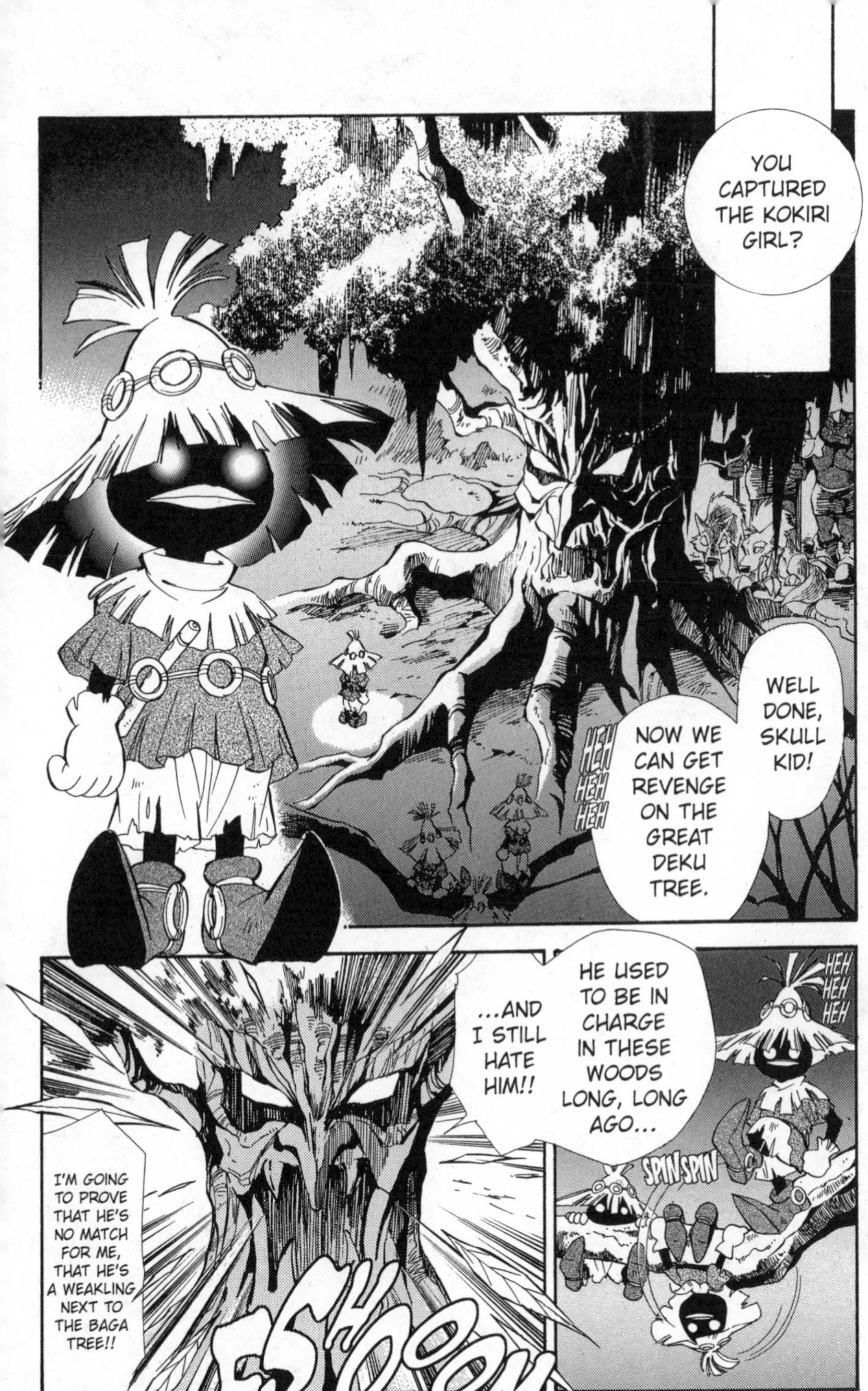
YOU CAPTURED THE KOKIRI GIRL?
WELL DONE, SKULL KID!
NOW WE CAN GET REVENGE ON THE GREAT DEKU TREE.
HEH HEH HEH
HE USED TO BE IN CHARGE IN THESE WOODS LONG, LONG AGO...
HEH HEH HEH
SPIN SPIN
...AND I STILL HATE HIM!!
I'M GOING TO PROVE THAT HE'S NO MATCH FOR ME, THAT HE'S A WEAKLING NEXT TO THE BAGA TREE!!
FSHOOOM

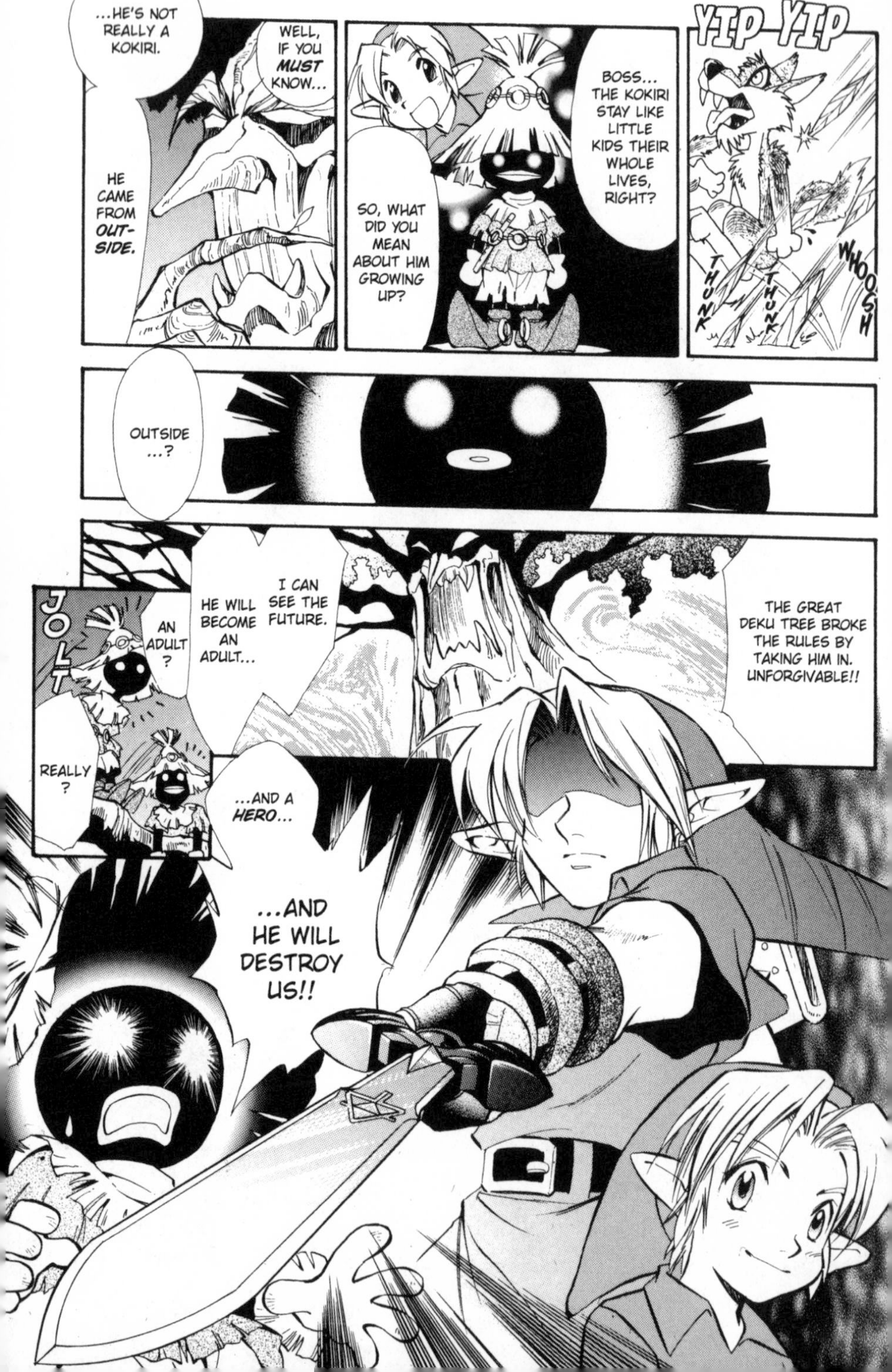
YIP YIP
WHOOOSH
THUNK
THUNK
BOSS... THE KOKIRI STAY LIKE LITTLE KIDS THEIR WHOLE LIVES, RIGHT?
SO, WHAT DID YOU MEAN ABOUT HIM GROWING UP?
WELL, IF YOU MUST KNOW...
...HE'S NOT REALLY A KOKIRI.
HE CAME FROM OUTSIDE.
OUTSIDE ...?
THE GREAT DEKU TREE BROKE THE RULES BY TAKING HIM IN. UNFORGIVABLE!!
I CAN SEE THE FUTURE.
HE WILL BECOME AN ADULT...
JOLT
AN ADULT?
REALLY?
...AND A HERO...
...AND HE WILL DESTROY US!!

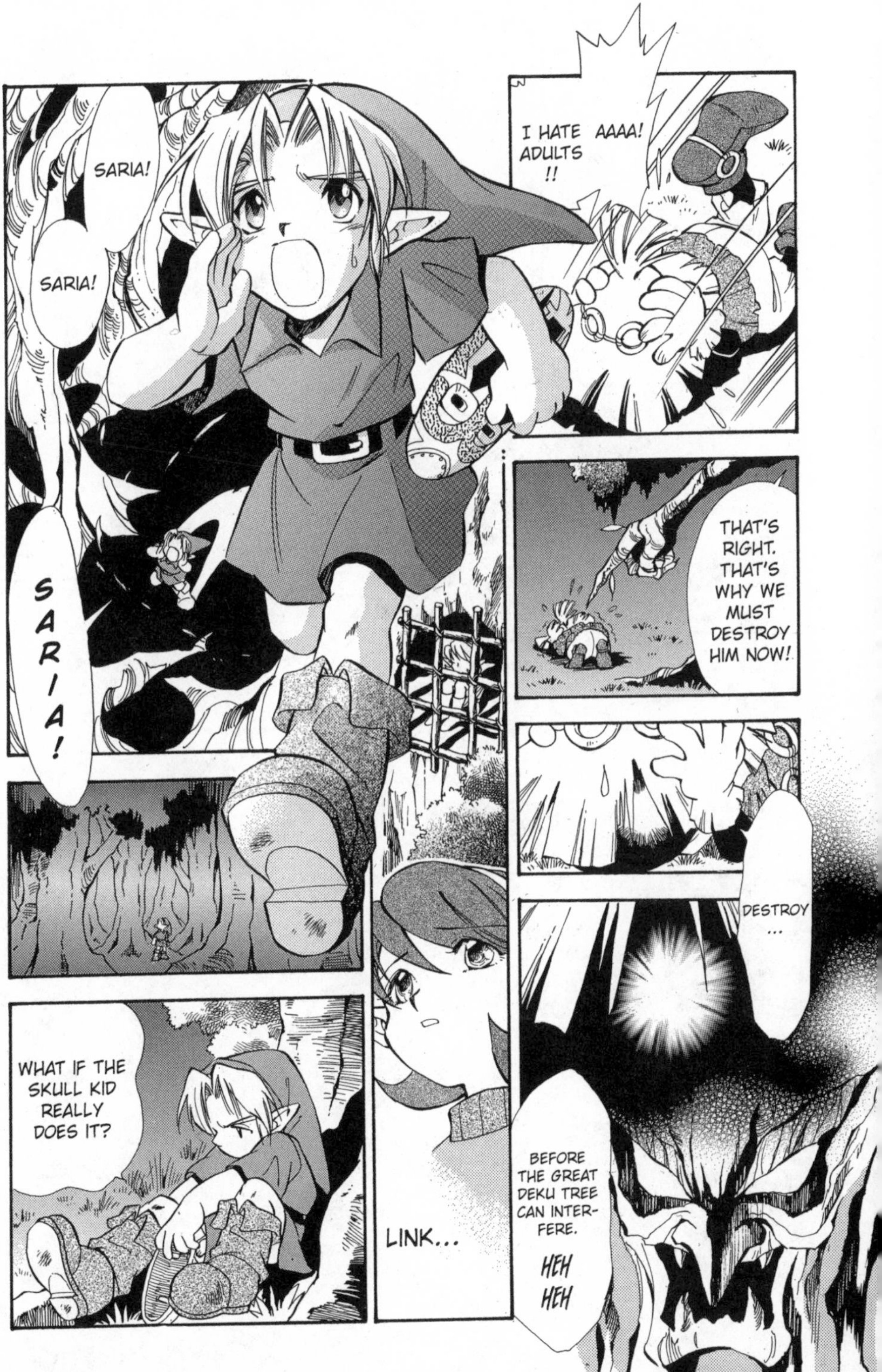
AAAA!
I HATE ADULTS!!
THAT'S RIGHT. THAT'S WHY WE MUST DESTROY HIM NOW!
DESTROY...
BEFORE THE GREAT DEKU TREE CAN INTER-FERE.
HEH HEH
SARIA!
SARIA!
SARIA!
LINK...
WHAT IF THE SKULL KID REALLY DOES IT?

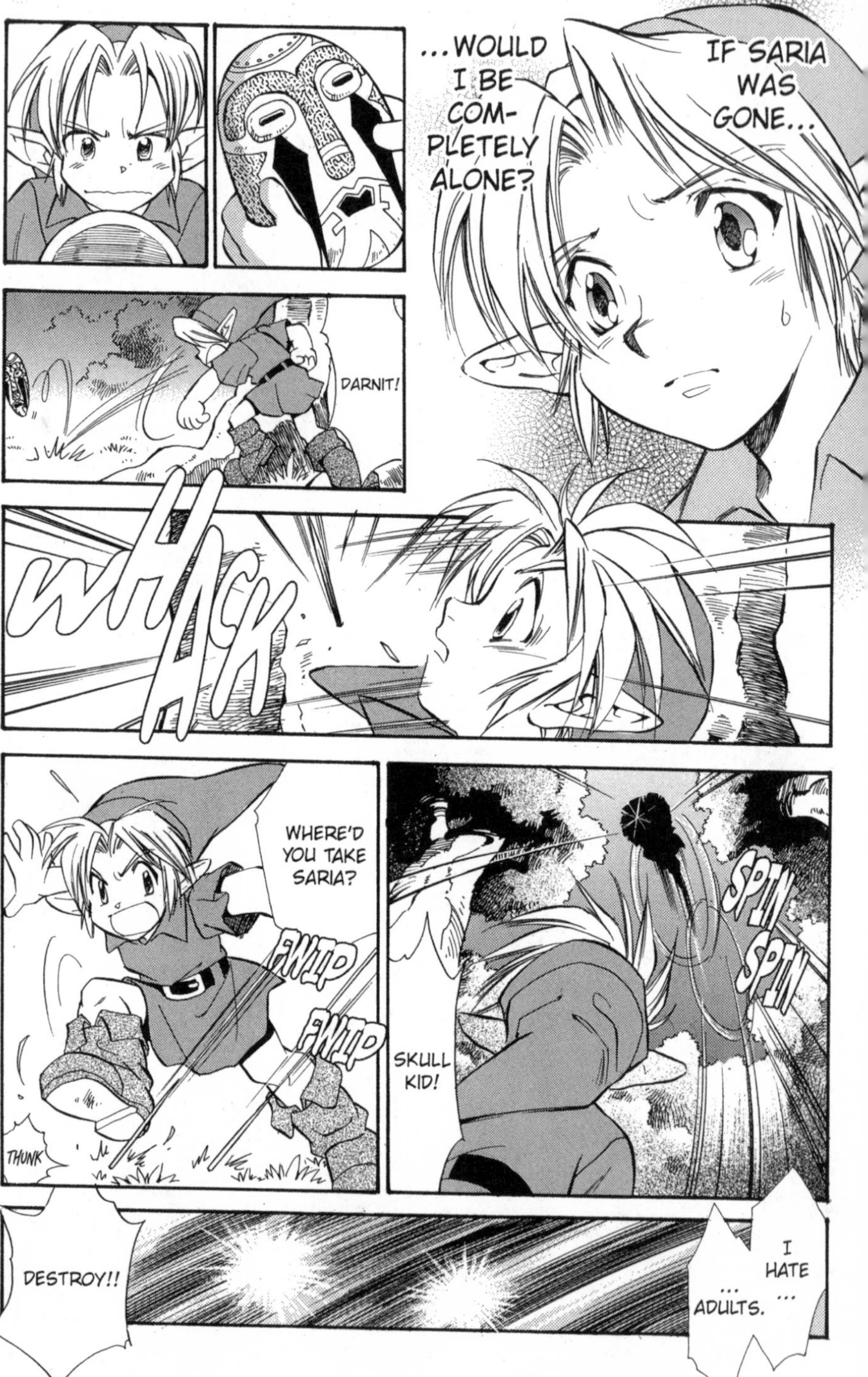
IF SARIA WAS GONE...
...WOULD I BE COM-PLETELY ALONE?
DARNIT!
WHACK
SPIN
SPIN
SKULL KID!
WHERE'D YOU TAKE SARIA?
FWIP
FWIP
THUNK
I HATE ... ADULTS.
DESTROY!!

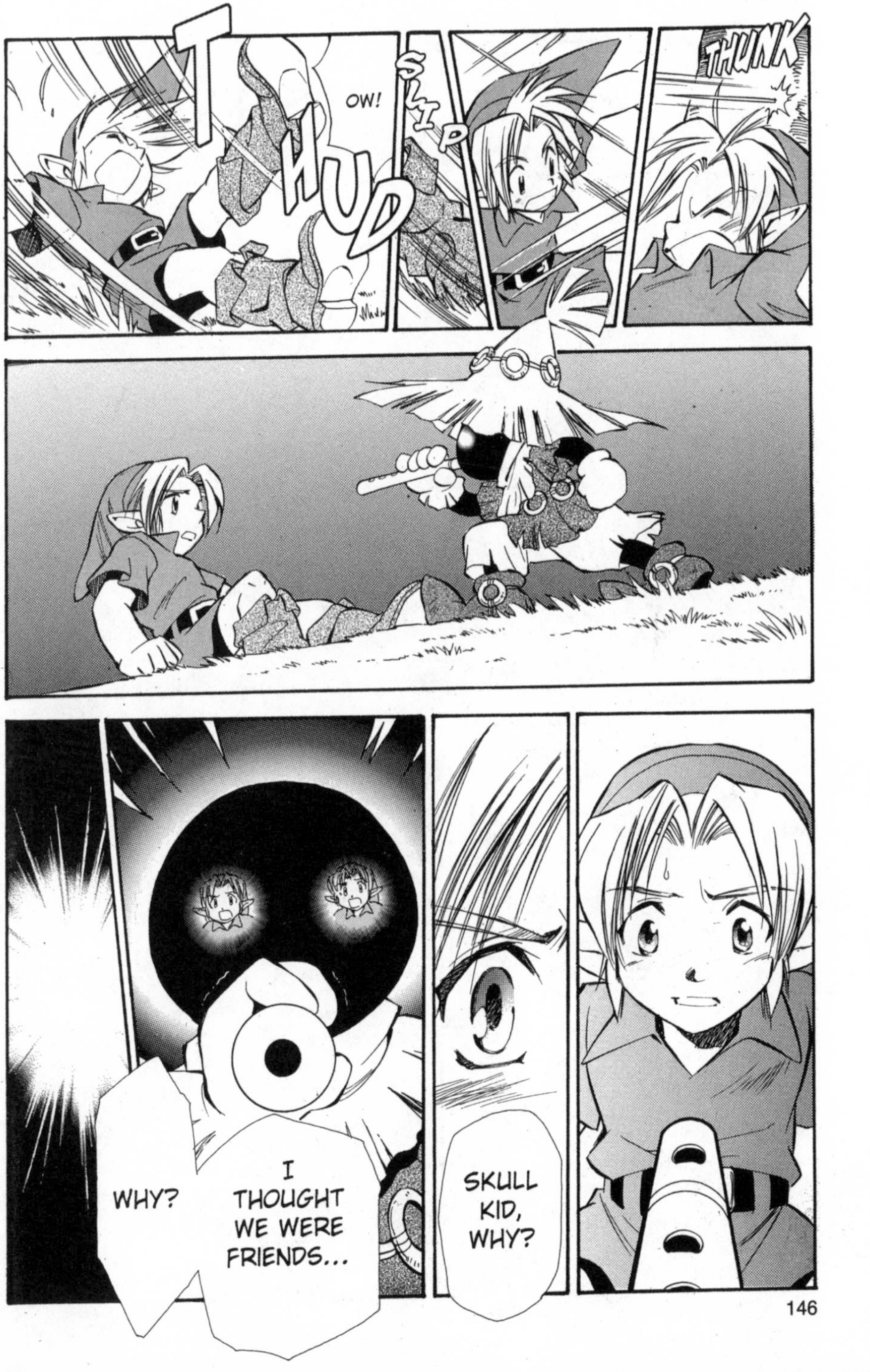
THUNK
SLIP
OW!
THUD
SKULL KID, WHY?
I THOUGHT WE WERE FRIENDS...
WHY?

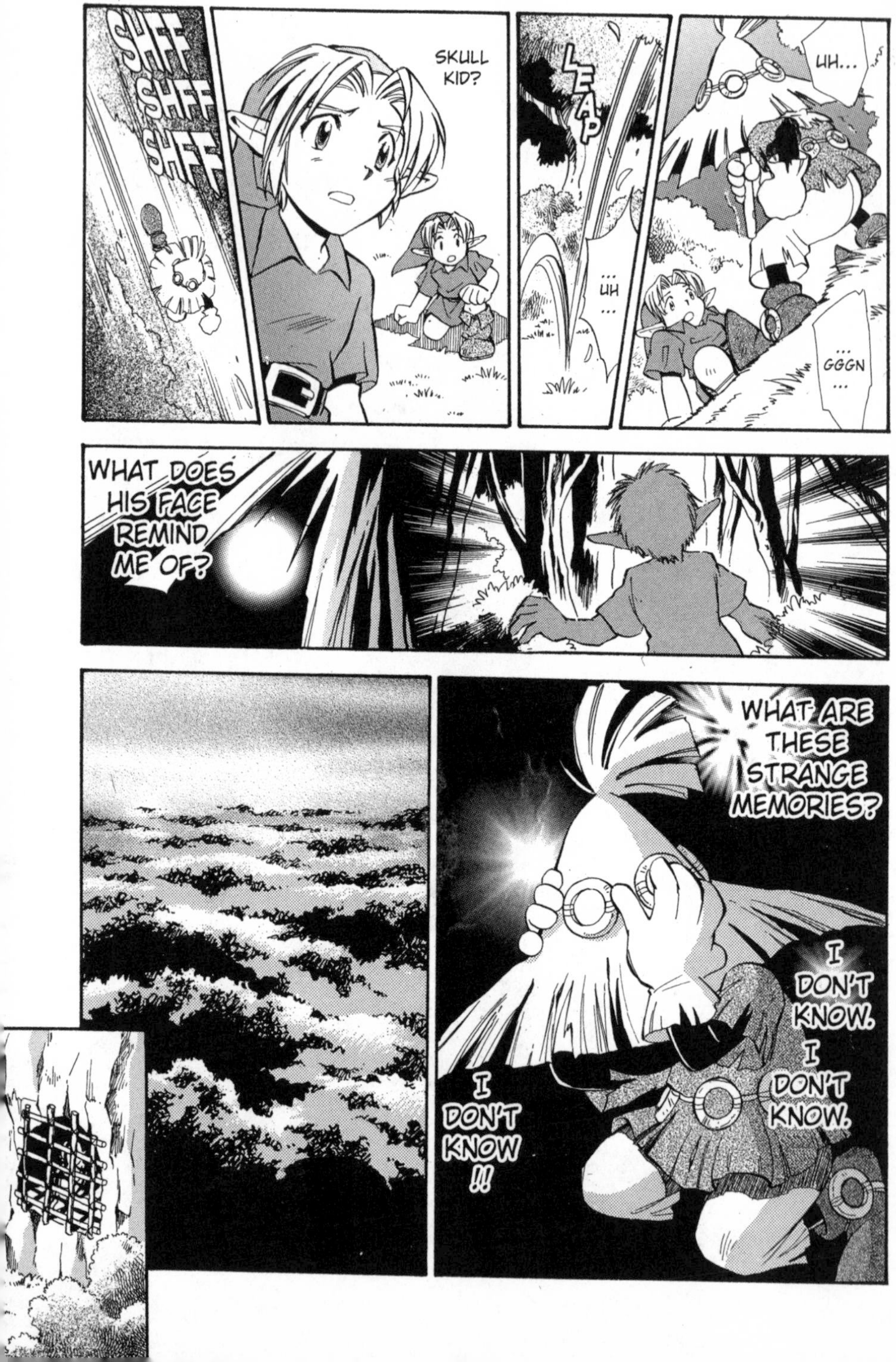
UH...
...GGGN...
LEAP
...UH...
SKULL KID?
SHFF
SHFF
SHFF
WHAT DOES HIS FACE REMIND ME OF?
WHAT ARE THESE STRANGE MEMORIES?
I DON'T KNOW.
I DON'T KNOW.
I DON'T KNOW!!

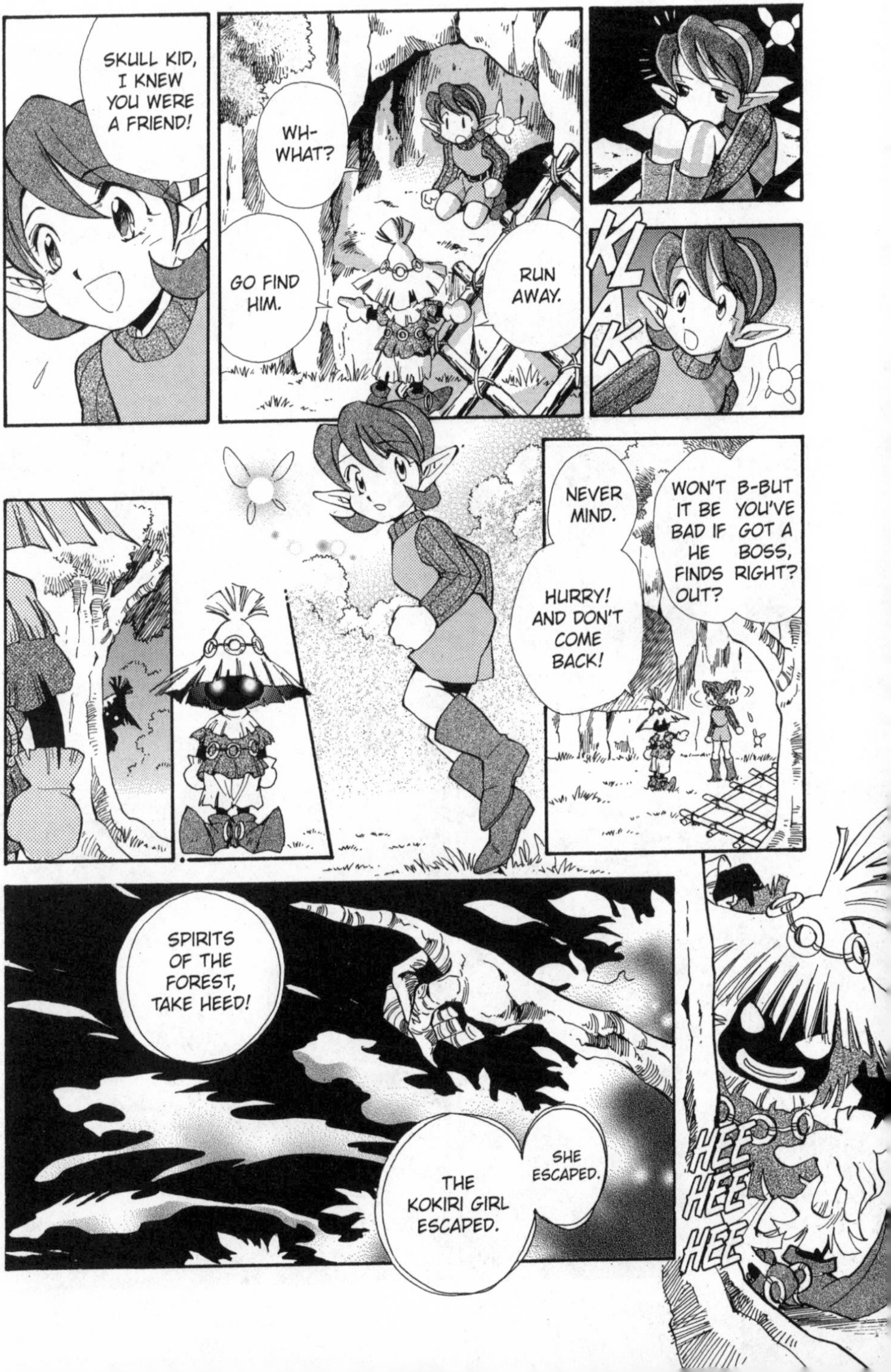
KLAK
WH-WHAT?
RUN AWAY.
GO FIND HIM.
SKULL KID, I KNEW YOU WERE A FRIEND!
B-BUT YOU'VE GOT A BOSS, RIGHT?
WON'T IT BE BAD IF HE FINDS OUT?
NEVER MIND.
HURRY! AND DON'T COME BACK!
HEE HEE HEE
SPIRITS OF THE FOREST, TAKE HEED!
SHE ESCAPED.
THE KOKIRI GIRL ESCAPED.

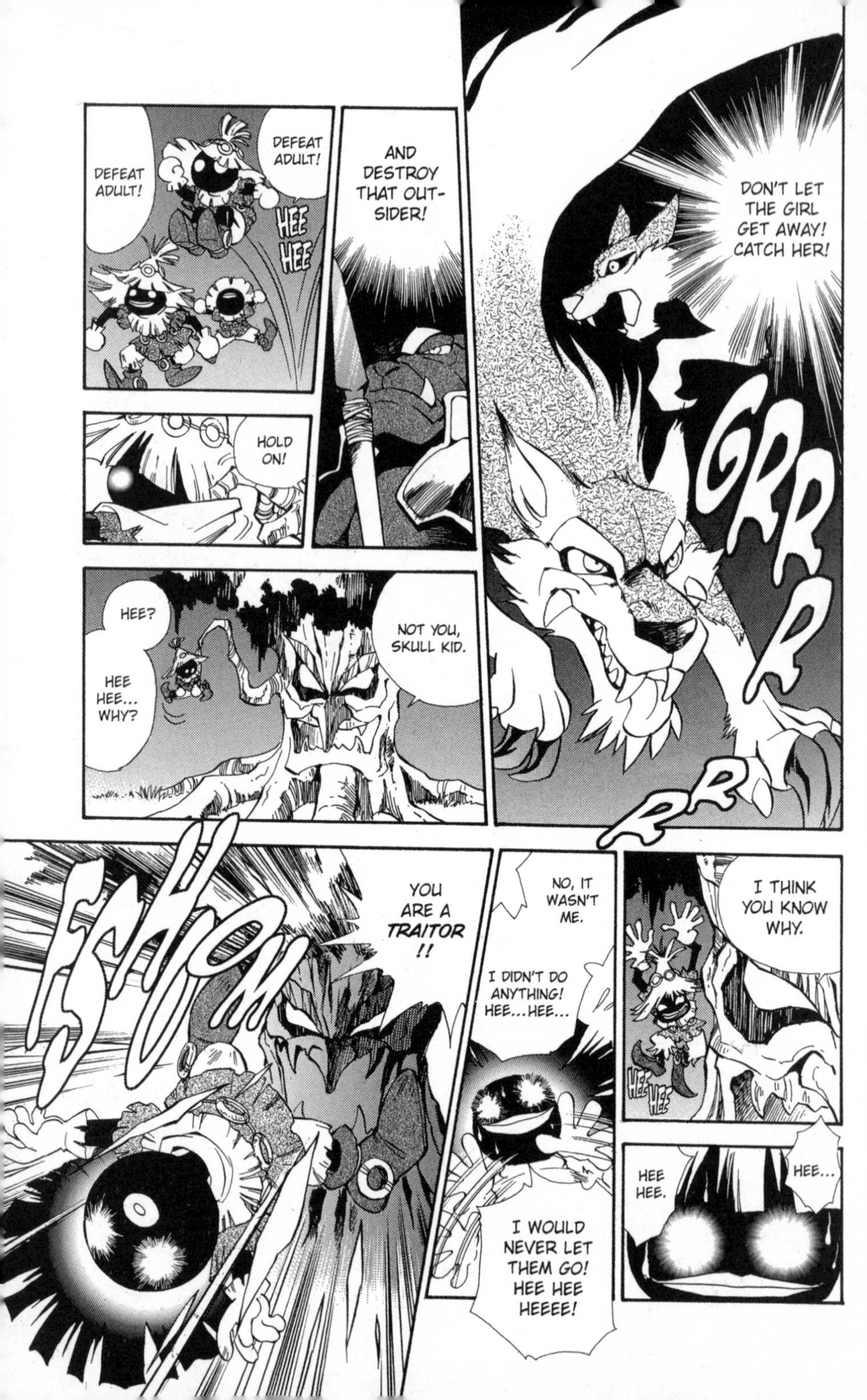
DON'T LET THE GIRL GET AWAY! CATCH HER!
GRRRRR
AND DESTROY THAT OUT-SIDER!
DEFEAT ADULT!
DEFEAT ADULT!
HEE HEE
HOLD ON!
NOT YOU, SKULL KID.
HEE?
HEE HEE... WHY?
I THINK YOU KNOW WHY.
HEE HEE
HEE...
HEE HEE.
NO, IT WASN'T ME.
I DIDN'T DO ANYTHING! HEE...HEE...
I WOULD NEVER LET THEM GO! HEE HEE HEEEE!
YOU ARE A TRAITOR!!

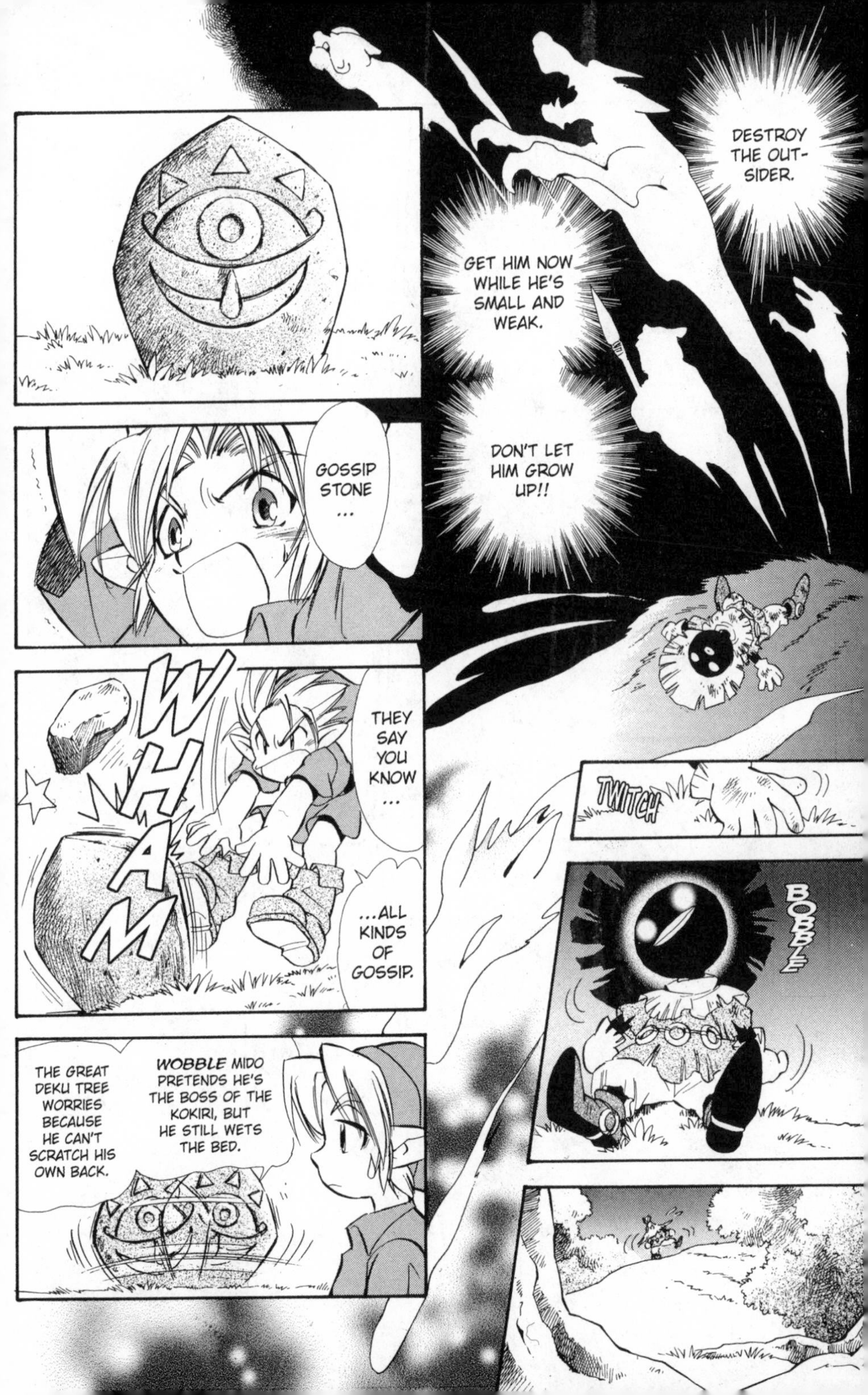
DESTROY THE OUT-SIDER.
GET HIM NOW WHILE HE'S SMALL AND WEAK.
DON'T LET HIM GROW UP!!
TWITCH
BOBBLE
GOSSIP STONE ...
THEY SAY YOU KNOW ...
WHAM
...ALL KINDS OF GOSSIP.
WOBBLE MIDO PRETENDS HE'S THE BOSS OF THE KOKIRI, BUT HE STILL WETS THE BED.
THE GREAT DEKU TREE WORRIES BECAUSE HE CAN'T SCRATCH HIS OWN BACK.

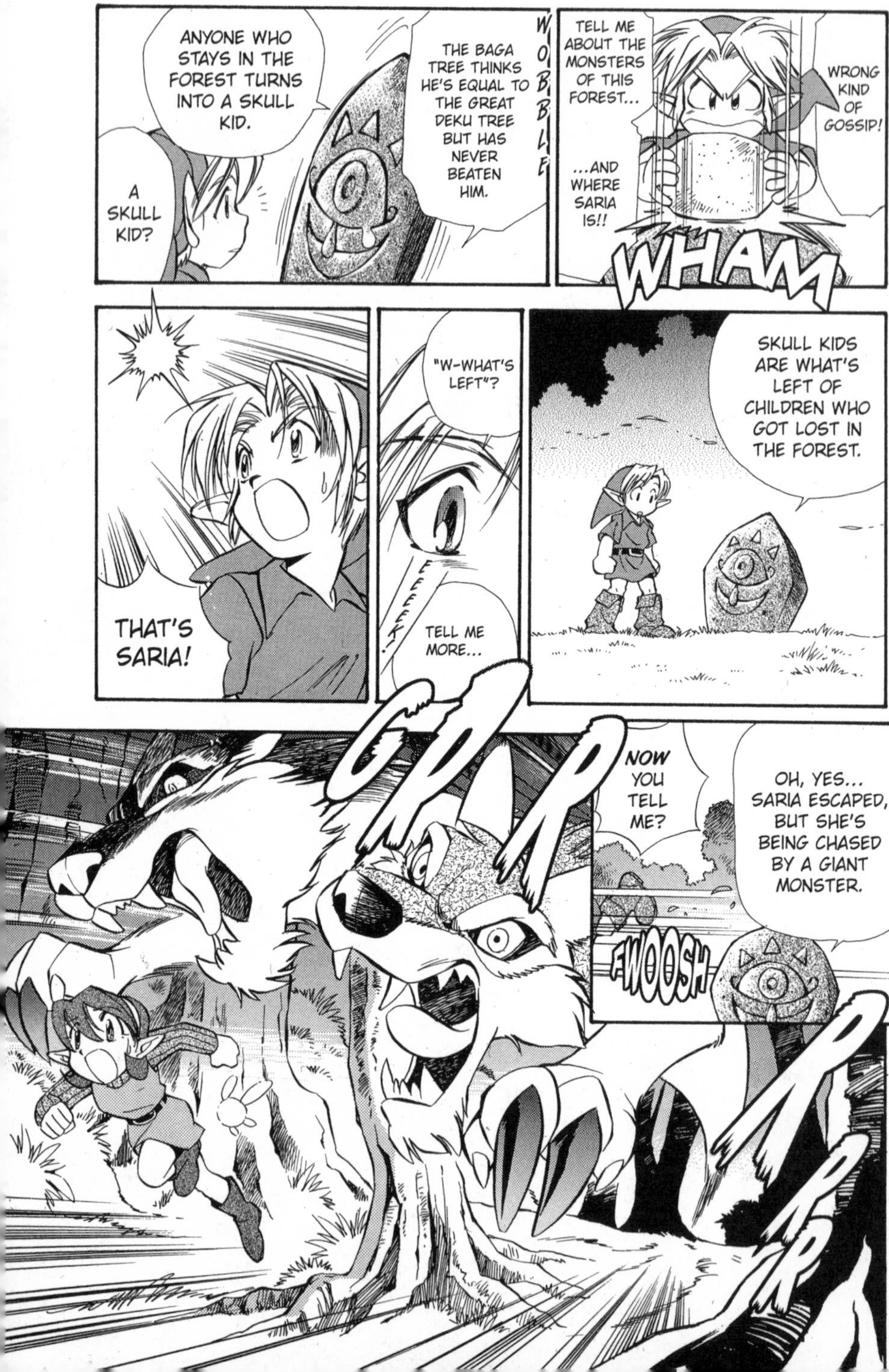

TELL ME ABOUT THE MONSTERS OF THIS FOREST...
...AND WHERE SARIA IS!!
WRONG KIND OF GOSSIP!
WHAM
WOBBLE
THE BAGA TREE THINKS HE'S EQUAL TO THE GREAT DEKU TREE BUT HAS NEVER BEATEN HIM.
ANYONE WHO STAYS IN THE FOREST TURNS INTO A SKULL KID.
A SKULL KID?
SKULL KIDS ARE WHAT'S LEFT OF CHILDREN WHO GOT LOST IN THE FOREST.
"W-WHAT'S LEFT"?
EEEEEK!
TELL ME MORE...
THAT'S SARIA!
OH, YES... SARIA ESCAPED, BUT SHE'S BEING CHASED BY A GIANT MONSTER.
NOW YOU TELL ME?
FWOOSH
GRRRRR

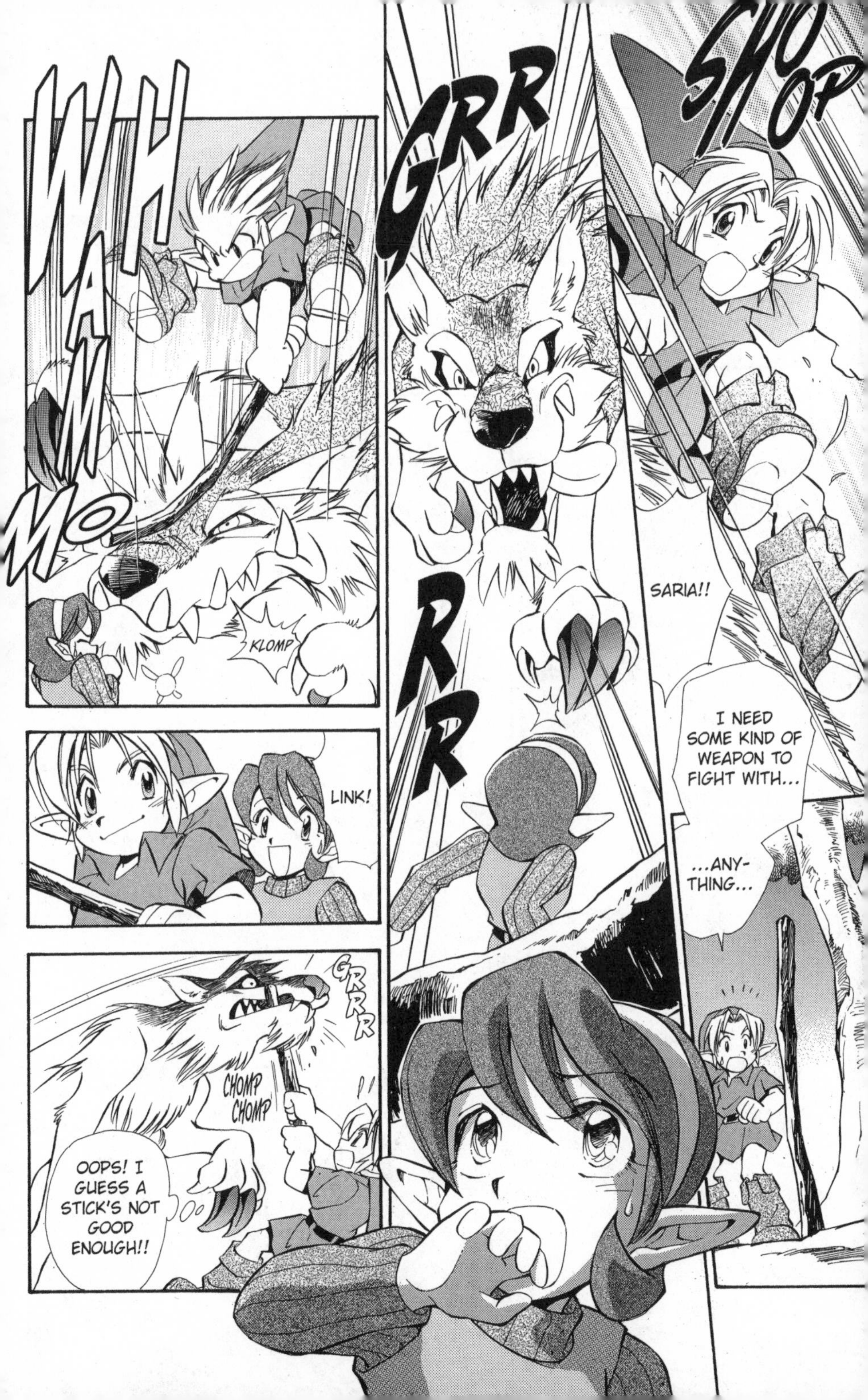
SHOOP
SARIA!!
I NEED SOME KIND OF WEAPON TO FIGHT WITH...
...ANY-THING...
GRRRRR
WHAMMO
KLOMP
LINK!
GRRR
CHOMP CHOMP
OOPS! I GUESS A STICK'S NOT GOOD ENOUGH!!

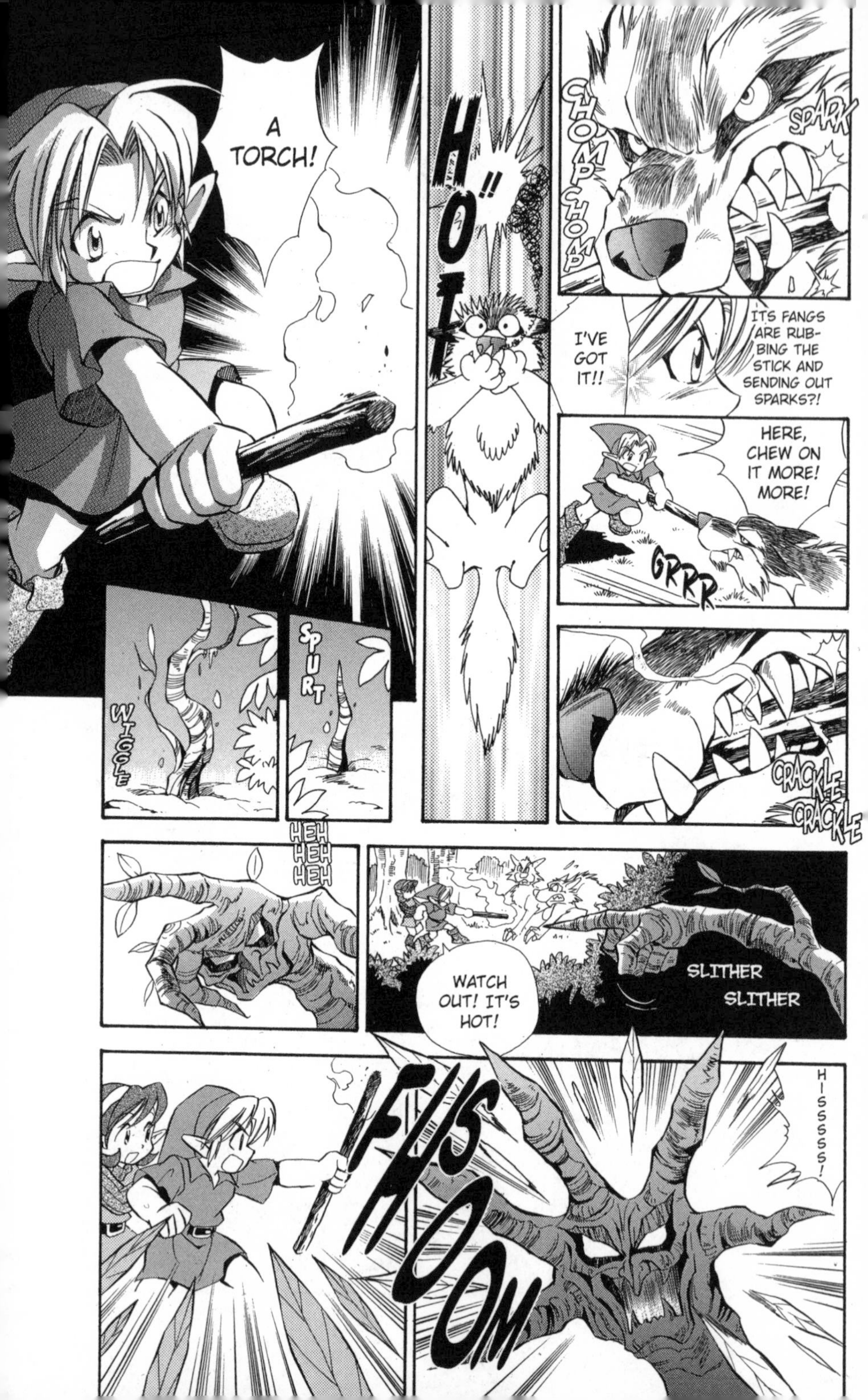
CHOMP CHOMP CHOMP
SPARK
IT'S FANGS ARE RUB-BING THE STICK AND SENDING OUT SPARKS?!
I'VE GOT IT!!
HERE, CHEW ON IT MORE! MORE!
GRRR
CRACKLE CRACKLE
HOT!!
A TORCH!
SPURT
WIGGLE
SLITHER SLITHER
WATCH OUT! IT'S HOT!
HEH HEH HEH
HISSSSS!
FWOOM

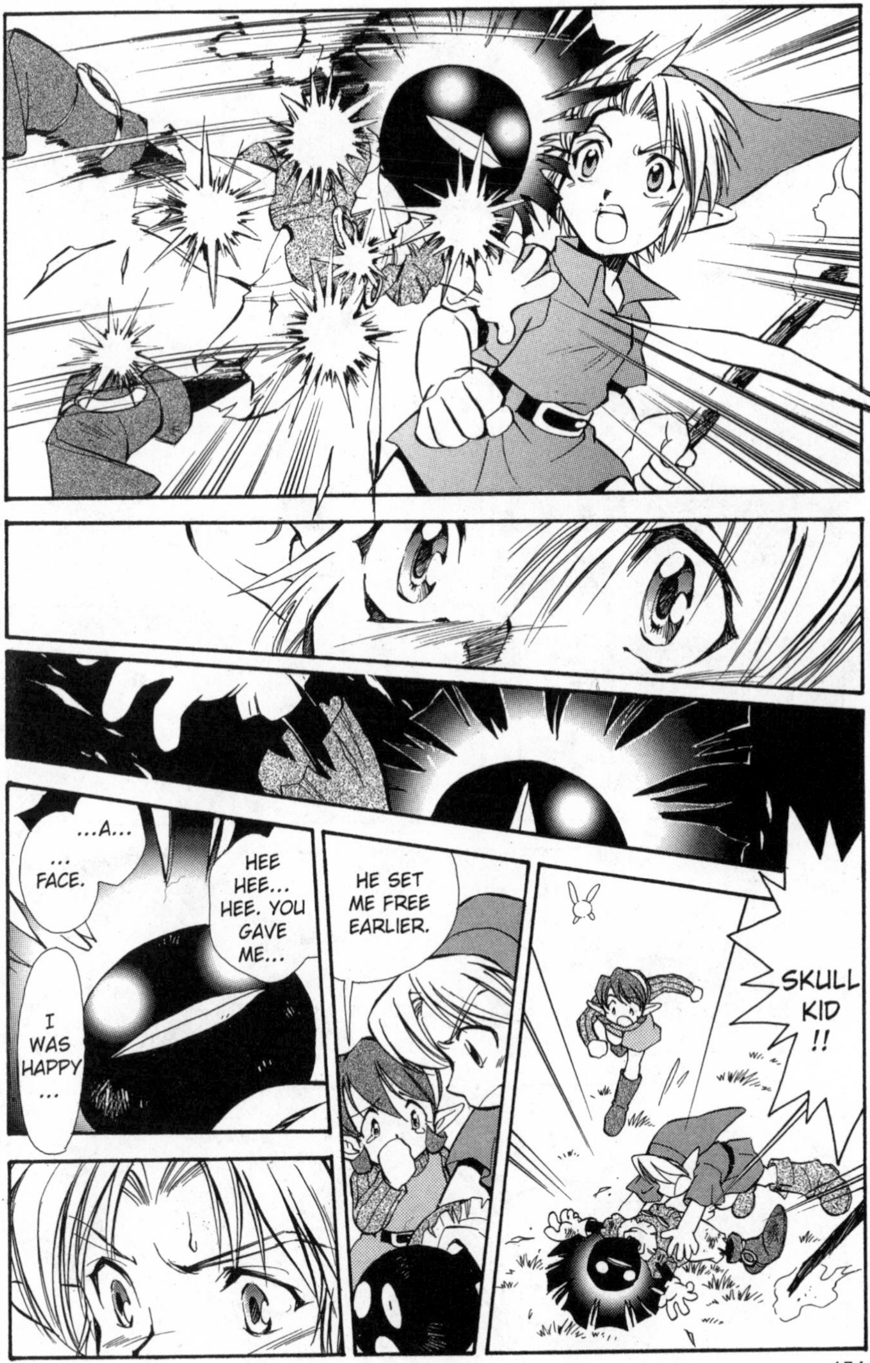
SKULL KID !!
HE SET ME FREE EARLIER.
HEE HEE... HEE. YOU GAVE ME...
...A... ...FACE.
I WAS HAPPY ...

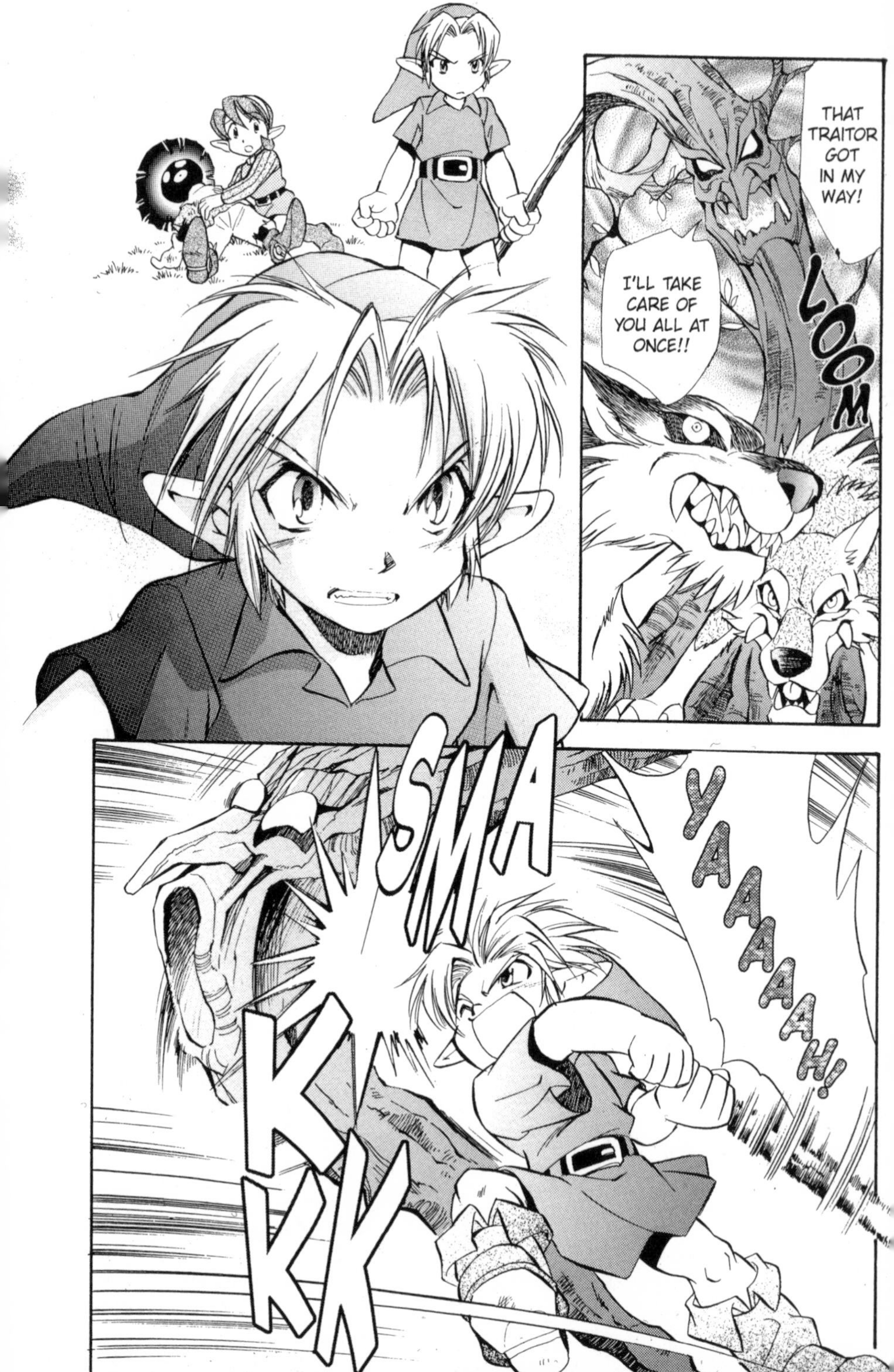
THAT TRAITOR GOT IN MY WAY!
LOOOM
I'LL TAKE CARE OF YOU ALL AT ONCE!!
YAAAAAAH!
SMAKKK

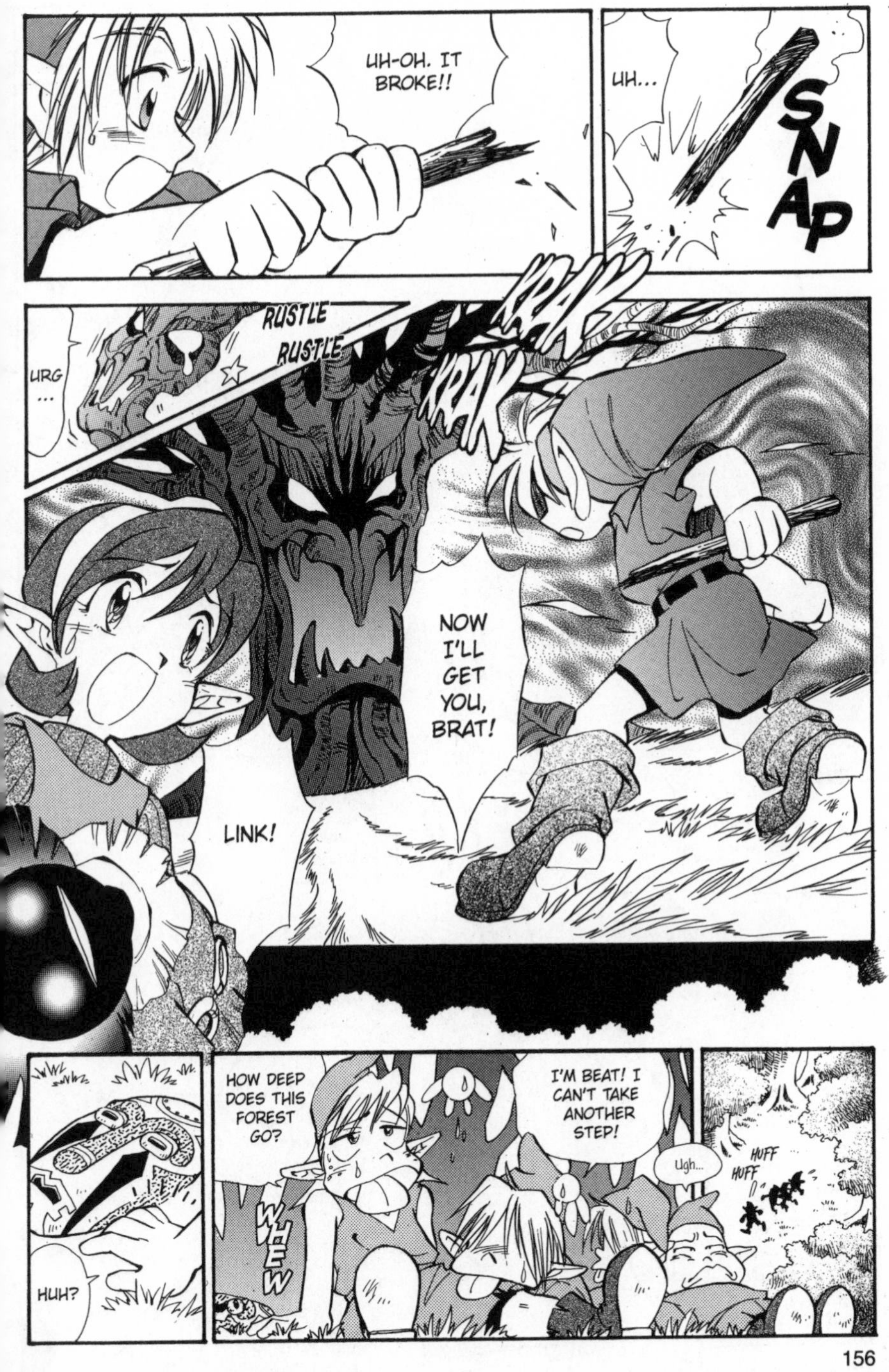
UH...
SNAP
UH-OH. IT BROKE!!
KRAK
KRAK
RUSTLE
RUSTLE
URG ...
NOW I'LL GET YOU, BRAT!
LINK!
HUFF HUFF
I'M BEAT! I CAN'T TAKE ANOTHER STEP!
Ugh...
HOW DEEP DOES THIS FOREST GO?
WHEW
HUH?

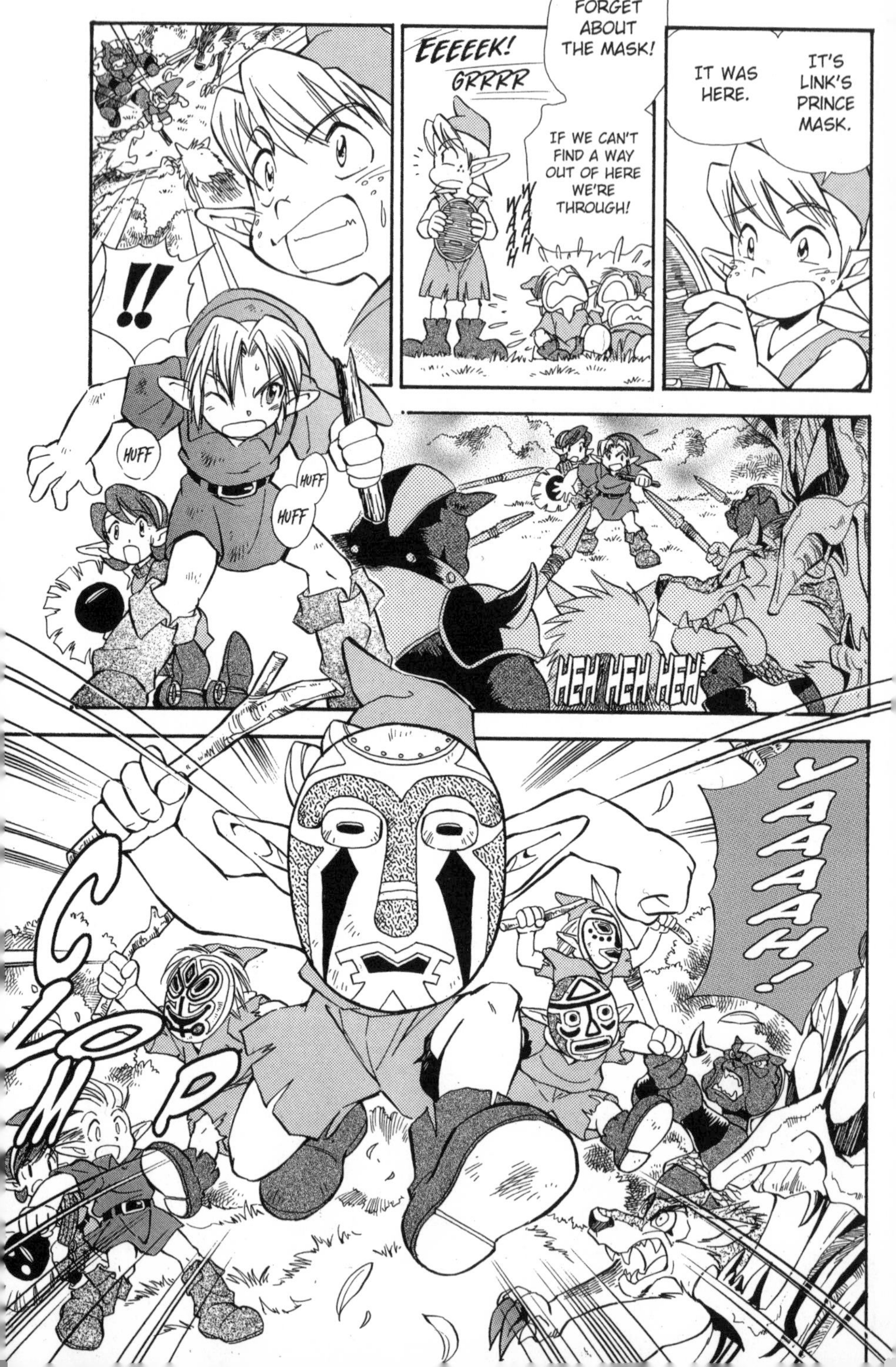
IT'S LINK'S PRINCE MASK.
IT WAS HERE.
FORGET ABOUT THE MASK!
EEEEEK!
GRRRR
IF WE CAN'T FIND A WAY OUT OF HERE WE'RE THROUGH!
WAAAAH
!!
HUFF
HUFF
HUFF
HEH HEH HEH
YAAAAAH!
CLOMP

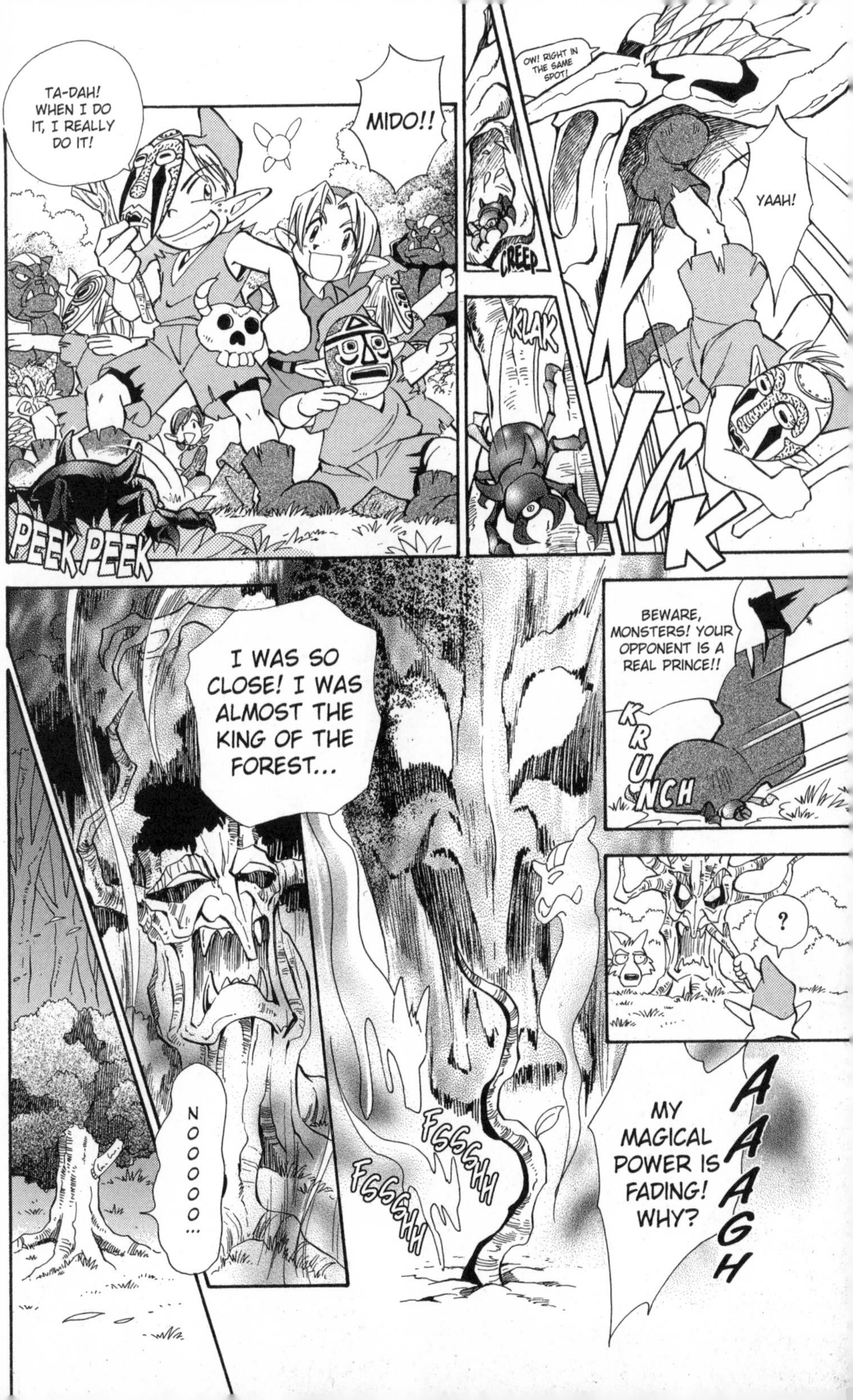
YAAH!
KICK
OW! RIGHT IN THE SAME SPOT!
CREEP
KLAK
MIDO!!
TA-DAH! WHEN I DO IT, I REALLY DO IT!
PEEK PEEK
BEWARE, MONSTERS! YOUR OPPONENT IS A REAL PRINCE!!
KRUNCH
?
AAAGH
MY MAGICAL POWER IS FADING! WHY?
I WAS SO CLOSE! I WAS ALMOST THE KING OF THE FOREST...
FSSGHH
FSSGHH
NOOOOOO...

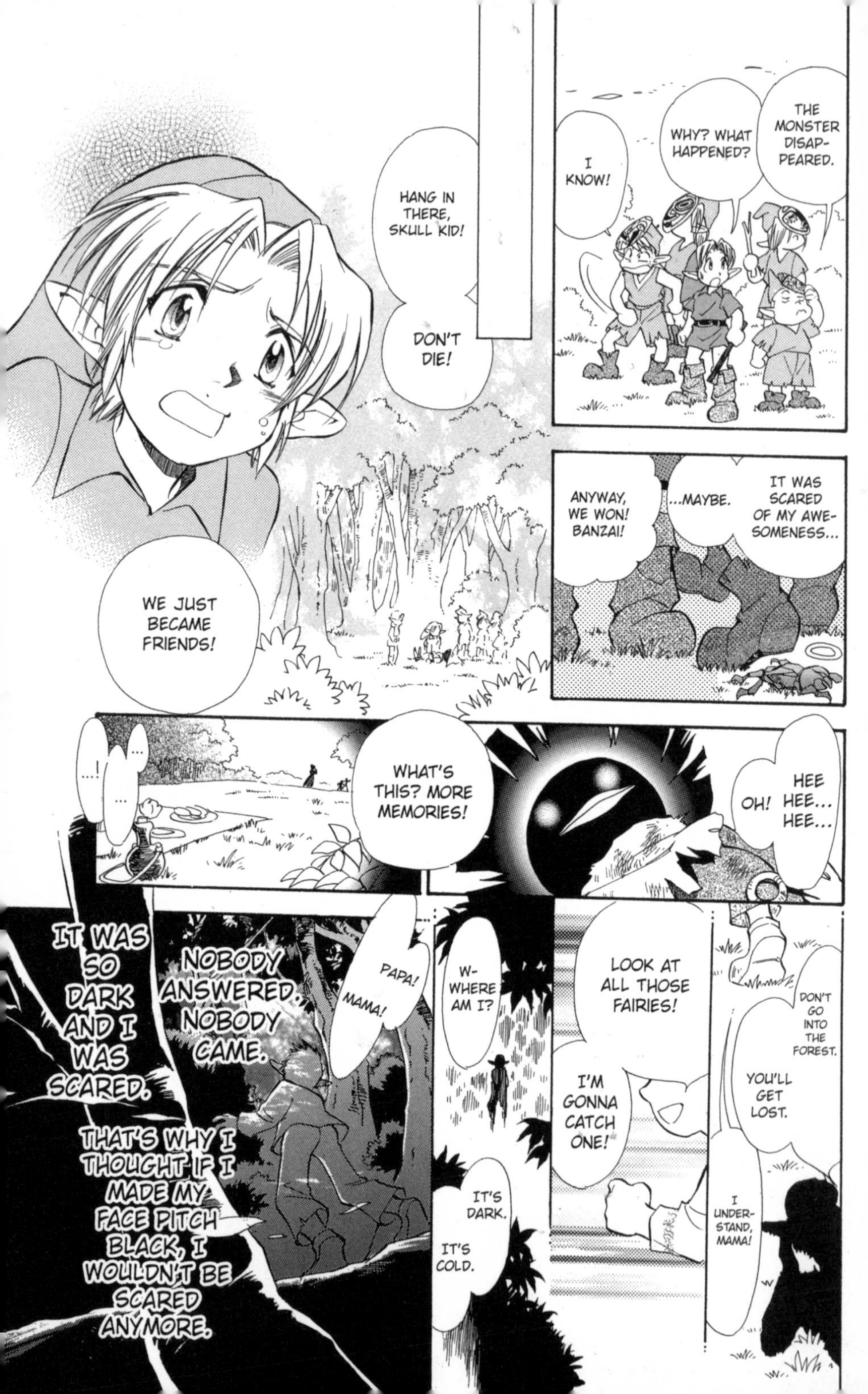
THE MONSTER DISAPPEARED.
WHY? WHAT HAPPENED?
I KNOW!
IT WAS SCARED OF MY AWESOMENESS...
...MAYBE.
ANYWAY, WE WON! BANZAI!
HANG IN THERE, SKULL KID!
DON'T DIE!
WE JUST BECAME FRIENDS!
HEE HEE... HEE...
OH!
WHAT'S THIS? MORE MEMORIES!
...
...!
...
DON'T GO INTO THE FOREST.
YOU'LL GET LOST.
I UNDERSTAND, MAMA!
LOOK AT ALL THOSE FAIRIES!
I'M GONNA CATCH ONE!
W-WHERE AM I?
IT'S DARK.
IT'S COLD.
PAPA!
MAMA!
NOBODY ANSWERED. NOBODY CAME.
IT WAS SO DARK AND I WAS SCARED.
THAT'S WHY I THOUGHT IF I MADE MY FACE PITCH BLACK, I WOULDN'T BE SCARED ANYMORE.

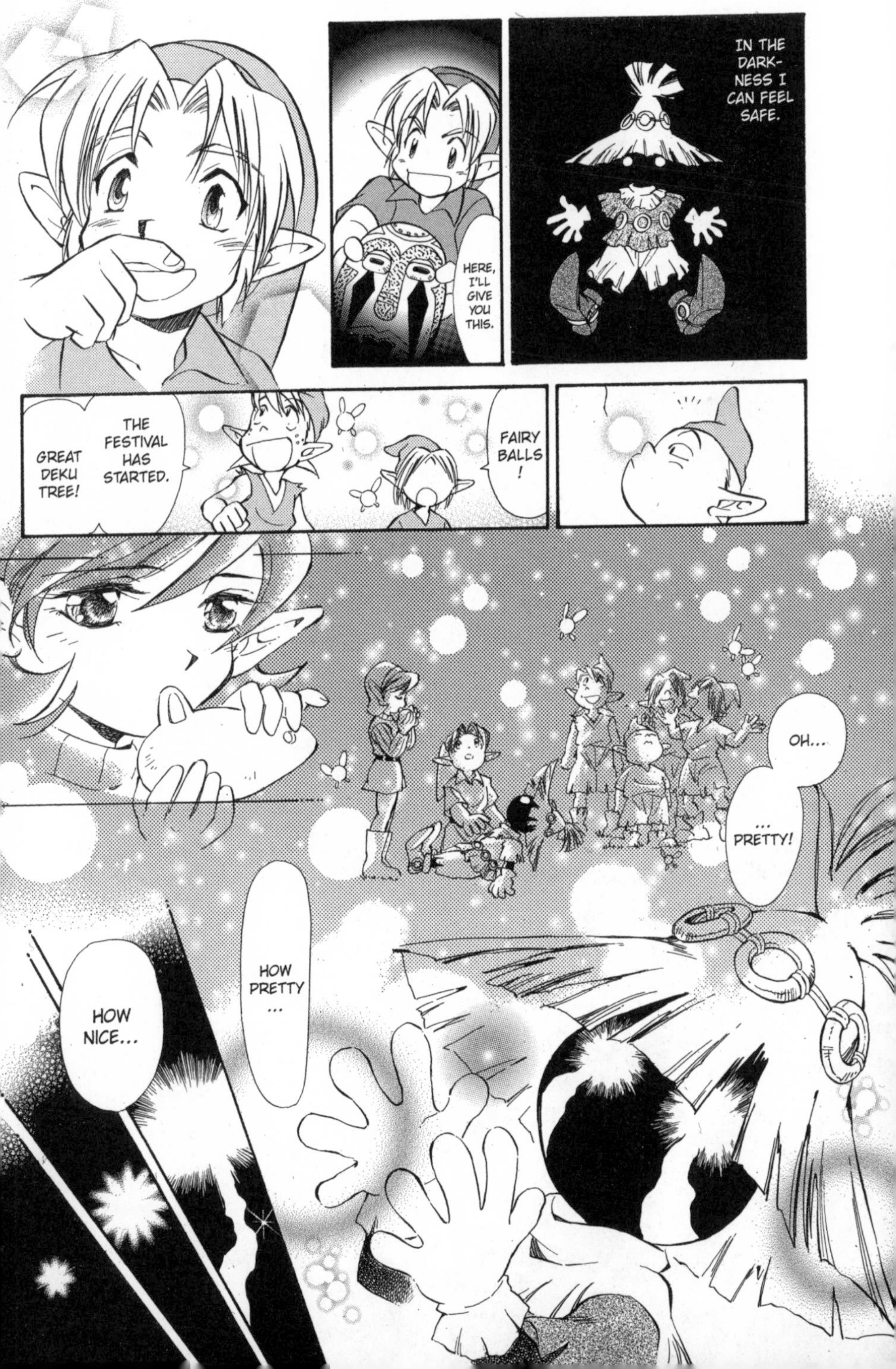
IN THE DARKNESS I CAN FEEL SAFE.
HERE, I'LL GIVE YOU THIS.
FAIRY BALLS!
THE FESTIVAL HAS STARTED.
GREAT DEKU TREE!
OH...
...PRETTY!
HOW PRETTY...
HOW NICE...

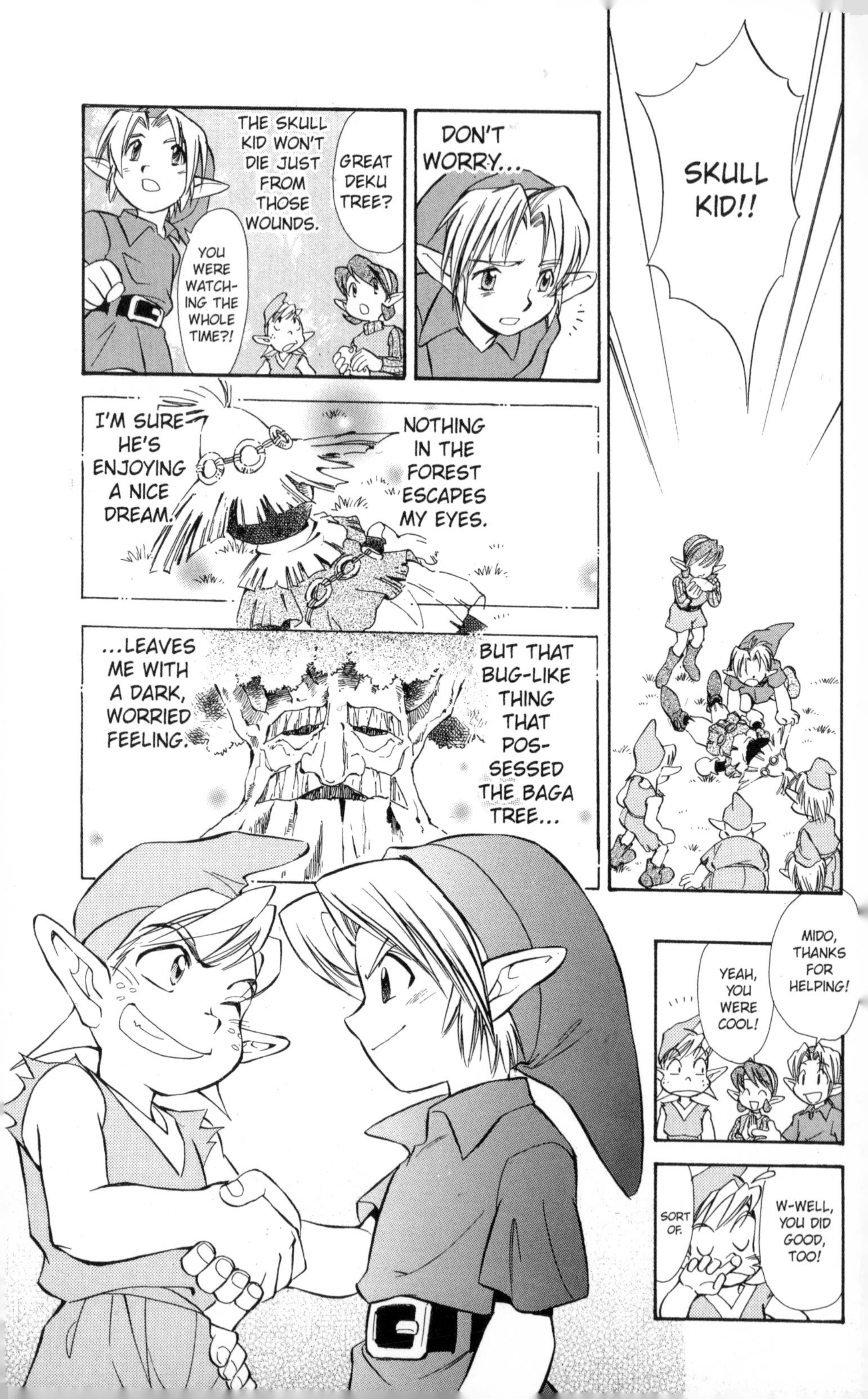
SKULL KID!!
DON'T WORRY...
THE SKULL KID WON'T DIE JUST FROM THOSE WOUNDS.
GREAT DEKU TREE?
YOU WERE WATCHING THE WHOLE TIME?!
NOTHING IN THE FOREST ESCAPES MY EYES.
I'M SURE HE'S ENJOYING A NICE DREAM.
BUT THAT BUG-LIKE THING THAT POS-SESSED THE BAGA TREE...
...LEAVES ME WITH A DARK, WORRIED FEELING.
MIDO, THANKS FOR HELPING!
YEAH, YOU WERE COOL!
W-WELL, YOU DID GOOD, TOO!
SORT OF.

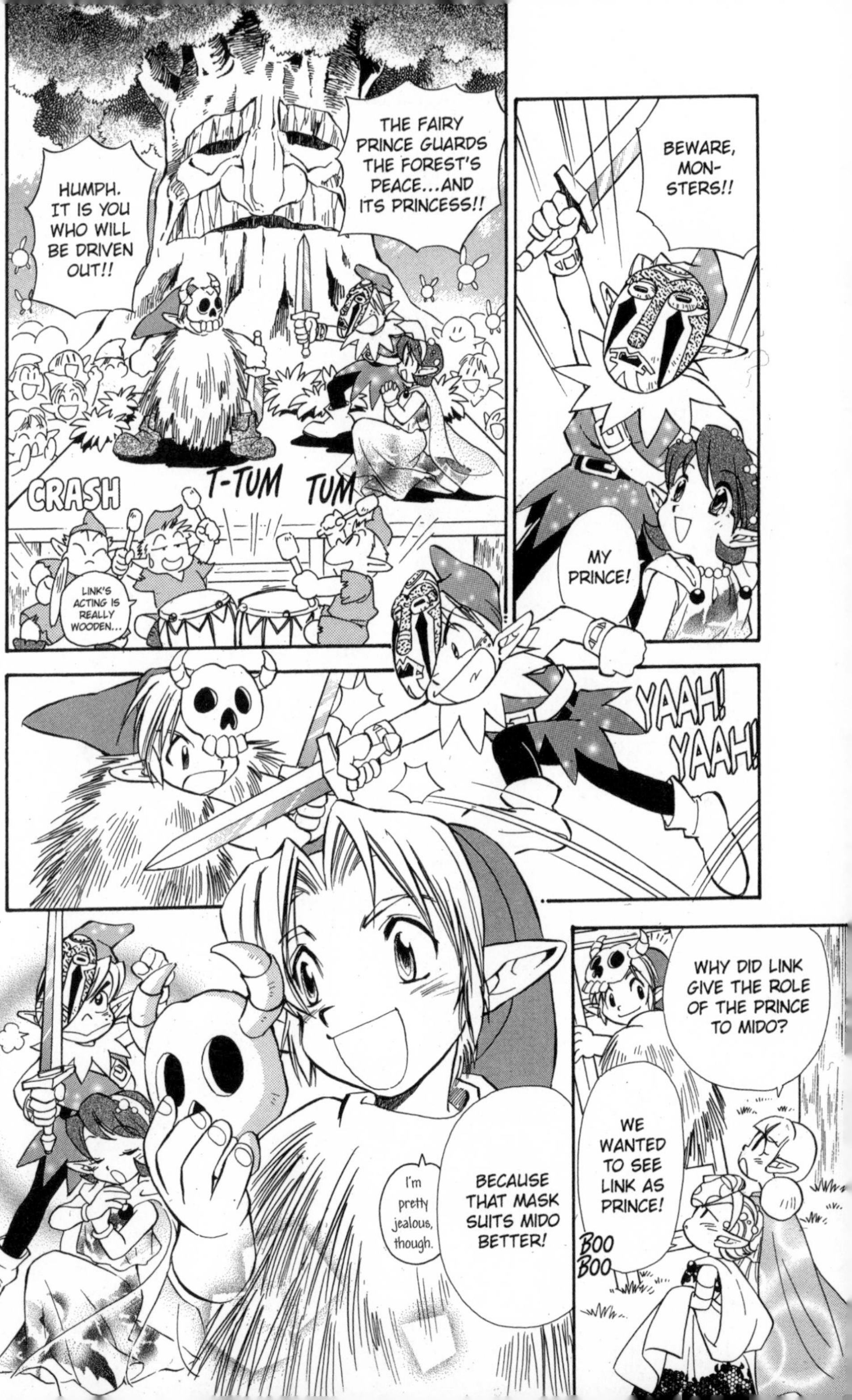
BEWARE, MON-STERS!!
MY PRINCE!
THE FAIRY PRINCE GUARDS THE FOREST'S PEACE...AND ITS PRINCESS!!
HUMPH. IT IS YOU WHO WILL BE DRIVEN OUT!!
CRASH
T-TUM TUM
LINK'S ACTING IS REALLY WOODEN...
YAAH! YAAH!
WHY DID LINK GIVE THE ROLE OF THE PRINCE TO MIDO?
WE WANTED TO SEE LINK AS PRINCE!
BOO BOO
BECAUSE THAT MASK SUITS MIDO BETTER!
I'm pretty jealous, though.

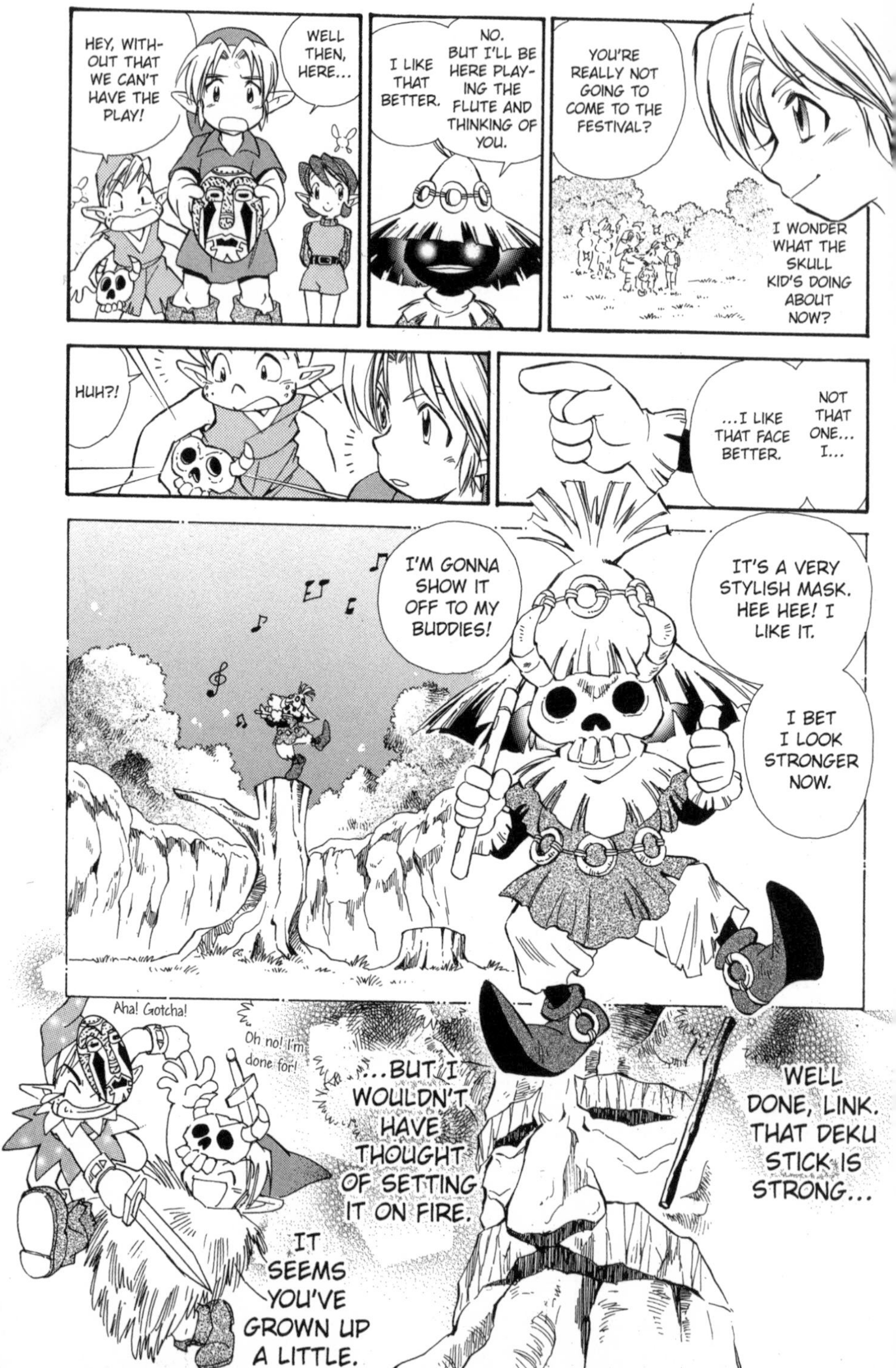
YOU'RE REALLY NOT GOING TO COME TO THE FESTIVAL?
I WONDER WHAT THE SKULL KID'S DOING ABOUT NOW?
NO. BUT I'LL BE HERE PLAYING THE FLUTE AND THINKING OF YOU.
I LIKE THAT BETTER.
WELL THEN, HERE...
HEY, WITHOUT THAT WE CAN'T HAVE THE PLAY!
NOT THAT ONE... I...
...I LIKE THAT FACE BETTER.
HUH?!
IT'S A VERY STYLISH MASK. HEE HEE! I LIKE IT.
I BET I LOOK STRONGER NOW.
I'M GONNA SHOW IT OFF TO MY BUDDIES!
WELL DONE, LINK. THAT DEKU STICK IS STRONG...
...BUT I WOULDN'T HAVE THOUGHT OF SETTING IT ON FIRE.
IT SEEMS YOU'VE GROWN UP A LITTLE.
Oh no! I'm done for!
Aha! Gotcha!

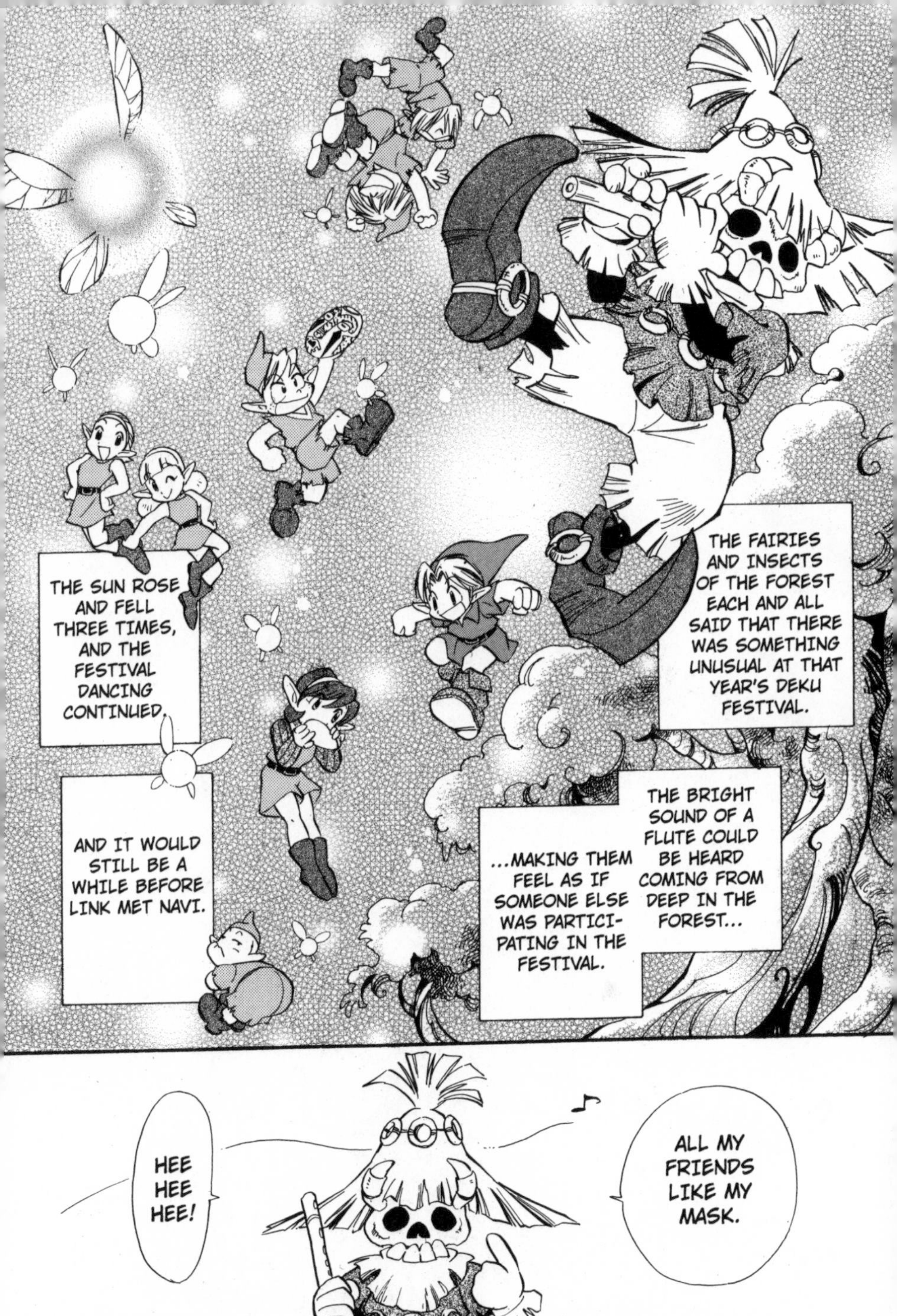
THE FAIRIES AND INSECTS OF THE FOREST EACH AND ALL SAID THAT THERE WAS SOMETHING UNUSUAL AT THAT YEAR'S DEKU FESTIVAL.
THE SUN ROSE AND FELL THREE TIMES, AND THE FESTIVAL DANCING CONTINUED.
THE BRIGHT SOUND OF A FLUTE COULD BE HEARD COMING FROM DEEP IN THE FOREST...
...MAKING THEM FEEL AS IF SOMEONE ELSE WAS PARTICI-PATING IN THE FESTIVAL.
AND IT WOULD STILL BE A WHILE BEFORE LINK MET NAVI.
ALL MY FRIENDS LIKE MY MASK.
HEE HEE HEE!

LEGEND OF ZELDA ~ OCARINA OF TIME ~ BONUS STORY ~ THE END

HERO *of* TIME

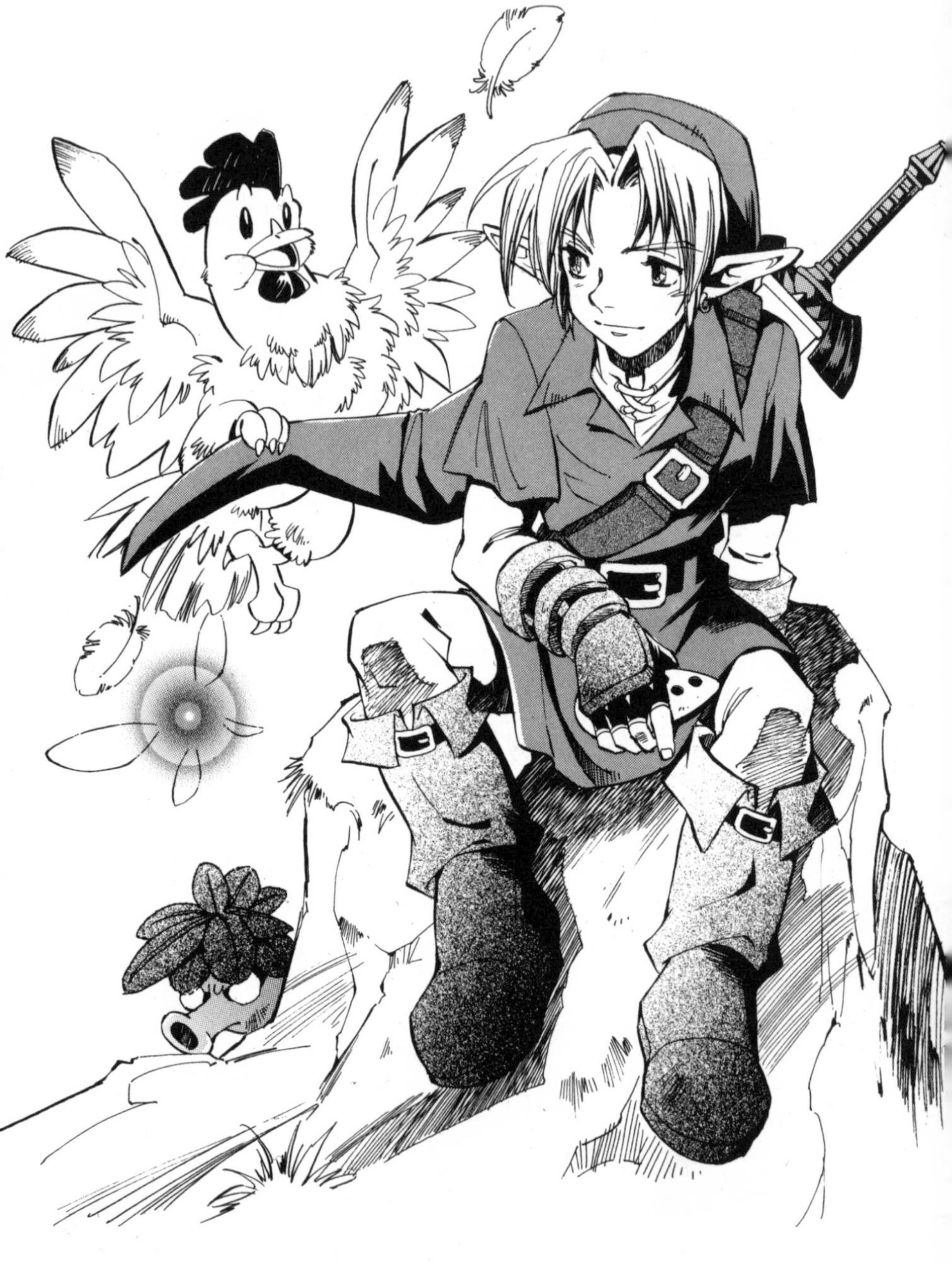

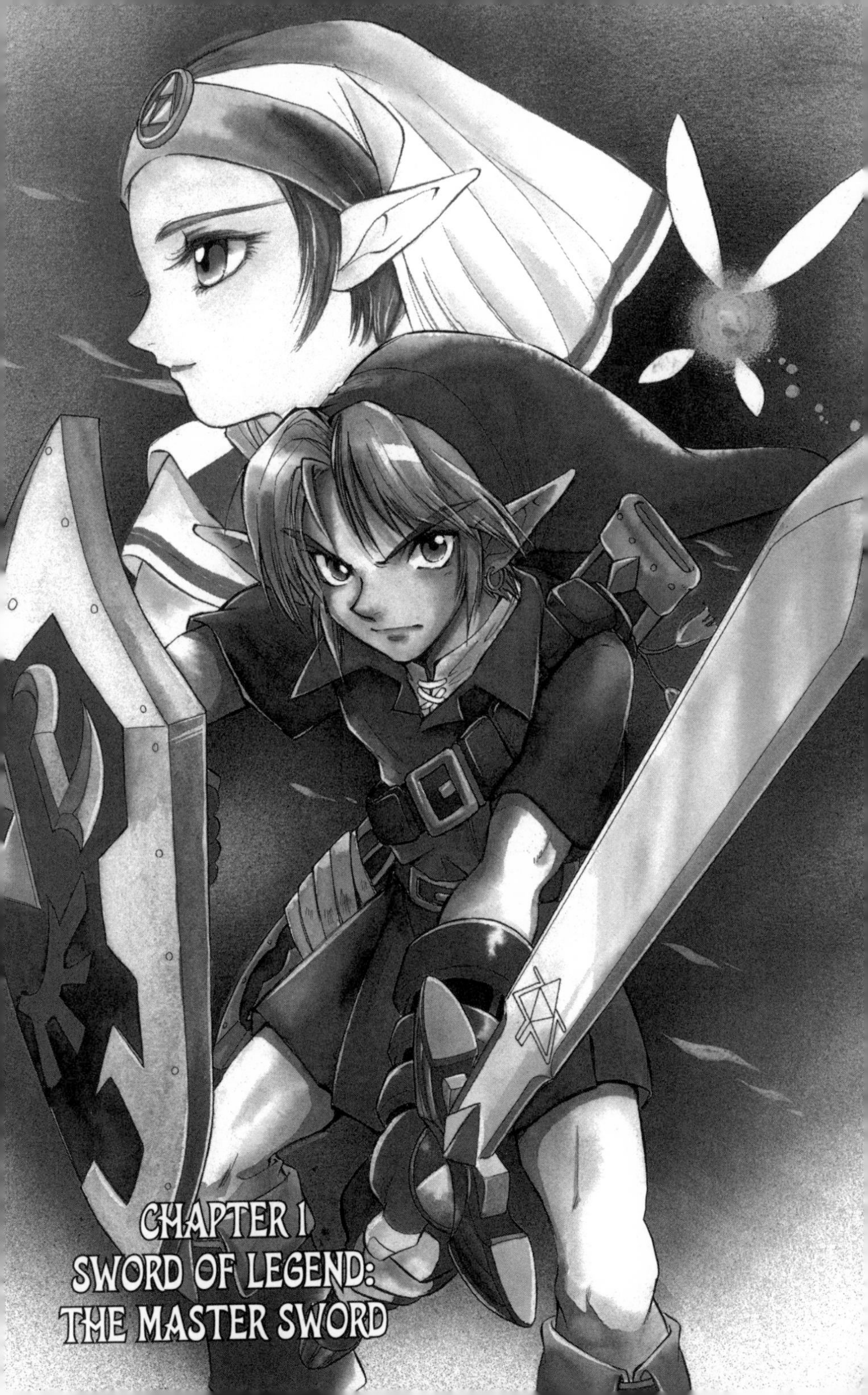

CHAPTER 1
SWORD OF LEGEND: THE MASTER SWORD

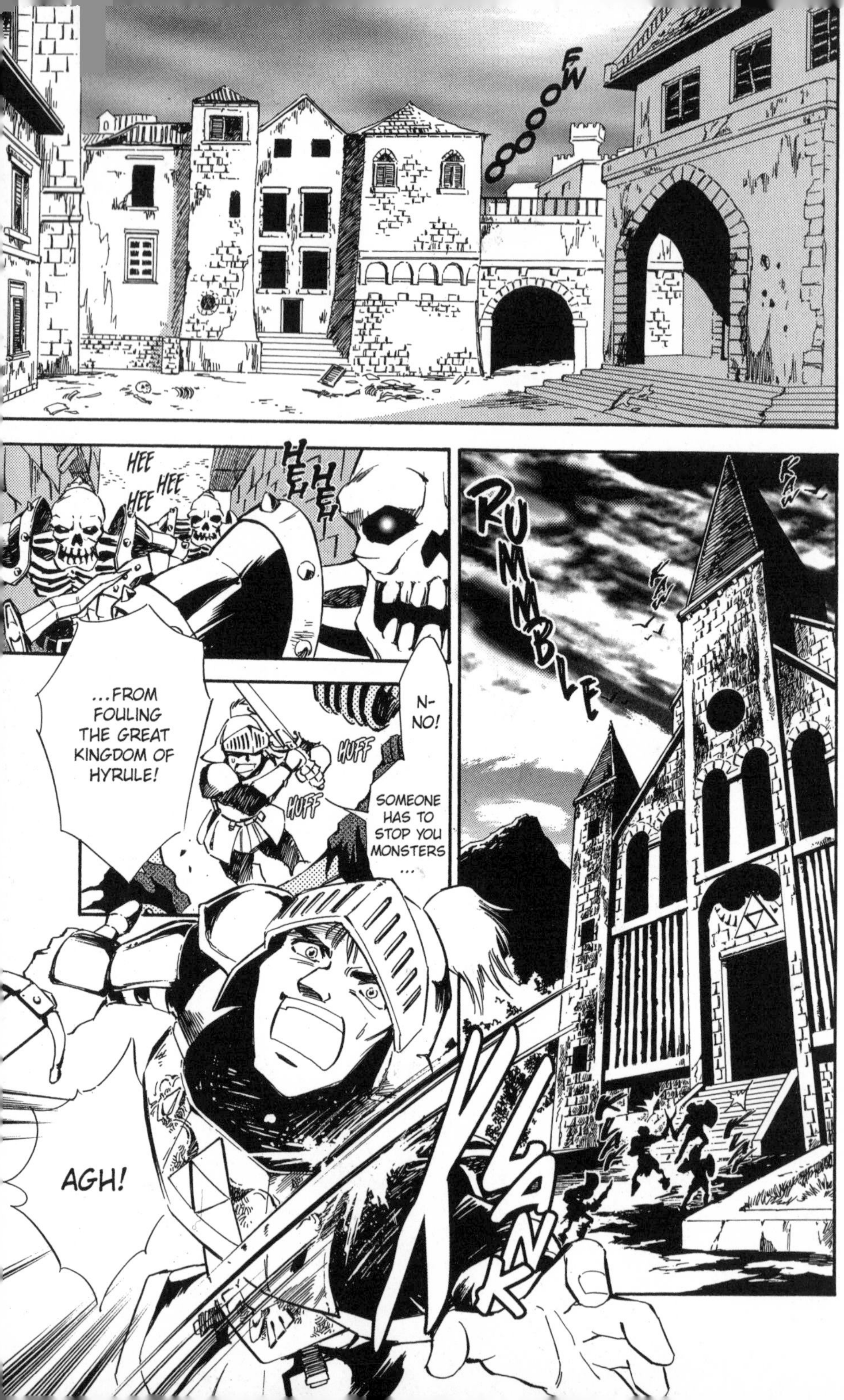
FWOOOOO
RUMMBLE
KAW
KAW
HEE
HEE
HEE
HEH HEH
N-
NO!
SOMEONE HAS TO STOP YOU MONSTERS ...
...FROM FOULING THE GREAT KINGDOM OF HYRULE!
HUFF
HUFF
KLANK
AGH!

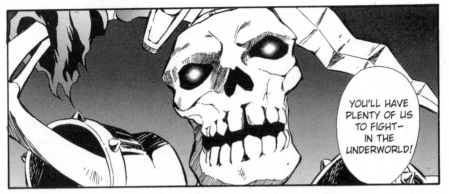

YOU'LL HAVE PLENTY OF US TO FIGHT— IN THE UNDERWORLD!

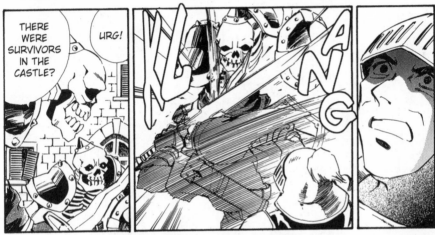

THERE WERE SURVIVORS IN THE CASTLE?

URG!

KLANG

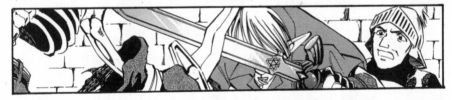

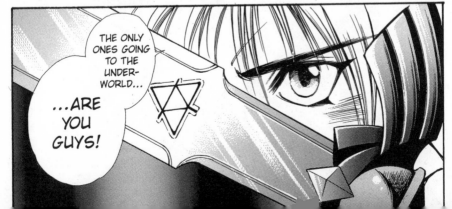

THE ONLY ONES GOING TO THE UNDER-WORLD...

...ARE YOU GUYS!

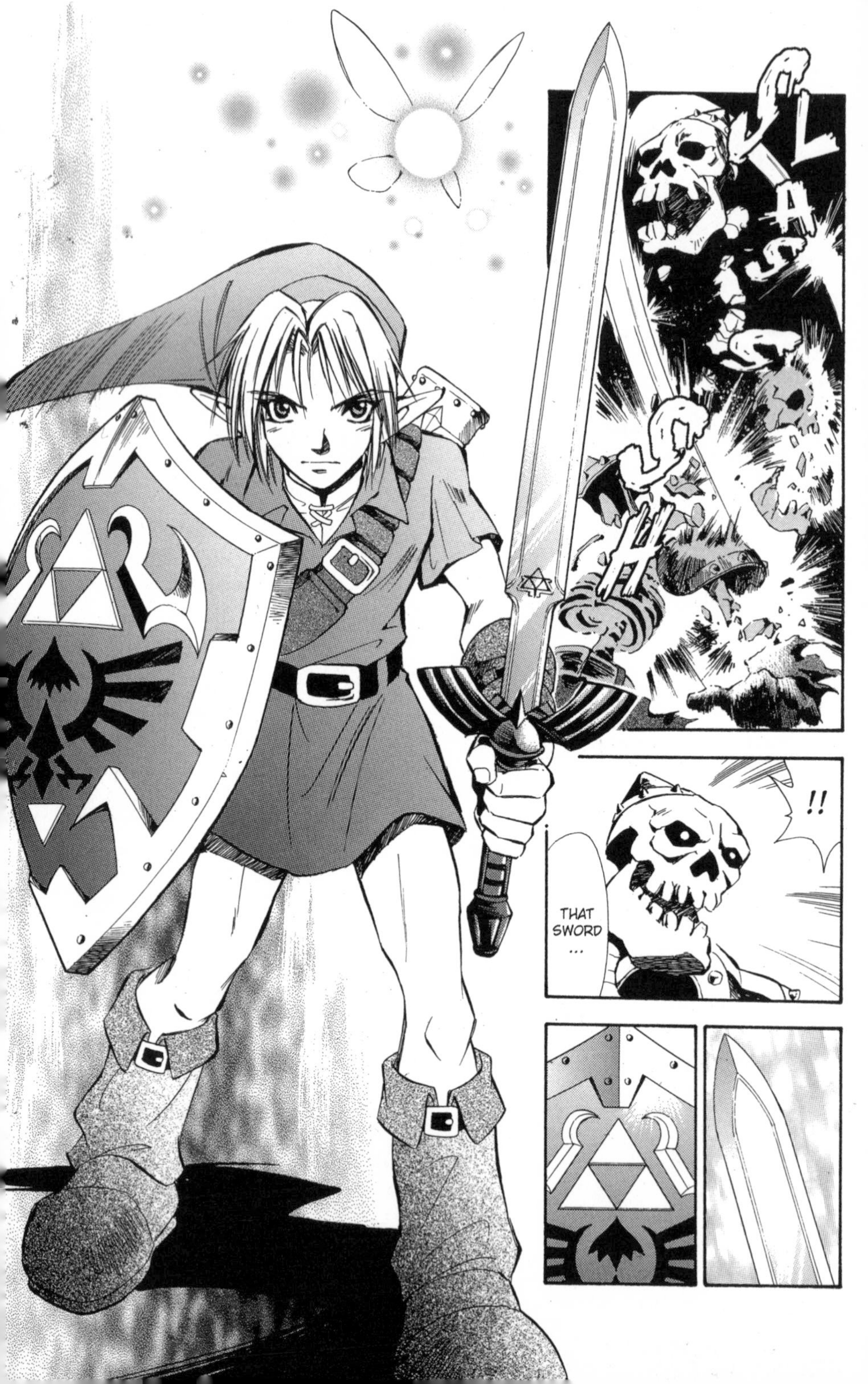
!!
THAT SWORD ...

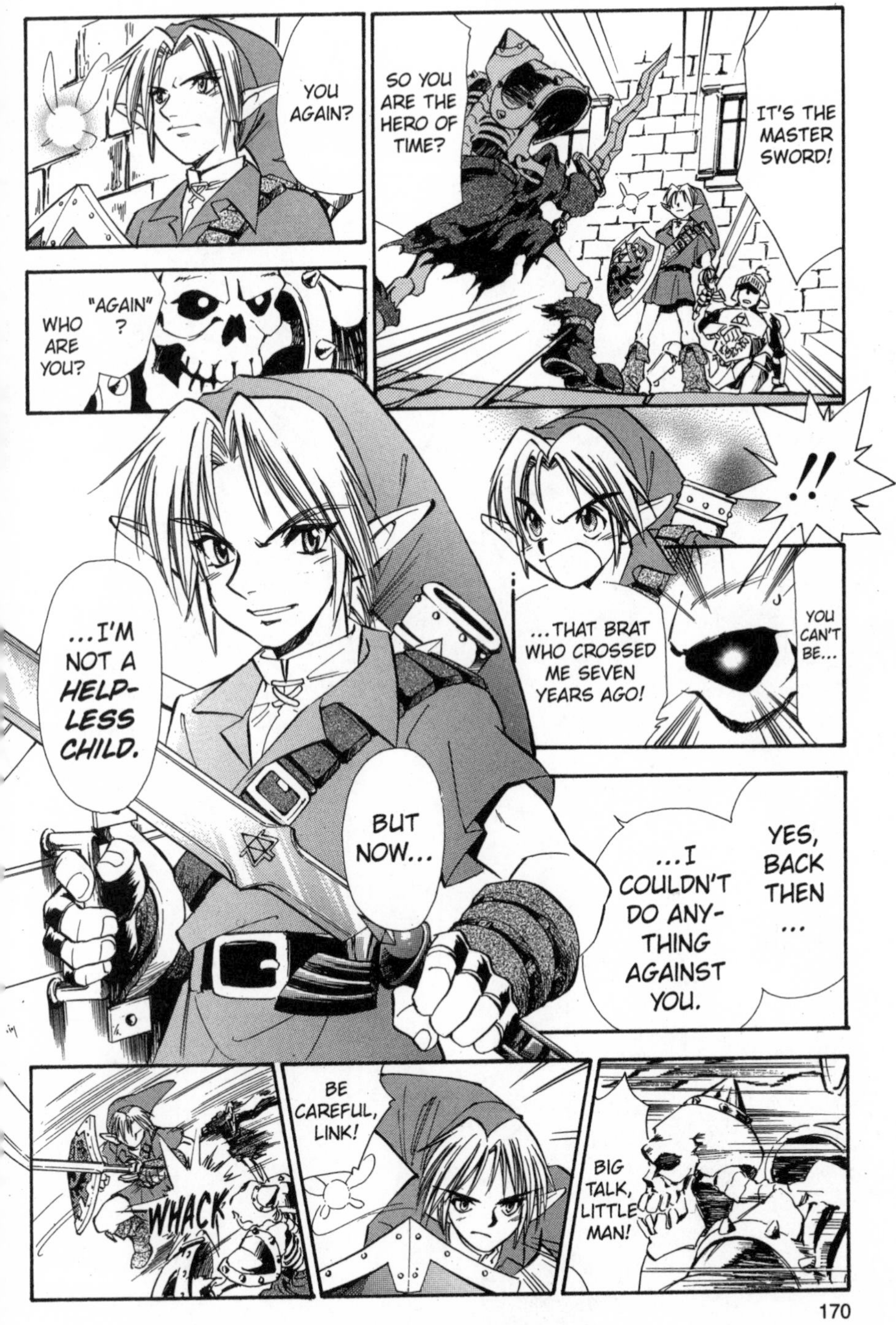
IT'S THE MASTER SWORD!
SO YOU ARE THE HERO OF TIME?
YOU AGAIN?
"AGAIN"?
WHO ARE YOU?
!!
YOU CAN'T BE...
...THAT BRAT WHO CROSSED ME SEVEN YEARS AGO!
YES, BACK THEN...
...I COULDN'T DO ANY-THING AGAINST YOU.
BUT NOW...
...I'M NOT A HELP-LESS CHILD.
BIG TALK, LITTLE MAN!
BE CAREFUL, LINK!
WHACK

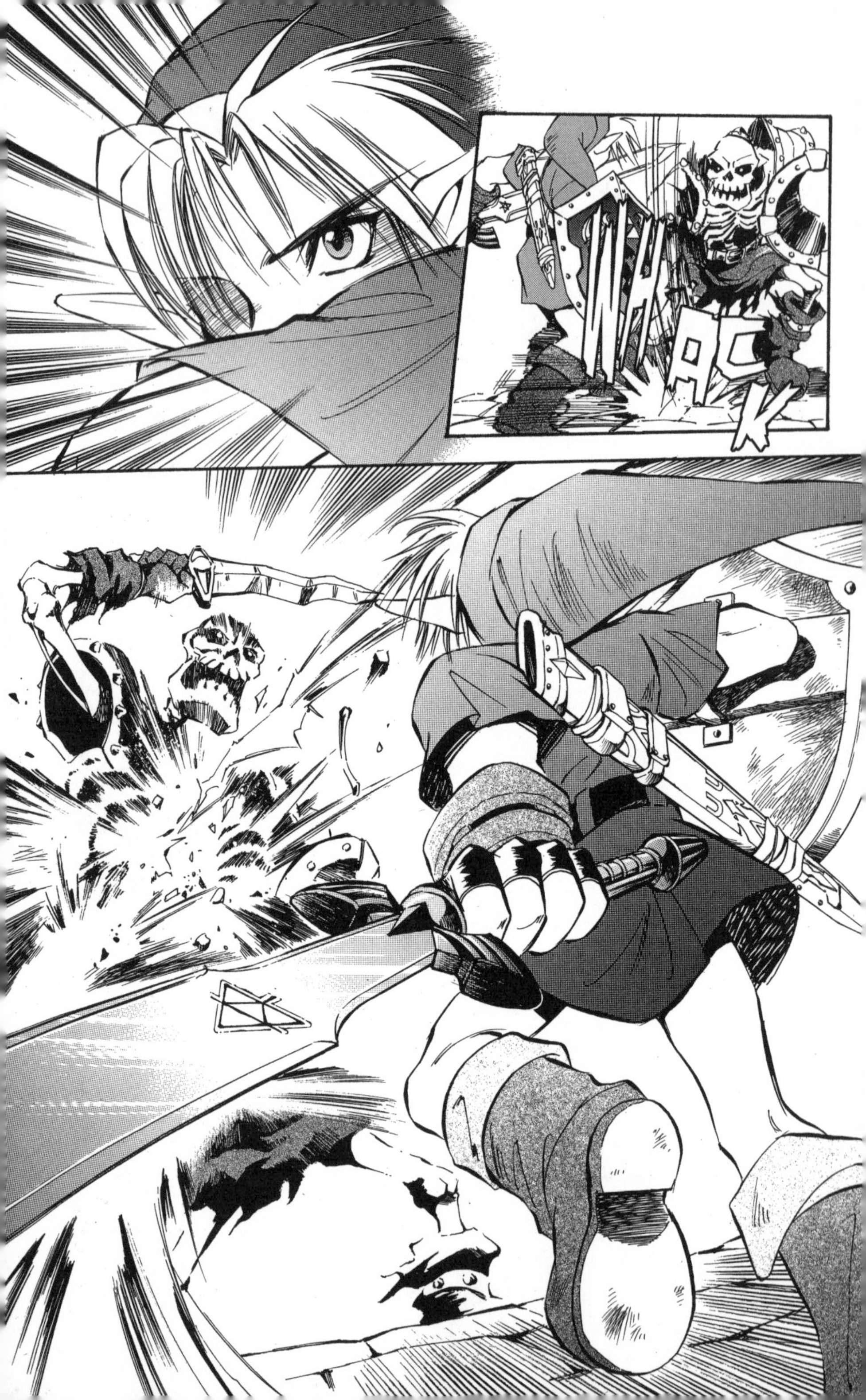
WHACK

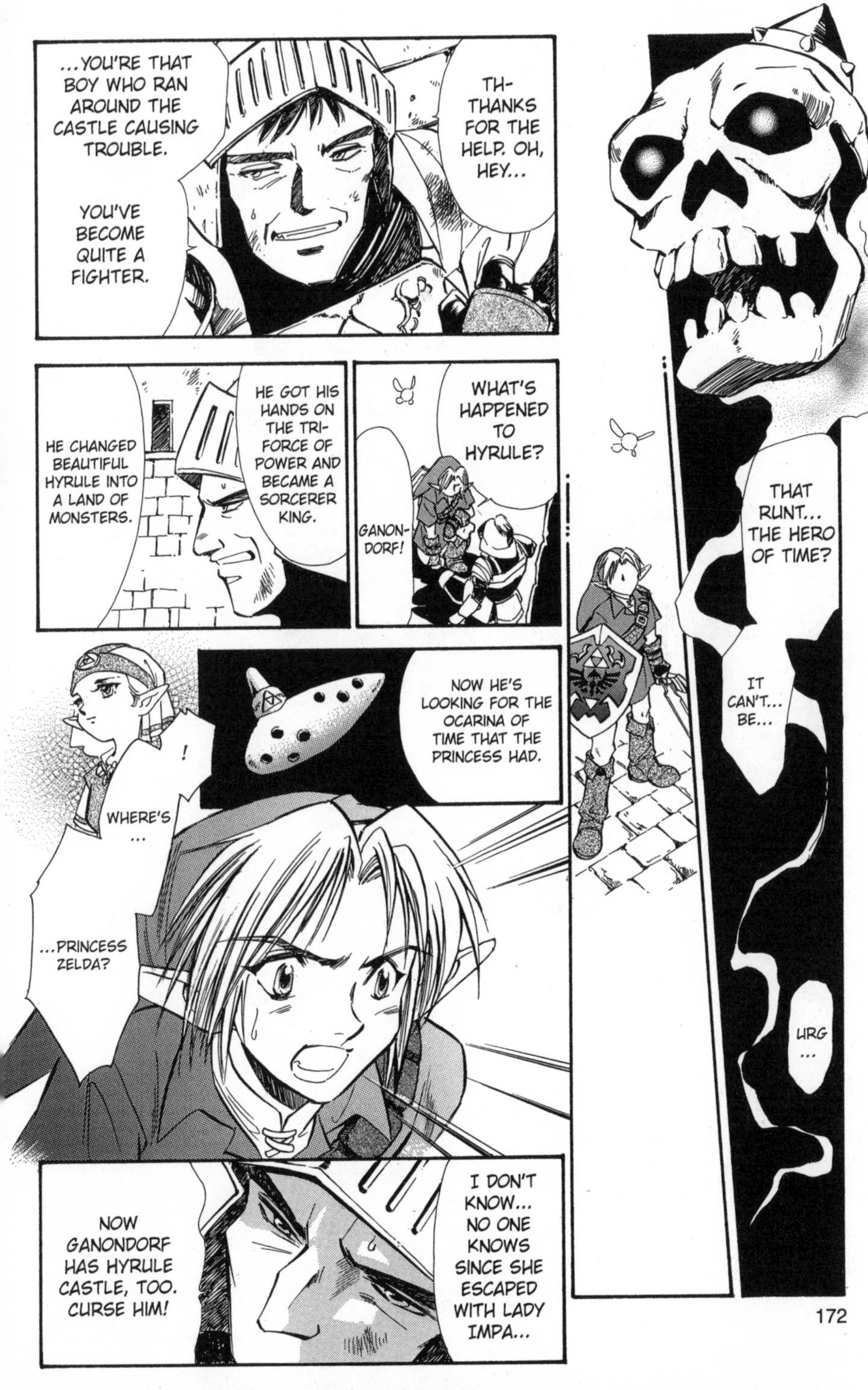
THAT RUNT... THE HERO OF TIME?
IT CAN'T... BE...
URG ...
TH- THANKS FOR THE HELP. OH, HEY...
...YOU'RE THAT BOY WHO RAN AROUND THE CASTLE CAUSING TROUBLE.
YOU'VE BECOME QUITE A FIGHTER.
WHAT'S HAPPENED TO HYRULE?
GANON- DORF!
HE GOT HIS HANDS ON THE TRI- FORCE OF POWER AND BECAME A SORCERER KING.
HE CHANGED BEAUTIFUL HYRULE INTO A LAND OF MONSTERS.
NOW HE'S LOOKING FOR THE OCARINA OF TIME THAT THE PRINCESS HAD.
!
WHERE'S ...
...PRINCESS ZELDA?
I DON'T KNOW... NO ONE KNOWS SINCE SHE ESCAPED WITH LADY IMPA...
NOW GANONDORF HAS HYRULE CASTLE, TOO. CURSE HIM!

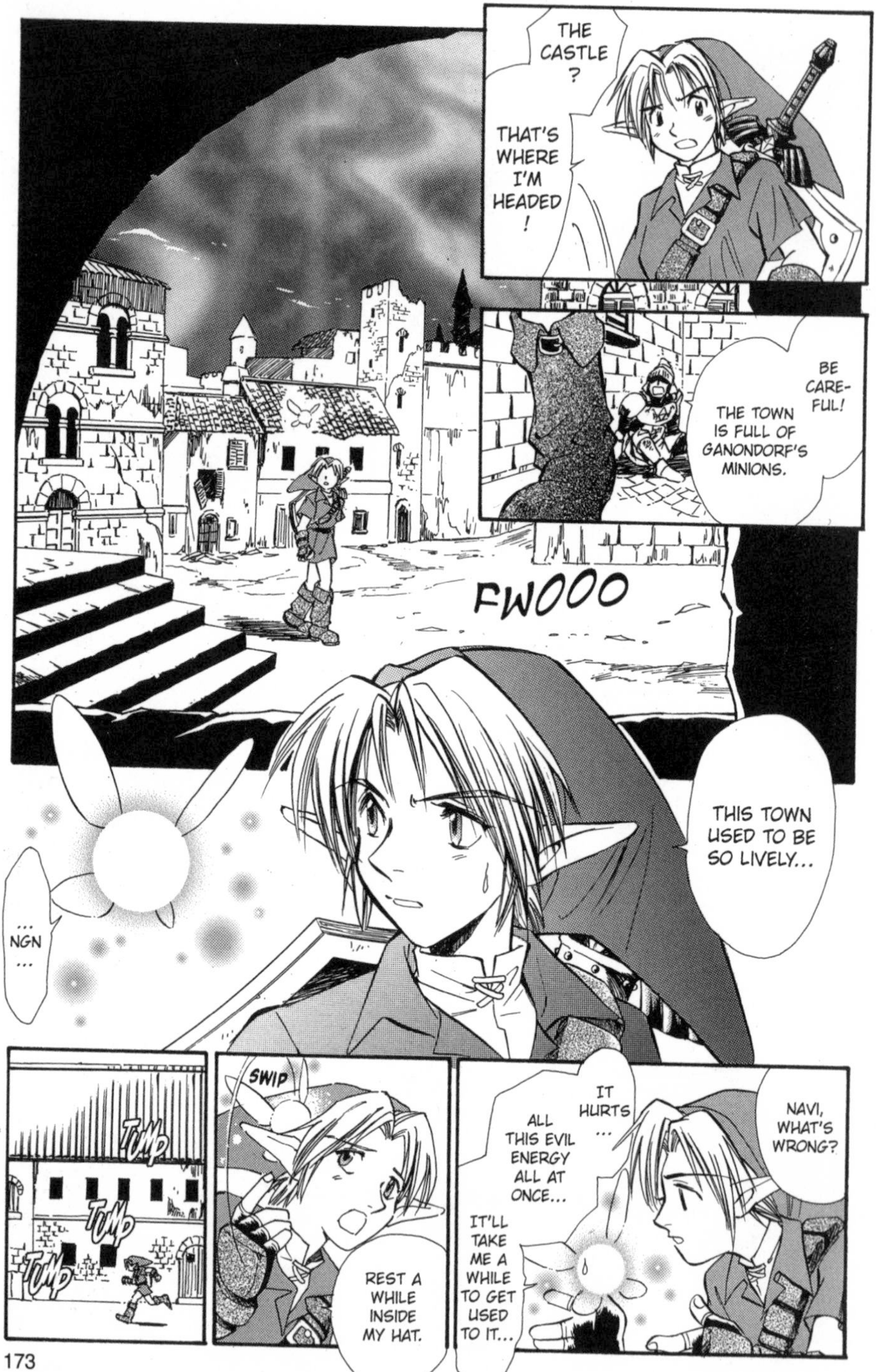
THE CASTLE?
THAT'S WHERE I'M HEADED!
BE CAREFUL!
THE TOWN IS FULL OF GANONDORF'S MINIONS.
FWOOO
THIS TOWN USED TO BE SO LIVELY...
...NGN...
NAVI, WHAT'S WRONG?
IT HURTS...
ALL THIS EVIL ENERGY ALL AT ONCE...
IT'LL TAKE ME A WHILE TO GET USED TO IT...
SWIP
REST A WHILE INSIDE MY HAT.
TUMP
TUMP
TUMP

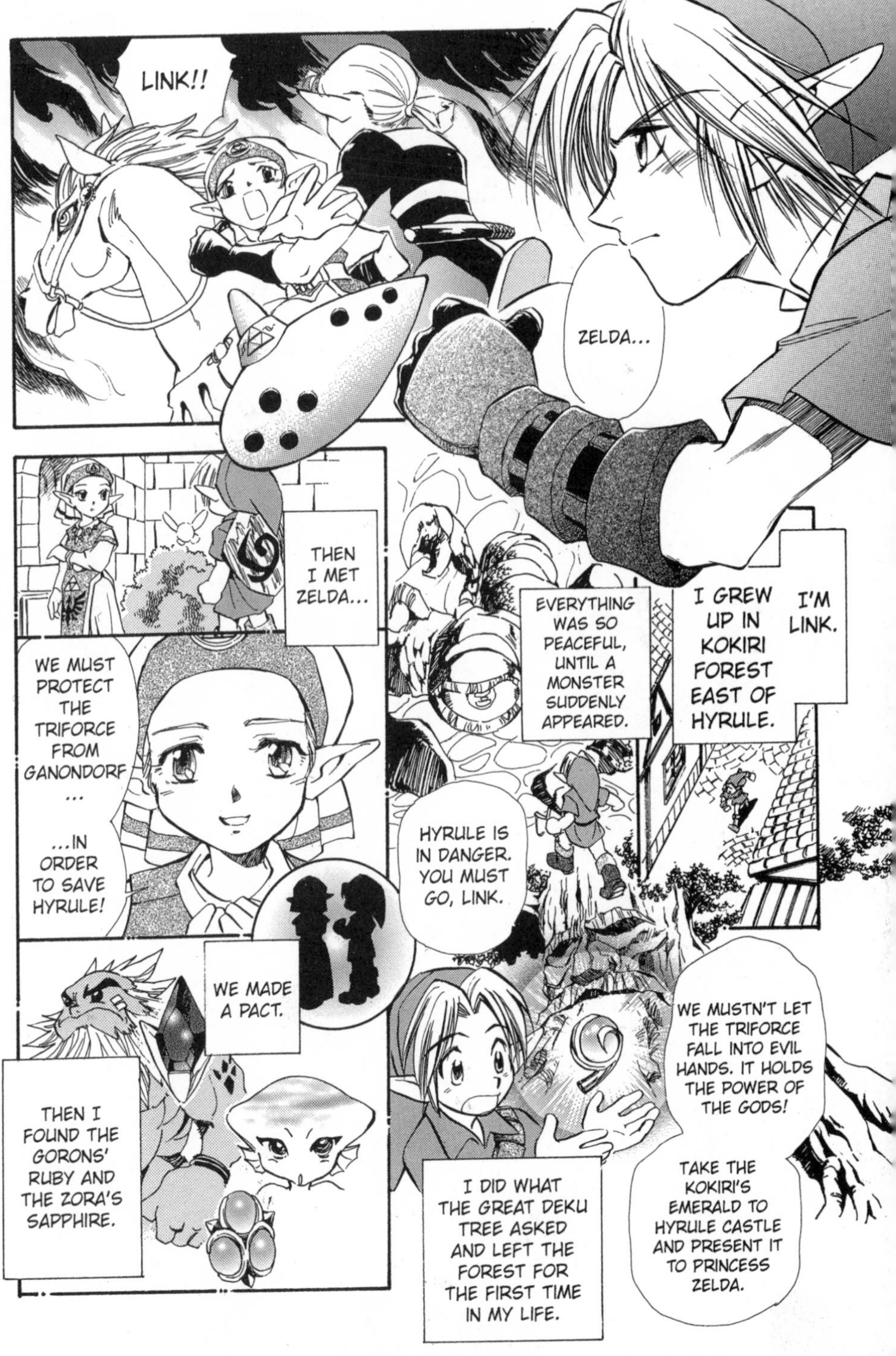
ZELDA...
LINK!!
I'M LINK.
I GREW UP IN KOKIRI FOREST EAST OF HYRULE.
EVERYTHING WAS SO PEACEFUL, UNTIL A MONSTER SUDDENLY APPEARED.
HYRULE IS IN DANGER. YOU MUST GO, LINK.
WE MUSTN'T LET THE TRIFORCE FALL INTO EVIL HANDS. IT HOLDS THE POWER OF THE GODS!
TAKE THE KOKIRI'S EMERALD TO HYRULE CASTLE AND PRESENT IT TO PRINCESS ZELDA.
I DID WHAT THE GREAT DEKU TREE ASKED AND LEFT THE FOREST FOR THE FIRST TIME IN MY LIFE.
THEN I MET ZELDA...
WE MUST PROTECT THE TRIFORCE FROM GANONDORF ...
...IN ORDER TO SAVE HYRULE!
WE MADE A PACT.
THEN I FOUND THE GORONS' RUBY AND THE ZORA'S SAPPHIRE.

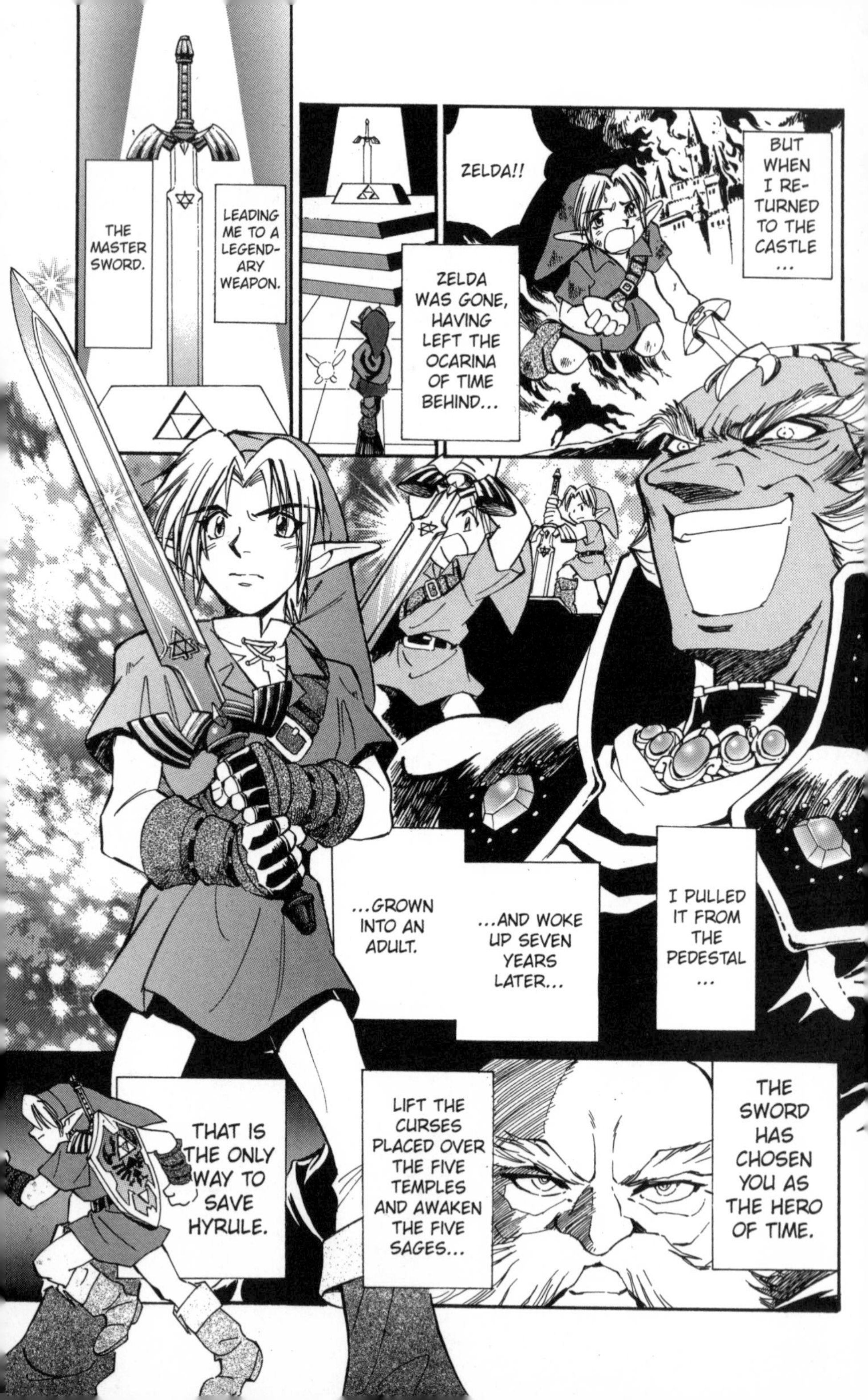
BUT WHEN I RETURNED TO THE CASTLE...
ZELDA!!
ZELDA WAS GONE, HAVING LEFT THE OCARINA OF TIME BEHIND...
LEADING ME TO A LEGENDARY WEAPON.
THE MASTER SWORD.
I PULLED IT FROM THE PEDESTAL...
...AND WOKE UP SEVEN YEARS LATER...
...GROWN INTO AN ADULT.
THE SWORD HAS CHOSEN YOU AS THE HERO OF TIME.
LIFT THE CURSES PLACED OVER THE FIVE TEMPLES AND AWAKEN THE FIVE SAGES...
THAT IS THE ONLY WAY TO SAVE HYRULE.

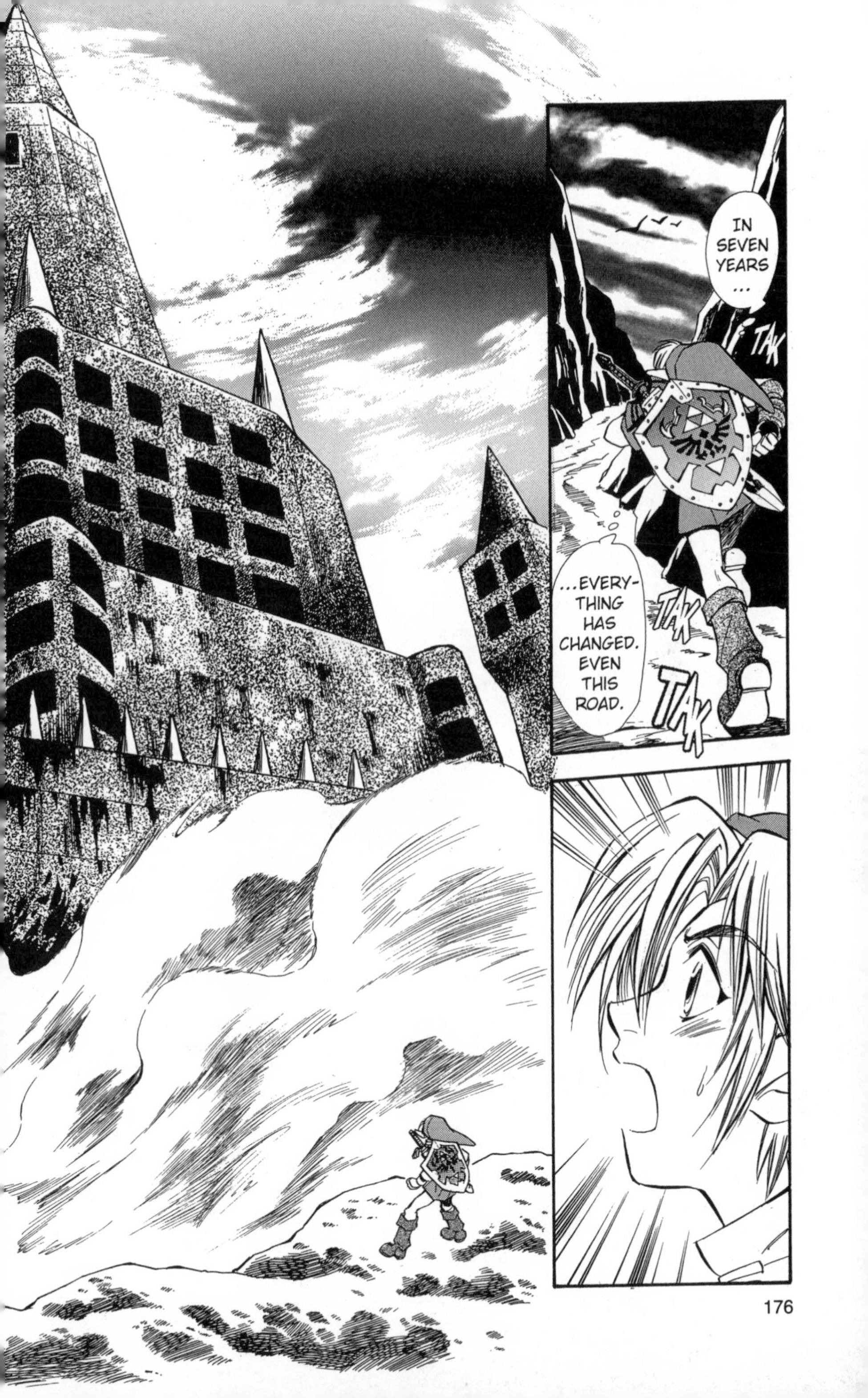
IN SEVEN YEARS ...
TAK
...EVERY-THING HAS CHANGED. EVEN THIS ROAD.
TAK
TAK

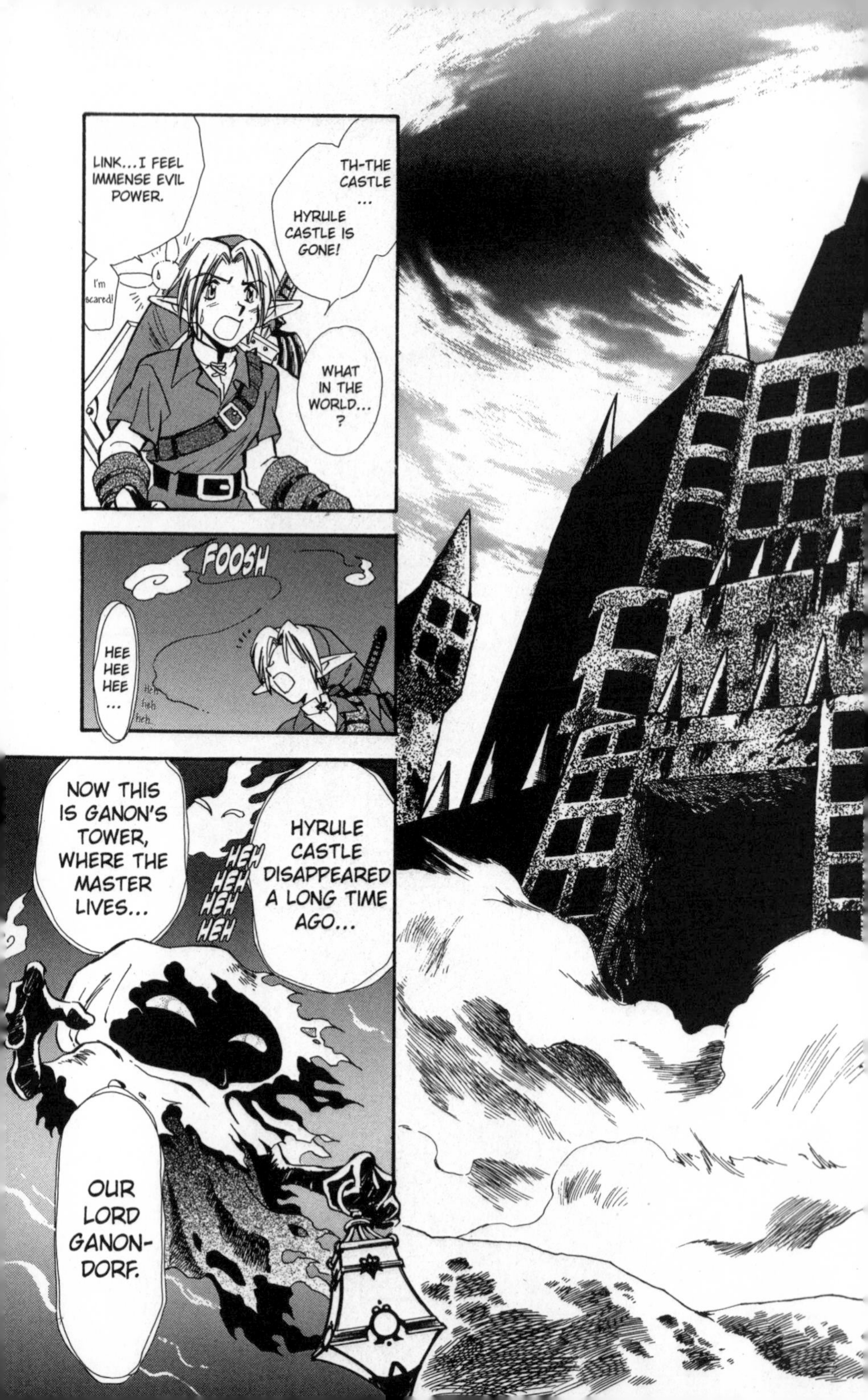
TH-THE CASTLE ...
HYRULE CASTLE IS GONE!
WHAT IN THE WORLD... ?
LINK...I FEEL IMMENSE EVIL POWER.
I'm scared!
FOOSH
HEE HEE HEE ...
Heh heh heh
HYRULE CASTLE DISAPPEARED A LONG TIME AGO...
HEH HEH HEH HEH
NOW THIS IS GANON'S TOWER, WHERE THE MASTER LIVES...
OUR LORD GANON-DORF.

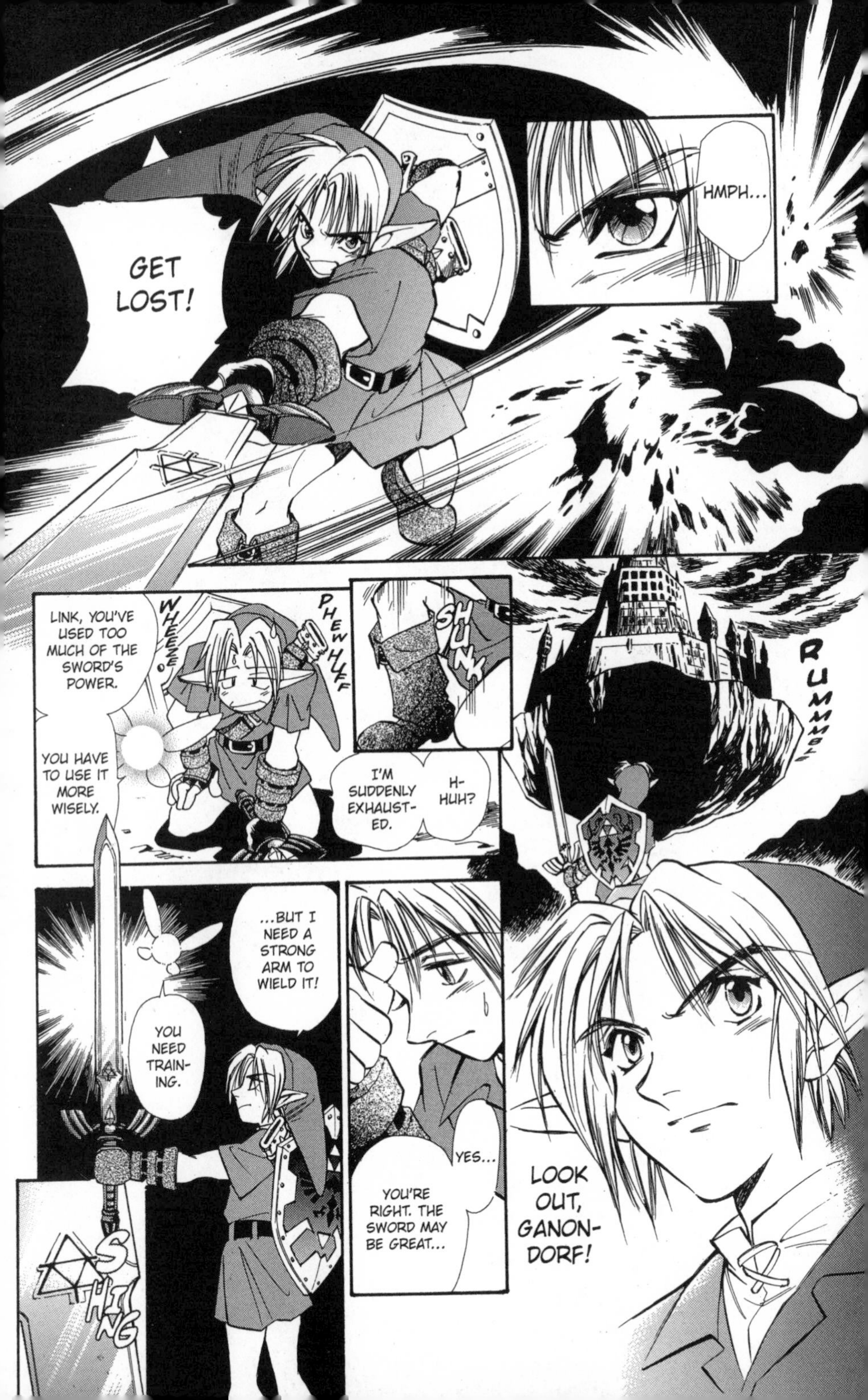

HMPH...
GET LOST!
RUMMMBLE
SHUNK
PHEW HUFF
WHEEZE
LINK, YOU'VE USED TOO MUCH OF THE SWORD'S POWER.
H-HUH?
I'M SUDDENLY EXHAUST-ED.
YOU HAVE TO USE IT MORE WISELY.
LOOK OUT, GANON-DORF!
YES...
YOU'RE RIGHT. THE SWORD MAY BE GREAT...
...BUT I NEED A STRONG ARM TO WIELD IT!
YOU NEED TRAIN-ING.
SHING

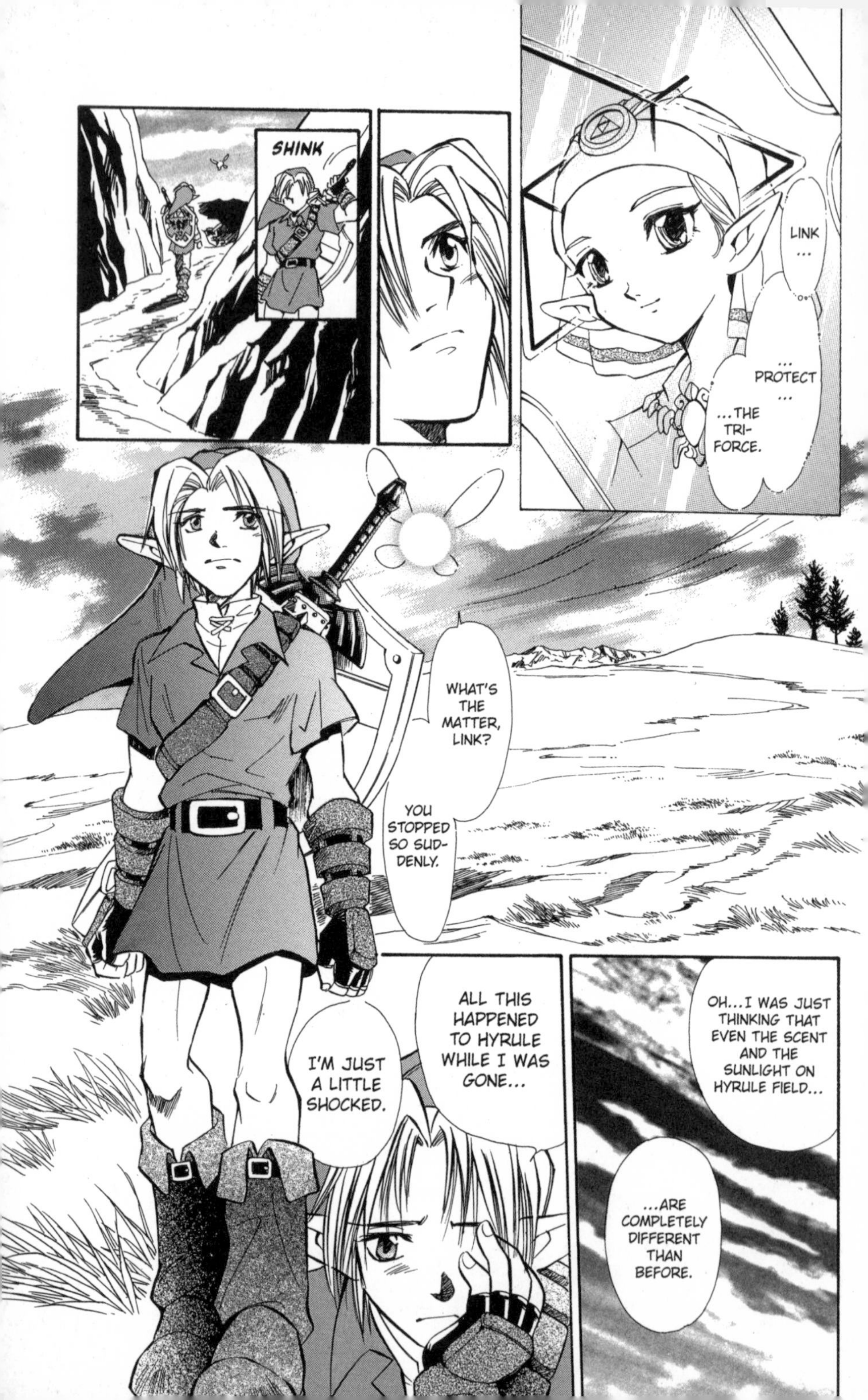
LINK ...
... PROTECT ...
...THE TRI-FORCE.
SHINK
WHAT'S THE MATTER, LINK?
YOU STOPPED SO SUD-DENLY.
OH...I WAS JUST THINKING THAT EVEN THE SCENT AND THE SUNLIGHT ON HYRULE FIELD...
...ARE COMPLETELY DIFFERENT THAN BEFORE.
ALL THIS HAPPENED TO HYRULE WHILE I WAS GONE...
I'M JUST A LITTLE SHOCKED.

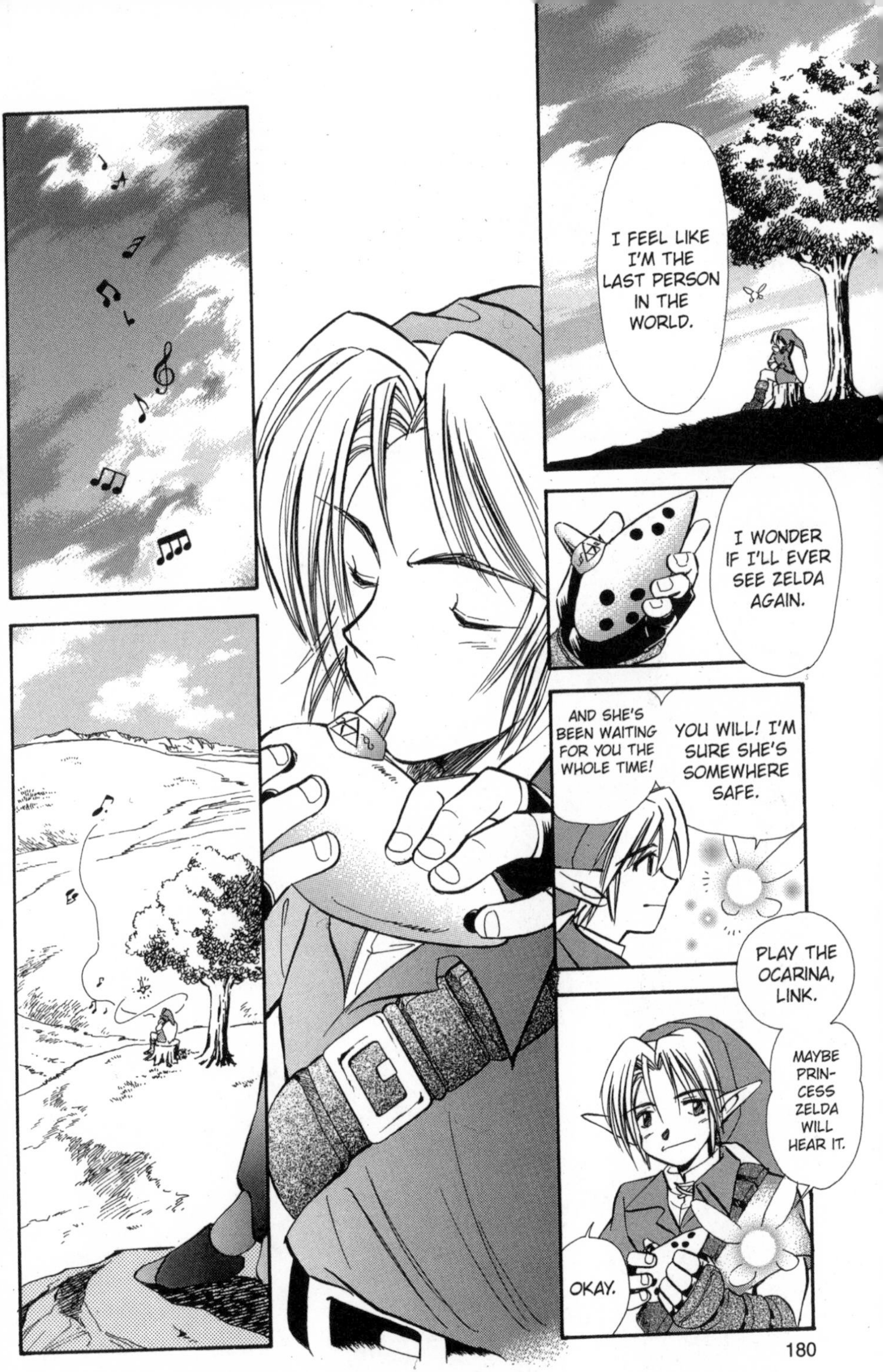
I FEEL LIKE I'M THE LAST PERSON IN THE WORLD.
I WONDER IF I'LL EVER SEE ZELDA AGAIN.
YOU WILL! I'M SURE SHE'S SOMEWHERE SAFE.
AND SHE'S BEEN WAITING FOR YOU THE WHOLE TIME!
PLAY THE OCARINA, LINK.
MAYBE PRINCESS ZELDA WILL HEAR IT.
OKAY.

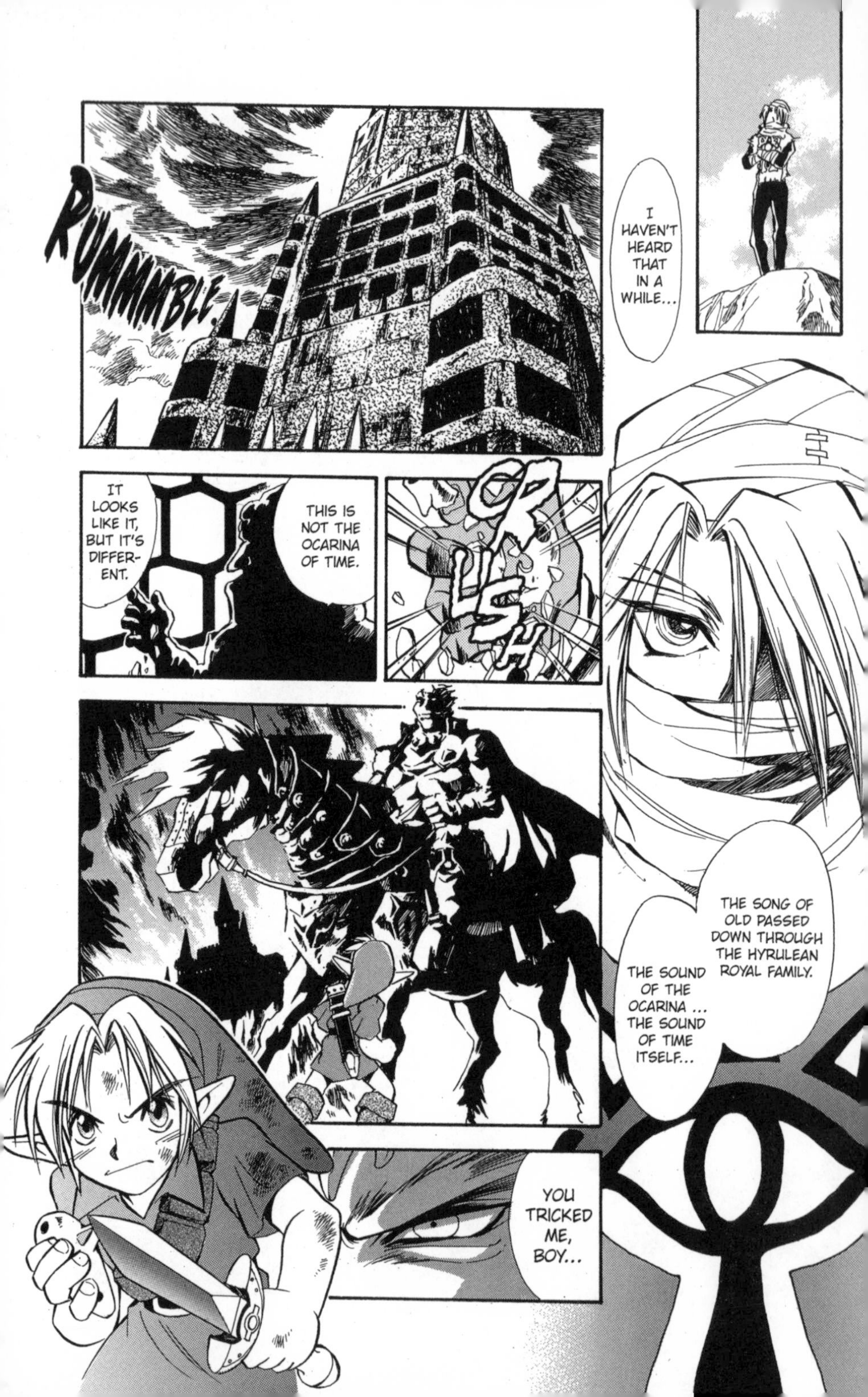
I HAVEN'T HEARD THAT IN A WHILE...
THE SONG OF OLD PASSED DOWN THROUGH THE HYRULEAN ROYAL FAMILY.
THE SOUND OF THE OCARINA ... THE SOUND OF TIME ITSELF...
RUMMMBLE
CRUSH
THIS IS NOT THE OCARINA OF TIME.
IT LOOKS LIKE IT, BUT IT'S DIFFERENT.
YOU TRICKED ME, BOY...

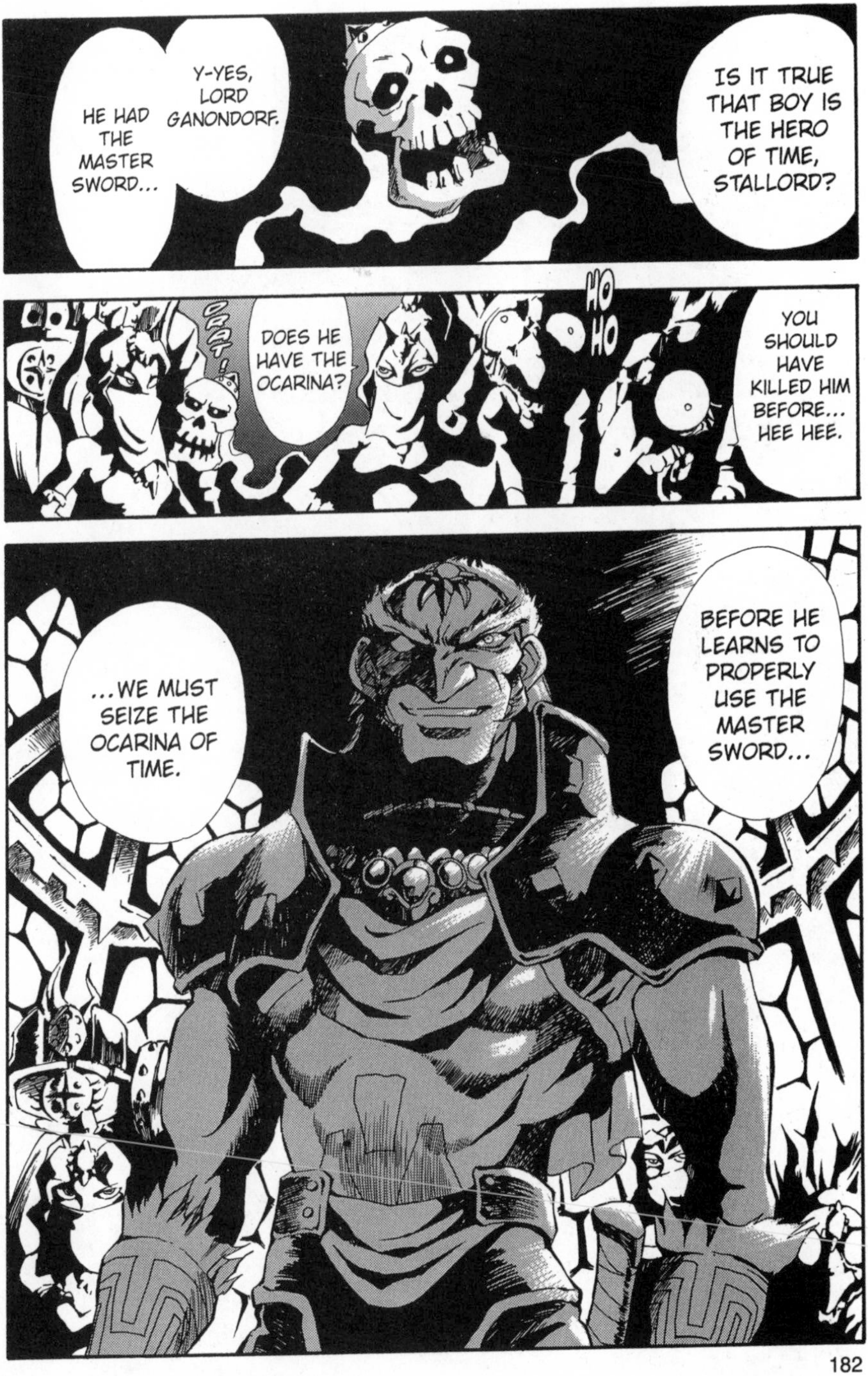
IS IT TRUE THAT BOY IS THE HERO OF TIME, STALLORD?
Y-YES, LORD GANONDORF.
HE HAD THE MASTER SWORD...
YOU SHOULD HAVE KILLED HIM BEFORE... HEE HEE.
HO HO
DOES HE HAVE THE OCARINA?
BEFORE HE LEARNS TO PROPERLY USE THE MASTER SWORD...
...WE MUST SEIZE THE OCARINA OF TIME.

CHAPTER 2 THE SAGE OF THE FOREST: SARIA

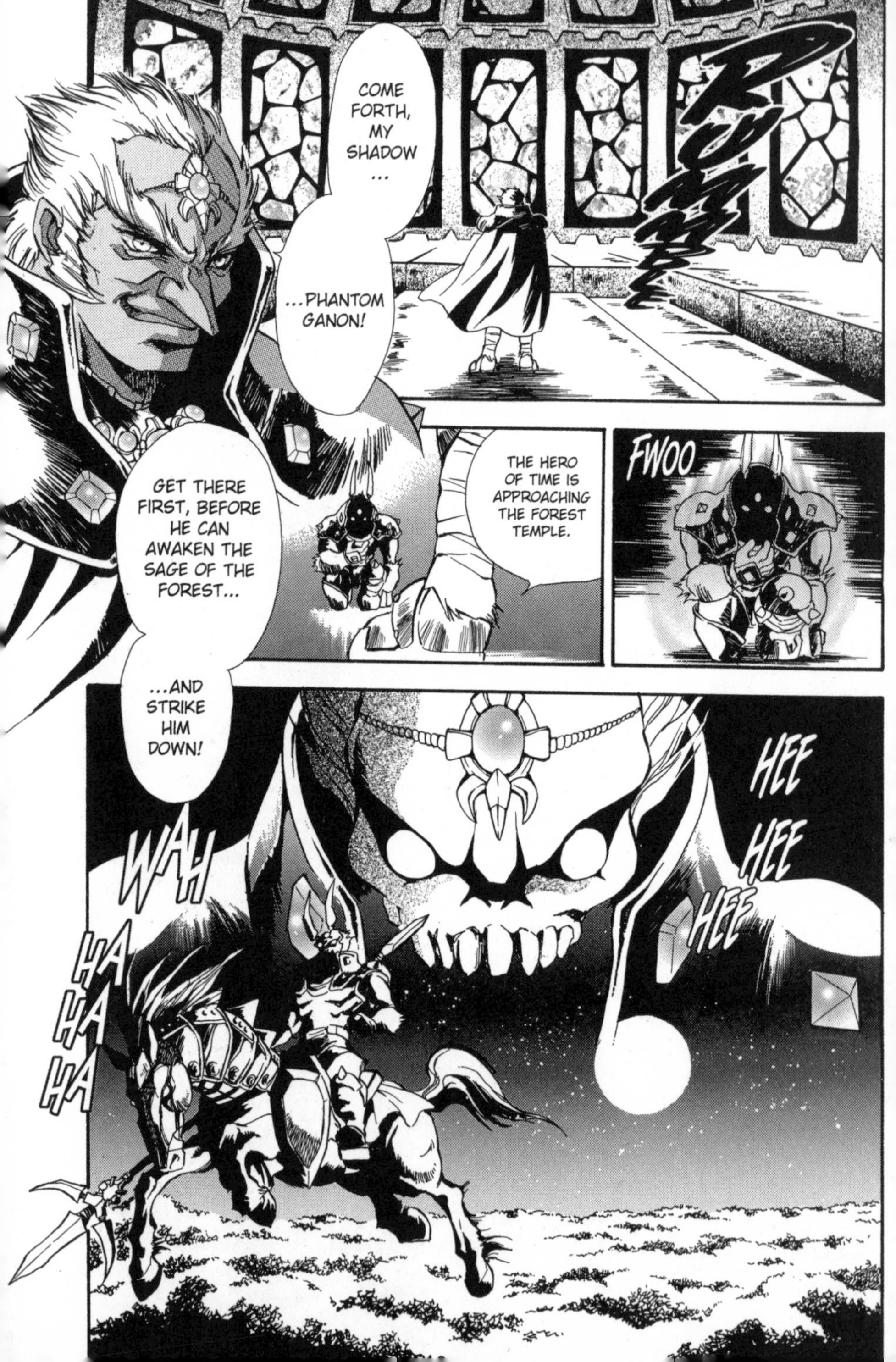
COME FORTH, MY SHADOW...
...PHANTOM GANON!
FWOO
THE HERO OF TIME IS APPROACHING THE FOREST TEMPLE.
GET THERE FIRST, BEFORE HE CAN AWAKEN THE SAGE OF THE FOREST...
...AND STRIKE HIM DOWN!
HEE HEE HEE
WAH HA HA HA HA

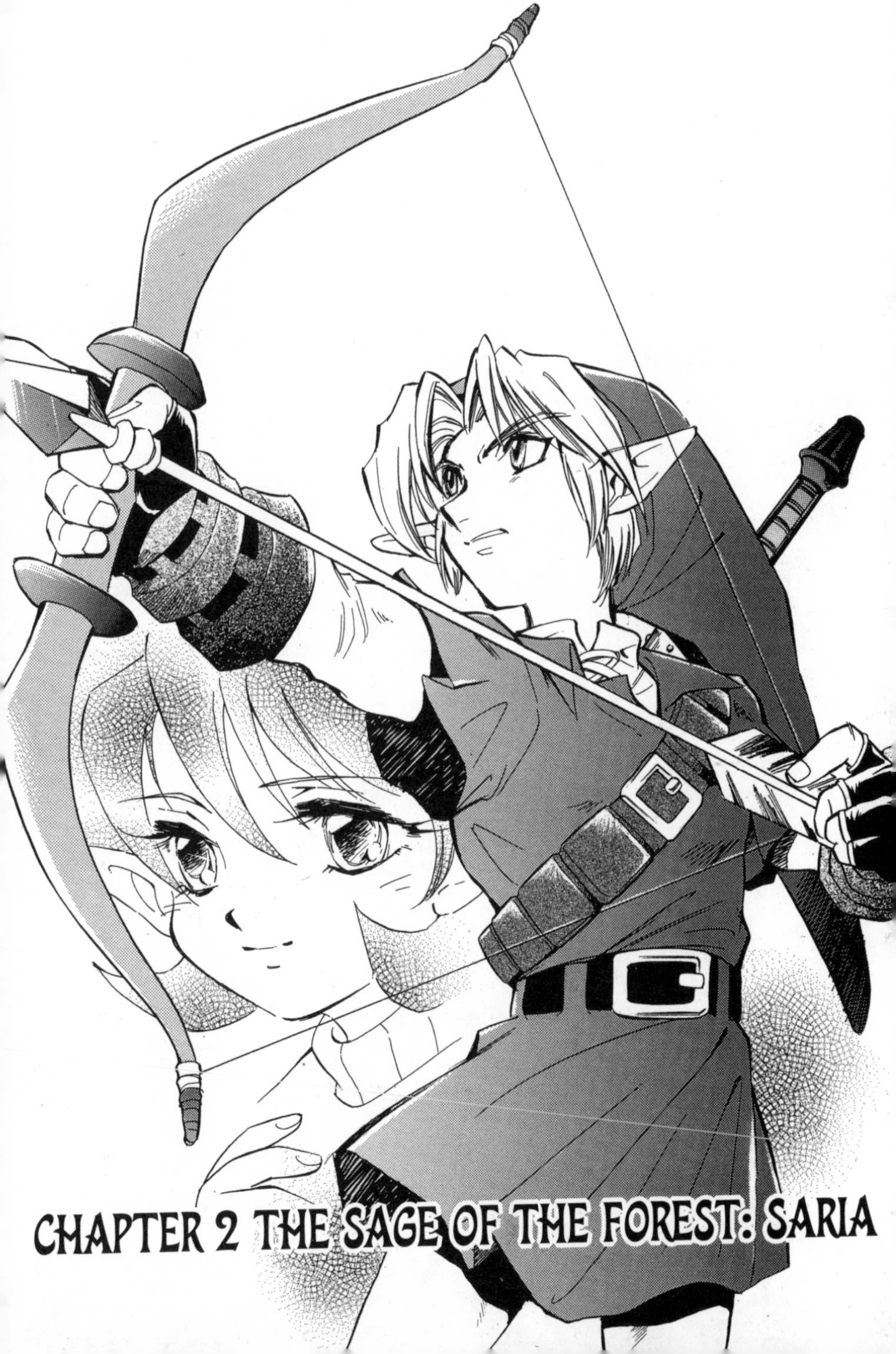

CHAPTER 2 THE SAGE OF THE FOREST: SARIA

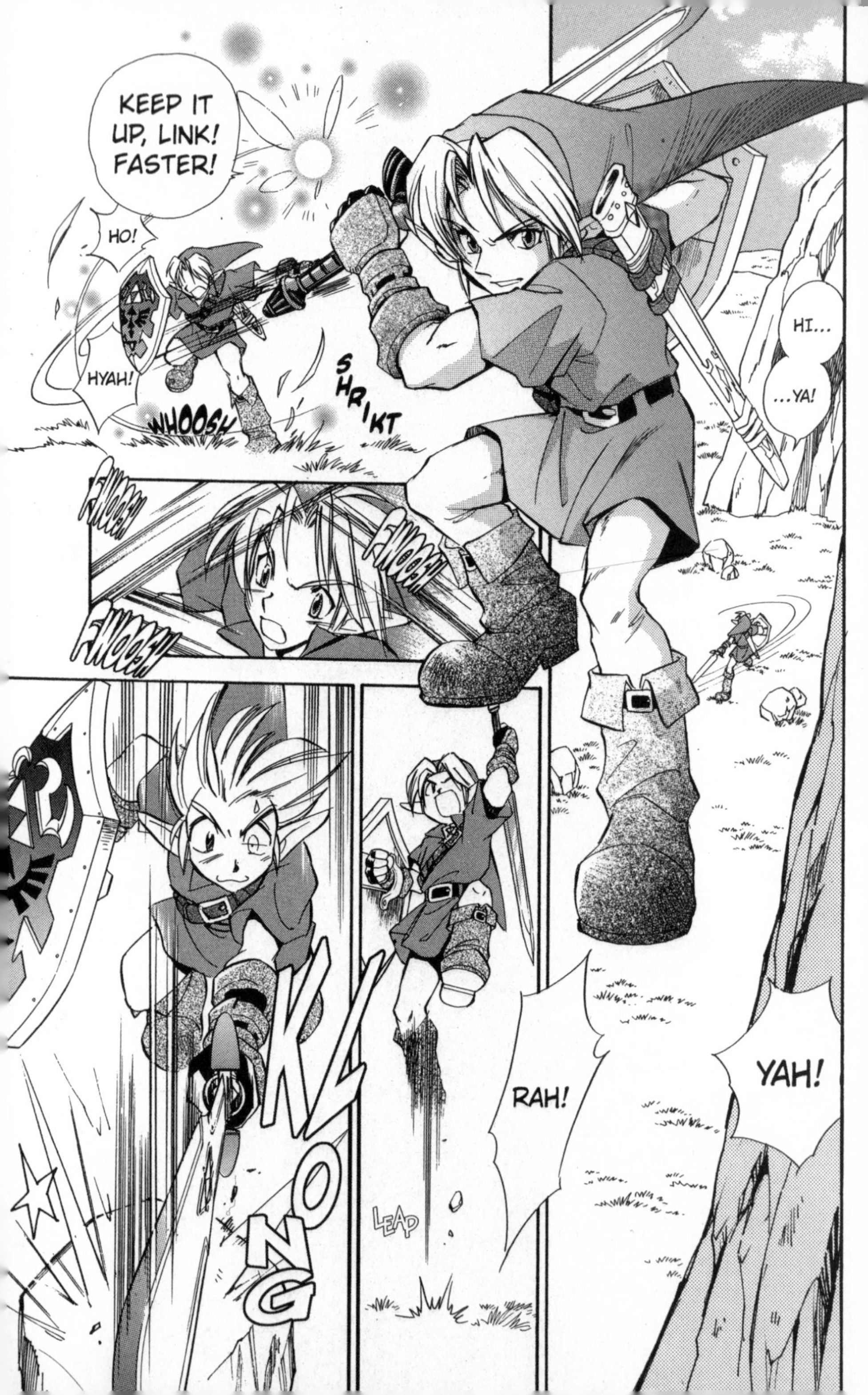
HI...
...YA!
KEEP IT UP, LINK! FASTER!
SHRIKT
HO!
HYAH!
WHOOSH
FWOOSH!!
FWOOSH!!
FWOOSH!!
YAH!
RAH!
LEAP
KWONG

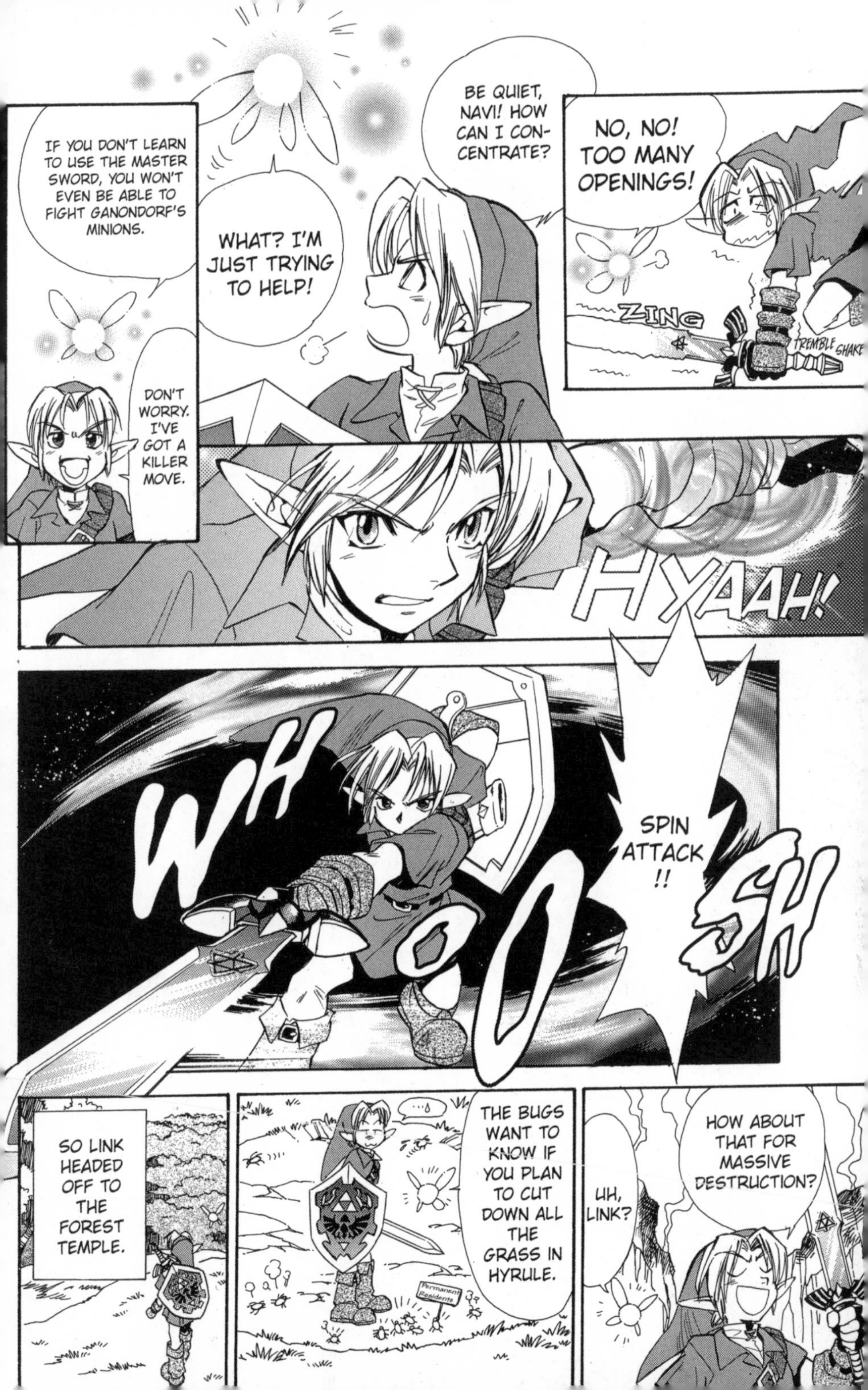

NO, NO! TOO MANY OPENINGS!
ZING
TREMBLE SHAKE
BE QUIET, NAVI! HOW CAN I CON-CENTRATE?
WHAT? I'M JUST TRYING TO HELP!
IF YOU DON'T LEARN TO USE THE MASTER SWORD, YOU WON'T EVEN BE ABLE TO FIGHT GANONDORF'S MINIONS.
DON'T WORRY. I'VE GOT A KILLER MOVE.
HYAAH!
SPIN ATTACK !!
WHOOSH
HOW ABOUT THAT FOR MASSIVE DESTRUCTION?
UH, LINK?
THE BUGS WANT TO KNOW IF YOU PLAN TO CUT DOWN ALL THE GRASS IN HYRULE.
...
Permanent Residents
SO LINK HEADED OFF TO THE FOREST TEMPLE.

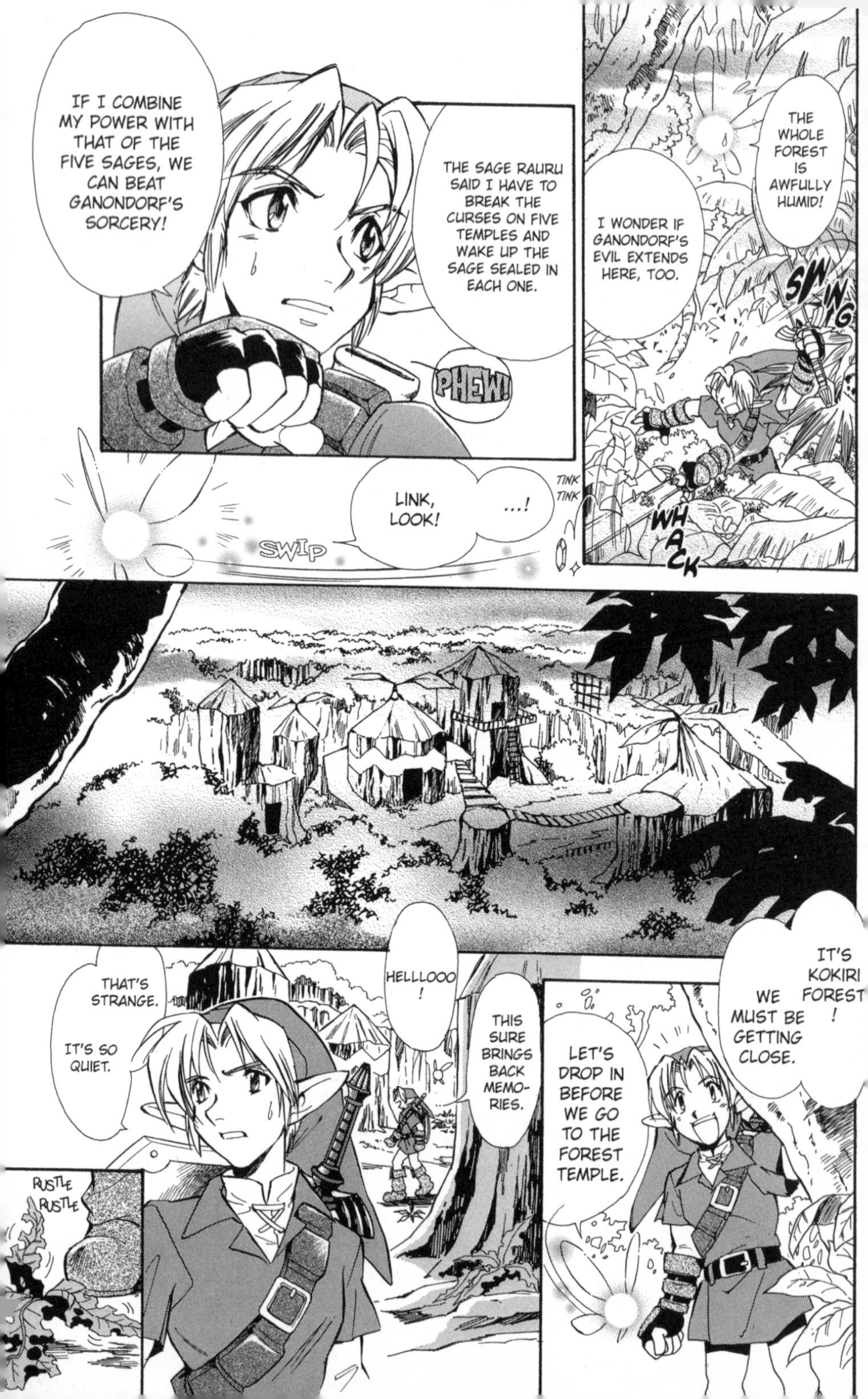
THE WHOLE FOREST IS AWFULLY HUMID!
I WONDER IF GANONDORF'S EVIL EXTENDS HERE, TOO.
SWING
TINK TINK
WHACK
THE SAGE RAURU SAID I HAVE TO BREAK THE CURSES ON FIVE TEMPLES AND WAKE UP THE SAGE SEALED IN EACH ONE.
IF I COMBINE MY POWER WITH THAT OF THE FIVE SAGES, WE CAN BEAT GANONDORF'S SORCERY!
PHEW!
...!
LINK, LOOK!
SWIP
IT'S KOKIRI FOREST!
WE MUST BE GETTING CLOSE.
LET'S DROP IN BEFORE WE GO TO THE FOREST TEMPLE.
THIS SURE BRINGS BACK MEMO-RIES.
HELLLOOO!
THAT'S STRANGE.
IT'S SO QUIET.
RUSTLE RUSTLE

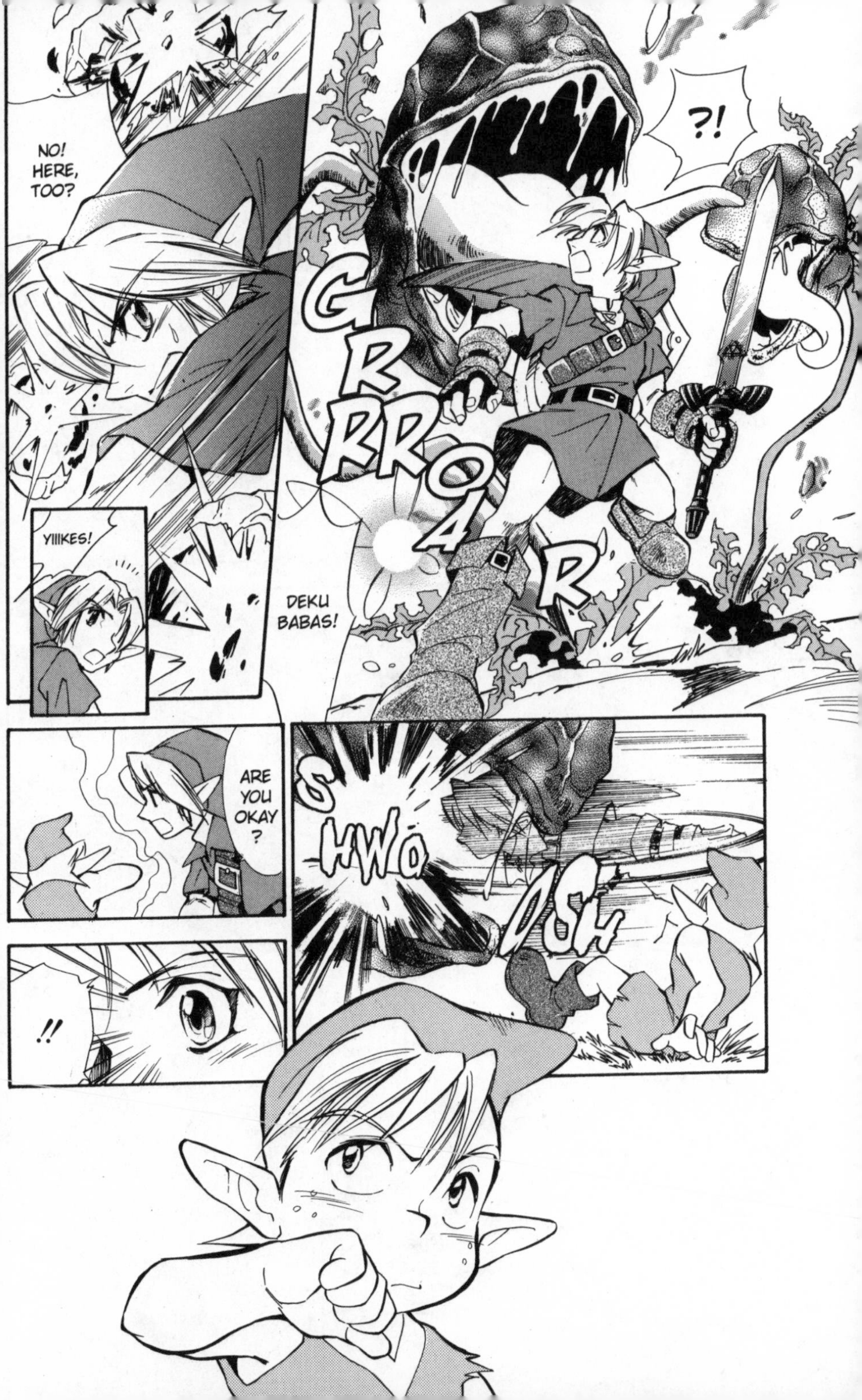
?!
GRRROAR
DEKU BABAS!
NO! HERE, TOO?
YIIIKES!
SHWOOSH
ARE YOU OKAY?
!!

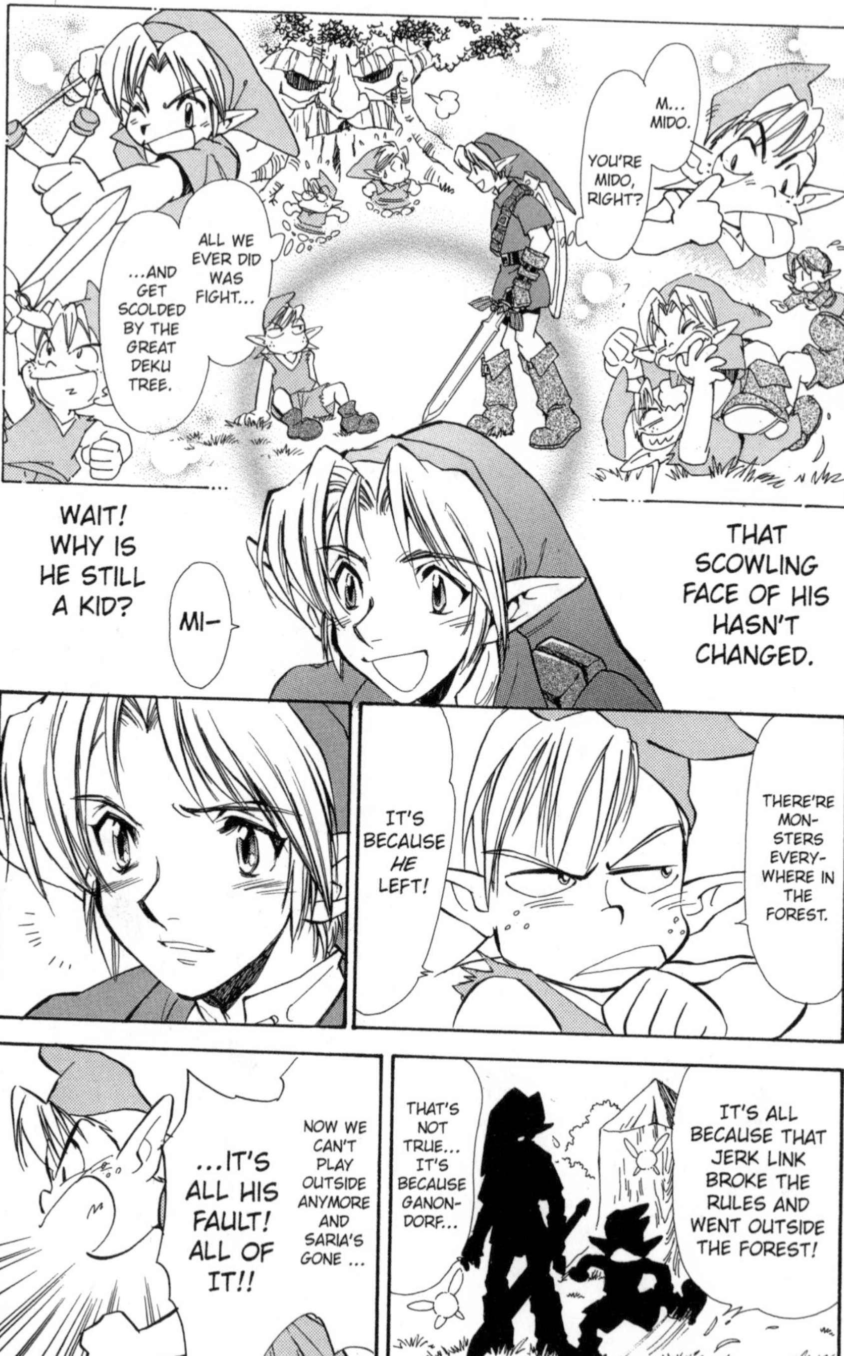
M... MIDO.
YOU'RE MIDO, RIGHT?
ALL WE EVER DID WAS FIGHT...
...AND GET SCOLDED BY THE GREAT DEKU TREE.
THAT SCOWLING FACE OF HIS HASN'T CHANGED.
MI–
WAIT! WHY IS HE STILL A KID?
THERE'RE MONSTERS EVERYWHERE IN THE FOREST.
IT'S BECAUSE *HE* LEFT!
IT'S ALL BECAUSE THAT JERK LINK BROKE THE RULES AND WENT OUTSIDE THE FOREST!
THAT'S NOT TRUE... IT'S BECAUSE GANONDORF...
NOW WE CAN'T PLAY OUTSIDE ANYMORE AND SARIA'S GONE ...
...IT'S ALL HIS FAULT! ALL OF IT!!

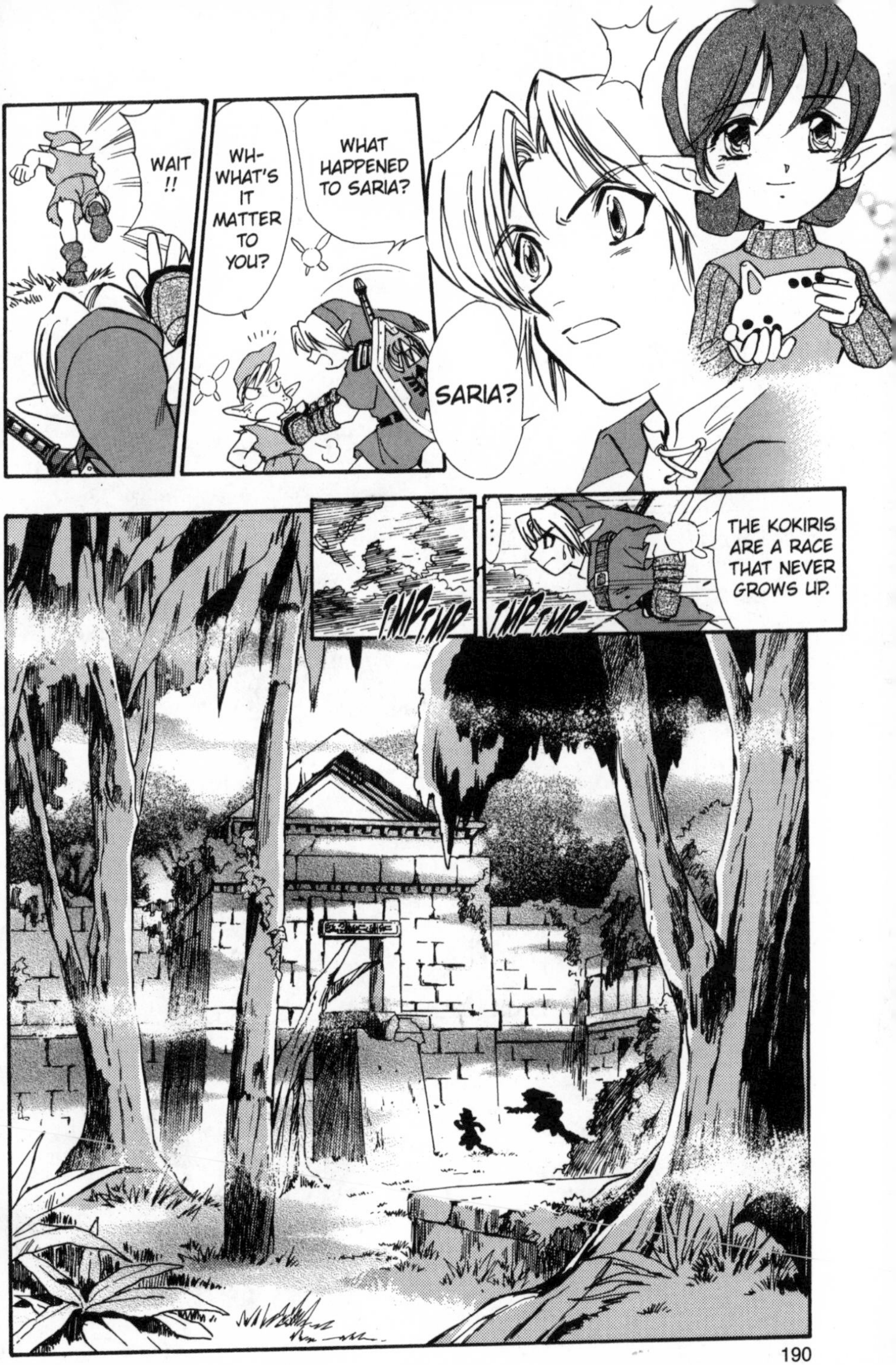
SARIA?
WHAT HAPPENED TO SARIA?
WH- WHAT'S IT MATTER TO YOU?
WAIT !!
THE KOKIRIS ARE A RACE THAT NEVER GROWS UP.
TMP TMP
TMP TMP

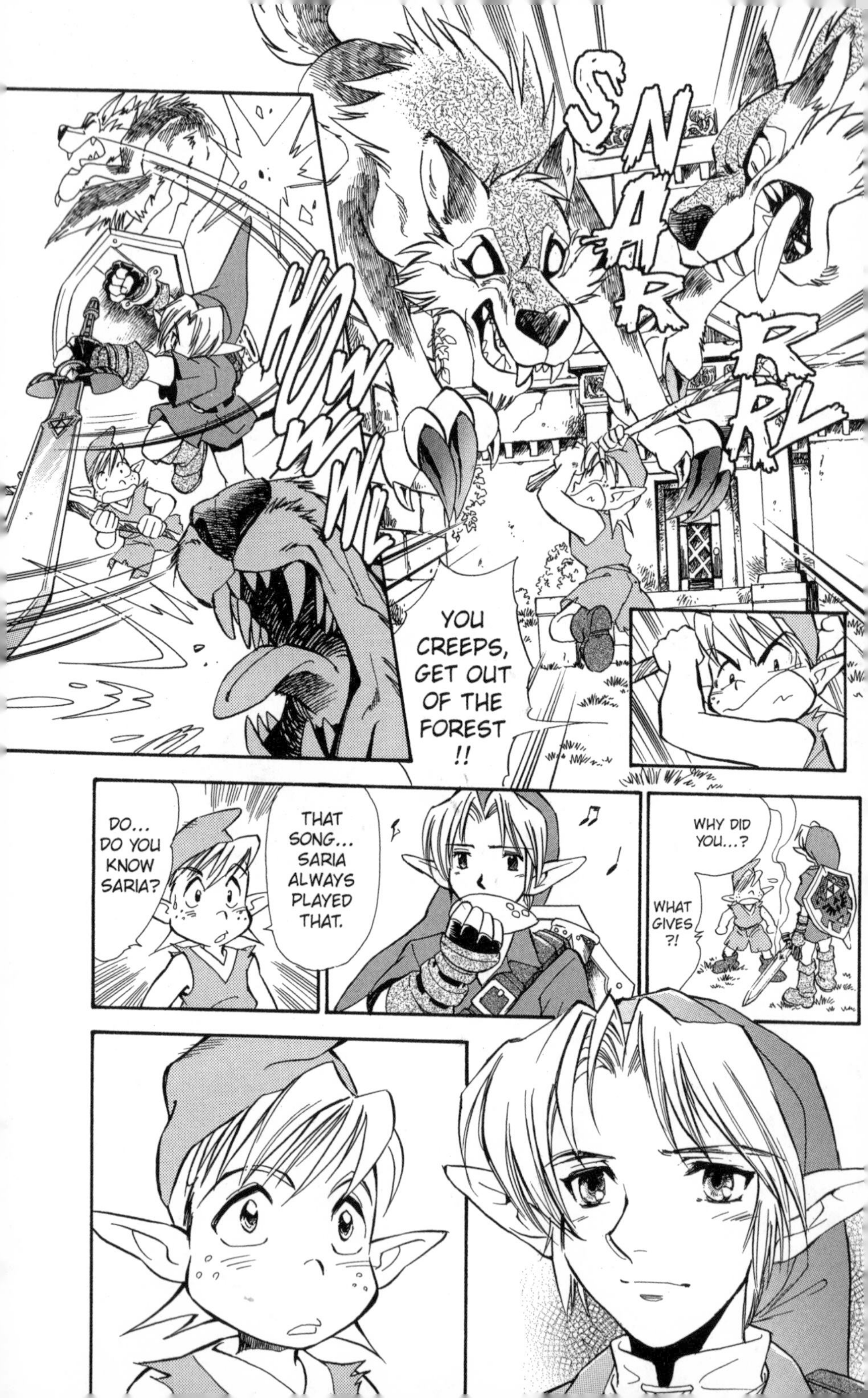
SNARRRL
HOWWWL
YOU CREEPS, GET OUT OF THE FOREST!!
WHY DID YOU...?
WHAT GIVES?!
THAT SONG... SARIA ALWAYS PLAYED THAT.
DO... DO YOU KNOW SARIA?

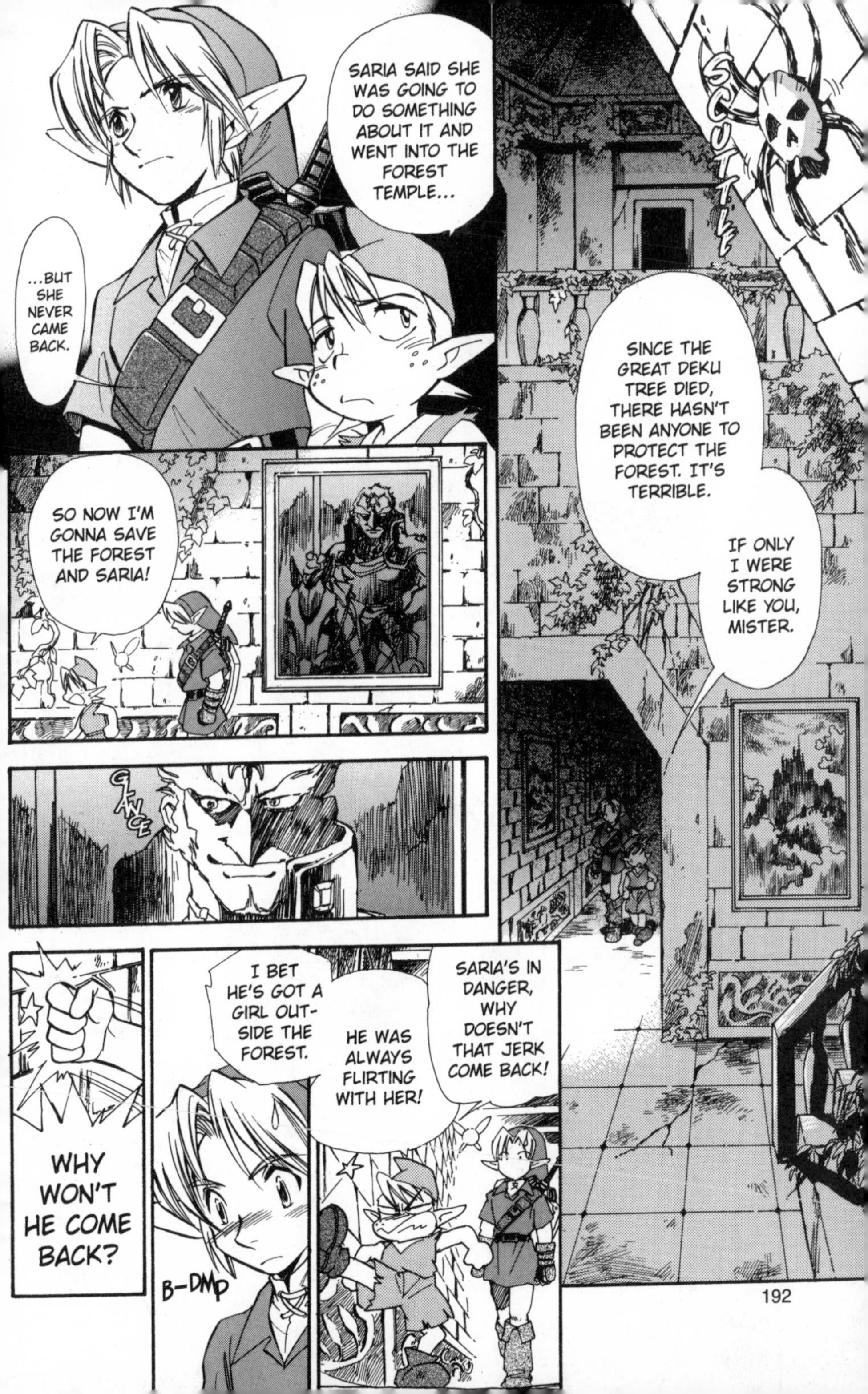
SCUTTLE
SINCE THE GREAT DEKU TREE DIED, THERE HASN'T BEEN ANYONE TO PROTECT THE FOREST. IT'S TERRIBLE.
IF ONLY I WERE STRONG LIKE YOU, MISTER.
SARIA SAID SHE WAS GOING TO DO SOMETHING ABOUT IT AND WENT INTO THE FOREST TEMPLE...
...BUT SHE NEVER CAME BACK.
SO NOW I'M GONNA SAVE THE FOREST AND SARIA!
GLANCE
SARIA'S IN DANGER, WHY DOESN'T THAT JERK COME BACK!
I BET HE'S GOT A GIRL OUT-SIDE THE FOREST.
HE WAS ALWAYS FLIRTING WITH HER!
B-DMP
WHY WON'T HE COME BACK?

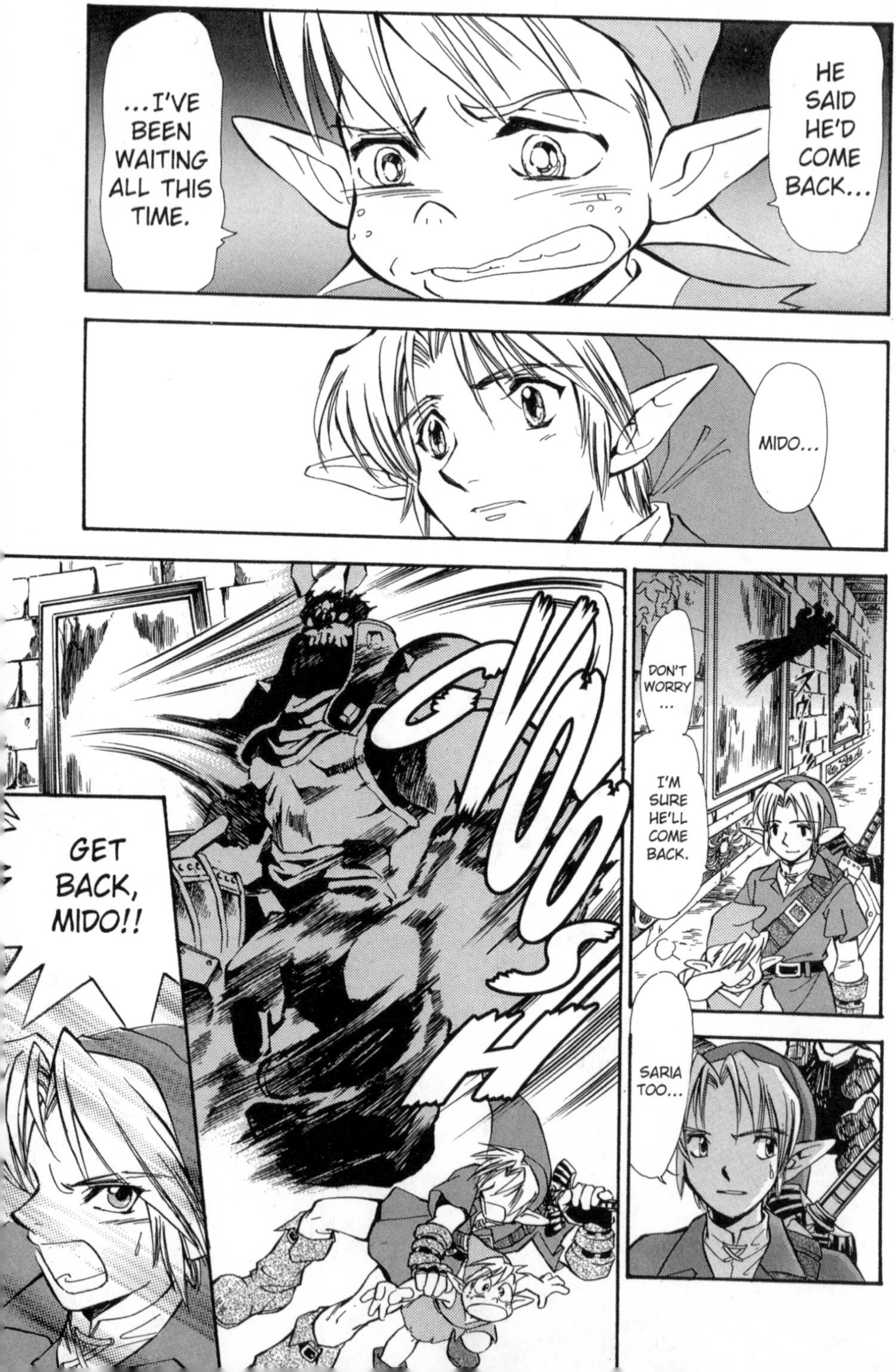
HE SAID HE'D COME BACK...
...I'VE BEEN WAITING ALL THIS TIME.
MIDO...
DON'T WORRY...
I'M SURE HE'LL COME BACK.
SARIA TOO...
WHOOOSH
GET BACK, MIDO!!

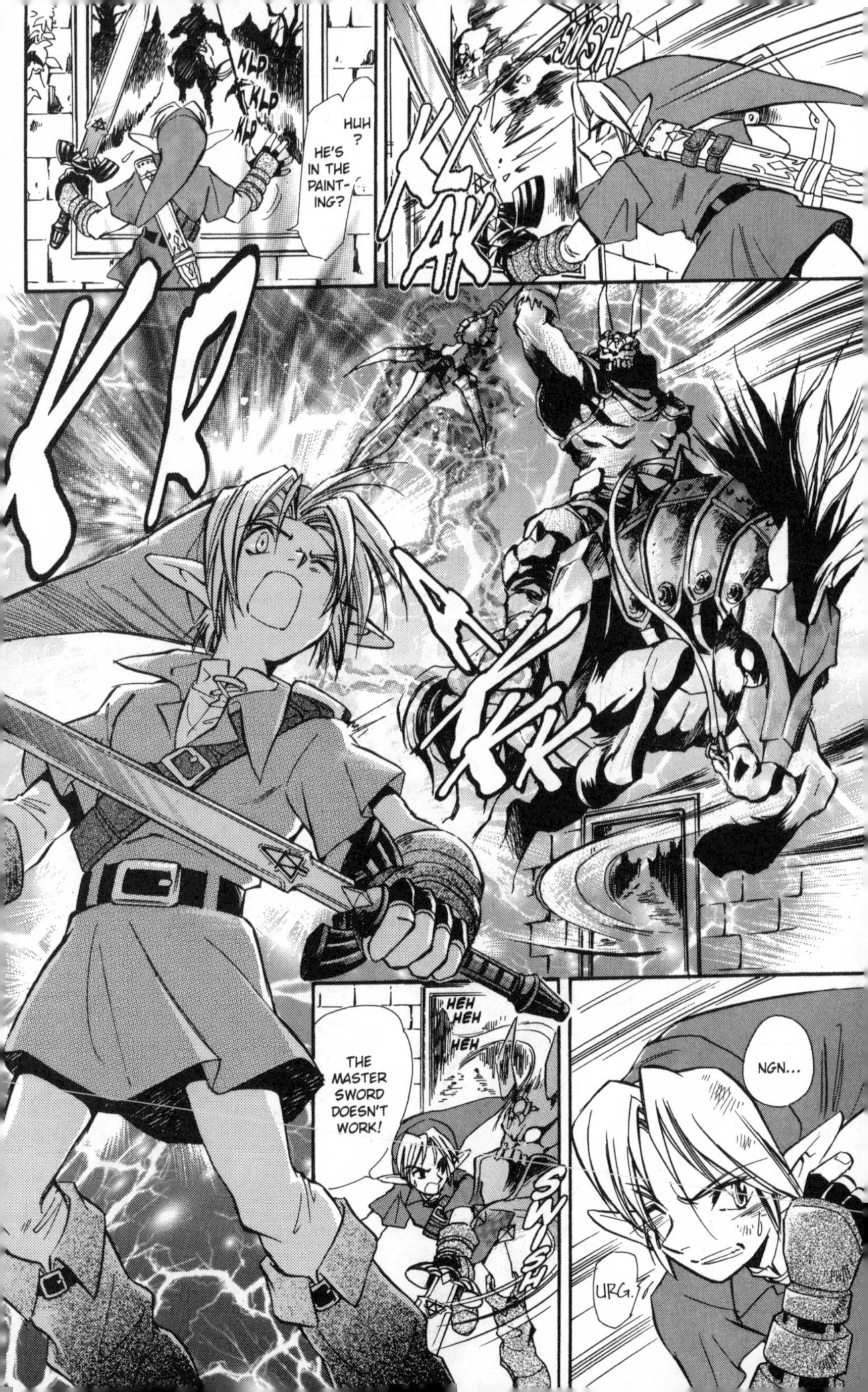
SWISH
KLLAK
KLP KLP KLP
HUH?
HE'S IN THE PAINTING?
KLP
NGN...
URG.
HEH HEH HEH
THE MASTER SWORD DOESN'T WORK!
SWISH

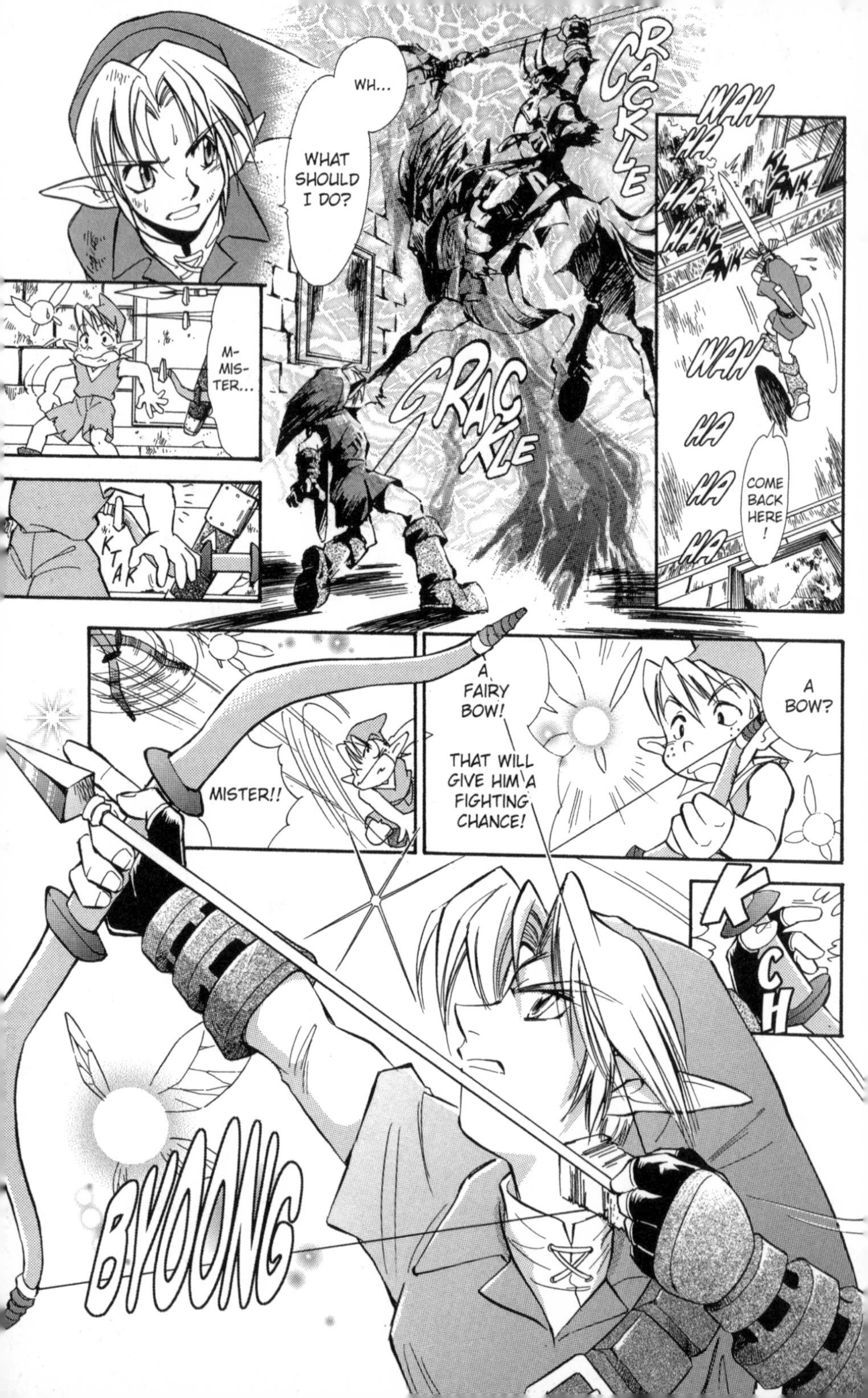
WAH HA HA HA
KWANK
WAH HA HA HA HA
COME BACK HERE!
CRACKLE
CRACKLE
WH...
WHAT SHOULD I DO?
M-MISTER...
KTAK
A BOW?
A FAIRY BOW!
THAT WILL GIVE HIM A FIGHTING CHANCE!
MISTER!!
KCH
BYOONG

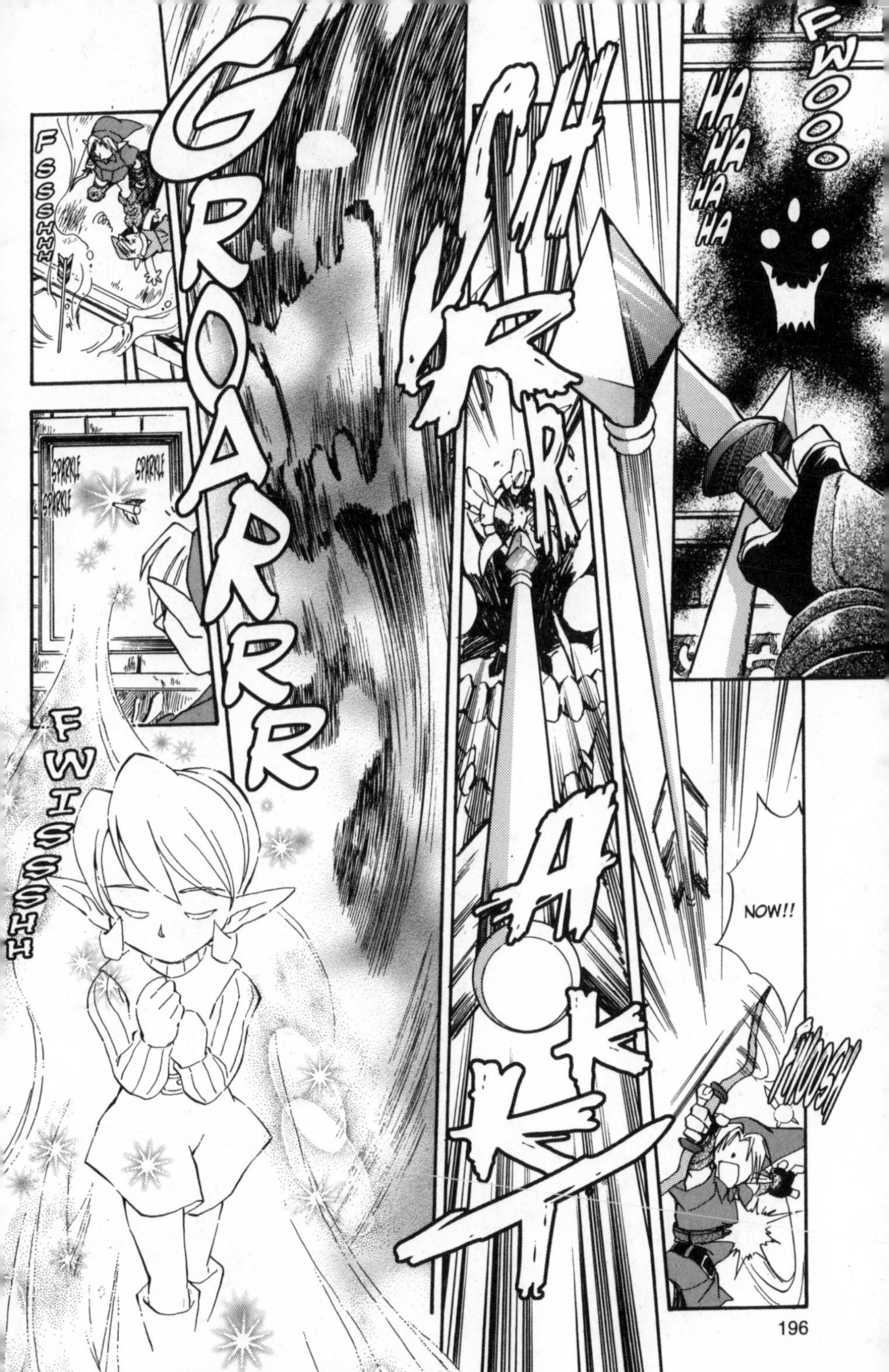
FWOOO
HA HA HA HA
CHKRAKK
FSSSHHH
SPARKLE
SPARKLE
SPARKLE
GROARRRR
FWISSSHH
NOW!!
FWOOSH

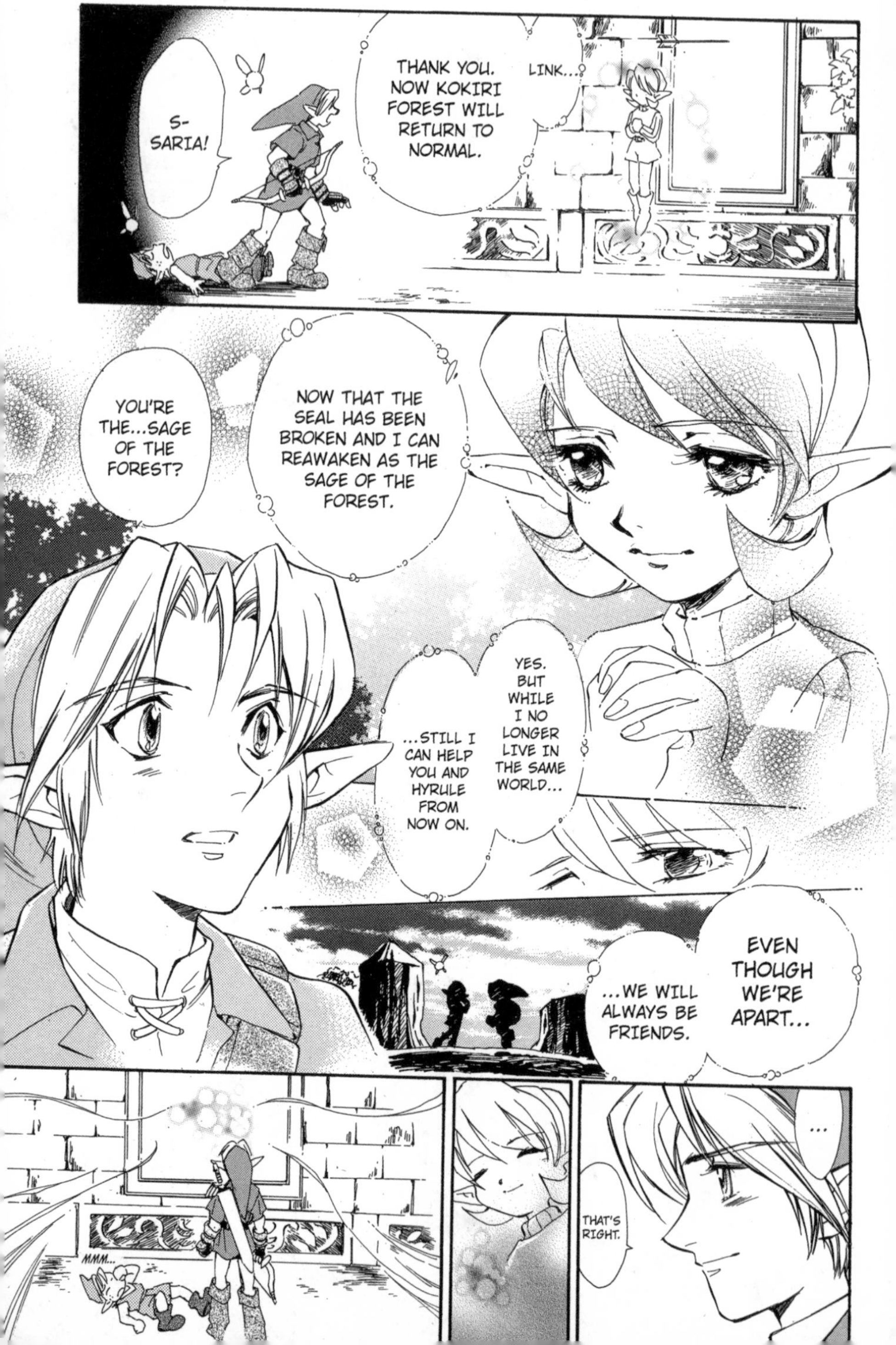
LINK...
THANK YOU. NOW KOKIRI FOREST WILL RETURN TO NORMAL.
S-SARIA!
NOW THAT THE SEAL HAS BEEN BROKEN AND I CAN REAWAKEN AS THE SAGE OF THE FOREST.
YOU'RE THE...SAGE OF THE FOREST?
YES. BUT WHILE I NO LONGER LIVE IN THE SAME WORLD...
...STILL I CAN HELP YOU AND HYRULE FROM NOW ON.
EVEN THOUGH WE'RE APART...
...WE WILL ALWAYS BE FRIENDS.
...
THAT'S RIGHT.
MMM...

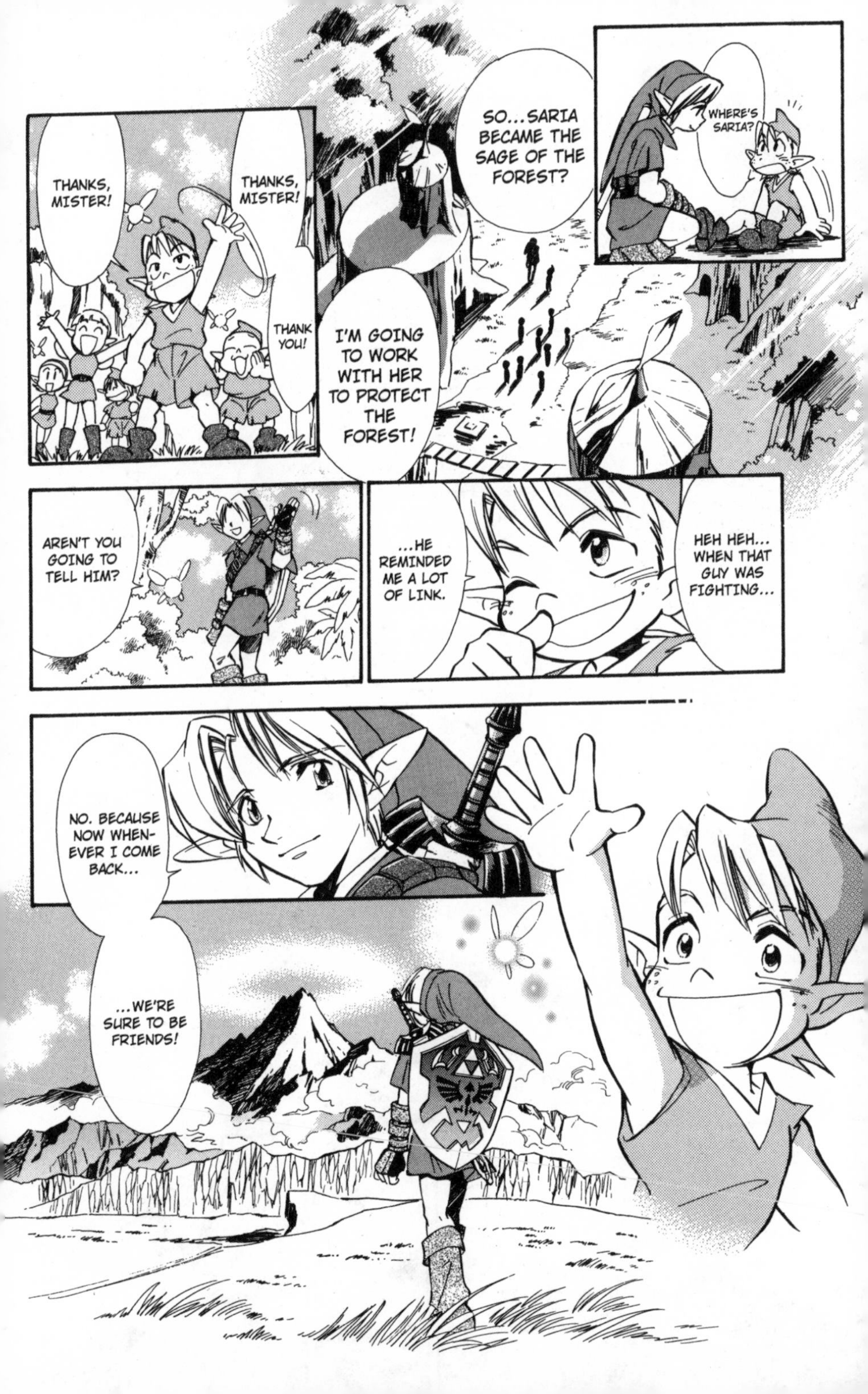
WHERE'S SARIA?
SO...SARIA BECAME THE SAGE OF THE FOREST?
I'M GOING TO WORK WITH HER TO PROTECT THE FOREST!
THANKS, MISTER!
THANK YOU!
THANKS, MISTER!
HEH HEH... WHEN THAT GUY WAS FIGHTING...
...HE REMINDED ME A LOT OF LINK.
AREN'T YOU GOING TO TELL HIM?
NO. BECAUSE NOW WHEN-EVER I COME BACK...
...WE'RE SURE TO BE FRIENDS!

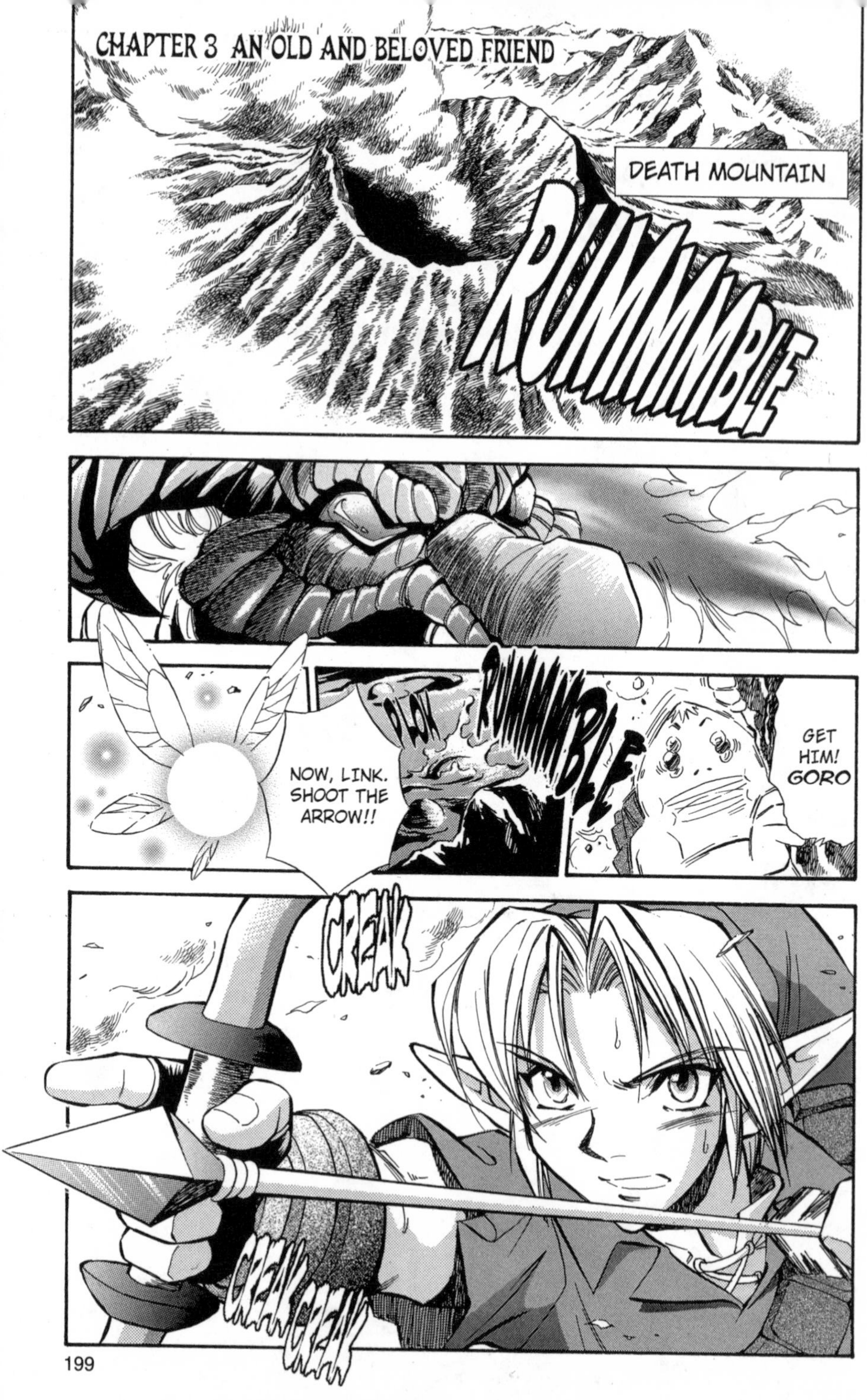
CHAPTER 3 AN OLD AND BELOVED FRIEND
DEATH MOUNTAIN
RUMMMBLE
GET HIM! GORO
RUMMMBLE
NOW, LINK. SHOOT THE ARROW!!
CREAK
CREAK CREAK

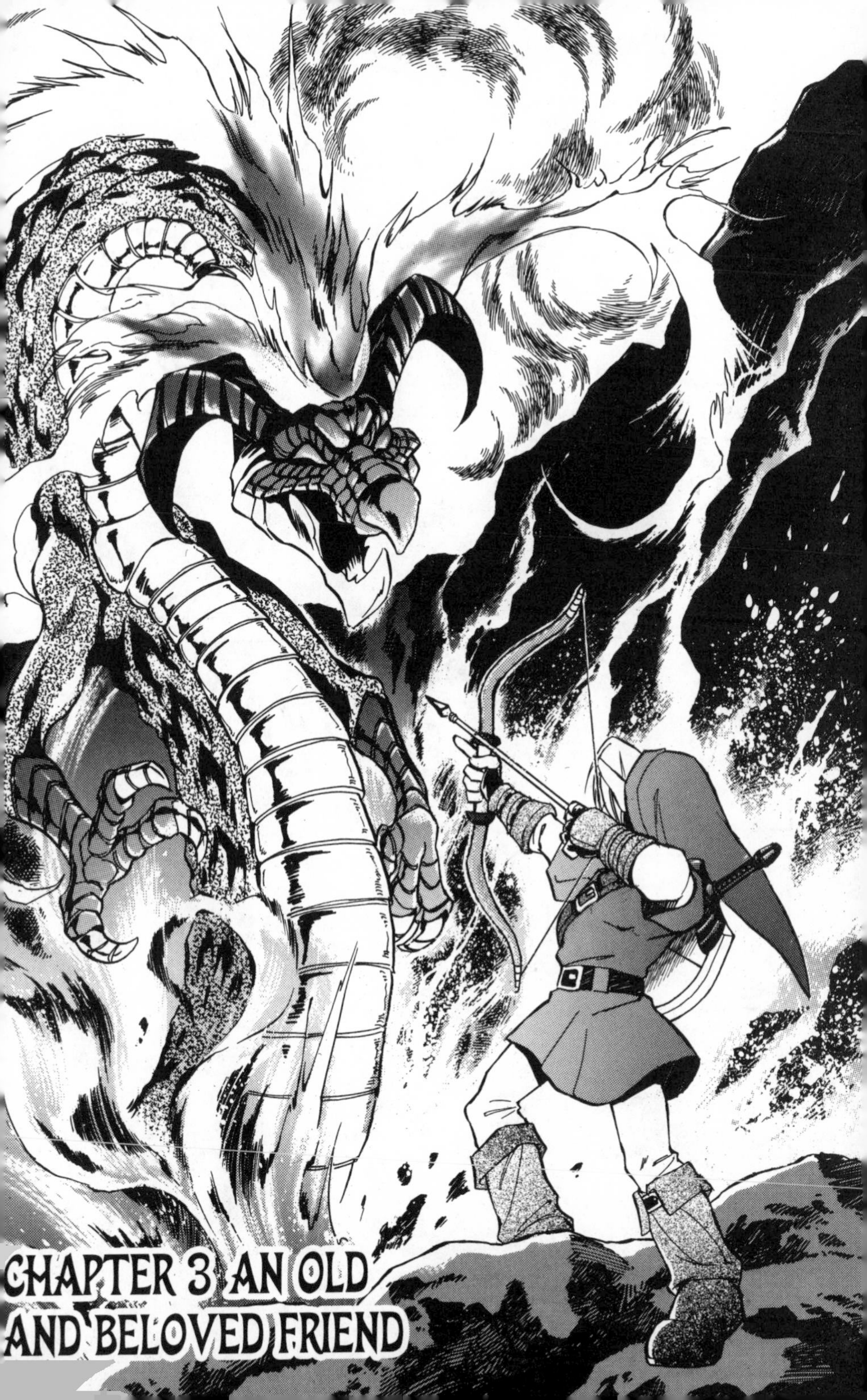
CHAPTER 3 AN OLD
AND BELOVED FRIEND

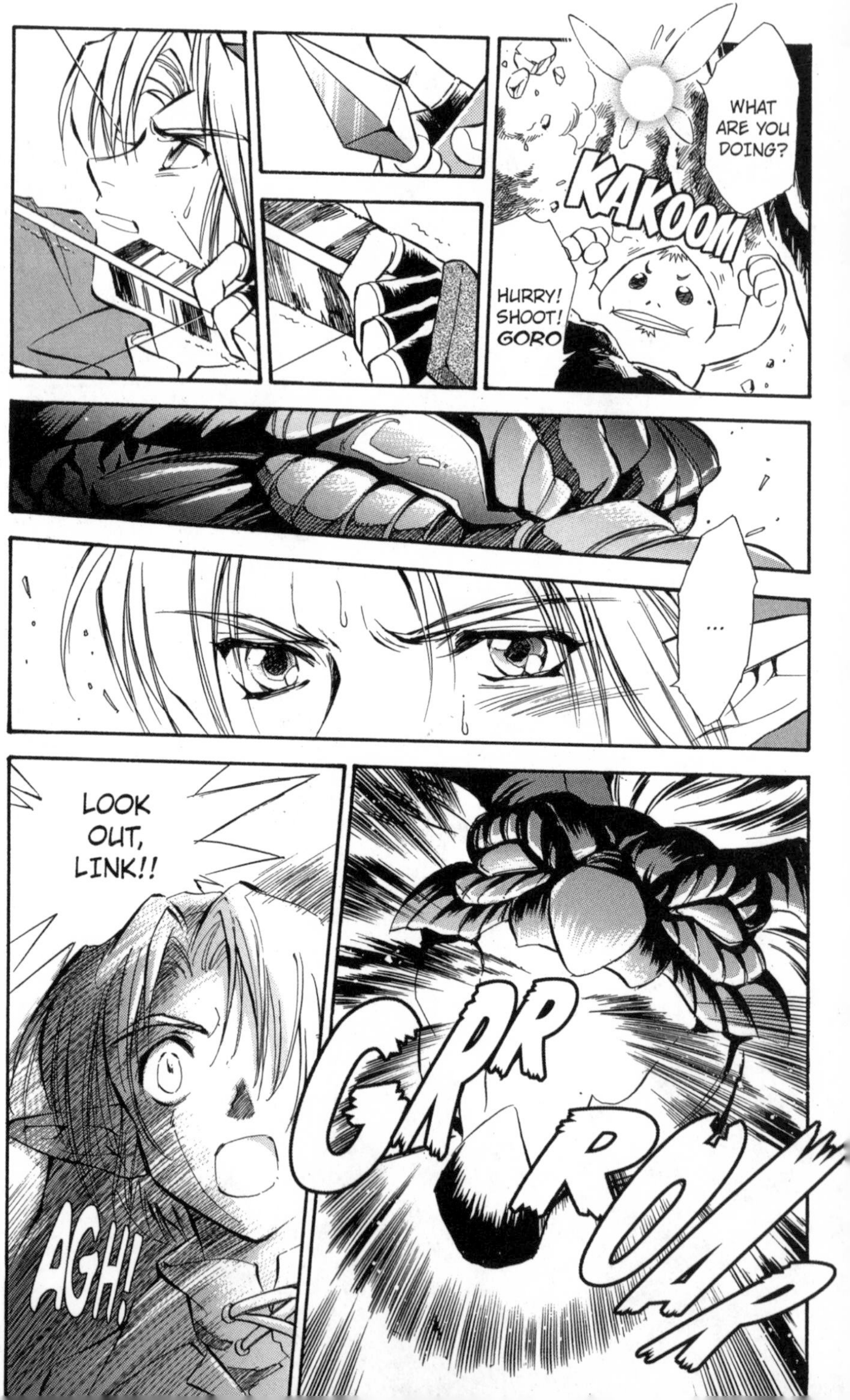
WHAT ARE YOU DOING?
KAKOOM
HURRY! SHOOT! GORO
...
GRROAR
LOOK OUT, LINK!!
AGH!

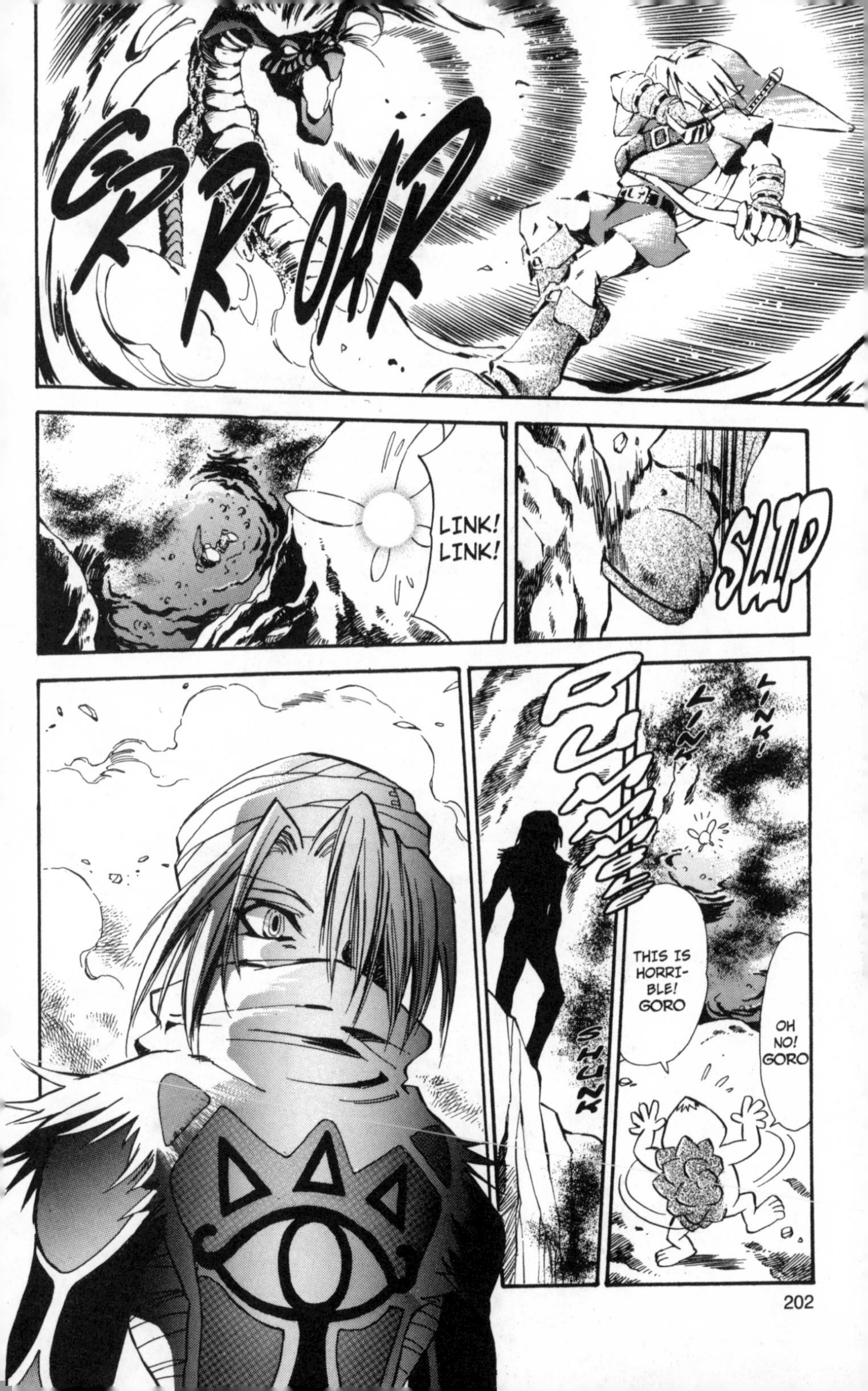
GRROAR
SLIP
LINK! LINK!
LINK! LINK!
OH NO! GORO
THIS IS HORRI-BLE! GORO
SHUNK

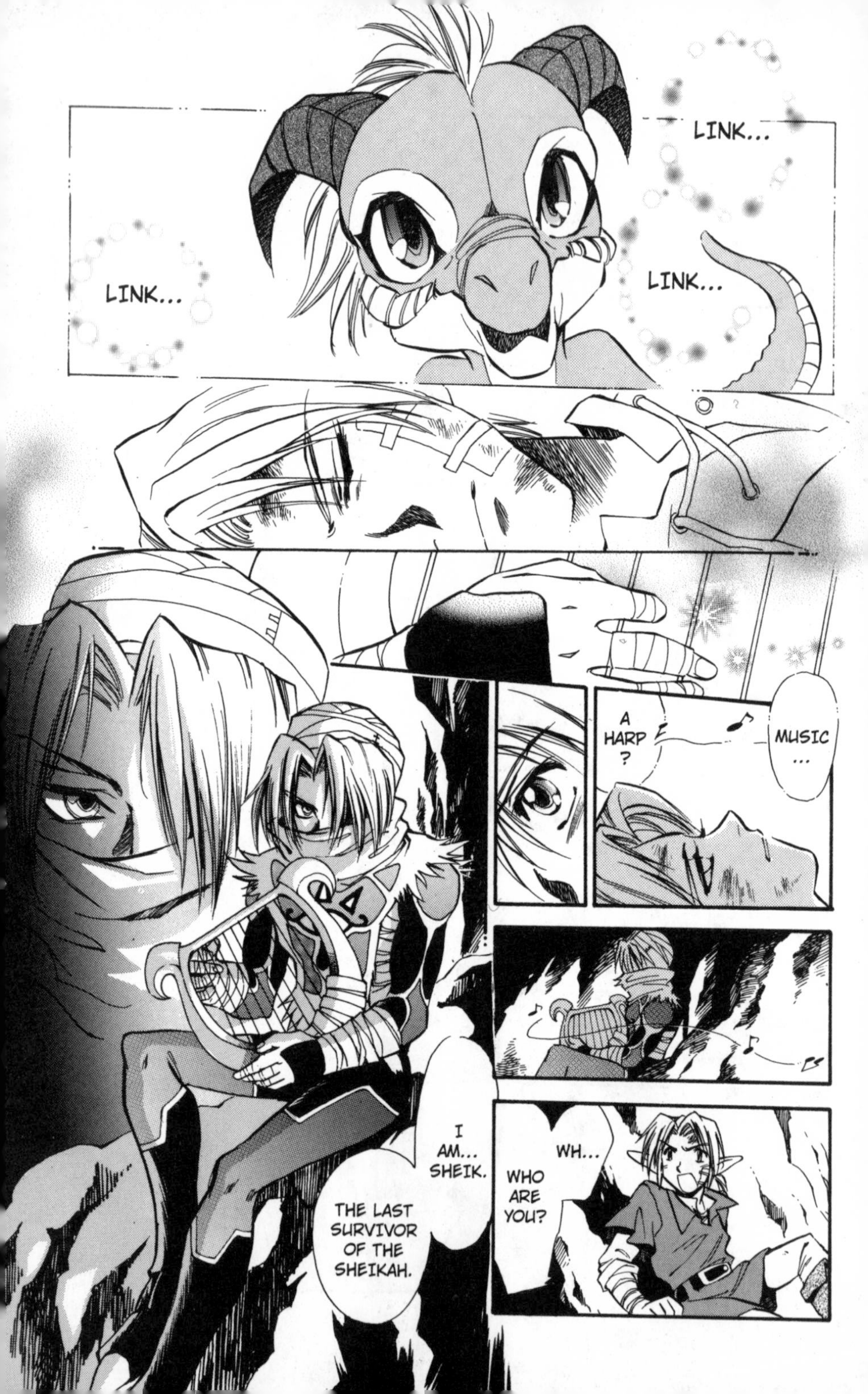
LINK...
LINK...
LINK...
MUSIC...
A HARP?
WH...
WHO ARE YOU?
I AM... SHEIK.
THE LAST SURVIVOR OF THE SHEIKAH.

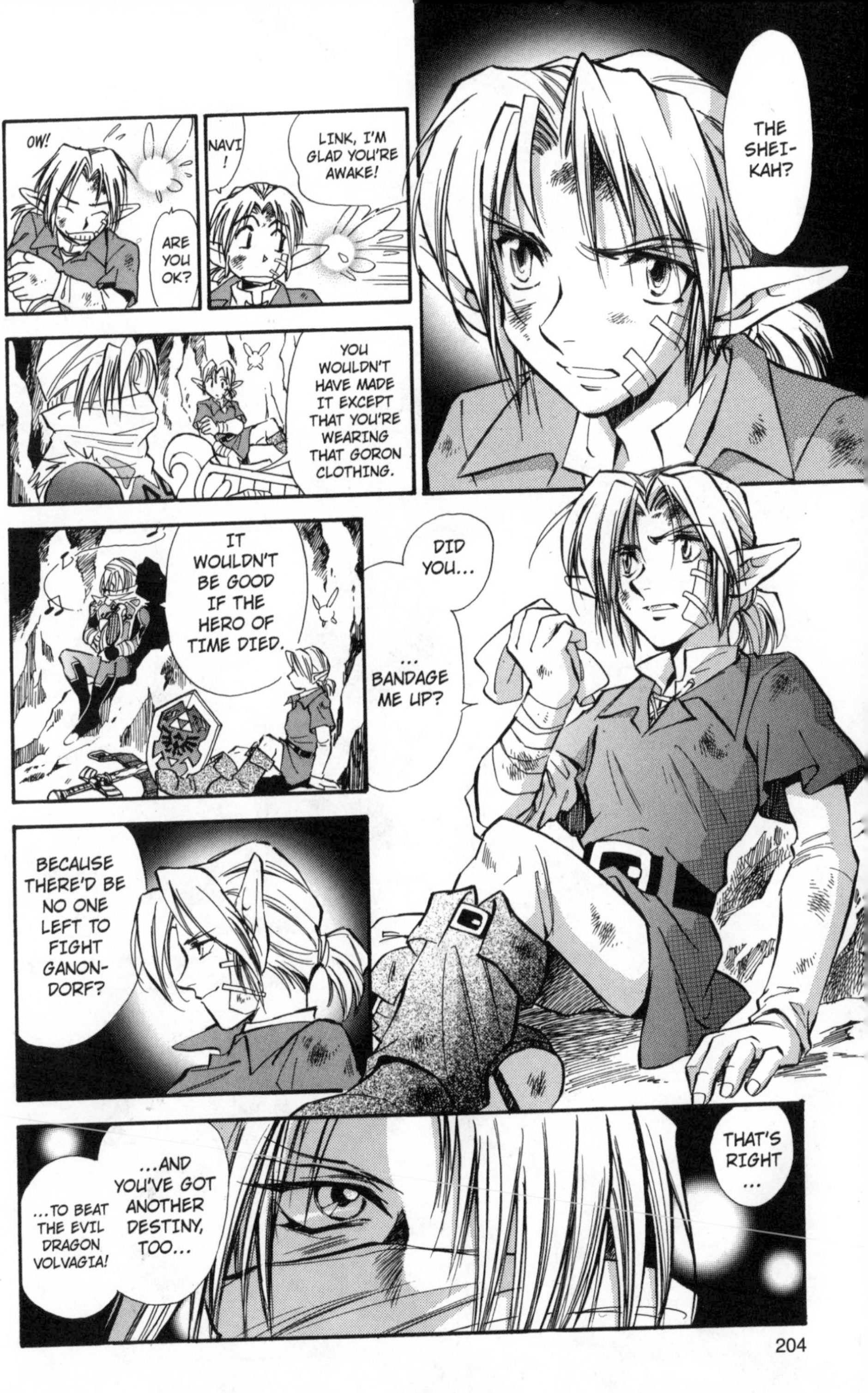
THE SHEI-KAH?
NAVI!
LINK, I'M GLAD YOU'RE AWAKE!
OW!
ARE YOU OK?
YOU WOULDN'T HAVE MADE IT EXCEPT THAT YOU'RE WEARING THAT GORON CLOTHING.
DID YOU...
...BANDAGE ME UP?
IT WOULDN'T BE GOOD IF THE HERO OF TIME DIED.
BECAUSE THERE'D BE NO ONE LEFT TO FIGHT GANON-DORF?
THAT'S RIGHT...
...AND YOU'VE GOT ANOTHER DESTINY, TOO...
...TO BEAT THE EVIL DRAGON VOLVAGIA!

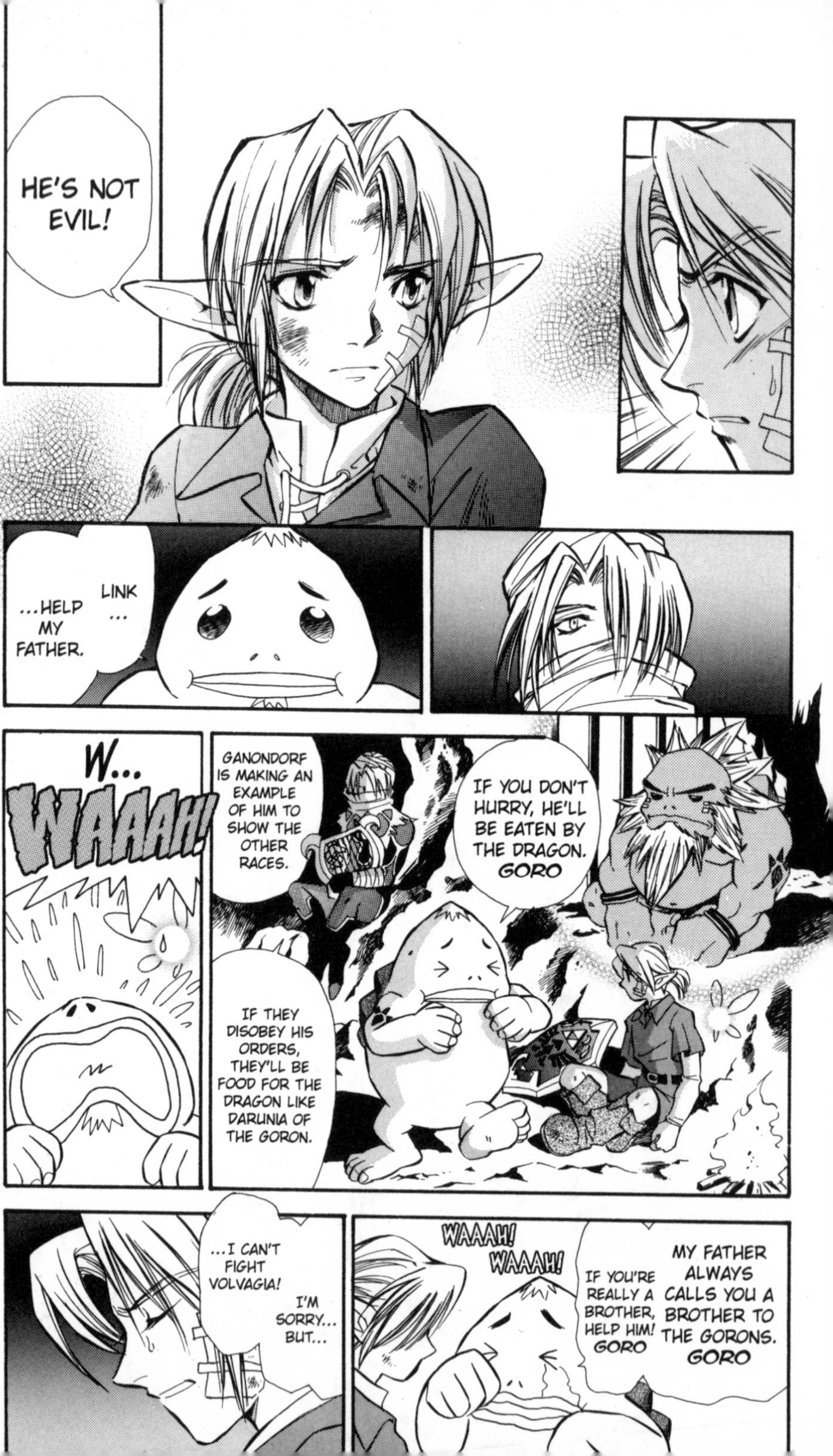
HE'S NOT EVIL!
LINK...
...HELP MY FATHER.
IF YOU DON'T HURRY, HE'LL BE EATEN BY THE DRAGON. GORO
GANONDORF IS MAKING AN EXAMPLE OF HIM TO SHOW THE OTHER RACES.
IF THEY DISOBEY HIS ORDERS, THEY'LL BE FOOD FOR THE DRAGON LIKE DARUNIA OF THE GORON.
W... WAAAH!
WAAAH! WAAAH!
MY FATHER ALWAYS CALLS YOU A BROTHER TO THE GORONS. GORO
IF YOU'RE REALLY A BROTHER, HELP HIM! GORO
...I CAN'T FIGHT VOLVAGIA!
I'M SORRY... BUT...

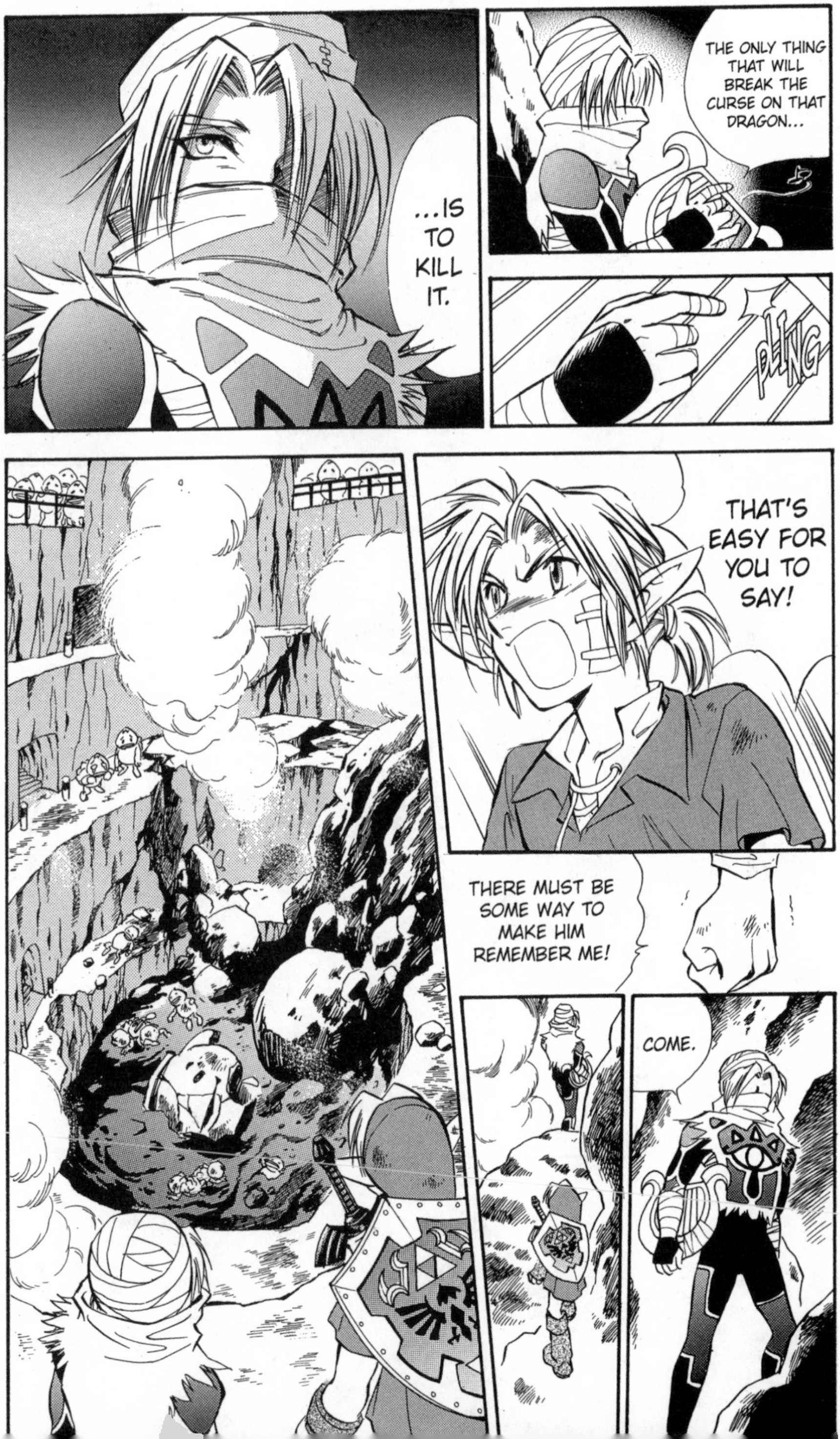
THE ONLY THING THAT WILL BREAK THE CURSE ON THAT DRAGON...
DLING
...IS TO KILL IT.
THAT'S EASY FOR YOU TO SAY!
THERE MUST BE SOME WAY TO MAKE HIM REMEMBER ME!
COME.

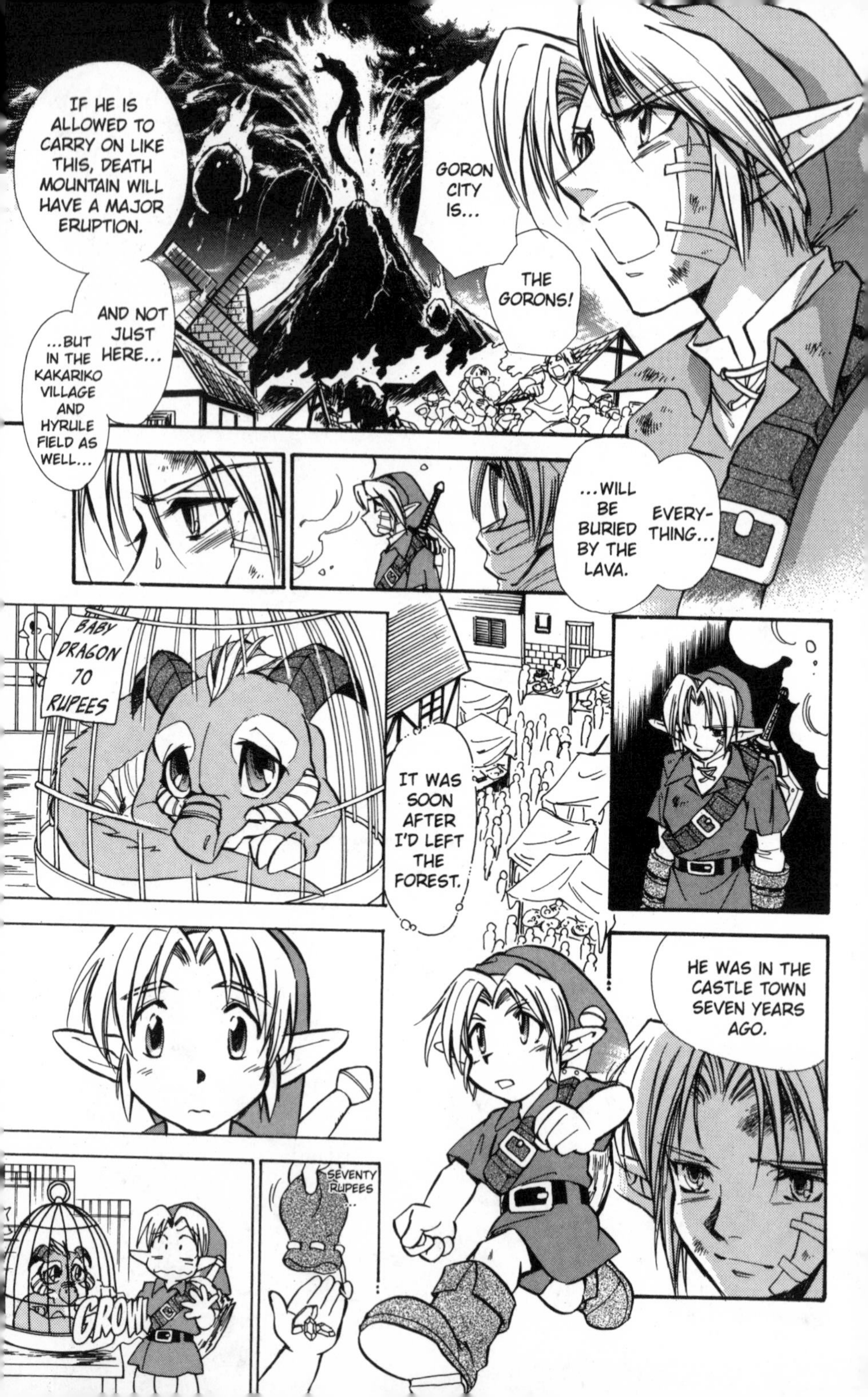
IF HE IS ALLOWED TO CARRY ON LIKE THIS, DEATH MOUNTAIN WILL HAVE A MAJOR ERUPTION.
GORON CITY IS...
THE GORONS!
AND NOT JUST HERE...
...BUT IN THE KAKARIKO VILLAGE AND HYRULE FIELD AS WELL...
EVERY-THING...
...WILL BE BURIED BY THE LAVA.
IT WAS SOON AFTER I'D LEFT THE FOREST.
BABY DRAGON 70 RUPEES
HE WAS IN THE CASTLE TOWN SEVEN YEARS AGO.
SEVENTY RUPEES...
GROWL

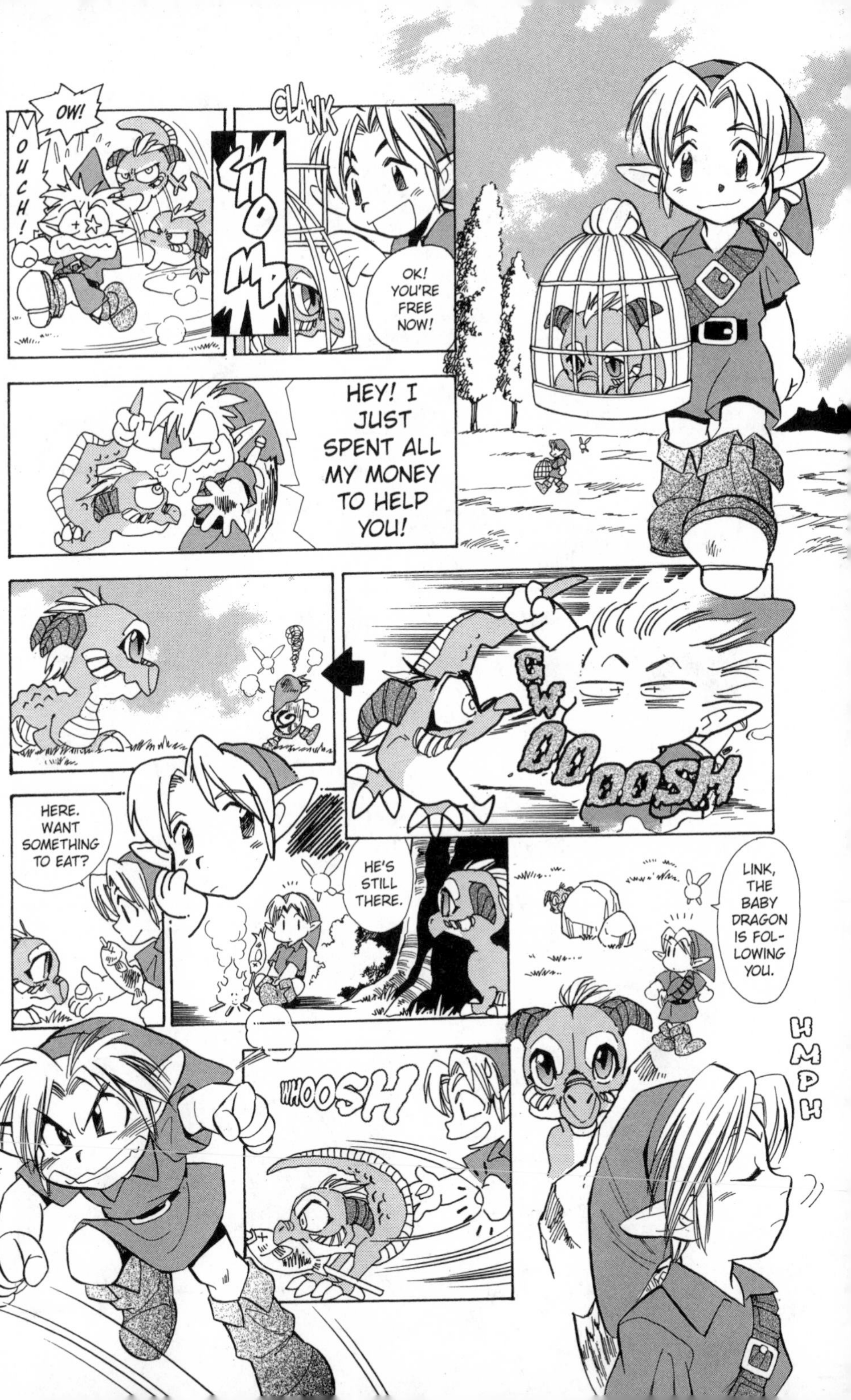

CLANK
CHOMP
OK! YOU'RE FREE NOW!
OW!
OUCH!
HEY! I JUST SPENT ALL MY MONEY TO HELP YOU!
GWOOOOSH
LINK, THE BABY DRAGON IS FOL-LOWING YOU.
HE'S STILL THERE.
HERE. WANT SOMETHING TO EAT?
HMPH
WHOOSH

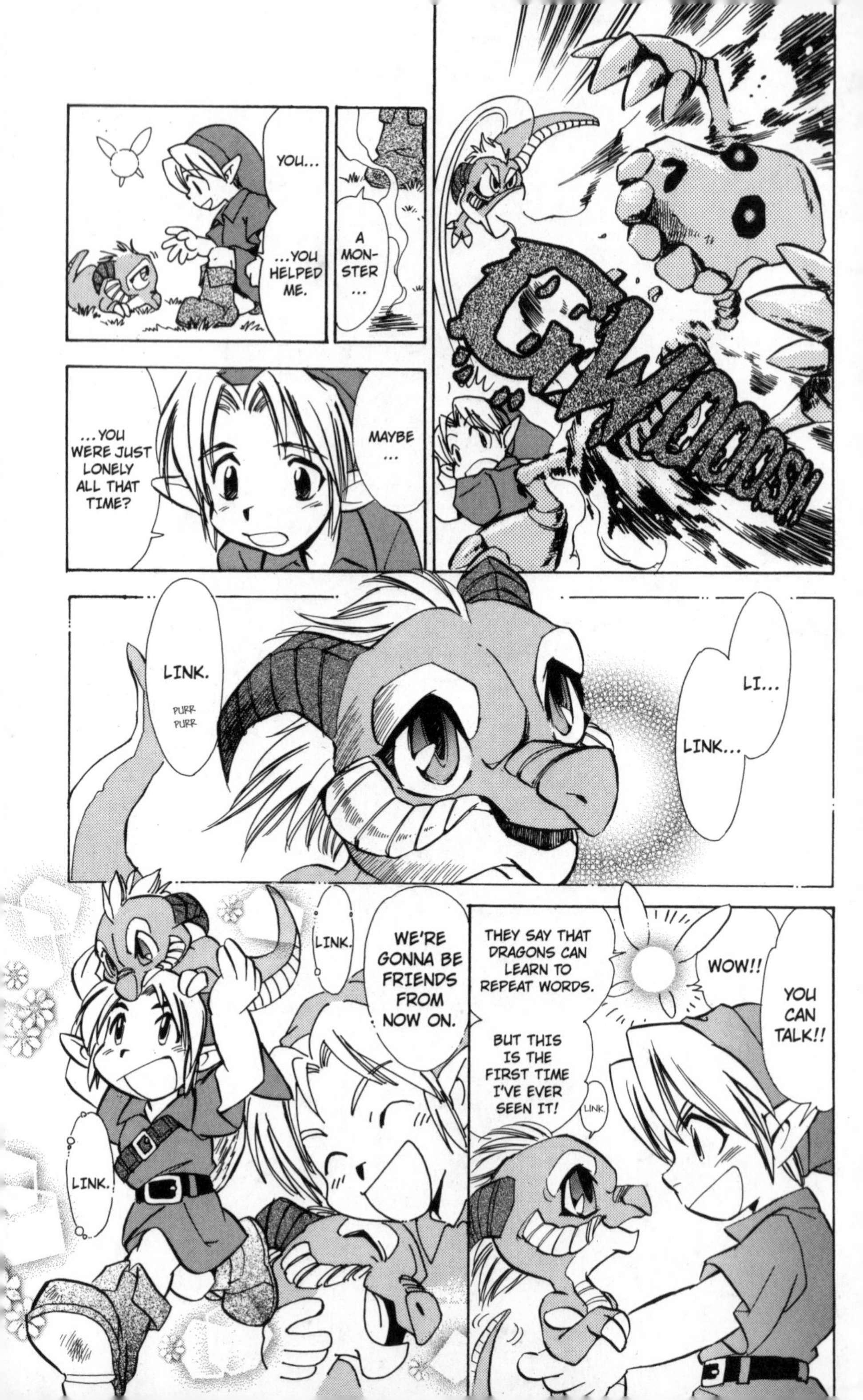
GWOOOSH
A MONSTER ...
YOU...
...YOU HELPED ME.
MAYBE ...
...YOU WERE JUST LONELY ALL THAT TIME?
LI...
LINK...
LINK.
PURR PURR
WOW!!
YOU CAN TALK!!
THEY SAY THAT DRAGONS CAN LEARN TO REPEAT WORDS.
BUT THIS IS THE FIRST TIME I'VE EVER SEEN IT!
LINK.
WE'RE GONNA BE FRIENDS FROM NOW ON.
LINK.
LINK.

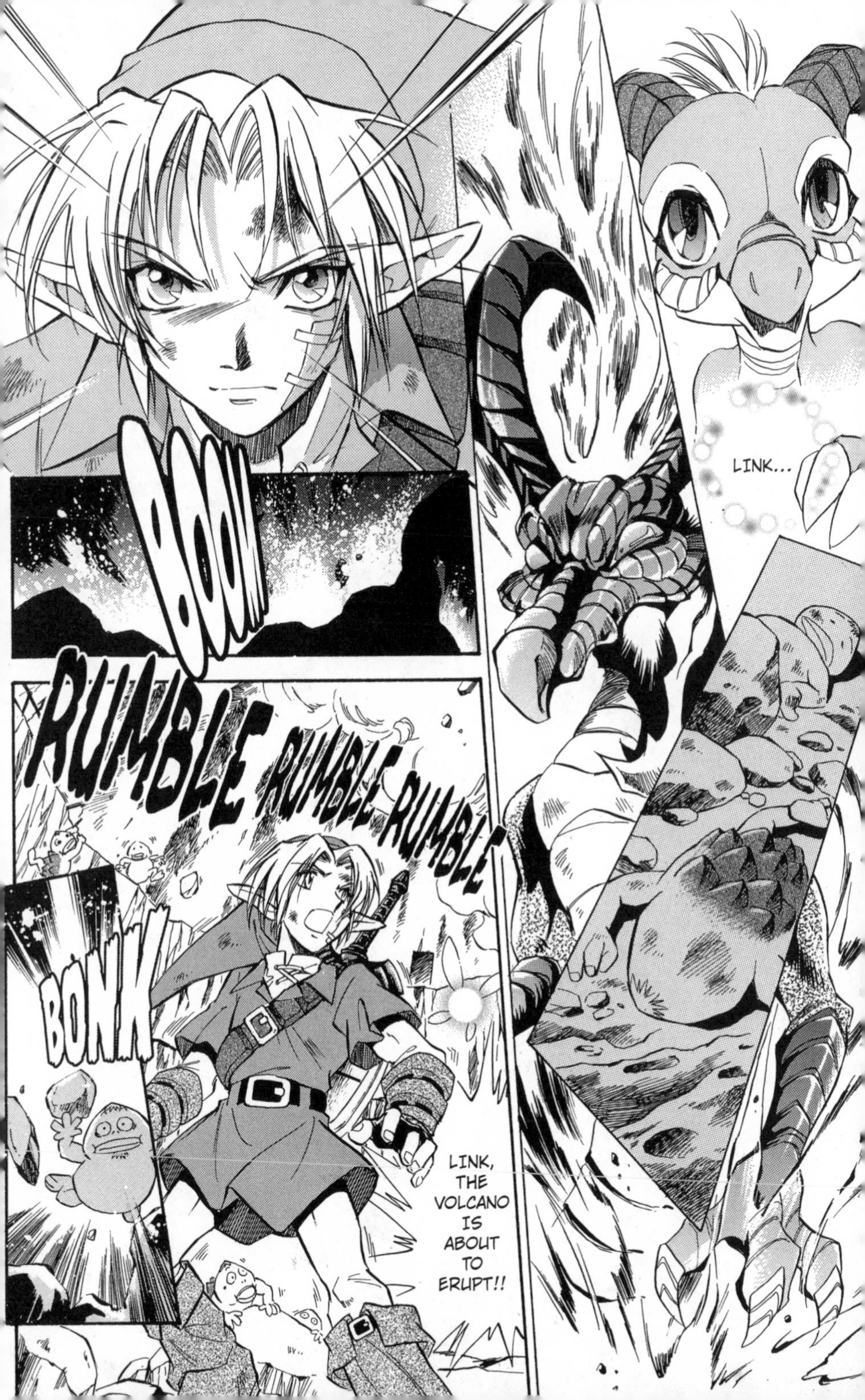

LINK...
BOOM
RUMBLE RUMBLE RUMBLE RUMBLE
BONK
LINK, THE VOLCANO IS ABOUT TO ERUPT!!

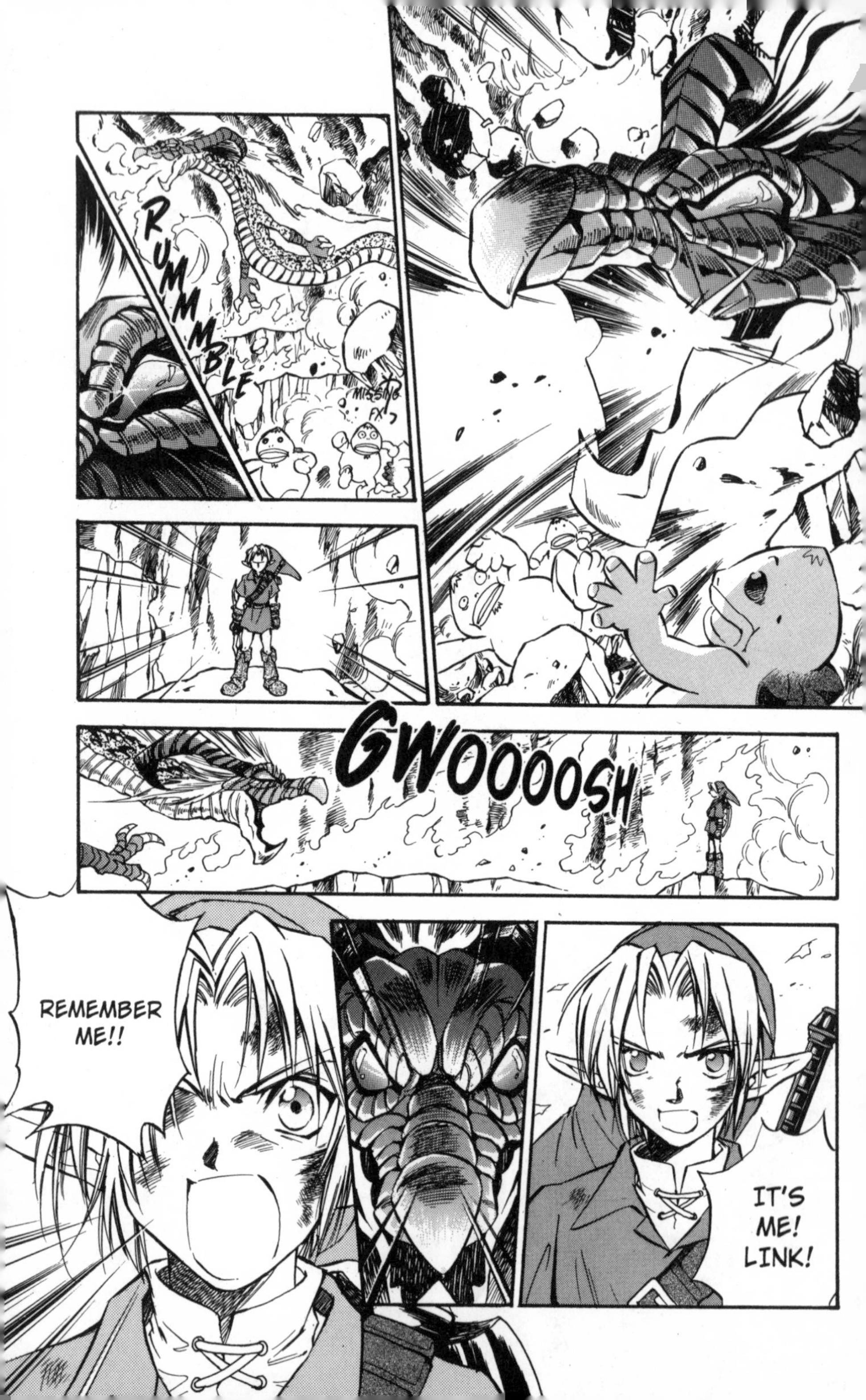
RUMMMBLE
MISSING FX
GWOOOOSH
IT'S ME! LINK!
REMEMBER ME!!

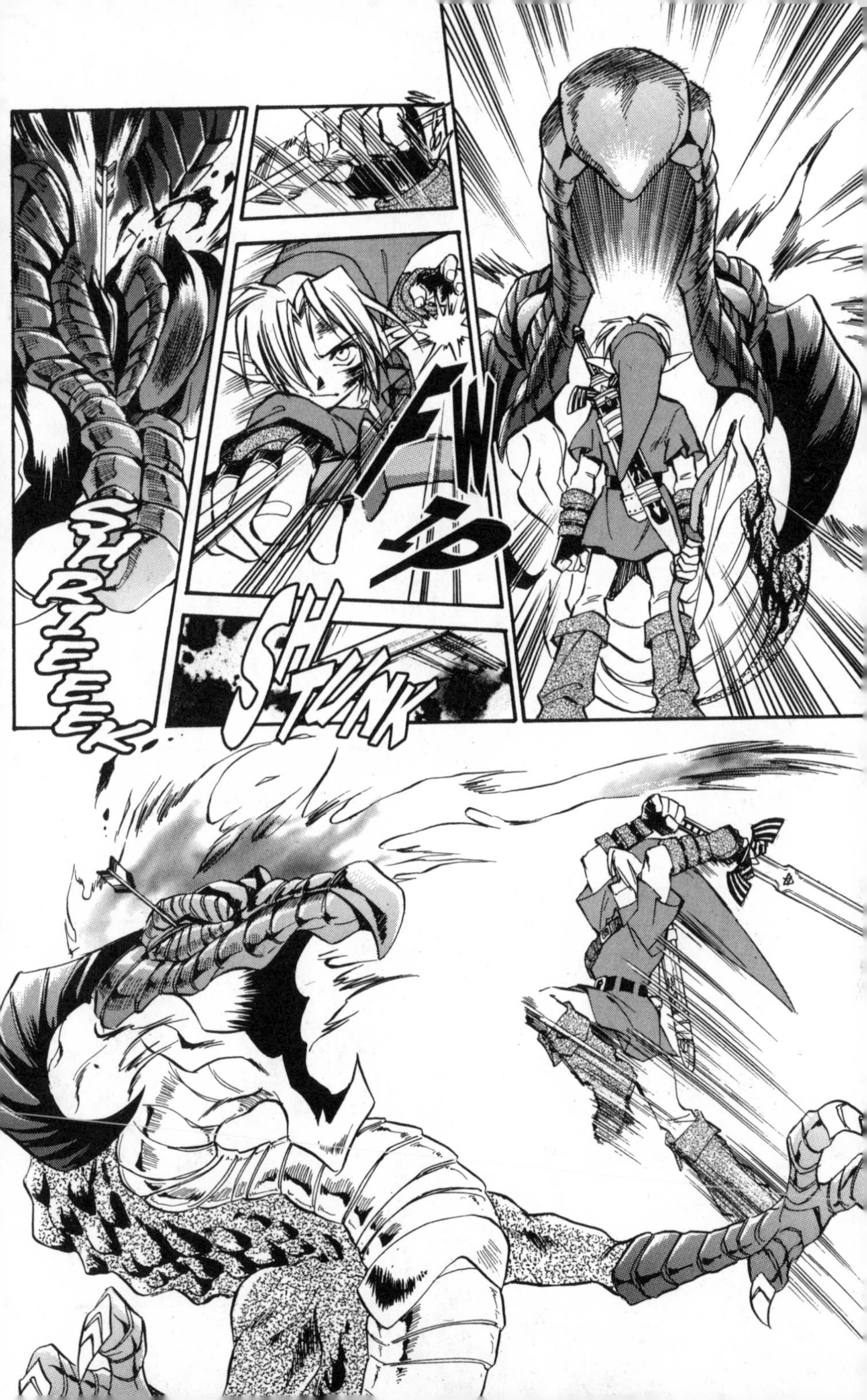
FWIP
SHTUNK
SHRIEEEK

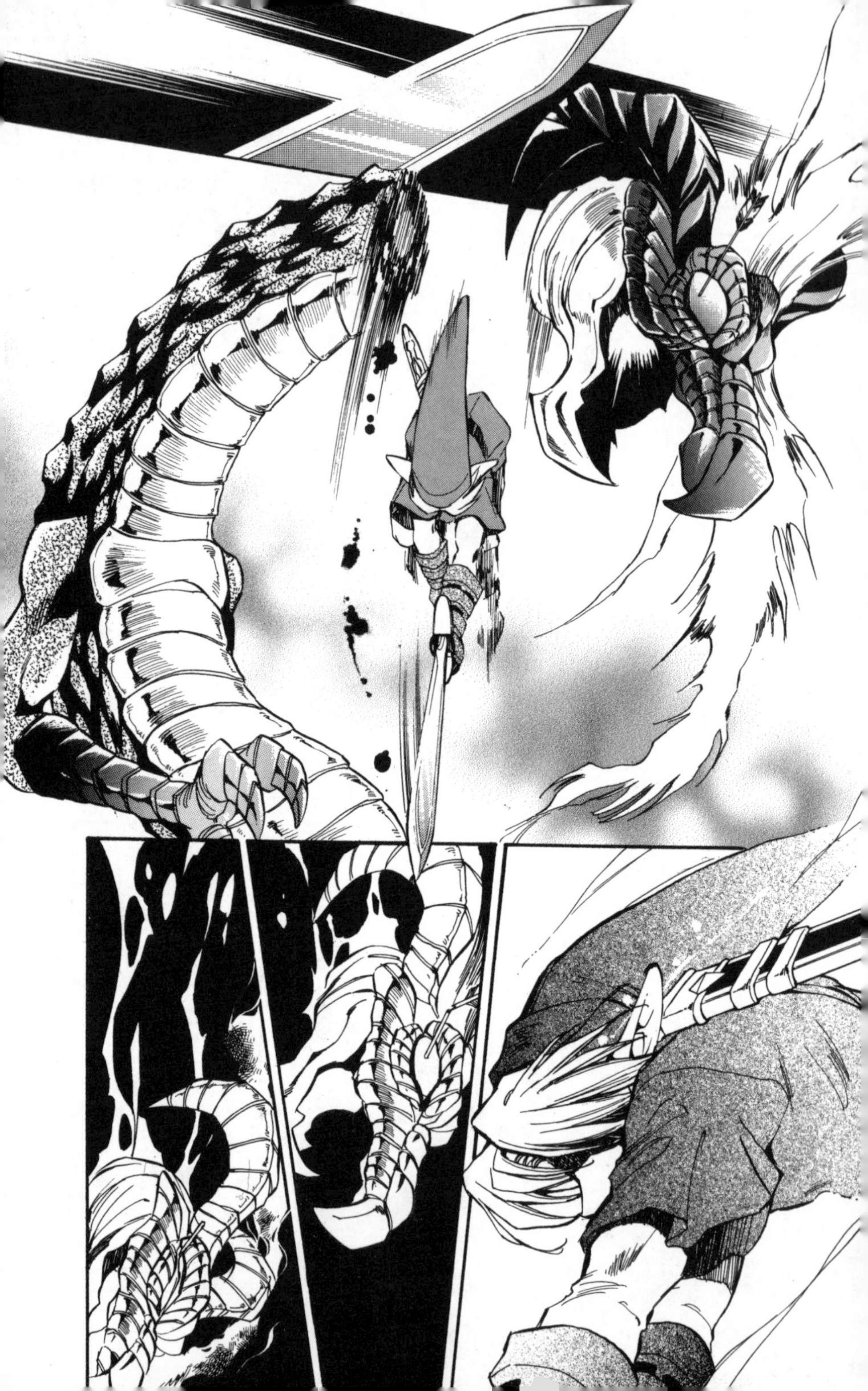

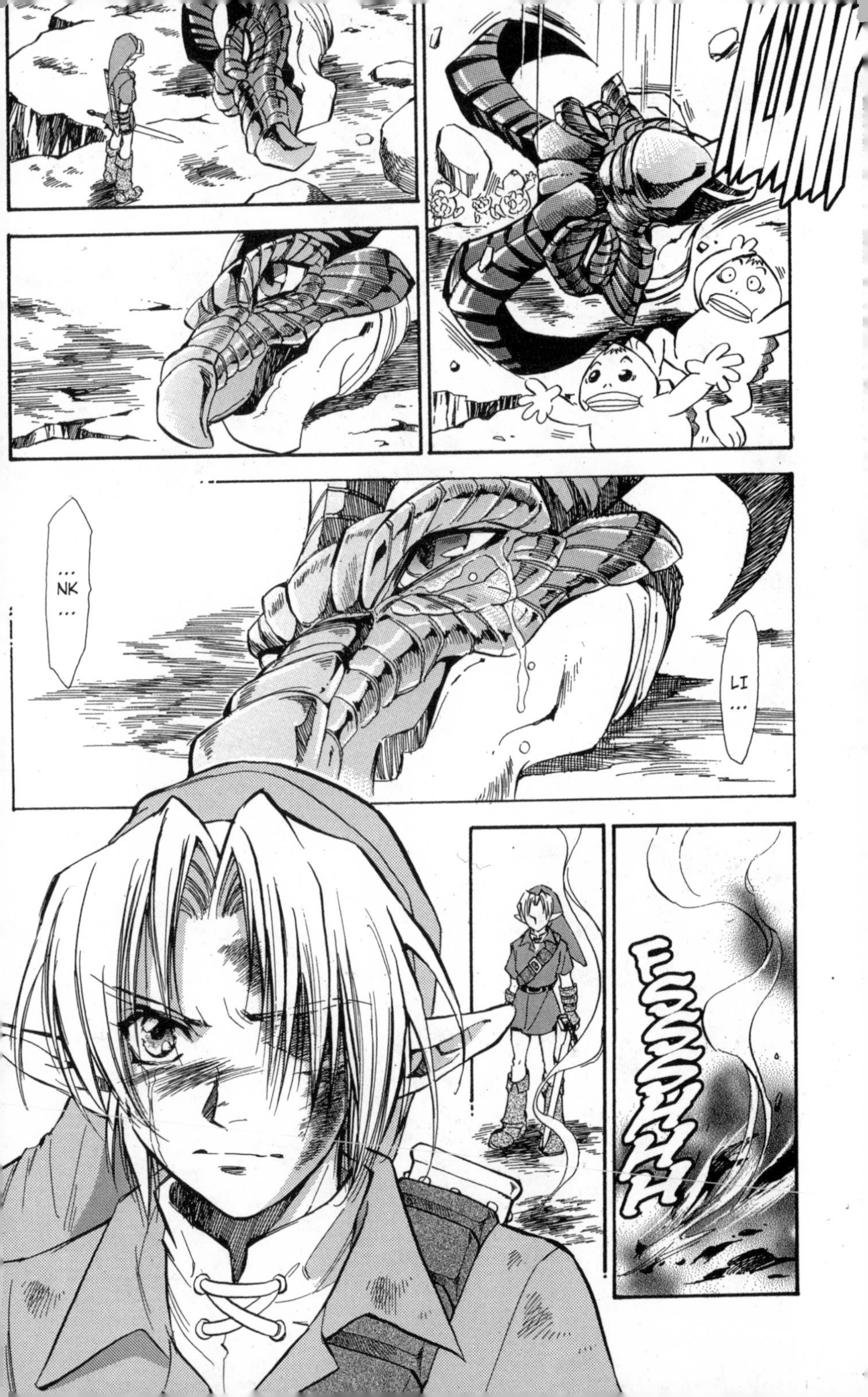
LI...
...NK...
FSSSSHHH

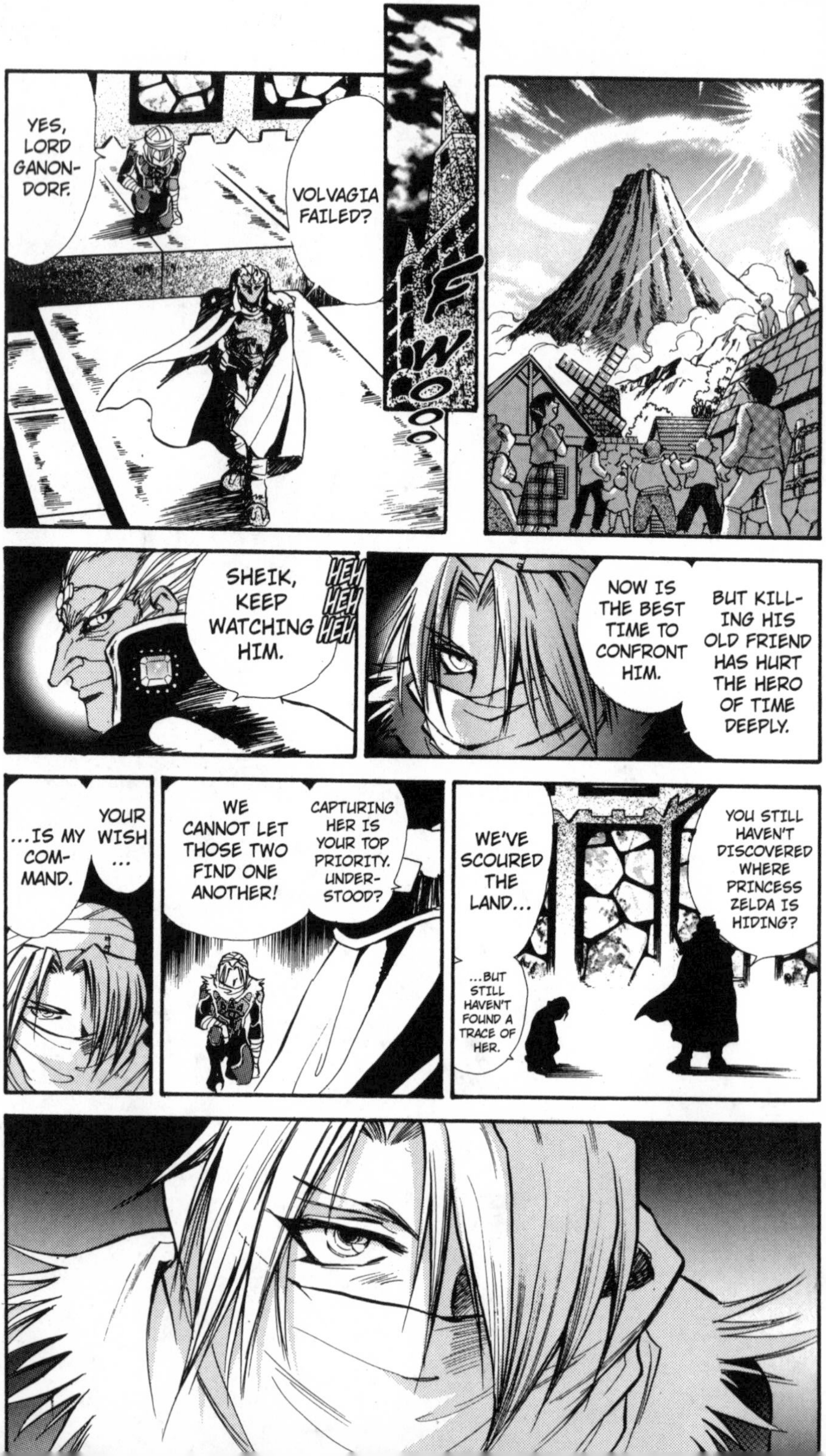
FWOOO
VOLVAGIA FAILED?
YES, LORD GANONDORF.
BUT KILLING HIS OLD FRIEND HAS HURT THE HERO OF TIME DEEPLY.
NOW IS THE BEST TIME TO CONFRONT HIM.
HEH HEH HEH
SHEIK, KEEP WATCHING HIM.
YOU STILL HAVEN'T DISCOVERED WHERE PRINCESS ZELDA IS HIDING?
WE'VE SCOURED THE LAND...
...BUT STILL HAVEN'T FOUND A TRACE OF HER.
CAPTURING HER IS YOUR TOP PRIORITY. UNDERSTOOD?
WE CANNOT LET THOSE TWO FIND ONE ANOTHER!
YOUR WISH...
...IS MY COMMAND.

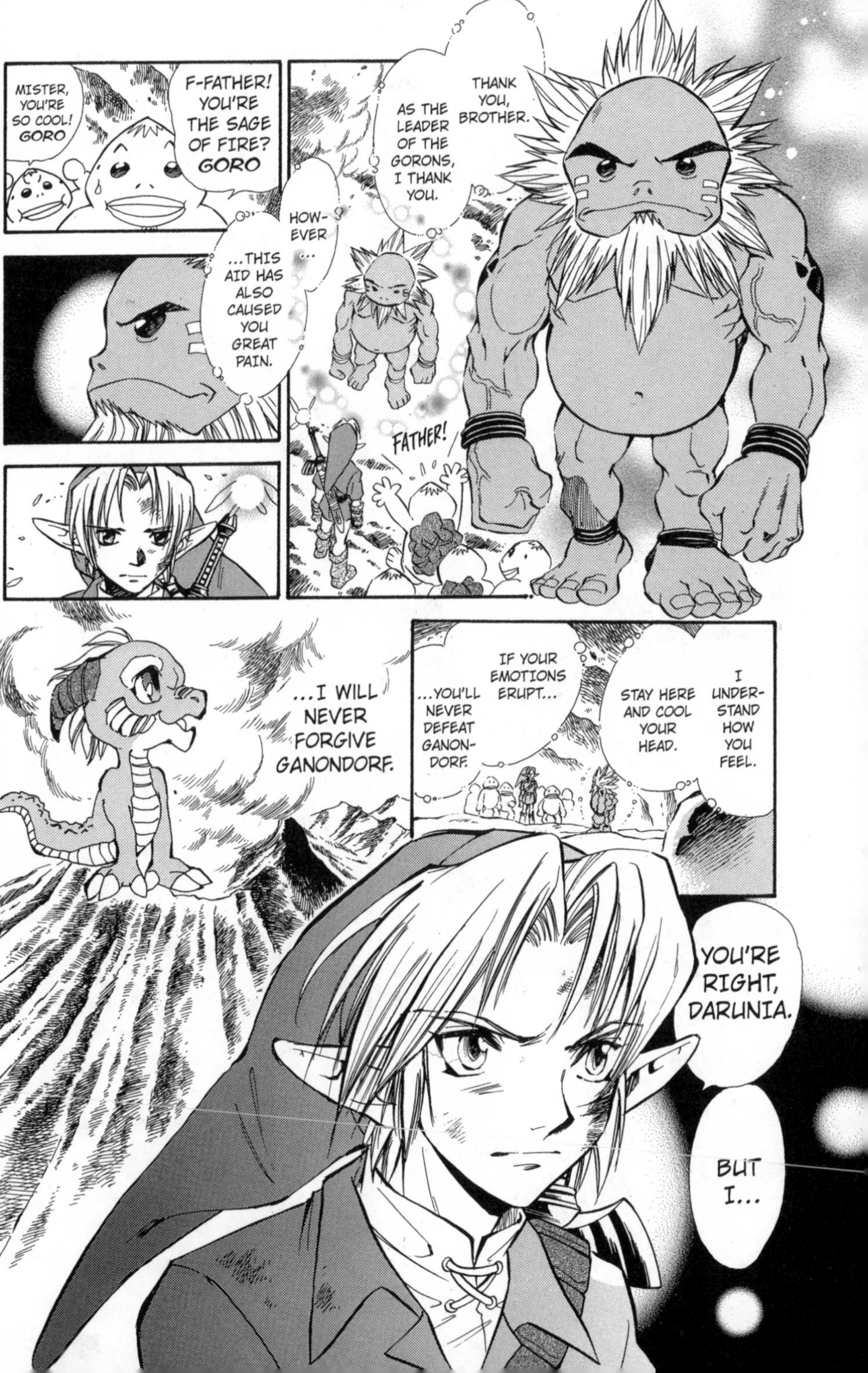
THANK YOU, BROTHER.
AS THE LEADER OF THE GORONS, I THANK YOU.
HOW-EVER...
...THIS AID HAS ALSO CAUSED YOU GREAT PAIN.
FATHER!
F-FATHER! YOU'RE THE SAGE OF FIRE? GORO
MISTER, YOU'RE SO COOL! GORO
I UNDER-STAND HOW YOU FEEL.
STAY HERE AND COOL YOUR HEAD.
IF YOUR EMOTIONS ERUPT...
...YOU'LL NEVER DEFEAT GANON-DORF.
...I WILL NEVER FORGIVE GANONDORF.
YOU'RE RIGHT, DARUNIA.
BUT I...

BONUS ILLUSTRATION 3

PRESENTING ANOTHER ROUGH SKETCH DONE BEFORE THE SERIES! IT'S UNUSUAL FOR HIM TO HOLD HIS SWORD IN HIS LEFT HAND.

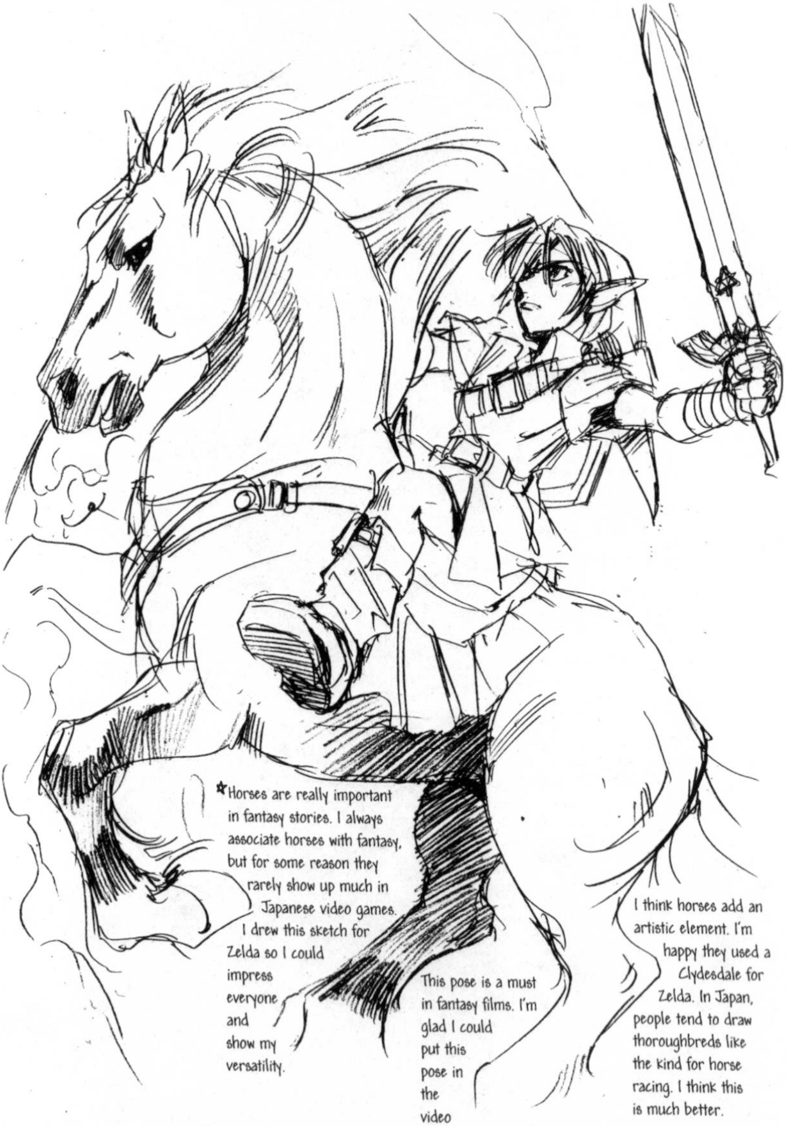

☆Horses are really important in fantasy stories. I always associate horses with fantasy, but for some reason they rarely show up much in Japanese video games. I drew this sketch for Zelda so I could impress everyone and show my versatility.
This pose is a must in fantasy films. I'm glad I could put this pose in the video game.
I think horses add an artistic element. I'm happy they used a Clydesdale for Zelda. In Japan, people tend to draw thoroughbreds like the kind for horse racing. I think this is much better.

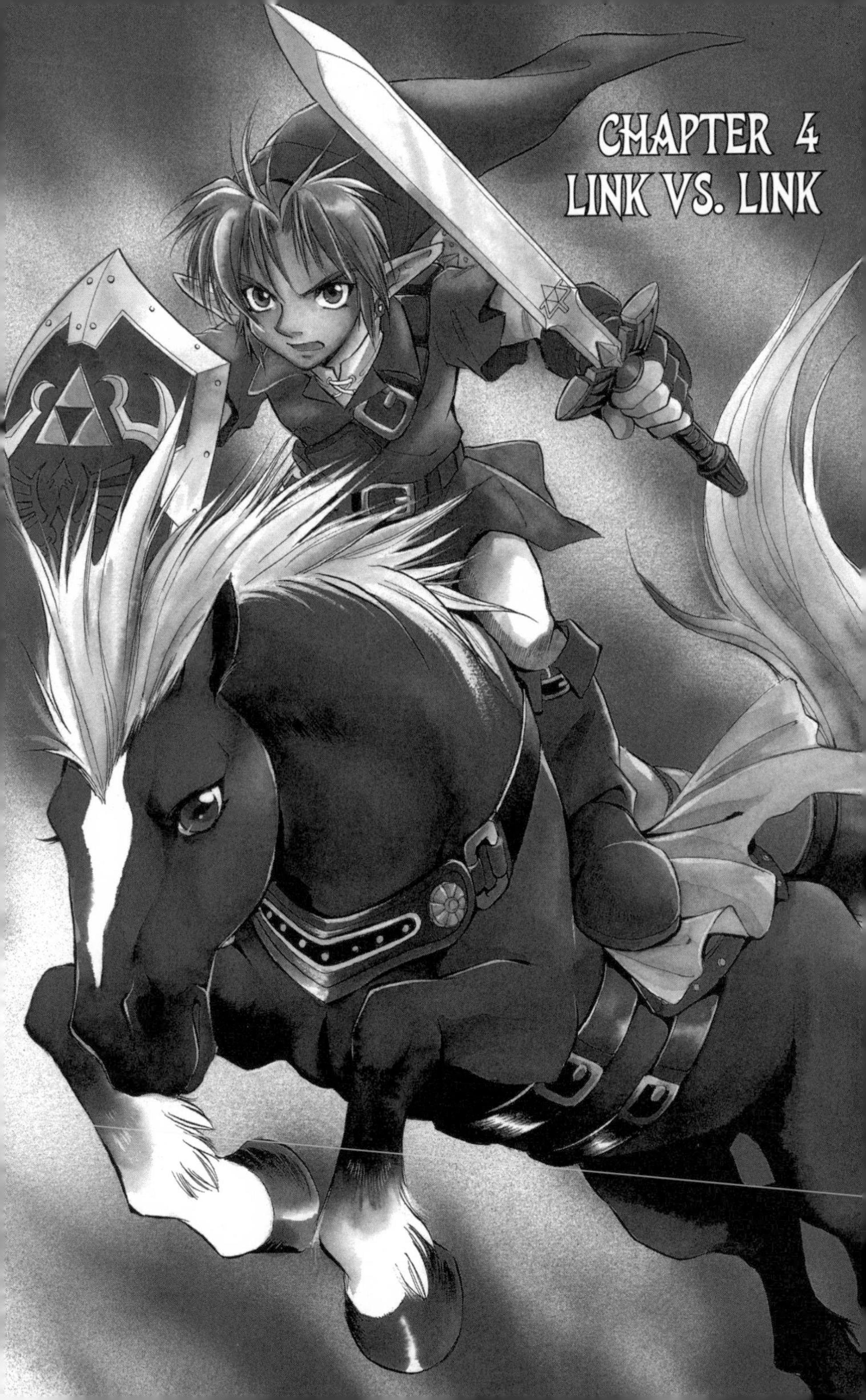
CHAPTER 4
LINK VS. LINK

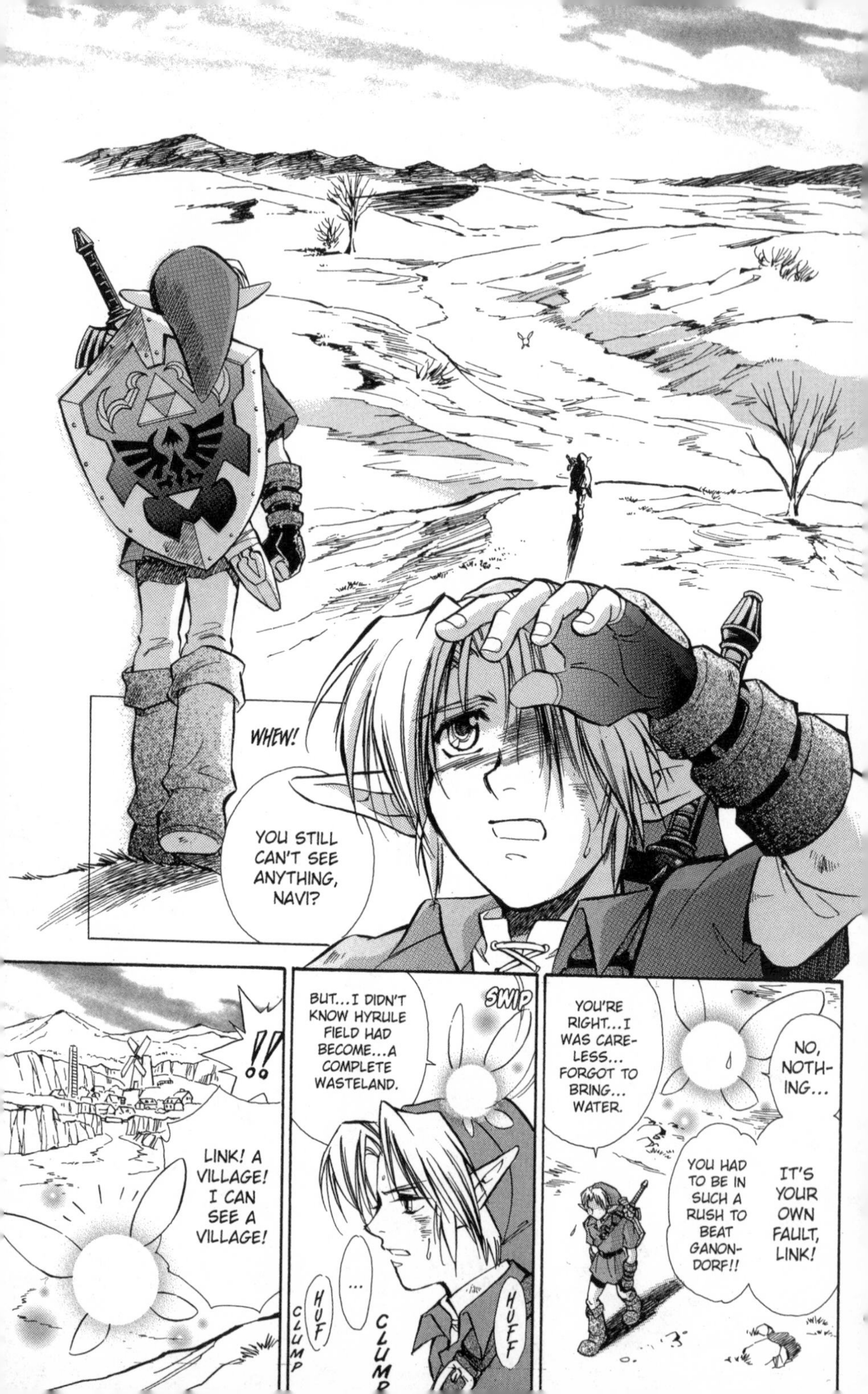
WHEW!
YOU STILL CAN'T SEE ANYTHING, NAVI?
NO, NOTHING...
IT'S YOUR OWN FAULT, LINK!
YOU HAD TO BE IN SUCH A RUSH TO BEAT GANONDORF!!
YOU'RE RIGHT...I WAS CARELESS... FORGOT TO BRING... WATER.
SWIP
BUT...I DIDN'T KNOW HYRULE FIELD HAD BECOME...A COMPLETE WASTELAND.
HUFF
...
HUF
CLUMP
CLUMP
!!
LINK! A VILLAGE! I CAN SEE A VILLAGE!

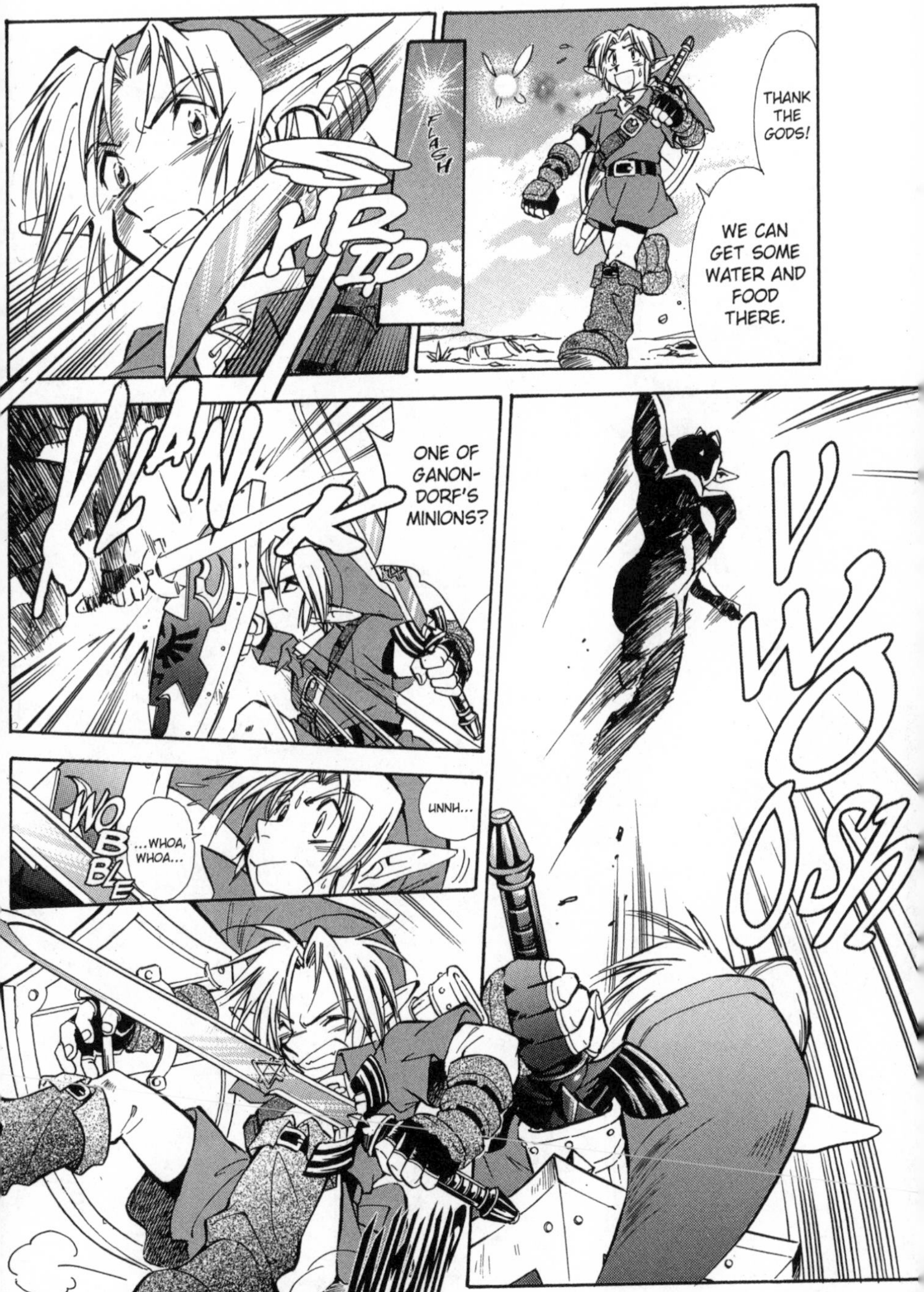
THANK THE GODS!
WE CAN GET SOME WATER AND FOOD THERE.
FLASH
SHRIP
VWOOSH
KLANK
ONE OF GANON-DORF'S MINIONS?
UNNH...
WOBBLE
...WHOA, WHOA...

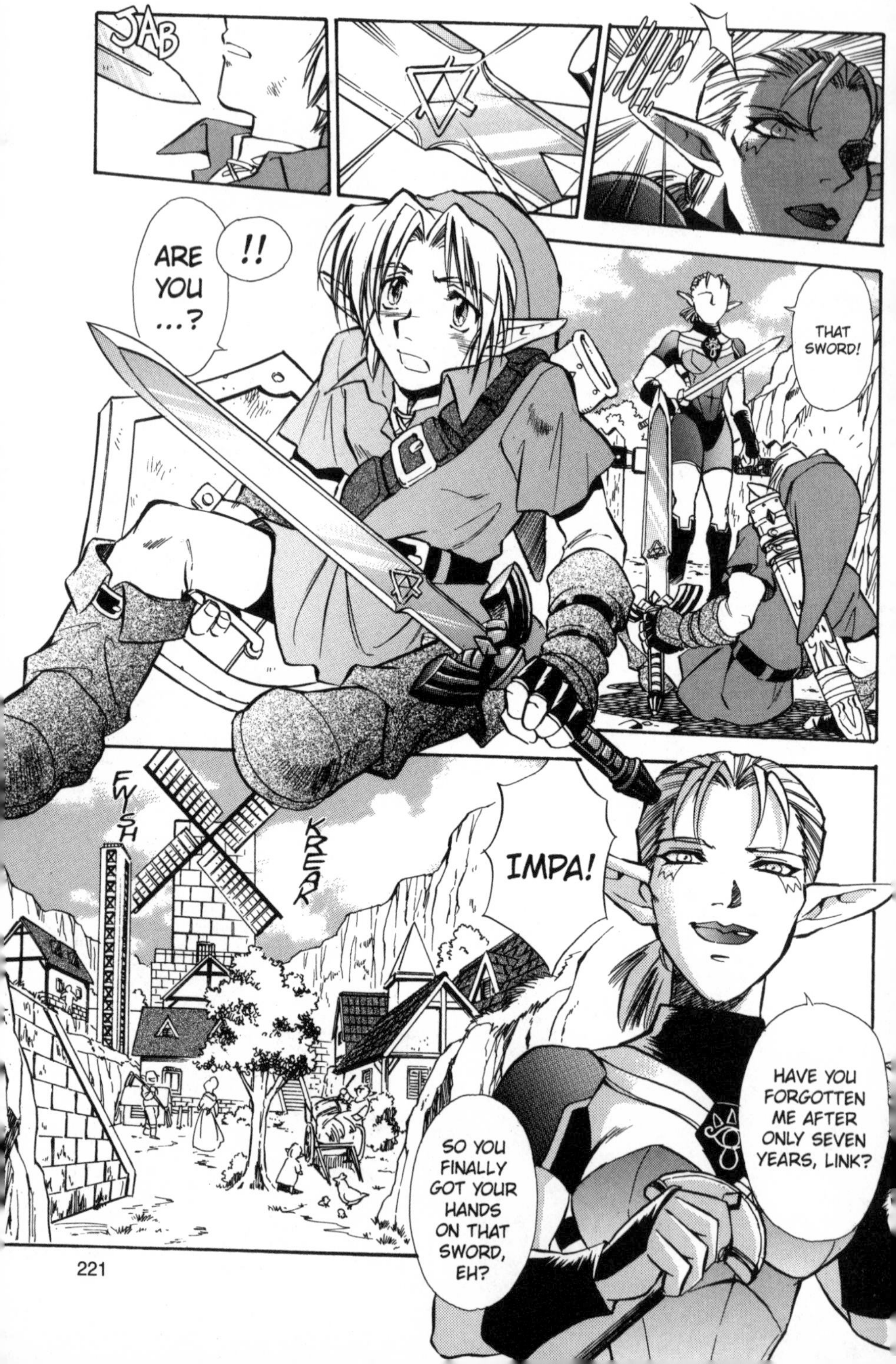
HUP
JAB
THAT SWORD!
!!
ARE YOU ...?
IMPA!
HAVE YOU FORGOTTEN ME AFTER ONLY SEVEN YEARS, LINK?
SO YOU FINALLY GOT YOUR HANDS ON THAT SWORD, EH?
KREAK
FWISH

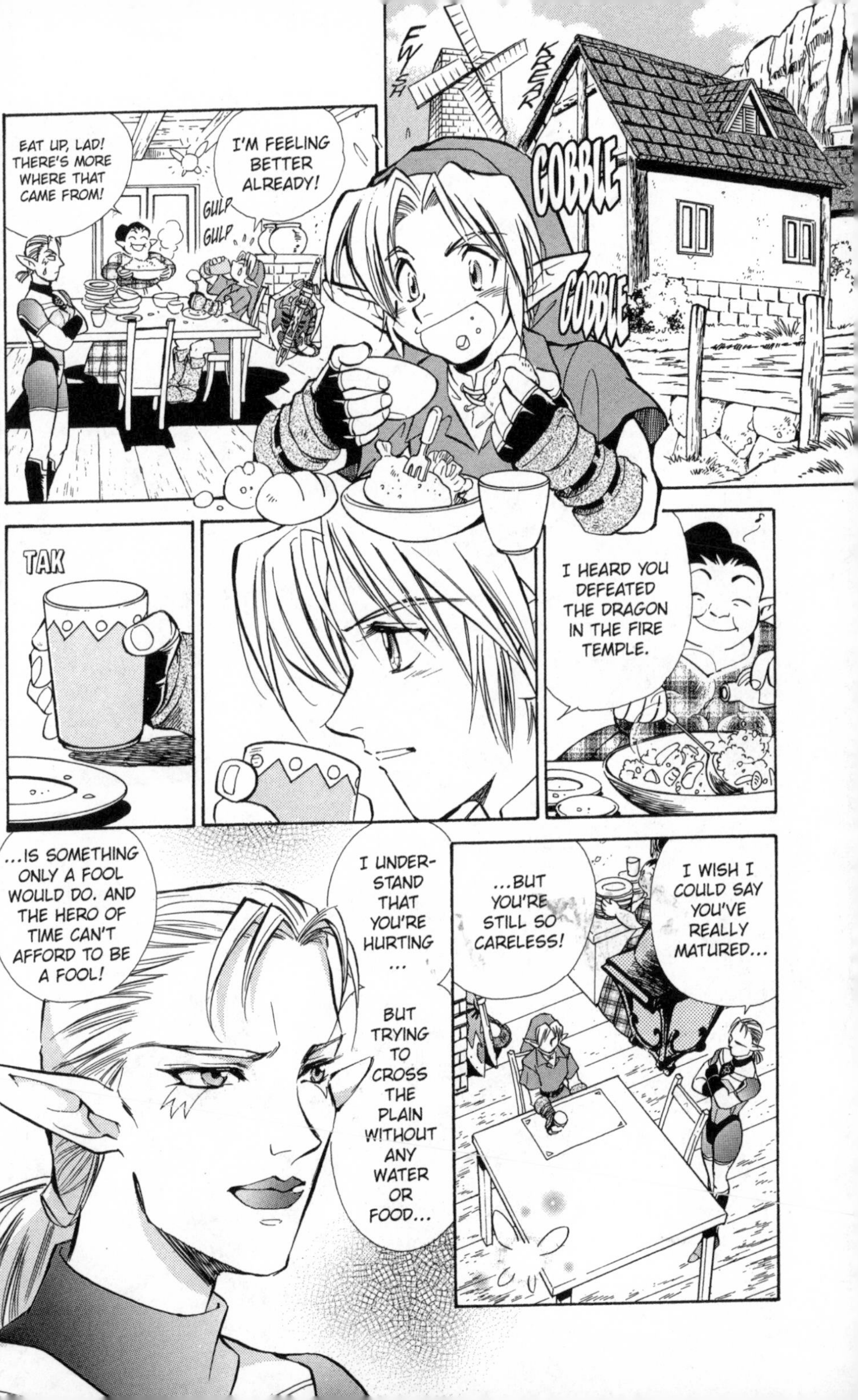
FWISH
KREAK
GOBBLE
GOBBLE
I'M FEELING BETTER ALREADY!
GULP GULP
EAT UP, LAD! THERE'S MORE WHERE THAT CAME FROM!
I HEARD YOU DEFEATED THE DRAGON IN THE FIRE TEMPLE.
TAK
I WISH I COULD SAY YOU'VE REALLY MATURED...
...BUT YOU'RE STILL SO CARELESS!
I UNDER-STAND THAT YOU'RE HURTING...
BUT TRYING TO CROSS THE PLAIN WITHOUT ANY WATER OR FOOD...
...IS SOMETHING ONLY A FOOL WOULD DO. AND THE HERO OF TIME CAN'T AFFORD TO BE A FOOL!

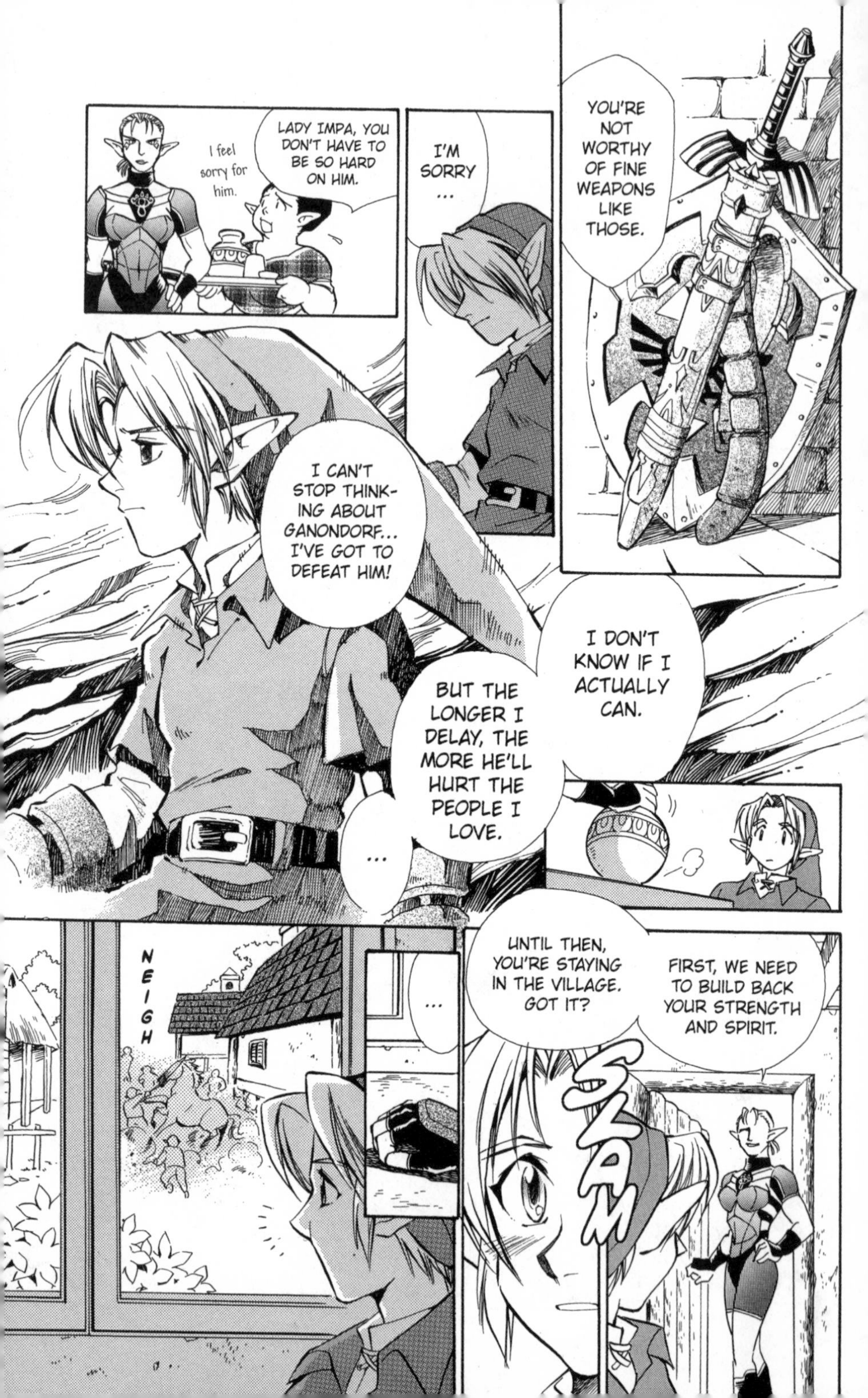
YOU'RE NOT WORTHY OF FINE WEAPONS LIKE THOSE.
I'M SORRY ...
LADY IMPA, YOU DON'T HAVE TO BE SO HARD ON HIM.
I feel sorry for him.
I CAN'T STOP THINK-ING ABOUT GANONDORF... I'VE GOT TO DEFEAT HIM!
I DON'T KNOW IF I ACTUALLY CAN.
BUT THE LONGER I DELAY, THE MORE HE'LL HURT THE PEOPLE I LOVE.
...
FIRST, WE NEED TO BUILD BACK YOUR STRENGTH AND SPIRIT.
UNTIL THEN, YOU'RE STAYING IN THE VILLAGE. GOT IT?
SLAM
...
NEIGH

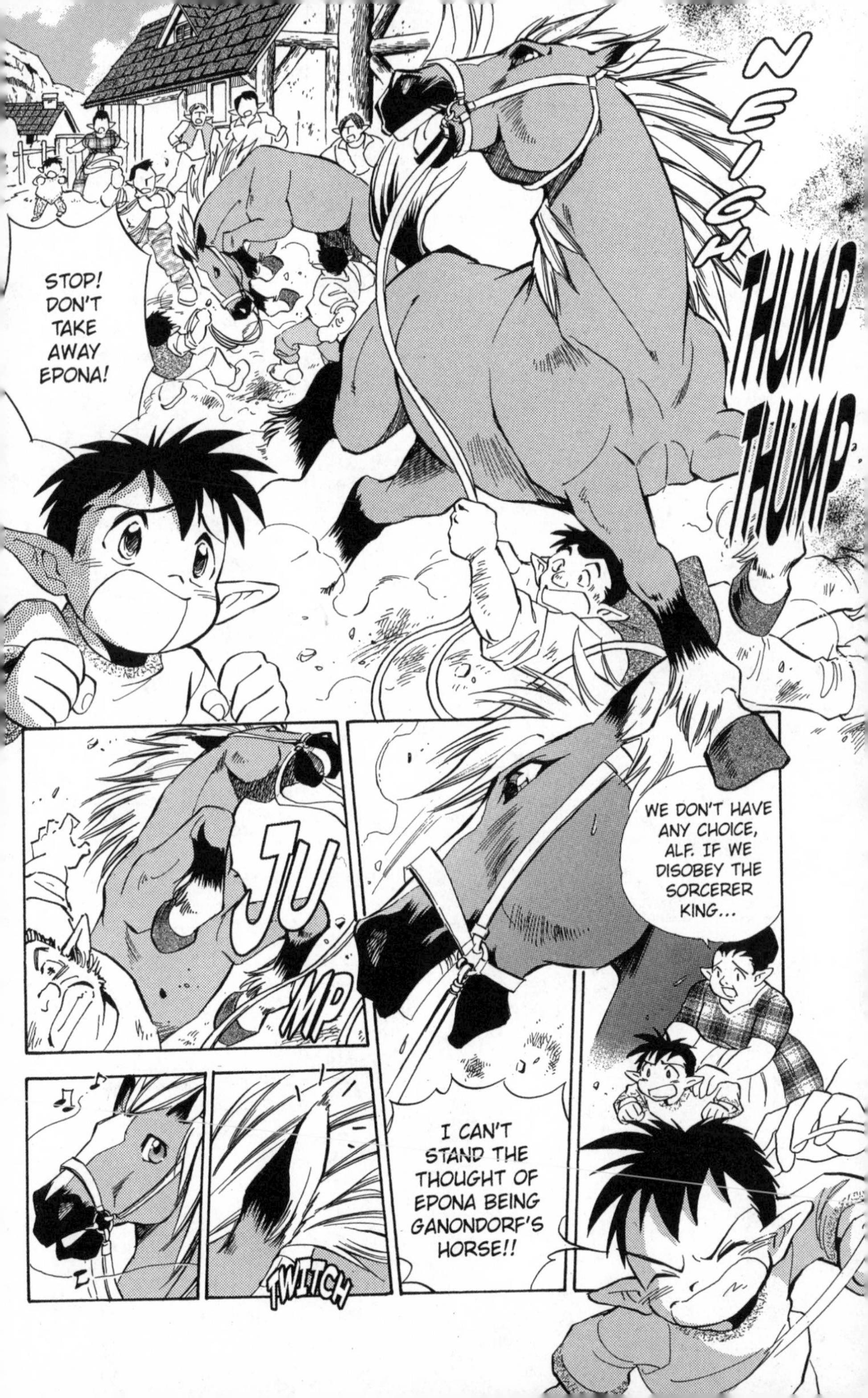
NEIGH
THUMP
THUMP
STOP! DON'T TAKE AWAY EPONA!
WE DON'T HAVE ANY CHOICE, ALF. IF WE DISOBEY THE SORCERER KING...
I CAN'T STAND THE THOUGHT OF EPONA BEING GANONDORF'S HORSE!!
JUMP
TWITCH

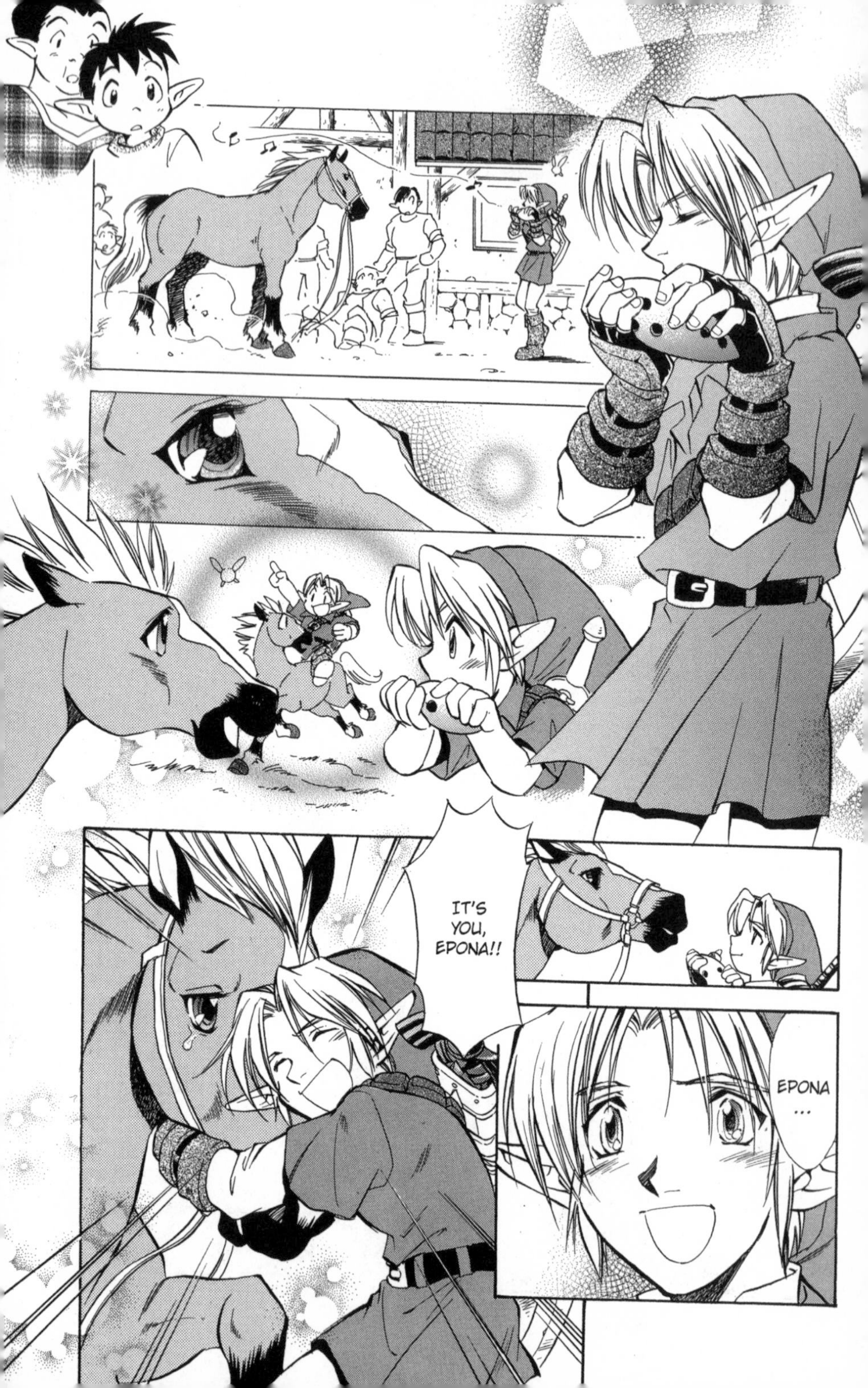
IT'S YOU, EPONA!!
EPONA ...

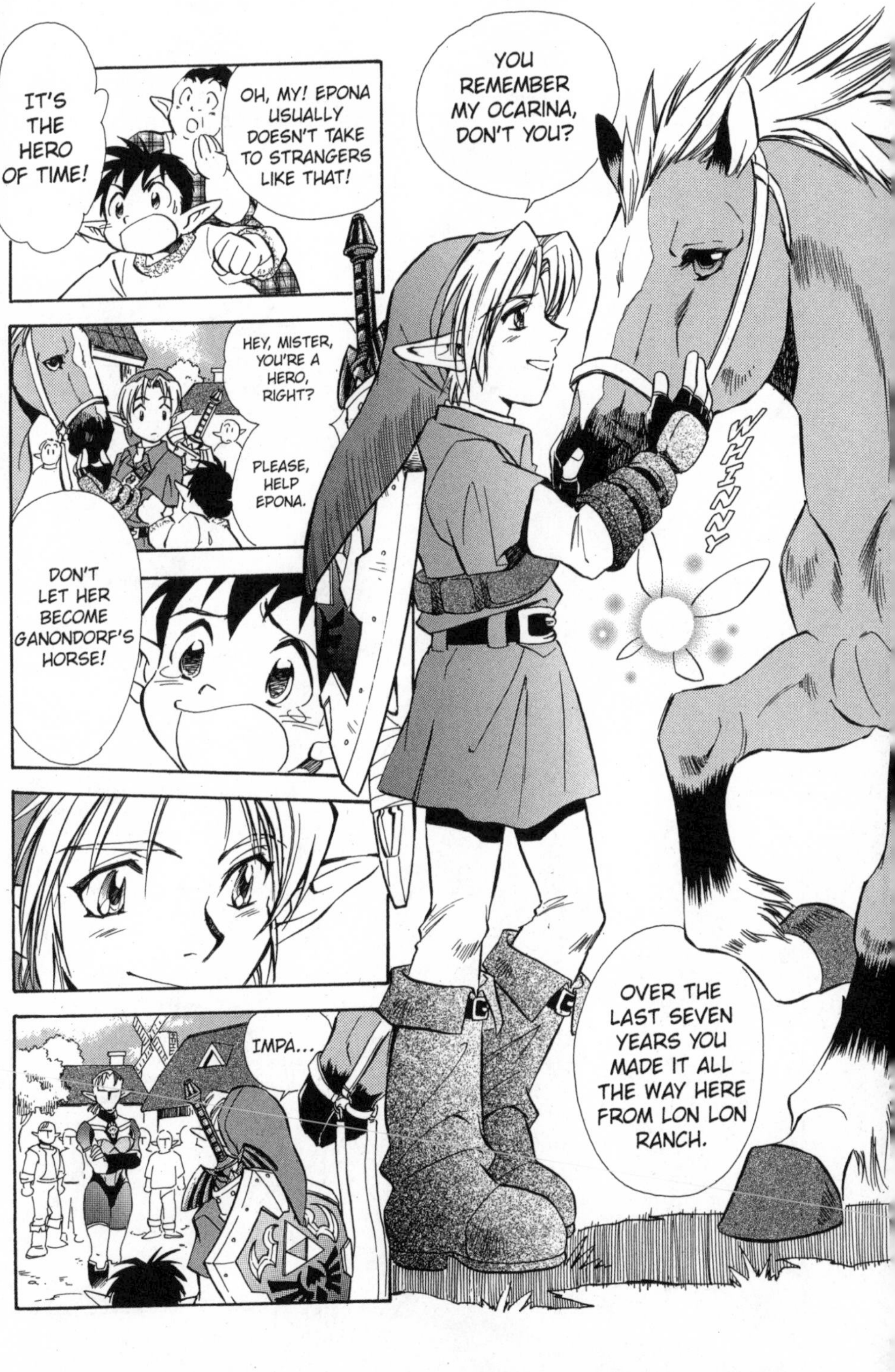
YOU REMEMBER MY OCARINA, DON'T YOU?
WHINNY
OVER THE LAST SEVEN YEARS YOU MADE IT ALL THE WAY HERE FROM LON LON RANCH.
OH, MY! EPONA USUALLY DOESN'T TAKE TO STRANGERS LIKE THAT!
IT'S THE HERO OF TIME!
HEY, MISTER, YOU'RE A HERO, RIGHT?
PLEASE, HELP EPONA.
DON'T LET HER BECOME GANONDORF'S HORSE!
IMPA...

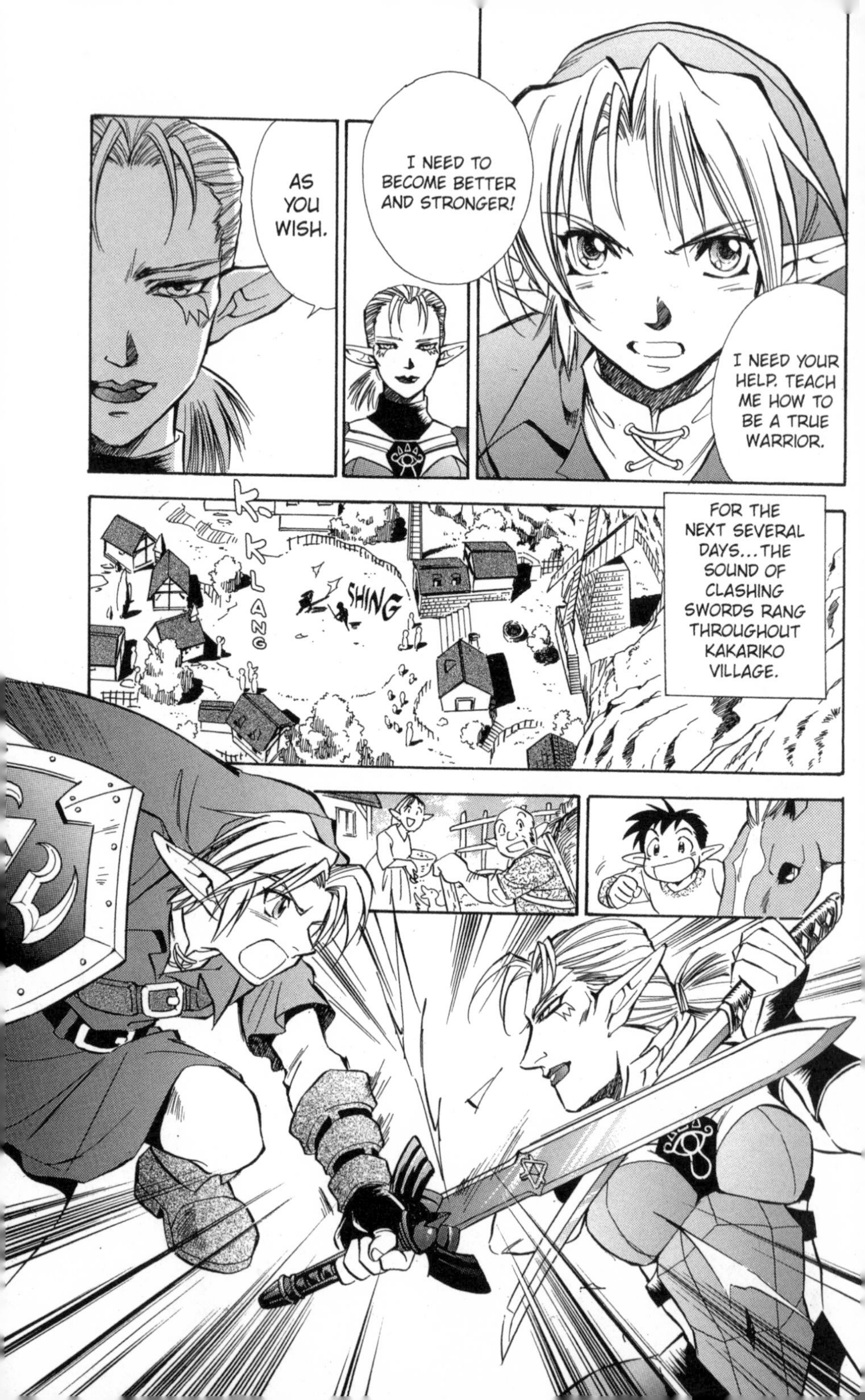
I NEED TO BECOME BETTER AND STRONGER!
I NEED YOUR HELP. TEACH ME HOW TO BE A TRUE WARRIOR.
AS YOU WISH.
FOR THE NEXT SEVERAL DAYS...THE SOUND OF CLASHING SWORDS RANG THROUGHOUT KAKARIKO VILLAGE.
SHING
K-KLANG

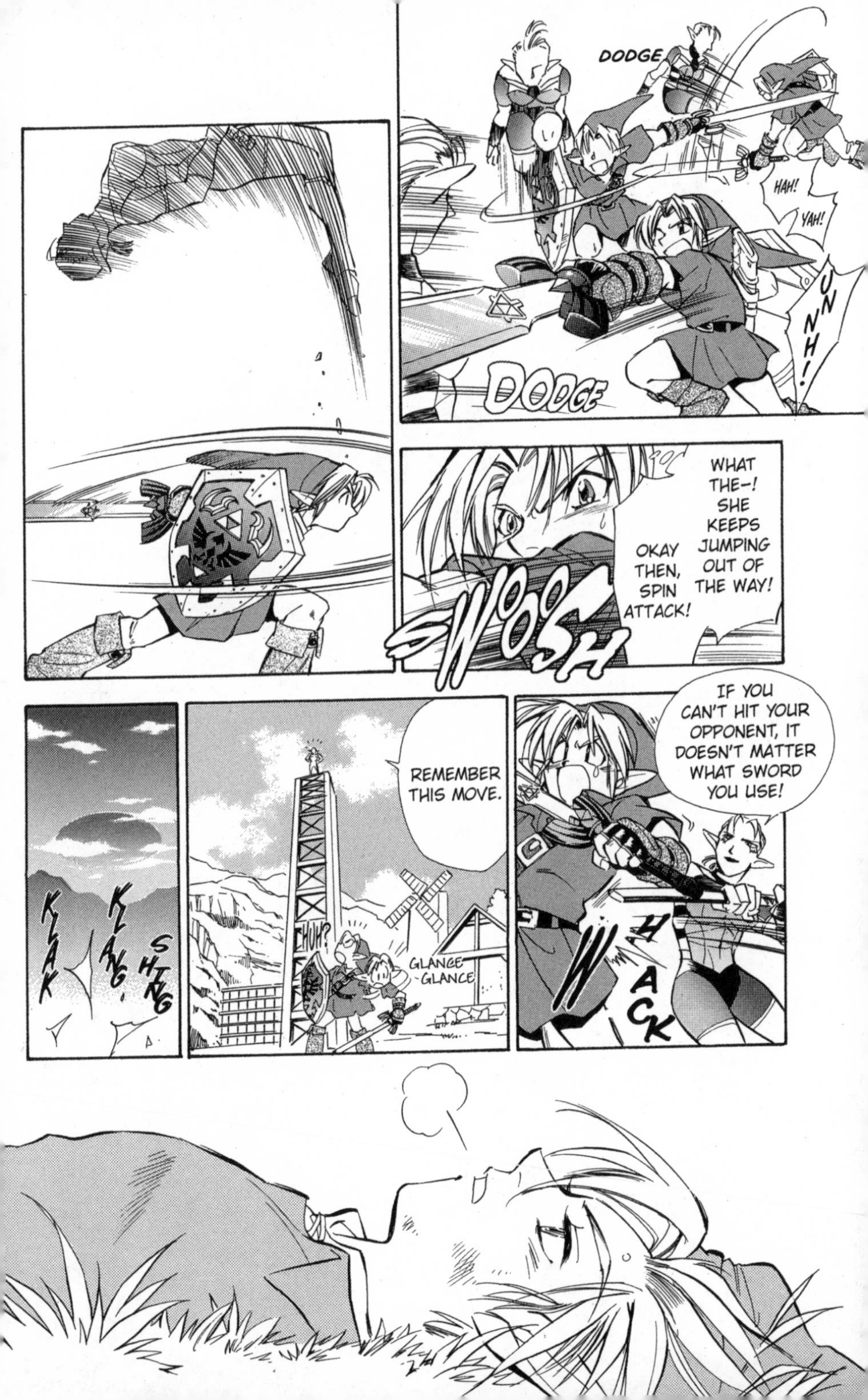
DODGE
HAH!
YAH!
UNNH!
DODGE
WHAT THE-! SHE KEEPS JUMPING OUT OF THE WAY!
OKAY THEN, SPIN ATTACK!
SWOOSH
IF YOU CAN'T HIT YOUR OPPONENT, IT DOESN'T MATTER WHAT SWORD YOU USE!
WHACK
REMEMBER THIS MOVE.
HUH?
GLANCE GLANCE
SHING
KLANG
KLAK

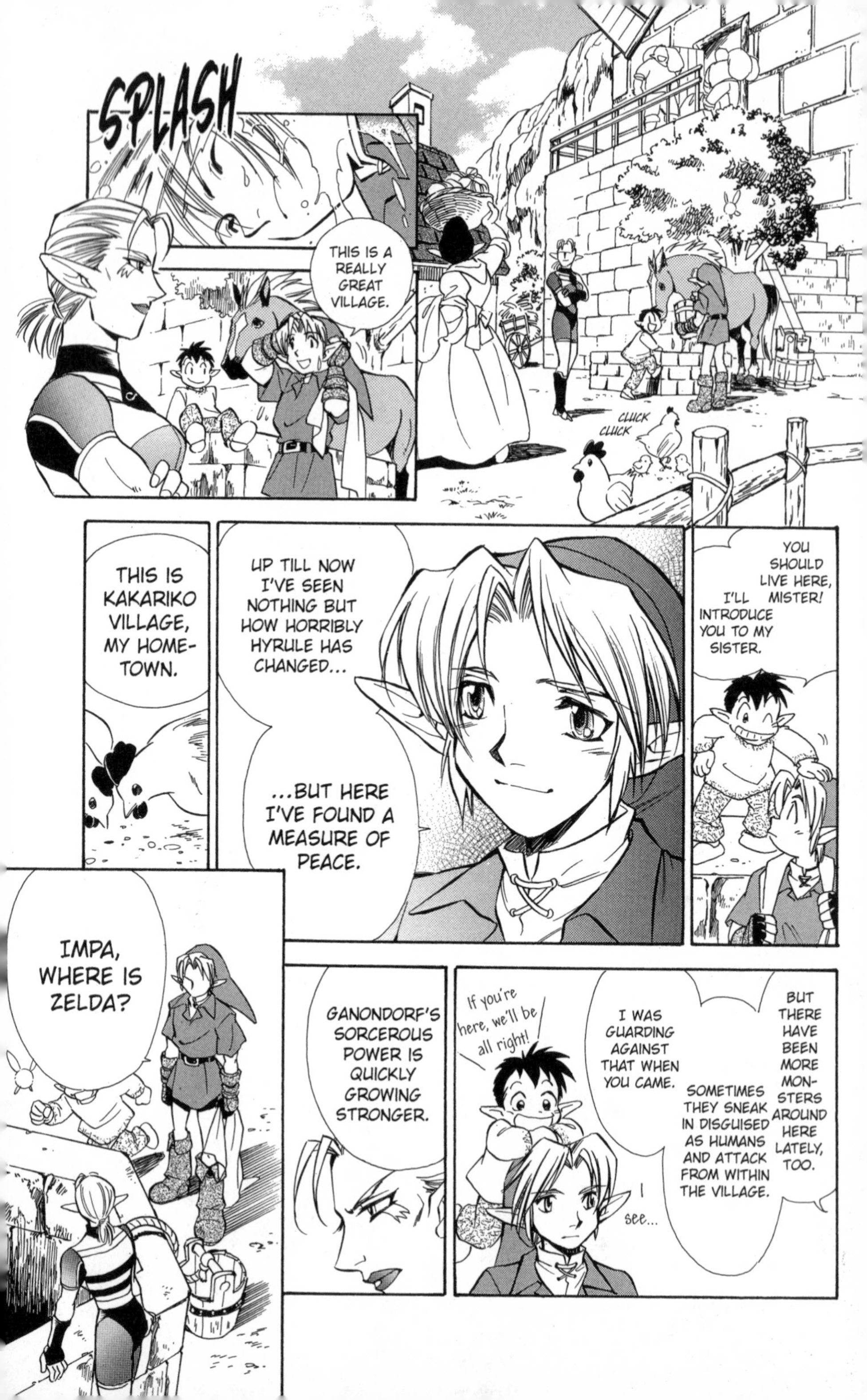
CLUCK CLUCK
THIS IS A REALLY GREAT VILLAGE.
SPLASH
YOU SHOULD LIVE HERE, MISTER!
I'LL INTRODUCE YOU TO MY SISTER.
UP TILL NOW I'VE SEEN NOTHING BUT HOW HORRIBLY HYRULE HAS CHANGED...
...BUT HERE I'VE FOUND A MEASURE OF PEACE.
THIS IS KAKARIKO VILLAGE, MY HOME-TOWN.
BUT THERE HAVE BEEN MORE MON-STERS AROUND HERE LATELY, TOO.
I WAS GUARDING AGAINST THAT WHEN YOU CAME.
SOMETIMES THEY SNEAK IN DISGUISED AS HUMANS AND ATTACK FROM WITHIN THE VILLAGE.
If you're here, we'll be all right!
I see...
GANONDORF'S SORCEROUS POWER IS QUICKLY GROWING STRONGER.
IMPA, WHERE IS ZELDA?

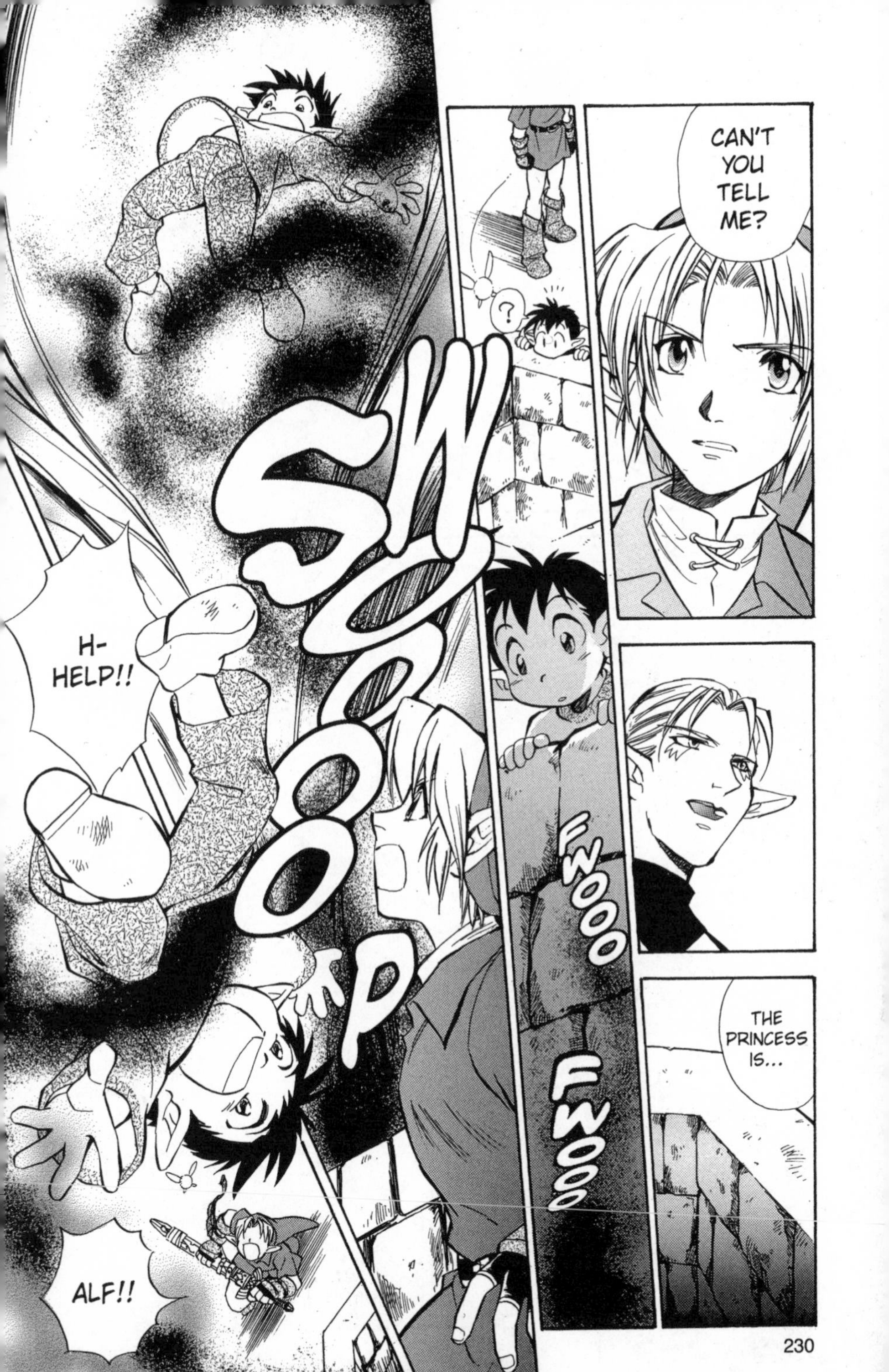
CAN'T YOU TELL ME?
?
THE PRINCESS IS...
FWOOO
FWOOO
SWOOOOP
H-HELP!!
ALF!!

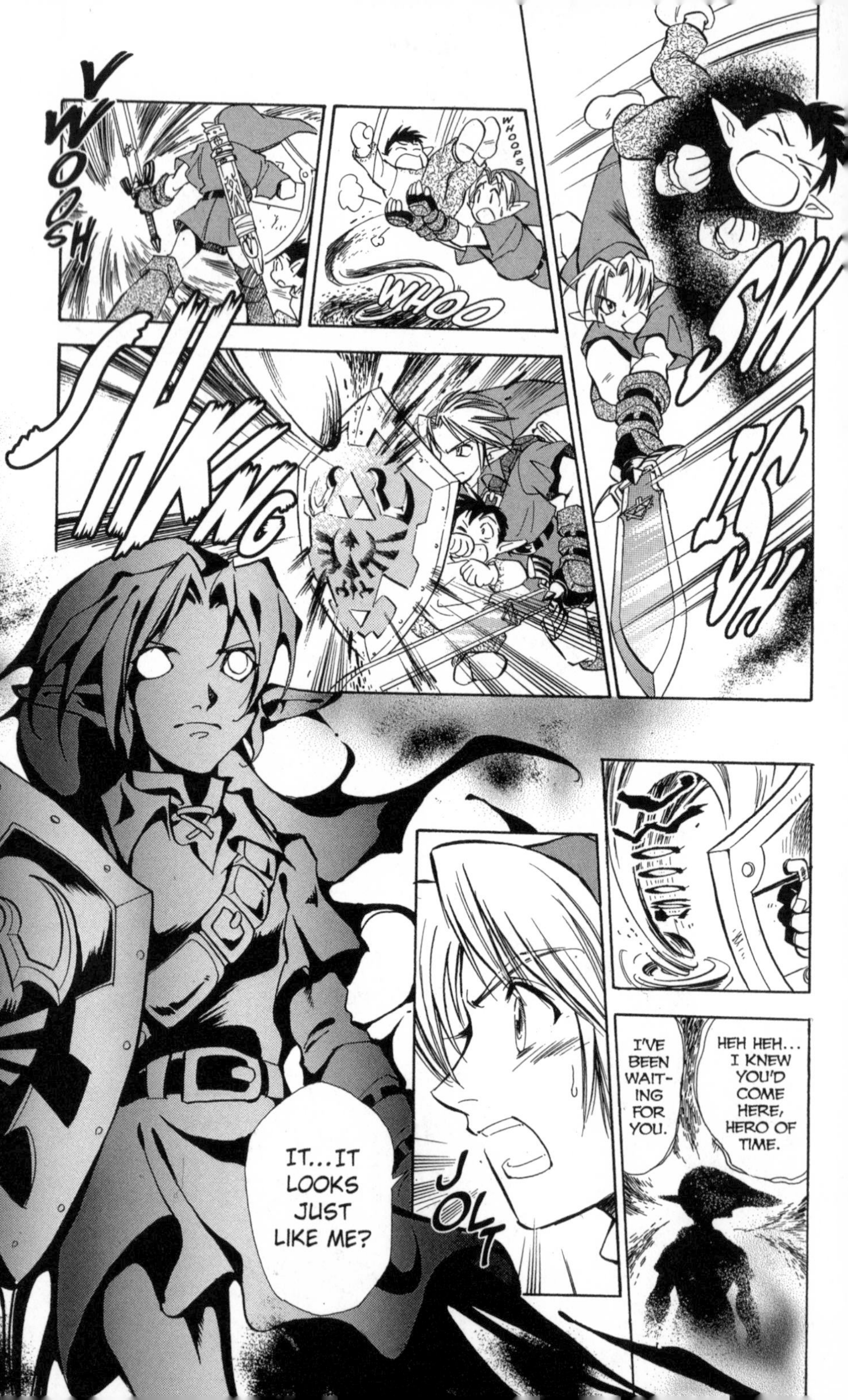
WHOOPS!
WHOO
VWOOOSH
SHKNG
HEH HEH... I KNEW YOU'D COME HERE, HERO OF TIME.
I'VE BEEN WAIT-ING FOR YOU.
JOLT
IT...IT LOOKS JUST LIKE ME?

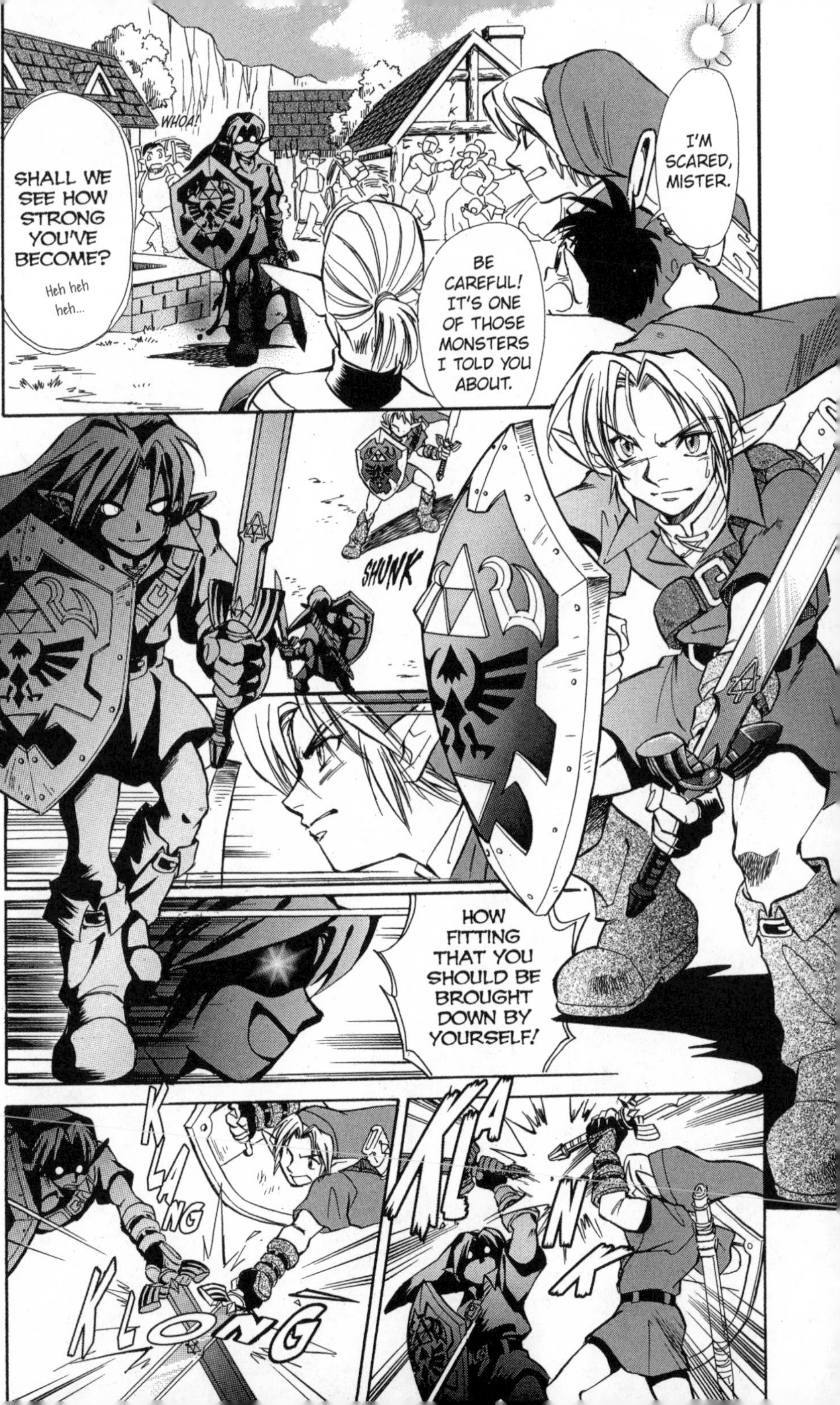
I'M SCARED, MISTER.
YIKES!
BE CAREFUL! IT'S ONE OF THOSE MONSTERS I TOLD YOU ABOUT.
WHOA!
SHALL WE SEE HOW STRONG YOU'VE BECOME?
Heh heh heh...
SHUNK
HOW FITTING THAT YOU SHOULD BE BROUGHT DOWN BY YOURSELF!
KLANK
KLANG
KLONG

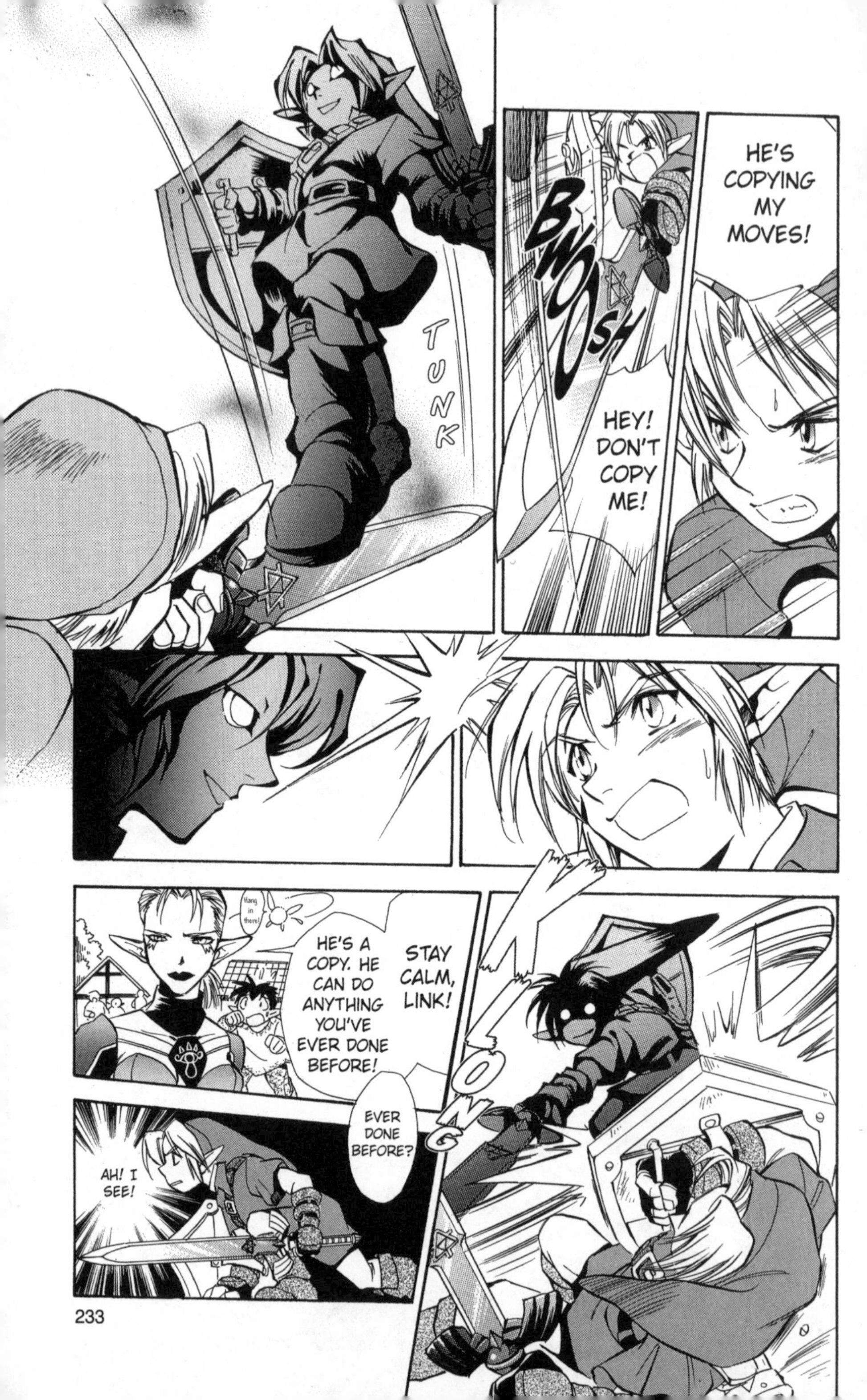

HE'S COPYING MY MOVES!
BWOOSH
HEY! DON'T COPY ME!
TUNK
STAY CALM, LINK!
HE'S A COPY. HE CAN DO ANYTHING YOU'VE EVER DONE BEFORE!
Hang in there!
EVER DONE BEFORE?
AH! I SEE!

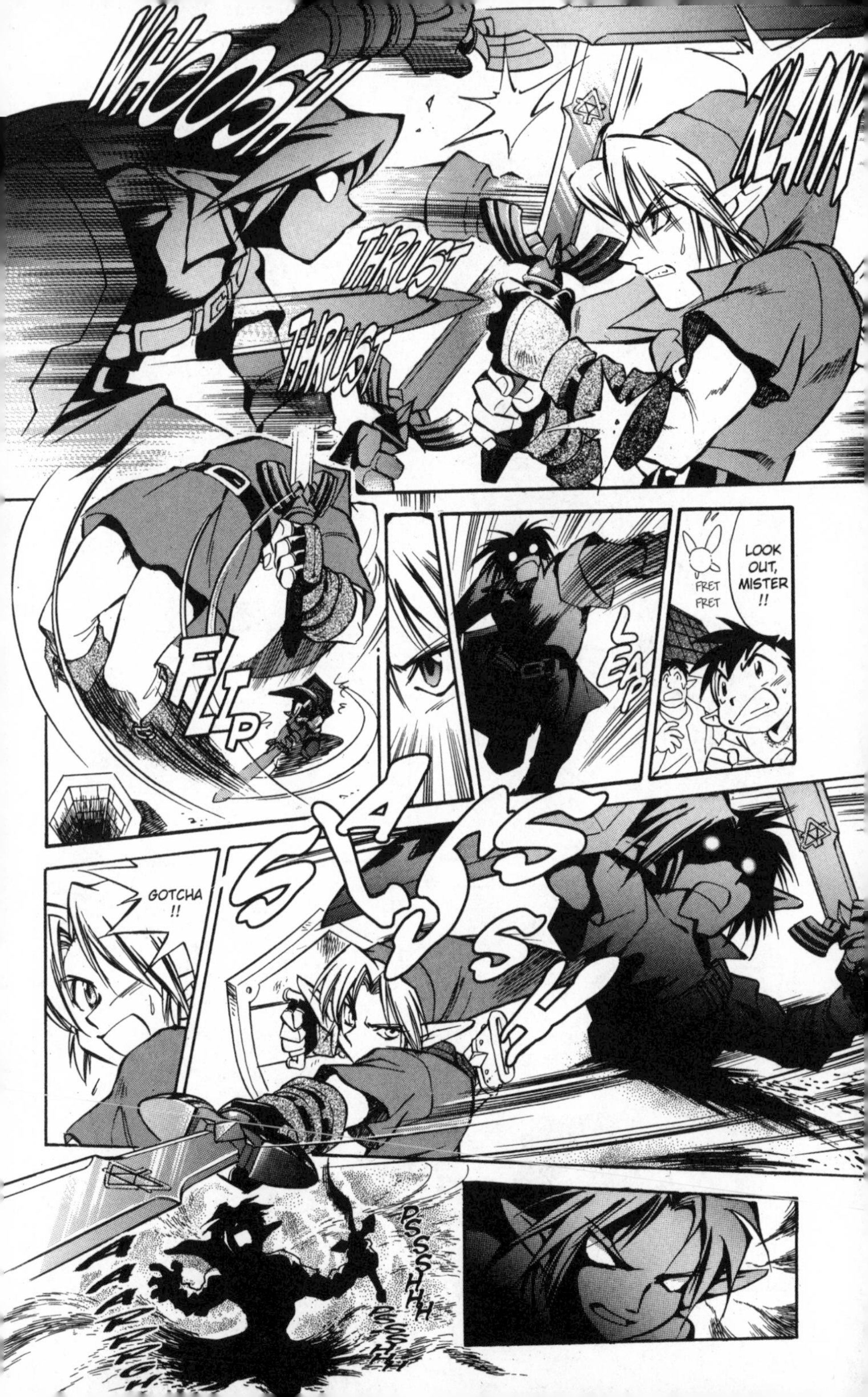
KLANK
WHOOSH
THRUST
THRUST
LOOK OUT, MISTER !!
FRET FRET
LEAP
FLIP
SLASSSH!
GOTCHA !!
PSSSHHH
PSSSHH
AAAAAGH

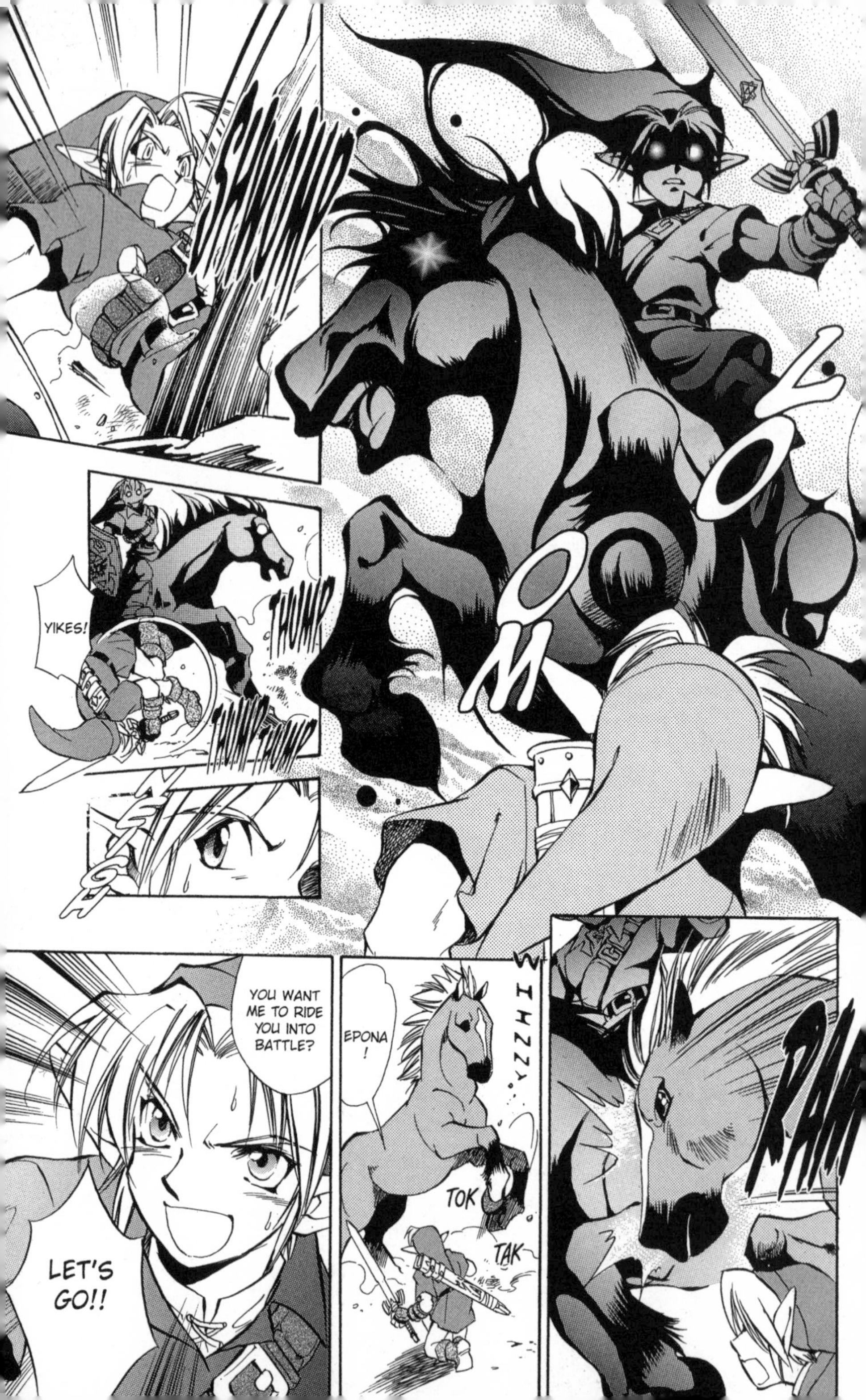
YIKES!
THUMP
THUMP THUMP
EPONA!
TOK
TAK
YOU WANT ME TO RIDE YOU INTO BATTLE?
LET'S GO!!

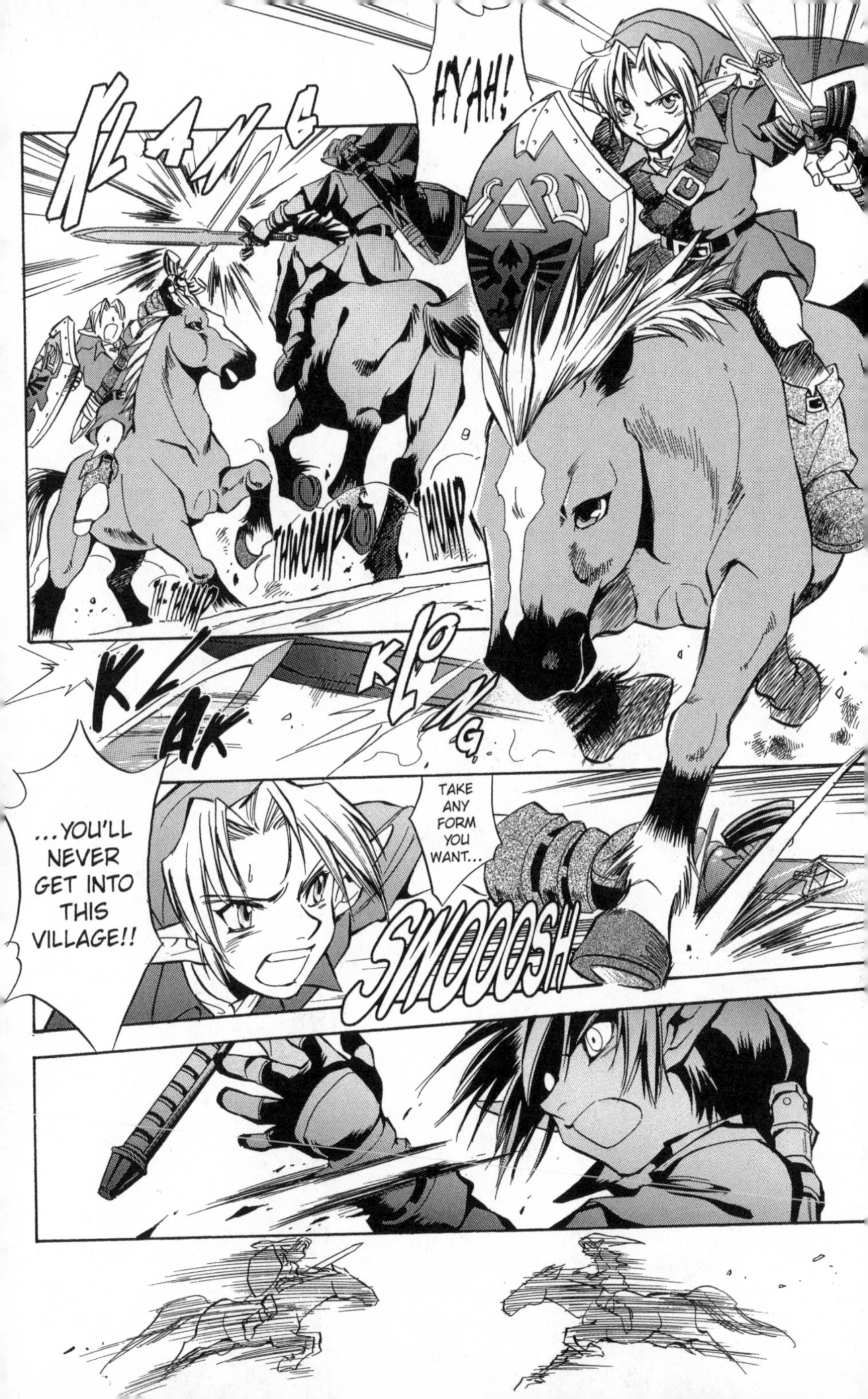
HYAH!
KLANG
THUMP
THWUMP
TH-THUMP
KLONG
KLAK
TAKE ANY FORM YOU WANT...
...YOU'LL NEVER GET INTO THIS VILLAGE!!
SWOOOSH

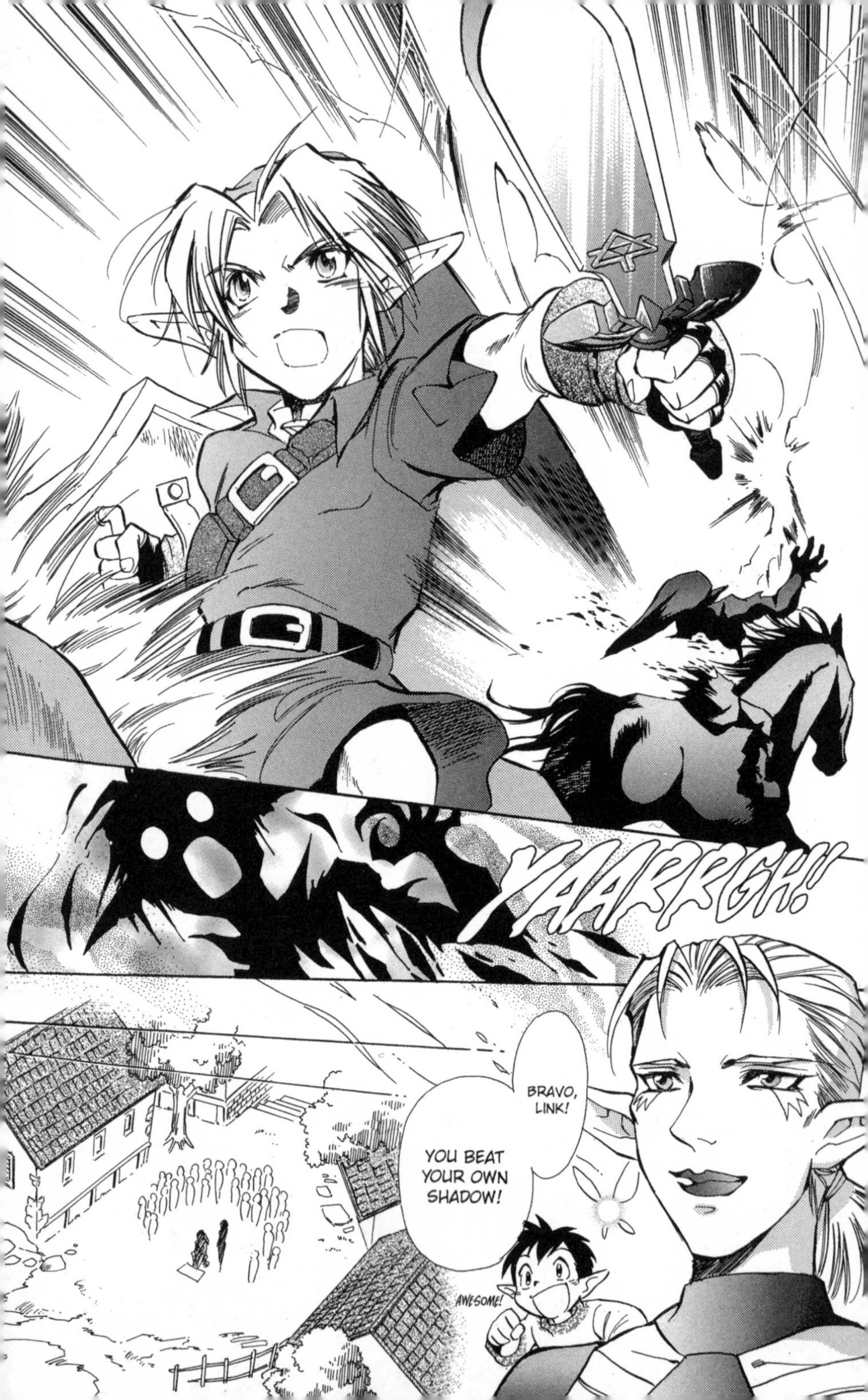
YAARRGH!
BRAVO, LINK!
YOU BEAT YOUR OWN SHADOW!
AWESOME!

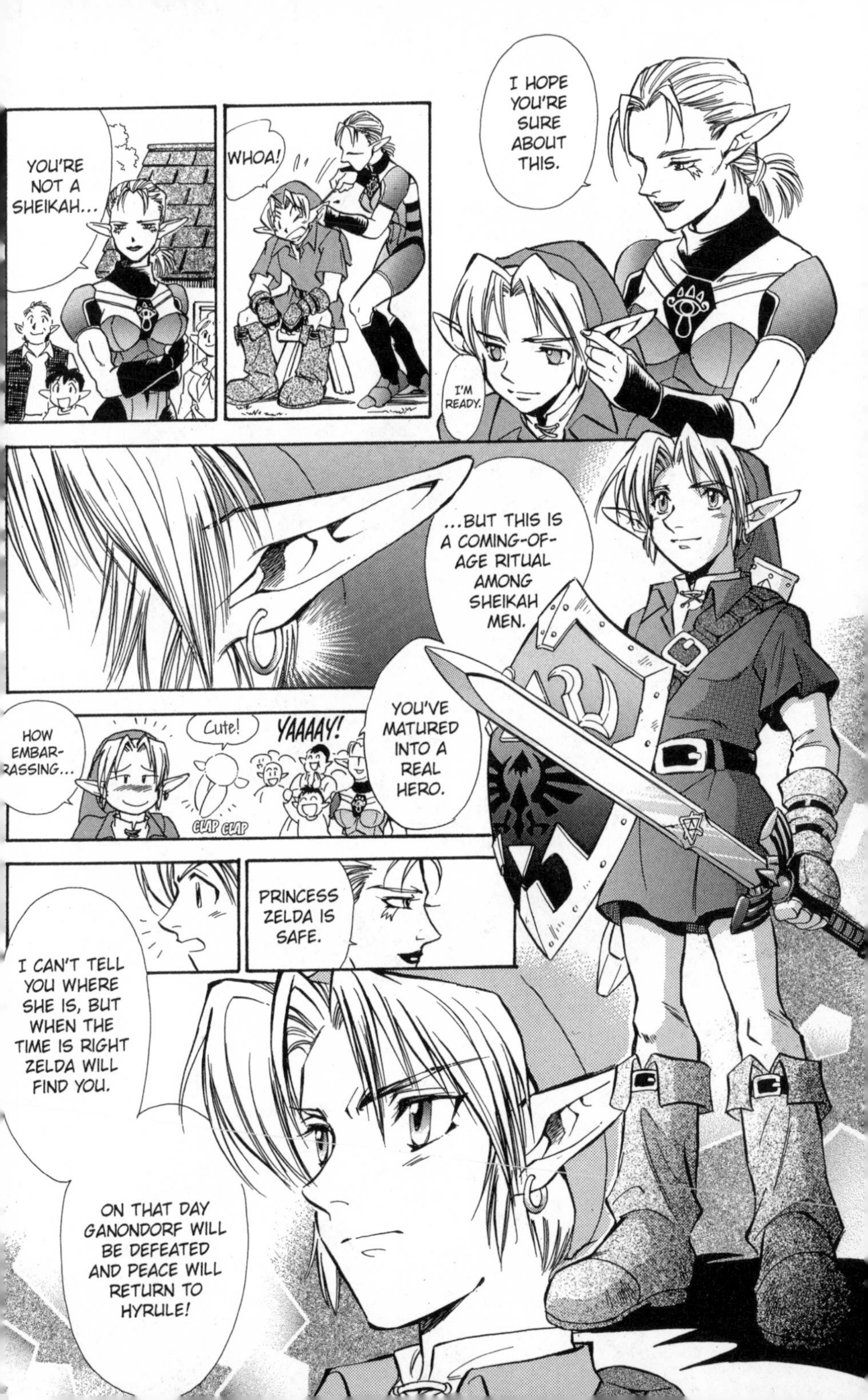

I HOPE YOU'RE SURE ABOUT THIS.
I'M READY.
WHOA!
YOU'RE NOT A SHEIKAH...
...BUT THIS IS A COMING-OF-AGE RITUAL AMONG SHEIKAH MEN.
YOU'VE MATURED INTO A REAL HERO.
YAAAAY!
Cute!
HOW EMBAR-RASSING...
CLAP CLAP
PRINCESS ZELDA IS SAFE.
I CAN'T TELL YOU WHERE SHE IS, BUT WHEN THE TIME IS RIGHT ZELDA WILL FIND YOU.
ON THAT DAY GANONDORF WILL BE DEFEATED AND PEACE WILL RETURN TO HYRULE!

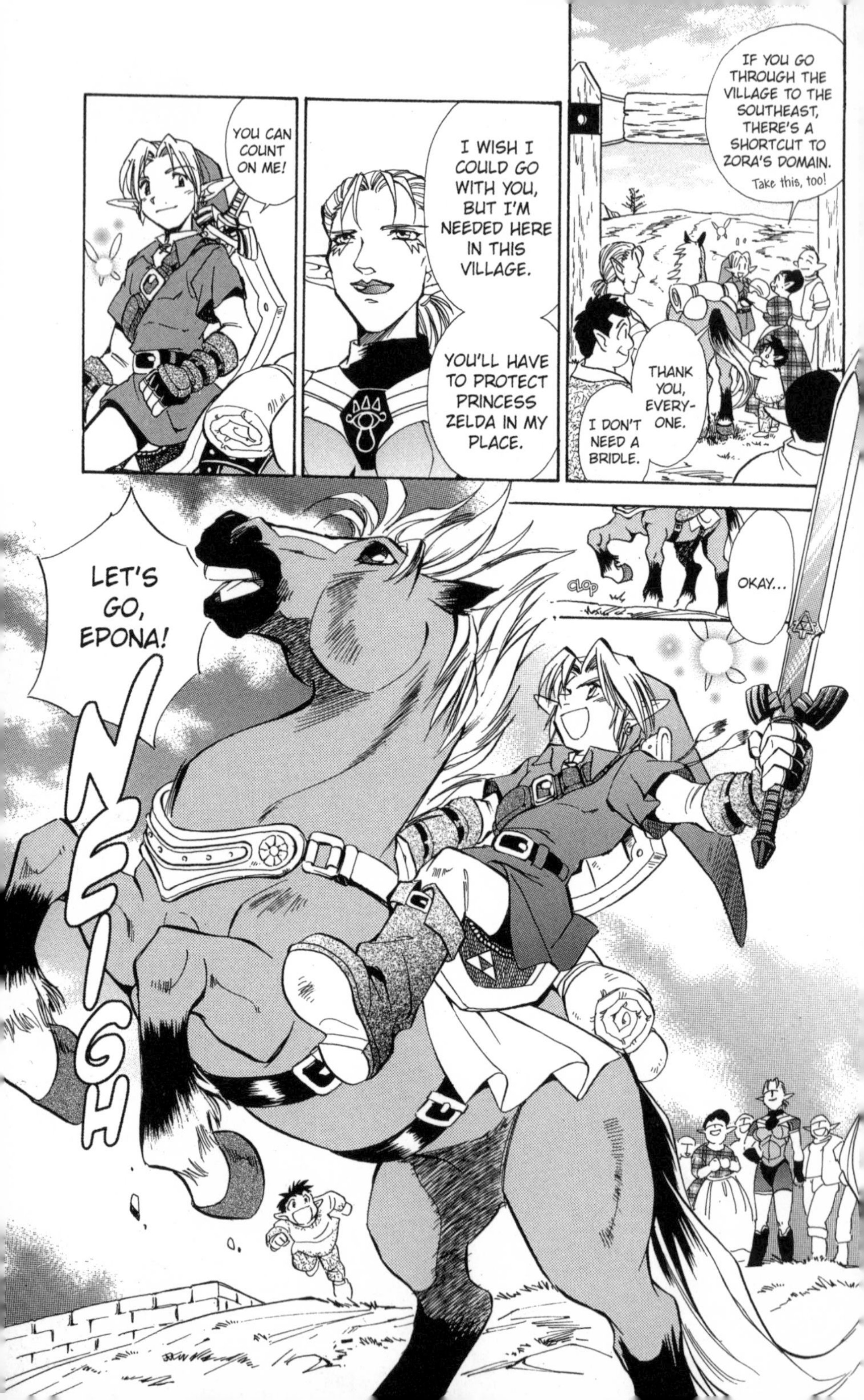
IF YOU GO THROUGH THE VILLAGE TO THE SOUTHEAST, THERE'S A SHORTCUT TO ZORA'S DOMAIN.
Take this, too!
THANK YOU, EVERY-ONE.
I DON'T NEED A BRIDLE.
I WISH I COULD GO WITH YOU, BUT I'M NEEDED HERE IN THIS VILLAGE.
YOU'LL HAVE TO PROTECT PRINCESS ZELDA IN MY PLACE.
YOU CAN COUNT ON ME!
OKAY...
CLOP
LET'S GO, EPONA!
NEIGH

CHAPTER 5
SHADOW GUIDE: SHEIK

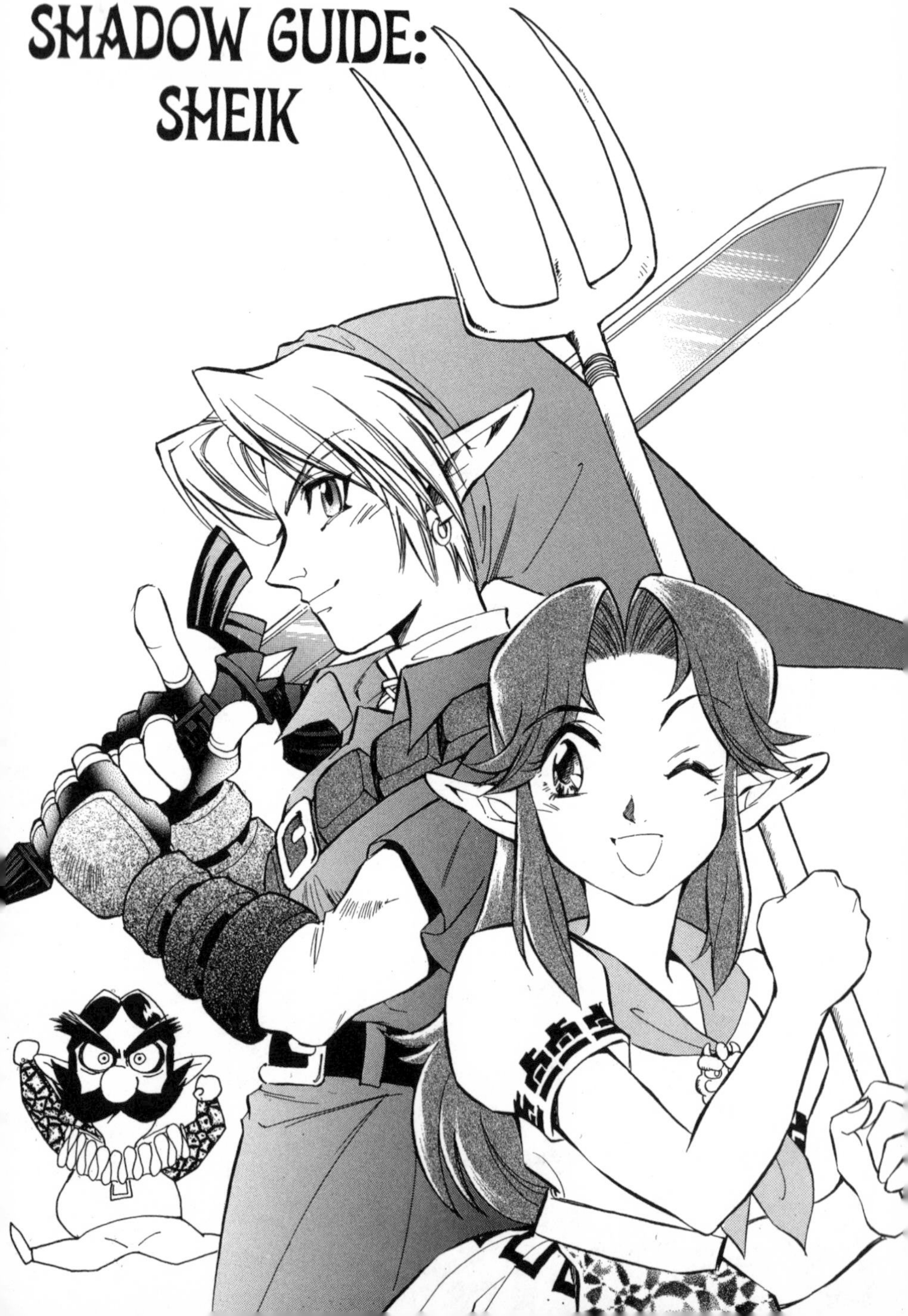

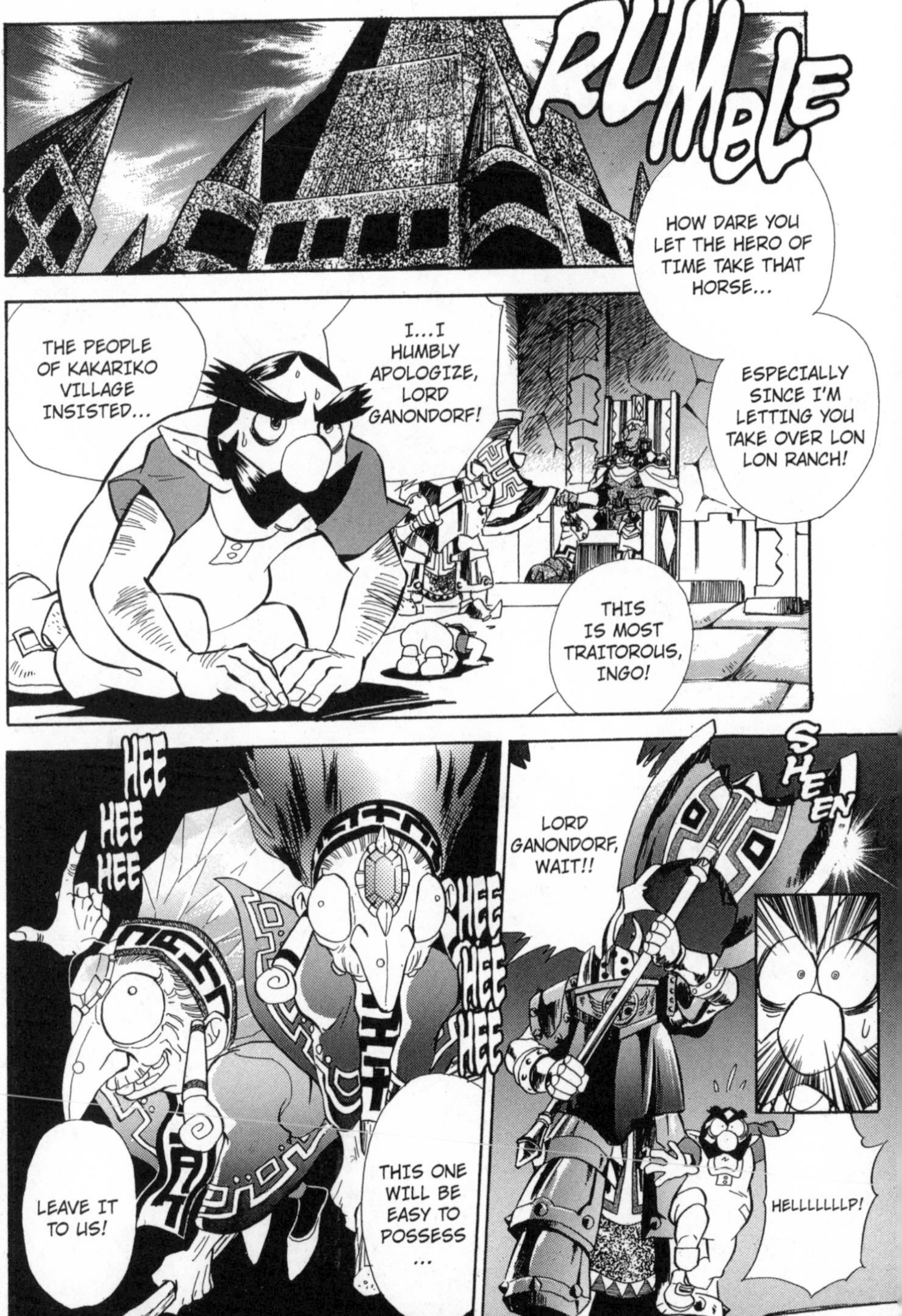
RUMBLE
HOW DARE YOU LET THE HERO OF TIME TAKE THAT HORSE...
ESPECIALLY SINCE I'M LETTING YOU TAKE OVER LON LON RANCH!
THIS IS MOST TRAITOROUS, INGO!
I...I HUMBLY APOLOGIZE, LORD GANONDORF!
THE PEOPLE OF KAKARIKO VILLAGE INSISTED...
SHEEN
LORD GANONDORF, WAIT!!
HELLLLLLLLP!
HEE HEE HEE
HEE HEE HEE
THIS ONE WILL BE EASY TO POSSESS...
LEAVE IT TO US!

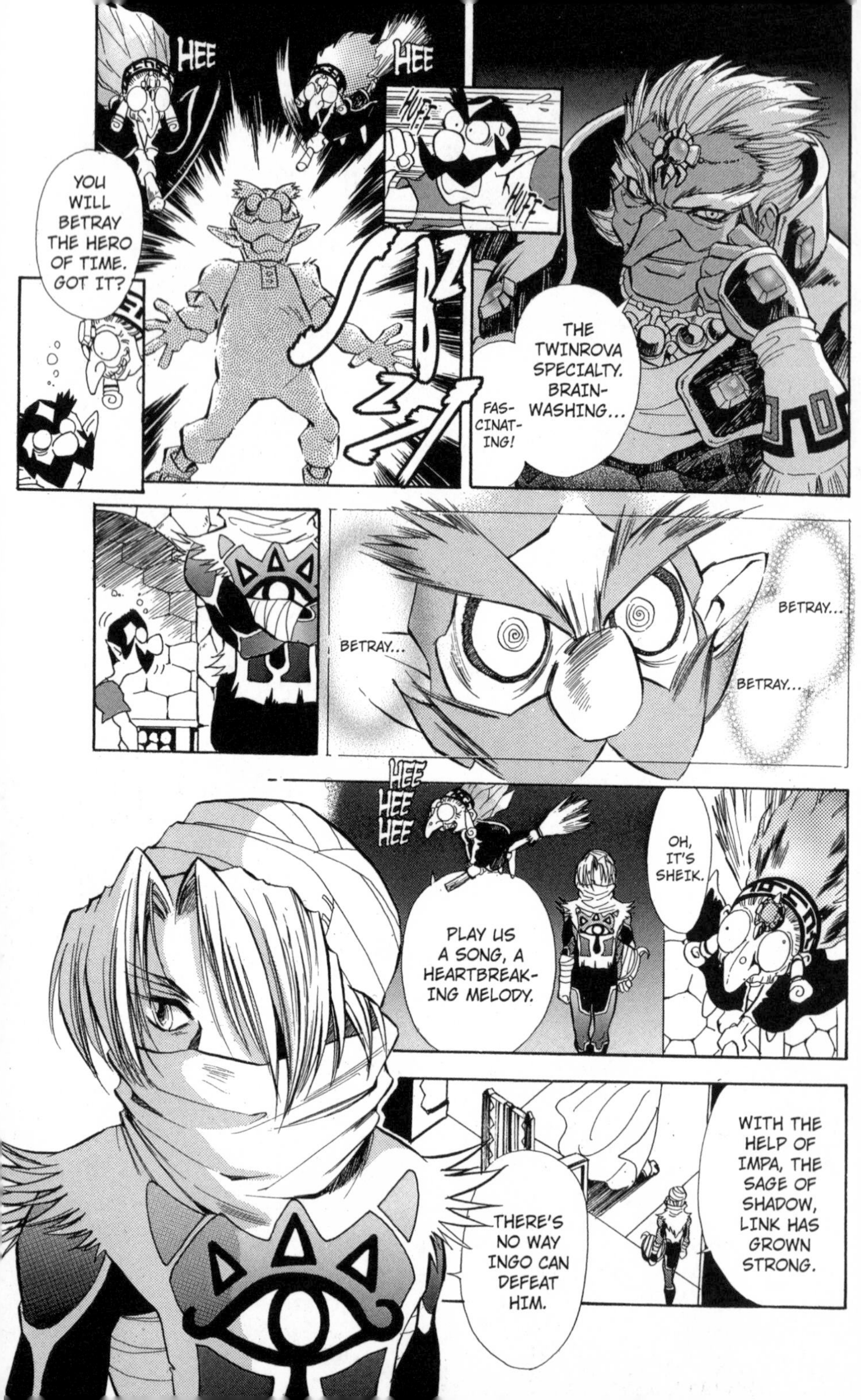
THE TWINROVA SPECIALTY. BRAIN-WASHING...
FAS-CINAT-ING!
HUFF
HUFF
HEE
HEE
YOU WILL BETRAY THE HERO OF TIME. GOT IT?
BZZ
BETRAY...
BETRAY...
BETRAY...
OH, IT'S SHEIK.
HEE HEE HEE
PLAY US A SONG, A HEARTBREAK-ING MELODY.
WITH THE HELP OF IMPA, THE SAGE OF SHADOW, LINK HAS GROWN STRONG.
THERE'S NO WAY INGO CAN DEFEAT HIM.

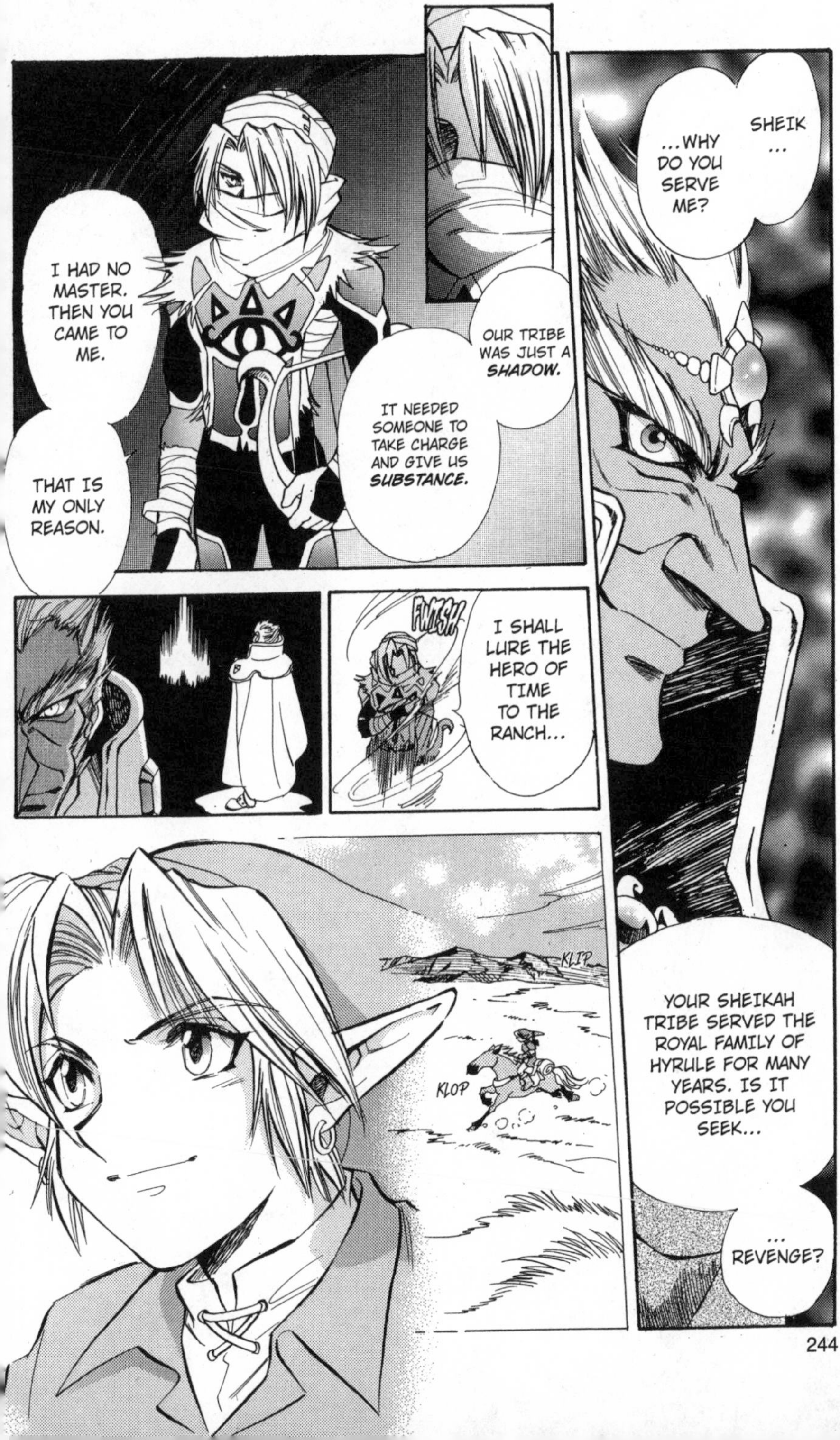
SHEIK...
...WHY DO YOU SERVE ME?
YOUR SHEIKAH TRIBE SERVED THE ROYAL FAMILY OF HYRULE FOR MANY YEARS. IS IT POSSIBLE YOU SEEK...
...REVENGE?
OUR TRIBE WAS JUST A SHADOW.
IT NEEDED SOMEONE TO TAKE CHARGE AND GIVE US SUBSTANCE.
I HAD NO MASTER. THEN YOU CAME TO ME.
THAT IS MY ONLY REASON.
FWISH
I SHALL LURE THE HERO OF TIME TO THE RANCH...
KLIP
KLOP

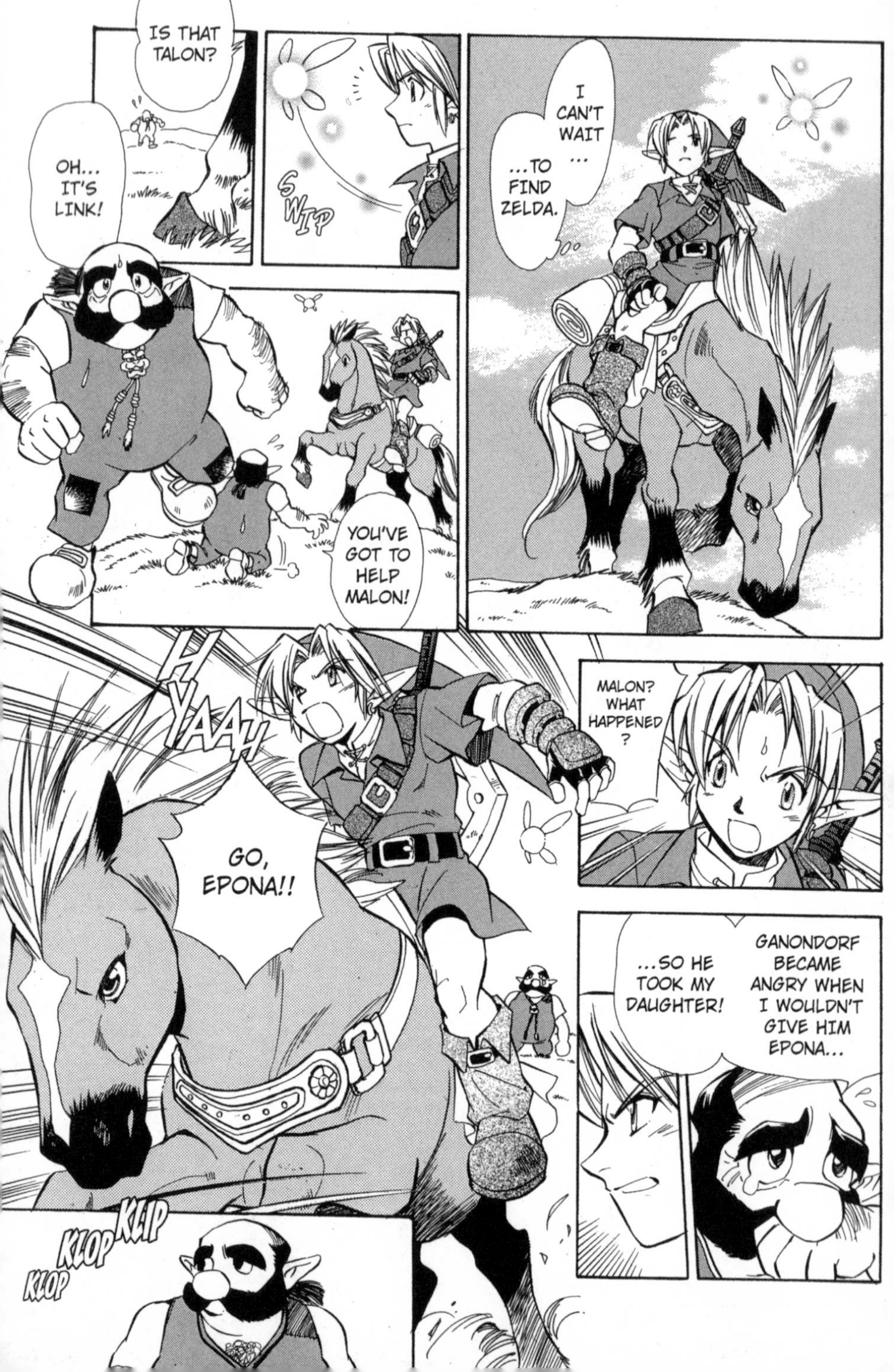
I CAN'T WAIT ...
...TO FIND ZELDA.
SWIP
IS THAT TALON?
OH... IT'S LINK!
YOU'VE GOT TO HELP MALON!
MALON? WHAT HAPPENED?
GANONDORF BECAME ANGRY WHEN I WOULDN'T GIVE HIM EPONA...
...SO HE TOOK MY DAUGHTER!
HYAAAH
GO, EPONA!!
KLIP
KLOP
KLOP

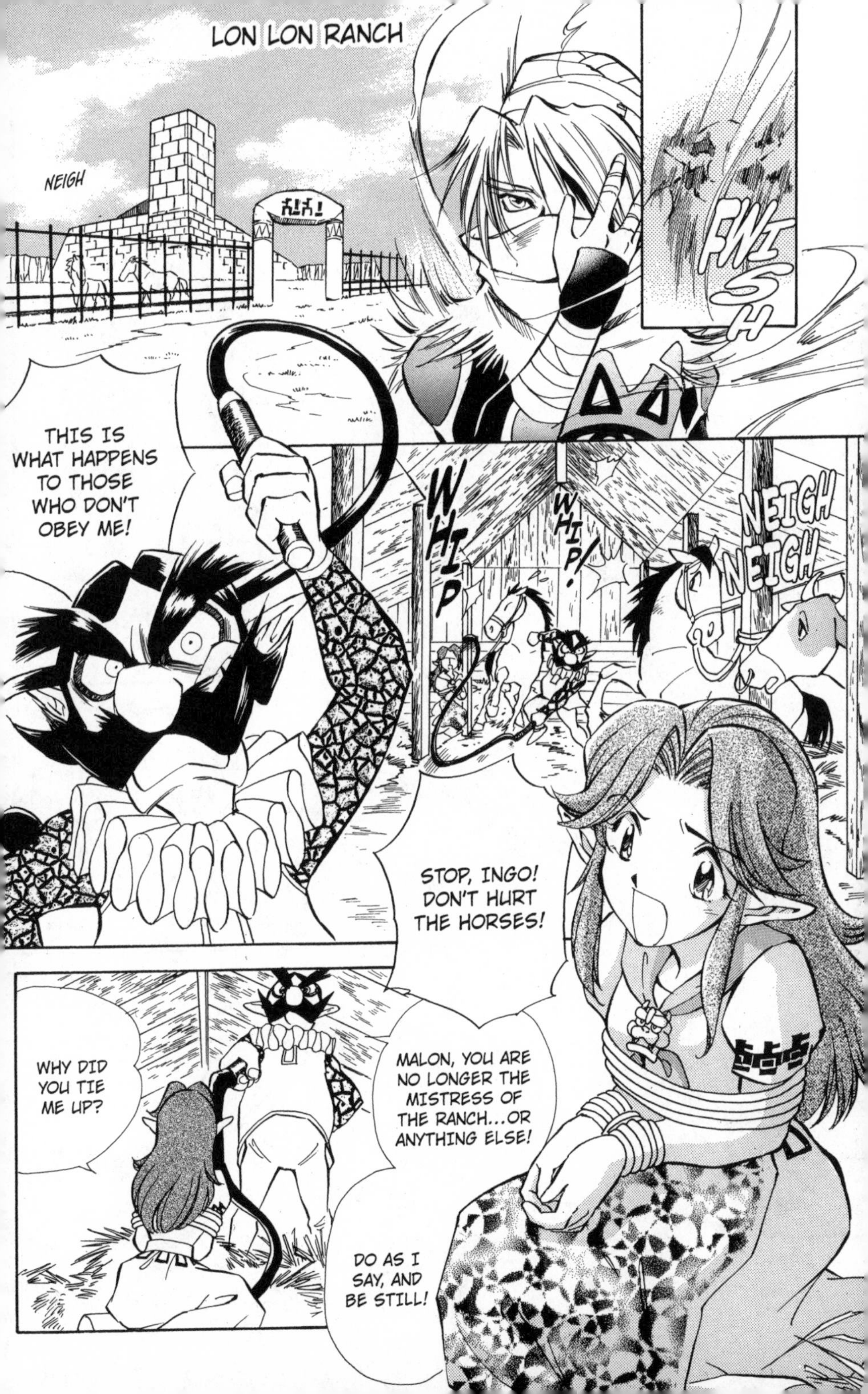
FWISH
LON LON RANCH
NEIGH
WHIP
WHIP!
NEIGH NEIGH
THIS IS WHAT HAPPENS TO THOSE WHO DON'T OBEY ME!
STOP, INGO! DON'T HURT THE HORSES!
WHY DID YOU TIE ME UP?
MALON, YOU ARE NO LONGER THE MISTRESS OF THE RANCH...OR ANYTHING ELSE!
DO AS I SAY, AND BE STILL!

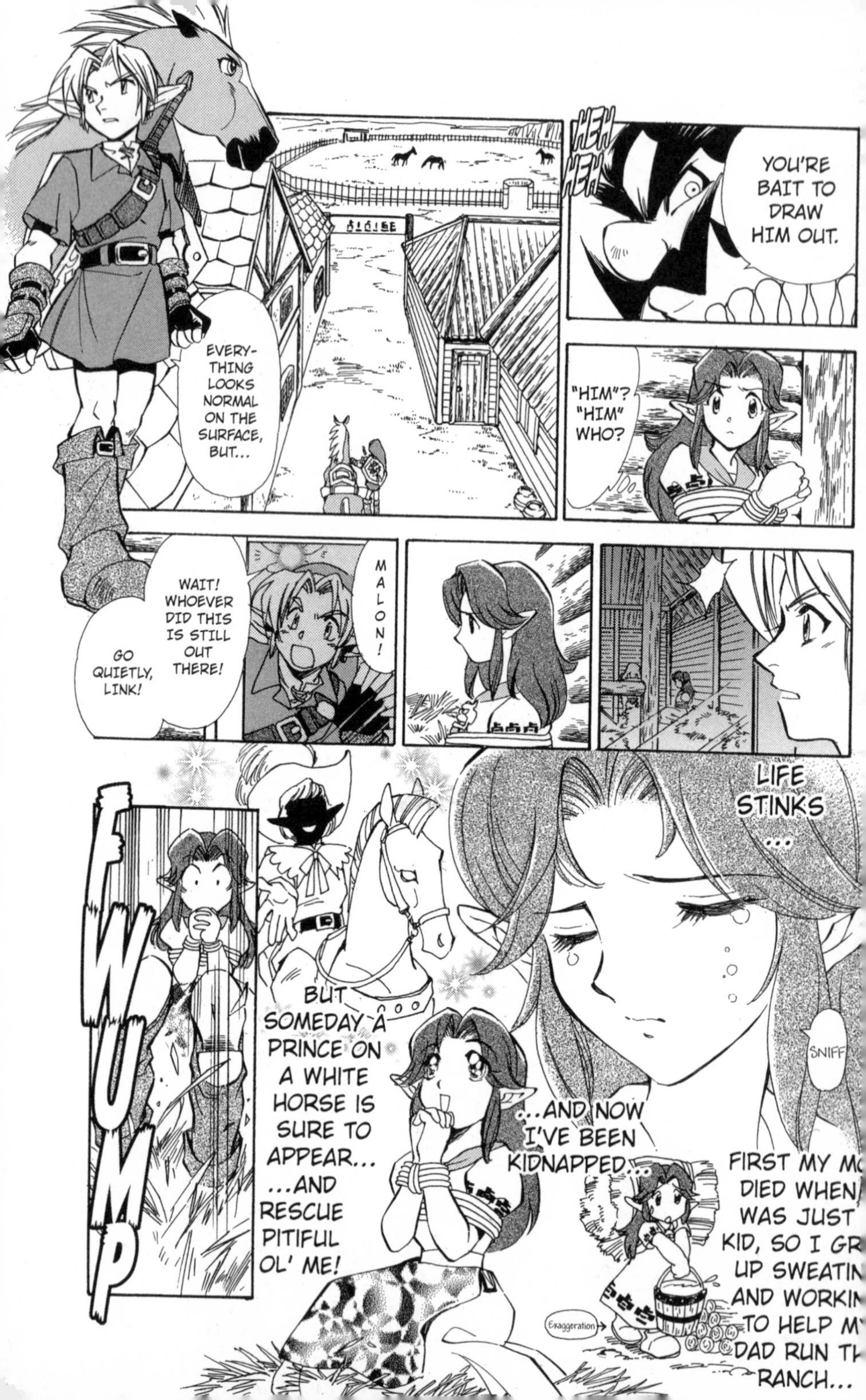
HEH HEH
YOU'RE BAIT TO DRAW HIM OUT.
"HIM"? "HIM" WHO?
EVERY-THING LOOKS NORMAL ON THE SURFACE, BUT...
MALON!
WAIT! WHOEVER DID THIS IS STILL OUT THERE!
GO QUIETLY, LINK!
LIFE STINKS...
SNIFF
FIRST MY M DIED WHEN WAS JUST KID, SO I GR UP SWEATIN AND WORKIN TO HELP M DAD RUN TH RANCH...
Exaggeration
...AND NOW I'VE BEEN KIDNAPPED...
BUT SOMEDAY A PRINCE ON A WHITE HORSE IS SURE TO APPEAR... ...AND RESCUE PITIFUL OL' ME!
WUMP

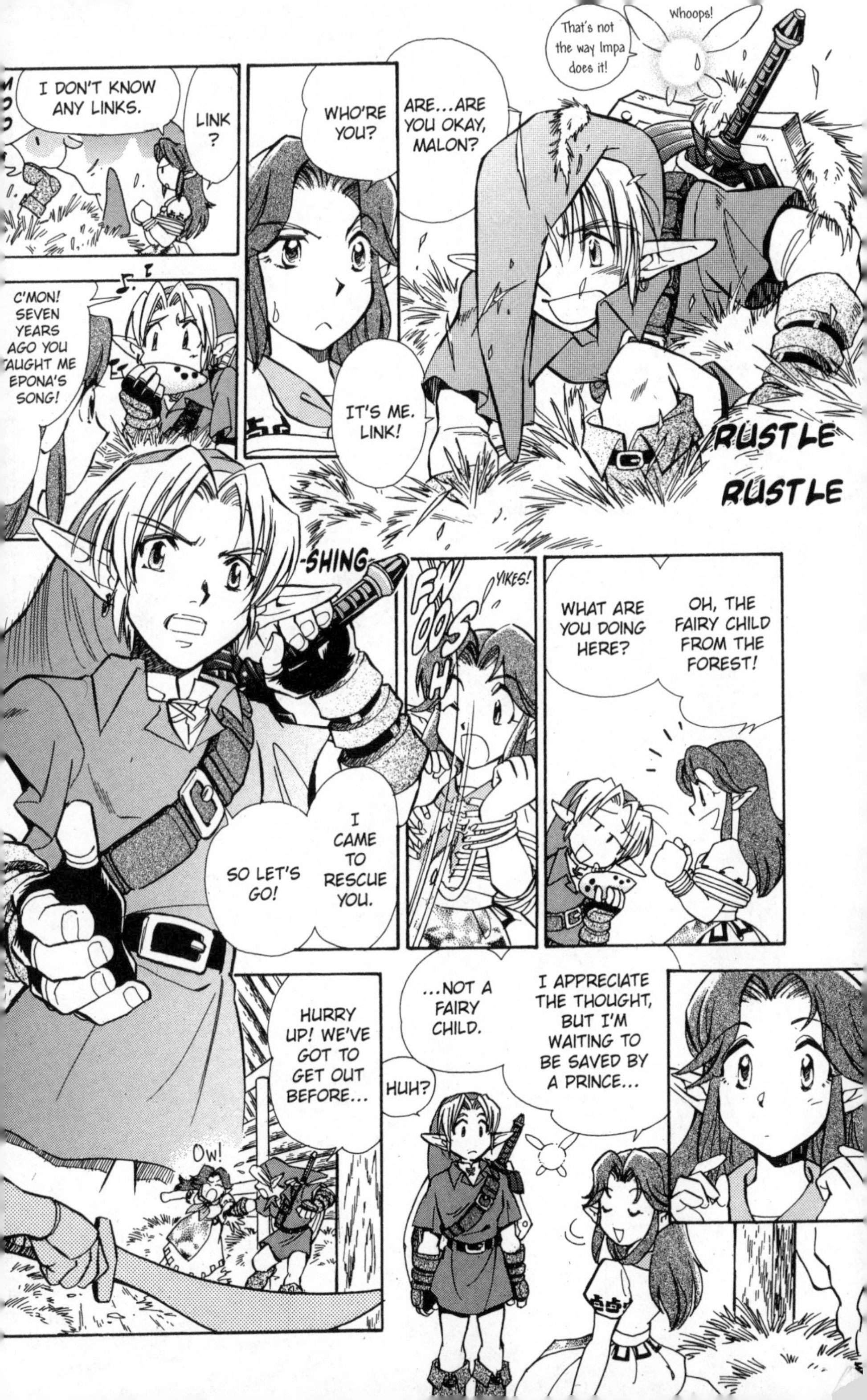

Whoops!
That's not the way Impa does it!
RUSTLE
RUSTLE
ARE...ARE YOU OKAY, MALON?
WHO'RE YOU?
IT'S ME. LINK!
LINK?
I DON'T KNOW ANY LINKS.
C'MON! SEVEN YEARS AGO YOU TAUGHT ME EPONA'S SONG!
OH, THE FAIRY CHILD FROM THE FOREST!
WHAT ARE YOU DOING HERE?
YIKES!
FWOOSH
-SHING
I CAME TO RESCUE YOU.
SO LET'S GO!
I APPRECIATE THE THOUGHT, BUT I'M WAITING TO BE SAVED BY A PRINCE...
...NOT A FAIRY CHILD.
HUH?
HURRY UP! WE'VE GOT TO GET OUT BEFORE...
OW!

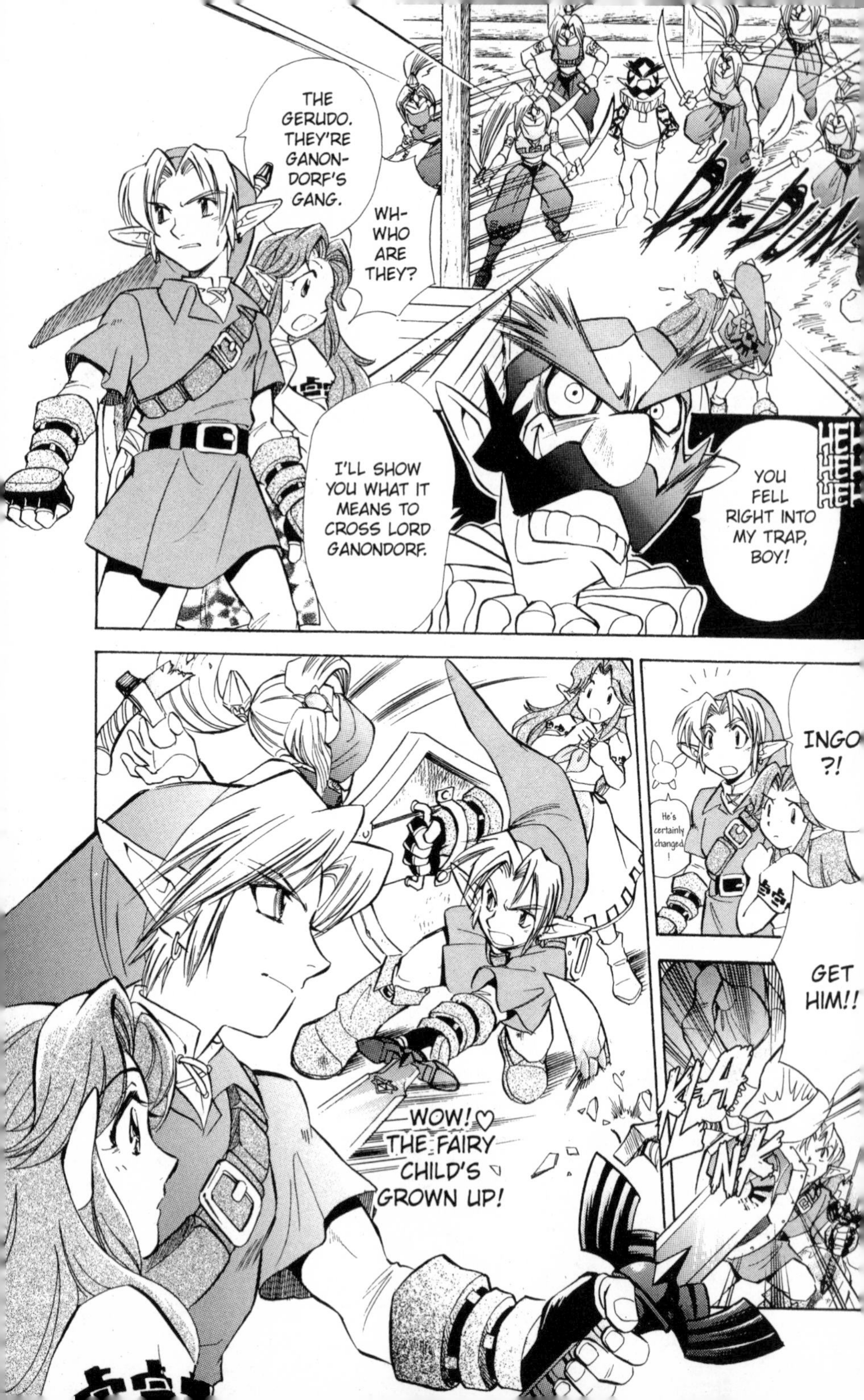
DA-DUM
HEH HEH HEH
YOU FELL RIGHT INTO MY TRAP, BOY!
I'LL SHOW YOU WHAT IT MEANS TO CROSS LORD GANONDORF.
WH- WHO ARE THEY?
THE GERUDO. THEY'RE GANON-DORF'S GANG.
INGO ?!
He's certainly changed!
GET HIM!!
KLANK
WOW! ♡ THE FAIRY CHILD'S GROWN UP!

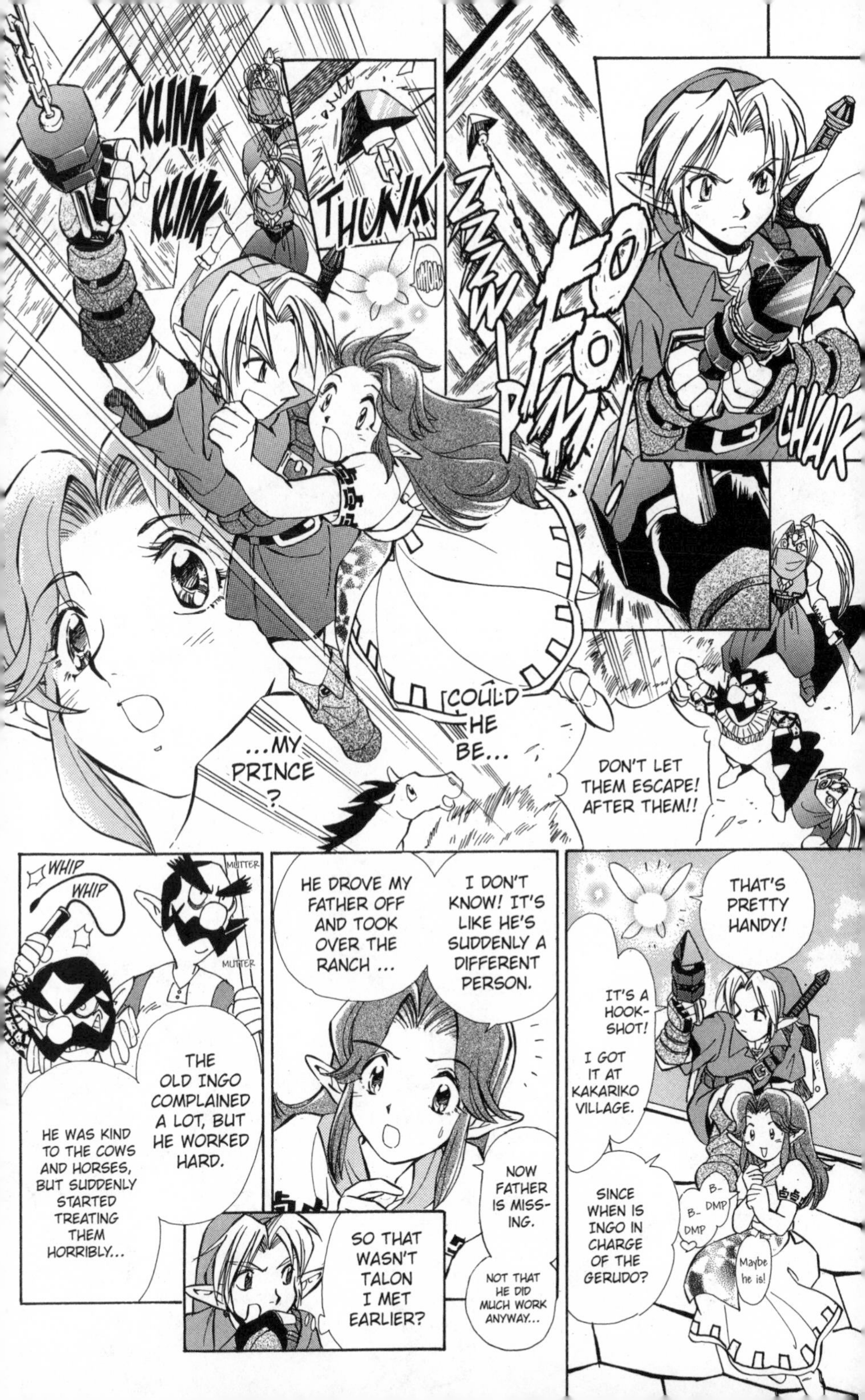

CHAK
FOOM
ZWIP
THUNK!
WHOA!
KLINK
KLINK
DON'T LET THEM ESCAPE! AFTER THEM!!
COULD HE BE...
...MY PRINCE?
THAT'S PRETTY HANDY!
IT'S A HOOK-SHOT!
I GOT IT AT KAKARIKO VILLAGE.
SINCE WHEN IS INGO IN CHARGE OF THE GERUDO?
B-DMP
B-DMP
Maybe he is!
I DON'T KNOW! IT'S LIKE HE'S SUDDENLY A DIFFERENT PERSON.
HE DROVE MY FATHER OFF AND TOOK OVER THE RANCH ...
NOW FATHER IS MISS-ING.
NOT THAT HE DID MUCH WORK ANYWAY...
SO THAT WASN'T TALON I MET EARLIER?
MUTTER
MUTTER
WHIP
WHIP
THE OLD INGO COMPLAINED A LOT, BUT HE WORKED HARD.
HE WAS KIND TO THE COWS AND HORSES, BUT SUDDENLY STARTED TREATING THEM HORRIBLY...

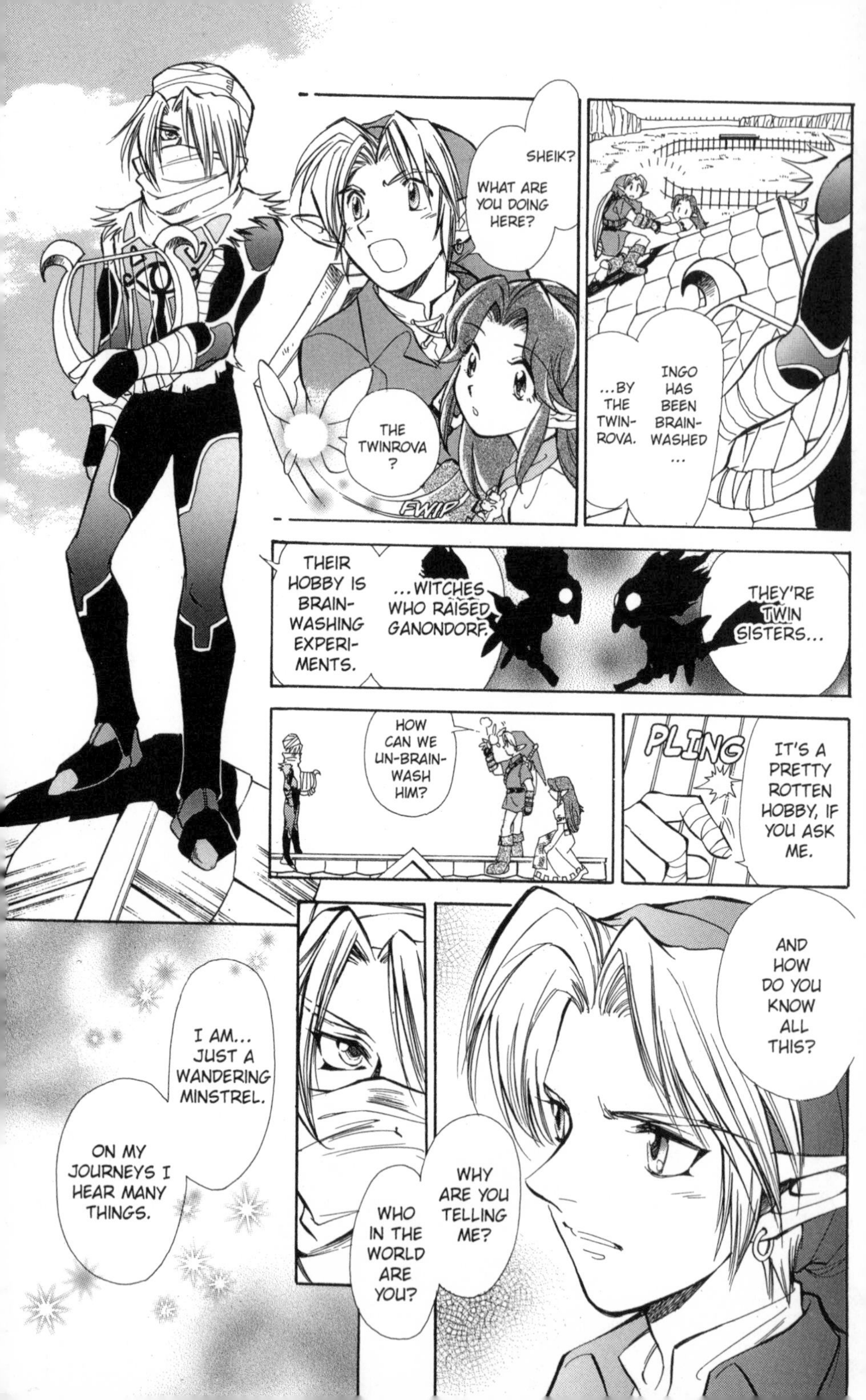
SHEIK?
WHAT ARE YOU DOING HERE?
INGO HAS BEEN BRAIN-WASHED…
…BY THE TWIN-ROVA.
THE TWINROVA?
FWIP
THEY'RE TWIN SISTERS…
…WITCHES WHO RAISED GANONDORF.
THEIR HOBBY IS BRAIN-WASHING EXPERI-MENTS.
IT'S A PRETTY ROTTEN HOBBY, IF YOU ASK ME.
PLING
HOW CAN WE UN-BRAIN-WASH HIM?
AND HOW DO YOU KNOW ALL THIS?
WHY ARE YOU TELLING ME?
WHO IN THE WORLD ARE YOU?
I AM… JUST A WANDERING MINSTREL.
ON MY JOURNEYS I HEAR MANY THINGS.

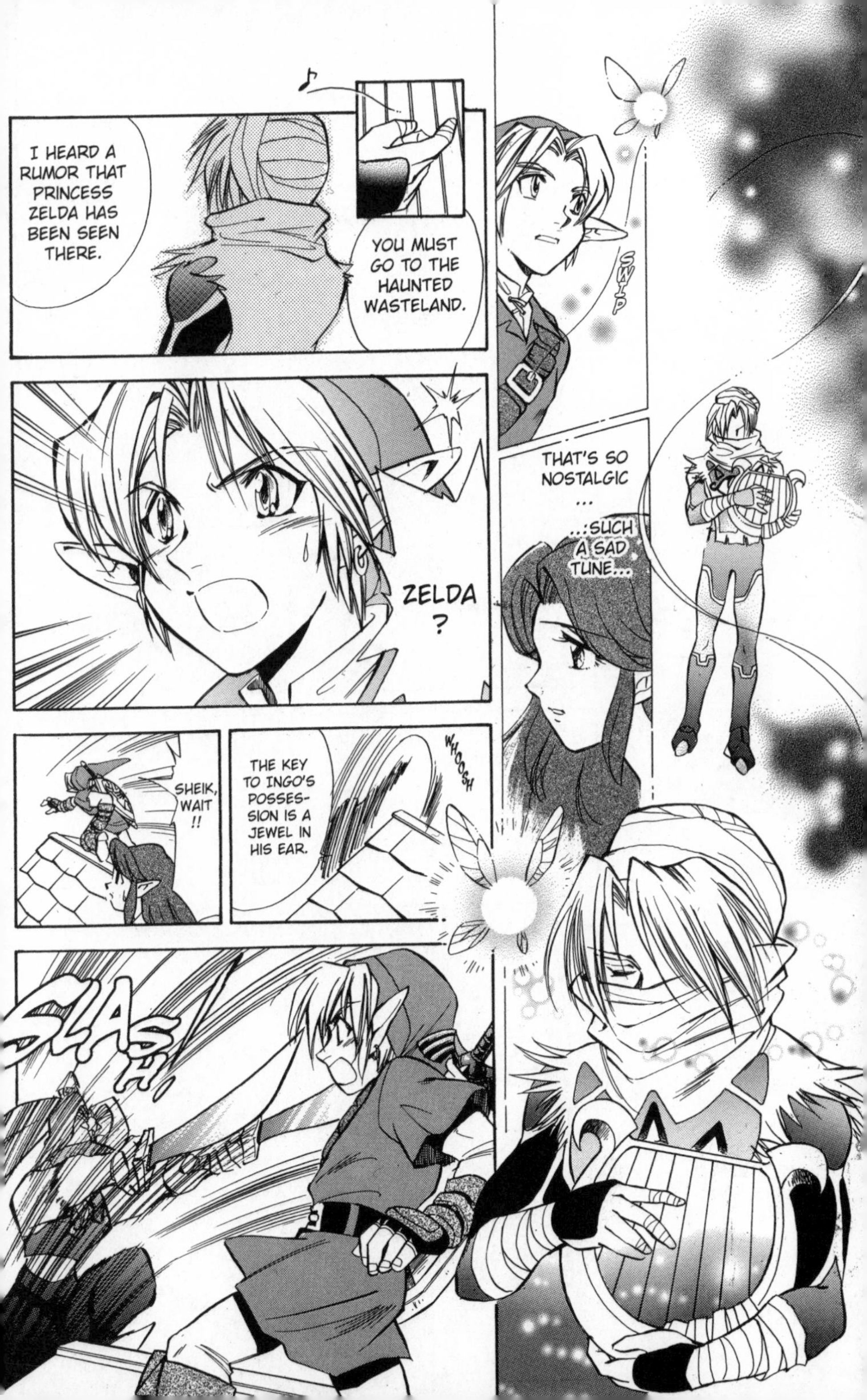
SWIP
THAT'S SO NOSTALGIC ...
...:SUCH A SAD TUNE...
YOU MUST GO TO THE HAUNTED WASTELAND.
I HEARD A RUMOR THAT PRINCESS ZELDA HAS BEEN SEEN THERE.
ZELDA ?
WHOOSH
THE KEY TO INGO'S POSSES-SION IS A JEWEL IN HIS EAR.
SHEIK, WAIT !!
SLASH!

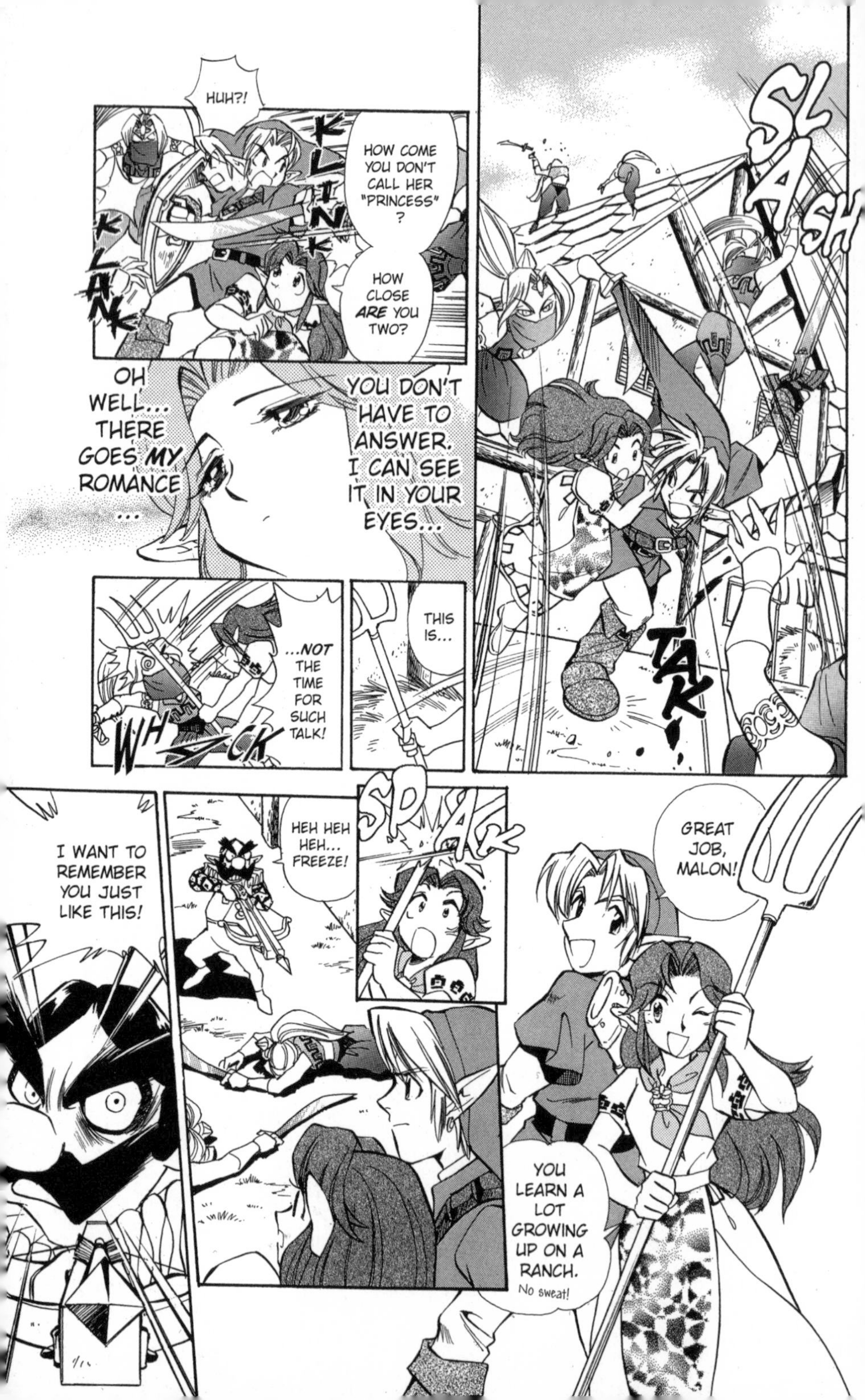
SLASH
TAK
HUH?!
KLINK
HOW COME YOU DON'T CALL HER "PRINCESS" ?
HOW CLOSE **ARE** YOU TWO?
KLANK
YOU DON'T HAVE TO ANSWER. I CAN SEE IT IN YOUR EYES...
OH WELL... THERE GOES **MY** ROMANCE ...
THIS IS...
...**NOT** THE TIME FOR SUCH TALK!
WHACK
GREAT JOB, MALON!
YOU LEARN A LOT GROWING UP ON A RANCH.
No sweat!
SPAK
HEH HEH HEH... FREEZE!
I WANT TO REMEMBER YOU JUST LIKE THIS!

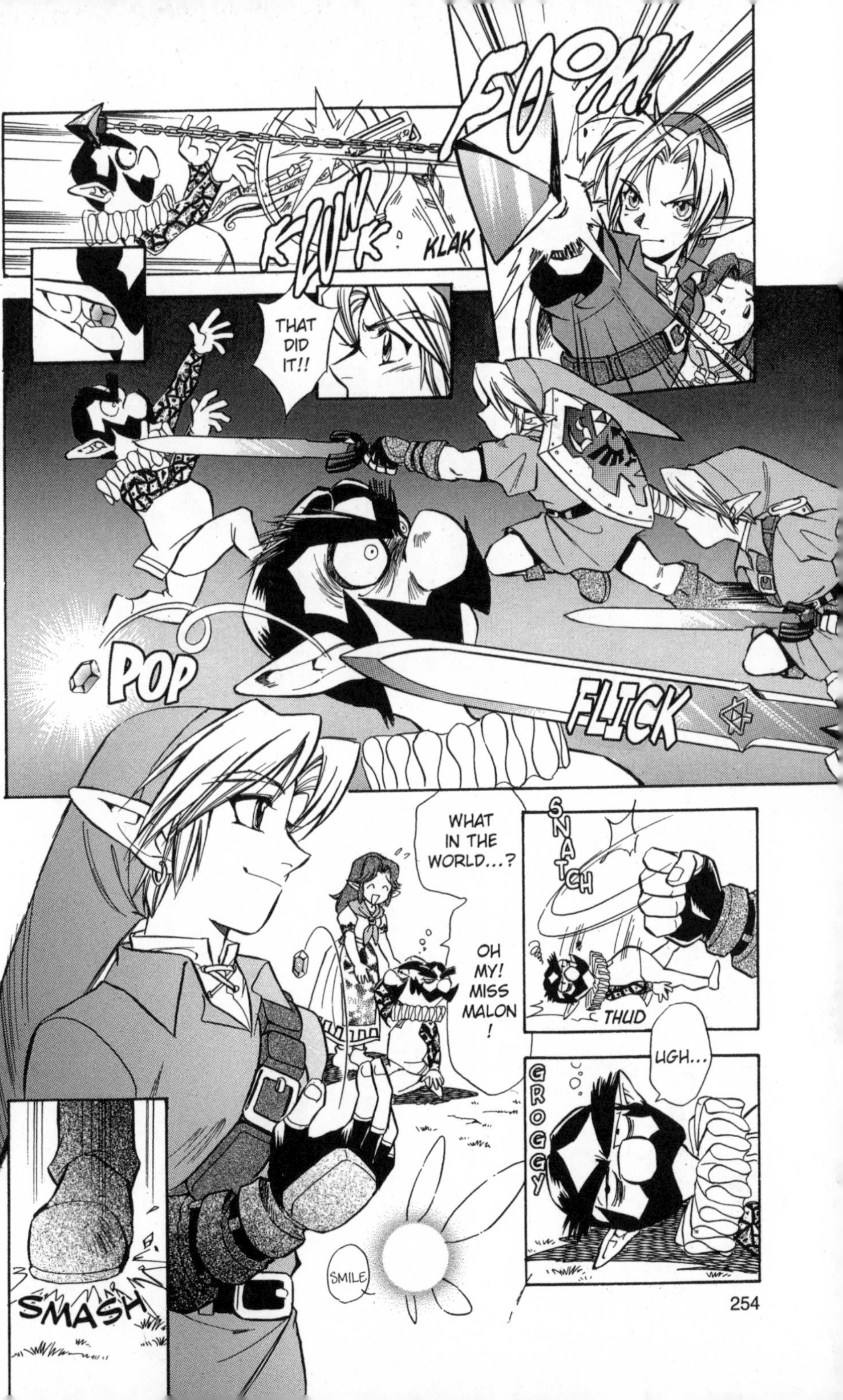

FOOM!
KLAK
KLINK
THAT DID IT!!
POP
FLICK
SNATCH
THUD
WHAT IN THE WORLD...?
OH MY! MISS MALON!
UGH...
GROGGY
SMILE
SMASH

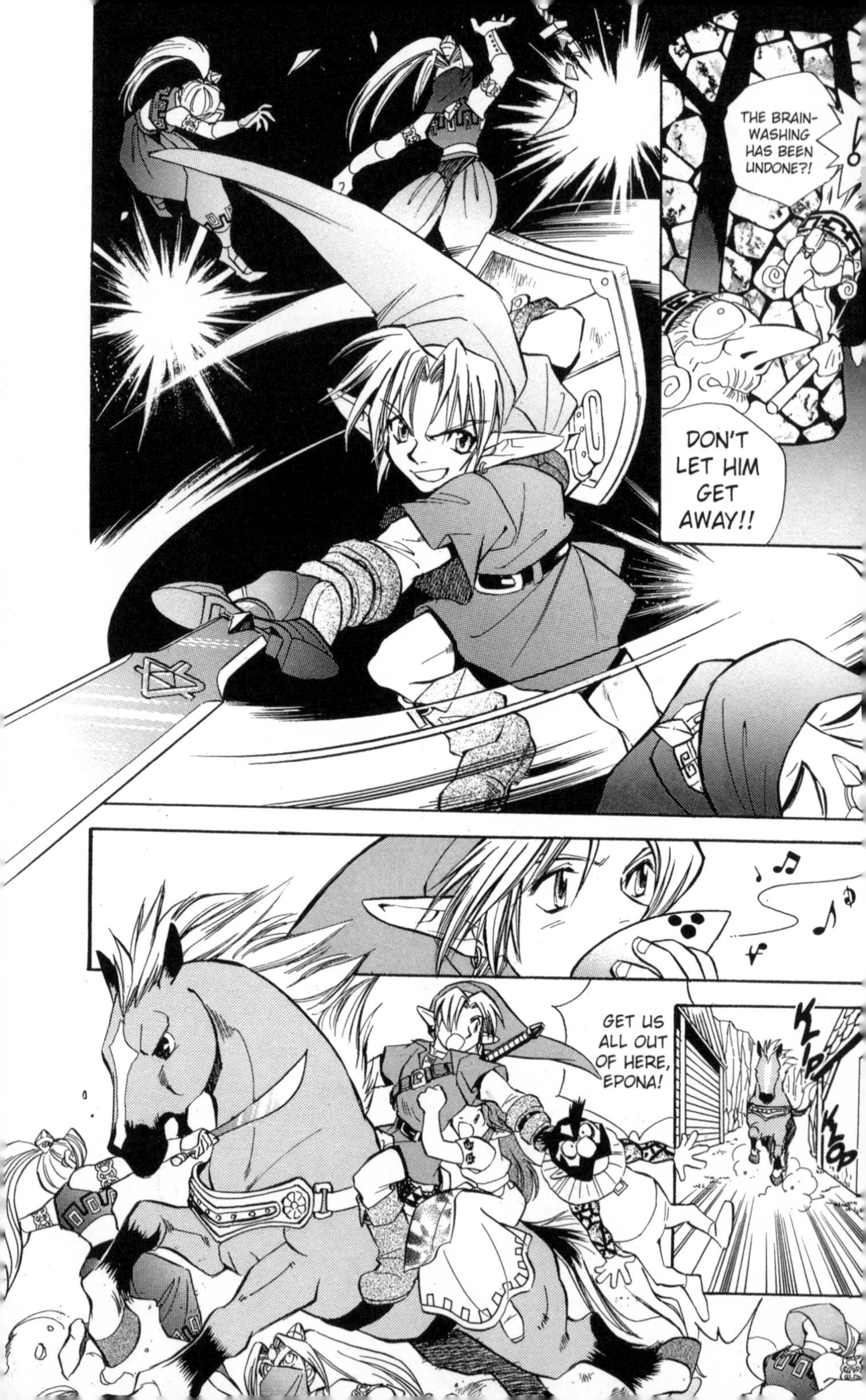
THE BRAIN-WASHING HAS BEEN UNDONE?!
DON'T LET HIM GET AWAY!!
KLIP
KLOP
GET US ALL OUT OF HERE, EPONA!

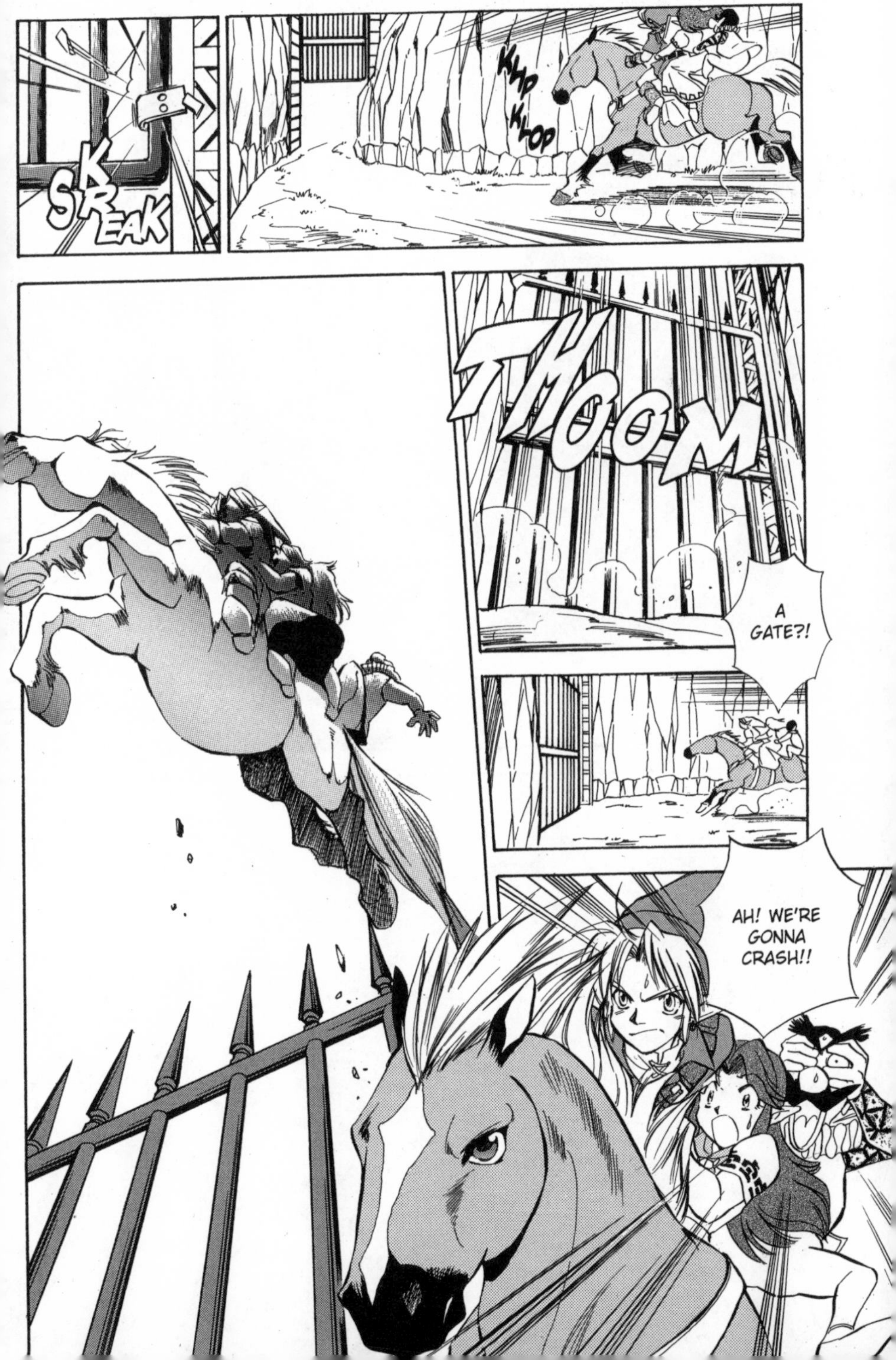
KLIP KLOP
SKREAK
THOOM
A GATE?!
AH! WE'RE GONNA CRASH!!

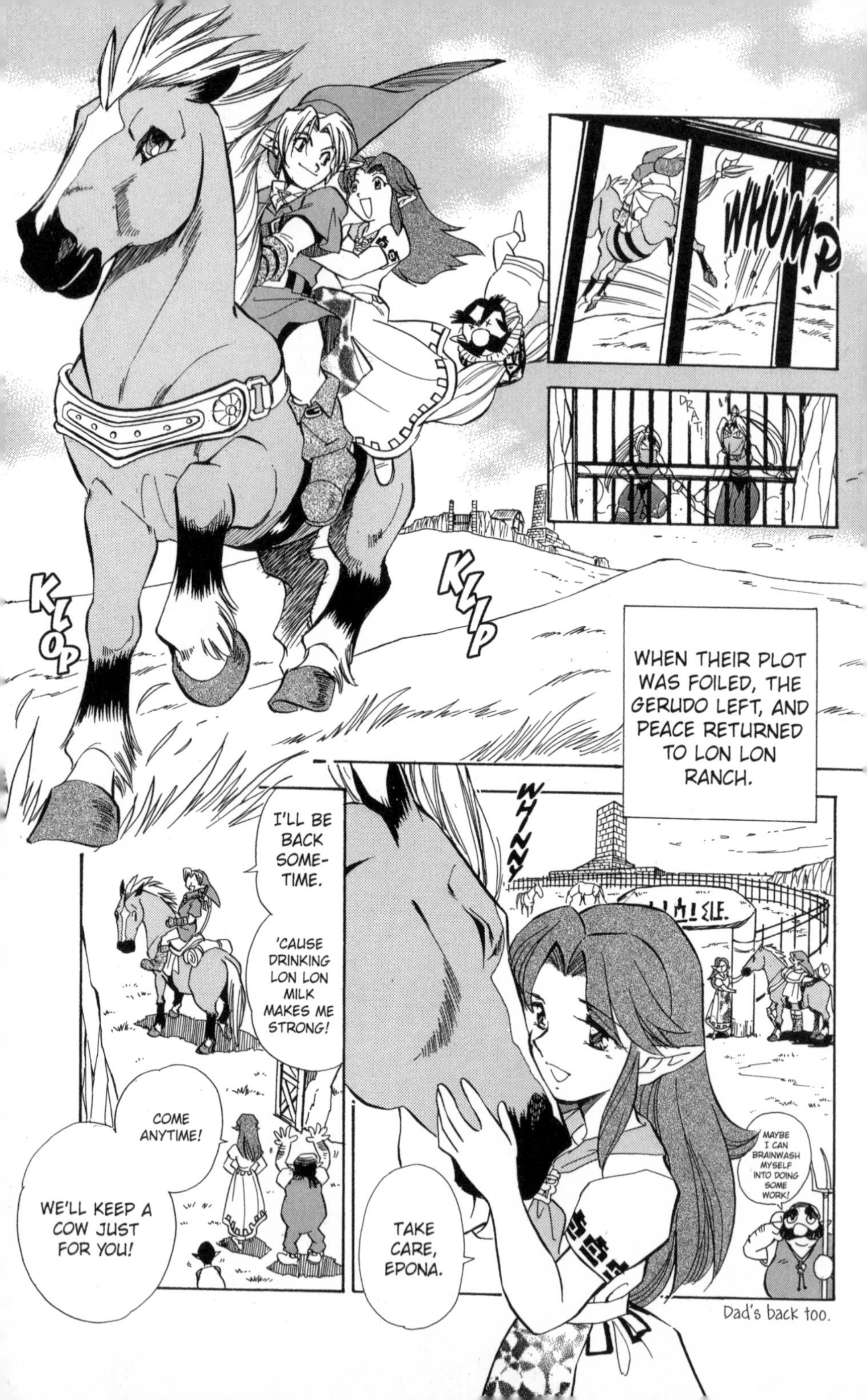
WHUMP
DRAT!
KLIP
KLOP
WHEN THEIR PLOT WAS FOILED, THE GERUDO LEFT, AND PEACE RETURNED TO LON LON RANCH.
WHINNY
TAKE CARE, EPONA.
MAYBE I CAN BRAINWASH MYSELF INTO DOING SOME WORK!
I'LL BE BACK SOME- TIME.
'CAUSE DRINKING LON LON MILK MAKES ME STRONG!
COME ANYTIME!
WE'LL KEEP A COW JUST FOR YOU!
Dad's back too.

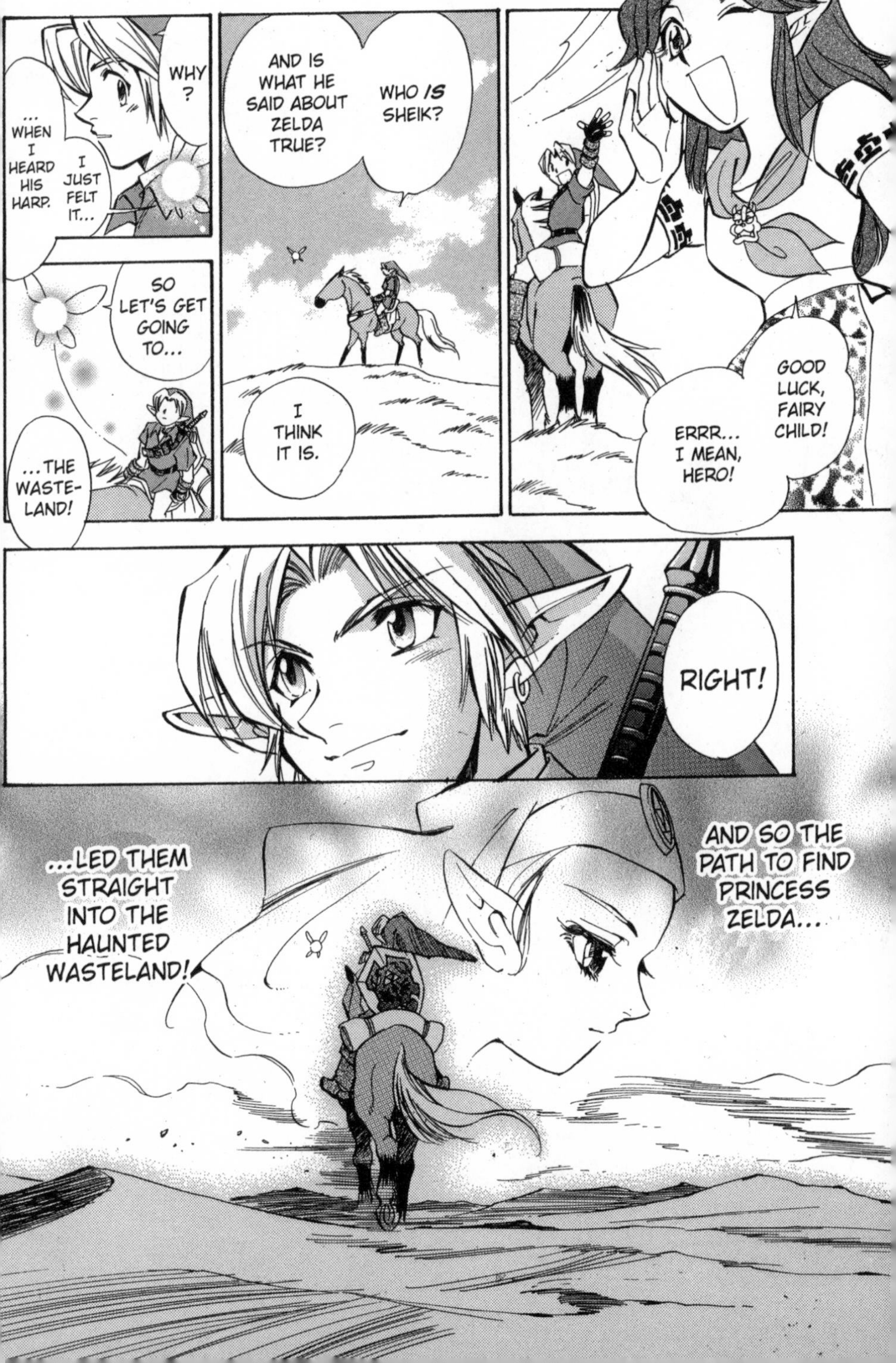
GOOD LUCK, FAIRY CHILD!
ERRR... I MEAN, HERO!
WHO *IS* SHEIK?
AND IS WHAT HE SAID ABOUT ZELDA TRUE?
I THINK IT IS.
WHY?
...WHEN I HEARD HIS HARP.
I JUST FELT IT...
SO LET'S GET GOING TO...
...THE WASTE-LAND!
RIGHT!
AND SO THE PATH TO FIND PRINCESS ZELDA...
...LED THEM STRAIGHT INTO THE HAUNTED WASTELAND!

CHAPTER 6
THE HAUNTED WASTELAND

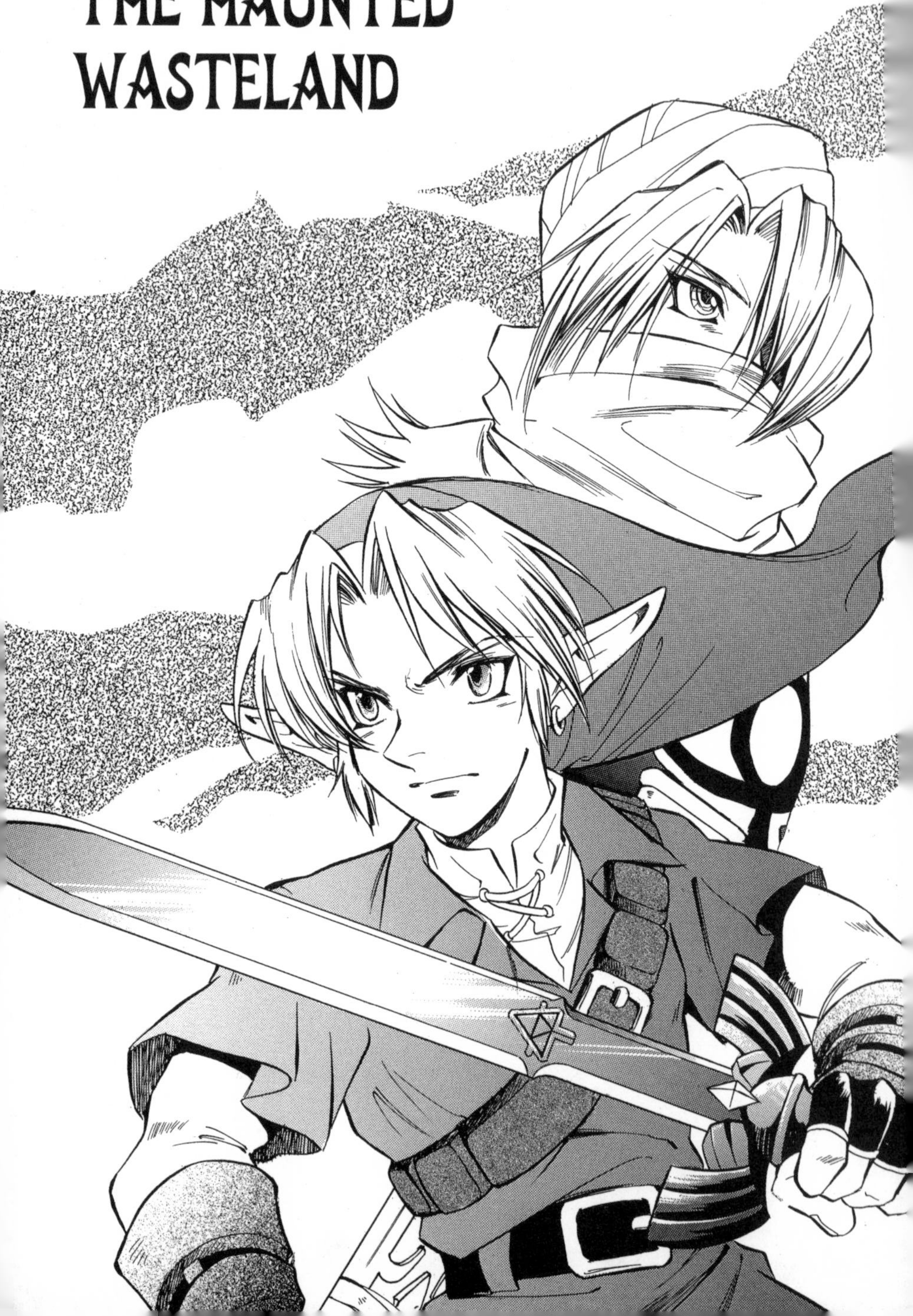

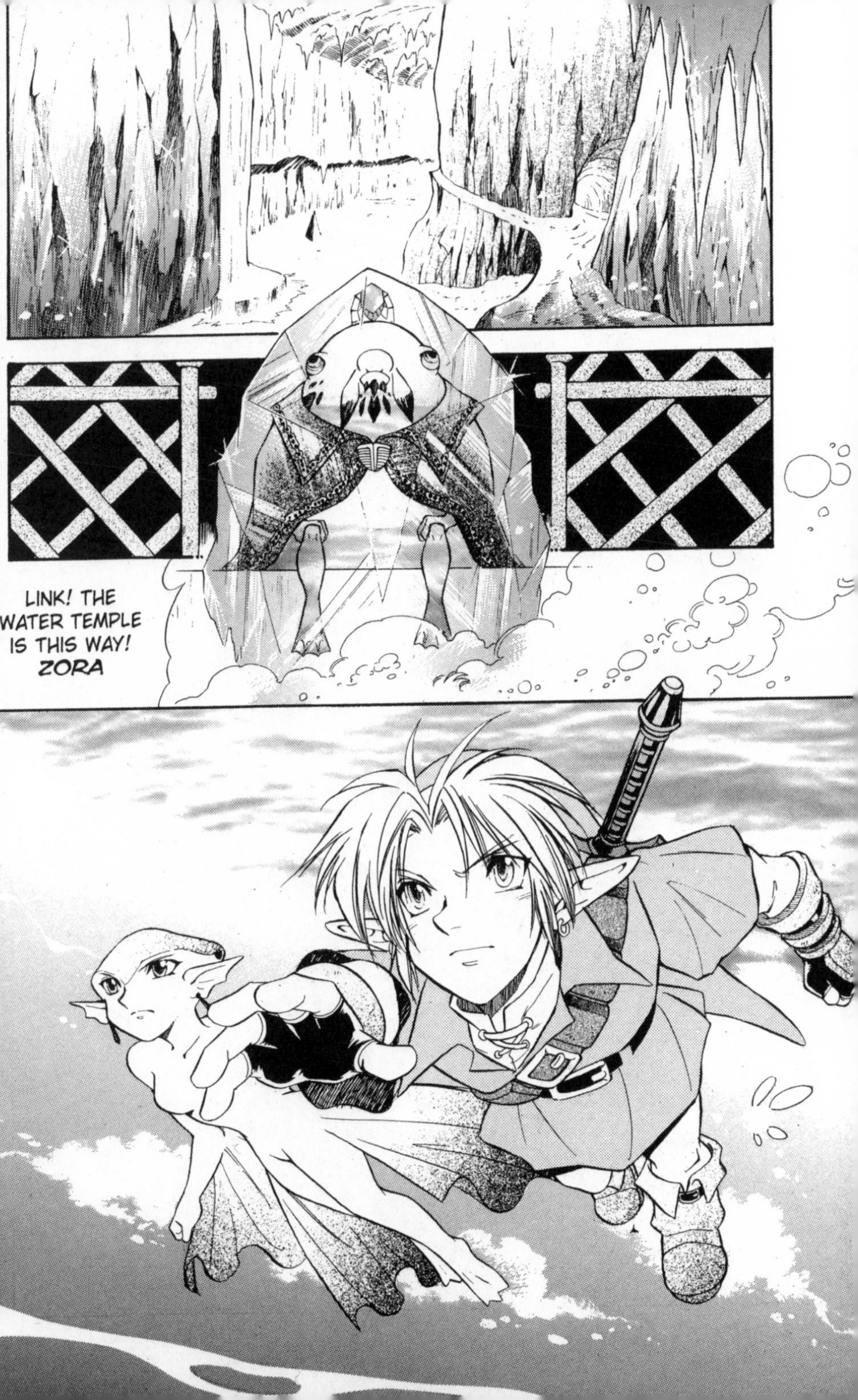
LINK! THE WATER TEMPLE IS THIS WAY!
ZORA

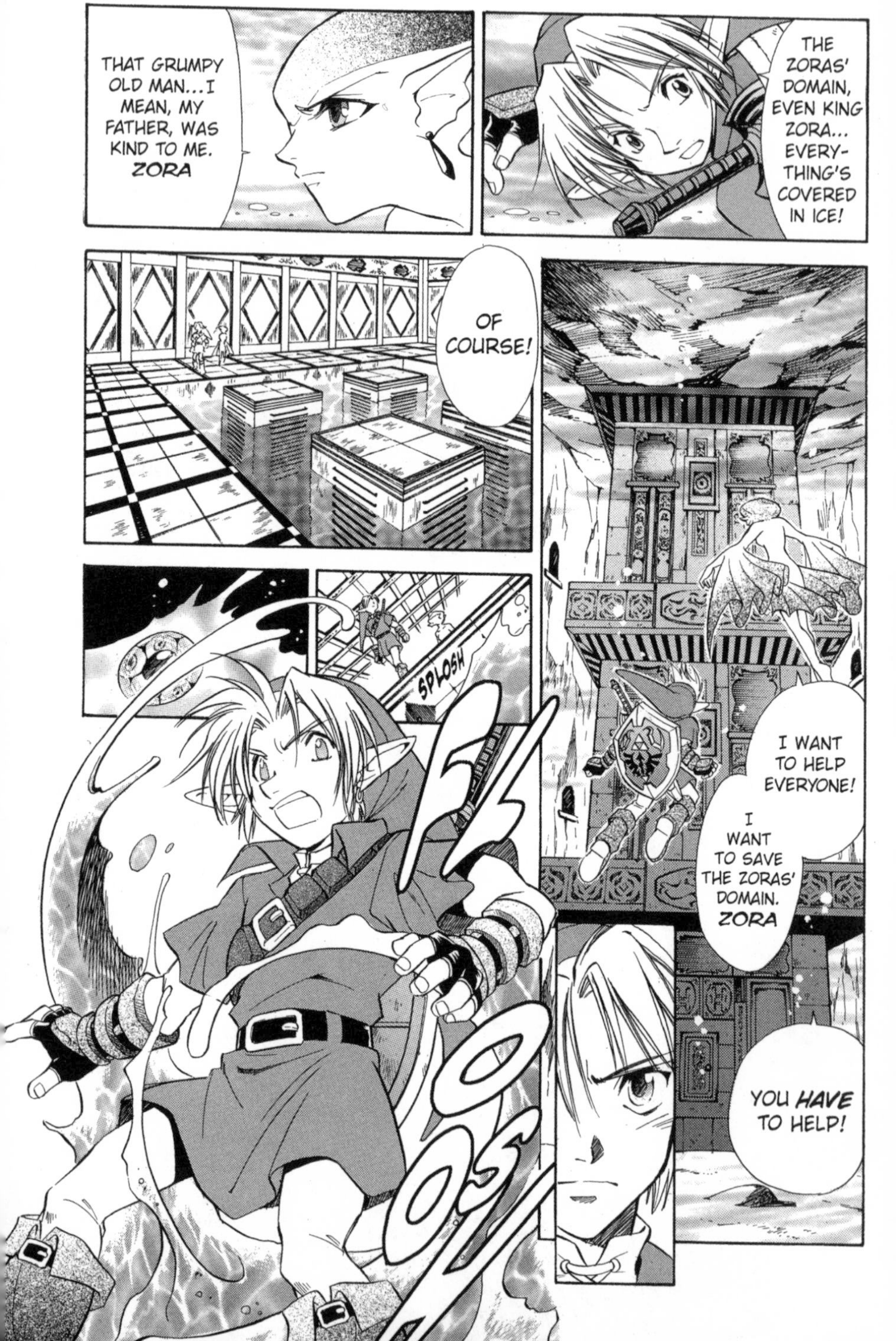
THE ZORAS' DOMAIN, EVEN KING ZORA... EVERY-THING'S COVERED IN ICE!
THAT GRUMPY OLD MAN...I MEAN, MY FATHER, WAS KIND TO ME. **ZORA**
OF COURSE!
I WANT TO HELP EVERYONE!
I WANT TO SAVE THE ZORAS' DOMAIN. **ZORA**
YOU ***HAVE*** TO HELP!
SPLOSH

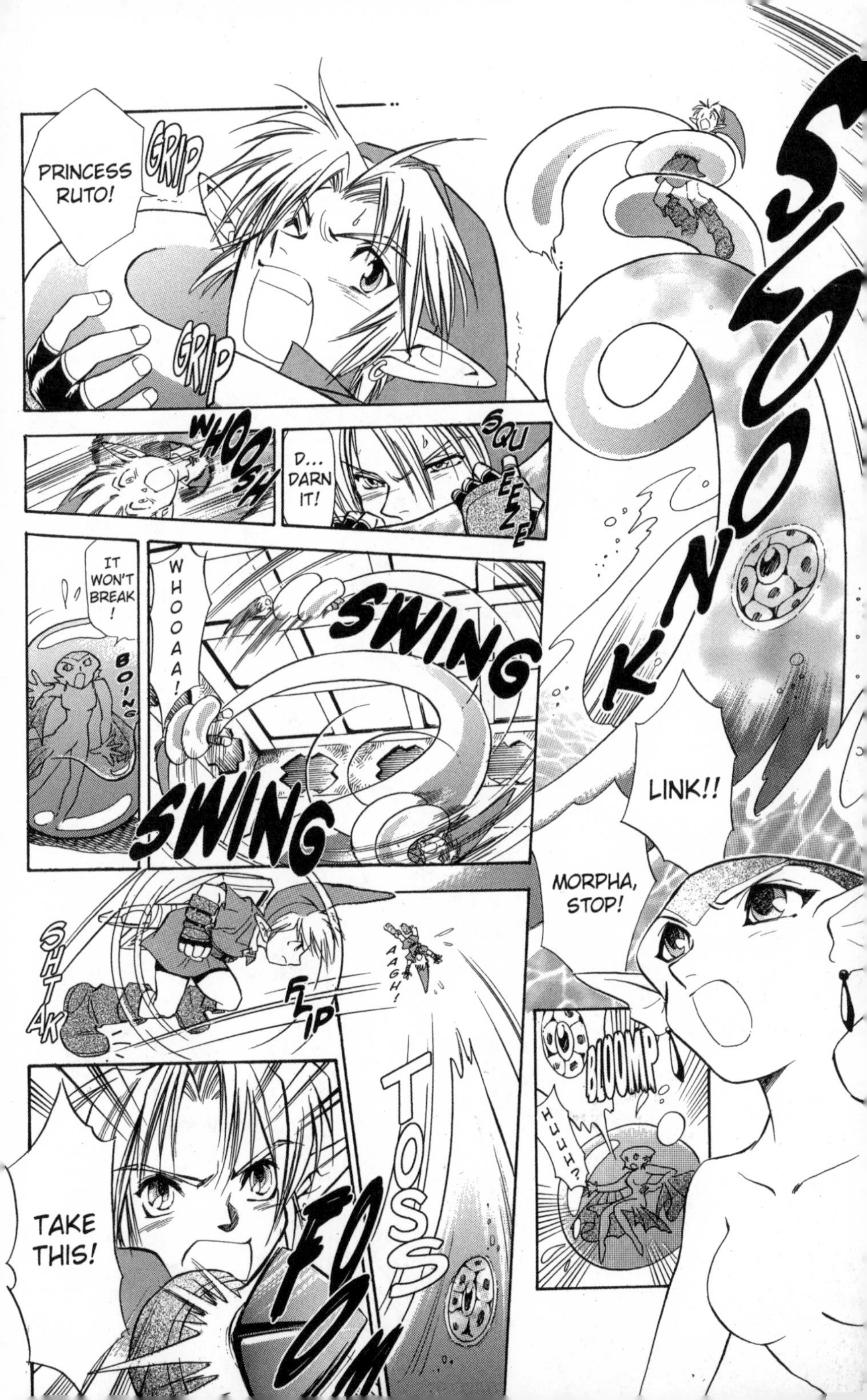
LINK!!
MORPHA, STOP!
BLOOMP
HUUUH?
PRINCESS RUTO!
GRIP
GRIP
D... DARN IT!
SQUEEZE
WHOOSH
IT WON'T BREAK!
BOING
WHOOAAA!
SWING
SWING
AAGH!
FLIP
SHTAK
TOSS
TAKE THIS!
FOOM

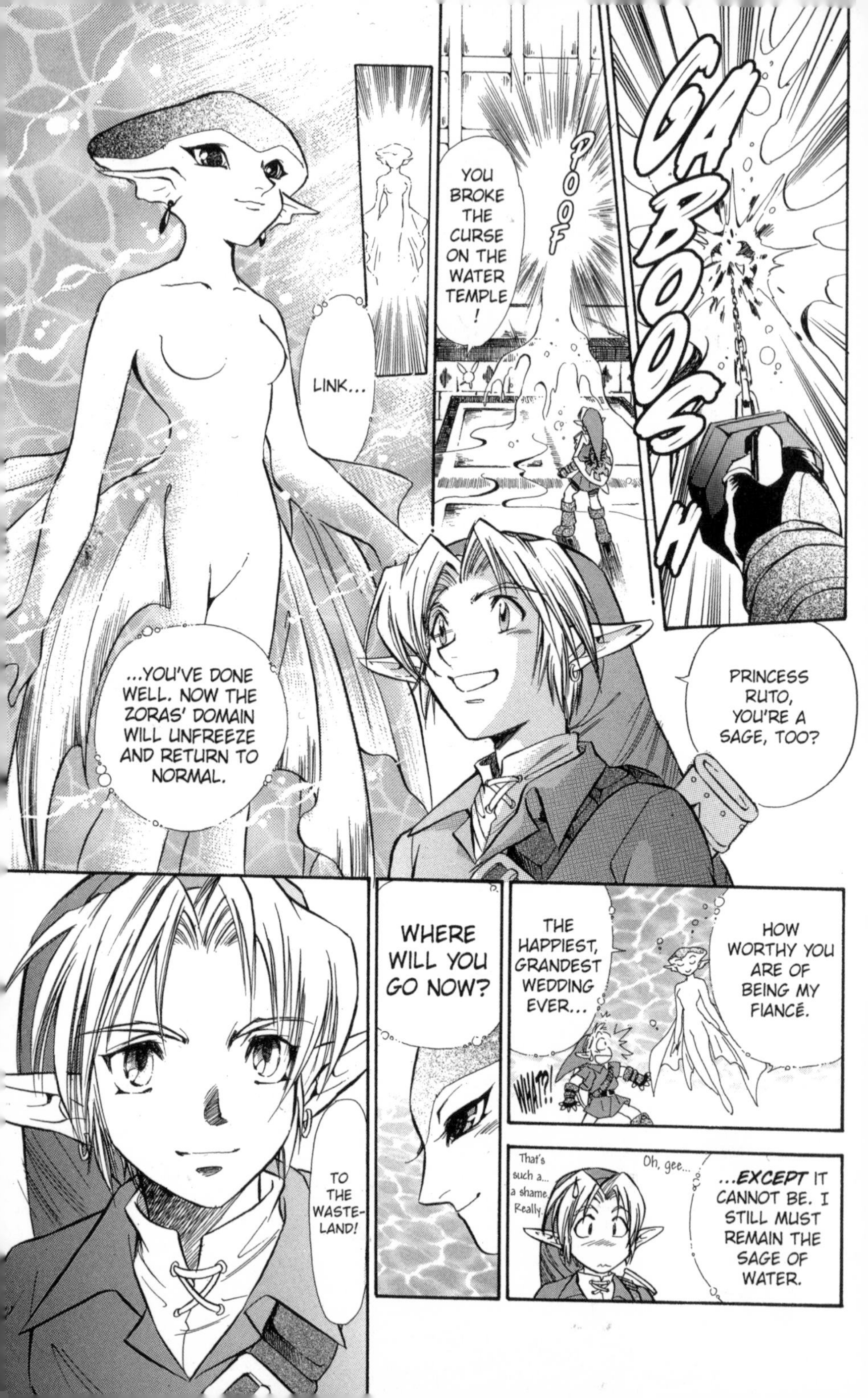
GABOOOSH
POOF
YOU BROKE THE CURSE ON THE WATER TEMPLE!
LINK...
...YOU'VE DONE WELL. NOW THE ZORAS' DOMAIN WILL UNFREEZE AND RETURN TO NORMAL.
PRINCESS RUTO, YOU'RE A SAGE, TOO?
HOW WORTHY YOU ARE OF BEING MY FIANCE.
THE HAPPIEST, GRANDEST WEDDING EVER...
WHAT?!
...*EXCEPT* IT CANNOT BE. I STILL MUST REMAIN THE SAGE OF WATER.
Oh, gee...
That's such a... a shame. Really.
WHERE WILL YOU GO NOW?
TO THE WASTE-LAND!

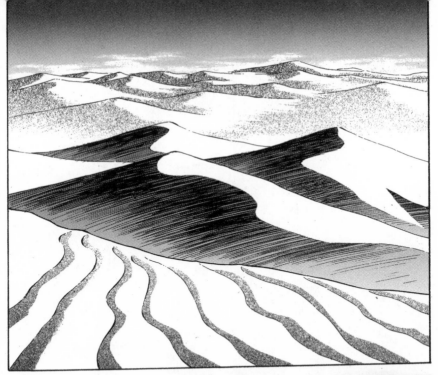

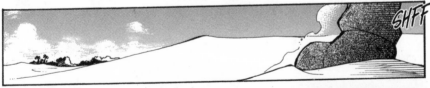

SHFF

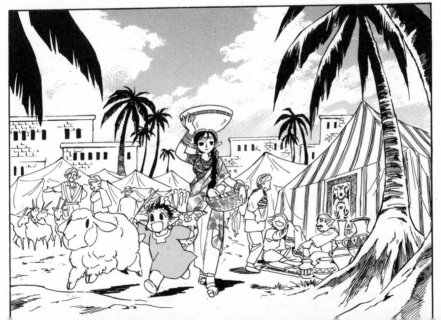

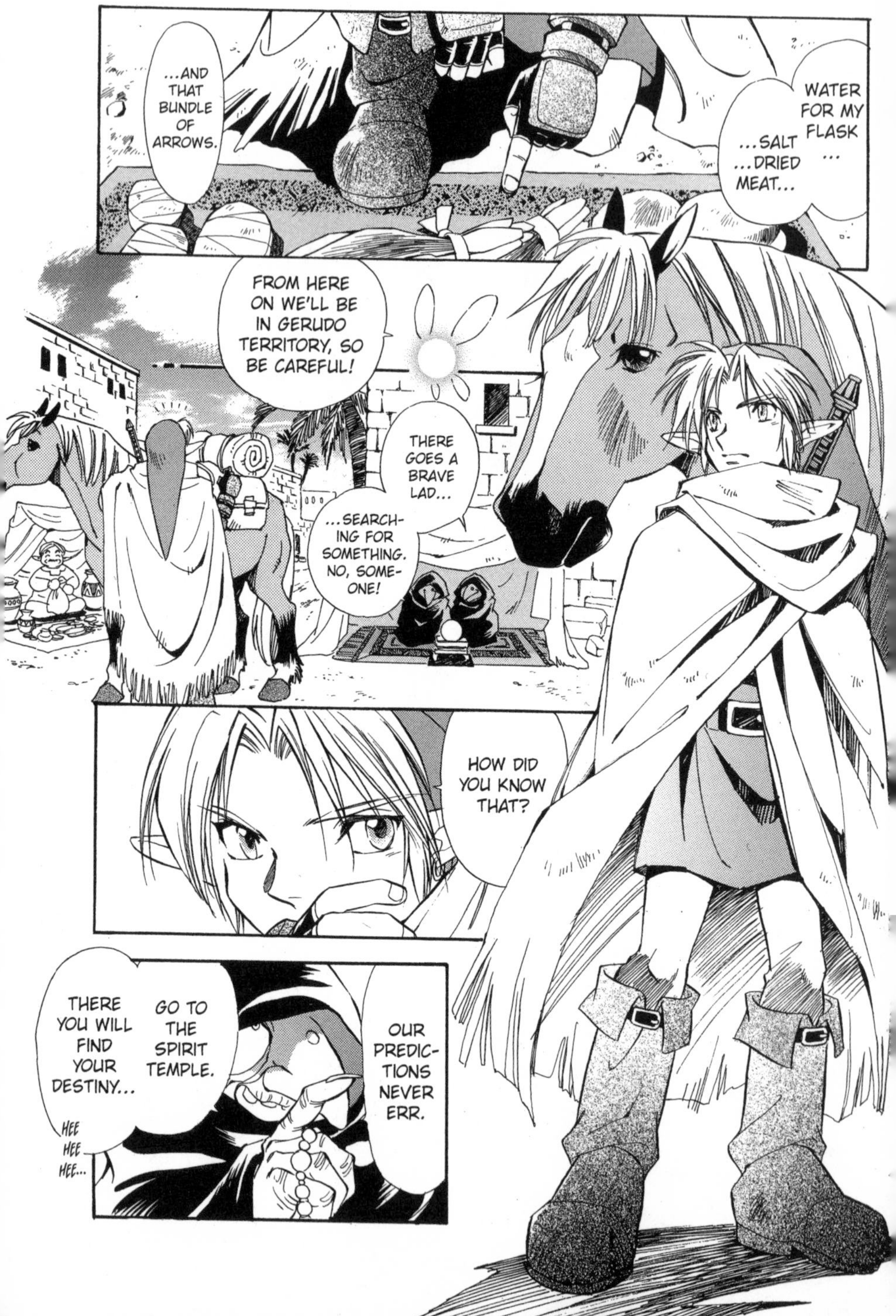
WATER FOR MY FLASK ...
...SALT ...DRIED MEAT...
...AND THAT BUNDLE OF ARROWS.
FROM HERE ON WE'LL BE IN GERUDO TERRITORY, SO BE CAREFUL!
THERE GOES A BRAVE LAD...
...SEARCHING FOR SOMETHING. NO, SOMEONE!
HOW DID YOU KNOW THAT?
OUR PREDICTIONS NEVER ERR.
GO TO THE SPIRIT TEMPLE.
THERE YOU WILL FIND YOUR DESTINY...
HEE HEE HEE...

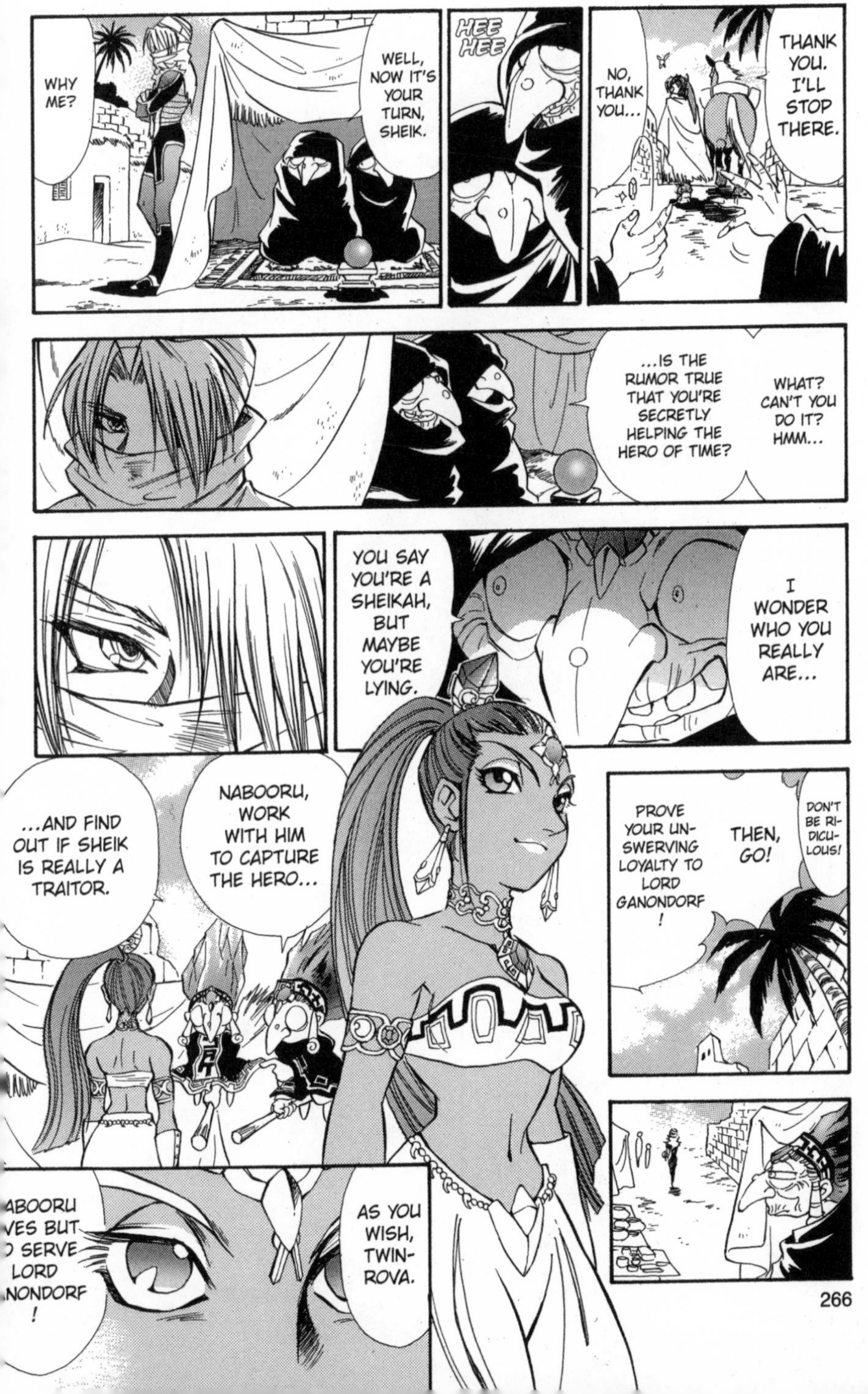
THANK YOU. I'LL STOP THERE.
NO, THANK YOU...
HEE HEE
WELL, NOW IT'S YOUR TURN, SHEIK.
WHY ME?
WHAT? CAN'T YOU DO IT? HMM...
...IS THE RUMOR TRUE THAT YOU'RE SECRETLY HELPING THE HERO OF TIME?
I WONDER WHO YOU REALLY ARE...
YOU SAY YOU'RE A SHEIKAH, BUT MAYBE YOU'RE LYING.
DON'T BE RIDICULOUS!
THEN, GO!
PROVE YOUR UNSWERVING LOYALTY TO LORD GANONDORF!
NABOORU, WORK WITH HIM TO CAPTURE THE HERO...
...AND FIND OUT IF SHEIK IS REALLY A TRAITOR.
AS YOU WISH, TWINROVA.
ABOORU VES BUT O SERVE LORD ANONDORF!

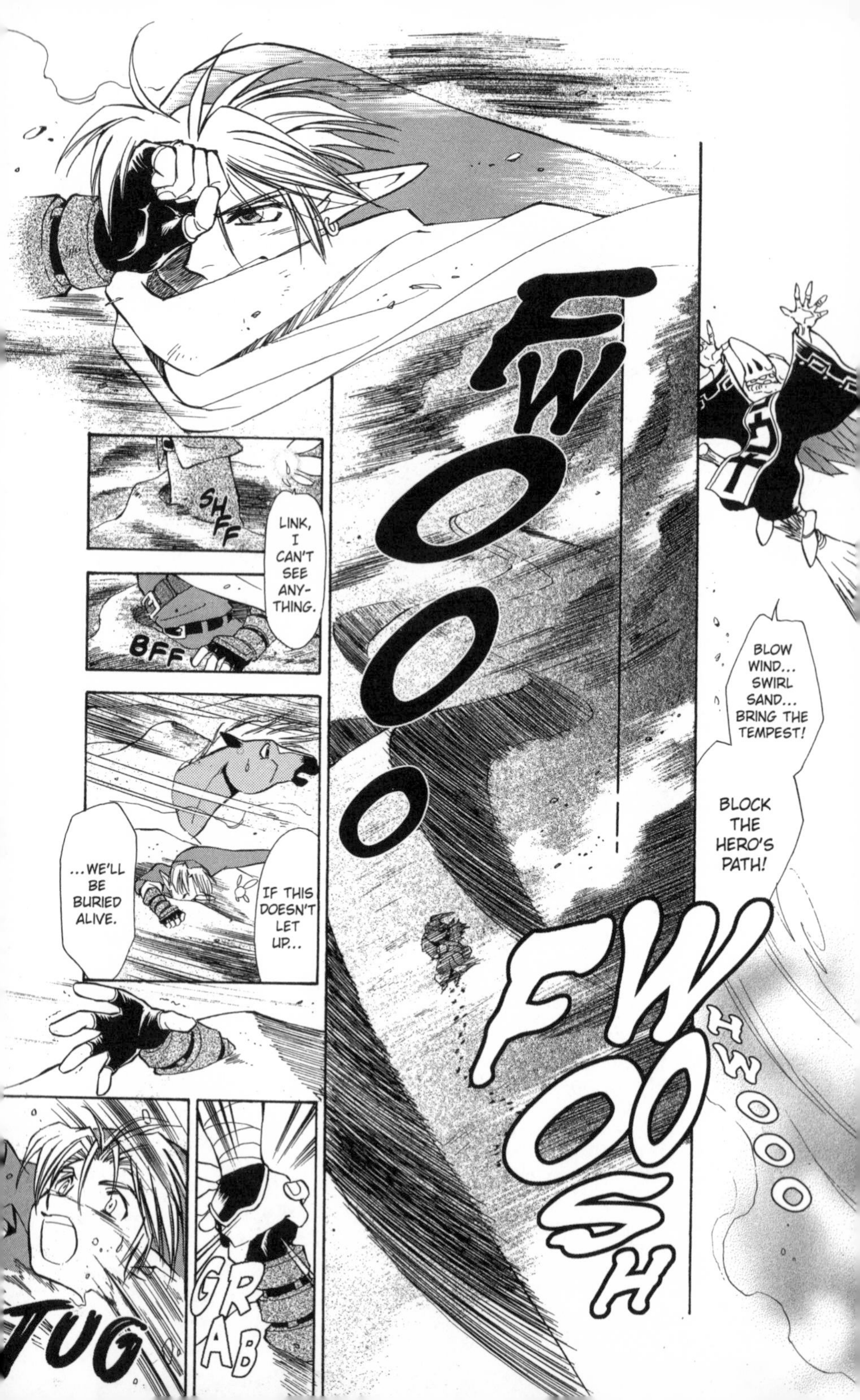
BLOW WIND... SWIRL SAND... BRING THE TEMPEST!
BLOCK THE HERO'S PATH!
FWOOSH
HWOOOO
FWOOOO
SHFF
LINK, I CAN'T SEE ANYTHING.
BFF
IF THIS DOESN'T LET UP...
...WE'LL BE BURIED ALIVE.
GRAB
TUG

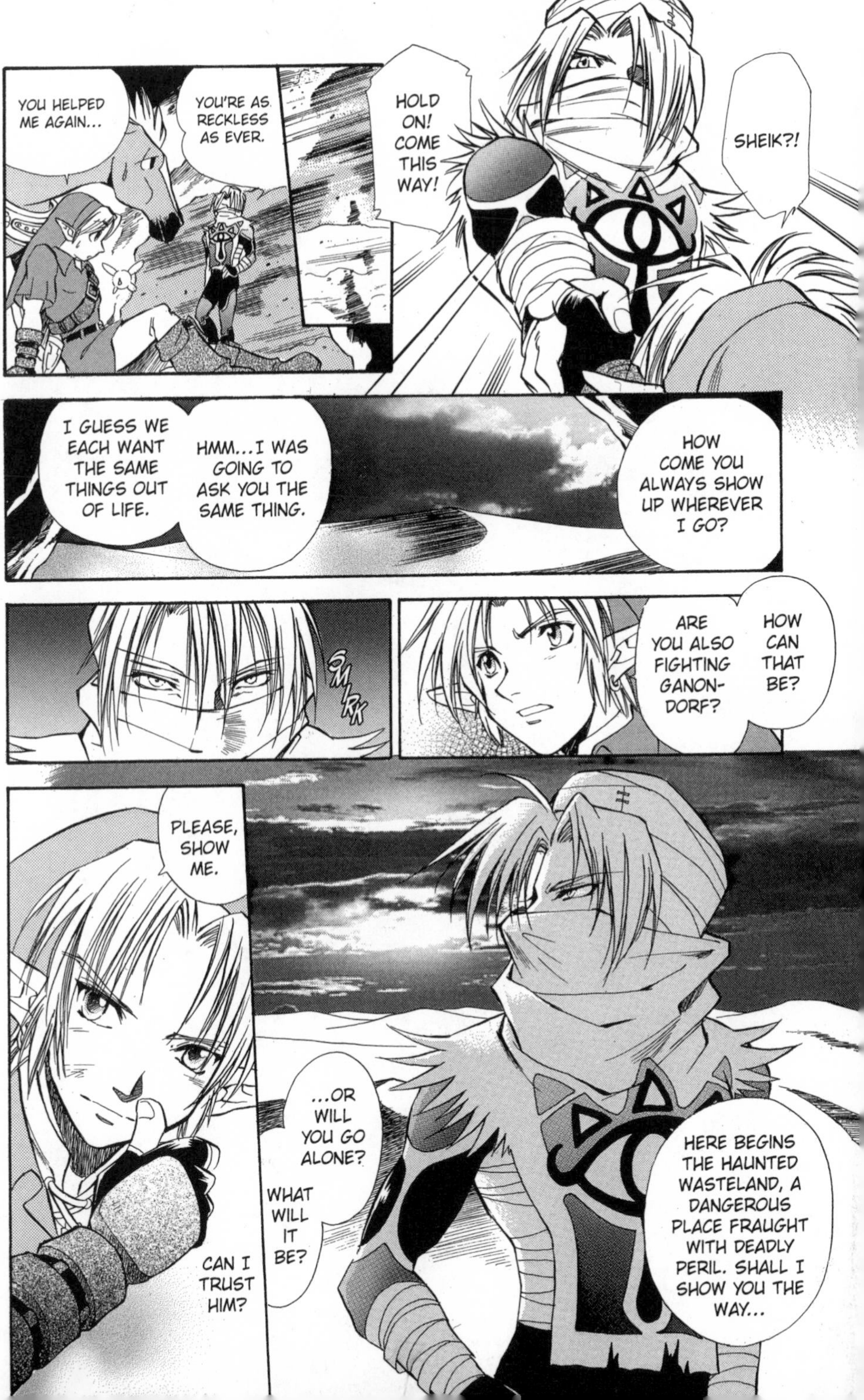
SHEIK?!
HOLD ON! COME THIS WAY!
YOU'RE AS RECKLESS AS EVER.
YOU HELPED ME AGAIN...
HOW COME YOU ALWAYS SHOW UP WHEREVER I GO?
HMM...I WAS GOING TO ASK YOU THE SAME THING.
I GUESS WE EACH WANT THE SAME THINGS OUT OF LIFE.
HOW CAN THAT BE?
ARE YOU ALSO FIGHTING GANON-DORF?
SMIRK
HERE BEGINS THE HAUNTED WASTELAND, A DANGEROUS PLACE FRAUGHT WITH DEADLY PERIL. SHALL I SHOW YOU THE WAY...
...OR WILL YOU GO ALONE?
WHAT WILL IT BE?
CAN I TRUST HIM?
PLEASE, SHOW ME.

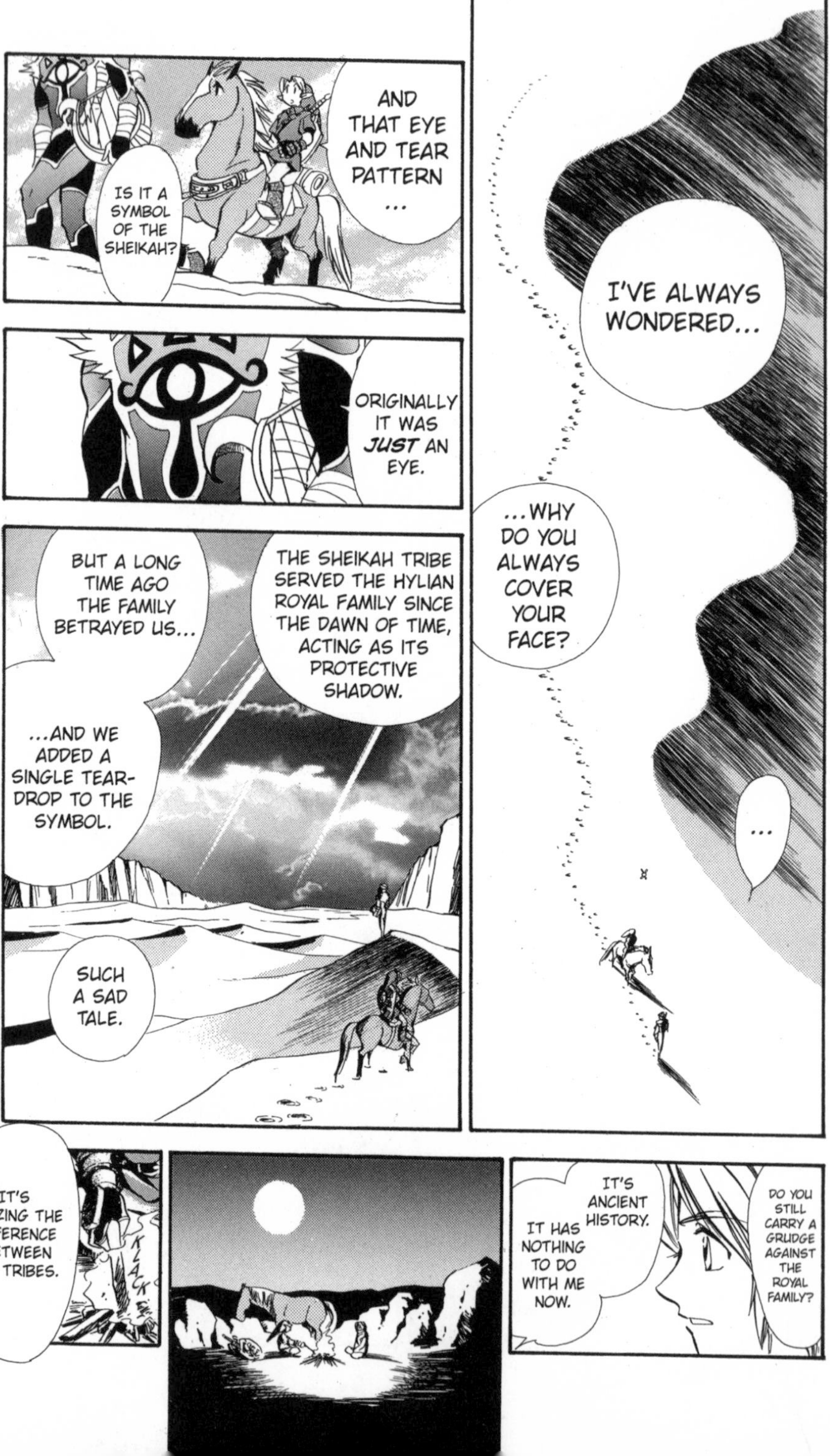
I'VE ALWAYS WONDERED...
...WHY DO YOU ALWAYS COVER YOUR FACE?
...
AND THAT EYE AND TEAR PATTERN...
IS IT A SYMBOL OF THE SHEIKAH?
ORIGINALLY IT WAS *JUST* AN EYE.
THE SHEIKAH TRIBE SERVED THE HYLIAN ROYAL FAMILY SINCE THE DAWN OF TIME, ACTING AS ITS PROTECTIVE SHADOW.
BUT A LONG TIME AGO THE FAMILY BETRAYED US...
...AND WE ADDED A SINGLE TEAR-DROP TO THE SYMBOL.
SUCH A SAD TALE.
DO YOU STILL CARRY A GRUDGE AGAINST THE ROYAL FAMILY?
IT'S ANCIENT HISTORY.
IT HAS NOTHING TO DO WITH ME NOW.
IT'S AMAZING THE DIFFERENCE BETWEEN THE TRIBES.
KLACK

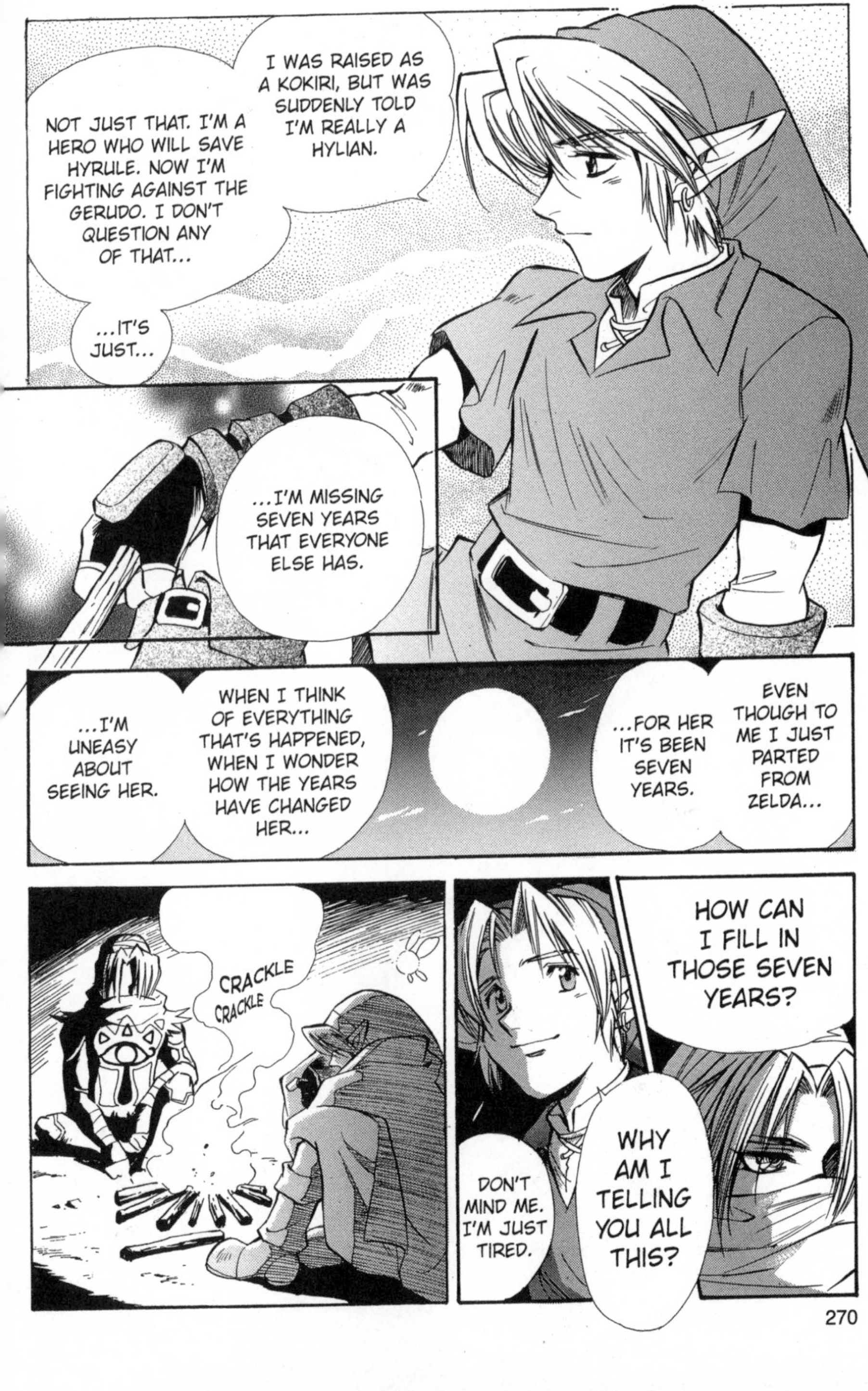
I WAS RAISED AS A KOKIRI, BUT WAS SUDDENLY TOLD I'M REALLY A HYLIAN.
NOT JUST THAT. I'M A HERO WHO WILL SAVE HYRULE. NOW I'M FIGHTING AGAINST THE GERUDO. I DON'T QUESTION ANY OF THAT...
...IT'S JUST...
...I'M MISSING SEVEN YEARS THAT EVERYONE ELSE HAS.
EVEN THOUGH TO ME I JUST PARTED FROM ZELDA...
...FOR HER IT'S BEEN SEVEN YEARS.
WHEN I THINK OF EVERYTHING THAT'S HAPPENED, WHEN I WONDER HOW THE YEARS HAVE CHANGED HER...
...I'M UNEASY ABOUT SEEING HER.
HOW CAN I FILL IN THOSE SEVEN YEARS?
WHY AM I TELLING YOU ALL THIS?
DON'T MIND ME. I'M JUST TIRED.
CRACKLE
CRACKLE

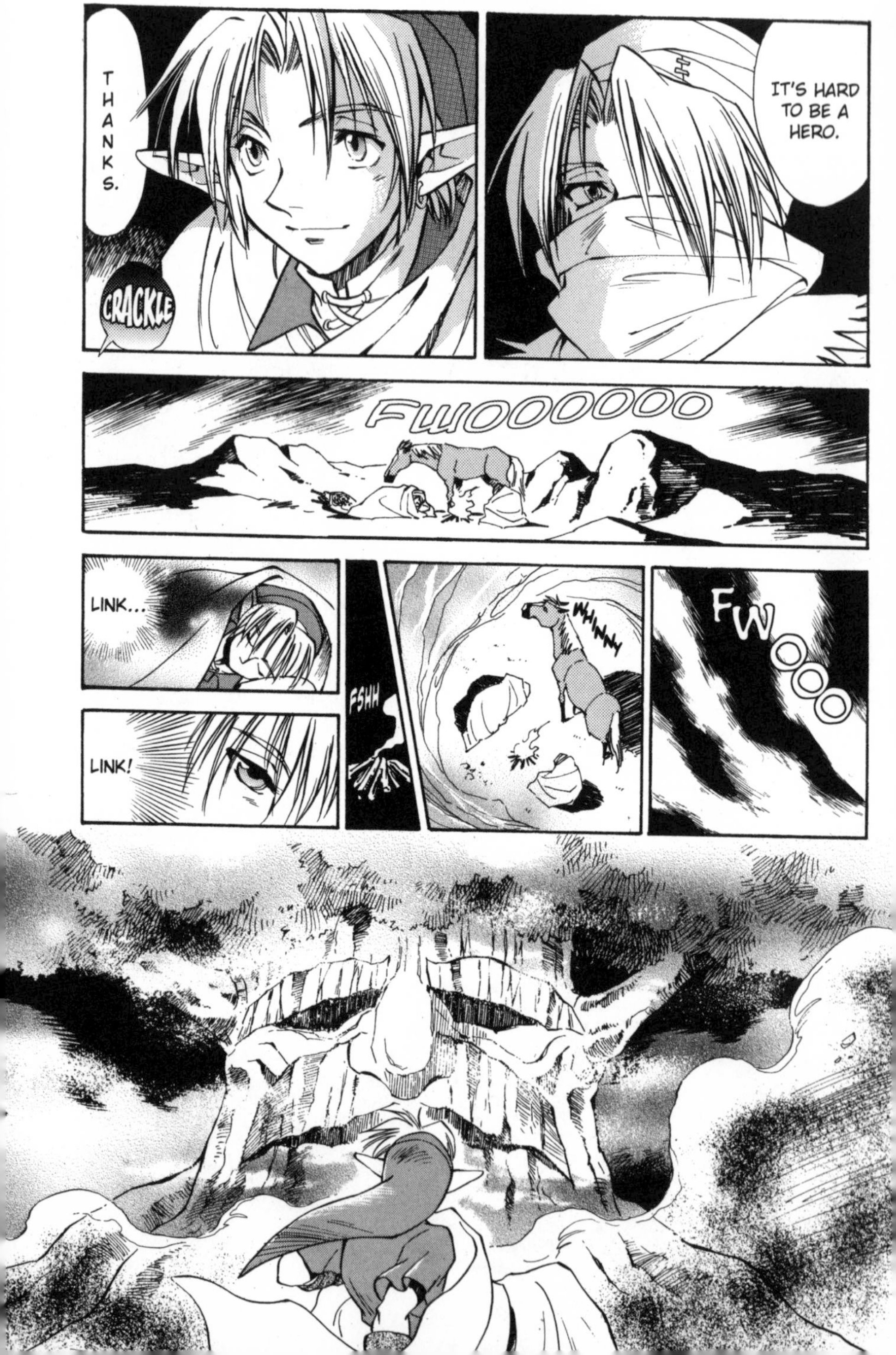
IT'S HARD TO BE A HERO.
THANKS.
CRACKLE
FWOOOOOOO
FWOOO
WHINNY
FSHH
LINK...
LINK!

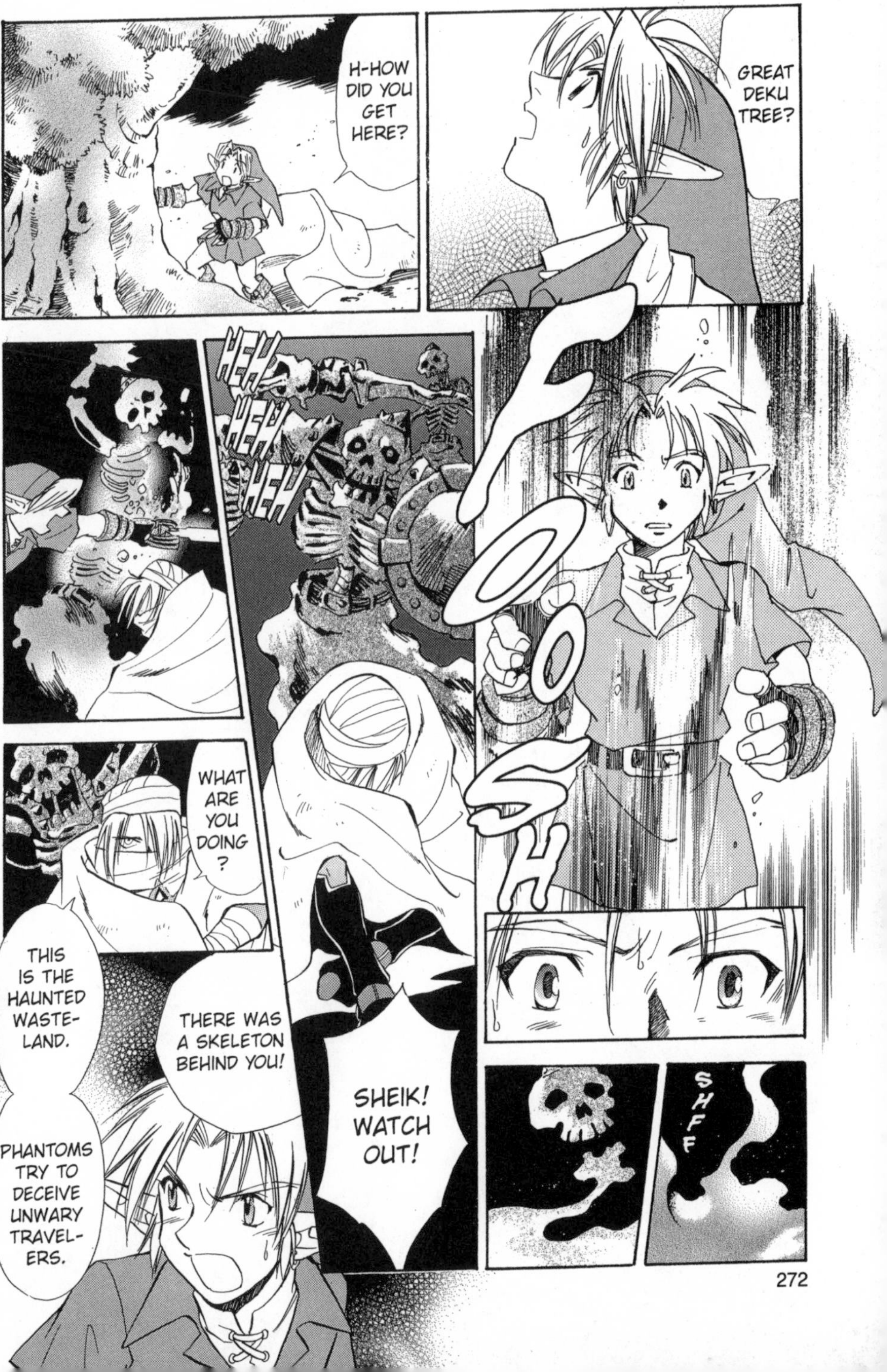
GREAT DEKU TREE?
H-HOW DID YOU GET HERE?
FOOOSH
HEH HEH HEH
SHEIK! WATCH OUT!
WHAT ARE YOU DOING?
THERE WAS A SKELETON BEHIND YOU!
SHFF
THIS IS THE HAUNTED WASTE-LAND.
PHANTOMS TRY TO DECEIVE UNWARY TRAVEL-ERS.

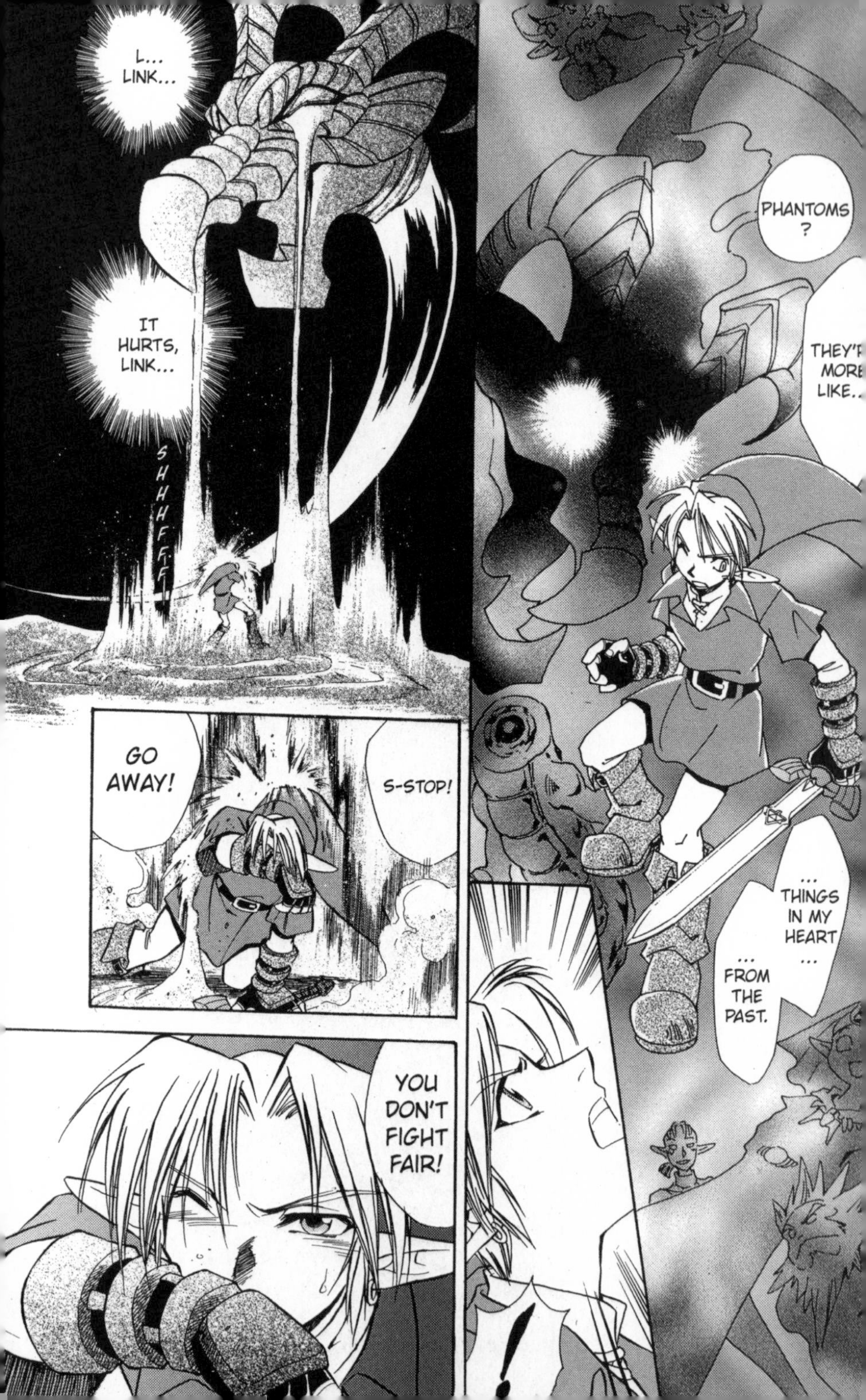

PHANTOMS?
THEY'R MORE LIKE..
...THINGS IN MY HEART...
...FROM THE PAST.
L... LINK...
IT HURTS, LINK...
SHHHFFF
S-STOP!
GO AWAY!
!
YOU DON'T FIGHT FAIR!

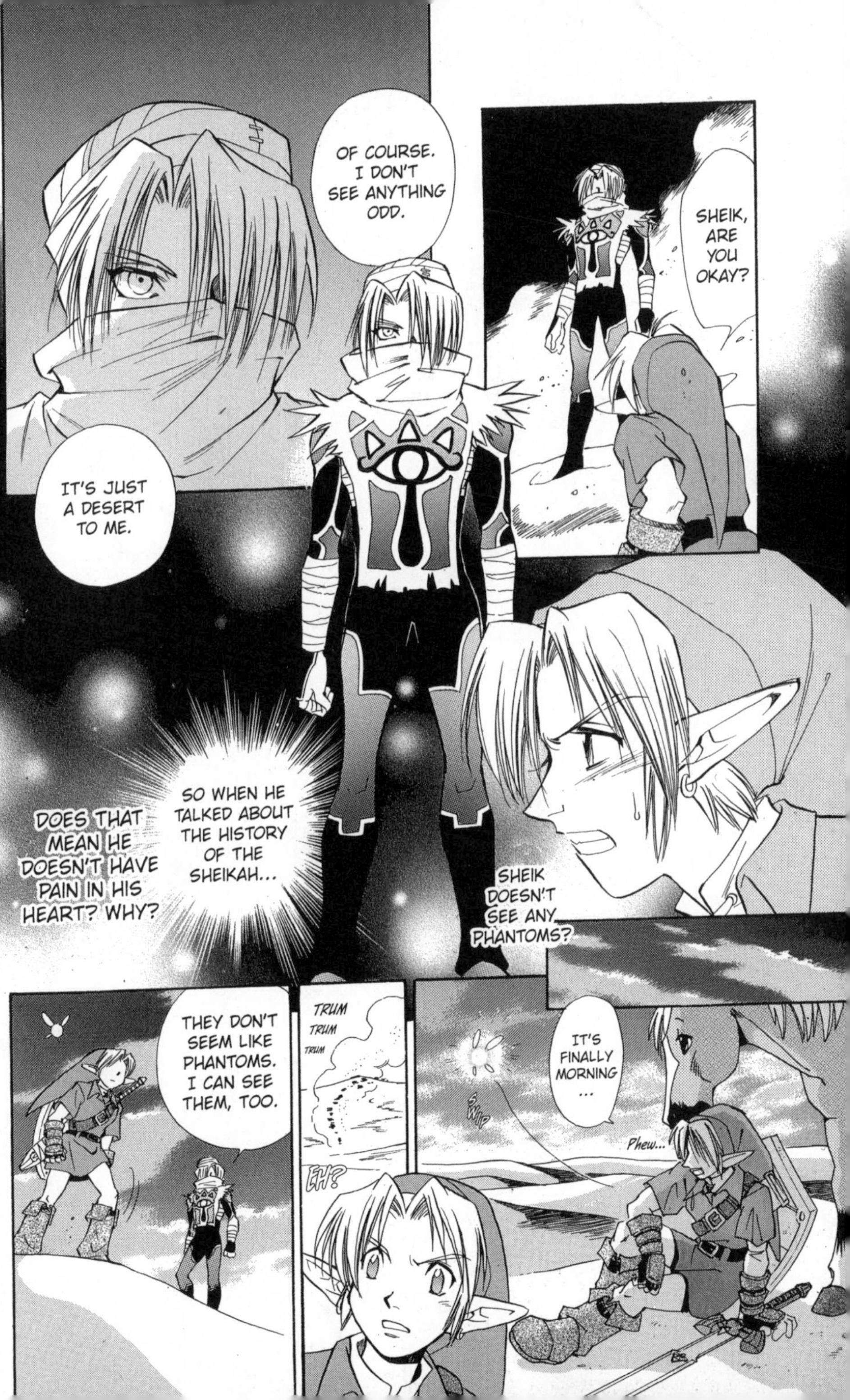
SHEIK, ARE YOU OKAY?
OF COURSE. I DON'T SEE ANYTHING ODD.
IT'S JUST A DESERT TO ME.
SHEIK DOESN'T SEE ANY PHANTOMS?
SO WHEN HE TALKED ABOUT THE HISTORY OF THE SHEIKAH...
DOES THAT MEAN HE DOESN'T HAVE PAIN IN HIS HEART? WHY?
IT'S FINALLY MORNING...
Phew...
SWIP
EH?
TRUM
TRUM
TRUM
THEY DON'T SEEM LIKE PHANTOMS. I CAN SEE THEM, TOO.

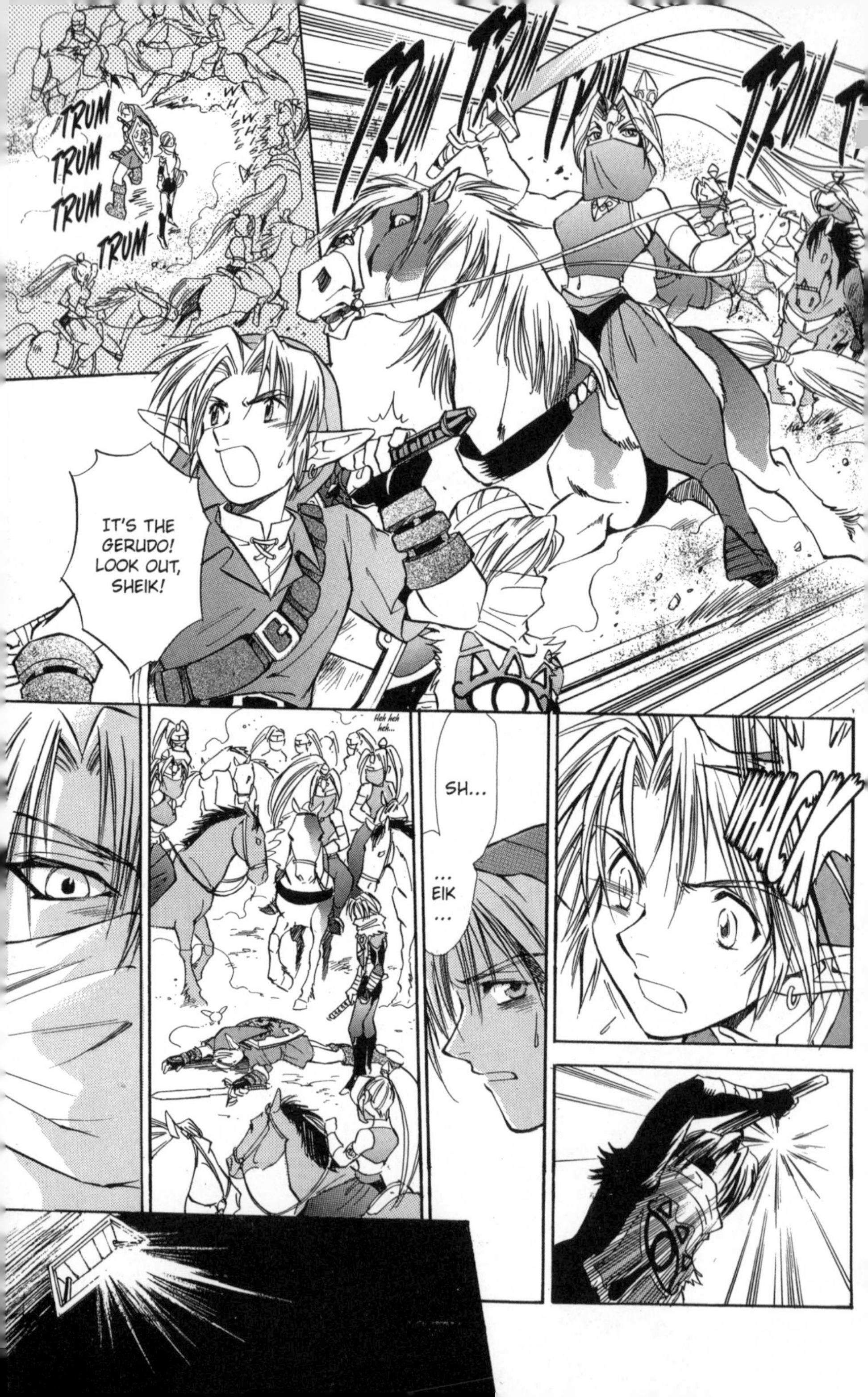
TRUM
TRUM
TRUM
TRUM
IT'S THE GERUDO! LOOK OUT, SHEIK!
WHACK
SH...
...EIK...
Heh heh heh...

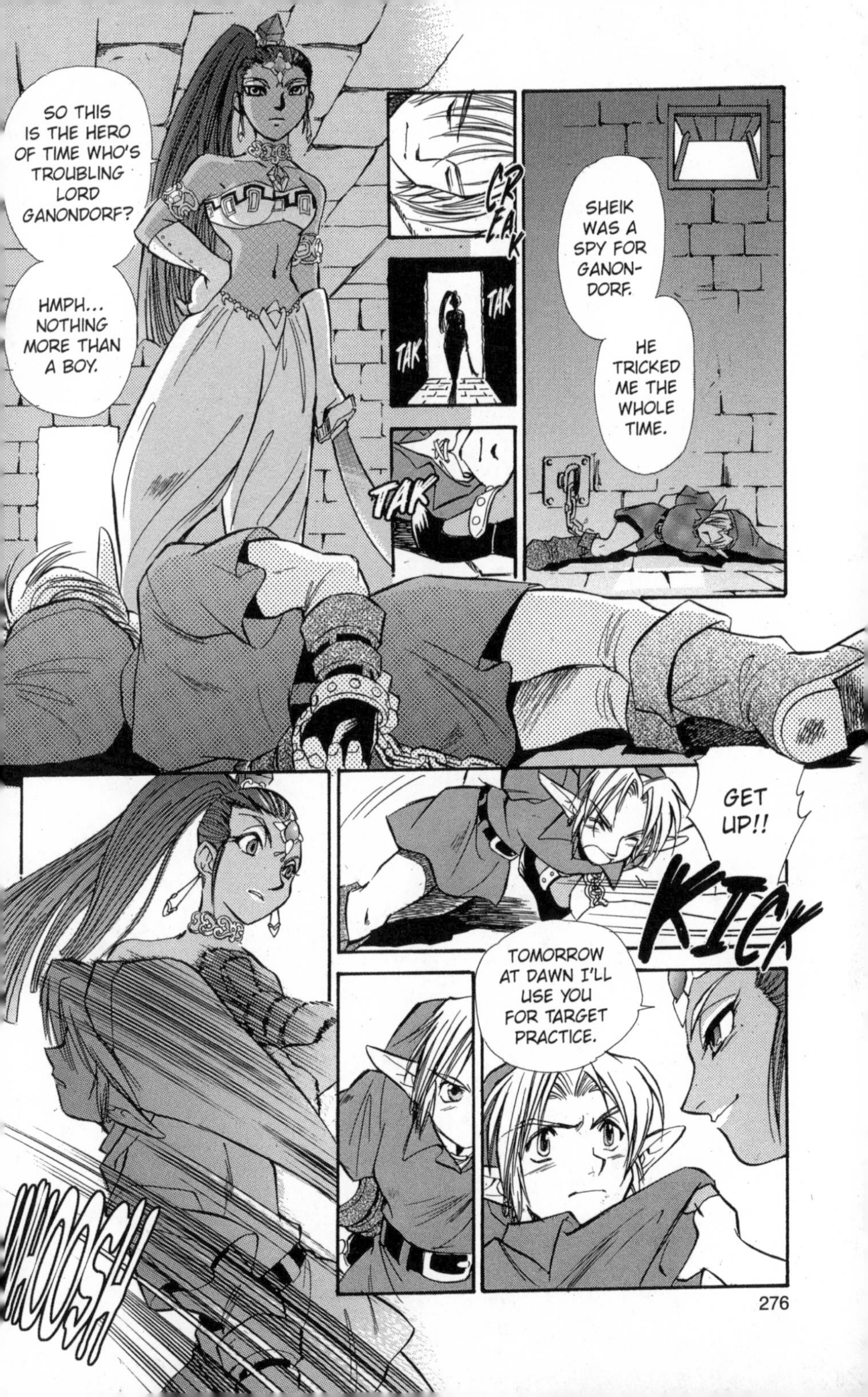
SHEIK WAS A SPY FOR GANON-DORF.
HE TRICKED ME THE WHOLE TIME.
CREAK
TAK
TAK
TAK
SO THIS IS THE HERO OF TIME WHO'S TROUBLING LORD GANONDORF?
HMPH... NOTHING MORE THAN A BOY.
GET UP!!
KICK
TOMORROW AT DAWN I'LL USE YOU FOR TARGET PRACTICE.
WHOOSH

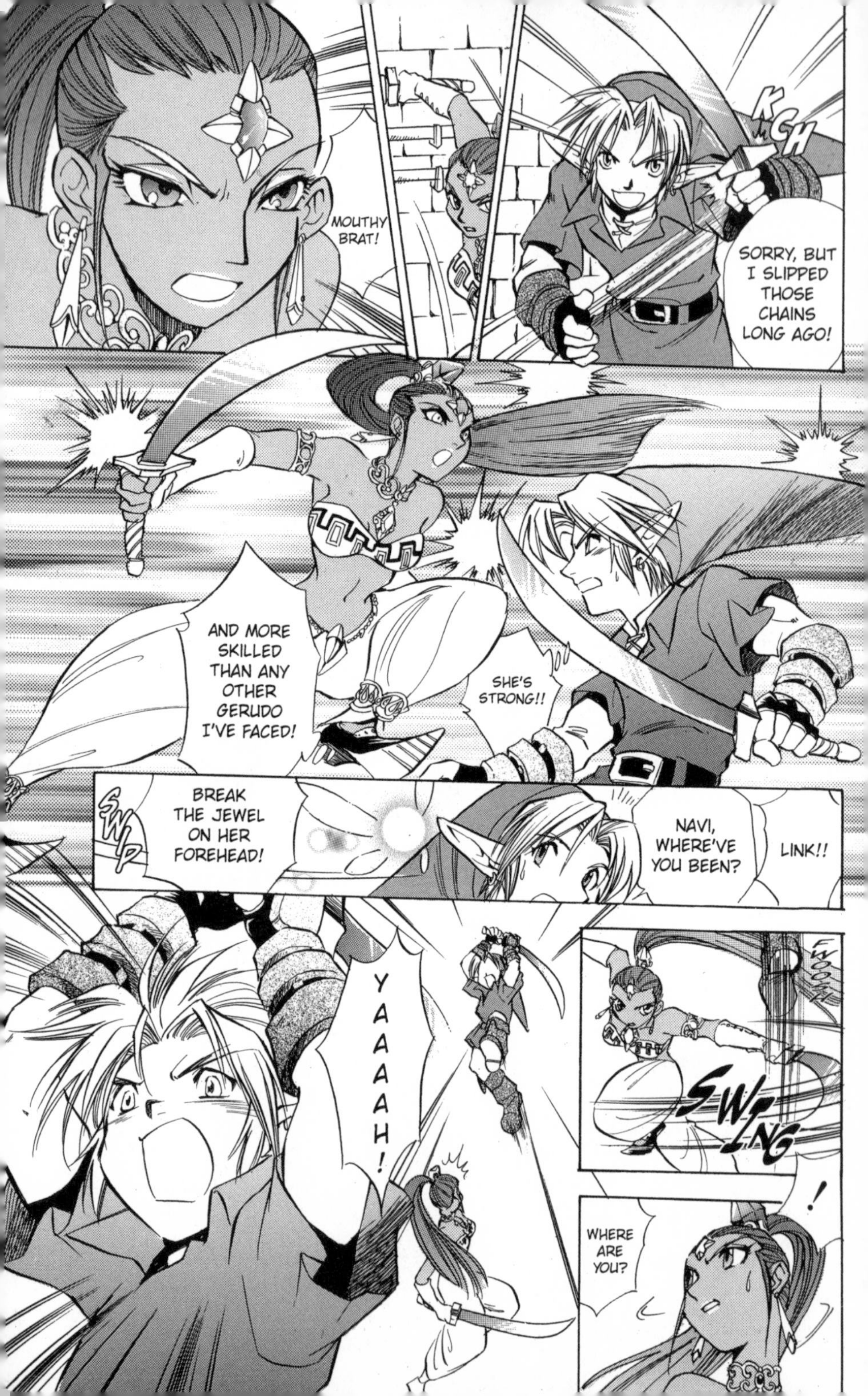
KCH
SORRY, BUT I SLIPPED THOSE CHAINS LONG AGO!
MOUTHY BRAT!
SHE'S STRONG!!
AND MORE SKILLED THAN ANY OTHER GERUDO I'VE FACED!
LINK!!
NAVI, WHERE'VE YOU BEEN?
BREAK THE JEWEL ON HER FOREHEAD!
SWIP
FWOOOSH
SWING
!
WHERE ARE YOU?
YAAAAAH!

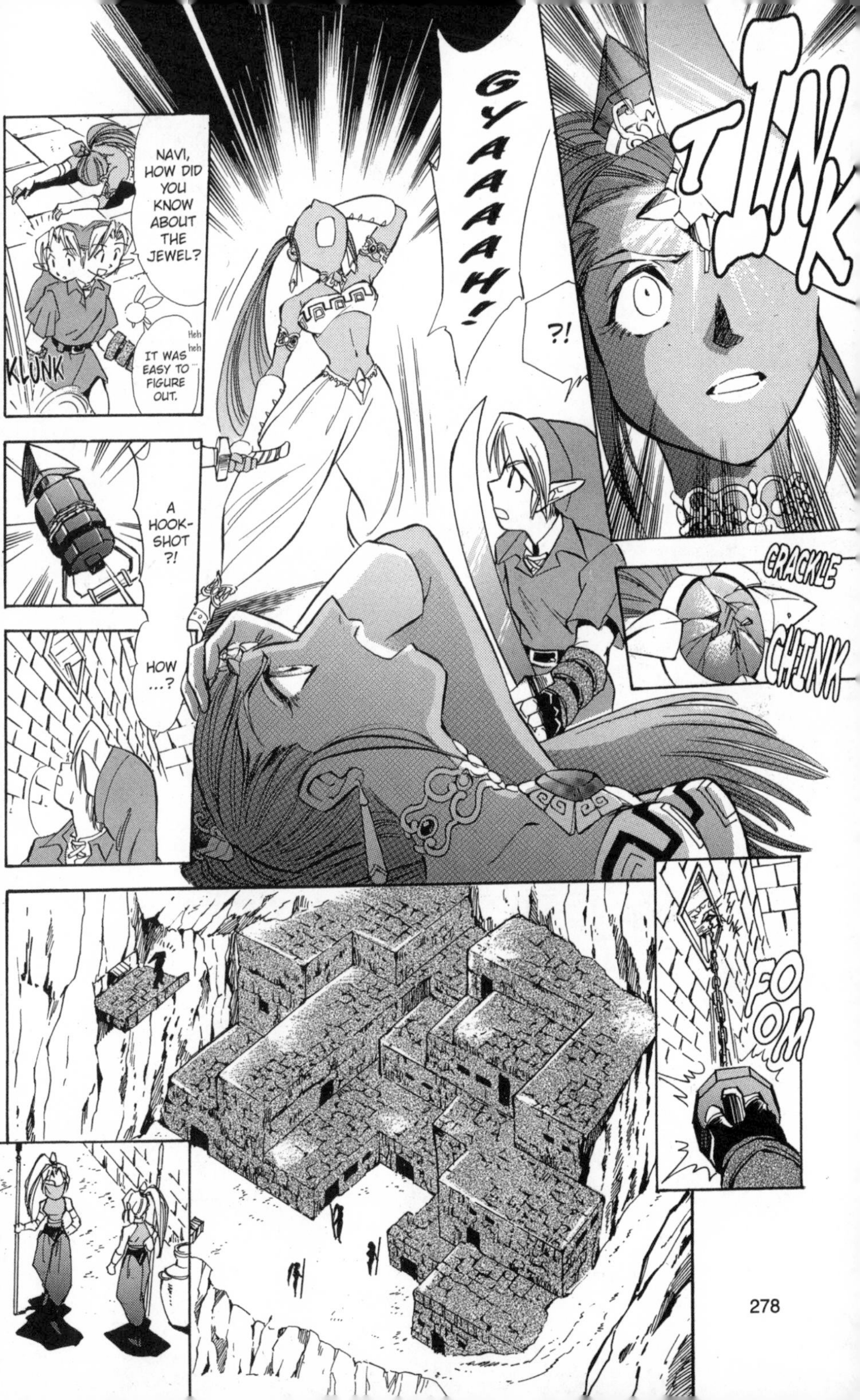
TINK
?!
CRACKLE
CHINK
GYAAAAAH!
NAVI, HOW DID YOU KNOW ABOUT THE JEWEL?
Heh heh...
IT WAS EASY TO FIGURE OUT.
KLUNK
A HOOK-SHOT ?!
HOW ...?
FOOOM

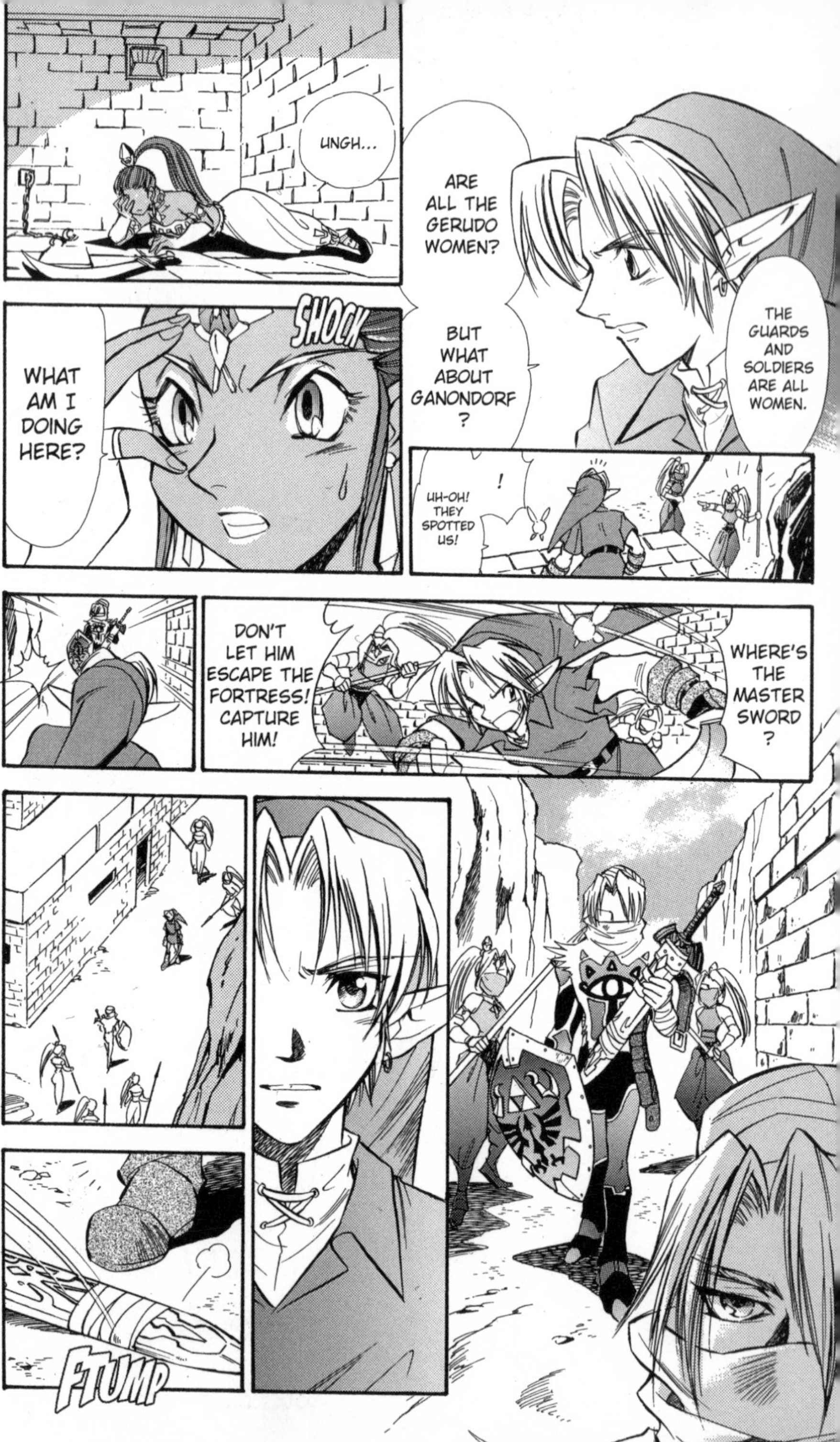
ARE ALL THE GERUDO WOMEN?
THE GUARDS AND SOLDIERS ARE ALL WOMEN.
BUT WHAT ABOUT GANONDORF?
UNGH...
SHOCK
WHAT AM I DOING HERE?
!
UH-OH! THEY SPOTTED US!
WHERE'S THE MASTER SWORD?
DON'T LET HIM ESCAPE THE FORTRESS! CAPTURE HIM!
FTUMP

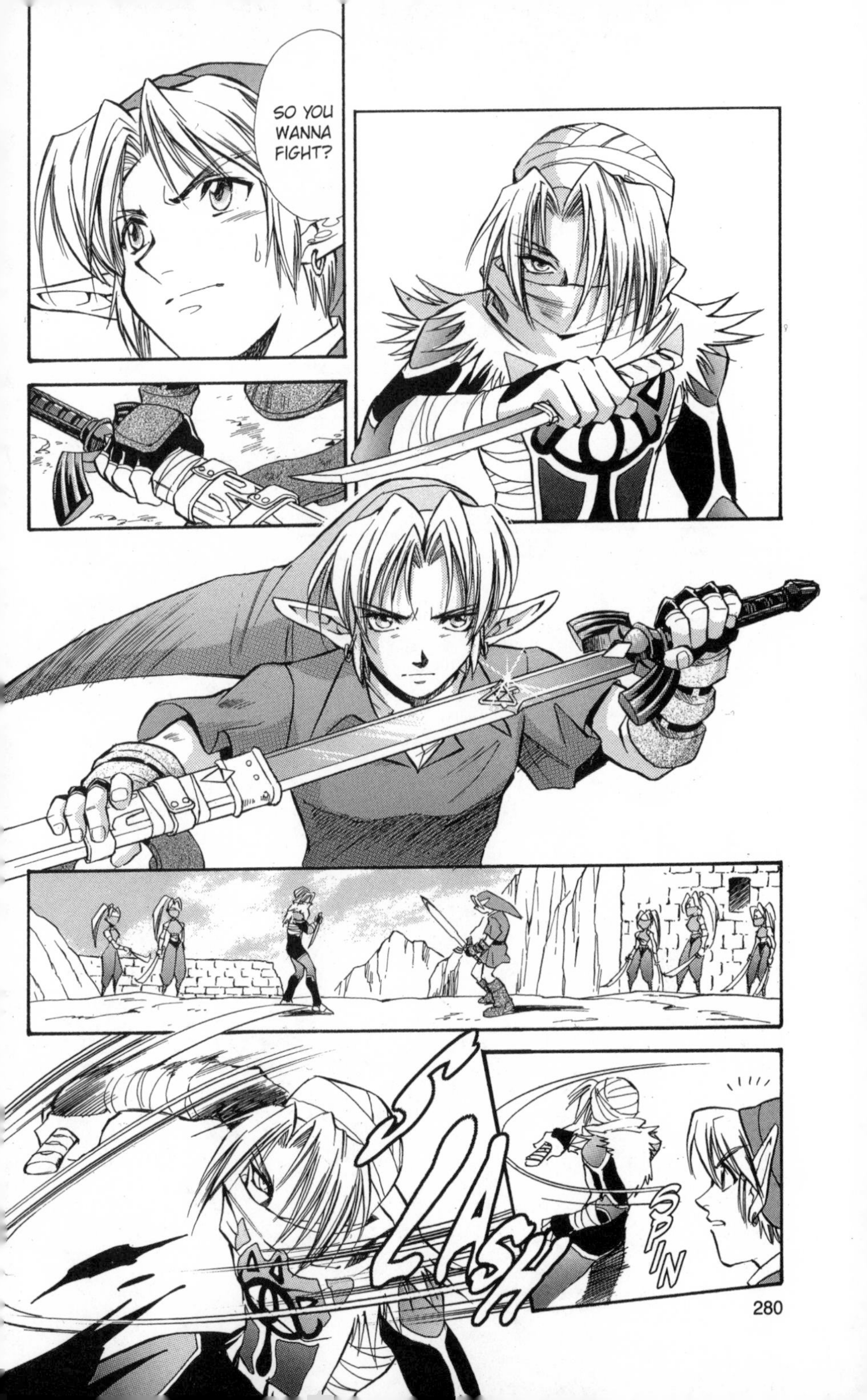
SO YOU WANNA FIGHT?
SPIN
CLASH

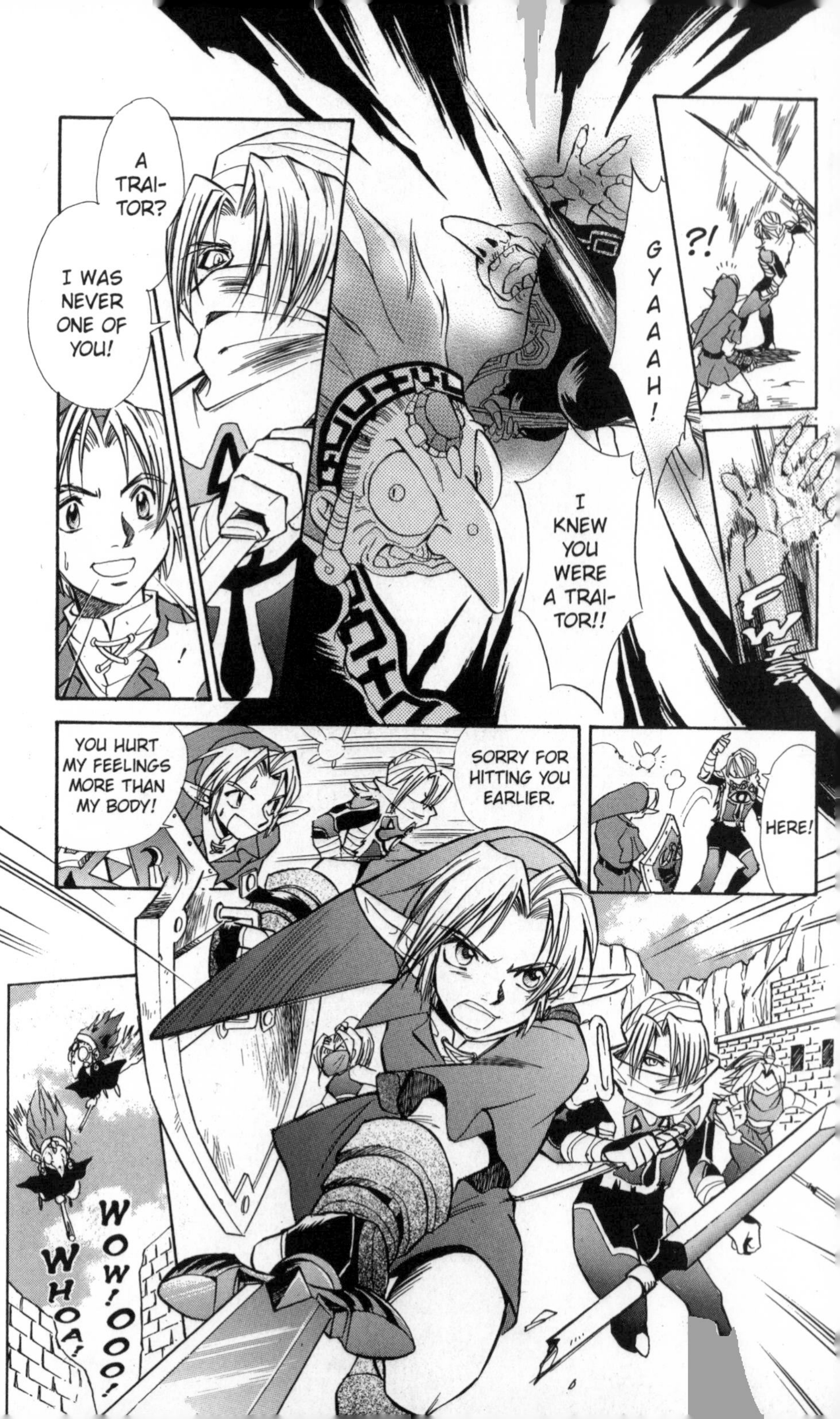
?!
GYAAAH!
I KNEW YOU WERE A TRAITOR!!
A TRAITOR?
I WAS NEVER ONE OF YOU!
HERE!
SORRY FOR HITTING YOU EARLIER.
YOU HURT MY FEELINGS MORE THAN MY BODY!
WOW! OOO!
WHOA!

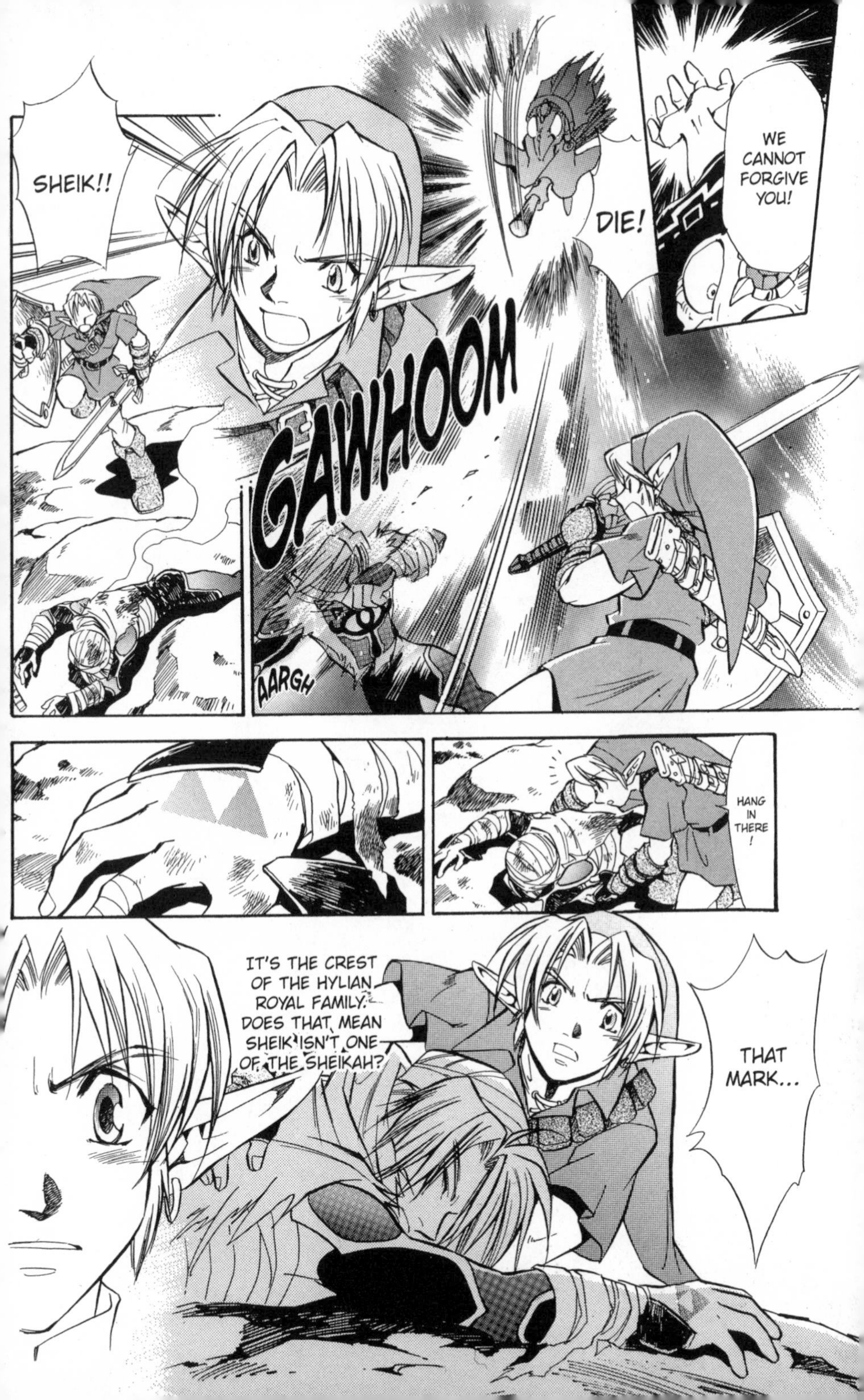
WE CANNOT FORGIVE YOU!
DIE!
SHEIK!!
GAWHOOM
AARGH
HANG IN THERE!
THAT MARK...
IT'S THE CREST OF THE HYLIAN ROYAL FAMILY. DOES THAT MEAN SHEIK ISN'T ONE OF THE SHEIKAH?

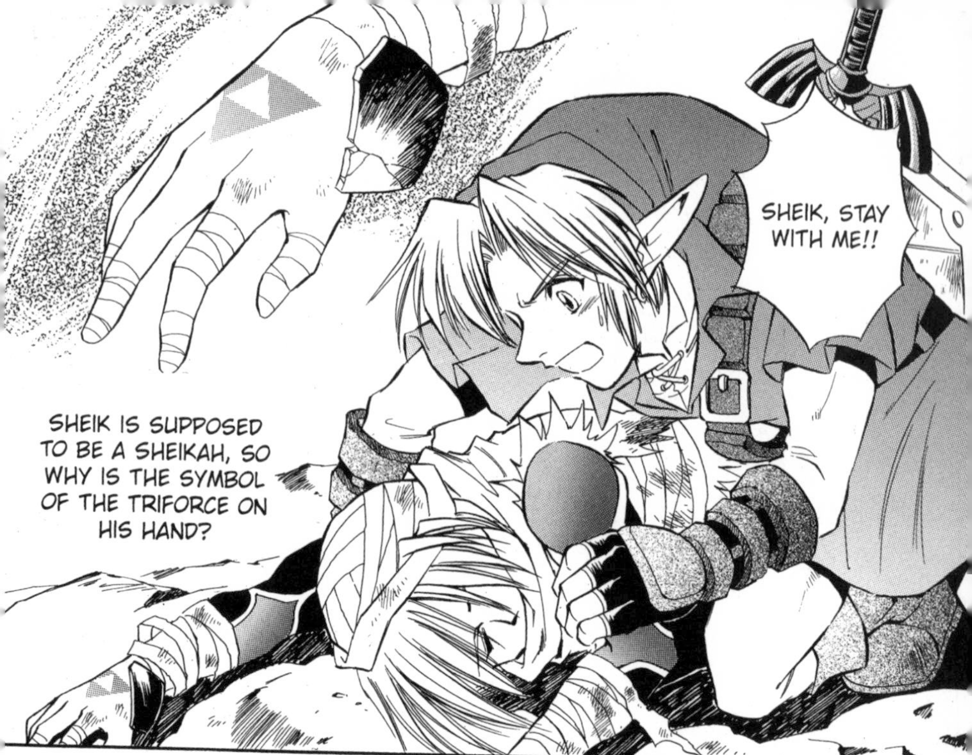
SHEIK, STAY WITH ME!!
SHEIK IS SUPPOSED TO BE A SHEIKAH, SO WHY IS THE SYMBOL OF THE TRIFORCE ON HIS HAND?

CHAPTER 7 A FATED REUNION

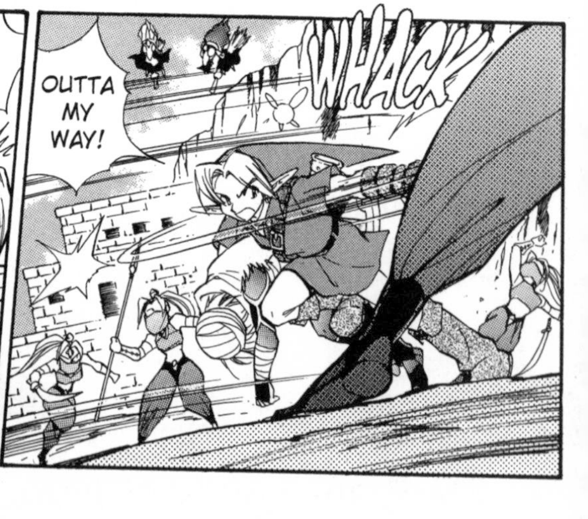
WHACK
OUTTA MY WAY!
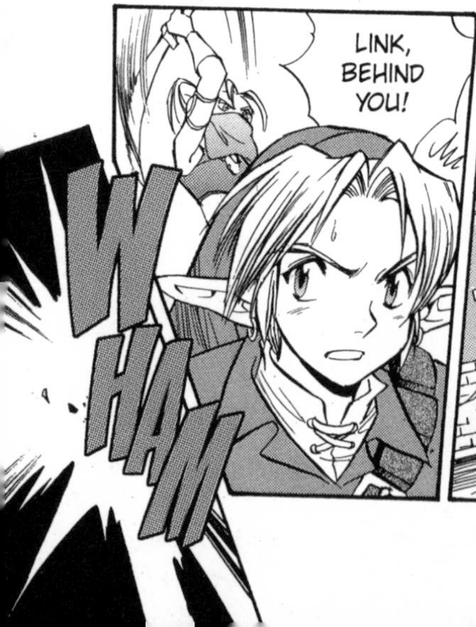
LINK, BEHIND YOU!
WHAM

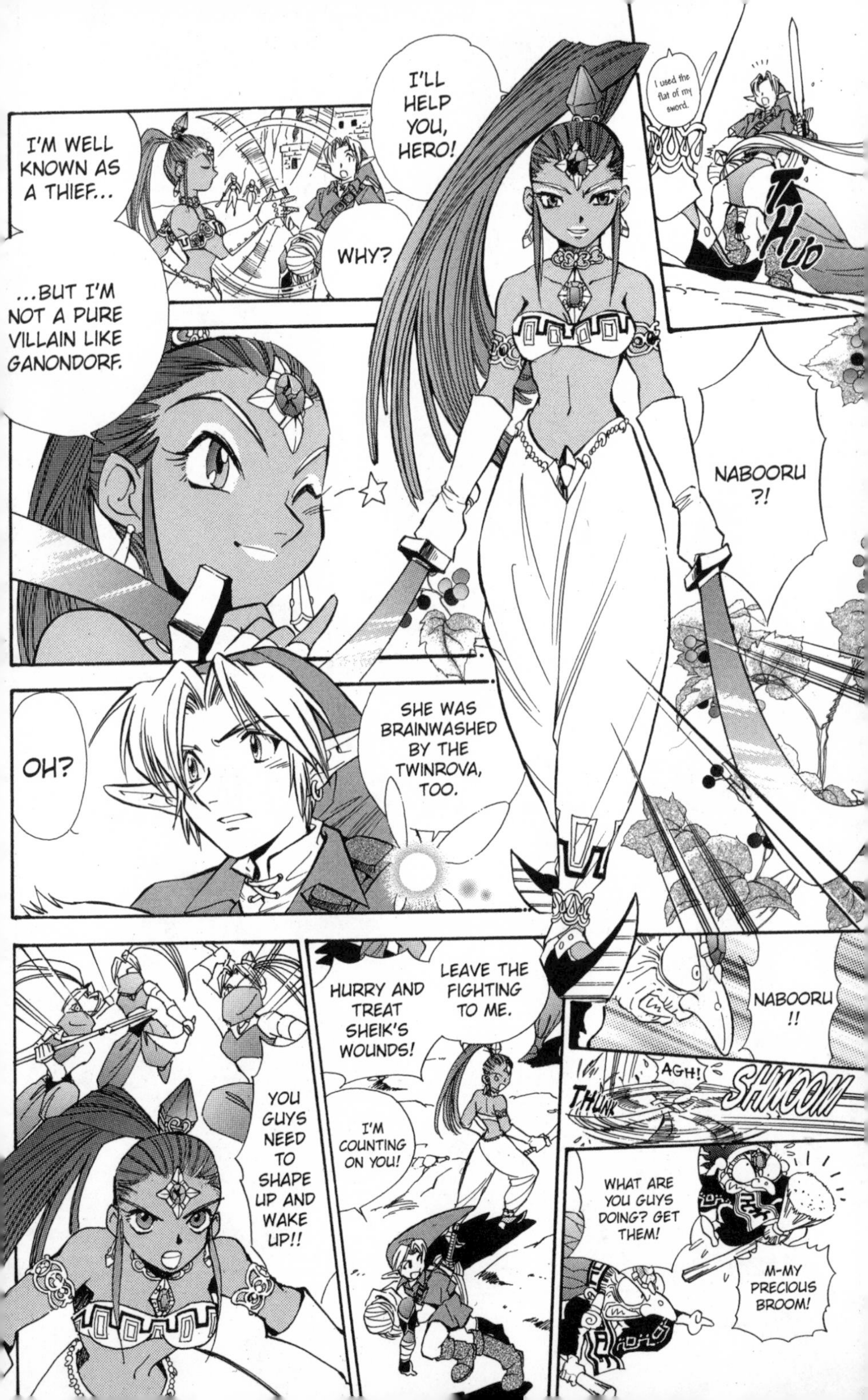
I used the flat of my sword.
THUD
NABOORU ?!
I'LL HELP YOU, HERO!
I'M WELL KNOWN AS A THIEF...
WHY?
...BUT I'M NOT A PURE VILLAIN LIKE GANONDORF.
SHE WAS BRAINWASHED BY THE TWINROVA, TOO.
OH?
NABOORU !!
AGH!
SHWOOM
THUNK
WHAT ARE YOU GUYS DOING? GET THEM!
M-MY PRECIOUS BROOM!
LEAVE THE FIGHTING TO ME.
HURRY AND TREAT SHEIK'S WOUNDS!
I'M COUNTING ON YOU!
YOU GUYS NEED TO SHAPE UP AND WAKE UP!!

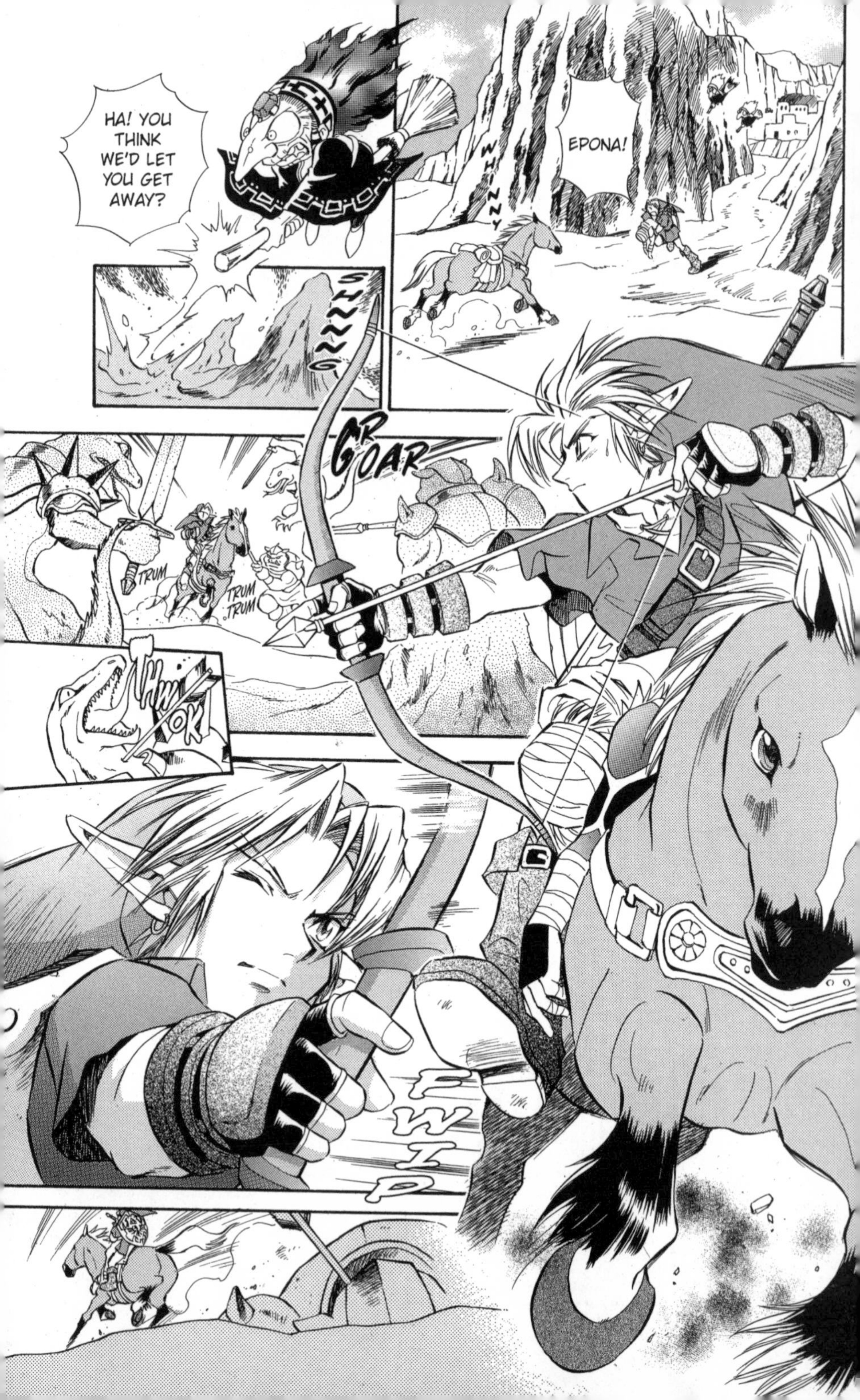
WHINNY
EPONA!
HA! YOU THINK WE'D LET YOU GET AWAY?
SHNNNG
GRGOAR
TRUM
TRUM TRUM
THWOK
FWIP

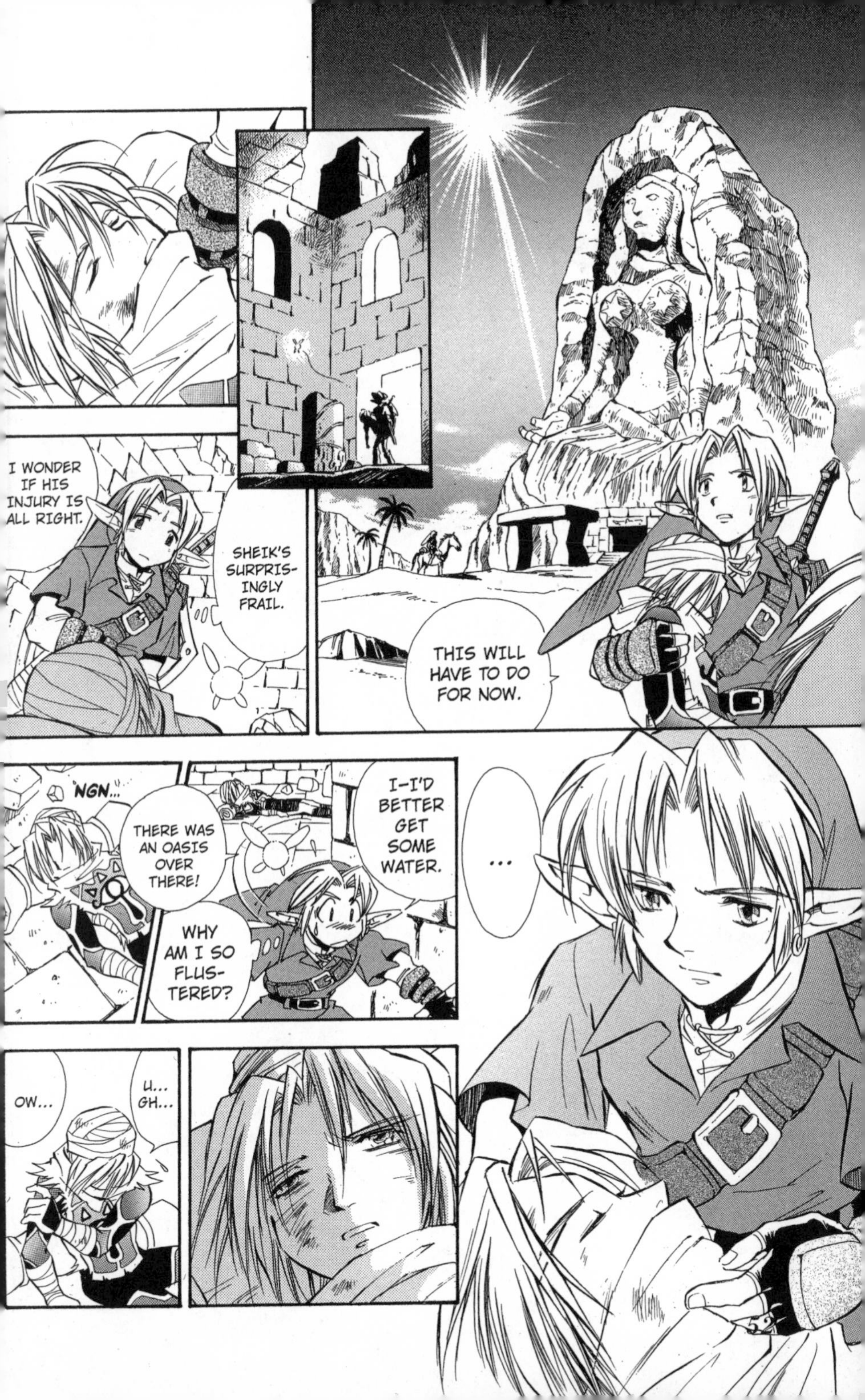
THIS WILL HAVE TO DO FOR NOW.
SHEIK'S SURPRIS-INGLY FRAIL.
I WONDER IF HIS INJURY IS ALL RIGHT.
...
I-I'D BETTER GET SOME WATER.
THERE WAS AN OASIS OVER THERE!
WHY AM I SO FLUS-TERED?
NGN...
U... GH...
OW...

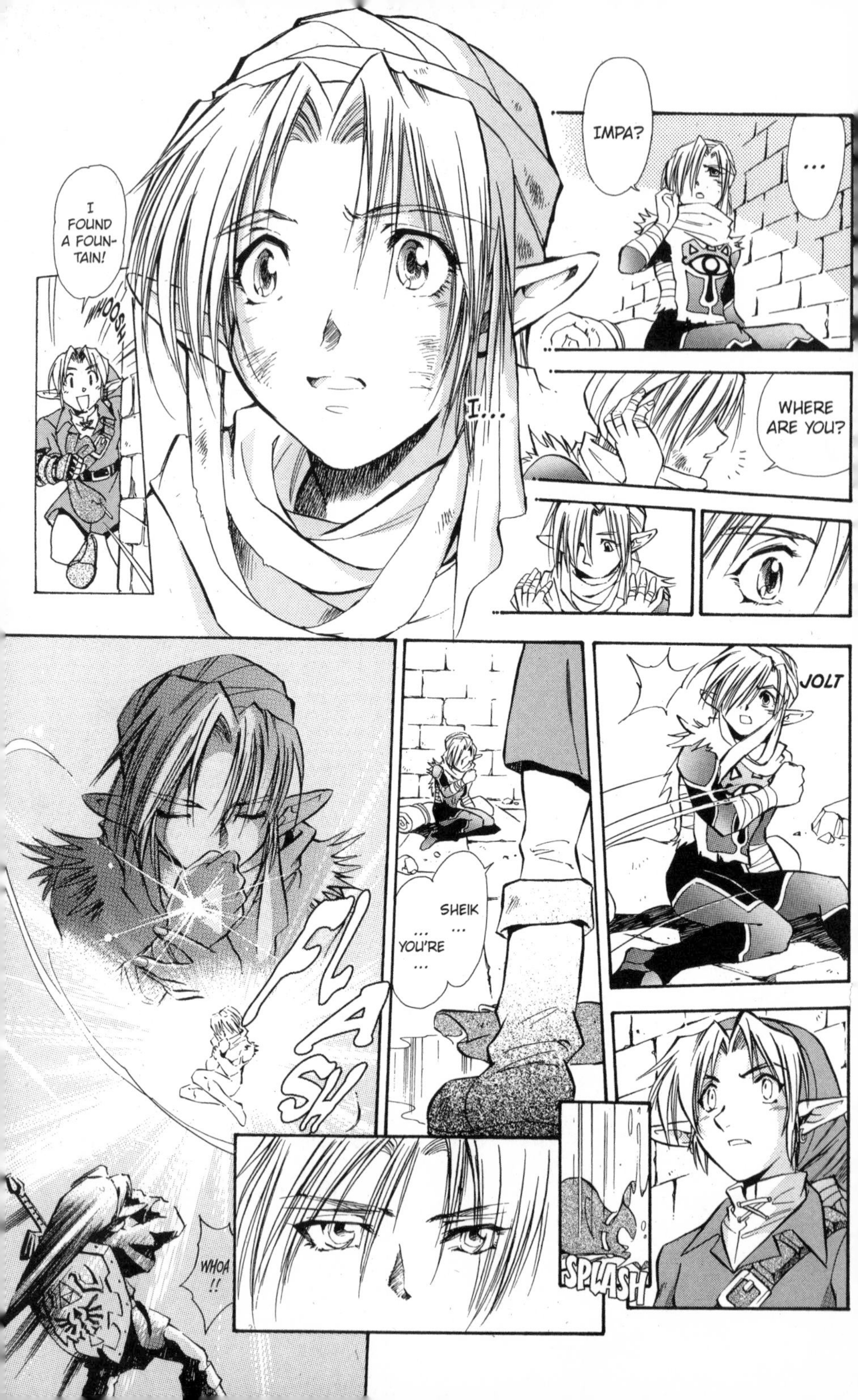
...
IMPA?
WHERE ARE YOU?
I...
I FOUND A FOUN-TAIN!
WHOOSH
JOLT
SHEIK ... ... YOU'RE ...
SPLASH
SLASH
WHOA !!

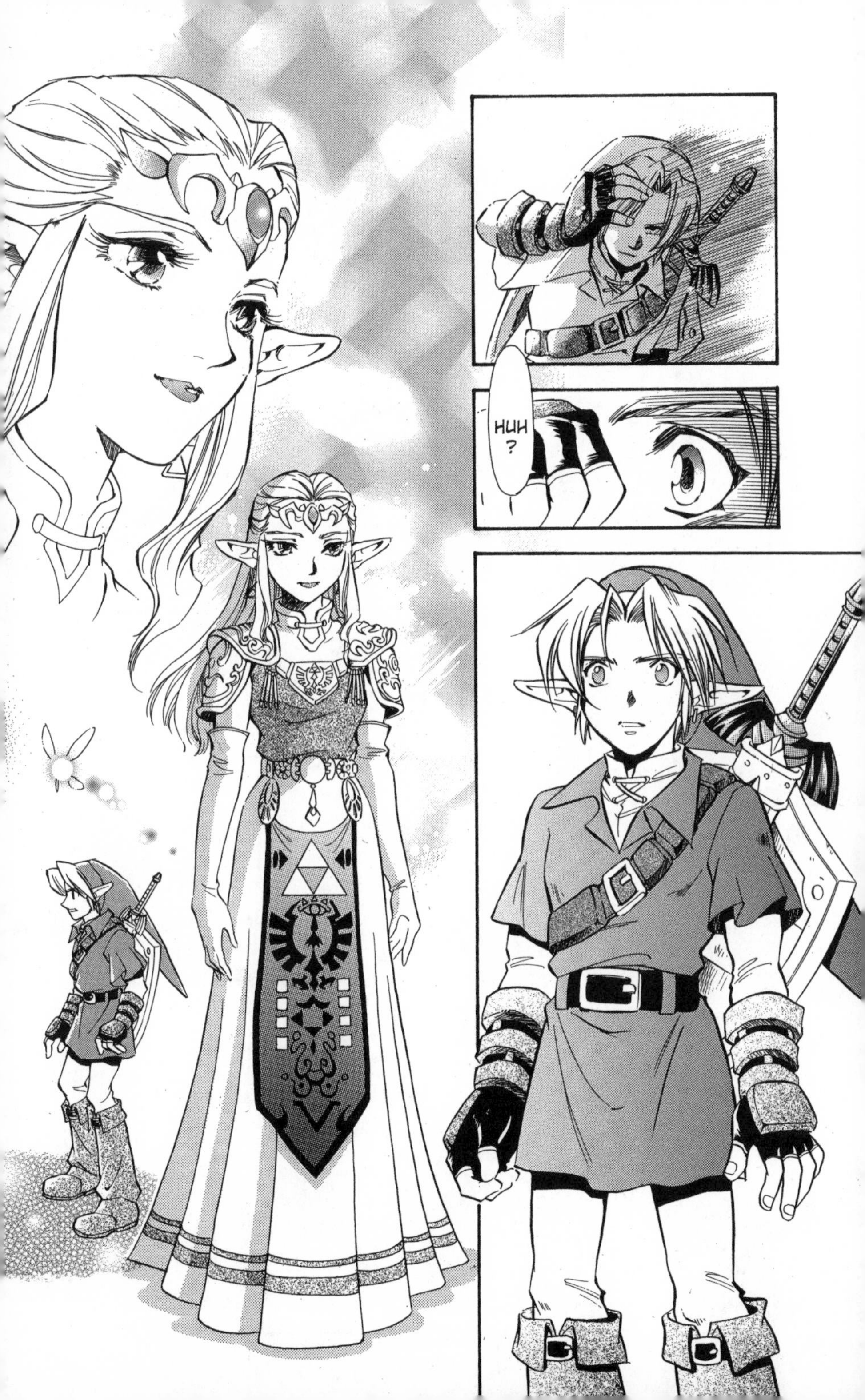
HUH?

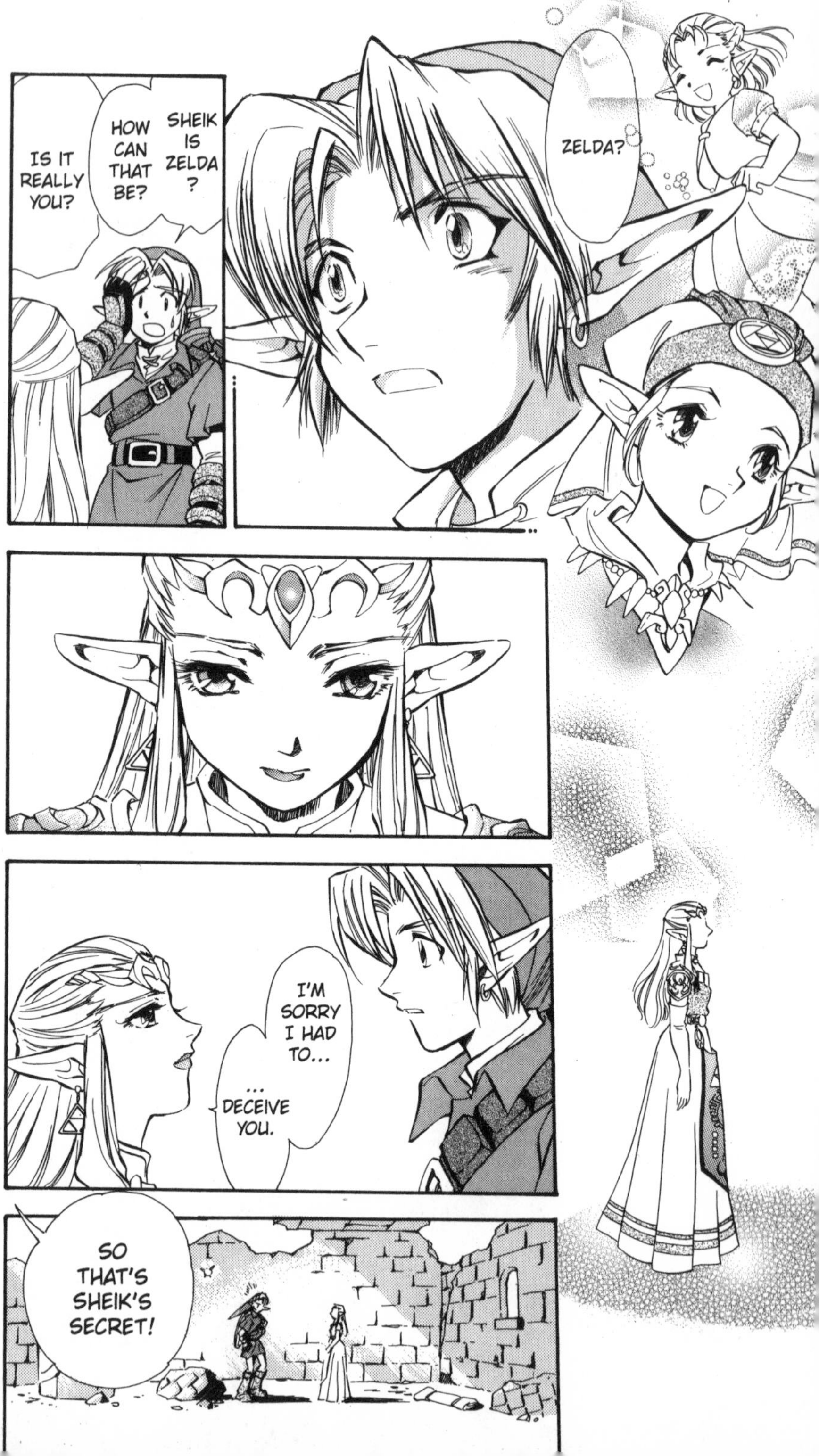
ZELDA?
SHEIK IS ZELDA?
HOW CAN THAT BE?
IS IT REALLY YOU?
I'M SORRY I HAD TO...
... DECEIVE YOU.
SO THAT'S SHEIK'S SECRET!

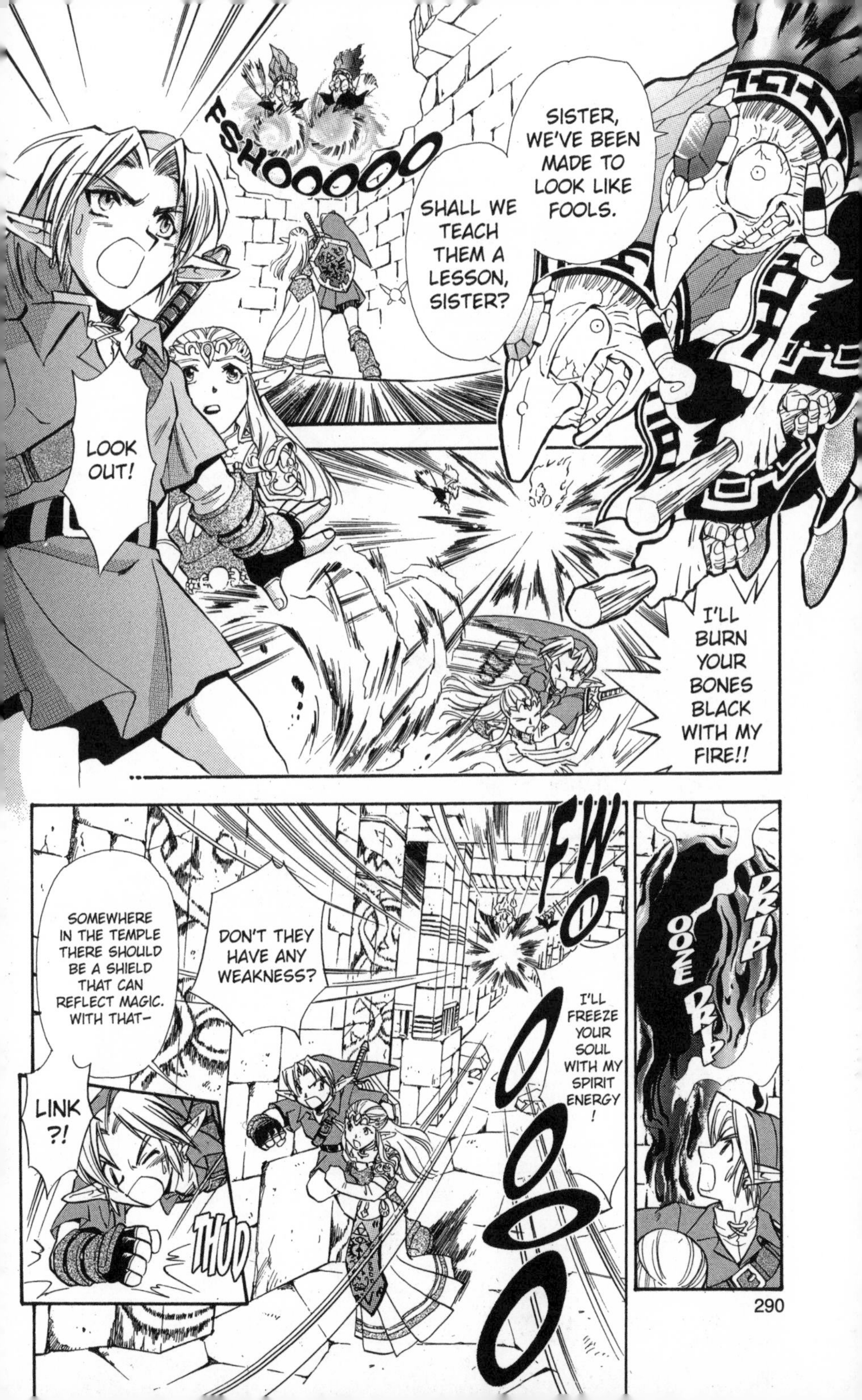
SISTER, WE'VE BEEN MADE TO LOOK LIKE FOOLS.
SHALL WE TEACH THEM A LESSON, SISTER?
FSHOOOOO
LOOK OUT!
I'LL BURN YOUR BONES BLACK WITH MY FIRE!!
DRIP
OOZE
DRIP
FWOOOOOO
I'LL FREEZE YOUR SOUL WITH MY SPIRIT ENERGY!
DON'T THEY HAVE ANY WEAKNESS?
SOMEWHERE IN THE TEMPLE THERE SHOULD BE A SHIELD THAT CAN REFLECT MAGIC. WITH THAT-
LINK?!
THUD

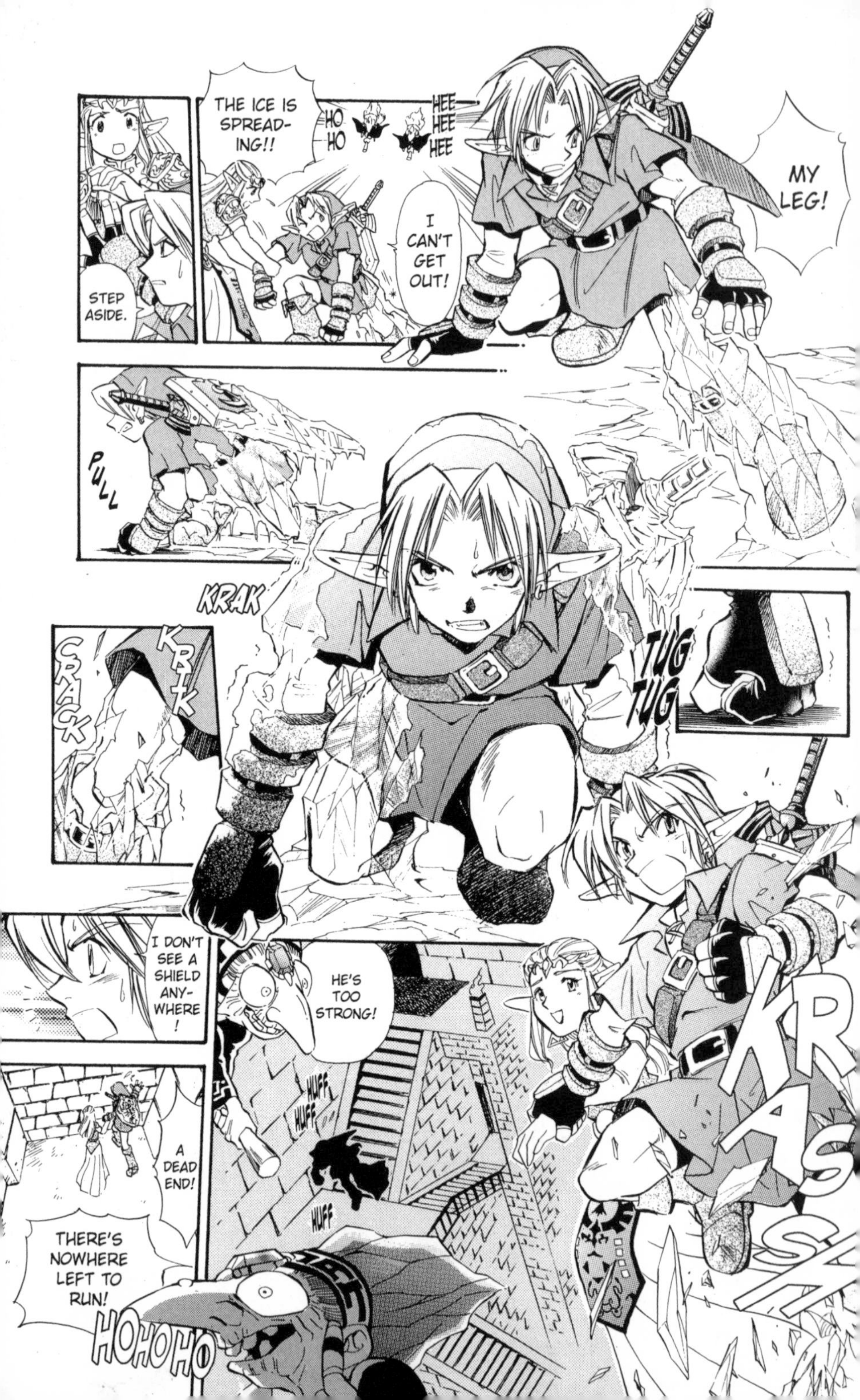
MY LEG!
THE ICE IS SPREADING!!
HO HO
HEE HEE HEE
I CAN'T GET OUT!
STEP ASIDE.
PULL
TUG TUG
KRAK
KRIK
CRACK
KRASH
HE'S TOO STRONG!
HUFF HUFF
HUFF
I DON'T SEE A SHIELD ANYWHERE!
A DEAD END!
THERE'S NOWHERE LEFT TO RUN!
HOHOHO

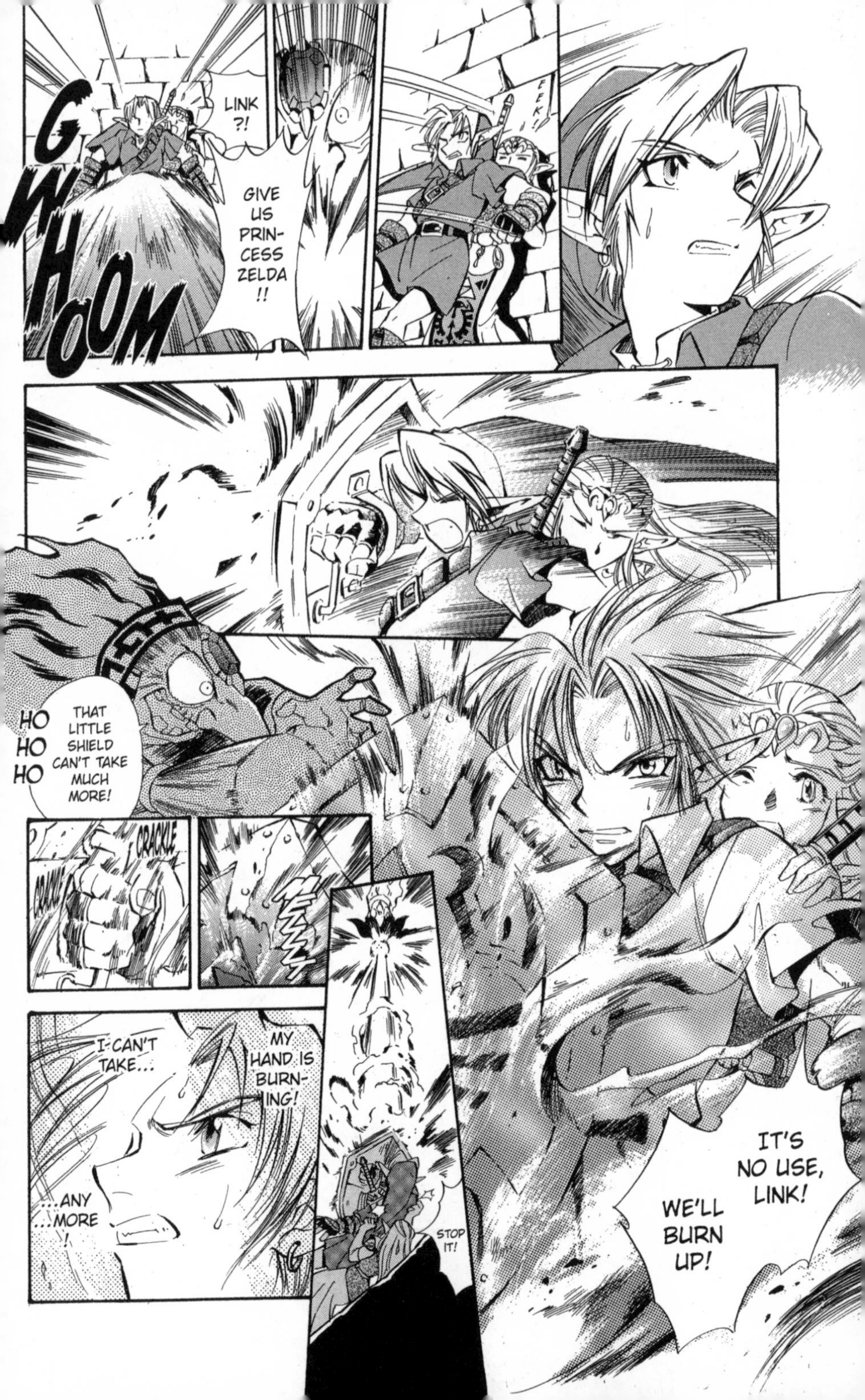
EEEK!
LINK ?!
GIVE US PRINCESS ZELDA !!
GWHOOM
HO HO HO
THAT LITTLE SHIELD CAN'T TAKE MUCH MORE!
IT'S NO USE, LINK!
WE'LL BURN UP!
CRACKLE
CRACKLE
STOP IT!
MY HAND IS BURNING!
I CAN'T TAKE...
...ANY ...MORE !

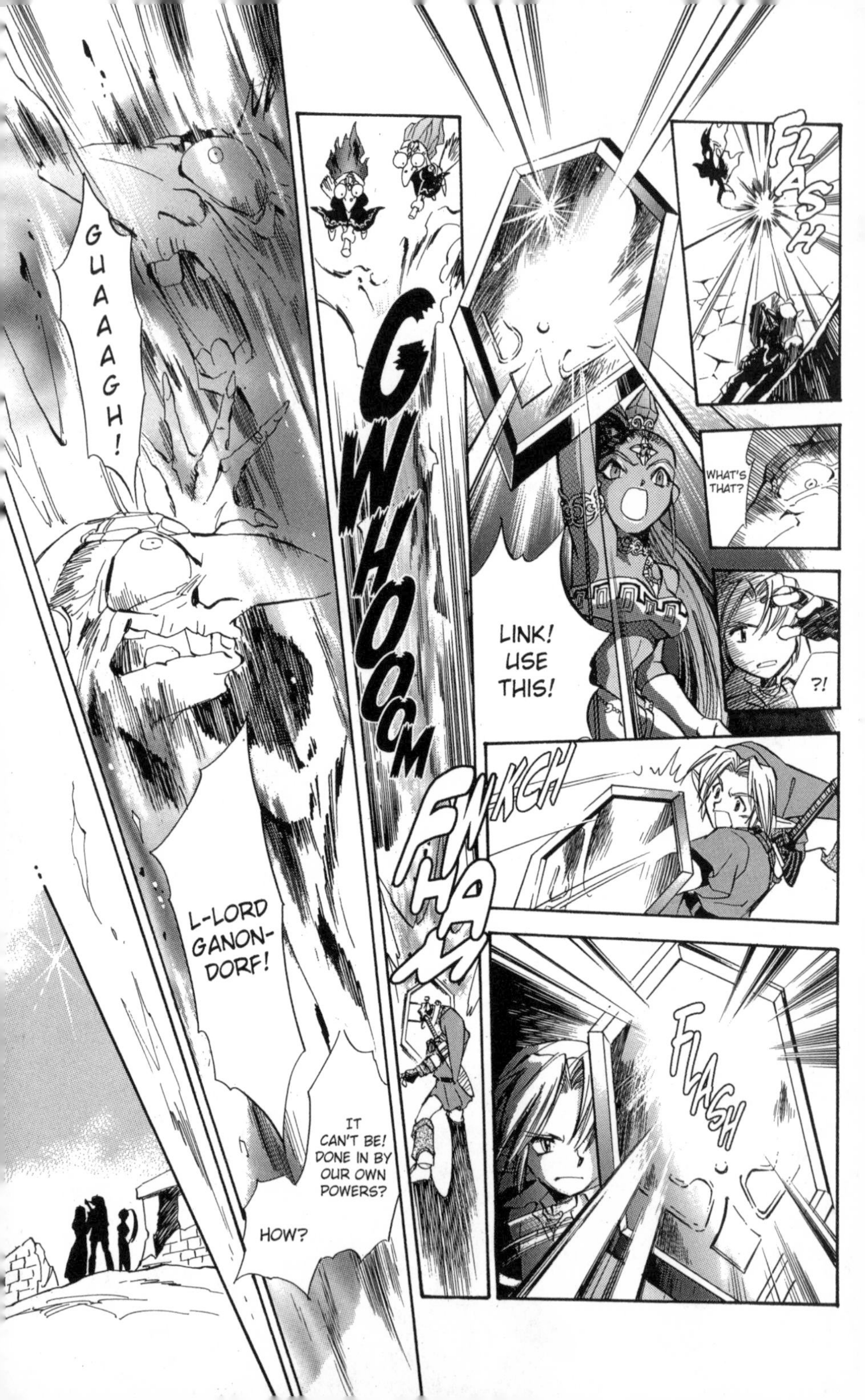
FLASH
WHAT'S THAT?
LINK! USE THIS!
?!
KCH
FLASH
GWHOOOM
FWHAM
GUAAAAGH!
L-LORD GANON-DORF!
IT CAN'T BE! DONE IN BY OUR OWN POWERS?
HOW?

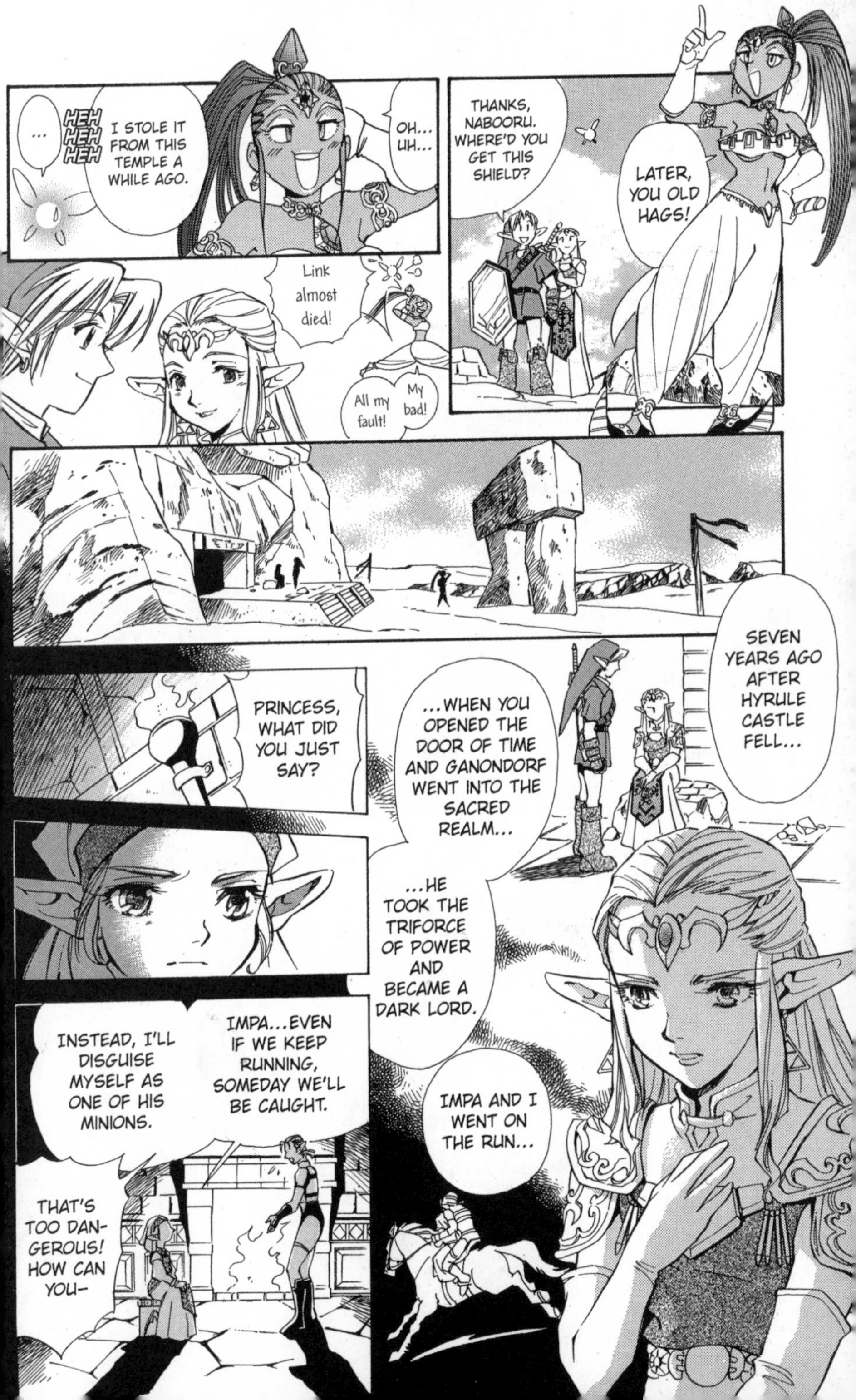
THANKS, NABOORU. WHERE'D YOU GET THIS SHIELD?
LATER, YOU OLD HAGS!
OH... UH...
I STOLE IT FROM THIS TEMPLE A WHILE AGO.
HEH HEH HEH
...
Link almost died!
My bad!
All my fault!
SEVEN YEARS AGO AFTER HYRULE CASTLE FELL...
...WHEN YOU OPENED THE DOOR OF TIME AND GANONDORF WENT INTO THE SACRED REALM...
PRINCESS, WHAT DID YOU JUST SAY?
...HE TOOK THE TRIFORCE OF POWER AND BECAME A DARK LORD.
IMPA AND I WENT ON THE RUN...
IMPA...EVEN IF WE KEEP RUNNING, SOMEDAY WE'LL BE CAUGHT.
INSTEAD, I'LL DISGUISE MYSELF AS ONE OF HIS MINIONS.
THAT'S TOO DAN-GEROUS! HOW CAN YOU-

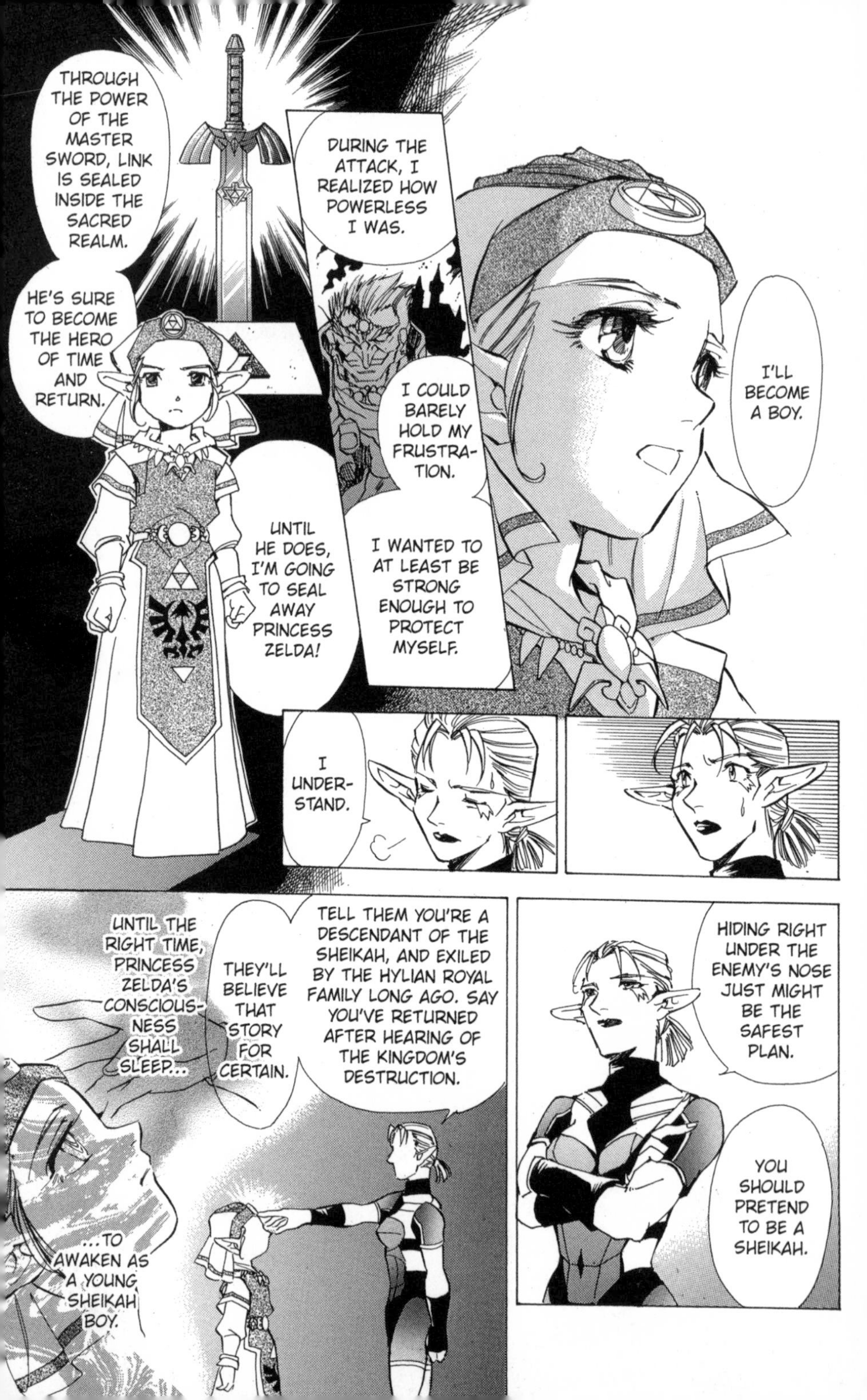
DURING THE ATTACK, I REALIZED HOW POWERLESS I WAS.
I COULD BARELY HOLD MY FRUSTRATION.
I WANTED TO AT LEAST BE STRONG ENOUGH TO PROTECT MYSELF.
I'LL BECOME A BOY.
I UNDERSTAND.
THROUGH THE POWER OF THE MASTER SWORD, LINK IS SEALED INSIDE THE SACRED REALM.
HE'S SURE TO BECOME THE HERO OF TIME AND RETURN.
UNTIL HE DOES, I'M GOING TO SEAL AWAY PRINCESS ZELDA!
HIDING RIGHT UNDER THE ENEMY'S NOSE JUST MIGHT BE THE SAFEST PLAN.
YOU SHOULD PRETEND TO BE A SHEIKAH.
TELL THEM YOU'RE A DESCENDANT OF THE SHEIKAH, AND EXILED BY THE HYLIAN ROYAL FAMILY LONG AGO. SAY YOU'VE RETURNED AFTER HEARING OF THE KINGDOM'S DESTRUCTION.
THEY'LL BELIEVE THAT STORY FOR CERTAIN.
UNTIL THE RIGHT TIME, PRINCESS ZELDA'S CONSCIOUSNESS SHALL SLEEP...
...TO AWAKEN AS A YOUNG SHEIKAH BOY.

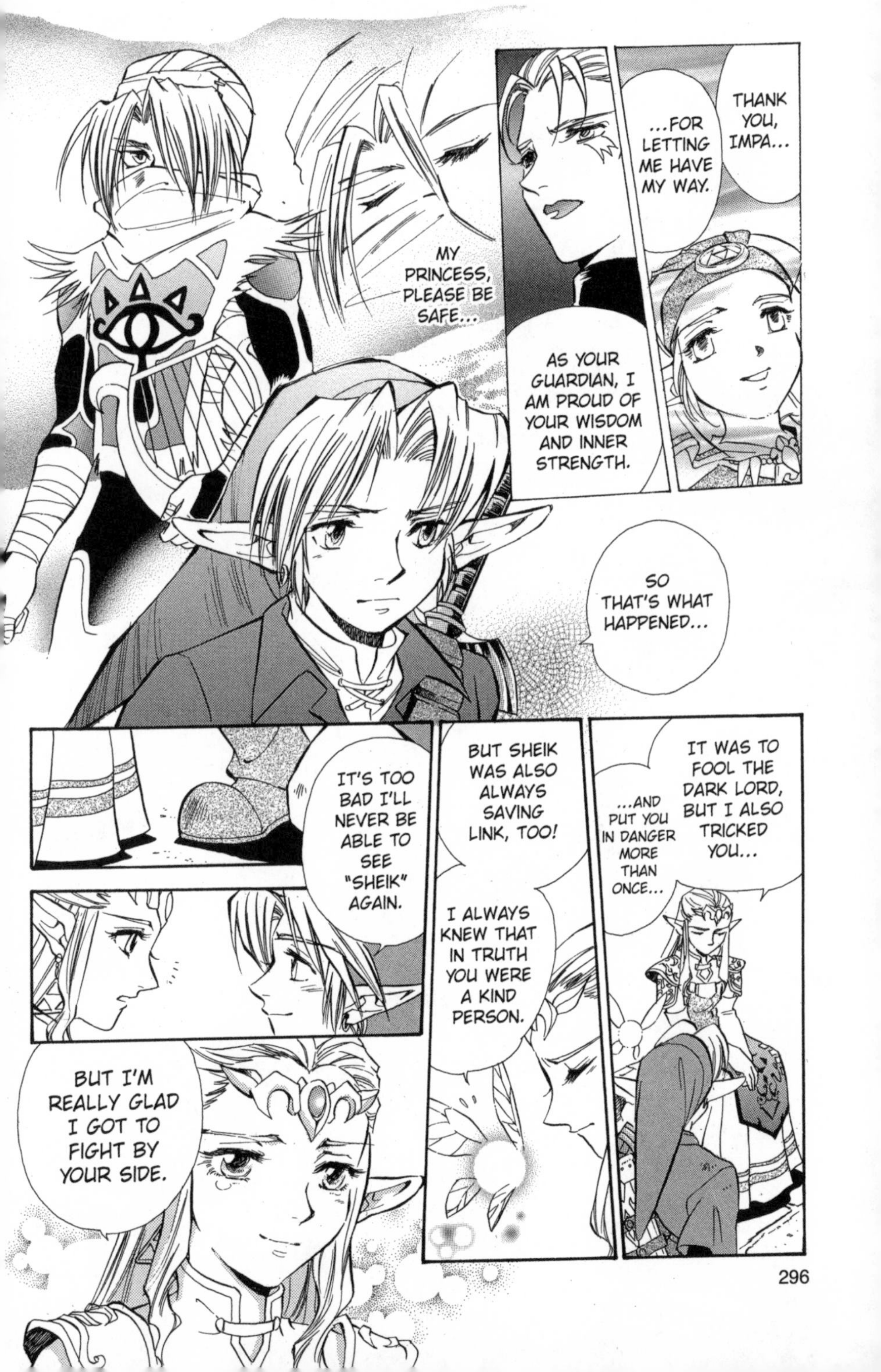
THANK YOU, IMPA...
...FOR LETTING ME HAVE MY WAY.
AS YOUR GUARDIAN, I AM PROUD OF YOUR WISDOM AND INNER STRENGTH.
MY PRINCESS, PLEASE BE SAFE...
SO THAT'S WHAT HAPPENED...
IT WAS TO FOOL THE DARK LORD, BUT I ALSO TRICKED YOU...
...AND PUT YOU IN DANGER MORE THAN ONCE...
BUT SHEIK WAS ALSO ALWAYS SAVING LINK, TOO!
I ALWAYS KNEW THAT IN TRUTH YOU WERE A KIND PERSON.
IT'S TOO BAD I'LL NEVER BE ABLE TO SEE "SHEIK" AGAIN.
BUT I'M REALLY GLAD I GOT TO FIGHT BY YOUR SIDE.

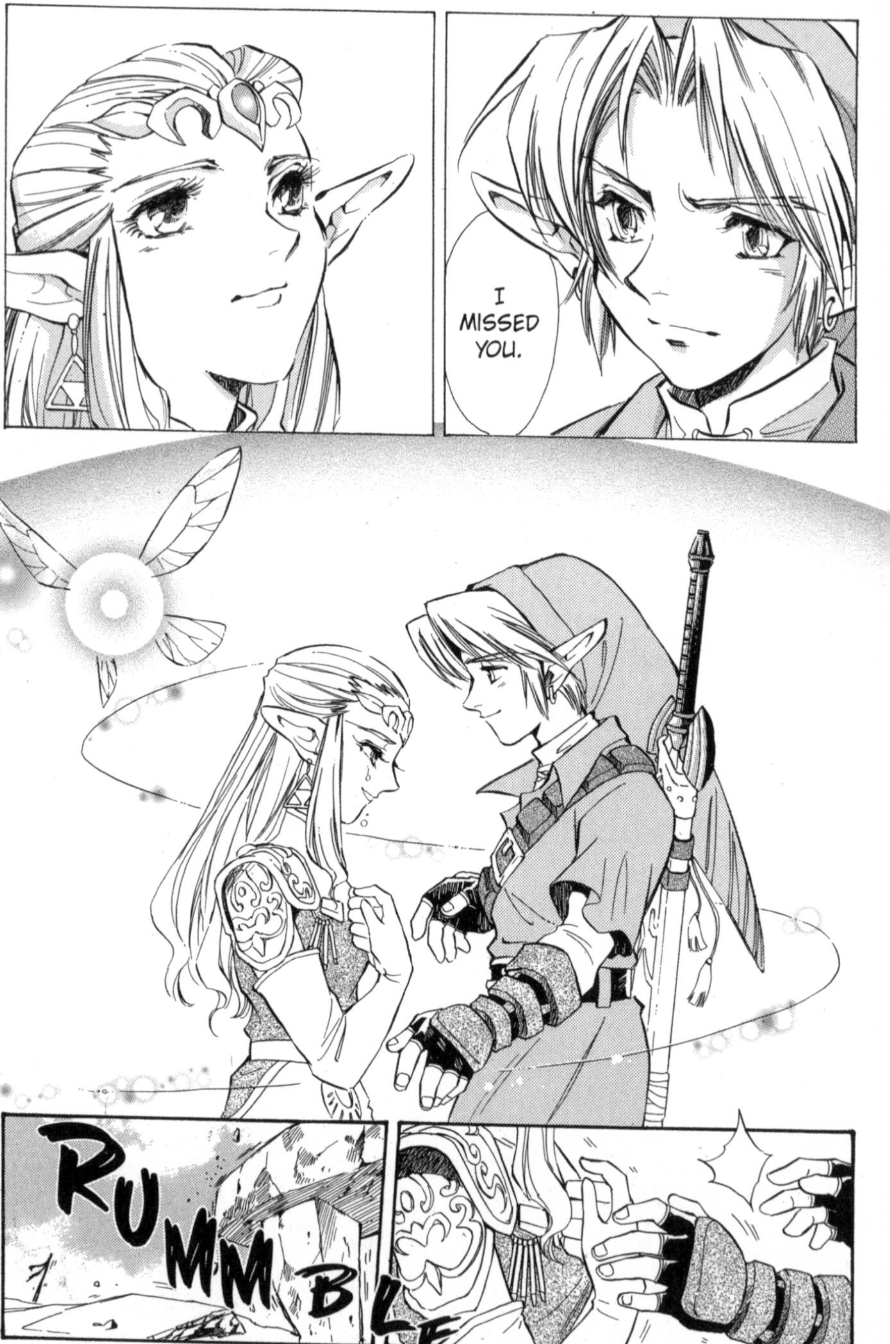
I MISSED YOU.
RUMMBLE

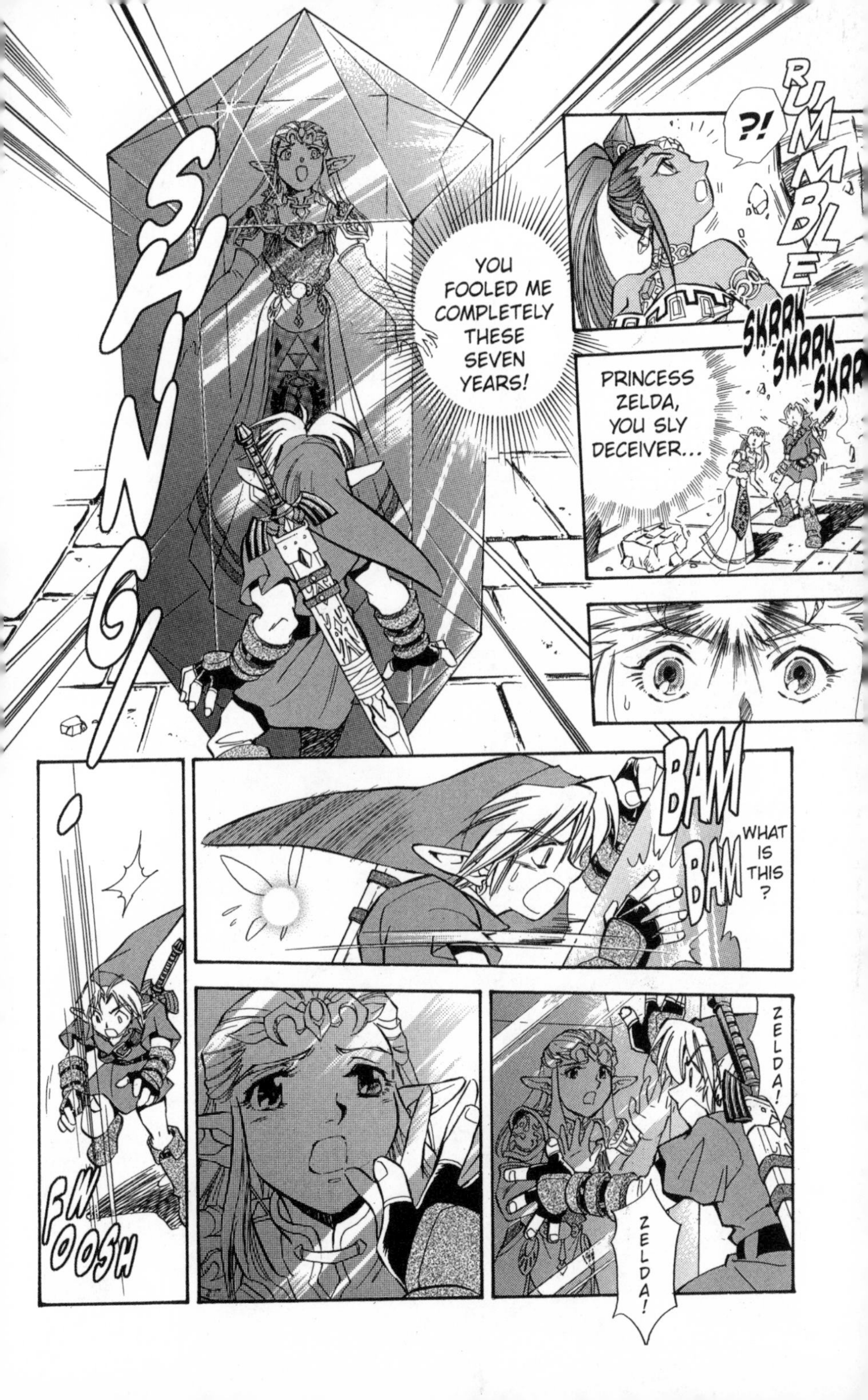
?!
RUMMBLE
SKRRK SKRRK SKRR
PRINCESS ZELDA, YOU SLY DECEIVER...
SHING!
YOU FOOLED ME COMPLETELY THESE SEVEN YEARS!
BAM BAM
WHAT IS THIS?
ZELDA!
ZELDA!
FWOOSH

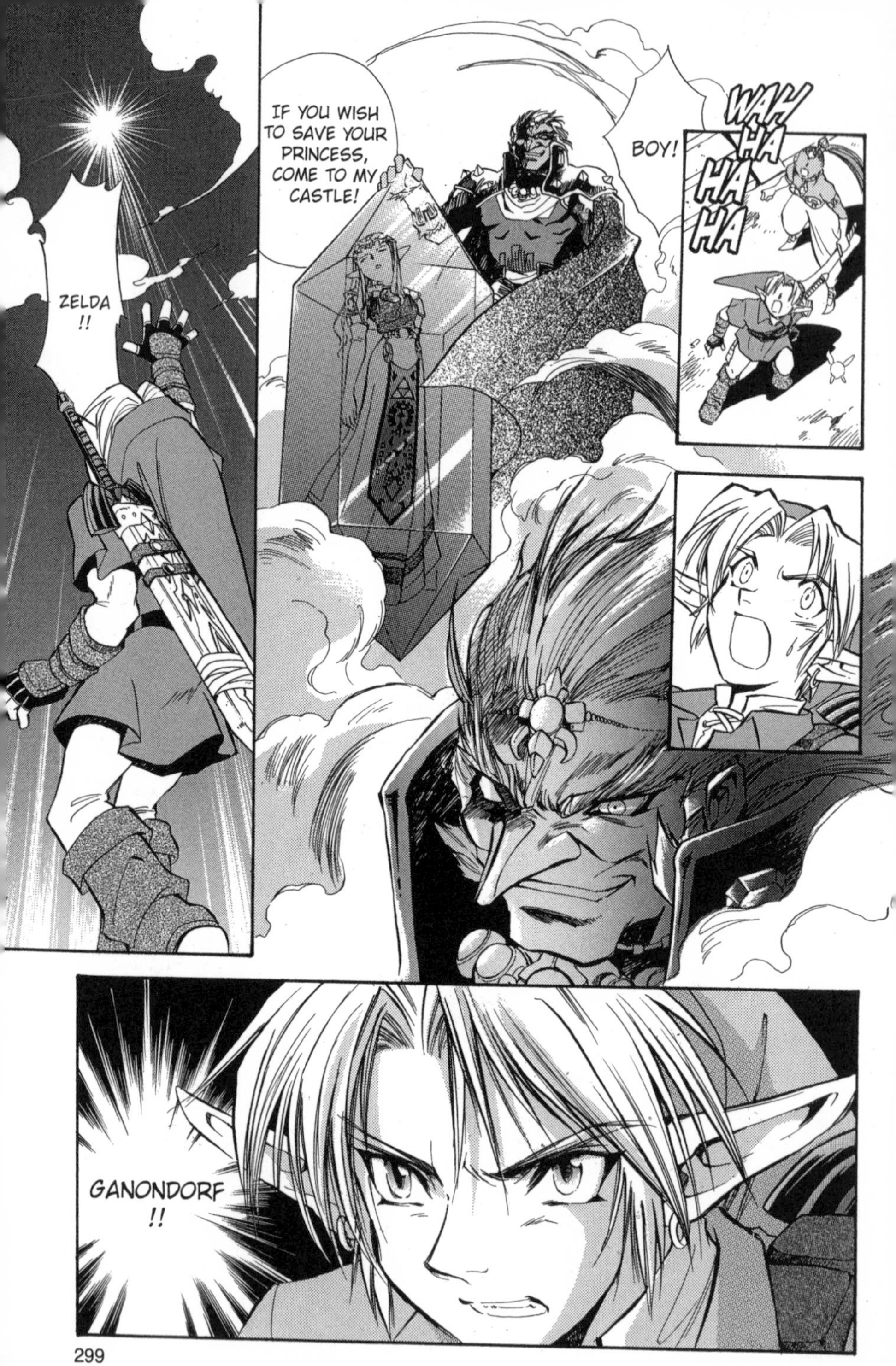
WAH HA HA HA
BOY!
IF YOU WISH TO SAVE YOUR PRINCESS, COME TO MY CASTLE!
ZELDA !!
GANONDORF !!

BONUS ILLUSTRATION 4

A ROUGH SKETCH HIMEKAWA SENSEI DREW BEFORE
BEGINNING WORK ON THE SERIES.

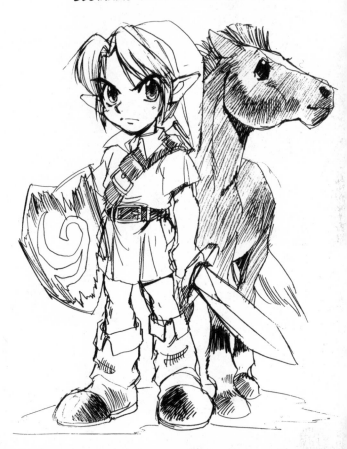

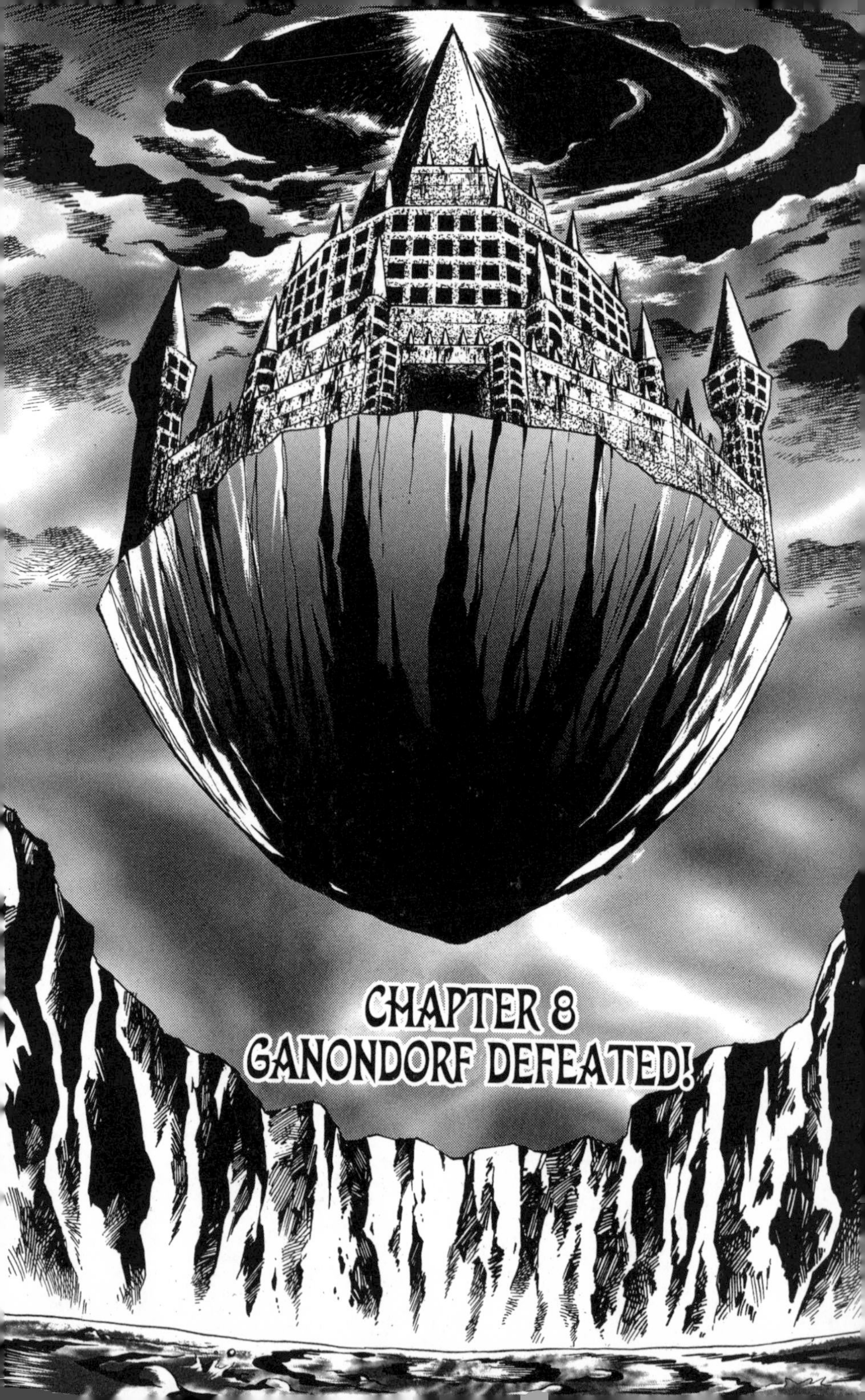
CHAPTER 8
GANONDORF DEFEATED!

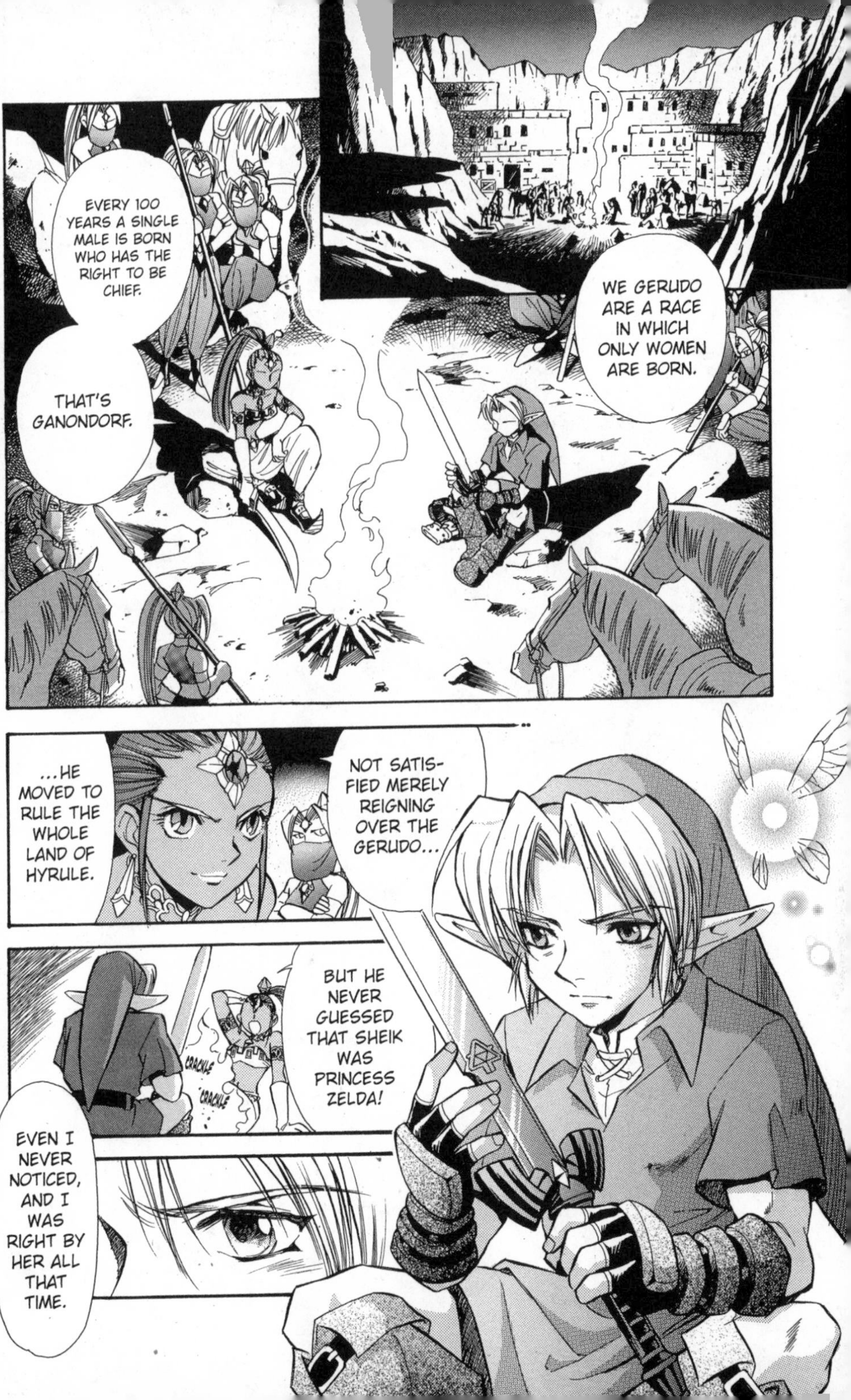
WE GERUDO ARE A RACE IN WHICH ONLY WOMEN ARE BORN.
EVERY 100 YEARS A SINGLE MALE IS BORN WHO HAS THE RIGHT TO BE CHIEF.
THAT'S GANONDORF.
NOT SATIS-FIED MERELY REIGNING OVER THE GERUDO...
...HE MOVED TO RULE THE WHOLE LAND OF HYRULE.
BUT HE NEVER GUESSED THAT SHEIK WAS PRINCESS ZELDA!
CRACKLE
CRACKLE
EVEN I NEVER NOTICED, AND I WAS RIGHT BY HER ALL THAT TIME.

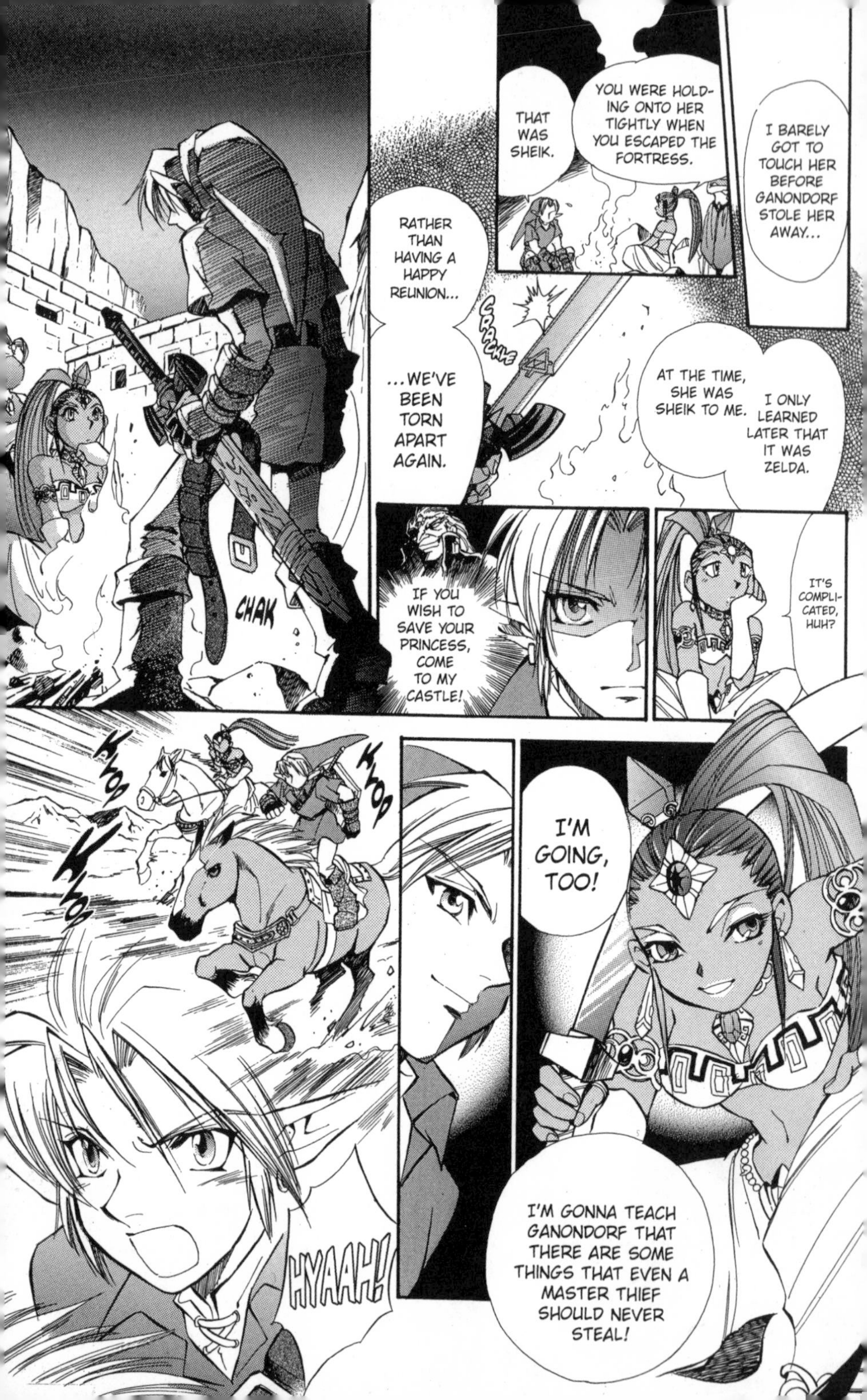

I BARELY GOT TO TOUCH HER BEFORE GANONDORF STOLE HER AWAY...
YOU WERE HOLDING ONTO HER TIGHTLY WHEN YOU ESCAPED THE FORTRESS.
THAT WAS SHEIK.
AT THE TIME, SHE WAS SHEIK TO ME.
I ONLY LEARNED LATER THAT IT WAS ZELDA.
CRACKLE
RATHER THAN HAVING A HAPPY REUNION...
...WE'VE BEEN TORN APART AGAIN.
IT'S COMPLICATED, HUH?
IF YOU WISH TO SAVE YOUR PRINCESS, COME TO MY CASTLE!
CHAK
I'M GOING, TOO!
I'M GONNA TEACH GANONDORF THAT THERE ARE SOME THINGS THAT EVEN A MASTER THIEF SHOULD NEVER STEAL!
KLOP
KLOP
KLOP
KLOP
HYAAH!

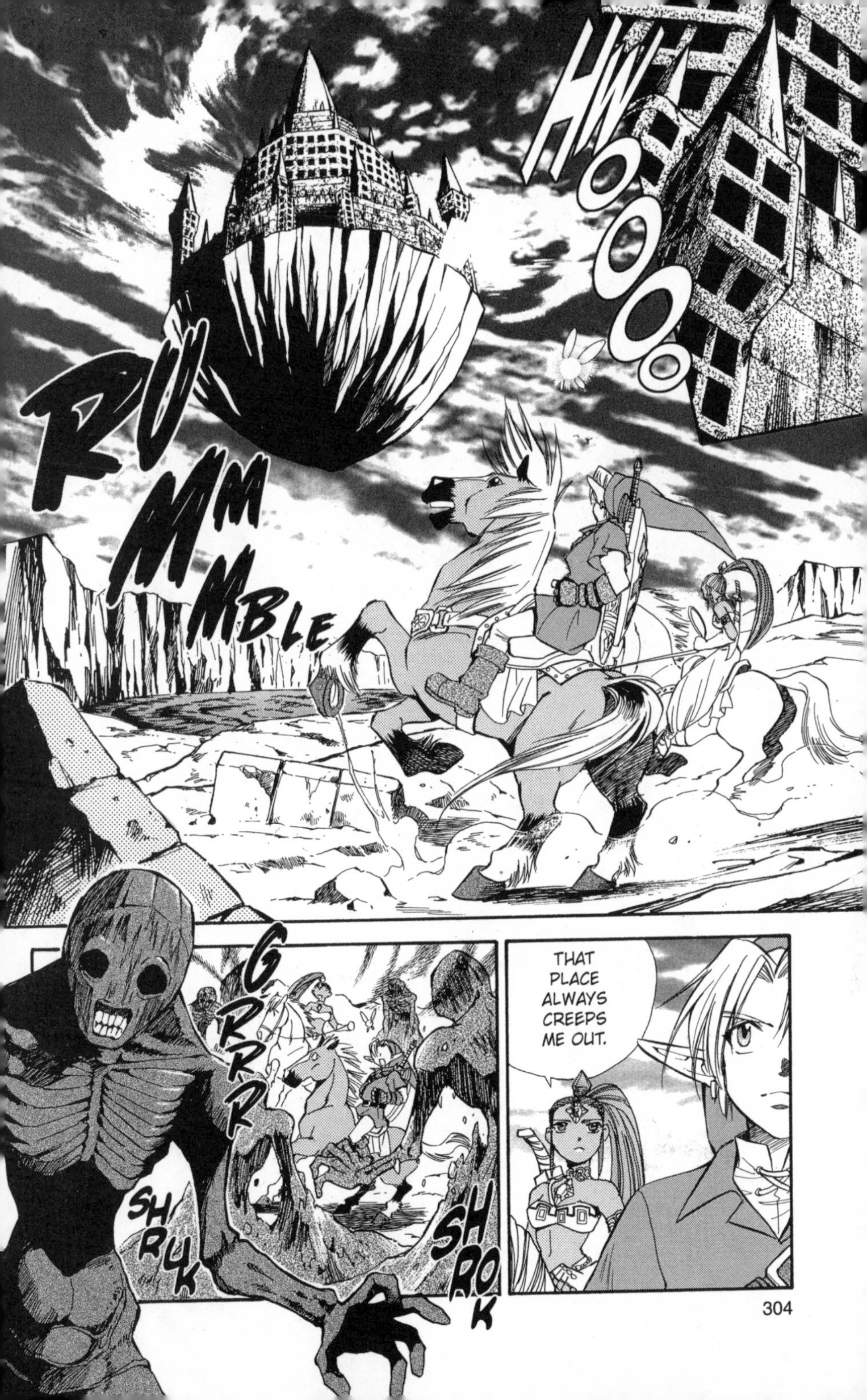
HWOOOOOO
RUMMMMBLE
THAT PLACE ALWAYS CREEPS ME OUT.
GRRRR
SHRUK
SHROK

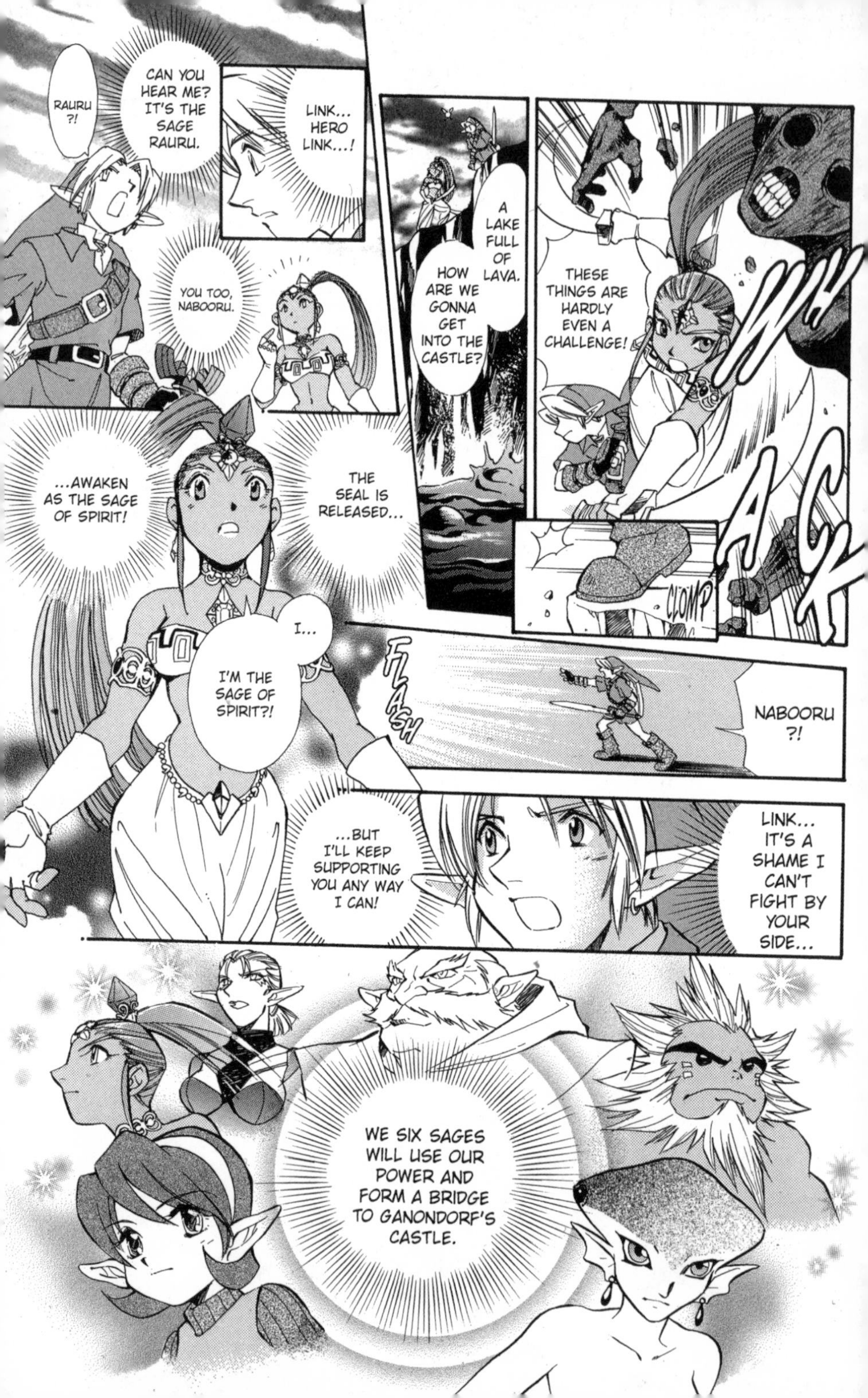
THESE THINGS ARE HARDLY EVEN A CHALLENGE!
WHACK
CLOMP
A LAKE FULL OF LAVA.
HOW ARE WE GONNA GET INTO THE CASTLE?
LINK... HERO LINK...!
CAN YOU HEAR ME? IT'S THE SAGE RAURU.
RAURU ?!
YOU TOO, NABOORU.
THE SEAL IS RELEASED...
...AWAKEN AS THE SAGE OF SPIRIT!
I...
I'M THE SAGE OF SPIRIT?!
FLASH
NABOORU ?!
LINK... IT'S A SHAME I CAN'T FIGHT BY YOUR SIDE...
...BUT I'LL KEEP SUPPORTING YOU ANY WAY I CAN!
WE SIX SAGES WILL USE OUR POWER AND FORM A BRIDGE TO GANONDORF'S CASTLE.

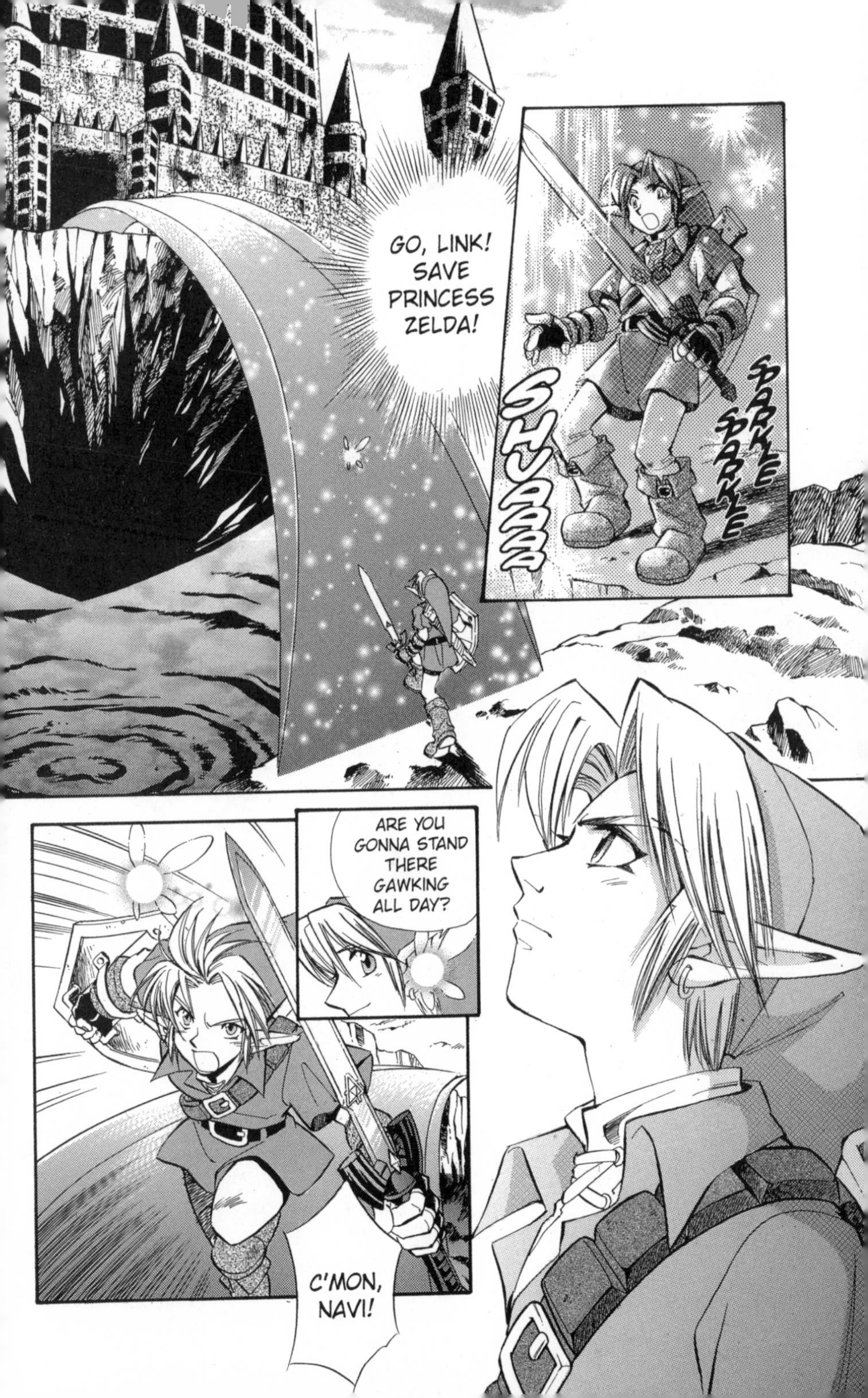
SHUAAAA
SPARKLE SPARKLE
GO, LINK! SAVE PRINCESS ZELDA!
ARE YOU GONNA STAND THERE GAWKING ALL DAY?
C'MON, NAVI!

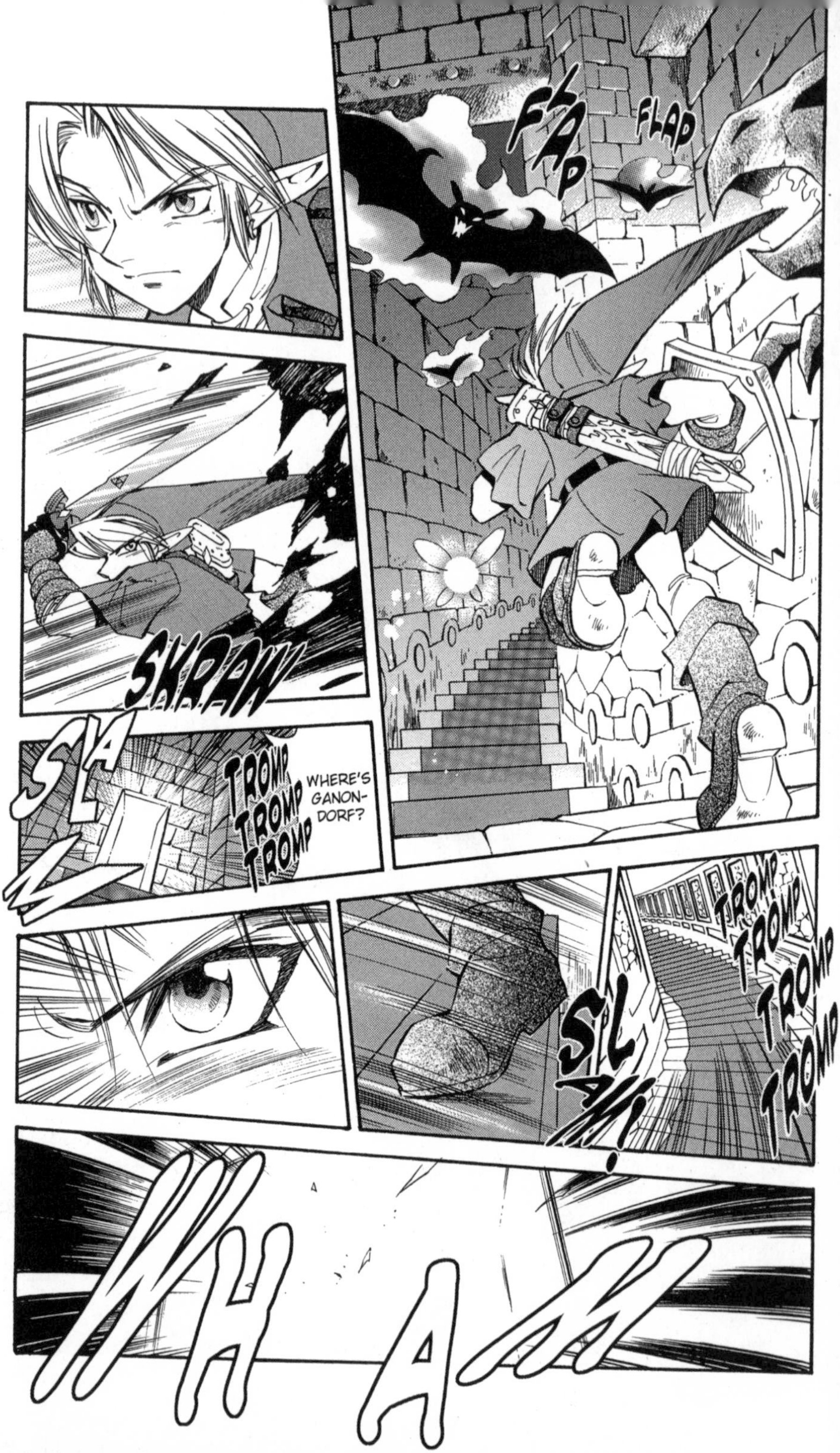
FLAP
FLAP
SKRAW
SLAM
TROMP TROMP TROMP
WHERE'S GANON-DORF?
TROMP TROMP TROMP TROMP
SLAM!
WHAM

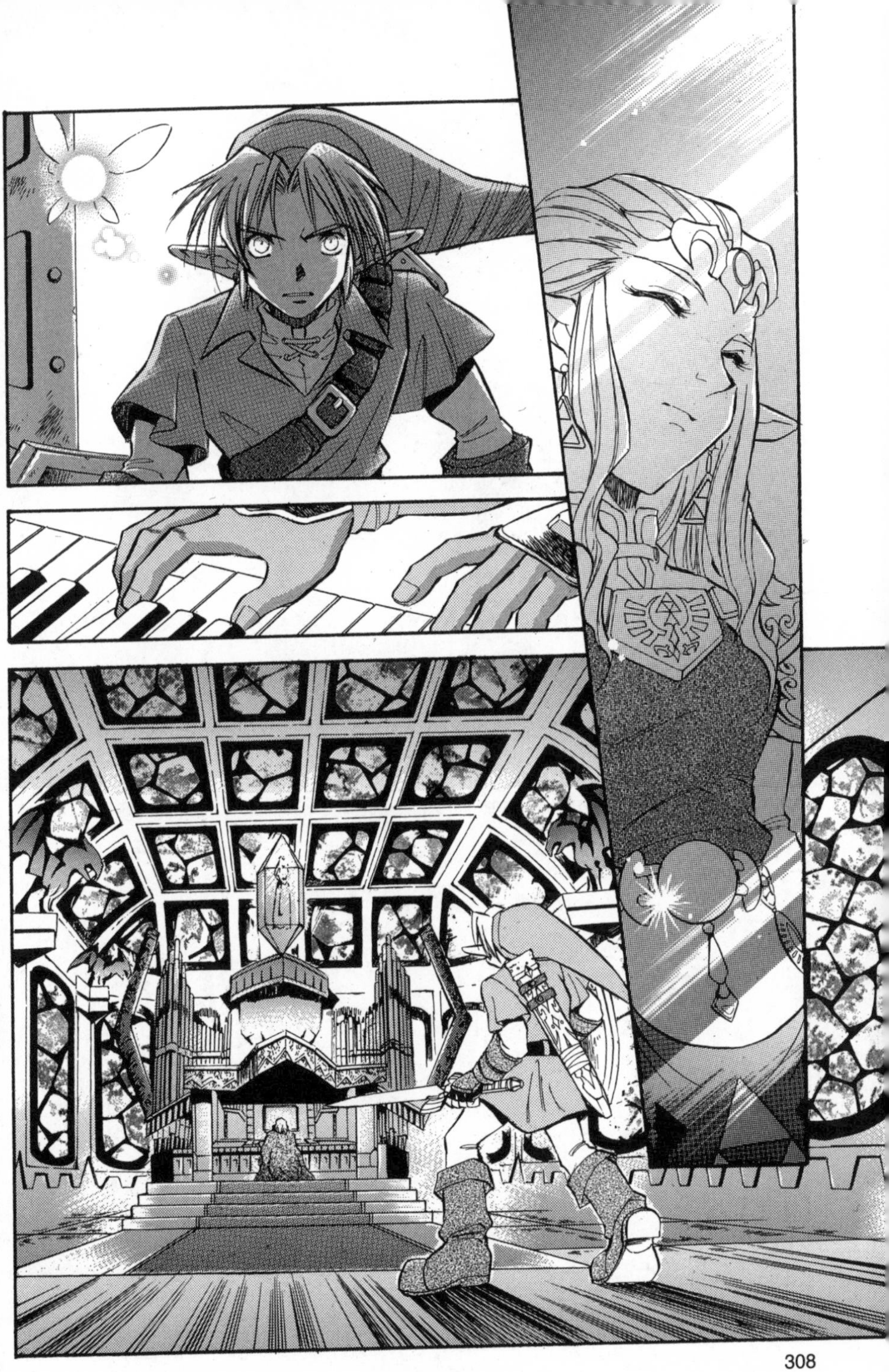

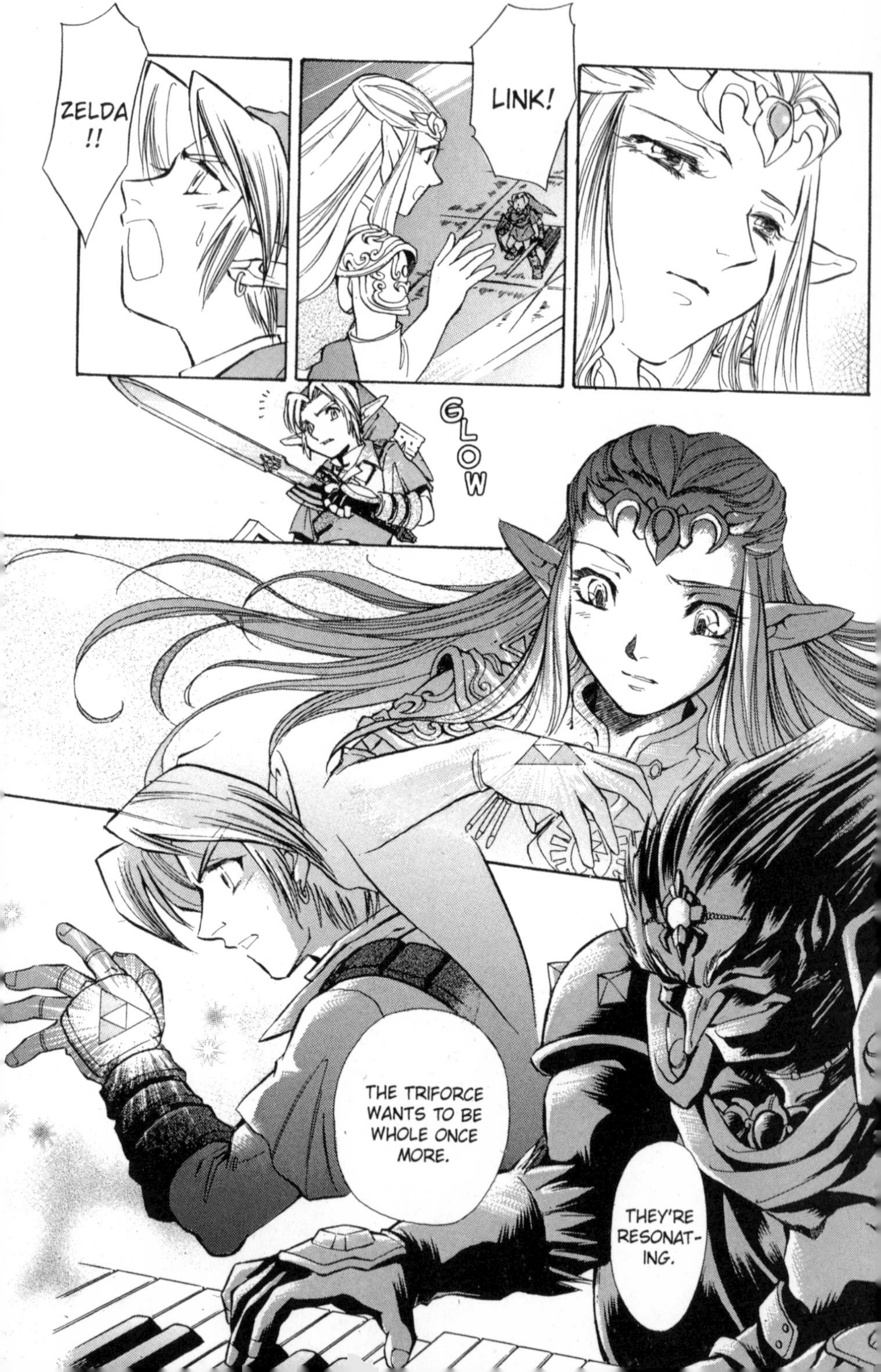
LINK!
ZELDA !!
GLOW
THE TRIFORCE WANTS TO BE WHOLE ONCE MORE.
THEY'RE RESONAT-ING.

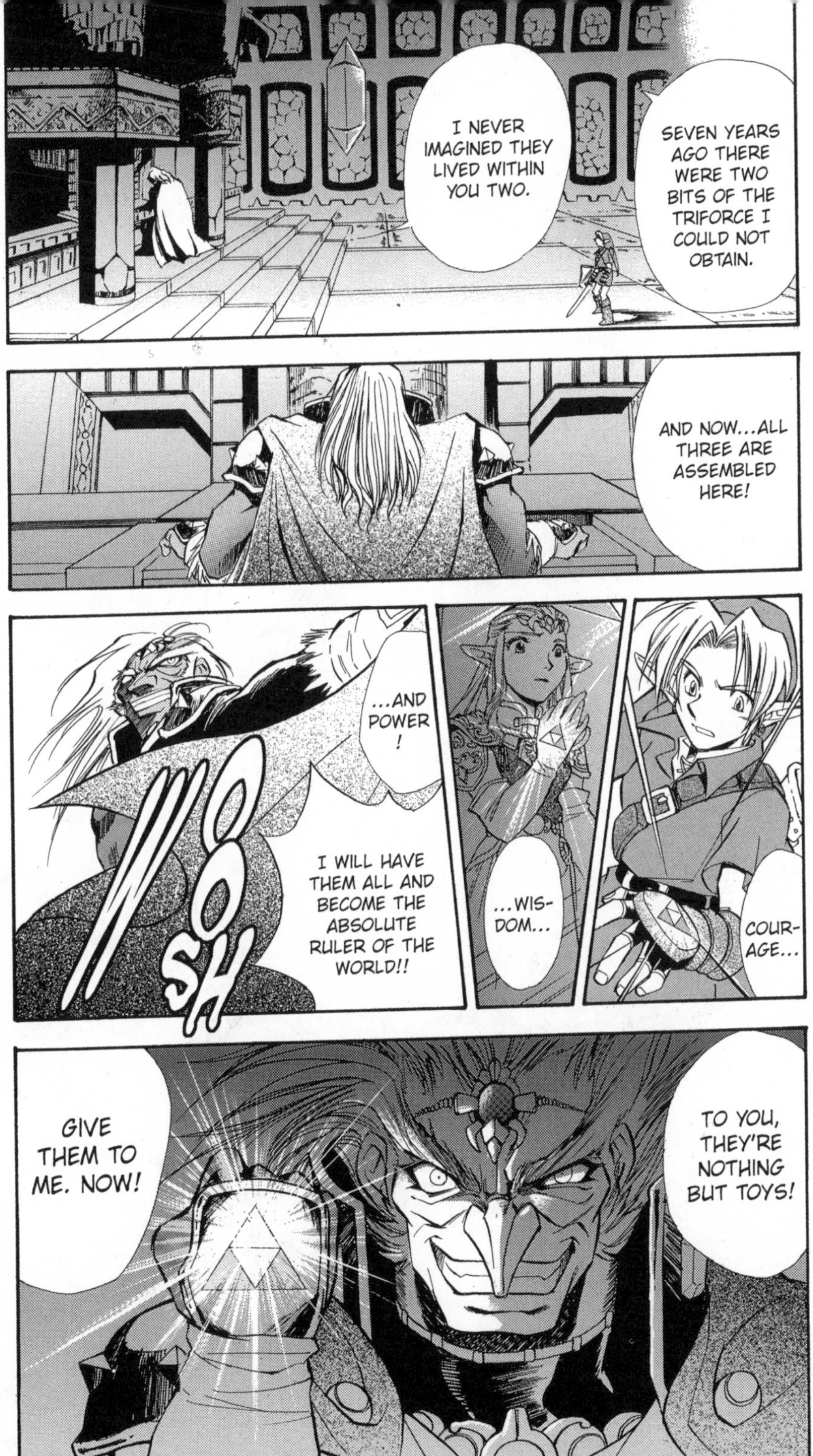
SEVEN YEARS AGO THERE WERE TWO BITS OF THE TRIFORCE I COULD NOT OBTAIN.
I NEVER IMAGINED THEY LIVED WITHIN YOU TWO.
AND NOW...ALL THREE ARE ASSEMBLED HERE!
COUR-AGE...
...WIS-DOM...
...AND POWER!
I WILL HAVE THEM ALL AND BECOME THE ABSOLUTE RULER OF THE WORLD!!
WOOSH
TO YOU, THEY'RE NOTHING BUT TOYS!
GIVE THEM TO ME. NOW!

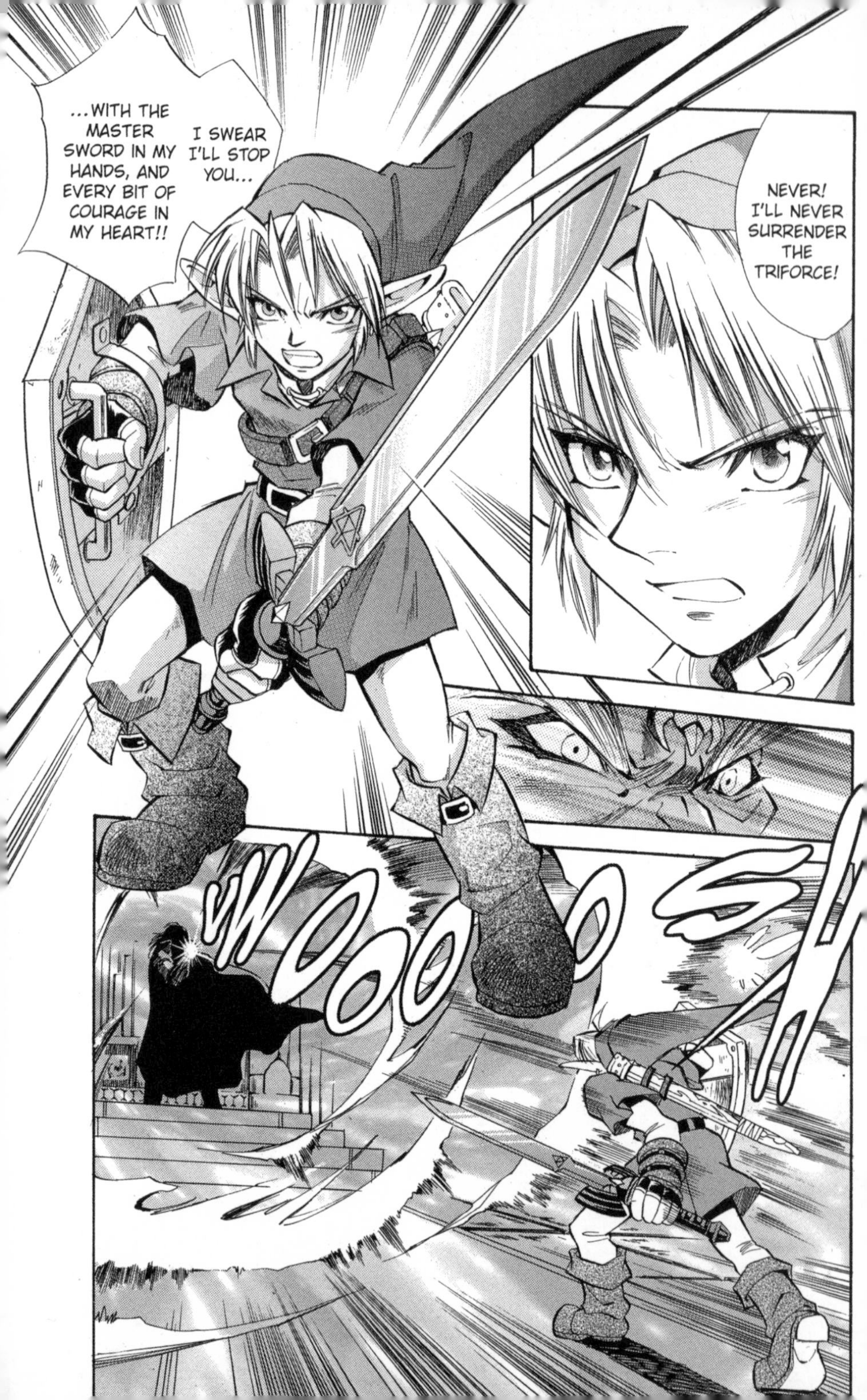
NEVER! I'LL NEVER SURRENDER THE TRIFORCE!
I SWEAR I'LL STOP YOU...
...WITH THE MASTER SWORD IN MY HANDS, AND EVERY BIT OF COURAGE IN MY HEART!!
WOOOOSH

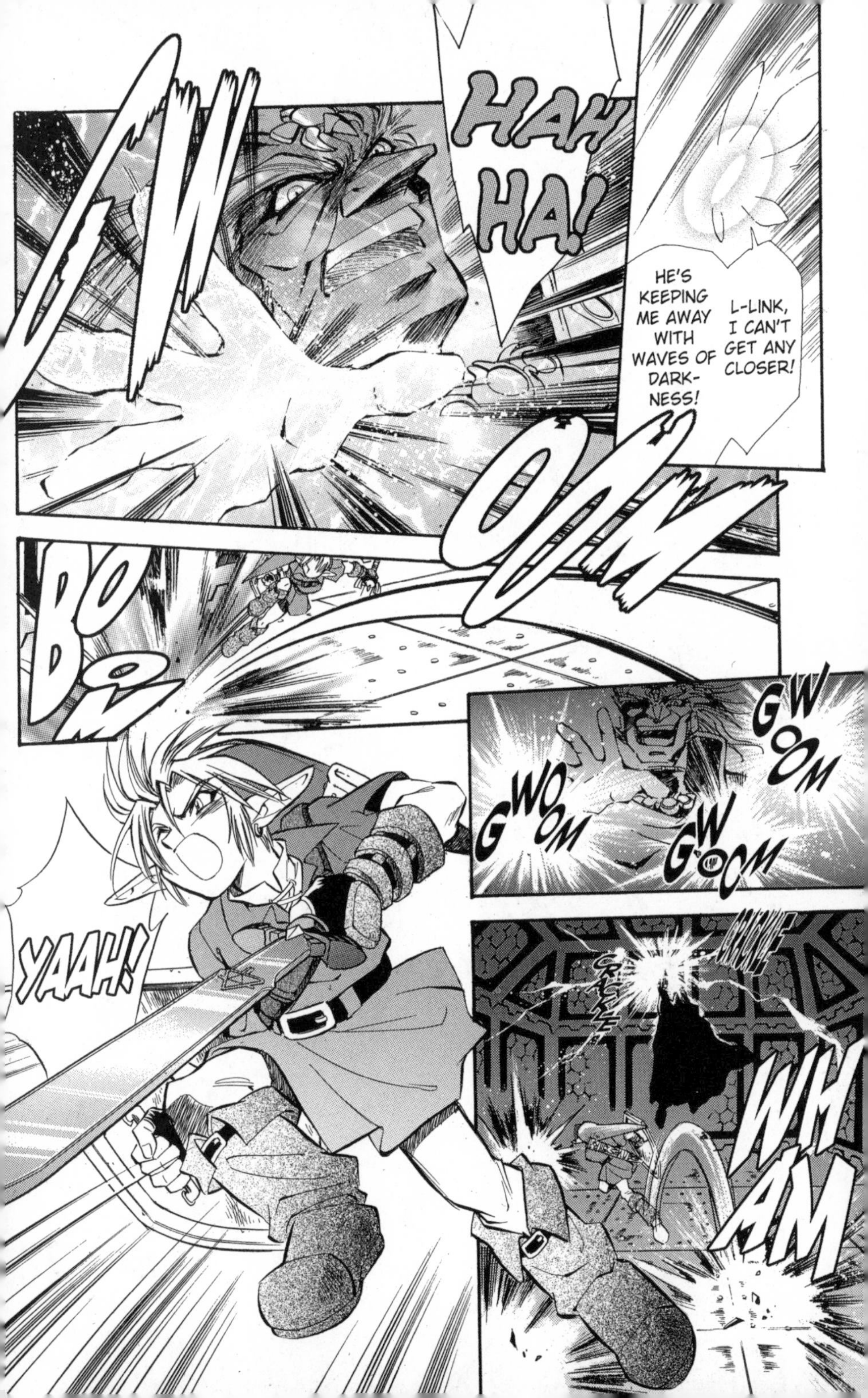
L-LINK, I CAN'T GET ANY CLOSER!
HE'S KEEPING ME AWAY WITH WAVES OF DARKNESS!
HAH HA!
GWOOM
GWOOM
GWOOM
YAAH!
CRACKLE
CRACKLE
WHAM

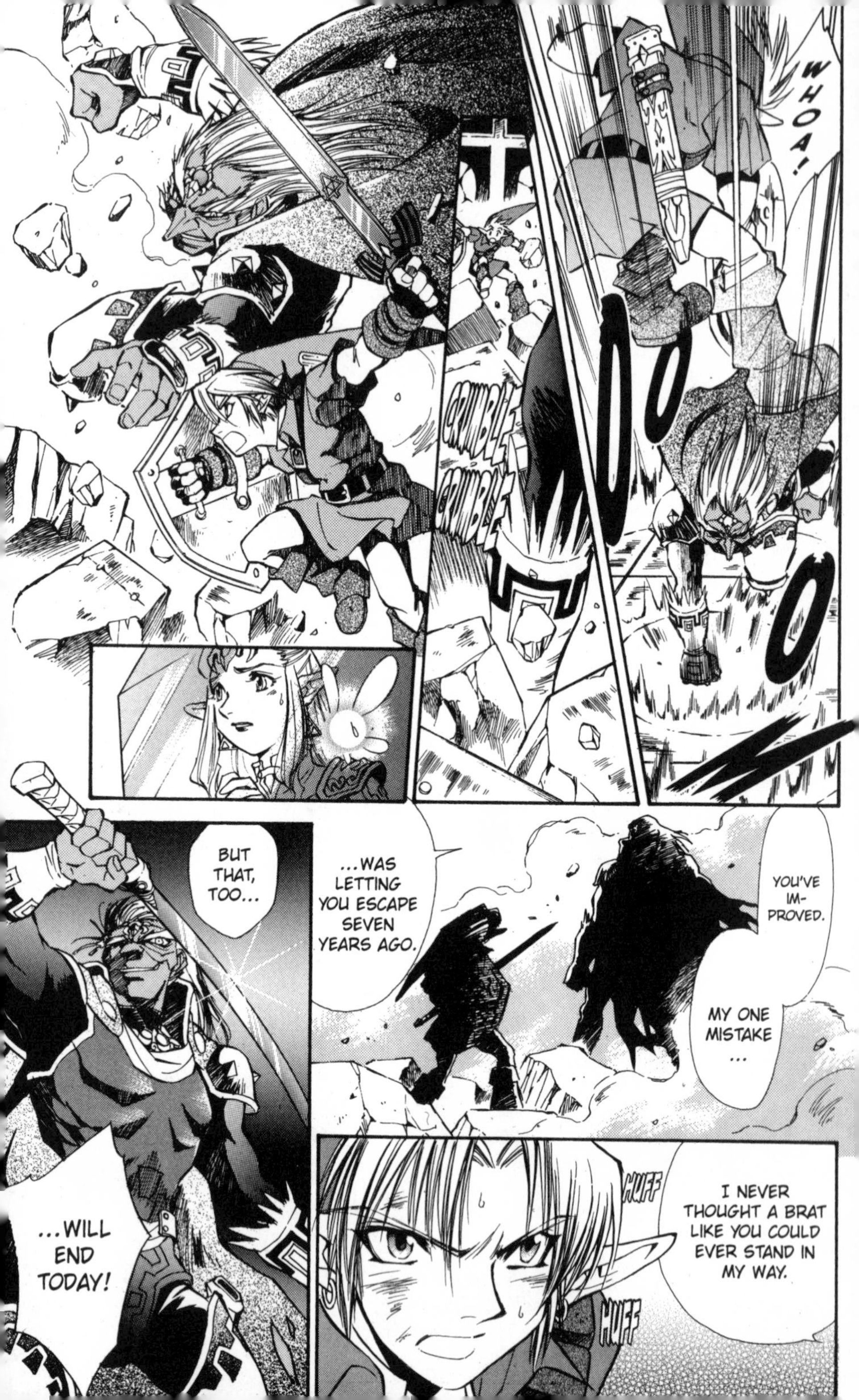
WHOA!
CRUMBLE
CRUMBLE
YOU'VE IM-PROVED.
MY ONE MISTAKE ...
...WAS LETTING YOU ESCAPE SEVEN YEARS AGO.
HUFF
I NEVER THOUGHT A BRAT LIKE YOU COULD EVER STAND IN MY WAY.
HUFF
BUT THAT, TOO...
...WILL END TODAY!

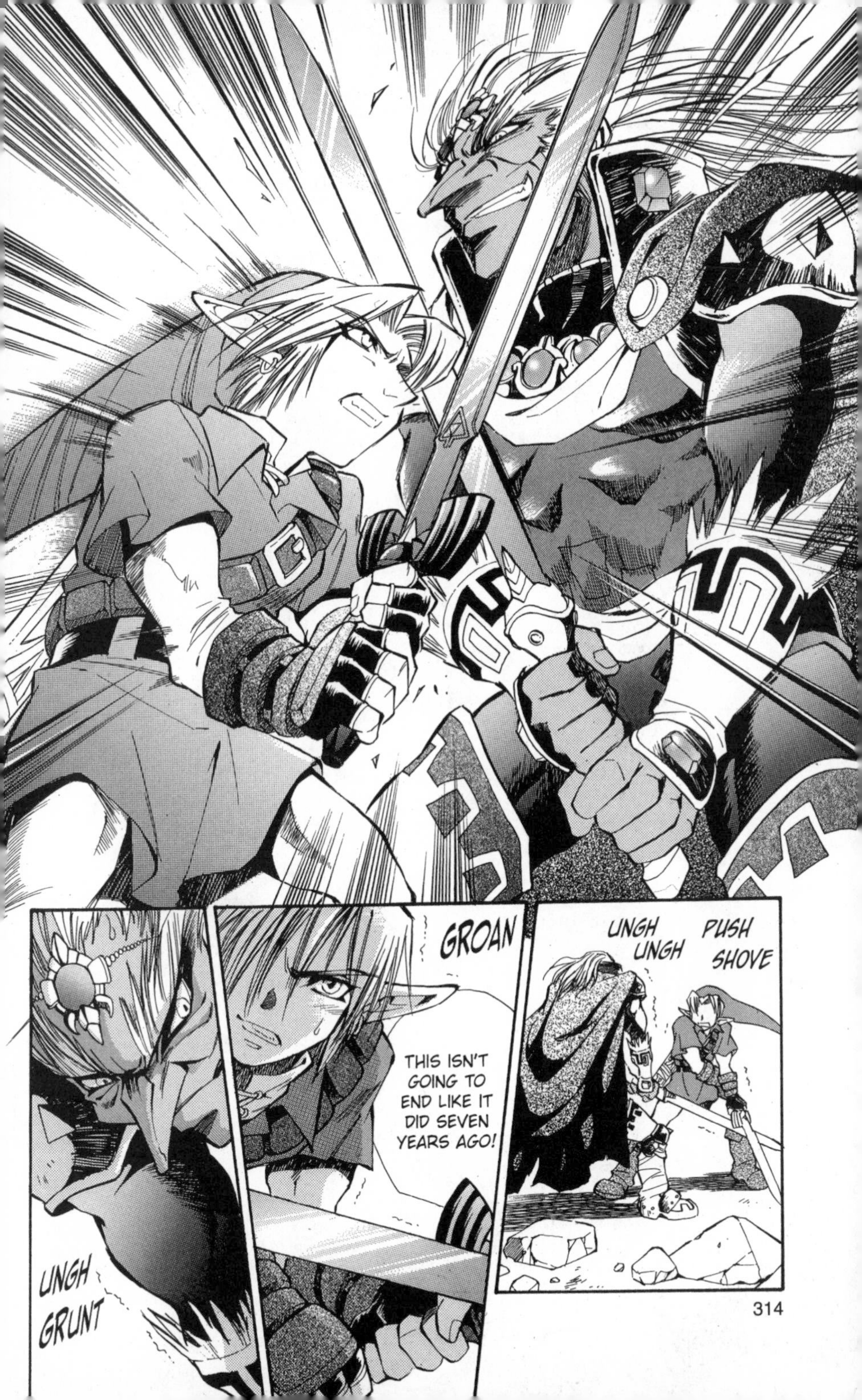
PUSH SHOVE
UNGH UNGH
GROAN
THIS ISN'T GOING TO END LIKE IT DID SEVEN YEARS AGO!
UNGH GRUNT

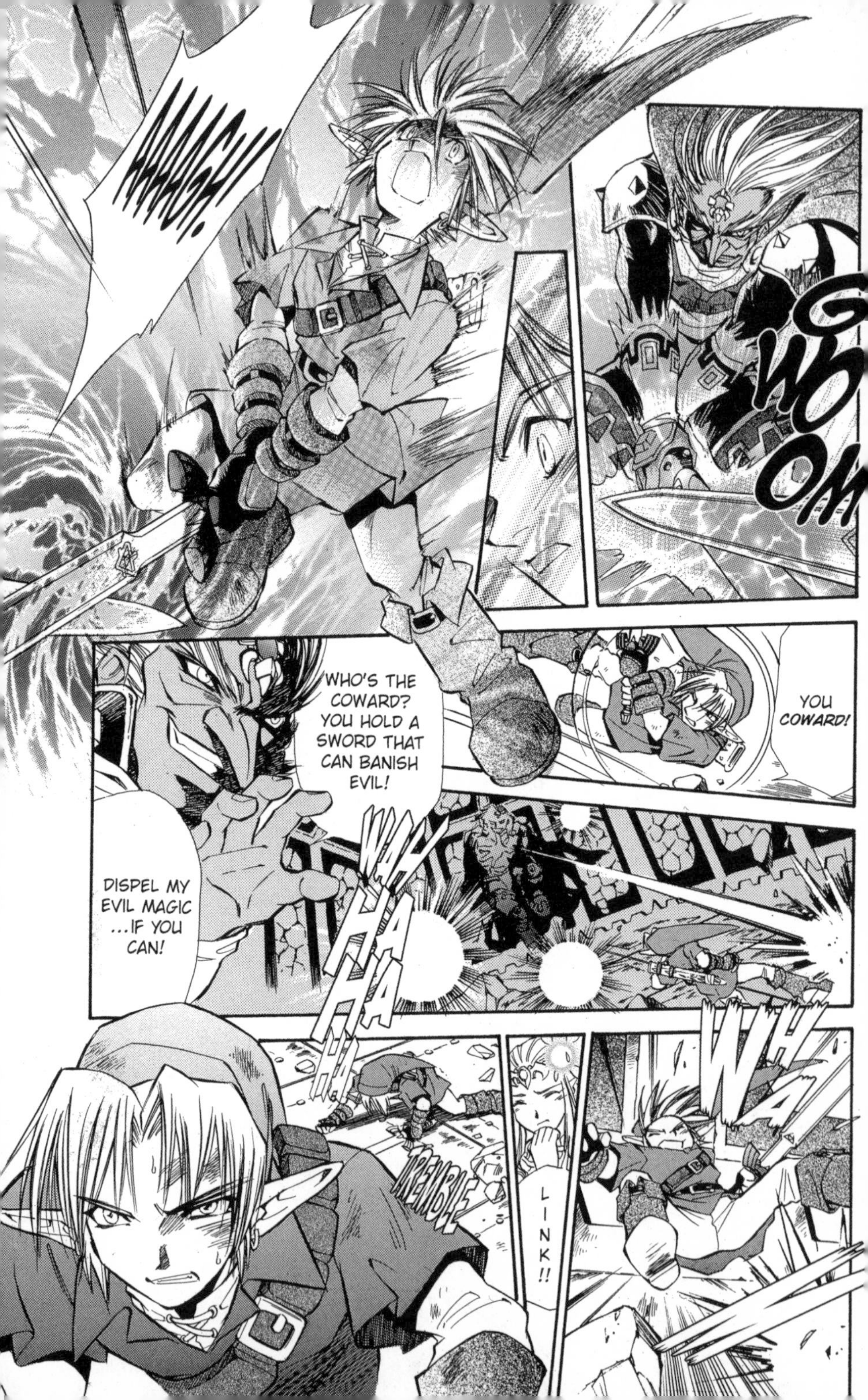
GWOOM
AAAGH!!
YOU COWARD!
WHO'S THE COWARD? YOU HOLD A SWORD THAT CAN BANISH EVIL!
DISPEL MY EVIL MAGIC ...IF YOU CAN!
WAH HA HA HA
WHA
LINK!!
TREMBLE

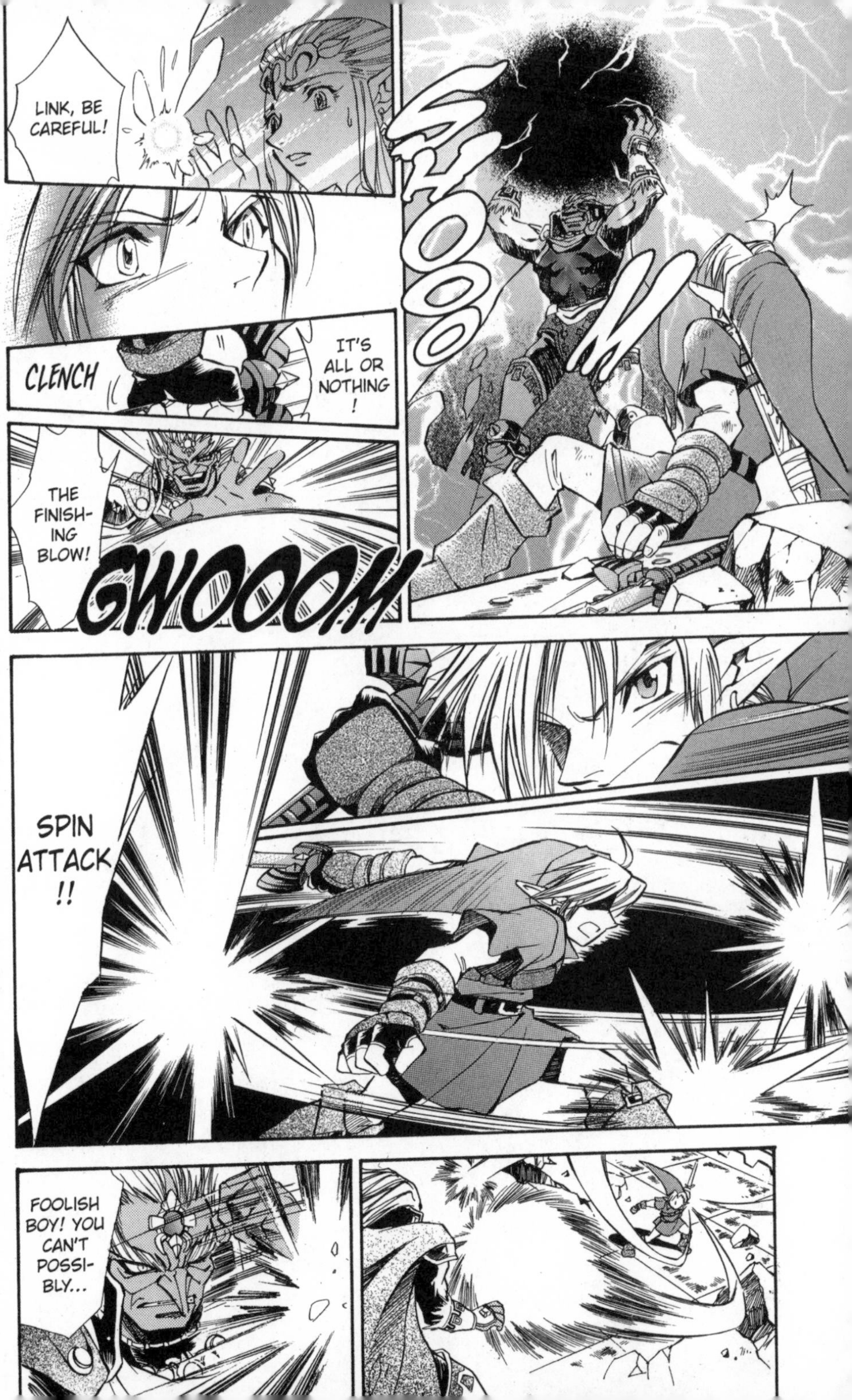
WHOOOM
LINK, BE CAREFUL!
IT'S ALL OR NOTHING!
CLENCH
THE FINISHING-ING BLOW!
GWOOOM
SPIN ATTACK!!
FOOLISH BOY! YOU CAN'T POSSI-BLY...

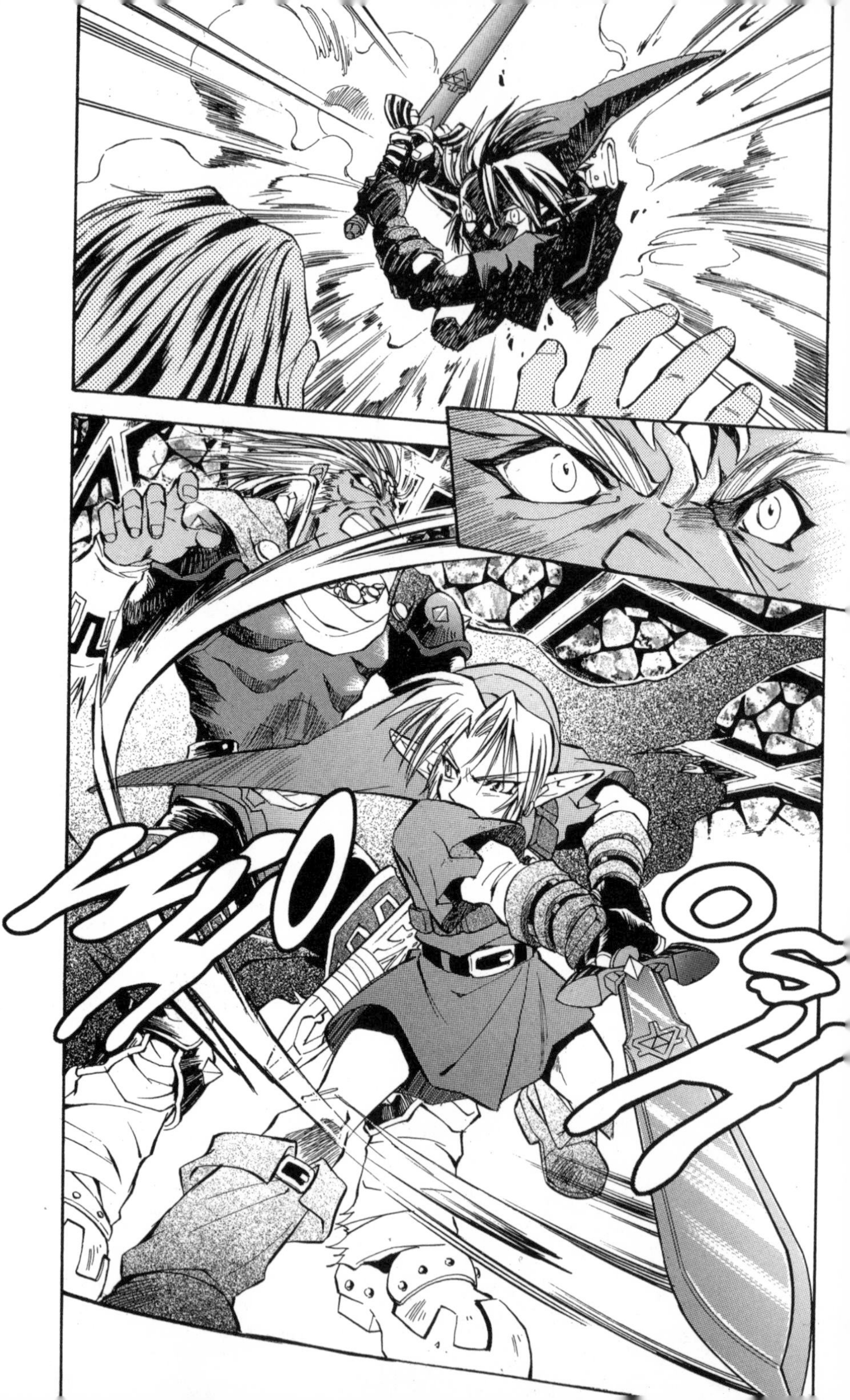
WHOOSH

BONUS ILLUSTRATION 5
A ROUGH SKETCH HIMEKAWA SENSEI DREW BEFORE WORKING ON THE SERIES.

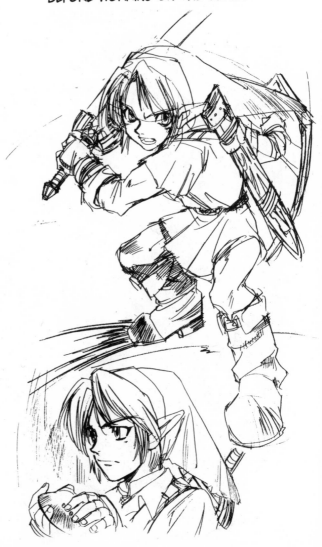

CHAPTER 9
A NEW JOURNEY BEGINS

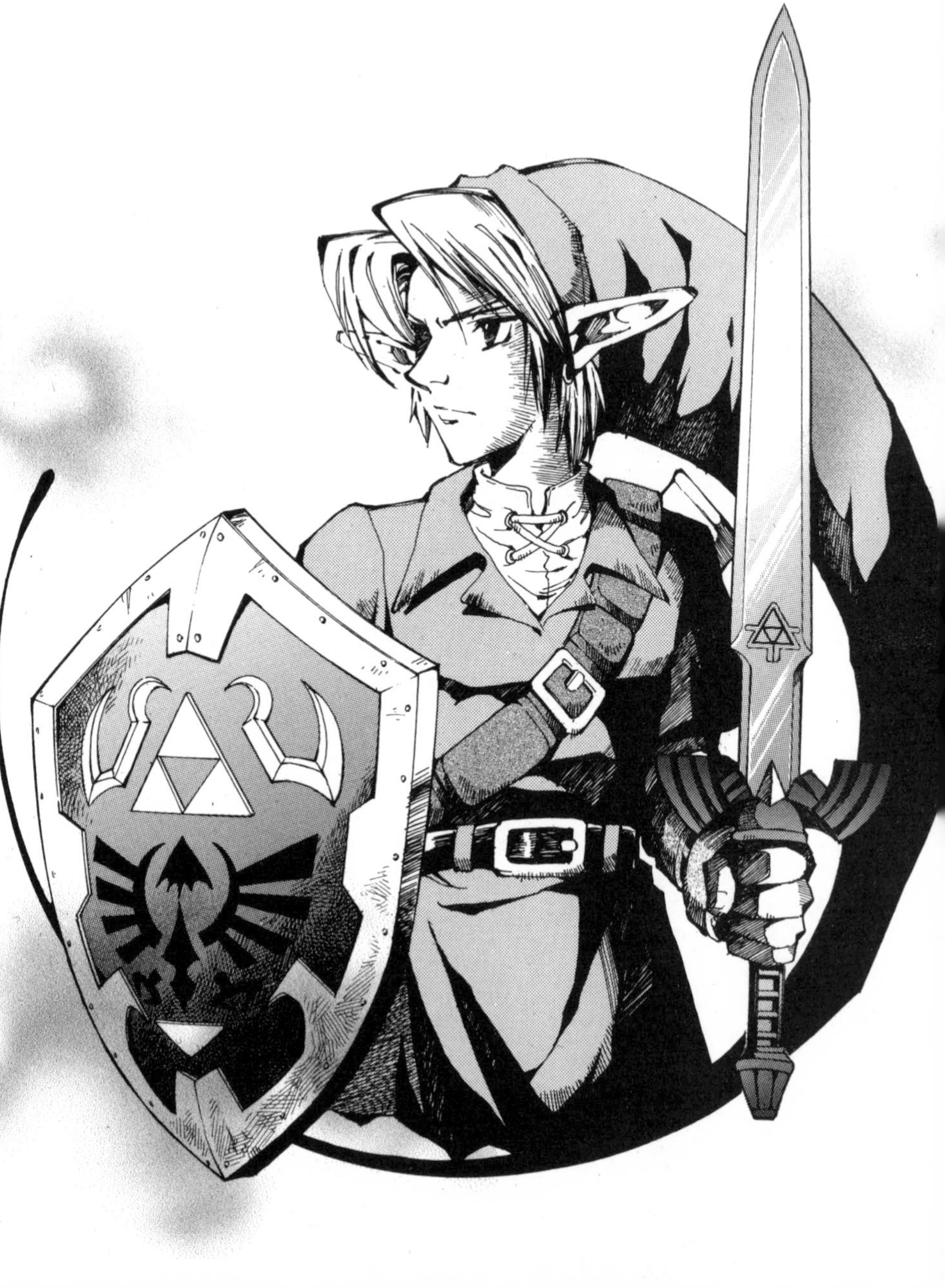

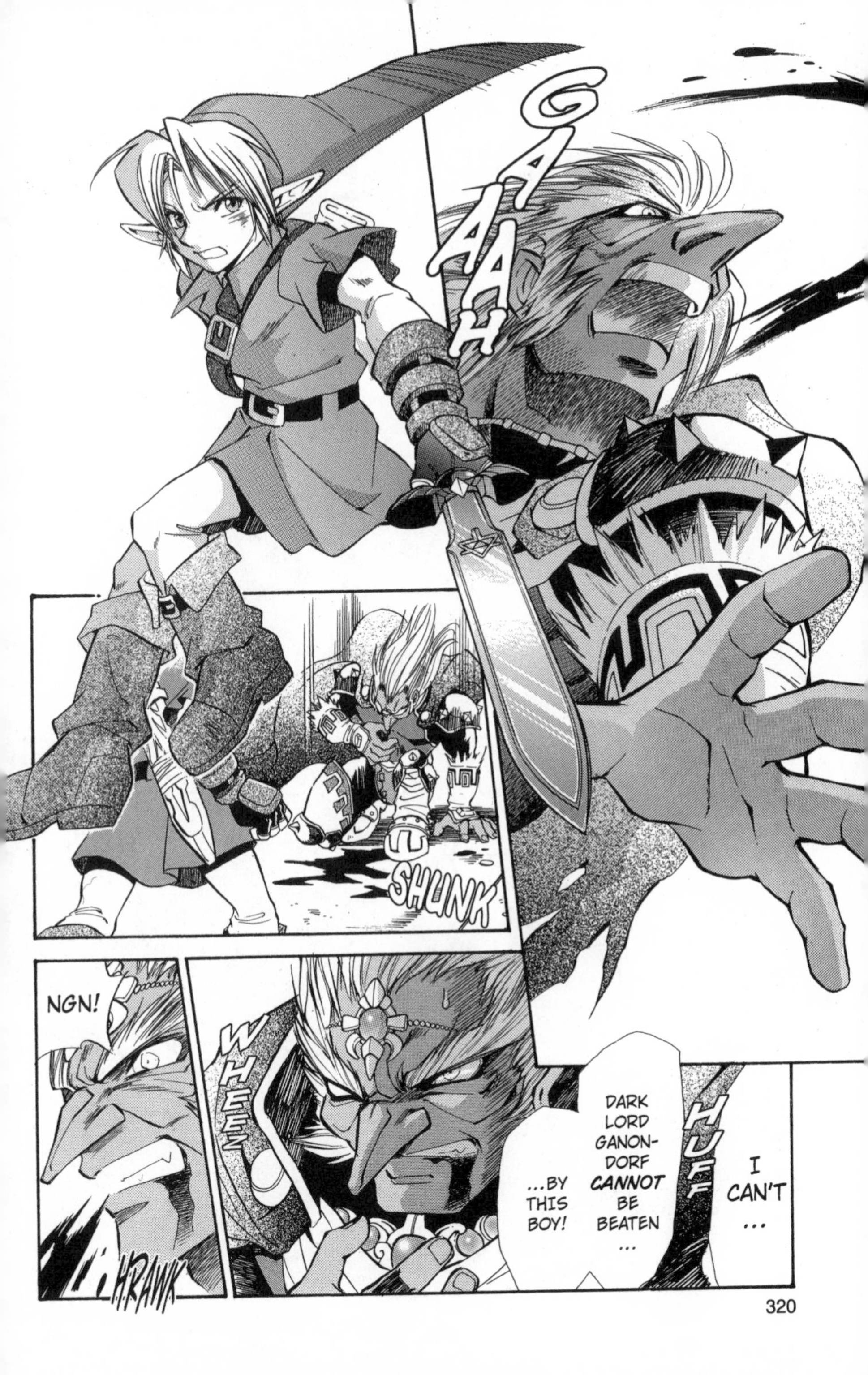
GAAAH
SHUNK
I CAN'T ...
HUFF
DARK LORD GANONDORF CANNOT BE BEATEN ...
...BY THIS BOY!
WHEEZ
NGN!
HRAWK

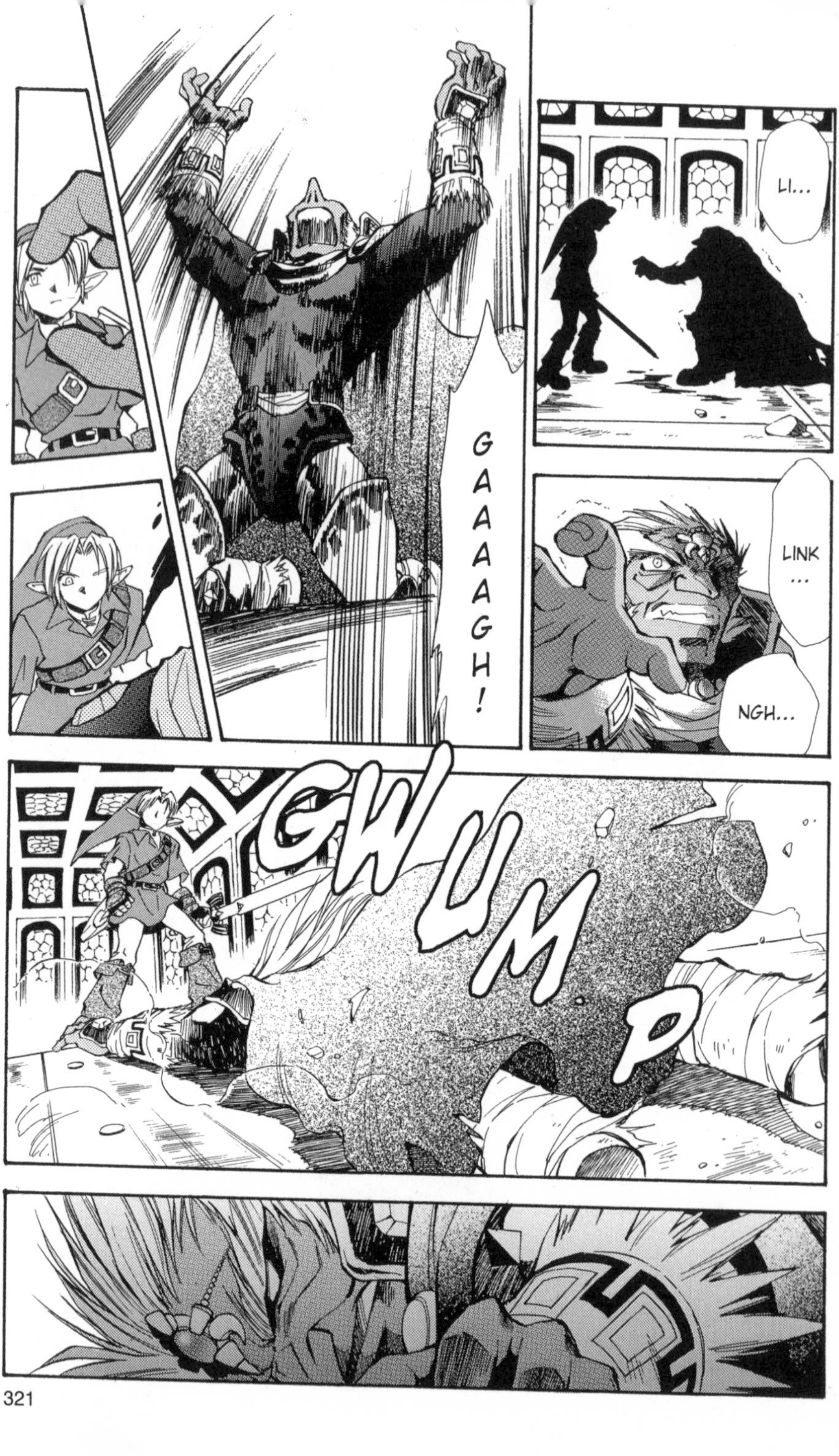
LI...
LINK ...
NGH...
GAAAAAGH!
GWUMP

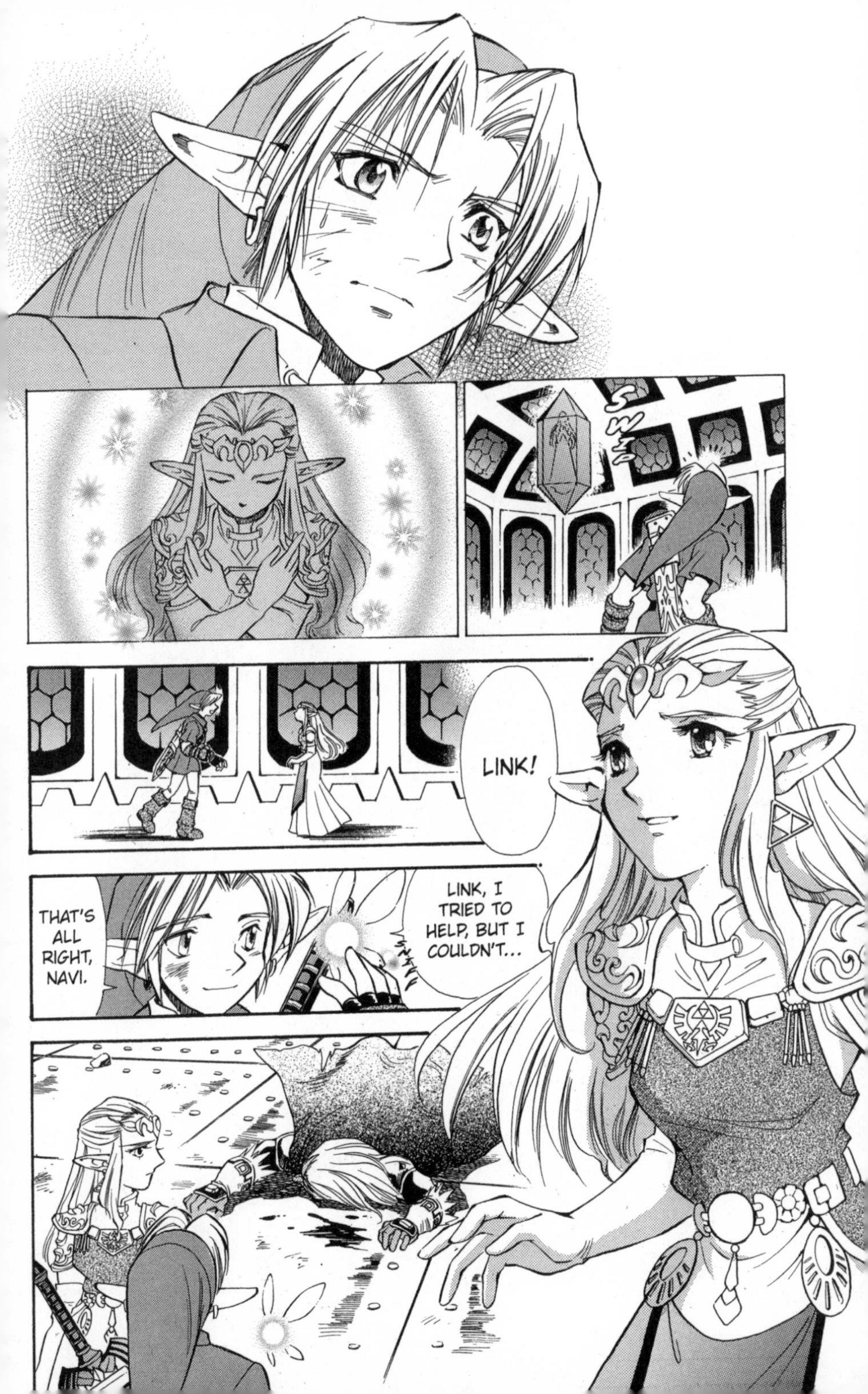
SWIP
LINK!
LINK, I TRIED TO HELP, BUT I COULDN'T...
SNIFF
THAT'S ALL RIGHT, NAVI.

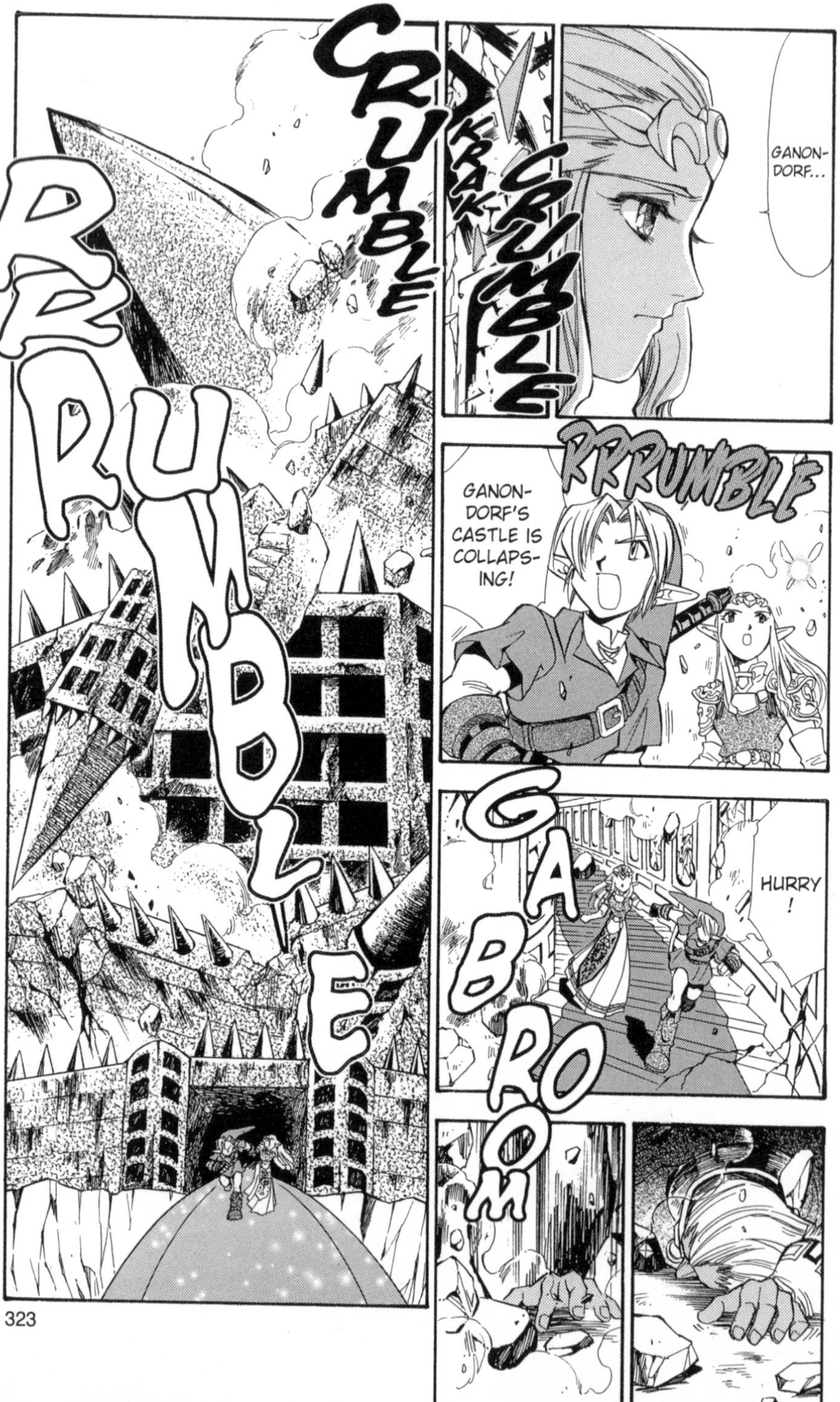
GANON-DORF...
CRUMBLE
KRAK
CRUMBLE
RRRUMBLE
GANON-DORF'S CASTLE IS COLLAPS-ING!
HURRY!
GABROOM
CRUMBLE
RRRUMBLE

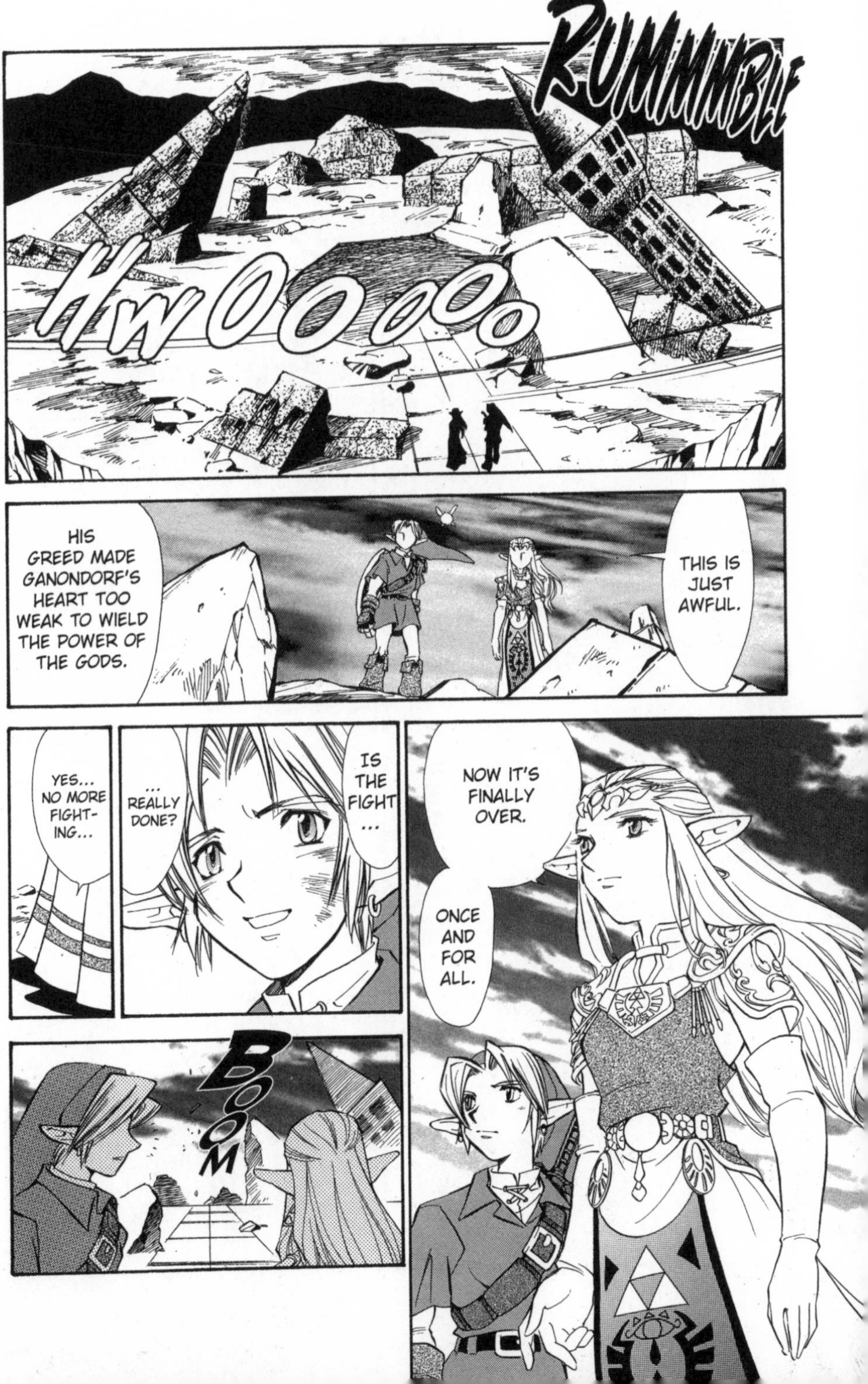
RUMMMBLE
HWOOOOO
THIS IS JUST AWFUL.
HIS GREED MADE GANONDORF'S HEART TOO WEAK TO WIELD THE POWER OF THE GODS.
NOW IT'S FINALLY OVER.
ONCE AND FOR ALL.
IS THE FIGHT...
...REALLY DONE?
YES... NO MORE FIGHT-ING...
BOOM

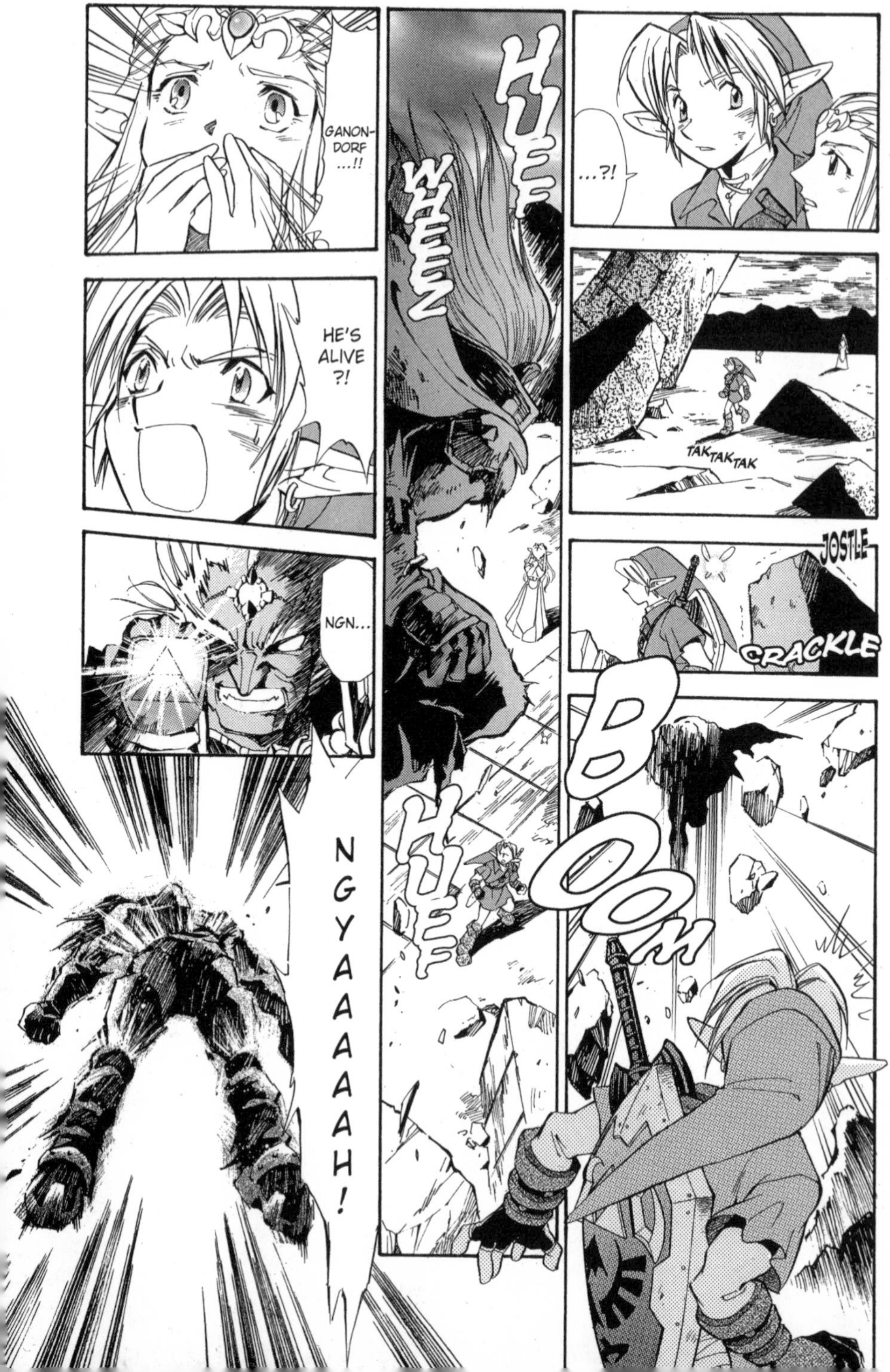
...?!
TAKTAKTAK
JOSTLE
CRACKLE
BOOM
HUFF
WHEEZ
HUFF
GANONDORF ...!!
HE'S ALIVE ?!
NGN...
NGYAAAAAAAH!

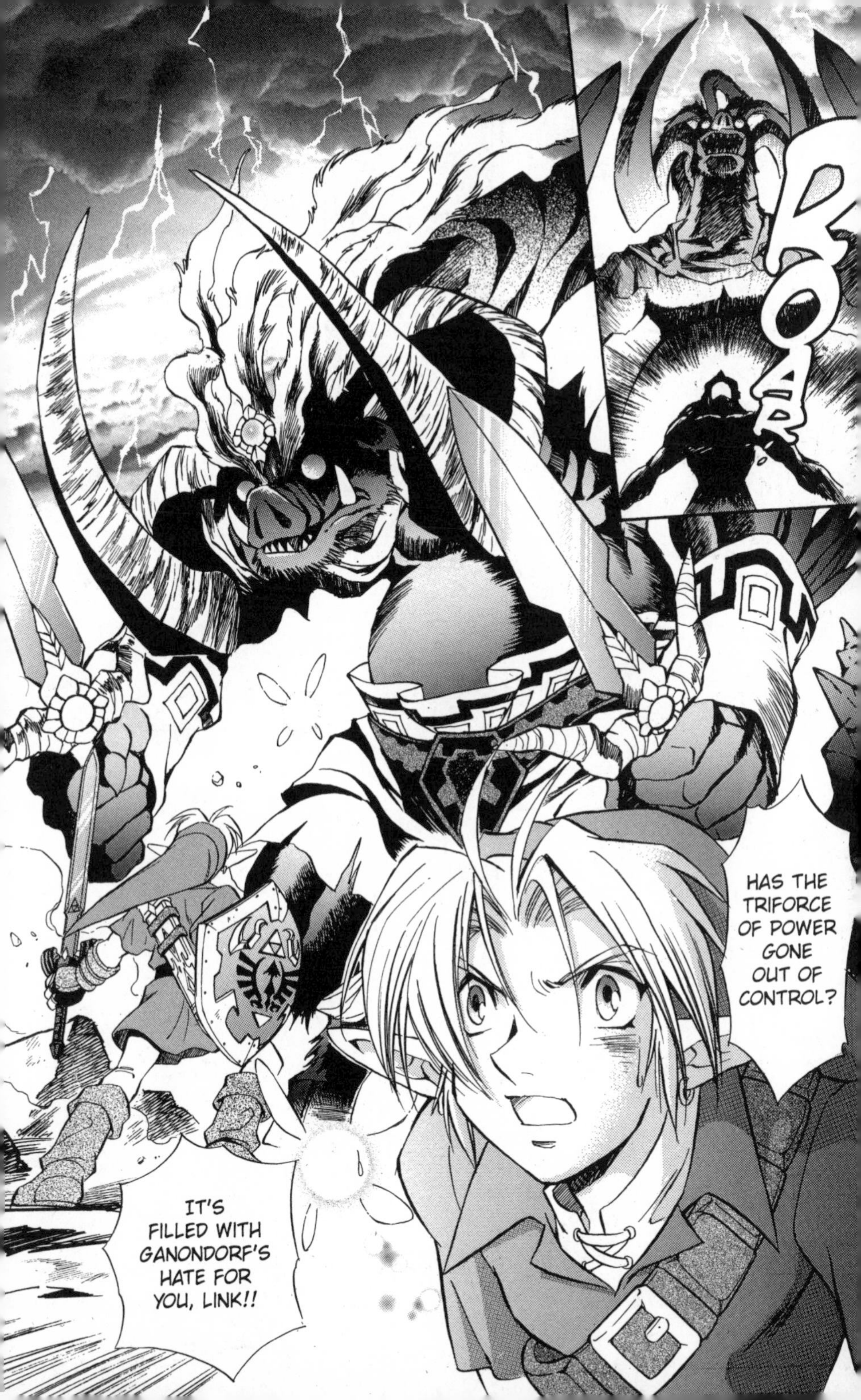
ROAR
HAS THE TRIFORCE OF POWER GONE OUT OF CONTROL?
IT'S FILLED WITH GANONDORF'S HATE FOR YOU, LINK!!

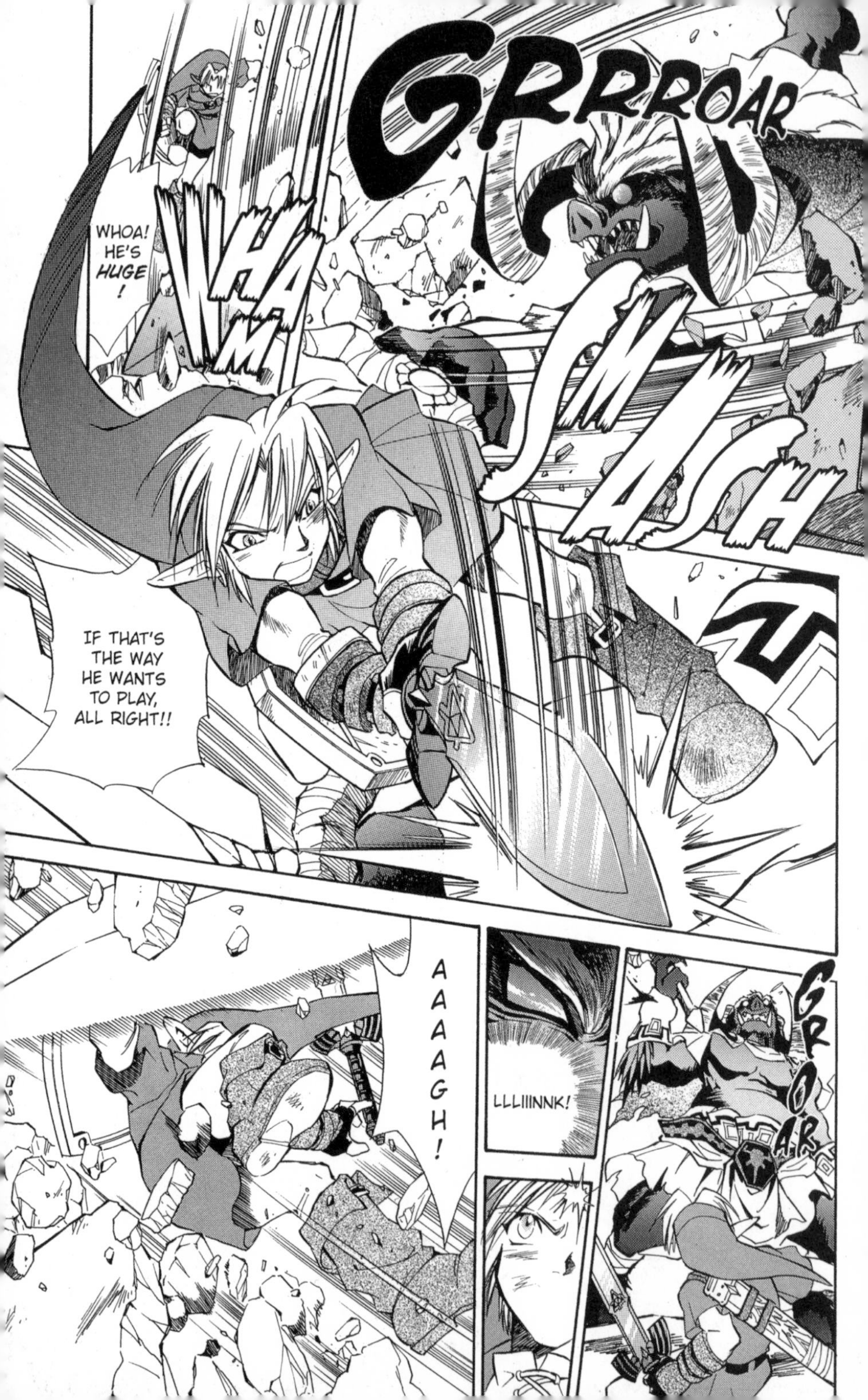
GRRROAR
SMASH
WHAM
WHOA! HE'S *HUGE*!
IF THAT'S THE WAY HE WANTS TO PLAY, ALL RIGHT!!
GROAR
LLLIIINNK!
AAAAGH!

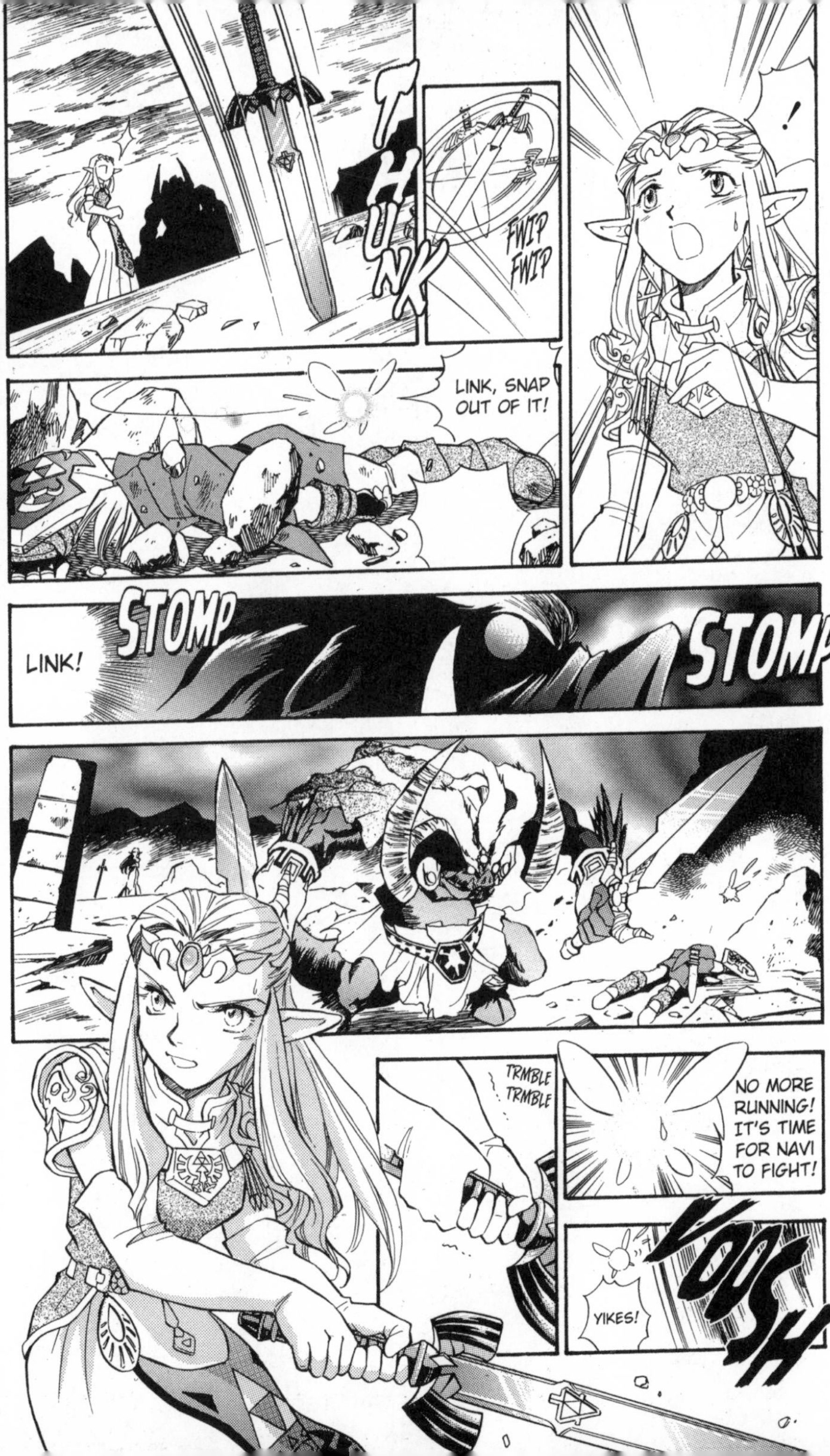
!
FWIP FWIP
THUNK
LINK, SNAP OUT OF IT!
STOMP
STOMP
LINK!
NO MORE RUNNING! IT'S TIME FOR NAVI TO FIGHT!
VOOSH
YIKES!
TRMBLE TRMBLE

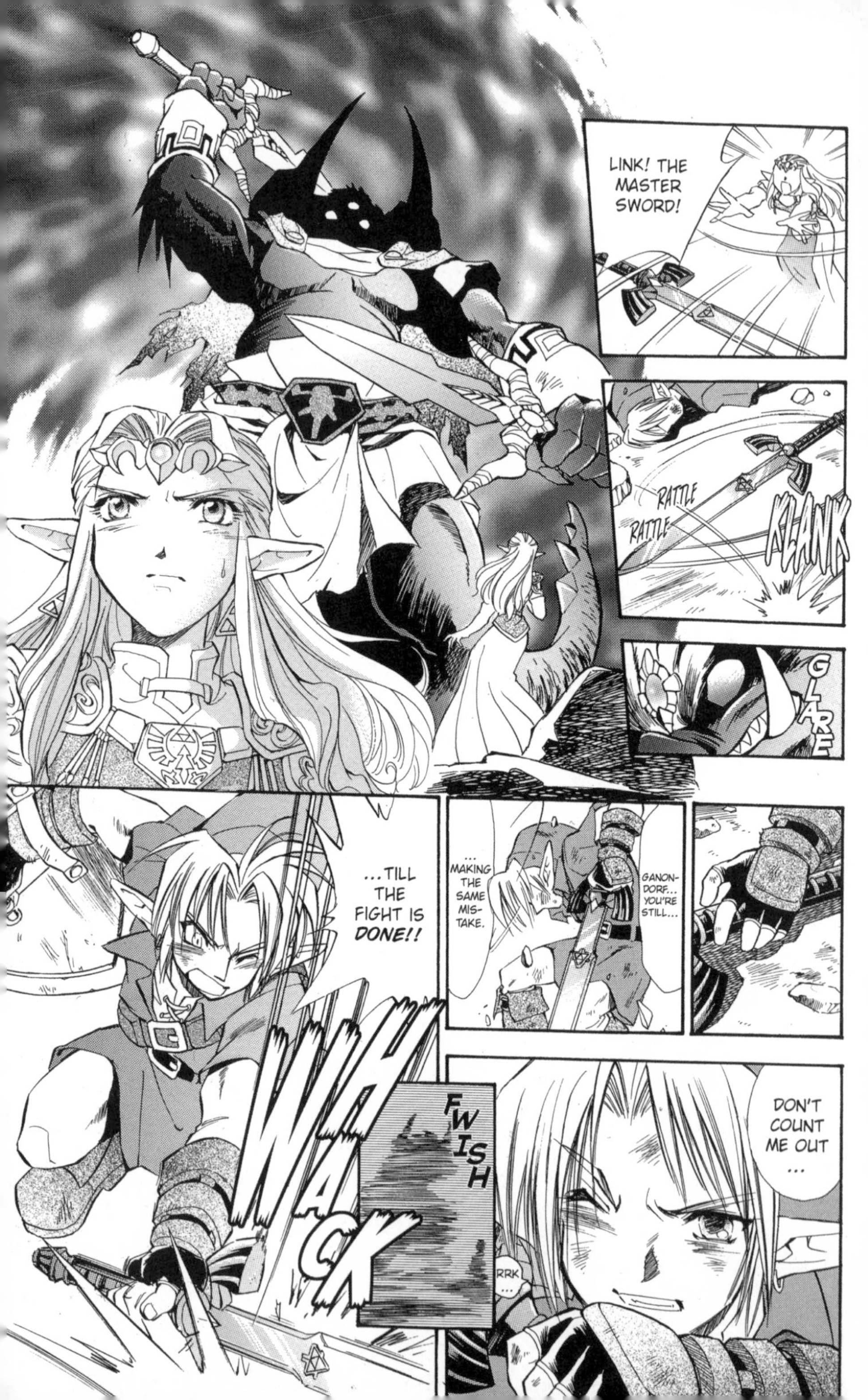
LINK! THE MASTER SWORD!
RATTLE
RATTLE
KLANK
GLARE
GANON-DORF... YOU'RE STILL...
...MAKING THE SAME MIS-TAKE.
DON'T COUNT ME OUT...
RRK...
...TILL THE FIGHT IS DONE!!
FWISH
WHACK

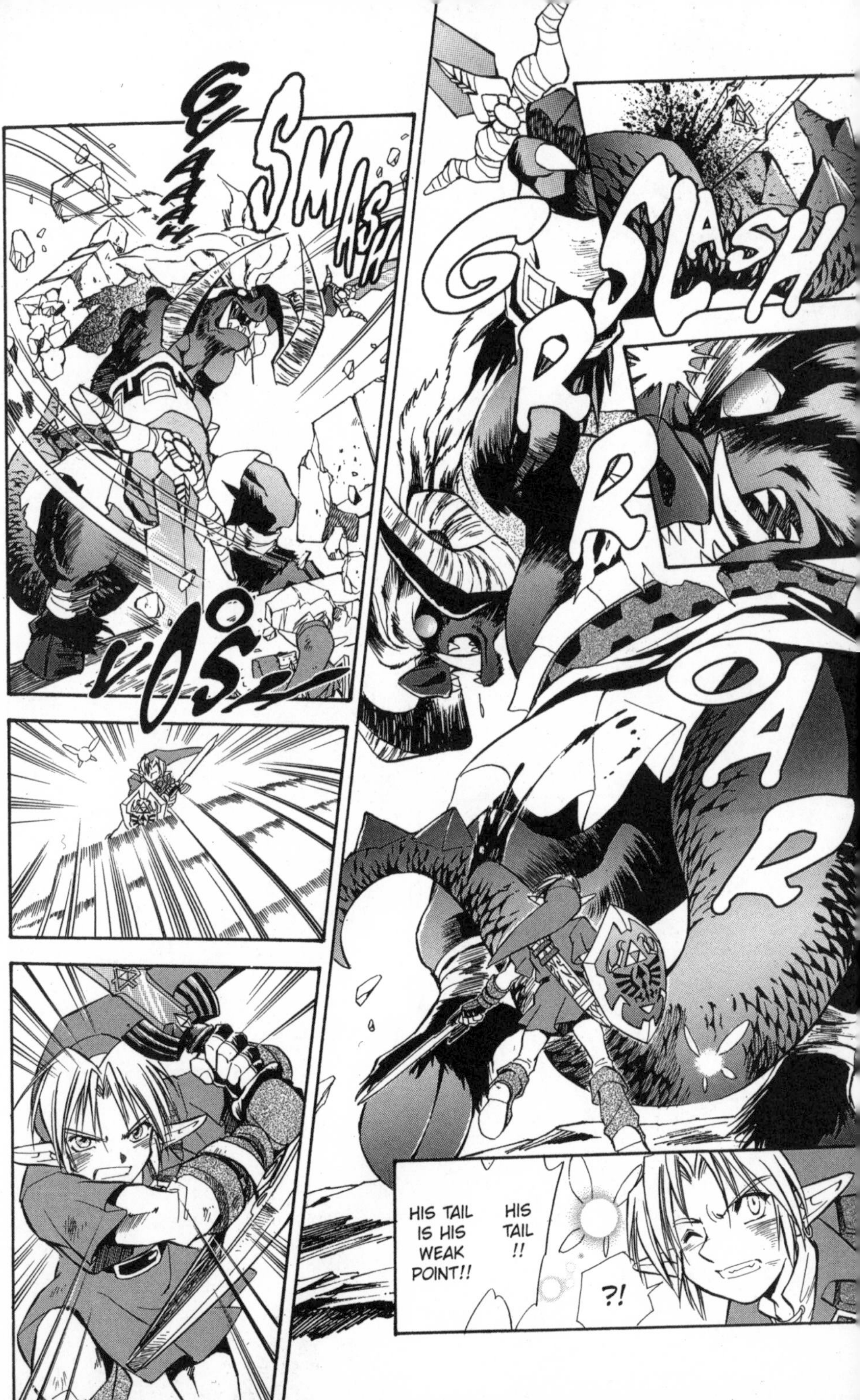
SLASH
GRROAR
HIS TAIL IS HIS WEAK POINT!!
HIS TAIL!!
?!
GYAAAH
SMASH
VOOSH

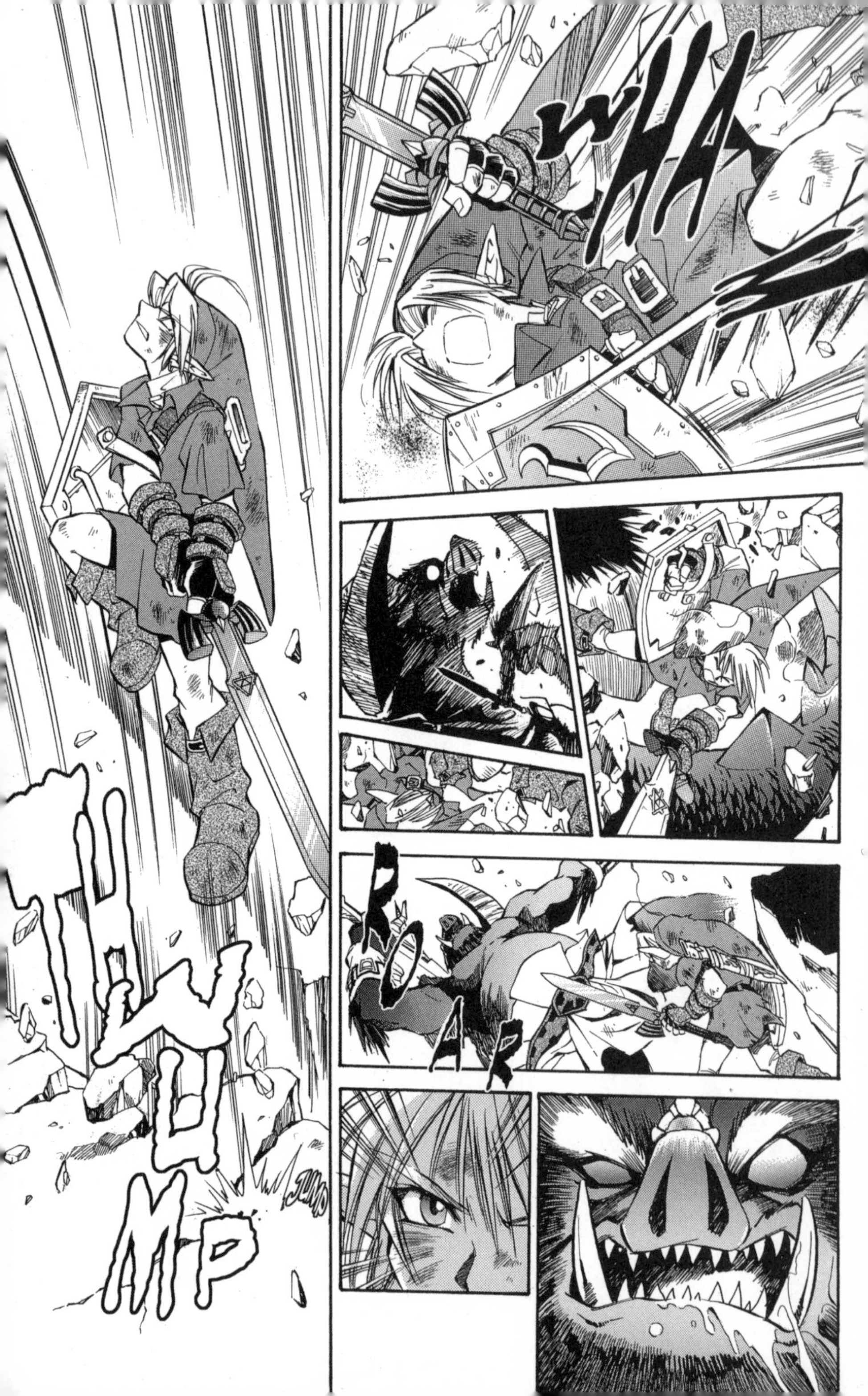
WHAA
ROAR
THUMP

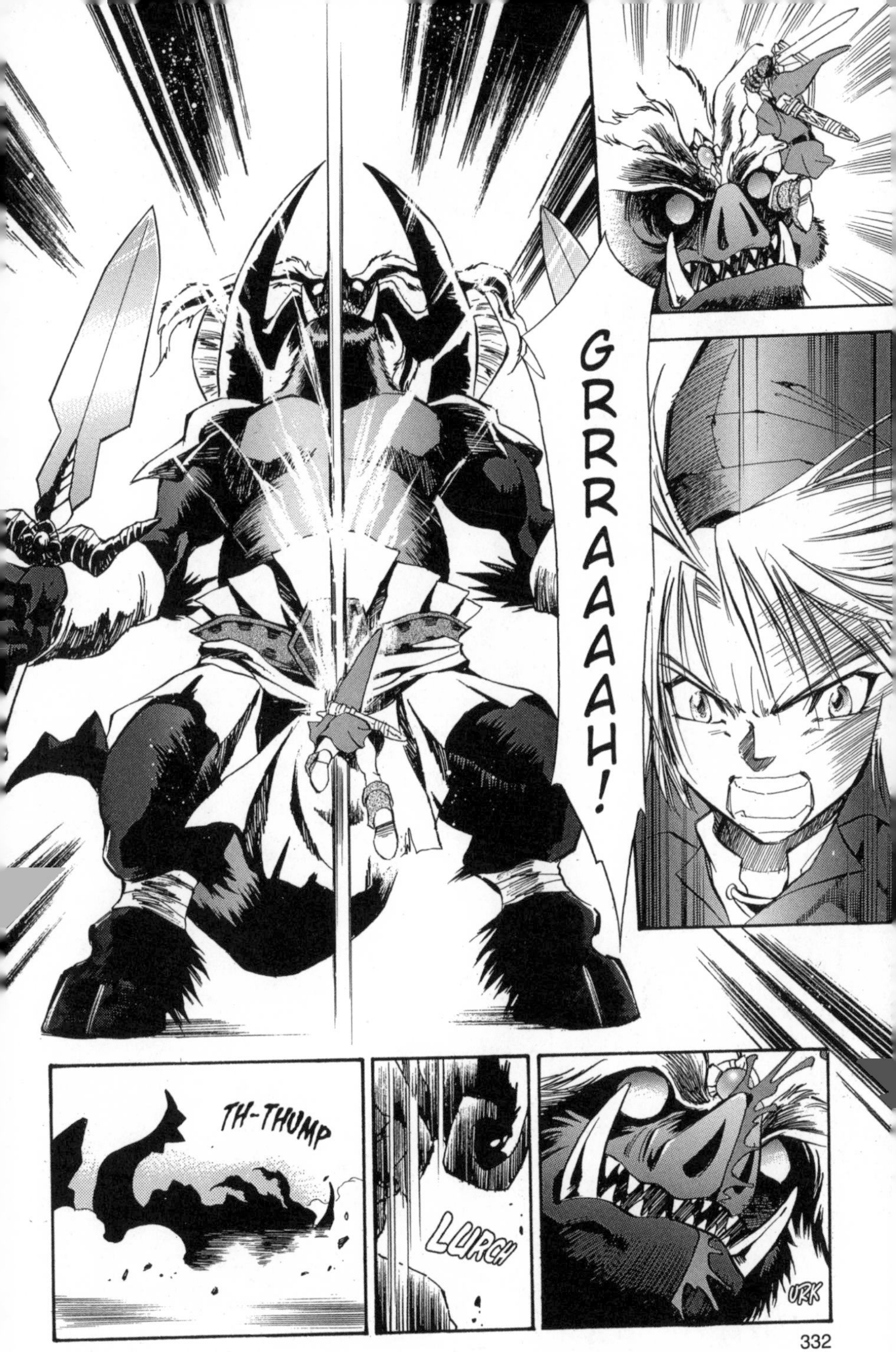
GRRRAAAAAH!
URK
LURCH
TH-THUMP

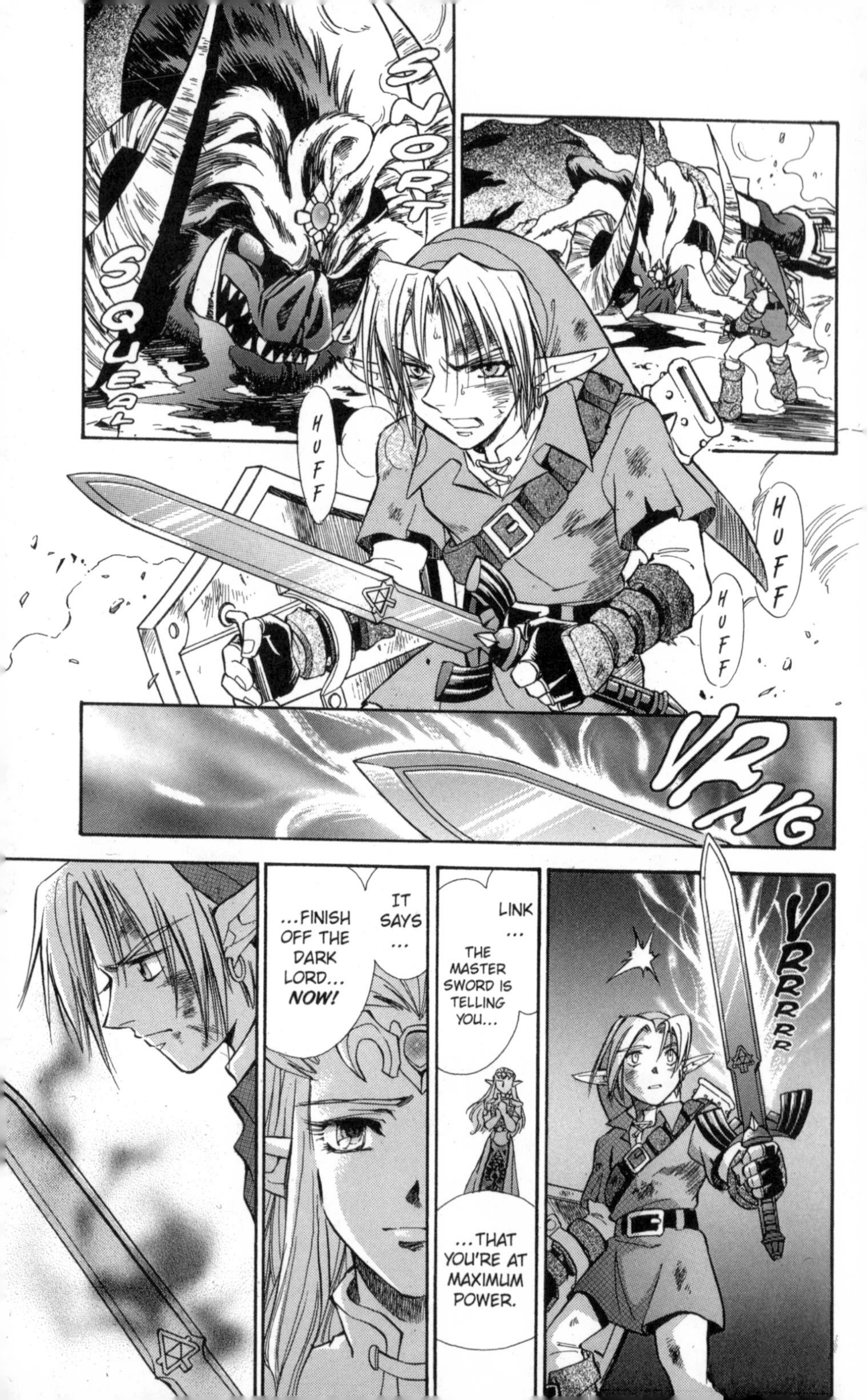
SNORT
SQUEAL
HUFF
HUFF
HUFF
VRNG
VRRRRR
LINK...
THE MASTER SWORD IS TELLING YOU...
...THAT YOU'RE AT MAXIMUM POWER.
IT SAYS...
...FINISH OFF THE DARK LORD... NOW!

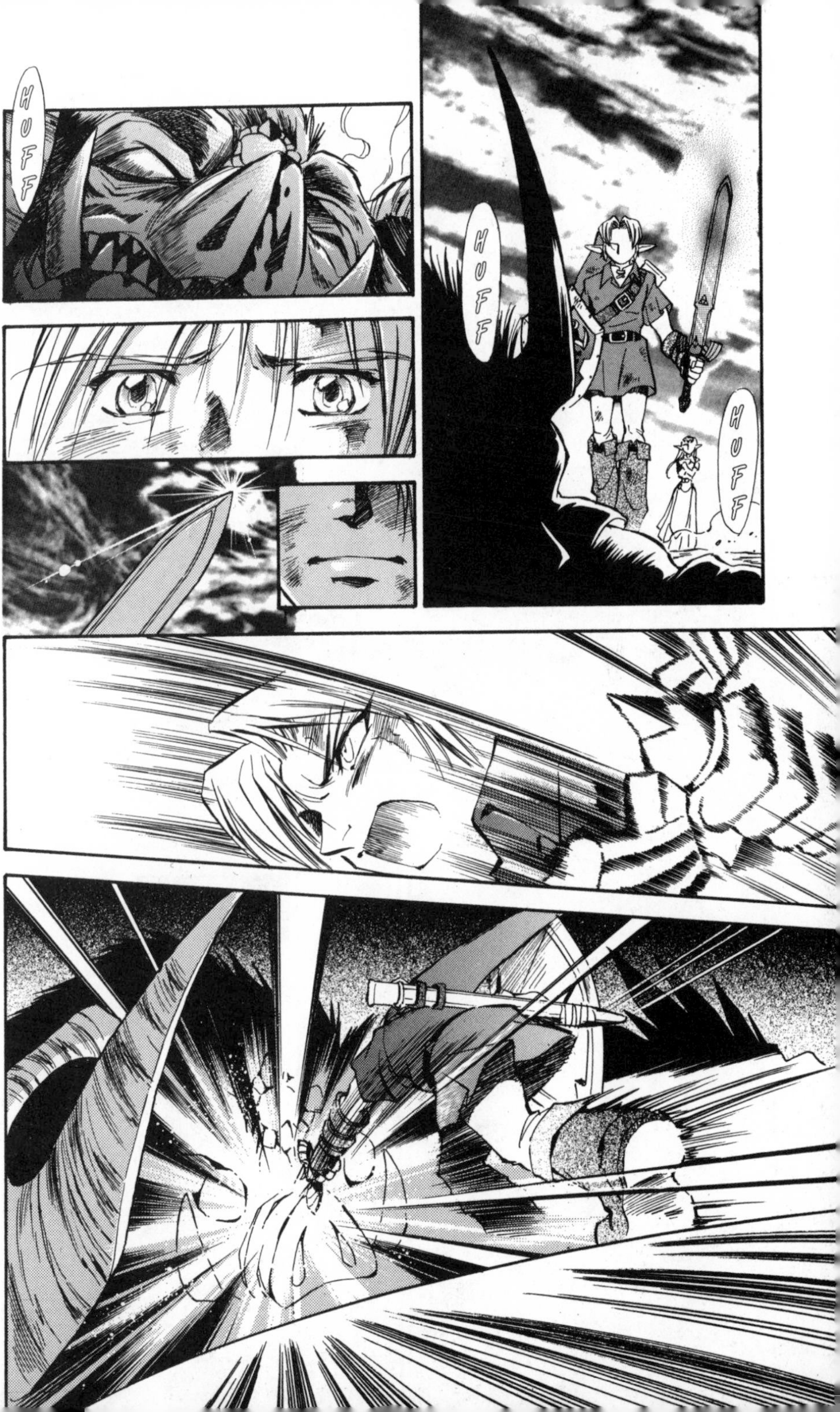
HUFF
HUFF
HUFF

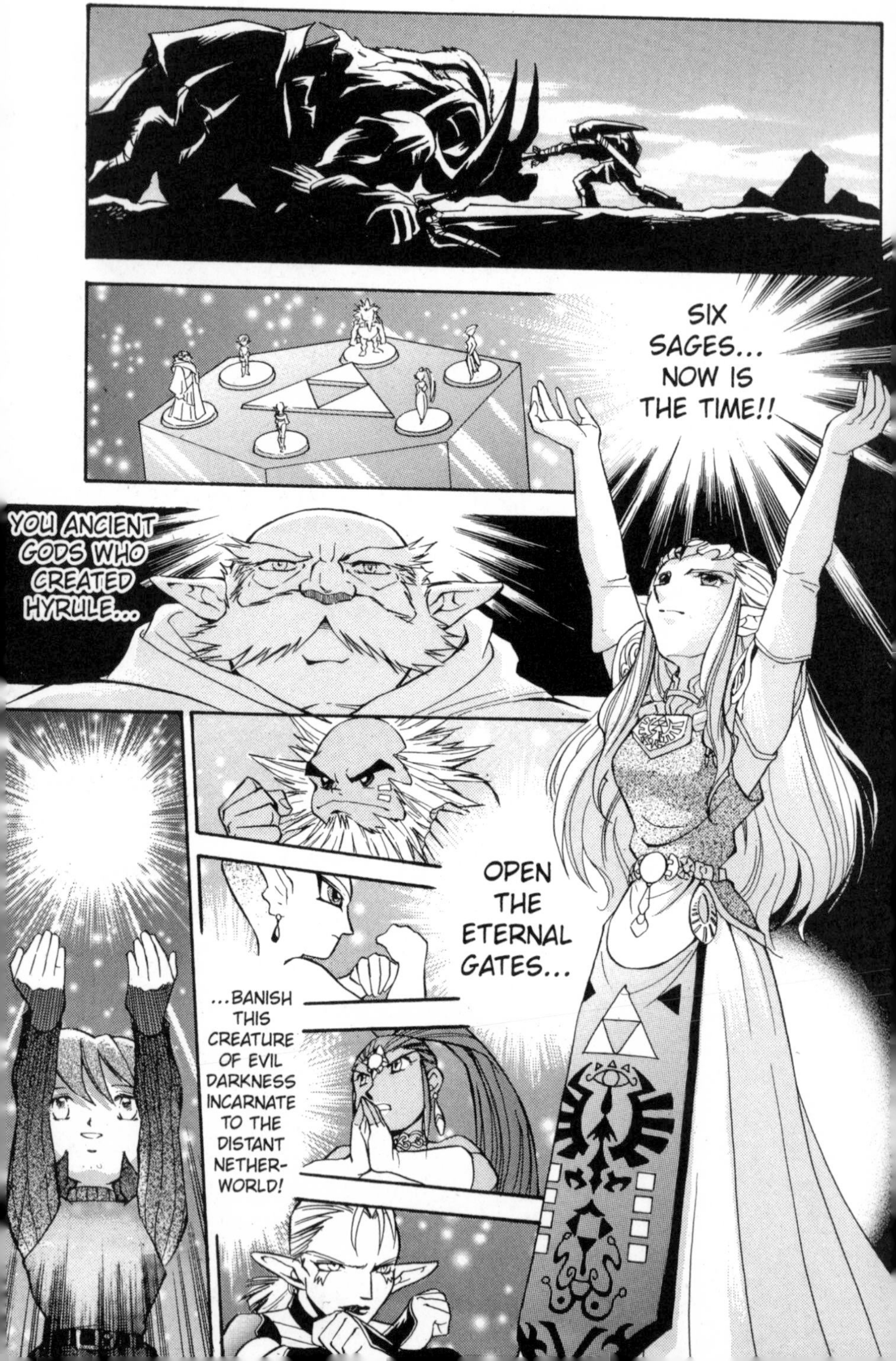
SIX SAGES... NOW IS THE TIME!!
YOU! ANCIENT GODS WHO CREATED HYRULE...
OPEN THE ETERNAL GATES...
...BANISH THIS CREATURE OF EVIL DARKNESS INCARNATE TO THE DISTANT NETHER-WORLD!

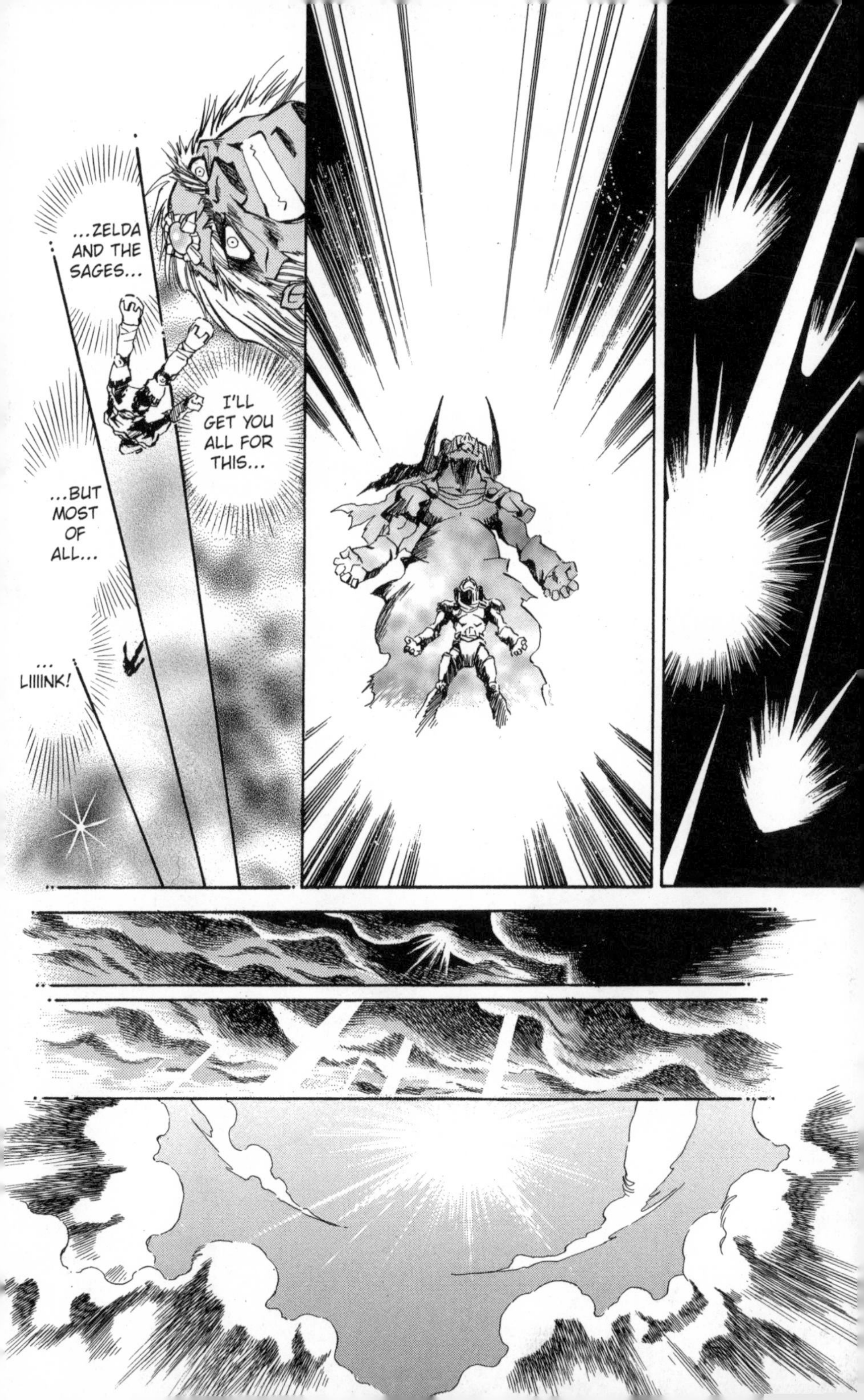
...ZELDA AND THE SAGES...
I'LL GET YOU ALL FOR THIS...
...BUT MOST OF ALL...
...LIIIINK!

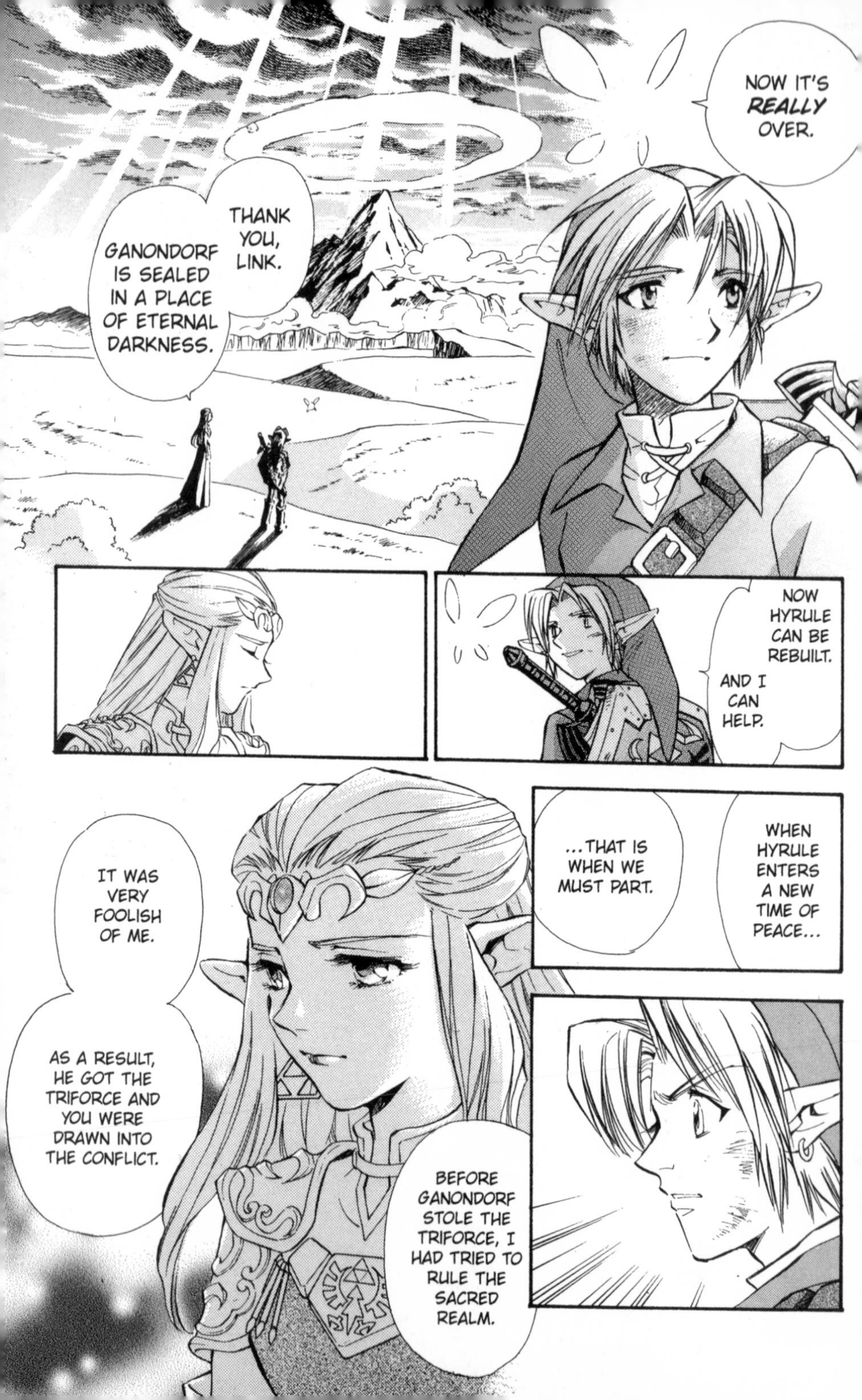
NOW IT'S ***REALLY*** OVER.
THANK YOU, LINK.
GANONDORF IS SEALED IN A PLACE OF ETERNAL DARKNESS.
NOW HYRULE CAN BE REBUILT.
AND I CAN HELP.
WHEN HYRULE ENTERS A NEW TIME OF PEACE...
...THAT IS WHEN WE MUST PART.
BEFORE GANONDORF STOLE THE TRIFORCE, I HAD TRIED TO RULE THE SACRED REALM.
IT WAS VERY FOOLISH OF ME.
AS A RESULT, HE GOT THE TRIFORCE AND YOU WERE DRAWN INTO THE CONFLICT.

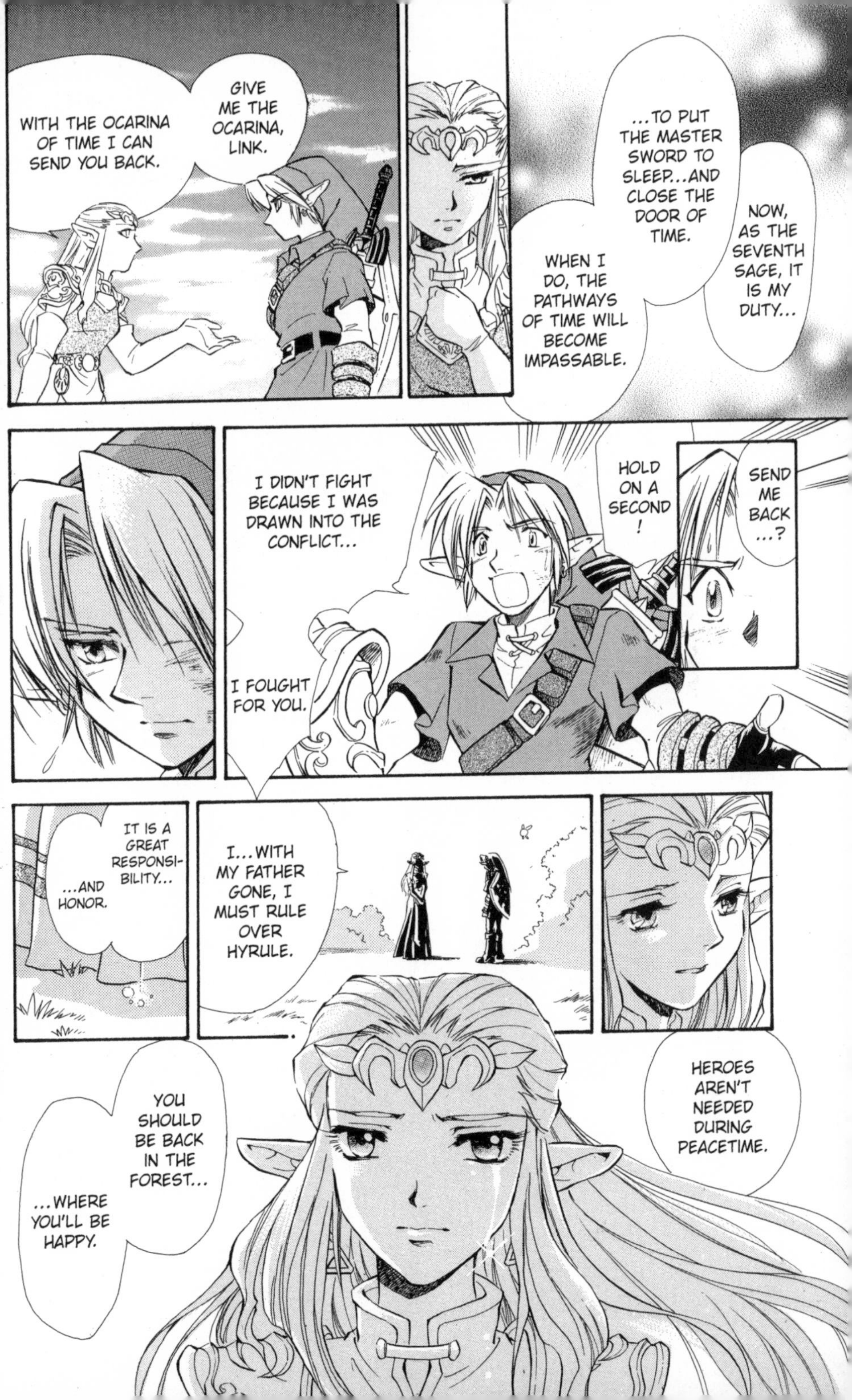
NOW, AS THE SEVENTH SAGE, IT IS MY DUTY...
...TO PUT THE MASTER SWORD TO SLEEP...AND CLOSE THE DOOR OF TIME.
WHEN I DO, THE PATHWAYS OF TIME WILL BECOME IMPASSABLE.
GIVE ME THE OCARINA, LINK.
WITH THE OCARINA OF TIME I CAN SEND YOU BACK.
SEND ME BACK ...?
HOLD ON A SECOND!
I DIDN'T FIGHT BECAUSE I WAS DRAWN INTO THE CONFLICT...
I FOUGHT FOR YOU.
I...WITH MY FATHER GONE, I MUST RULE OVER HYRULE.
IT IS A GREAT RESPONSIBILITY...
...AND HONOR.
HEROES AREN'T NEEDED DURING PEACETIME.
YOU SHOULD BE BACK IN THE FOREST...
...WHERE YOU'LL BE HAPPY.

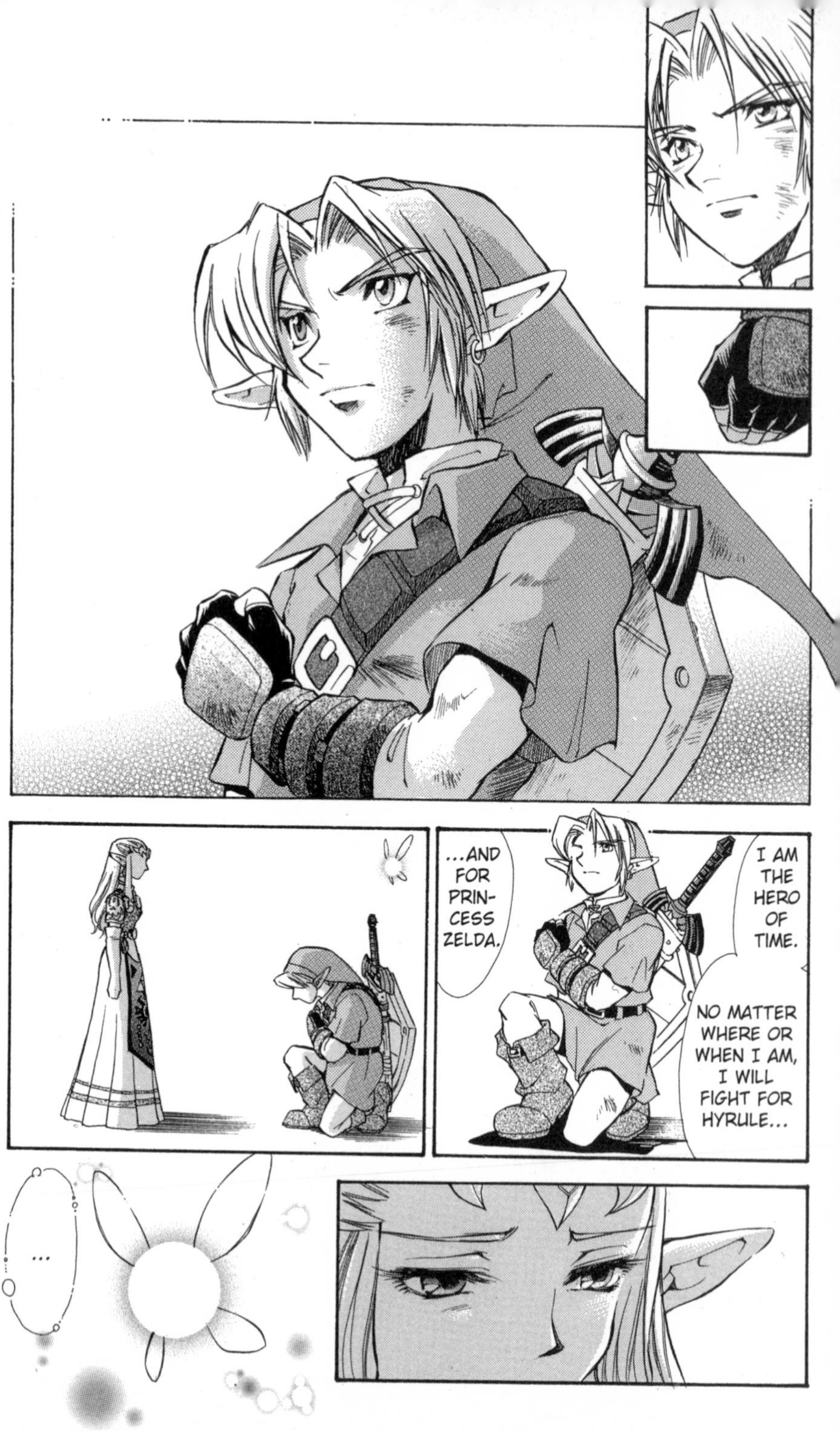
I AM THE HERO OF TIME.
NO MATTER WHERE OR WHEN I AM, I WILL FIGHT FOR HYRULE...
...AND FOR PRINCESS ZELDA.
...

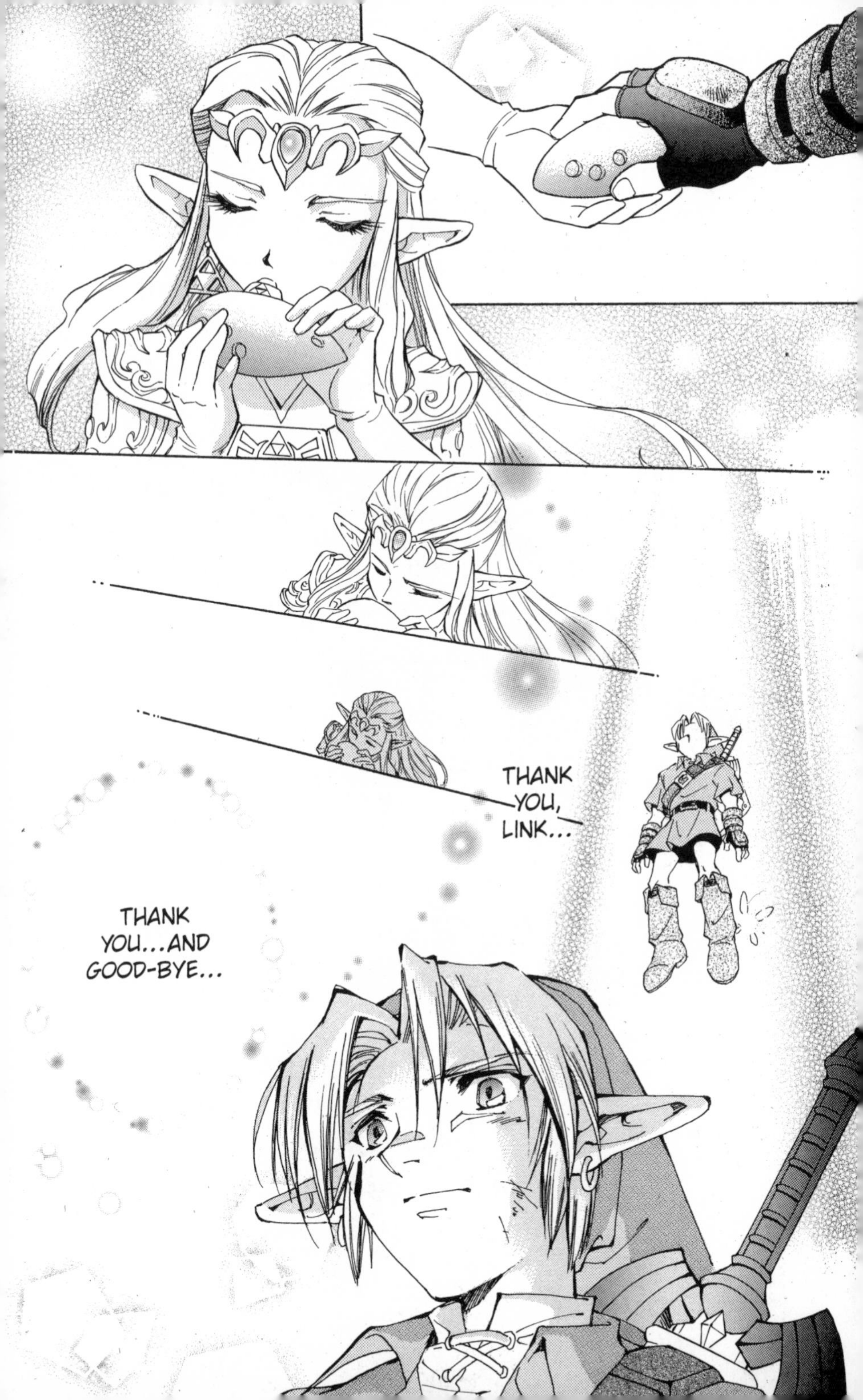
THANK YOU, LINK...
THANK YOU...AND GOOD-BYE...

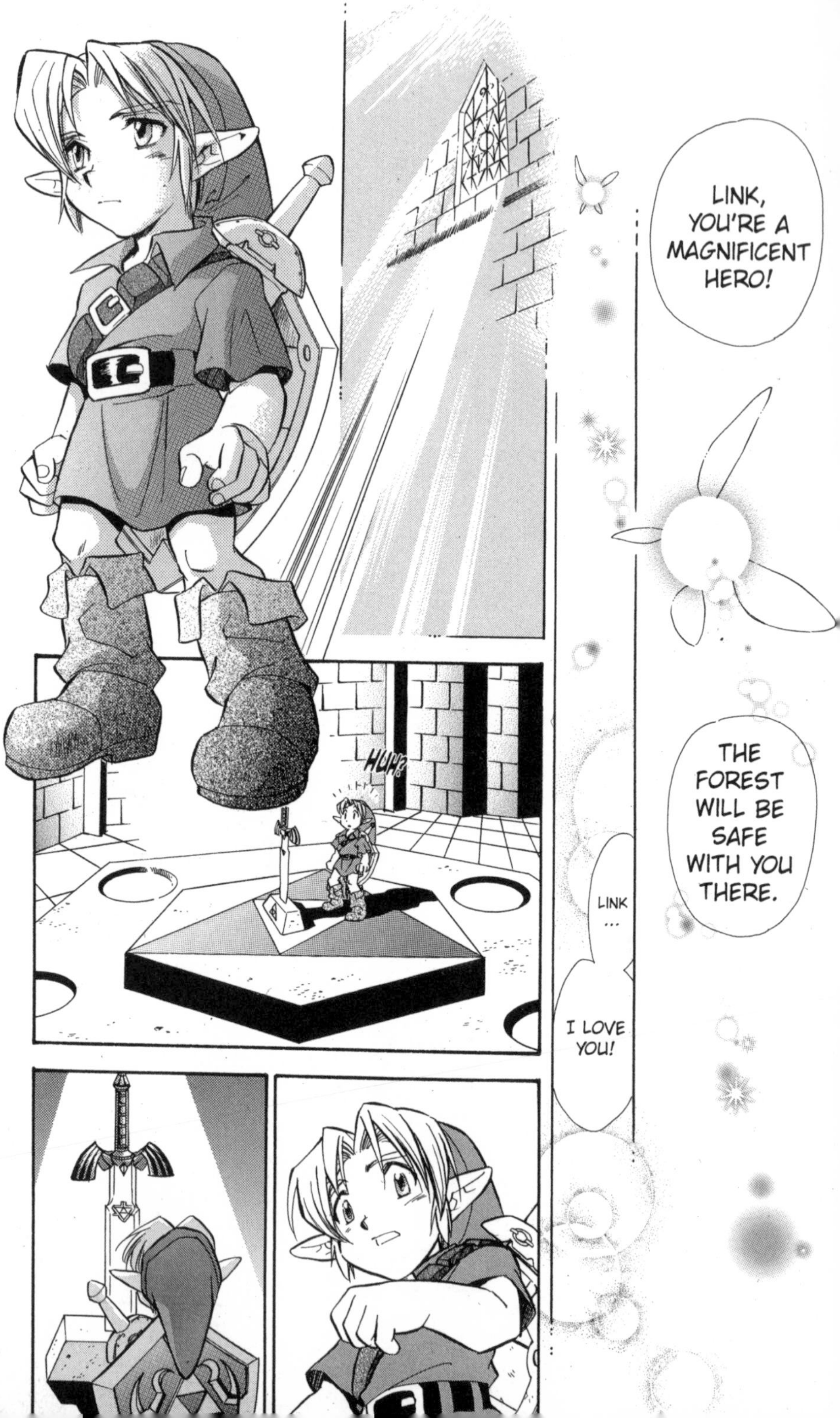
LINK, YOU'RE A MAGNIFICENT HERO!
THE FOREST WILL BE SAFE WITH YOU THERE.
LINK ...
I LOVE YOU!
HUH?

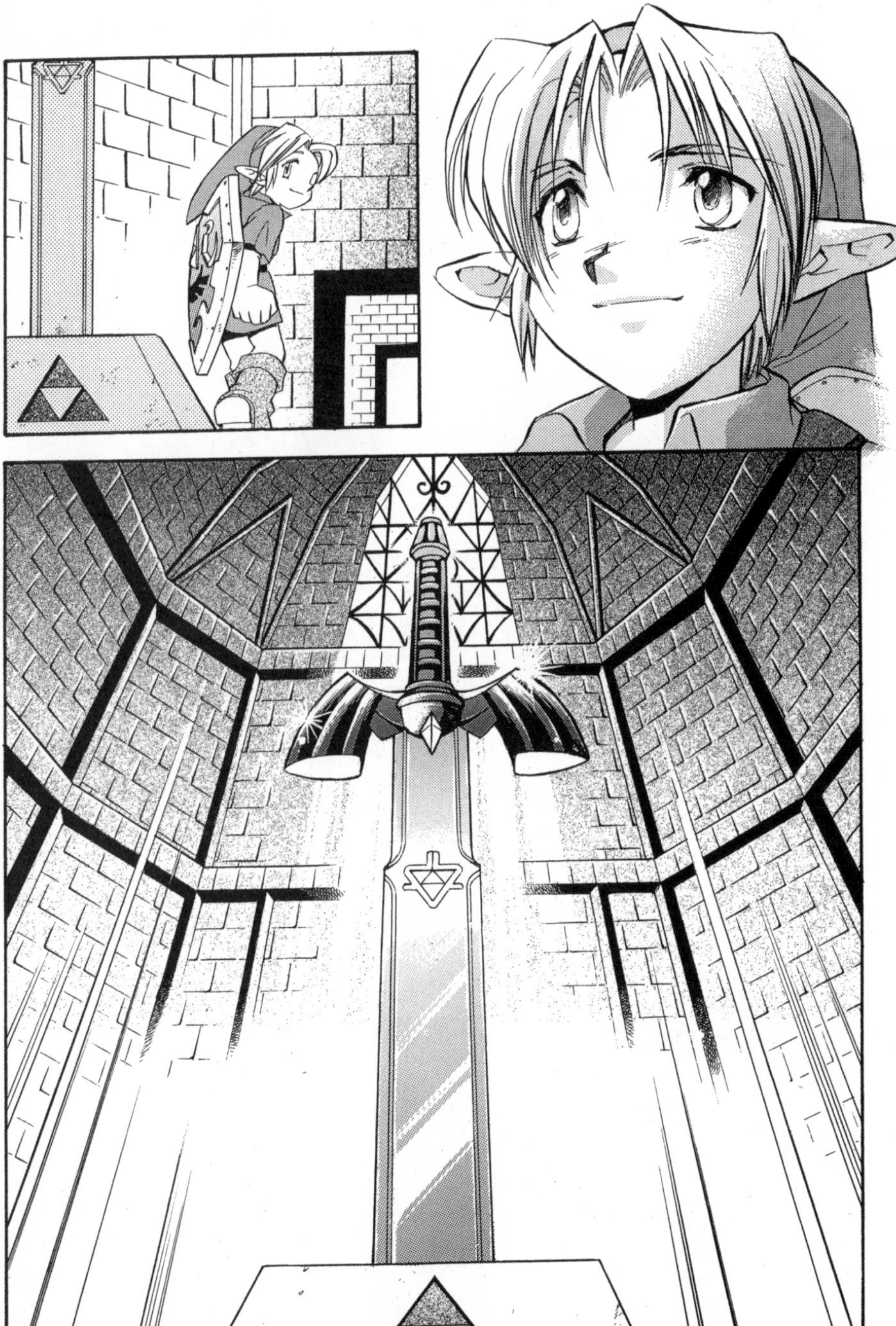

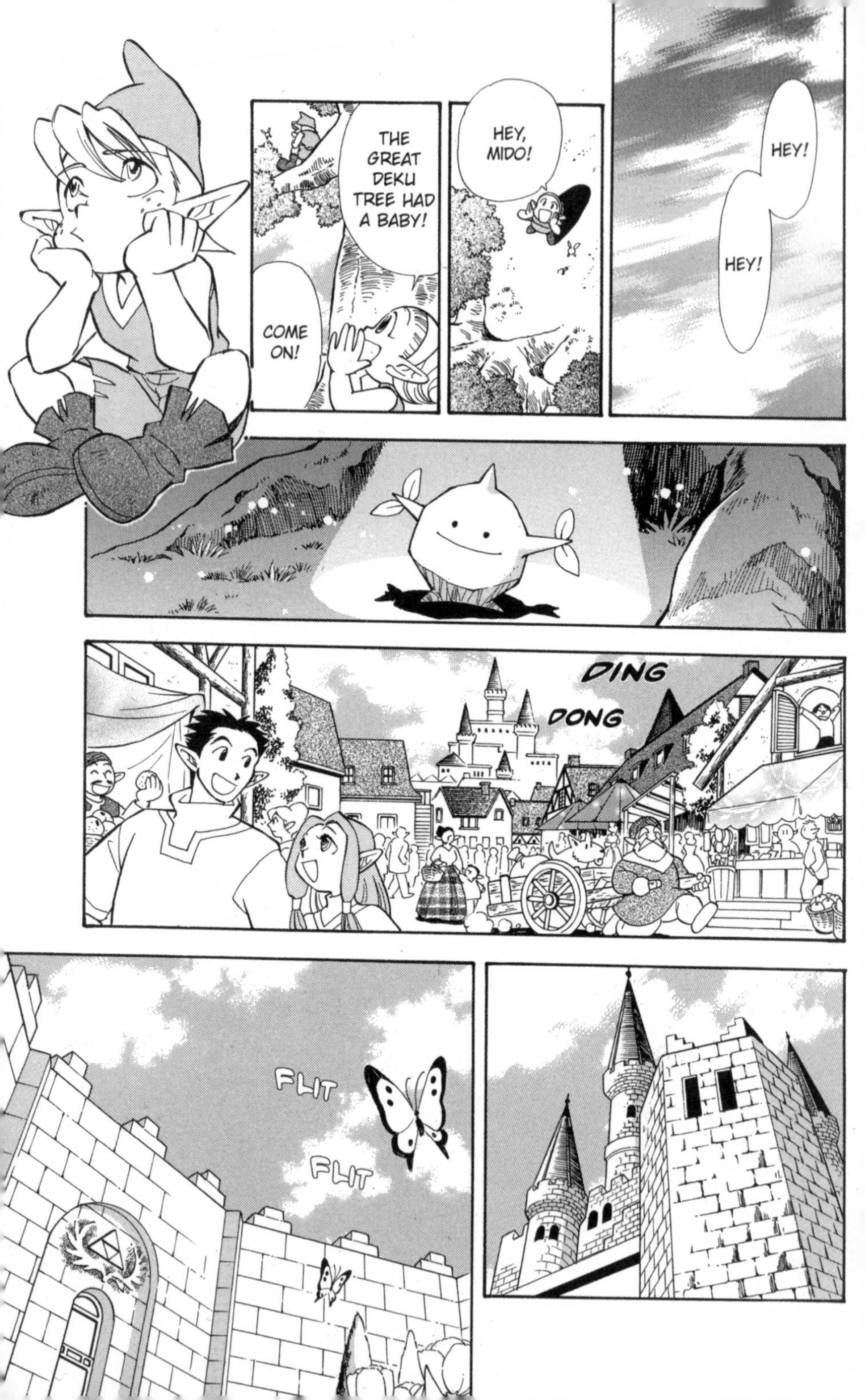
HEY!
HEY!
HEY, MIDO!
THE GREAT DEKU TREE HAD A BABY!
COME ON!
DING
DONG
FLIT
FLIT

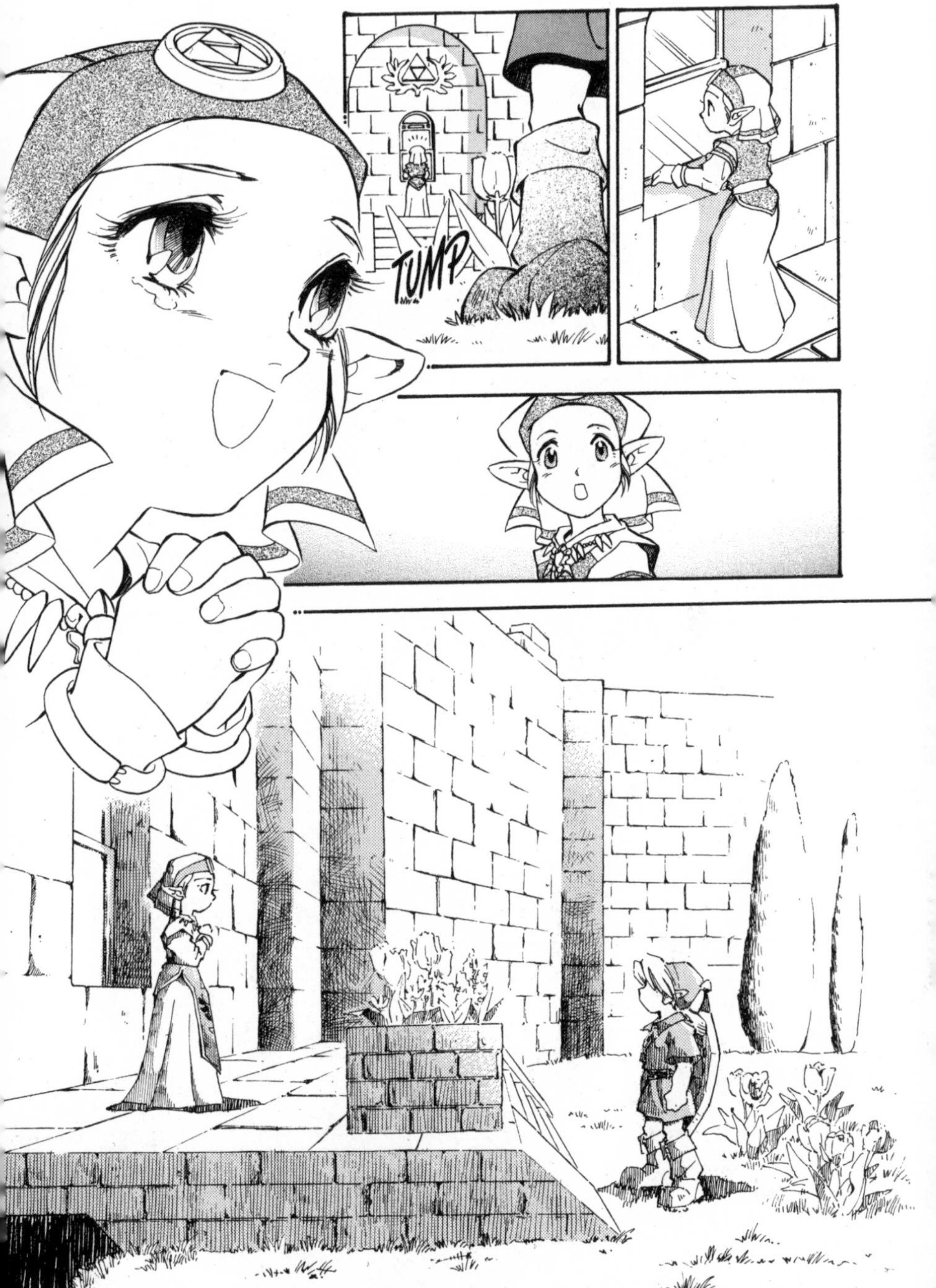
TUMP

OCARINA OF TIME/ADULT ARC (END)

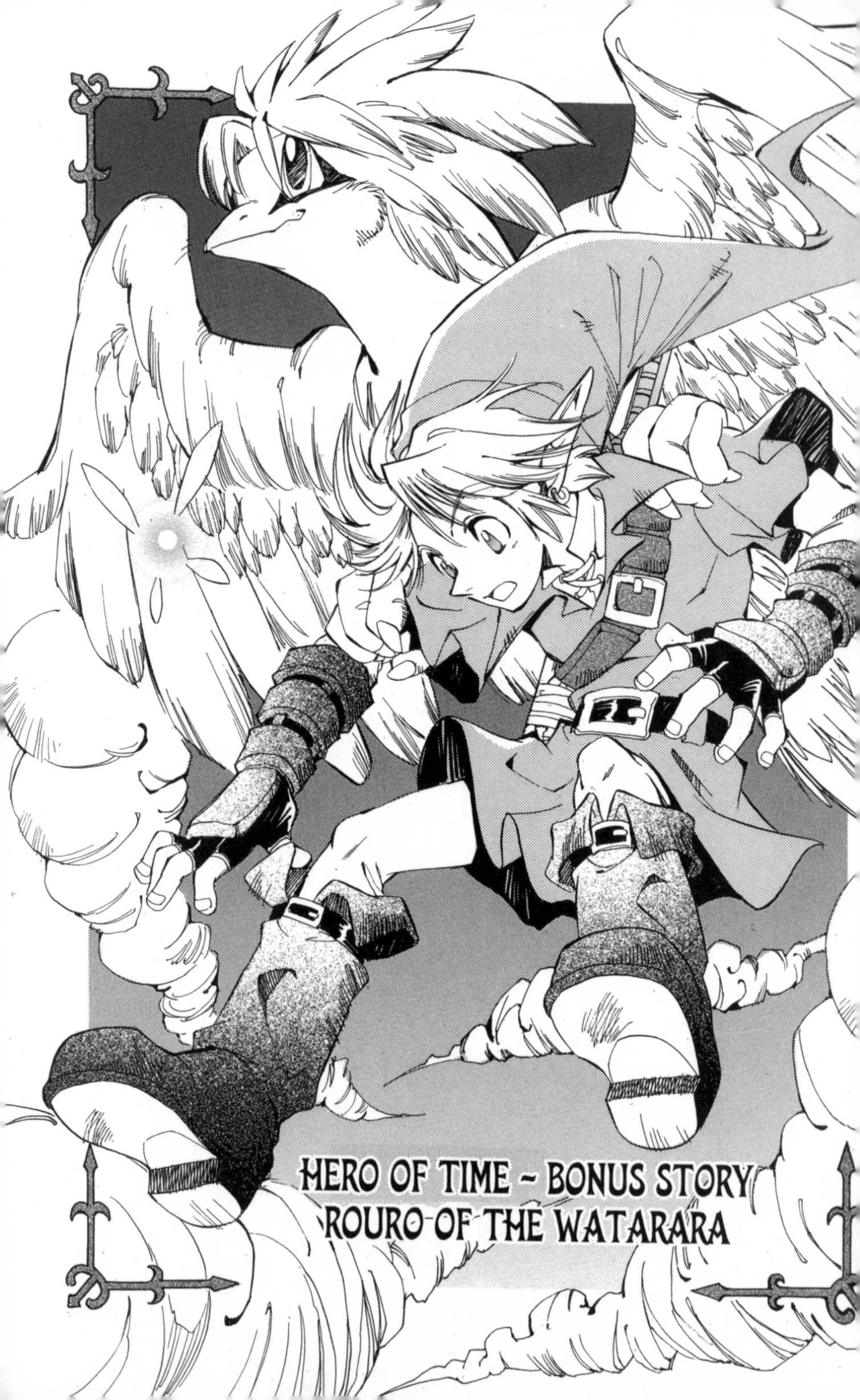
HERO OF TIME - BONUS STORY
ROURO OF THE WATARARA

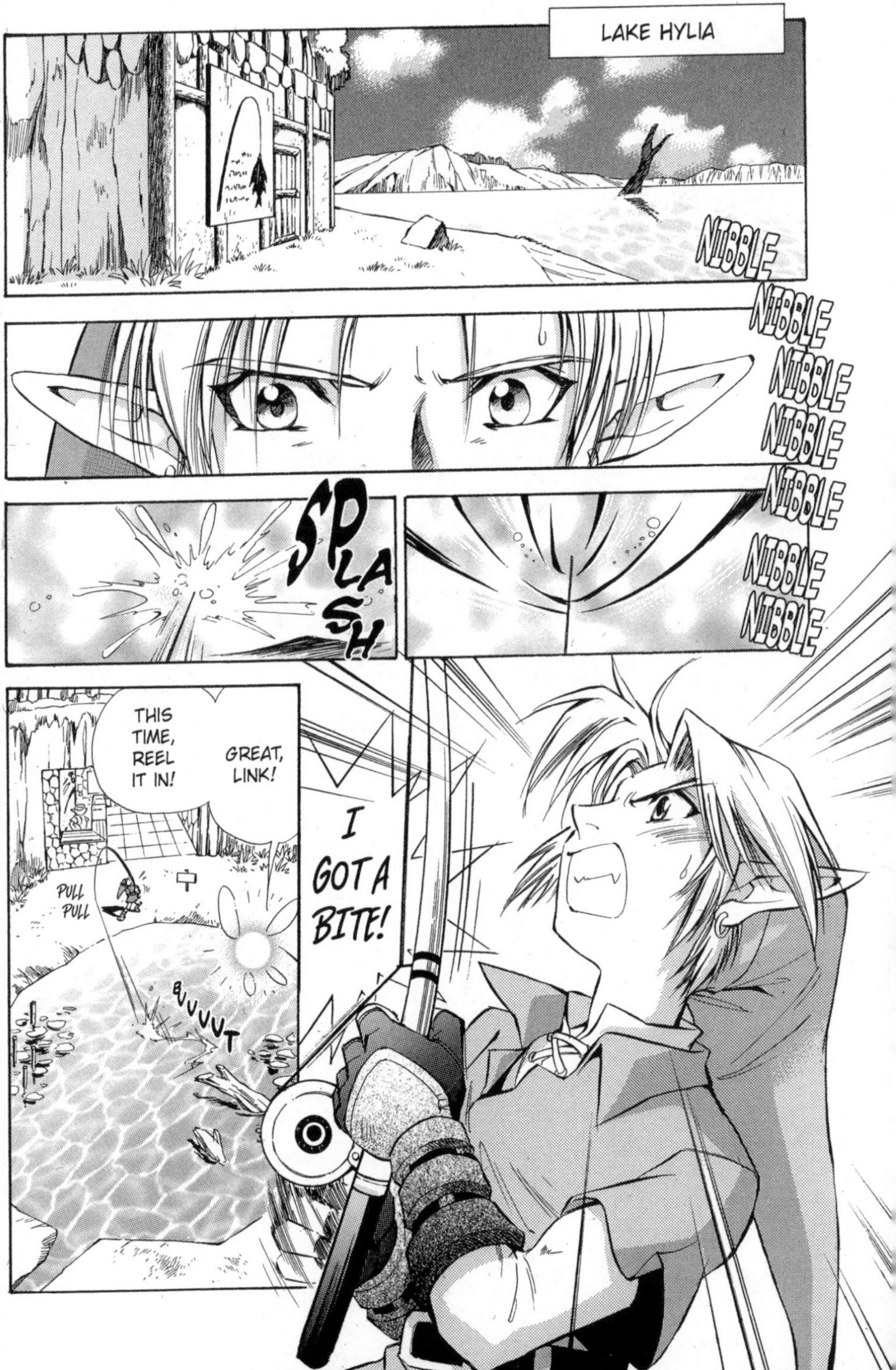
LAKE HYLIA
NIBBLE NIBBLE NIBBLE NIBBLE NIBBLE NIBBLE NIBBLE
SPLASH!
I GOT A BITE!
GREAT, LINK!
THIS TIME, REEL IT IN!
PULL PULL
BUUUUT

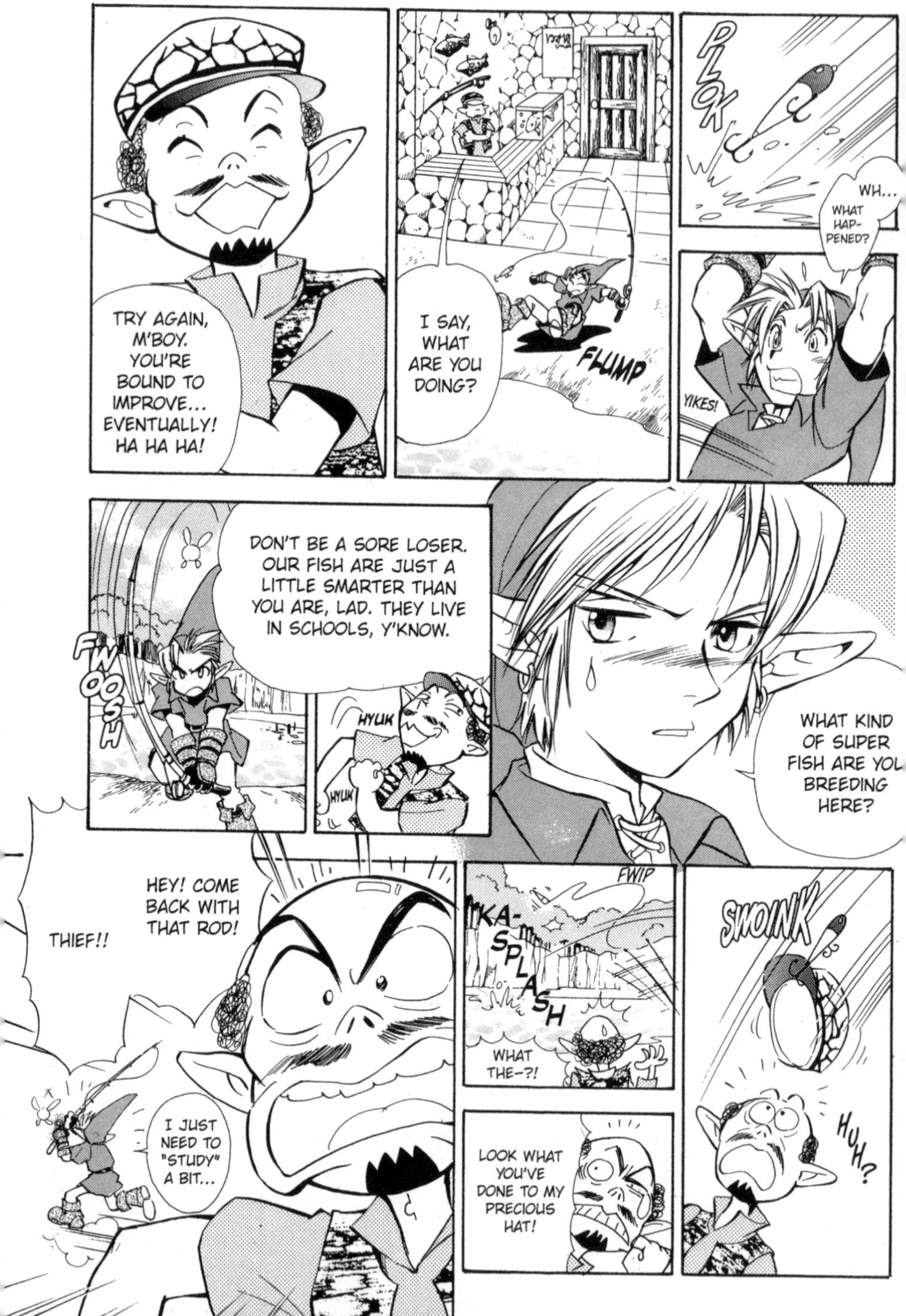
PLOK
WH... WHAT HAPPENED?
YIKES!
I SAY, WHAT ARE YOU DOING?
FLUMP
TRY AGAIN, M'BOY. YOU'RE BOUND TO IMPROVE... EVENTUALLY! HA HA HA!
WHAT KIND OF SUPER FISH ARE YOU BREEDING HERE?
DON'T BE A SORE LOSER. OUR FISH ARE JUST A LITTLE SMARTER THAN YOU ARE, LAD. THEY LIVE IN SCHOOLS, Y'KNOW.
HYUK
HYUK
FWOOSH
SWOINK
HUH?
FWIP
KA-SPLASH
WHAT THE-?!
LOOK WHAT YOU'VE DONE TO MY PRECIOUS HAT!
HEY! COME BACK WITH THAT ROD!
THIEF!!
I JUST NEED TO "STUDY" A BIT...

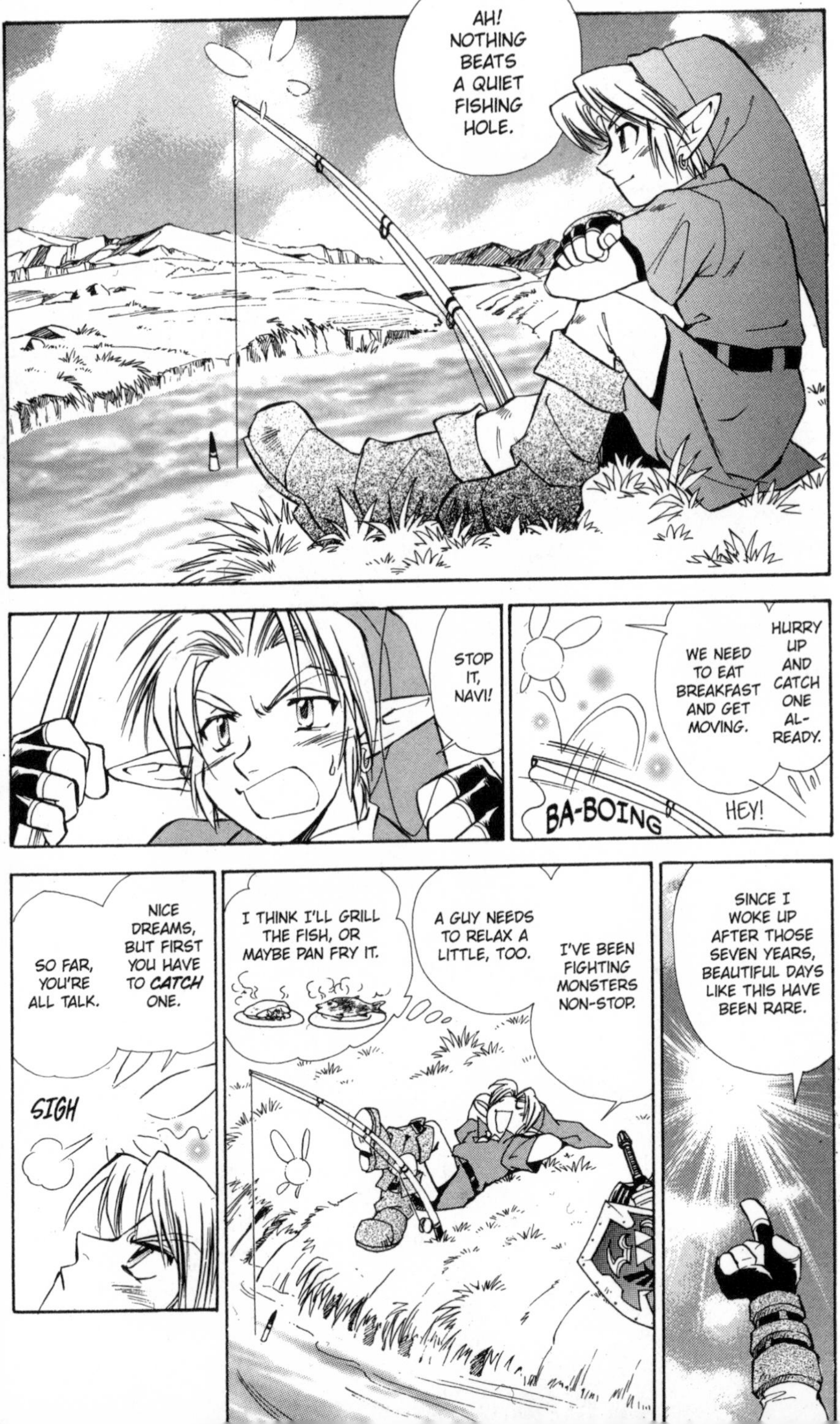
AH! NOTHING BEATS A QUIET FISHING HOLE.
HURRY UP AND CATCH ONE AL-READY.
WE NEED TO EAT BREAKFAST AND GET MOVING.
BA-BOING
HEY!
STOP IT, NAVI!
SINCE I WOKE UP AFTER THOSE SEVEN YEARS, BEAUTIFUL DAYS LIKE THIS HAVE BEEN RARE.
I'VE BEEN FIGHTING MONSTERS NON-STOP.
A GUY NEEDS TO RELAX A LITTLE, TOO.
I THINK I'LL GRILL THE FISH, OR MAYBE PAN FRY IT.
NICE DREAMS, BUT FIRST YOU HAVE TO *CATCH* ONE.
SO FAR, YOU'RE ALL TALK.
SIGH

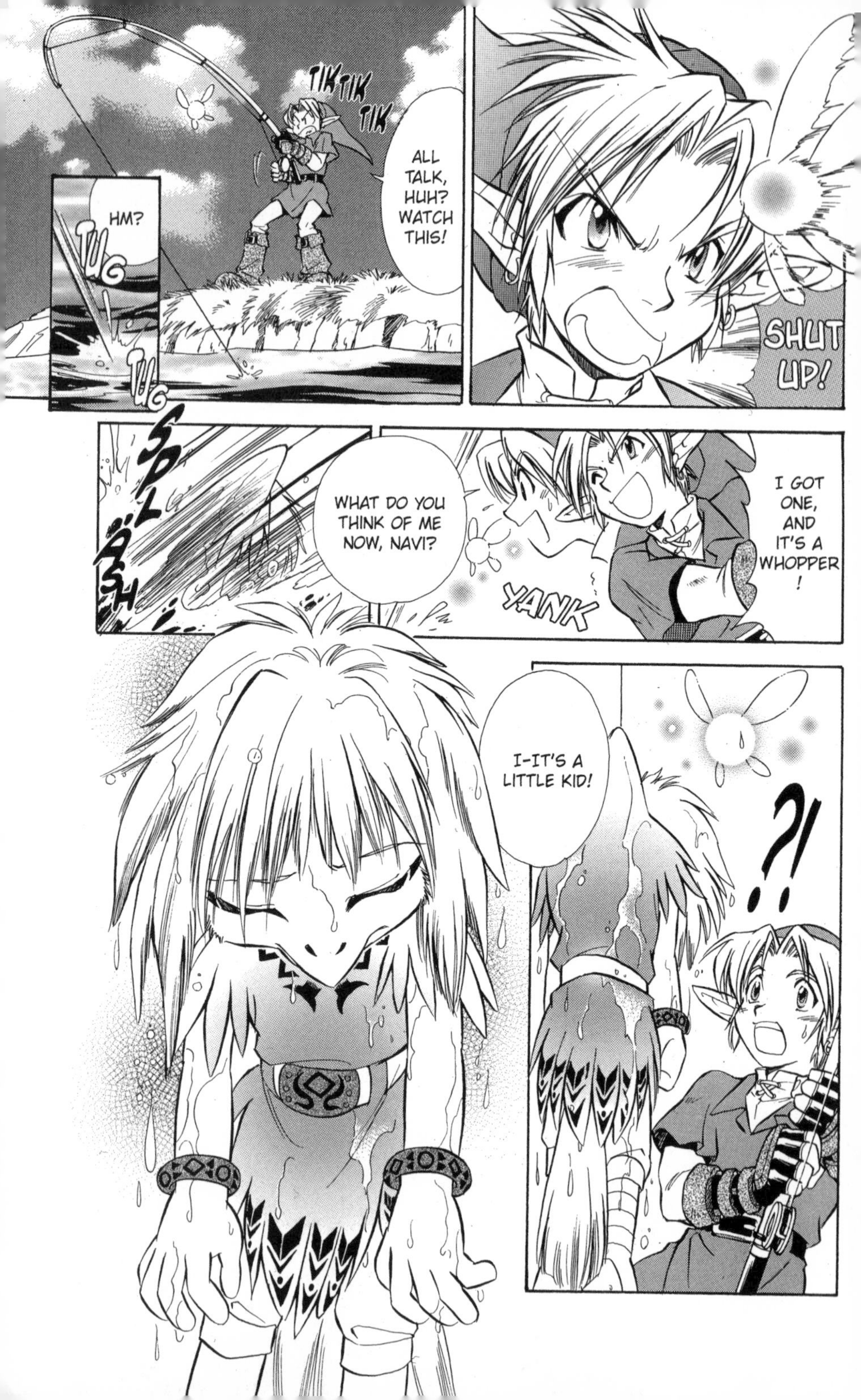
SHUT UP!
TIK TIK TIK
ALL TALK, HUH? WATCH THIS!
HM?
TUG
TUG
I GOT ONE, AND IT'S A WHOPPER!
WHAT DO YOU THINK OF ME NOW, NAVI?
YANK
SPLASH
?!
I-IT'S A LITTLE KID!

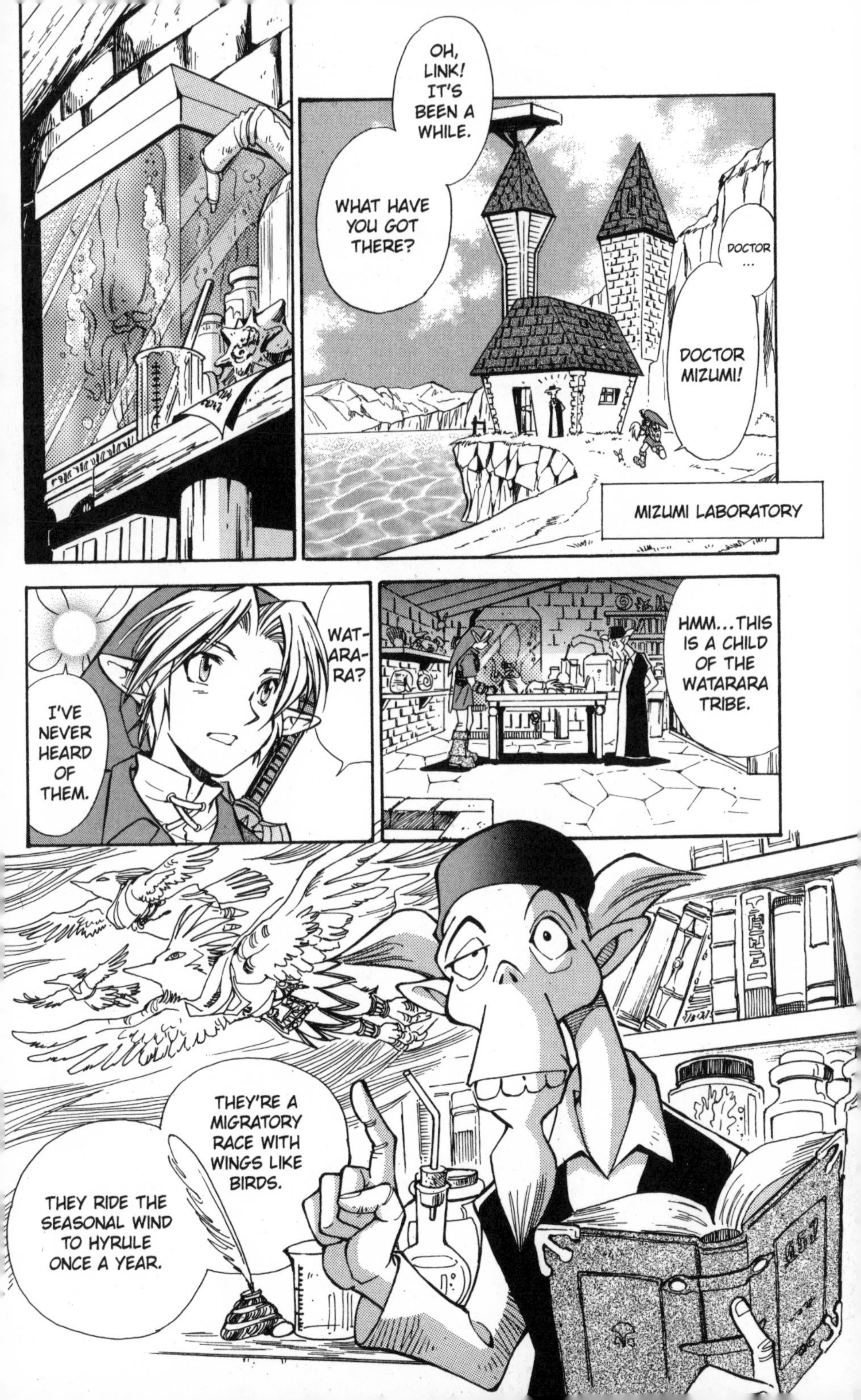
MIZUMI LABORATORY
DOCTOR ...
DOCTOR MIZUMI!
OH, LINK! IT'S BEEN A WHILE.
WHAT HAVE YOU GOT THERE?
HMM...THIS IS A CHILD OF THE WATARARA TRIBE.
WAT-ARA-RA?
I'VE NEVER HEARD OF THEM.
THEY'RE A MIGRATORY RACE WITH WINGS LIKE BIRDS.
THEY RIDE THE SEASONAL WIND TO HYRULE ONCE A YEAR.

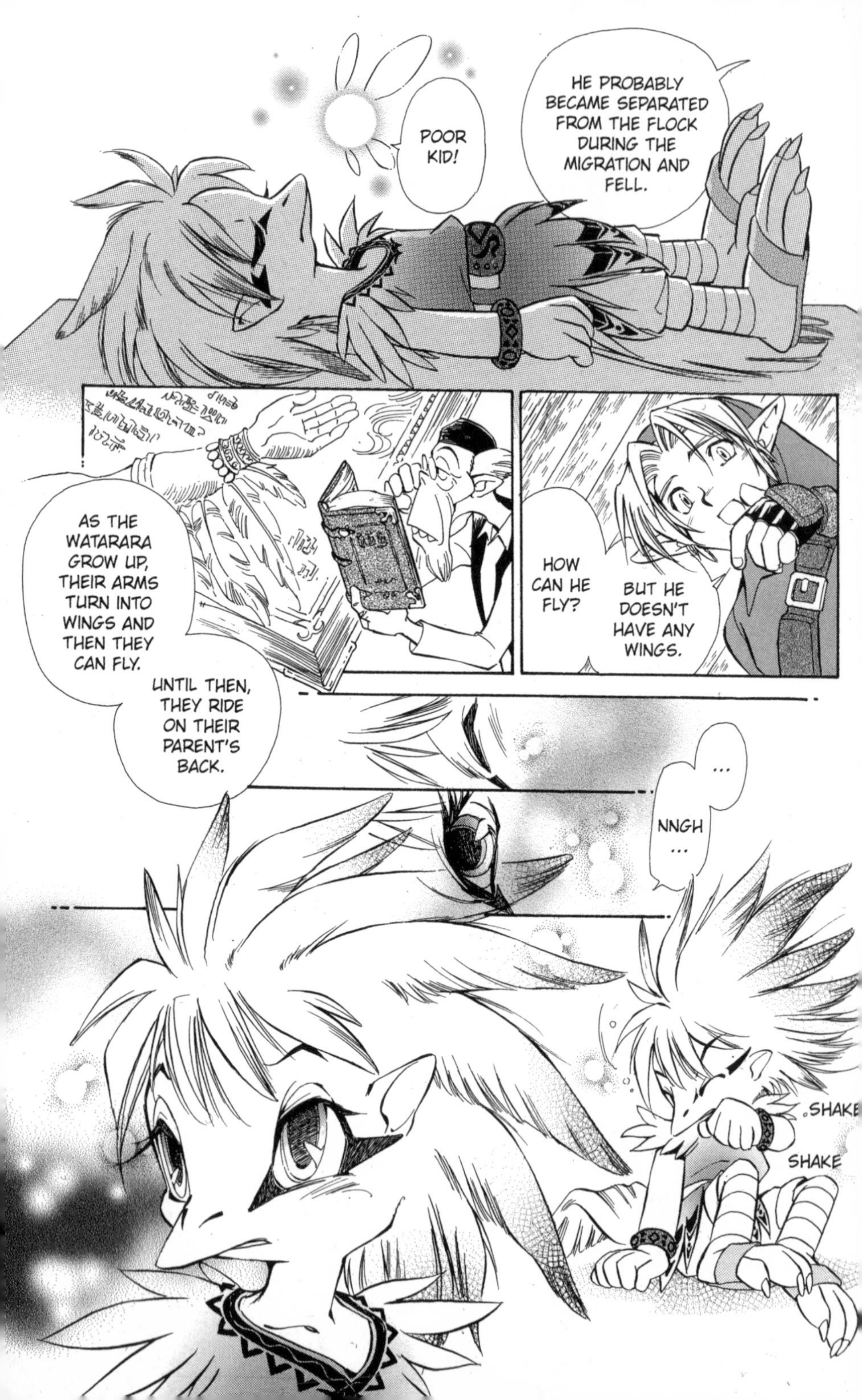

HE PROBABLY BECAME SEPARATED FROM THE FLOCK DURING THE MIGRATION AND FELL.
POOR KID!
BUT HE DOESN'T HAVE ANY WINGS.
HOW CAN HE FLY?
AS THE WATARARA GROW UP, THEIR ARMS TURN INTO WINGS AND THEN THEY CAN FLY.
UNTIL THEN, THEY RIDE ON THEIR PARENT'S BACK.
...
NNGH ...
SHAKE
SHAKE

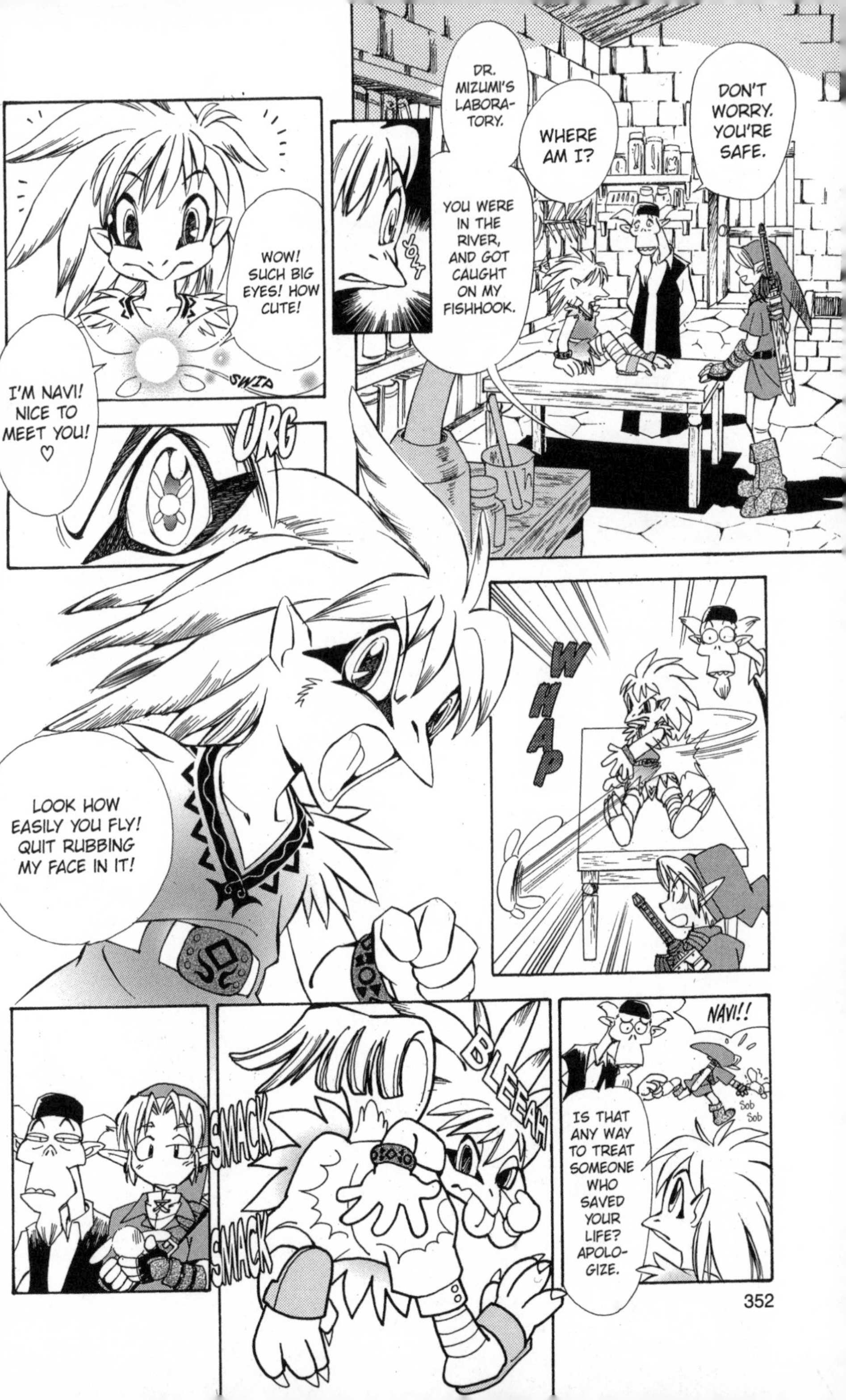
DON'T WORRY. YOU'RE SAFE.
WHERE AM I?
DR. MIZUMI'S LABORA-TORY.
YOU WERE IN THE RIVER, AND GOT CAUGHT ON MY FISHHOOK.
WOW! SUCH BIG EYES! HOW CUTE!
SWIP
I'M NAVI! NICE TO MEET YOU! ♡
URG
LOOK HOW EASILY YOU FLY! QUIT RUBBING MY FACE IN IT!
WHAP
NAVI!!
Sob Sob
IS THAT ANY WAY TO TREAT SOMEONE WHO SAVED YOUR LIFE? APOLO-GIZE.
BLEEAH
SMACK
SMACK

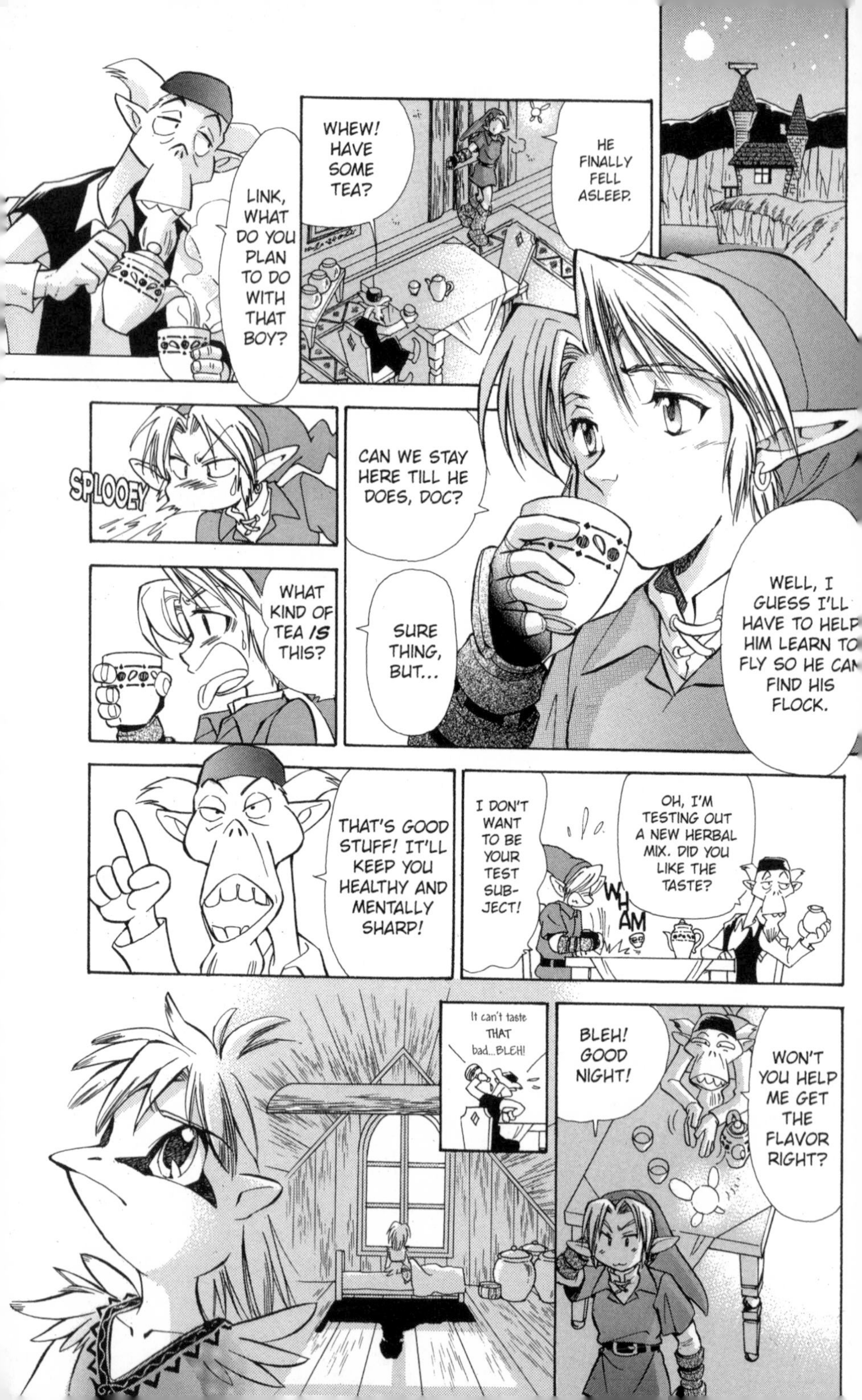
HE FINALLY FELL ASLEEP.
WHEW! HAVE SOME TEA?
LINK, WHAT DO YOU PLAN TO DO WITH THAT BOY?
WELL, I GUESS I'LL HAVE TO HELP HIM LEARN TO FLY SO HE CAN FIND HIS FLOCK.
CAN WE STAY HERE TILL HE DOES, DOC?
SURE THING, BUT...
SPLOOEY
WHAT KIND OF TEA IS THIS?
OH, I'M TESTING OUT A NEW HERBAL MIX. DID YOU LIKE THE TASTE?
I DON'T WANT TO BE YOUR TEST SUBJECT!
WHAM
THAT'S GOOD STUFF! IT'LL KEEP YOU HEALTHY AND MENTALLY SHARP!
WON'T YOU HELP ME GET THE FLAVOR RIGHT?
BLEH! GOOD NIGHT!
It can't taste THAT bad...BLEH!

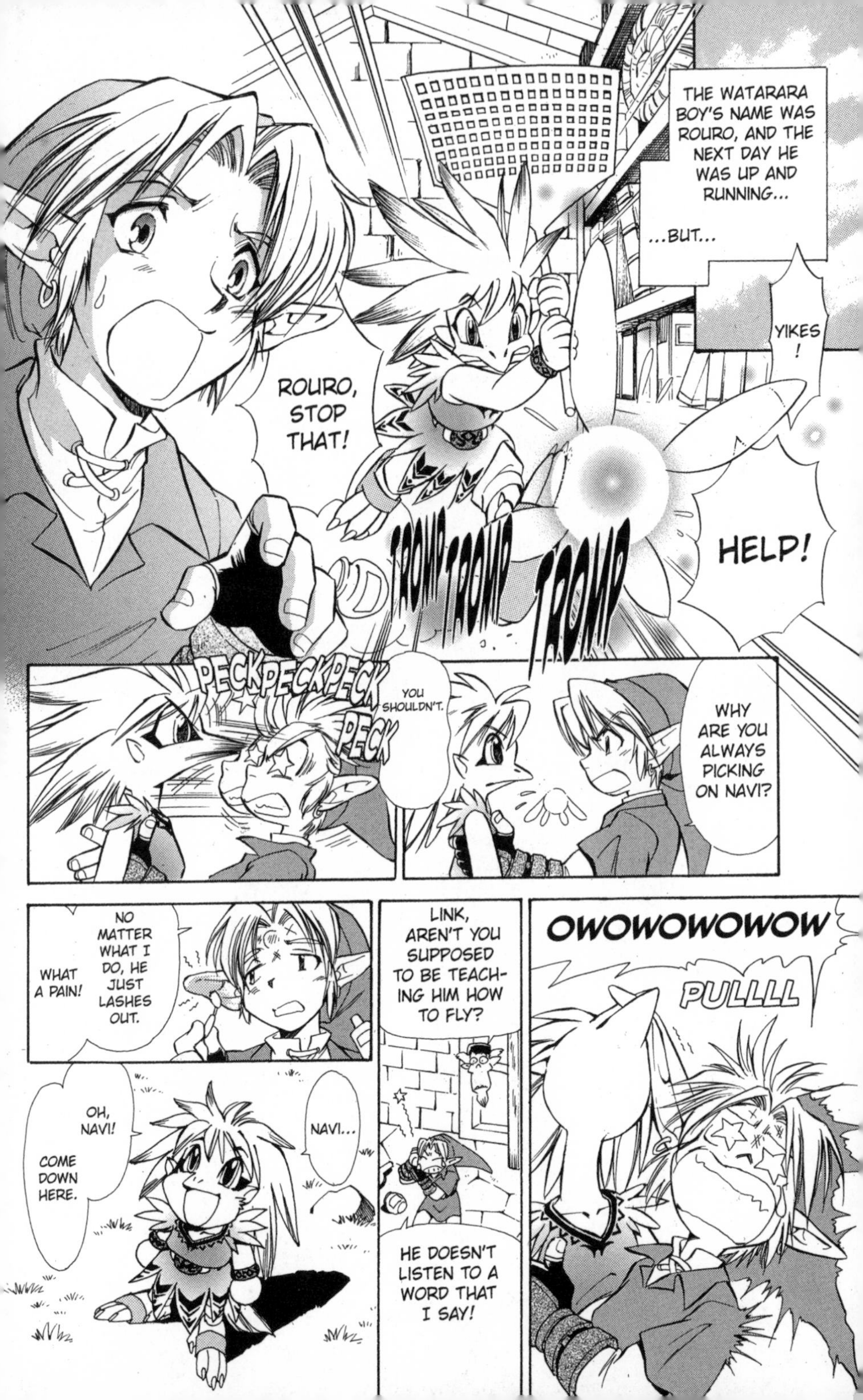
THE WATARARA BOY'S NAME WAS ROURO, AND THE NEXT DAY HE WAS UP AND RUNNING...
...BUT...
YIKES!
HELP!
TROMP TROMP TROMP
ROURO, STOP THAT!
WHY ARE YOU ALWAYS PICKING ON NAVI?
YOU SHOULDN'T.
PECKPECKPECK PECK
OWOWOWOWOW
PULLLL
LINK, AREN'T YOU SUPPOSED TO BE TEACHING HIM HOW TO FLY?
HE DOESN'T LISTEN TO A WORD THAT I SAY!
NO MATTER WHAT I DO, HE JUST LASHES OUT.
WHAT A PAIN!
NAVI...
OH, NAVI!
COME DOWN HERE.

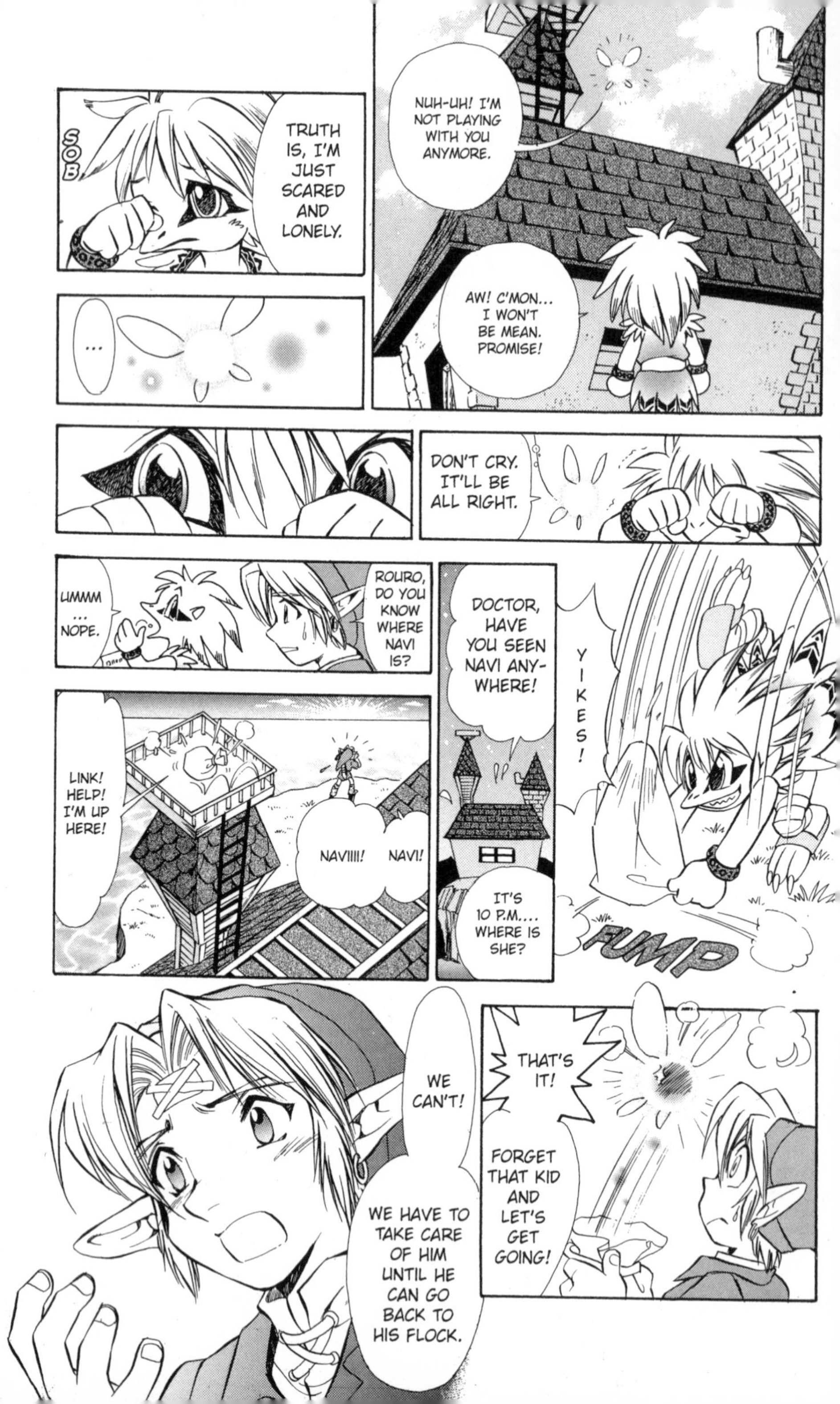
NUH-UH! I'M NOT PLAYING WITH YOU ANYMORE.
AW! C'MON... I WON'T BE MEAN. PROMISE!
TRUTH IS, I'M JUST SCARED AND LONELY.
SOB
...
DON'T CRY. IT'LL BE ALL RIGHT.
YIKES!
FUMP
DOCTOR, HAVE YOU SEEN NAVI ANY-WHERE!
IT'S 10 P.M.... WHERE IS SHE?
ROURO, DO YOU KNOW WHERE NAVI IS?
UMMM ... NOPE.
NAVI!
NAVIIII!
LINK! HELP! I'M UP HERE!
THAT'S IT!
FORGET THAT KID AND LET'S GET GOING!
WE CAN'T!
WE HAVE TO TAKE CARE OF HIM UNTIL HE CAN GO BACK TO HIS FLOCK.

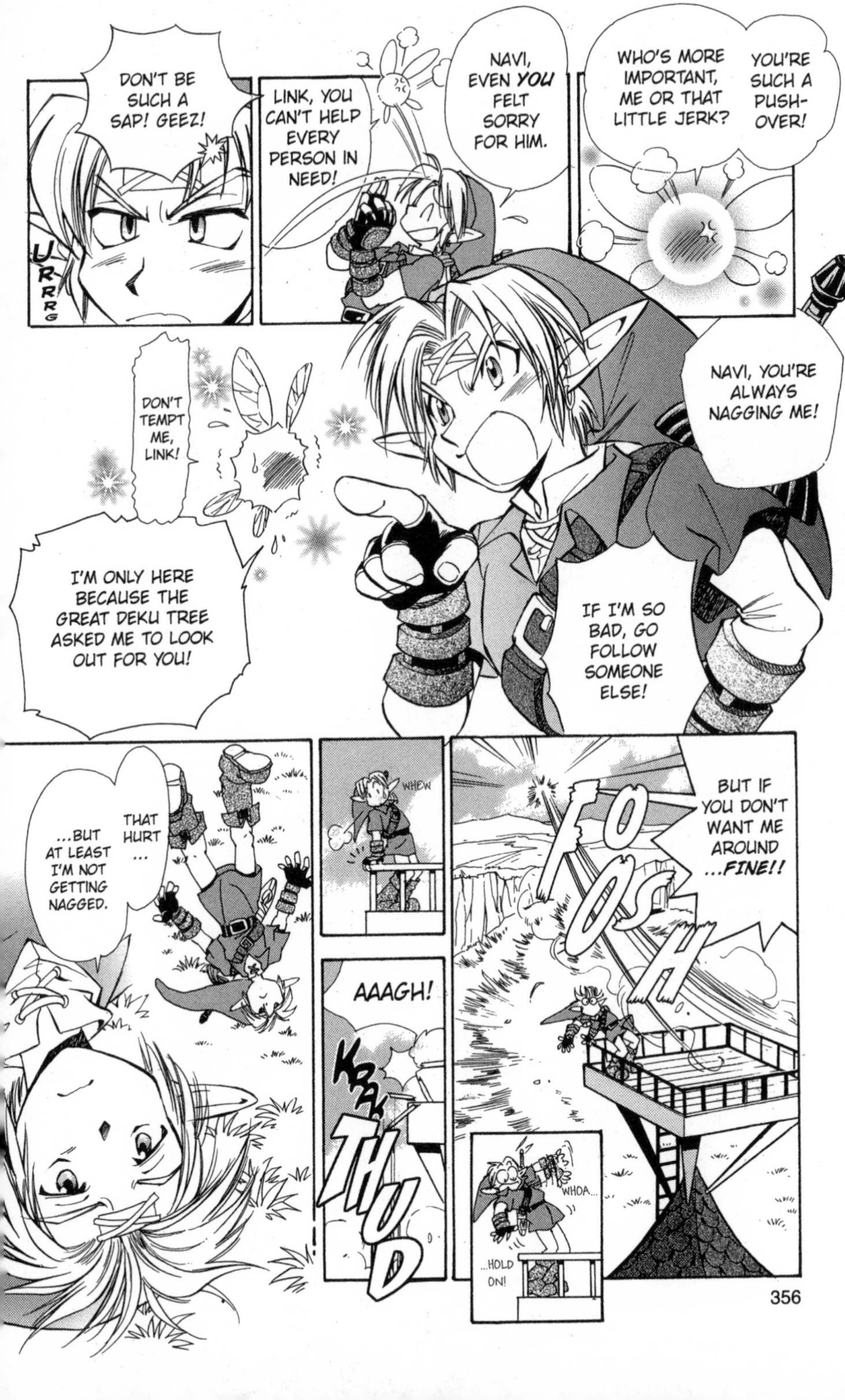
YOU'RE SUCH A PUSH-OVER!
WHO'S MORE IMPORTANT, ME OR THAT LITTLE JERK?
NAVI, EVEN *YOU* FELT SORRY FOR HIM.
LINK, YOU CAN'T HELP EVERY PERSON IN NEED!
DON'T BE SUCH A SAP! GEEZ!
URRRG
NAVI, YOU'RE ALWAYS NAGGING ME!
IF I'M SO BAD, GO FOLLOW SOMEONE ELSE!
DON'T TEMPT ME, LINK!
I'M ONLY HERE BECAUSE THE GREAT DEKU TREE ASKED ME TO LOOK OUT FOR YOU!
BUT IF YOU DON'T WANT ME AROUND ...*FINE!!*
FOOSH
WHOA...
...HOLD ON!
WHEW
AAAGH!
KRAK
THUD
THAT HURT...
...BUT AT LEAST I'M NOT GETTING NAGGED.

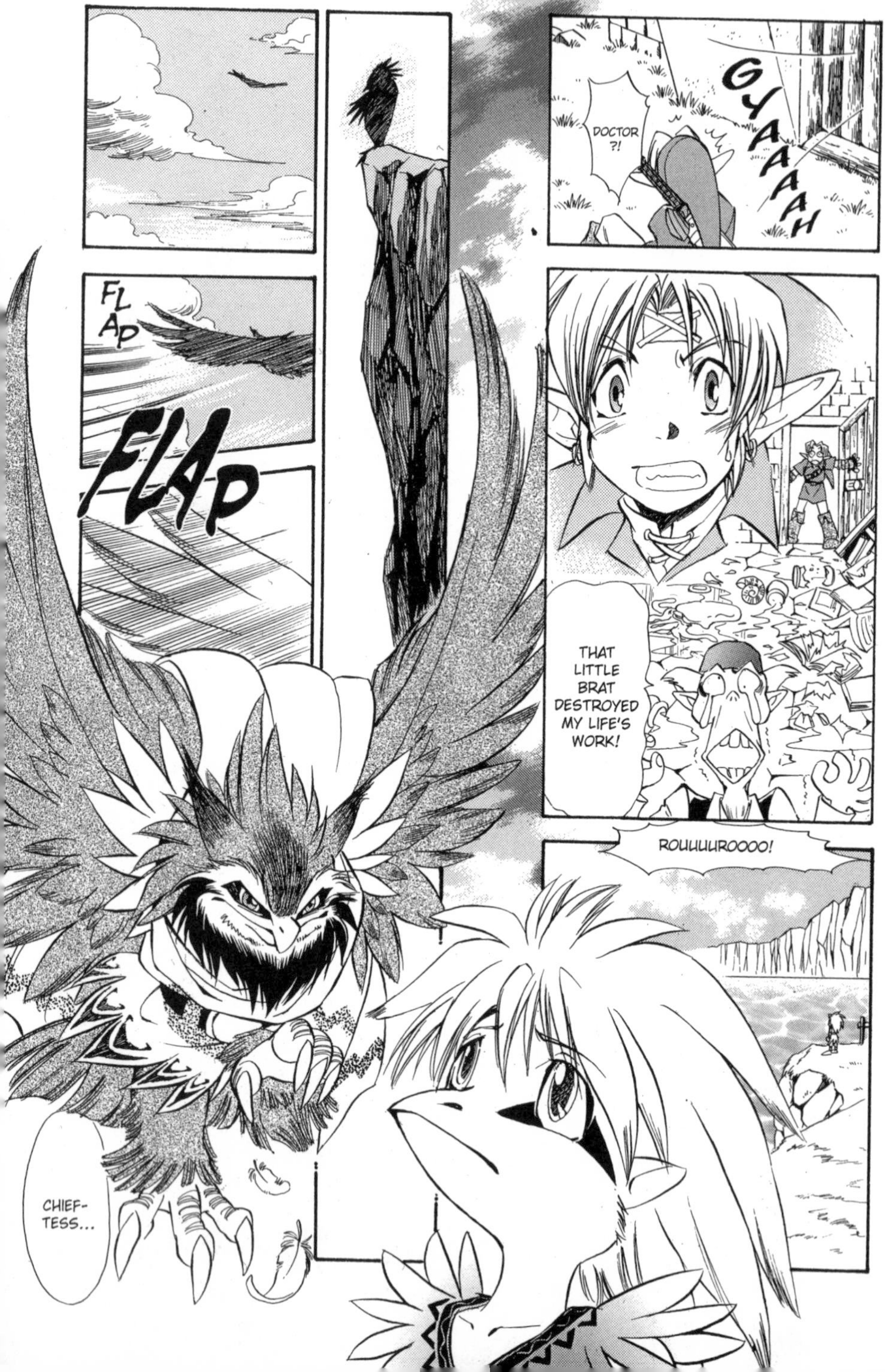
GYAAAAH
DOCTOR ?!
THAT LITTLE BRAT DESTROYED MY LIFE'S WORK!
ROUUUUROOOO!
FLAP
FLAP
CHIEF-TESS...

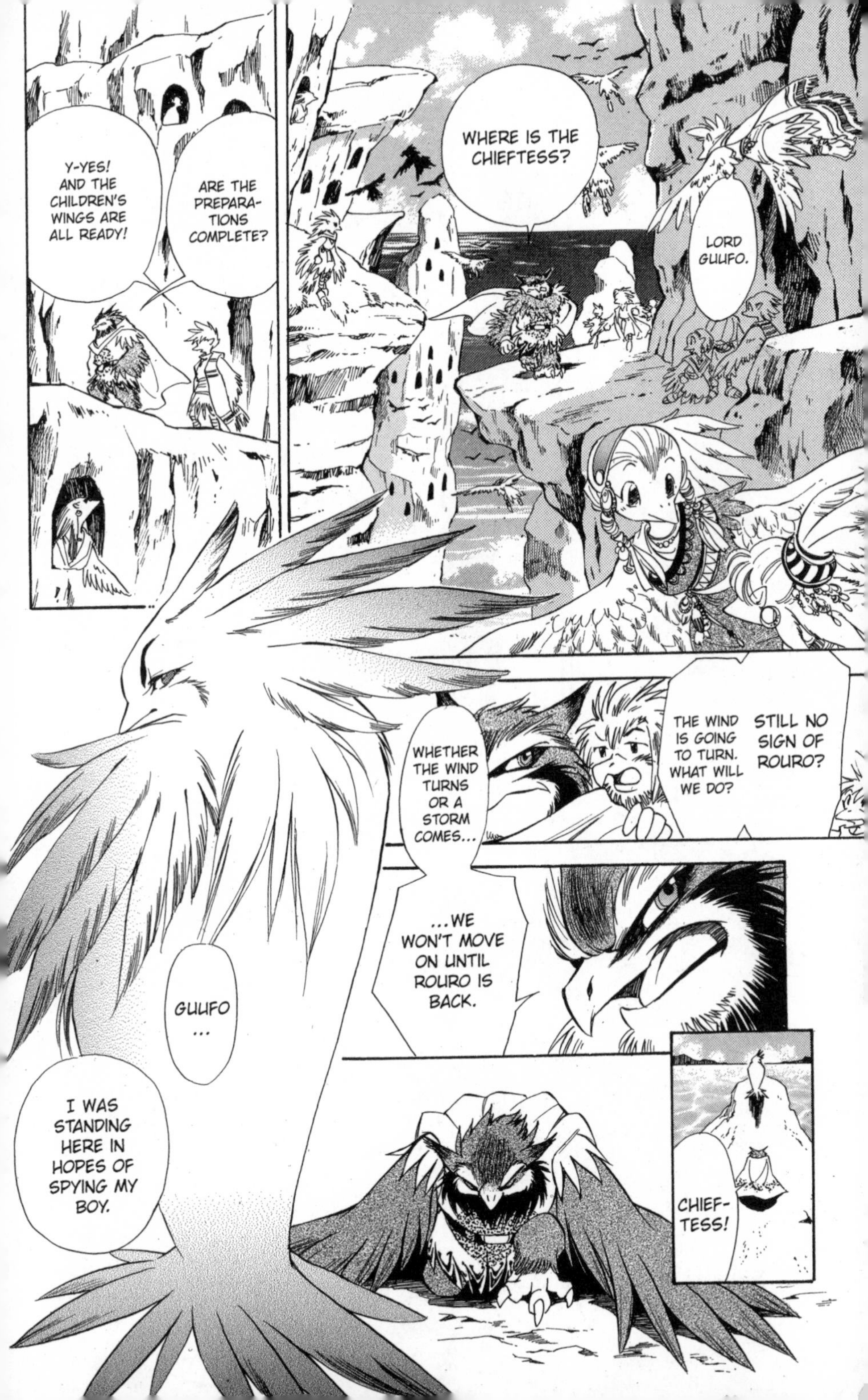
LORD GUUFO.
WHERE IS THE CHIEFTESS?
ARE THE PREPARATIONS COMPLETE?
Y-YES! AND THE CHILDREN'S WINGS ARE ALL READY!
STILL NO SIGN OF ROURO?
THE WIND IS GOING TO TURN. WHAT WILL WE DO?
WHETHER THE WIND TURNS OR A STORM COMES...
...WE WON'T MOVE ON UNTIL ROURO IS BACK.
CHIEF-TESS!
GUUFO...
I WAS STANDING HERE IN HOPES OF SPYING MY BOY.

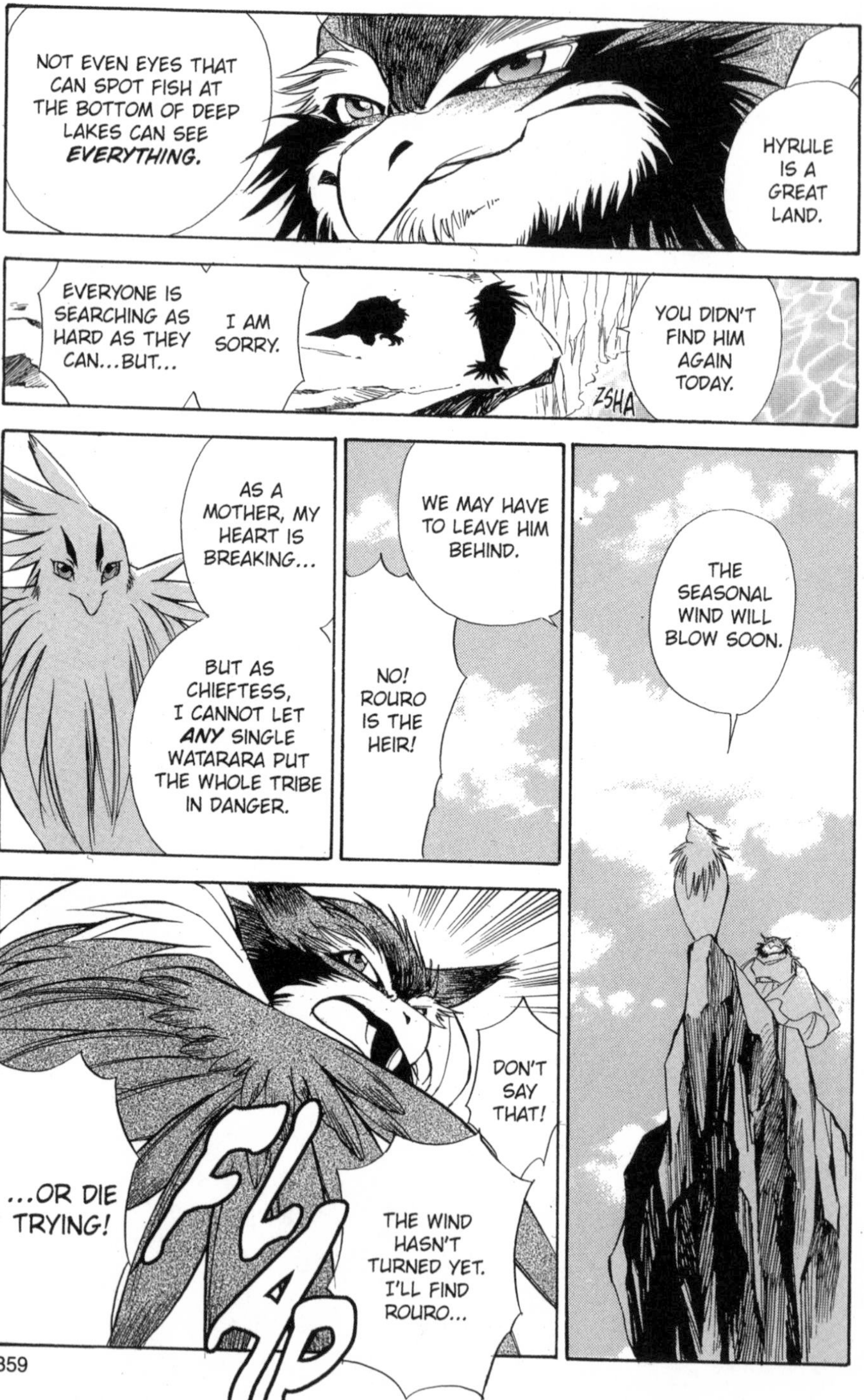
HYRULE IS A GREAT LAND.
NOT EVEN EYES THAT CAN SPOT FISH AT THE BOTTOM OF DEEP LAKES CAN SEE EVERYTHING.
YOU DIDN'T FIND HIM AGAIN TODAY.
ZSHA
I AM SORRY.
EVERYONE IS SEARCHING AS HARD AS THEY CAN...BUT...
THE SEASONAL WIND WILL BLOW SOON.
WE MAY HAVE TO LEAVE HIM BEHIND.
NO! ROURO IS THE HEIR!
AS A MOTHER, MY HEART IS BREAKING...
BUT AS CHIEFTESS, I CANNOT LET ANY SINGLE WATARARA PUT THE WHOLE TRIBE IN DANGER.
DON'T SAY THAT!
THE WIND HASN'T TURNED YET. I'LL FIND ROURO...
FLAP
...OR DIE TRYING!

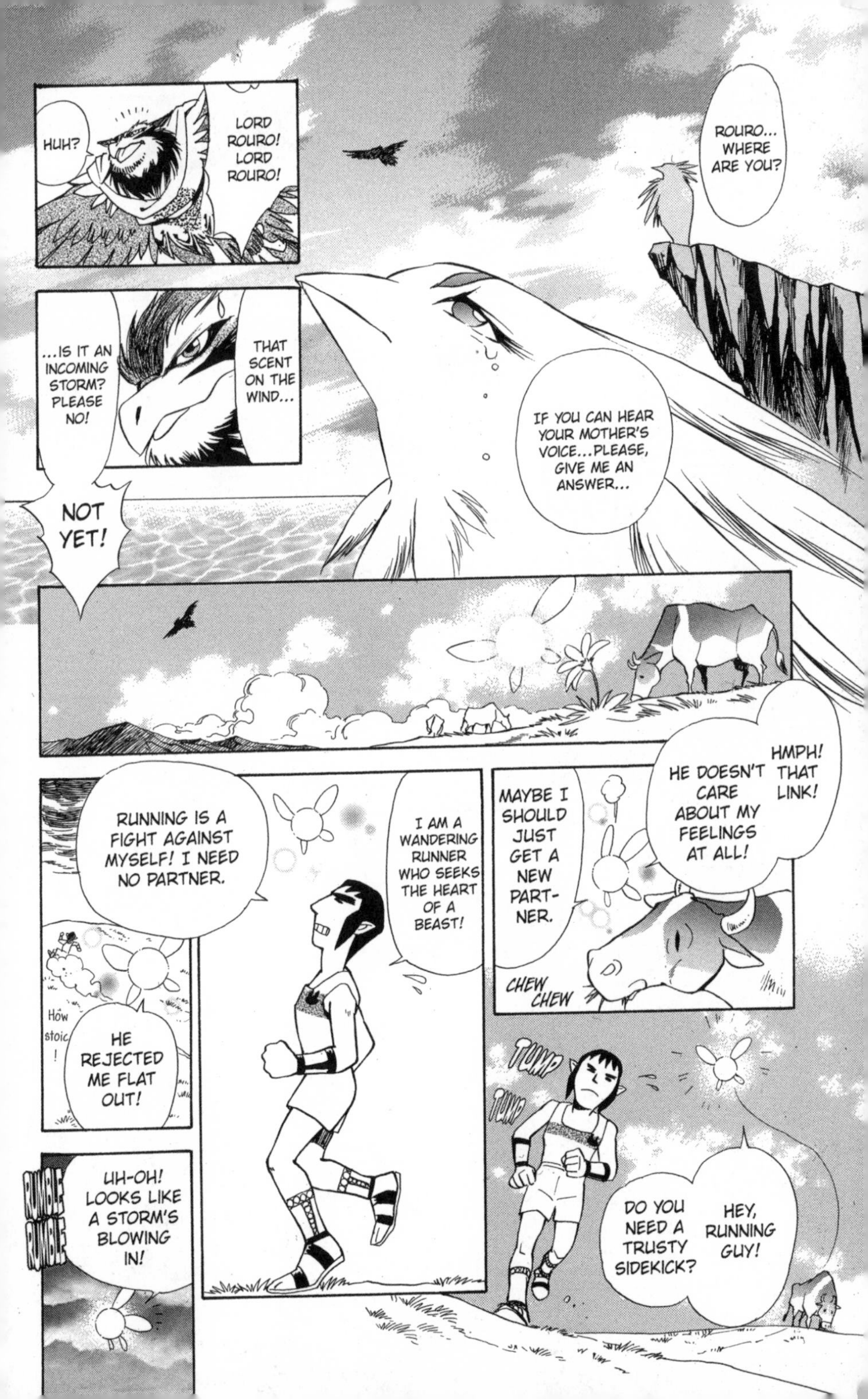
ROURO... WHERE ARE YOU?
IF YOU CAN HEAR YOUR MOTHER'S VOICE...PLEASE, GIVE ME AN ANSWER...
NOT YET!
LORD ROURO! LORD ROURO!
HUH?
THAT SCENT ON THE WIND...
...IS IT AN INCOMING STORM? PLEASE NO!
HMPH! THAT LINK!
HE DOESN'T CARE ABOUT MY FEELINGS AT ALL!
MAYBE I SHOULD JUST GET A NEW PART-NER.
CHEW CHEW
TUMP
TUMP
HEY, RUNNING GUY!
DO YOU NEED A TRUSTY SIDEKICK?
I AM A WANDERING RUNNER WHO SEEKS THE HEART OF A BEAST!
RUNNING IS A FIGHT AGAINST MYSELF! I NEED NO PARTNER.
HE REJECTED ME FLAT OUT!
How stoic!
RUMBLE RUMBLE
UH-OH! LOOKS LIKE A STORM'S BLOWING IN!

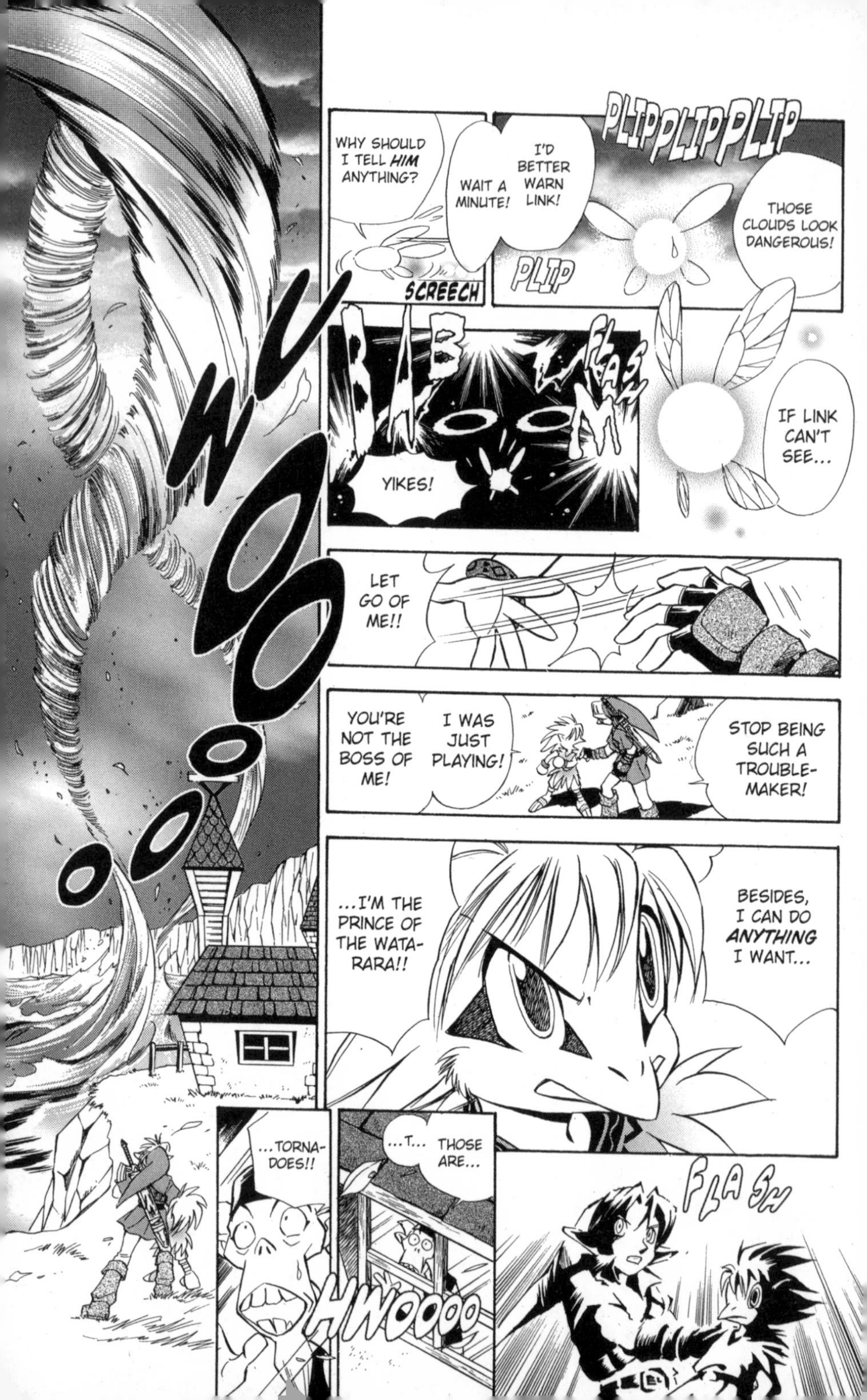
PLIPPLIPPLIP
THOSE CLOUDS LOOK DANGEROUS!
PLIP
I'D BETTER WARN LINK!
WAIT A MINUTE!
WHY SHOULD I TELL *HIM* ANYTHING?
SCREECH
IF LINK CAN'T SEE...
FLASH
BABOOM
YIKES!
LET GO OF ME!!
STOP BEING SUCH A TROUBLE-MAKER!
I WAS JUST PLAYING!
YOU'RE NOT THE BOSS OF ME!
BESIDES, I CAN DO ***ANYTHING*** I WANT...
...I'M THE PRINCE OF THE WATA-RARA!!
FLASH
...T... THOSE ARE...
...TORNA-DOES!!
HWOOOO
WHOOOOOOO

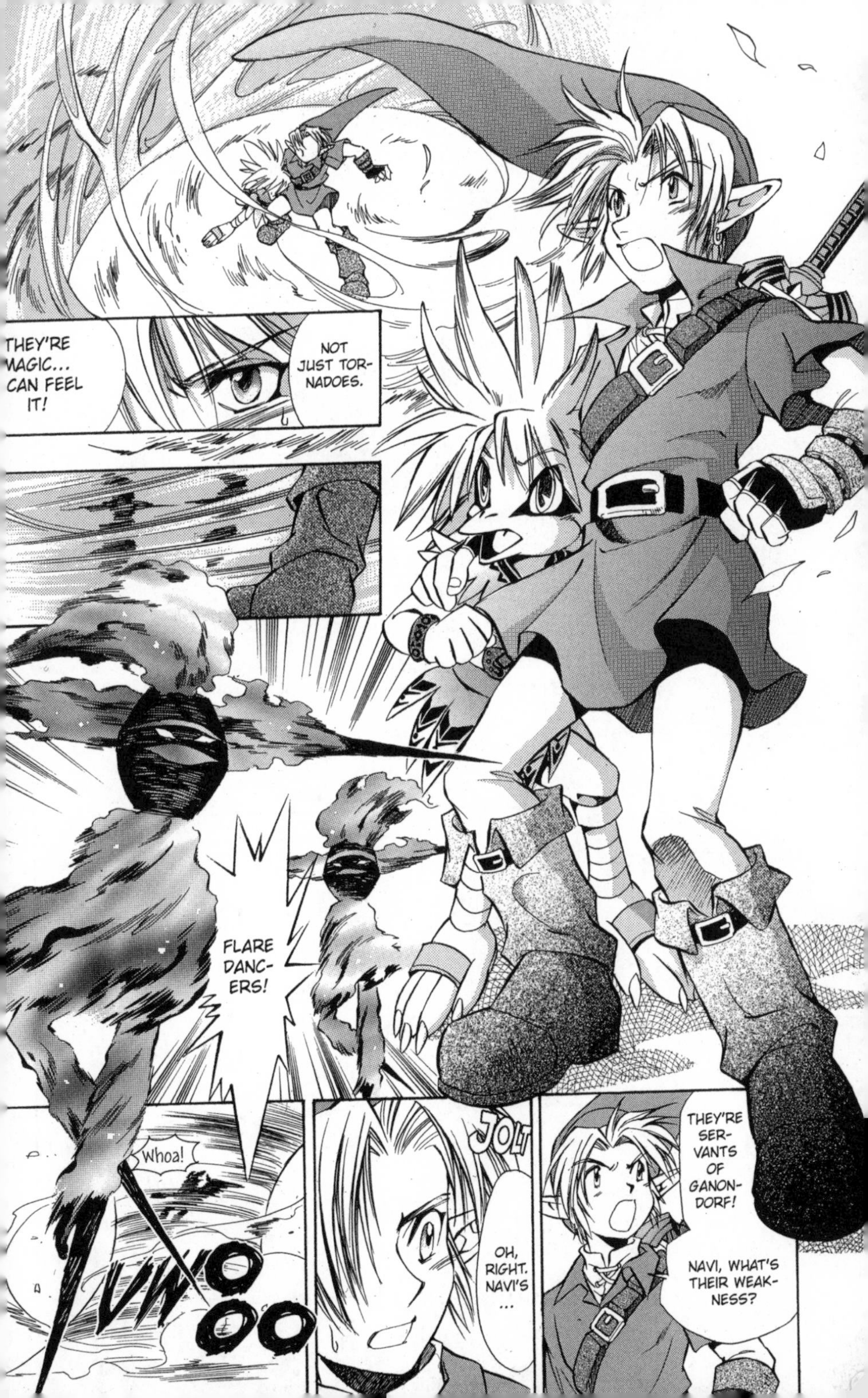
NOT JUST TOR-NADOES.
THEY'RE MAGIC... CAN FEEL IT!
FLARE DANCERS!
THEY'RE SER-VANTS OF GANON-DORF!
NAVI, WHAT'S THEIR WEAK-NESS?
JOLT
OH, RIGHT. NAVI'S ...
Whoa!
VWOOOO

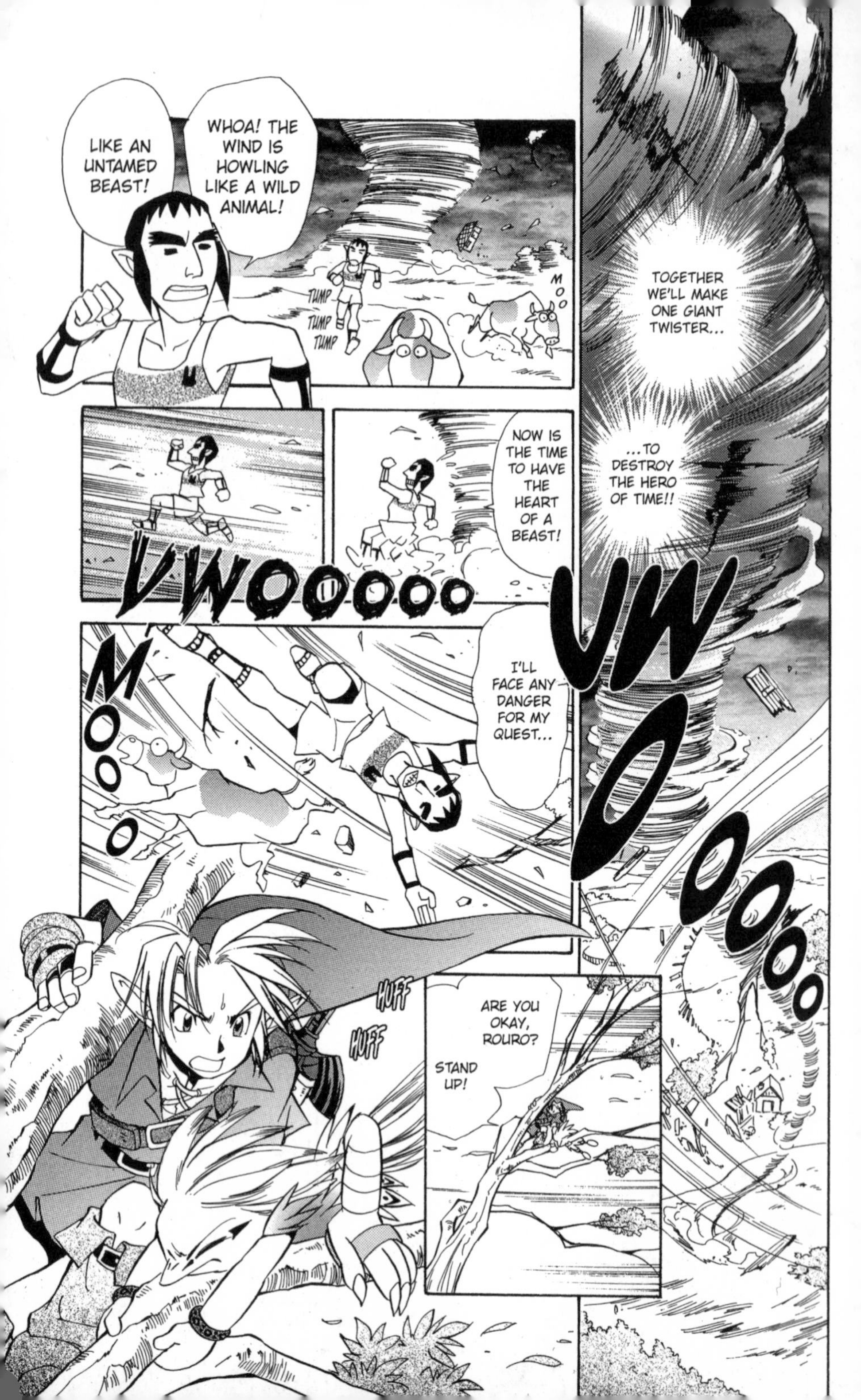
TOGETHER WE'LL MAKE ONE GIANT TWISTER...
...TO DESTROY THE HERO OF TIME!!
VWOOOOOO
WHOA! THE WIND IS HOWLING LIKE A WILD ANIMAL!
LIKE AN UNTAMED BEAST!
TUMP TUMP TUMP
MOO
NOW IS THE TIME TO HAVE THE HEART OF A BEAST!
VWOOOOOO
I'LL FACE ANY DANGER FOR MY QUEST...
MOOO
HUFF HUFF
ARE YOU OKAY, ROURO?
STAND UP!

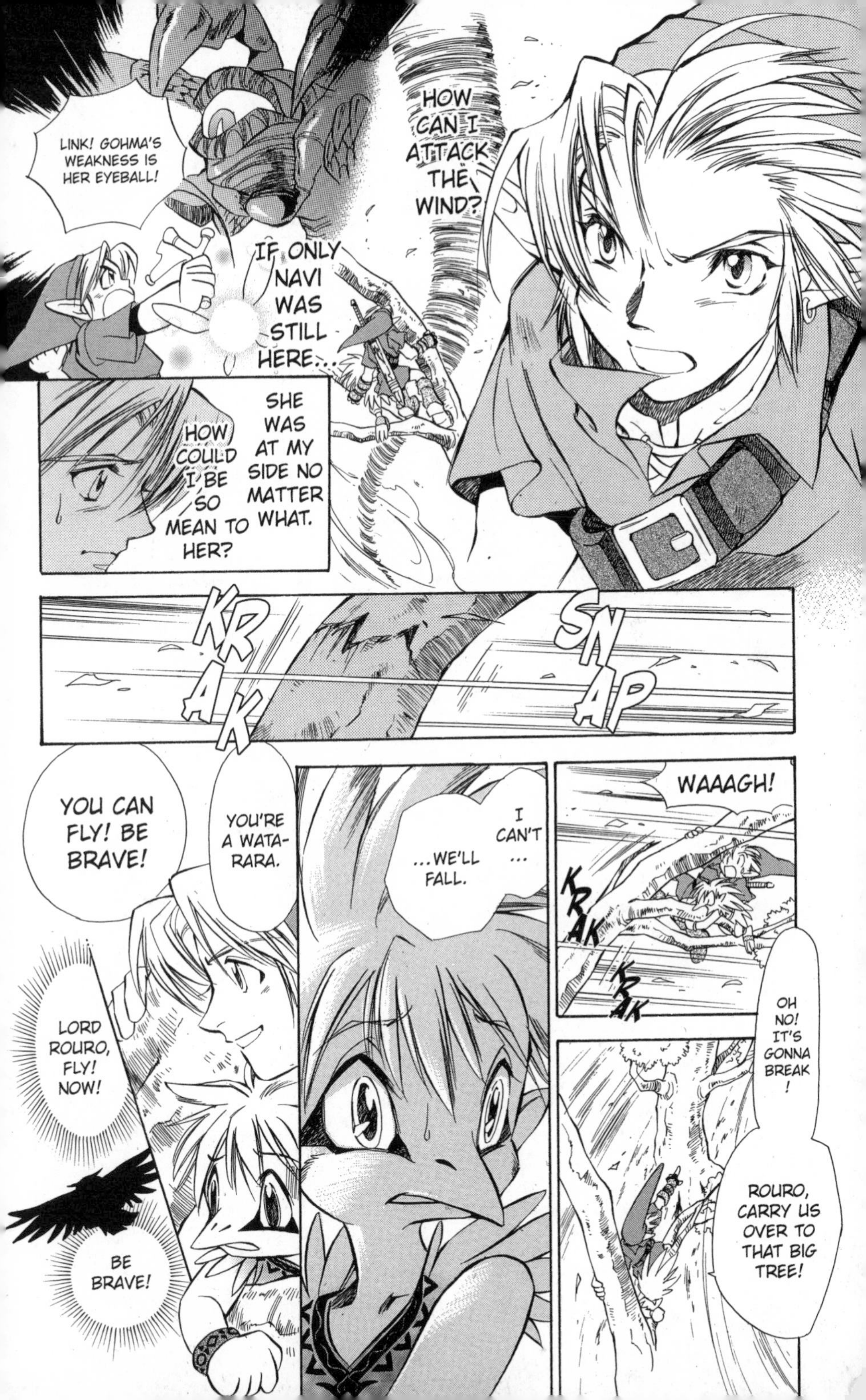
HOW CAN I ATTACK THE WIND?
IF ONLY NAVI WAS STILL HERE...
LINK! GOHMA'S WEAKNESS IS HER EYEBALL!
SHE WAS AT MY SIDE NO MATTER WHAT.
HOW COULD I BE SO MEAN TO HER?
SNAP
KRAK
WAAAGH!
KRAK
KRAK
OH NO! IT'S GONNA BREAK!
ROURO, CARRY US OVER TO THAT BIG TREE!
I CAN'T...
...WE'LL FALL.
YOU'RE A WATA-RARA.
YOU CAN FLY! BE BRAVE!
LORD ROURO, FLY! NOW!
BE BRAVE!

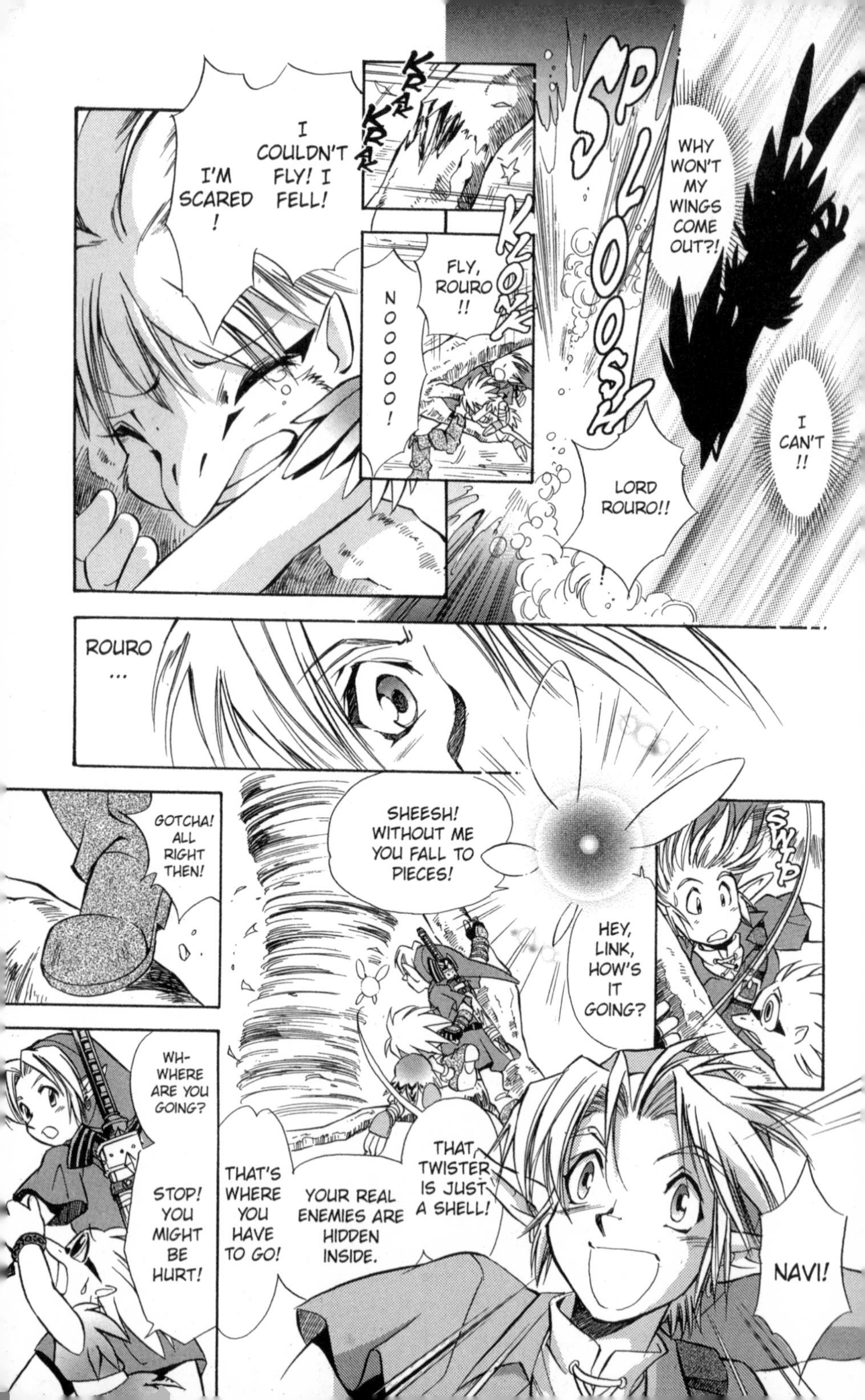

WHY WON'T MY WINGS COME OUT?!
I CAN'T !!
LORD ROURO!!
KRA KRA
FLY, ROURO !!
NOOOOOO!
I COULDN'T FLY! I FELL!
I'M SCARED !
ROURO ...
SWP
HEY, LINK, HOW'S IT GOING?
SHEESH! WITHOUT ME YOU FALL TO PIECES!
GOTCHA! ALL RIGHT THEN!
NAVI!
THAT TWISTER IS JUST A SHELL!
YOUR REAL ENEMIES ARE HIDDEN INSIDE.
THAT'S WHERE YOU HAVE TO GO!
WH-WHERE ARE YOU GOING?
STOP! YOU MIGHT BE HURT!

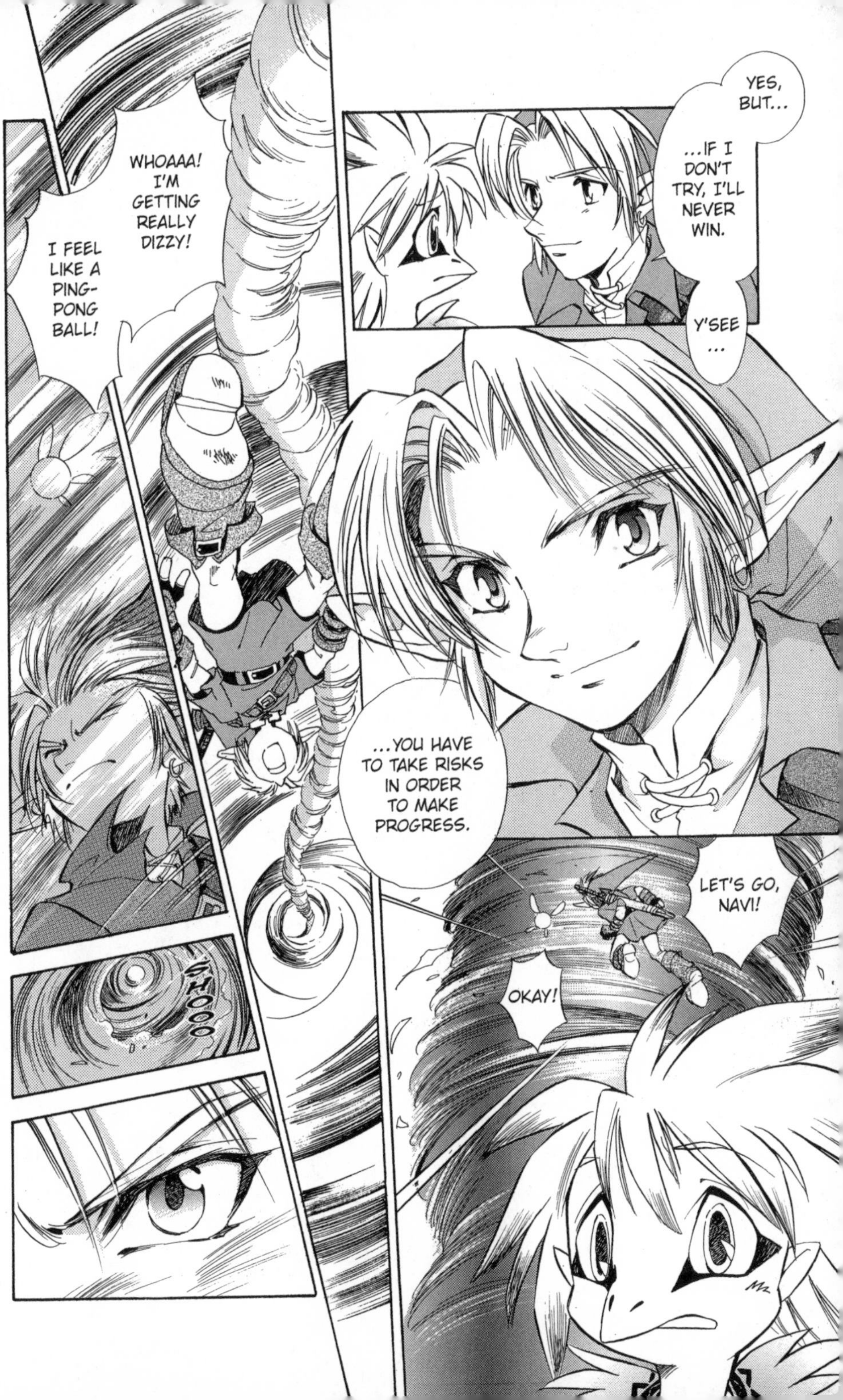
YES, BUT...
...IF I DON'T TRY, I'LL NEVER WIN.
Y'SEE...
...YOU HAVE TO TAKE RISKS IN ORDER TO MAKE PROGRESS.
WHOAAA! I'M GETTING REALLY DIZZY!
I FEEL LIKE A PING-PONG BALL!
LET'S GO, NAVI!
OKAY!
SHOOO

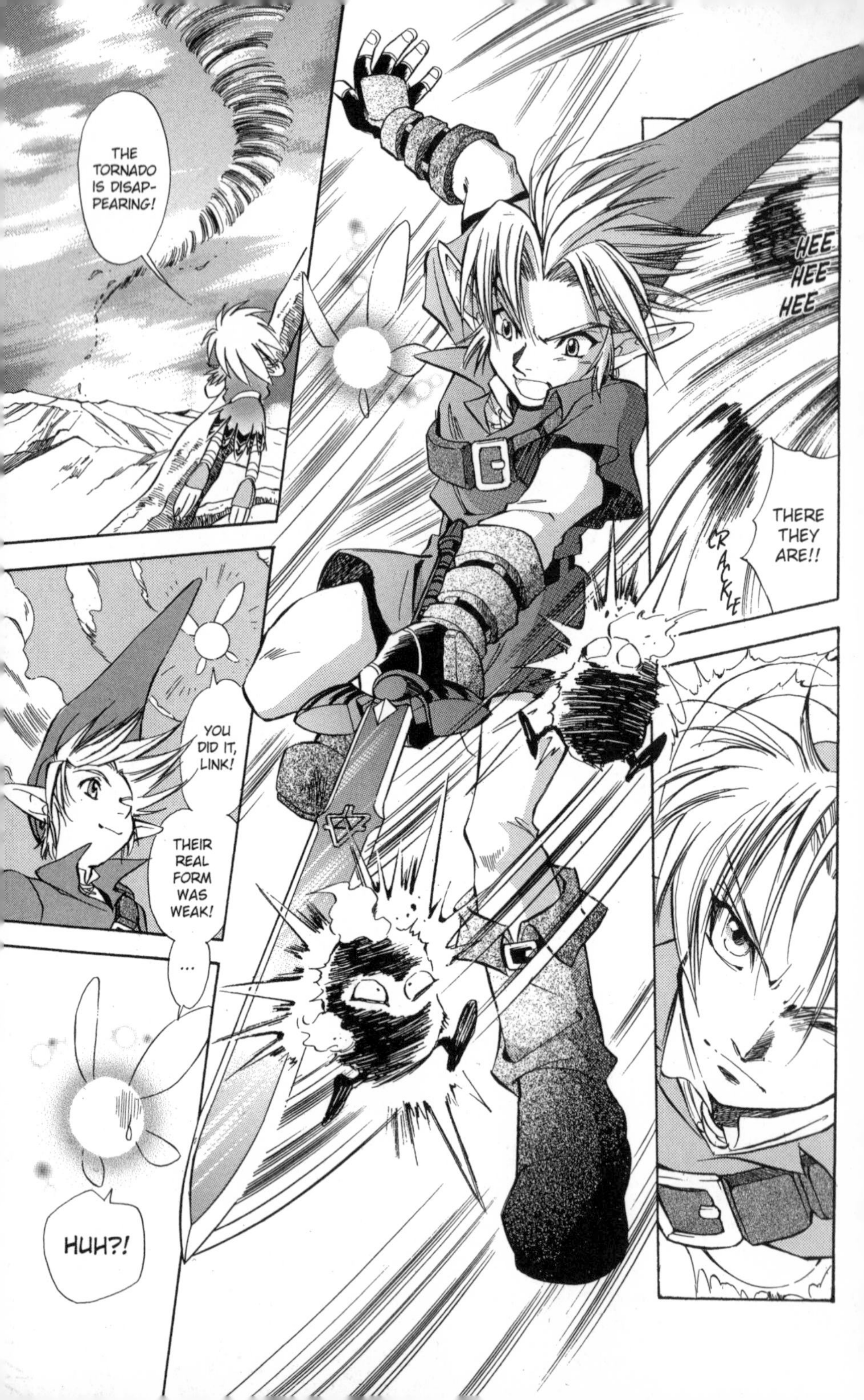
HEE HEE HEE
THERE THEY ARE!!
CRACKLE
THE TORNADO IS DISAPPEARING!
YOU DID IT, LINK!
THEIR REAL FORM WAS WEAK!
...
HUH?!

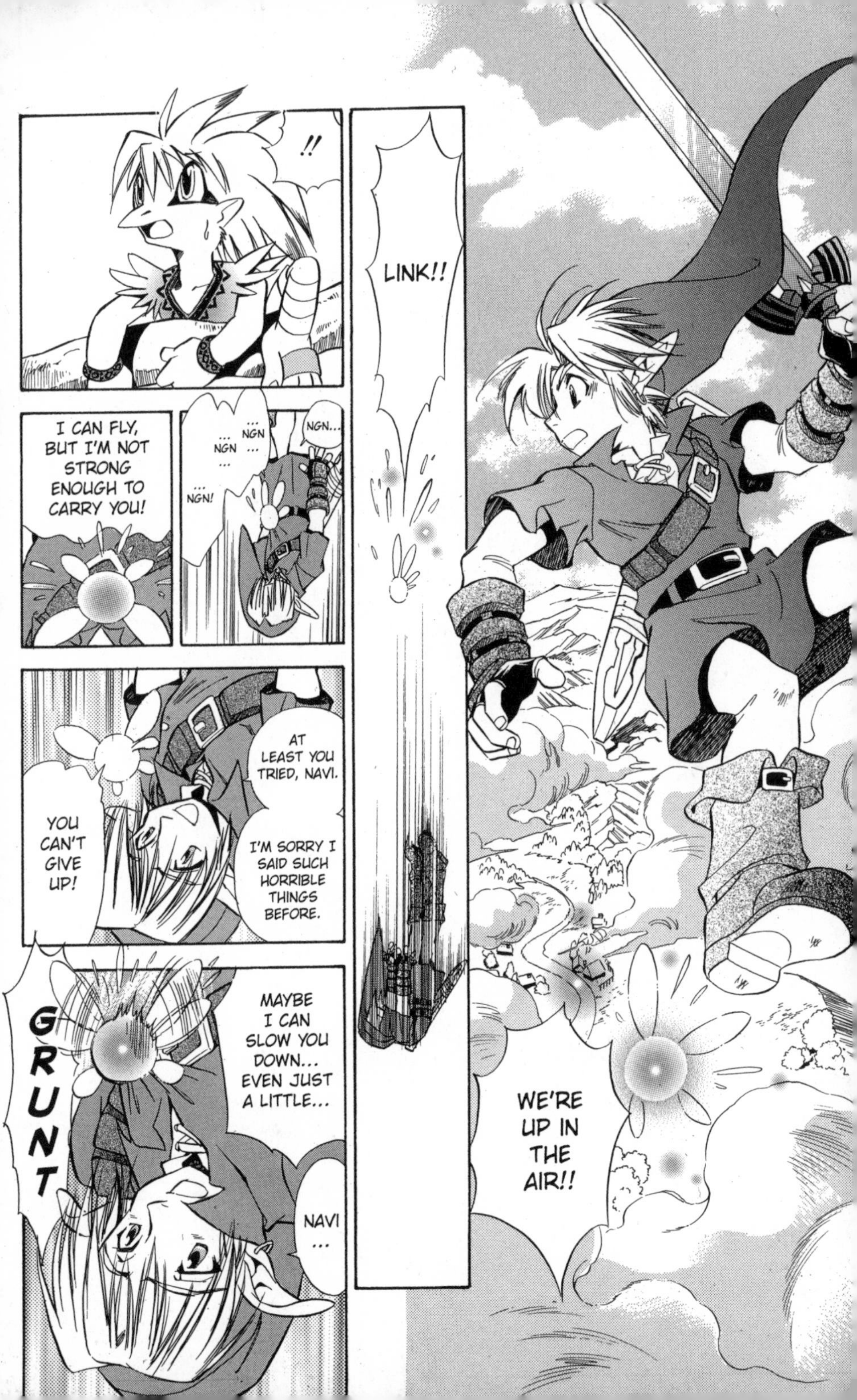
WE'RE UP IN THE AIR!!
LINK!!
!!
NGN...
... NGN ...
NGN ...
... NGN!
I CAN FLY, BUT I'M NOT STRONG ENOUGH TO CARRY YOU!
AT LEAST YOU TRIED, NAVI.
I'M SORRY I SAID SUCH HORRIBLE THINGS BEFORE.
YOU CAN'T GIVE UP!
MAYBE I CAN SLOW YOU DOWN... EVEN JUST A LITTLE...
NAVI ...
GRUNT

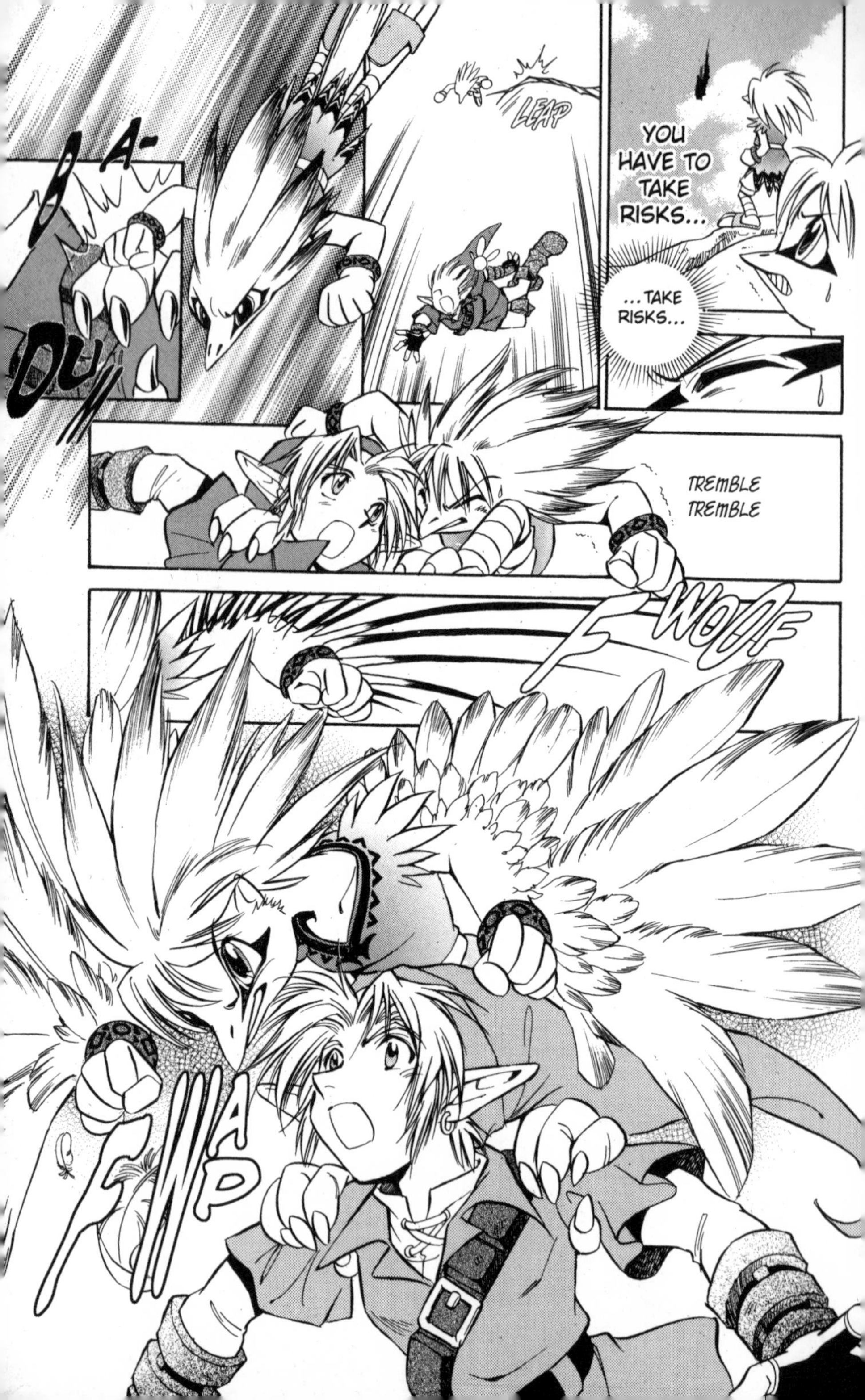
YOU HAVE TO TAKE RISKS...
...TAKE RISKS...
LEAP
DA-
DU
TREMBLE TREMBLE
FWOOF
FLAP

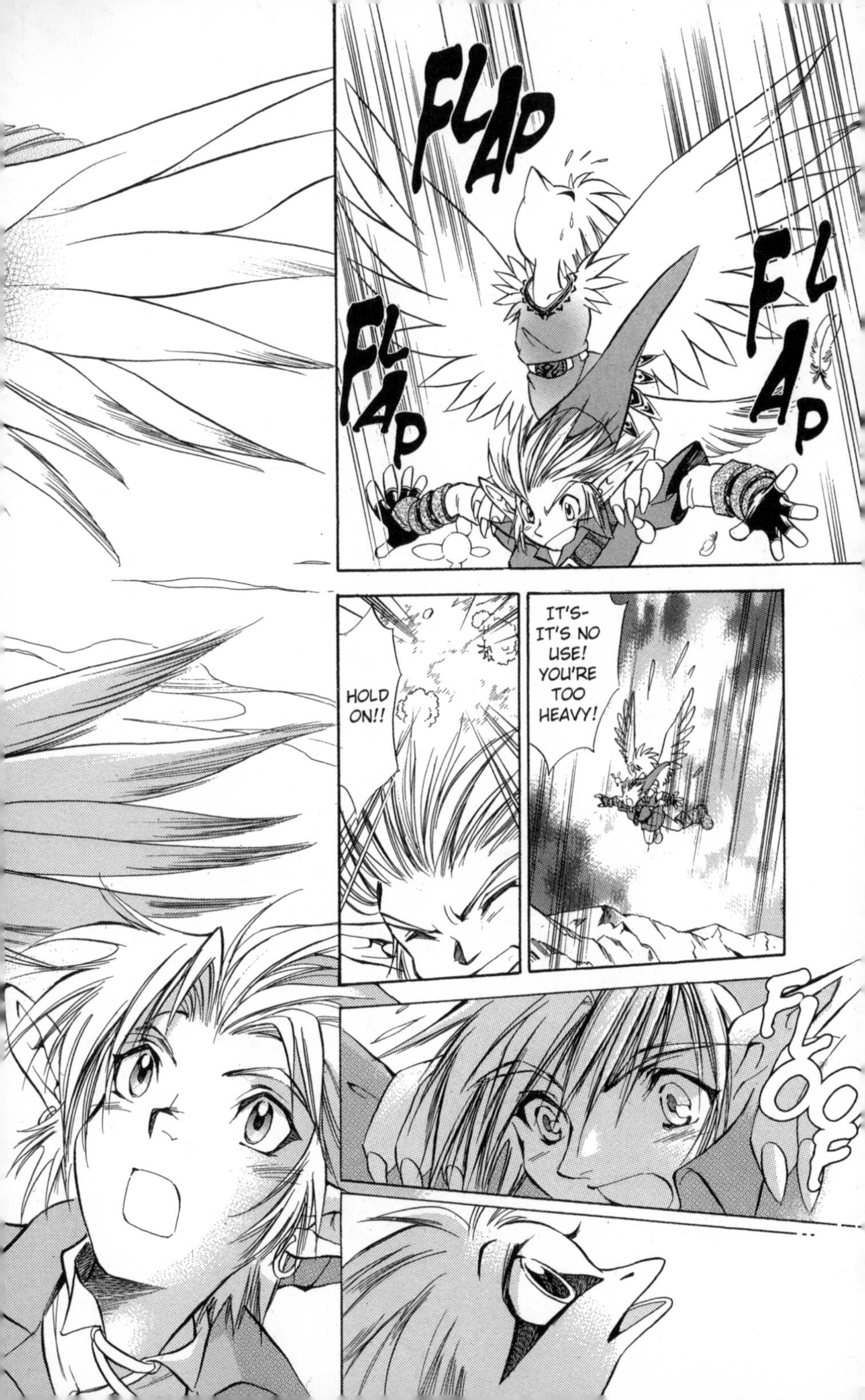
FLAP
FLAP
FLAP
IT'S- IT'S NO USE! YOU'RE TOO HEAVY!
HOLD ON!!
FLOOF

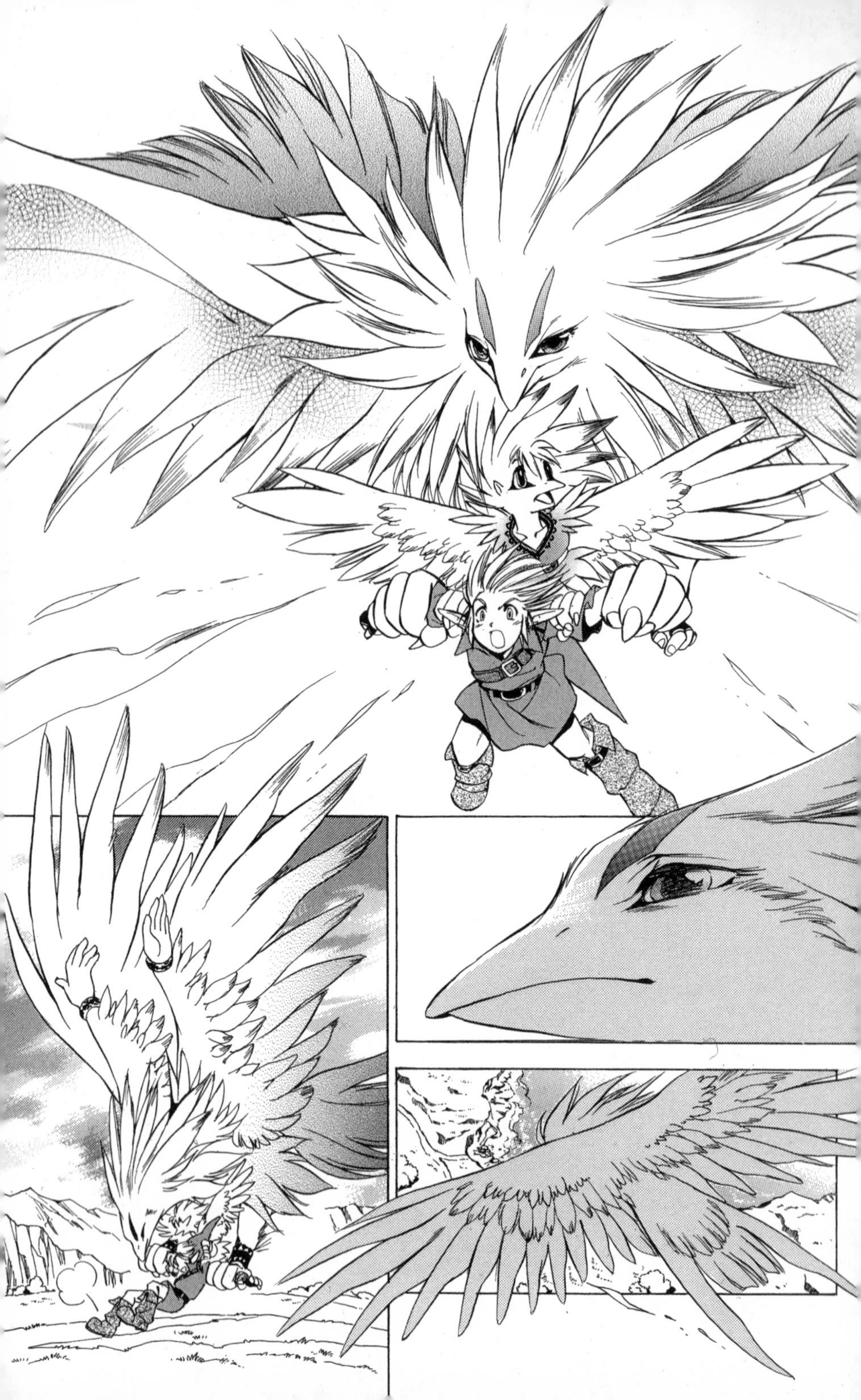

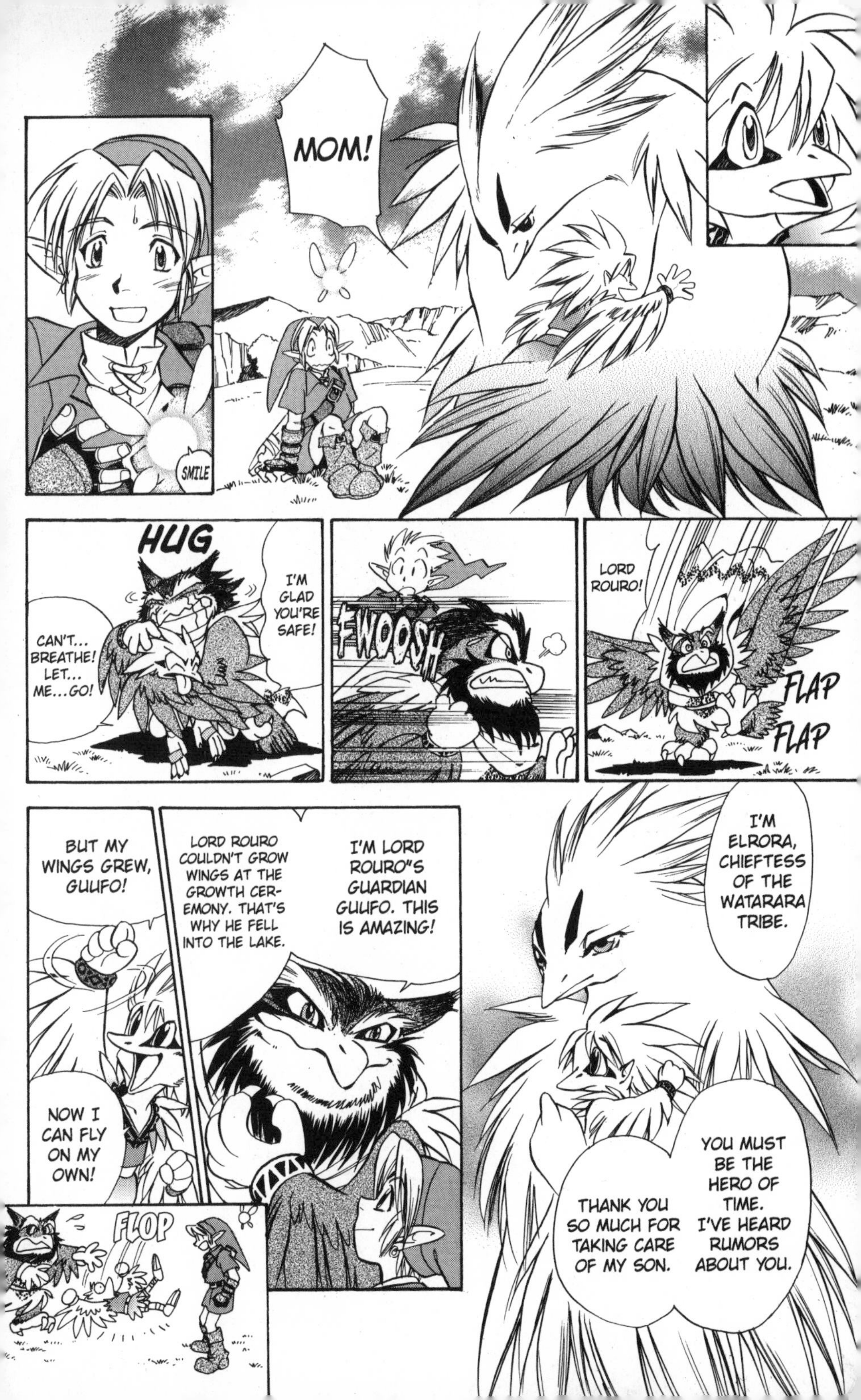
MOM!
SMILE
LORD ROURO!
FLAP
FLAP
FWOOSH
HUG
I'M GLAD YOU'RE SAFE!
CAN'T... BREATHE! LET... ME...GO!
I'M ELRORA, CHIEFTESS OF THE WATARARA TRIBE.
YOU MUST BE THE HERO OF TIME. I'VE HEARD RUMORS ABOUT YOU.
THANK YOU SO MUCH FOR TAKING CARE OF MY SON.
I'M LORD ROURO"S GUARDIAN GUUFO. THIS IS AMAZING!
LORD ROURO COULDN'T GROW WINGS AT THE GROWTH CER-EMONY. THAT'S WHY HE FELL INTO THE LAKE.
BUT MY WINGS GREW, GUUFO!
NOW I CAN FLY ON MY OWN!
FLOP

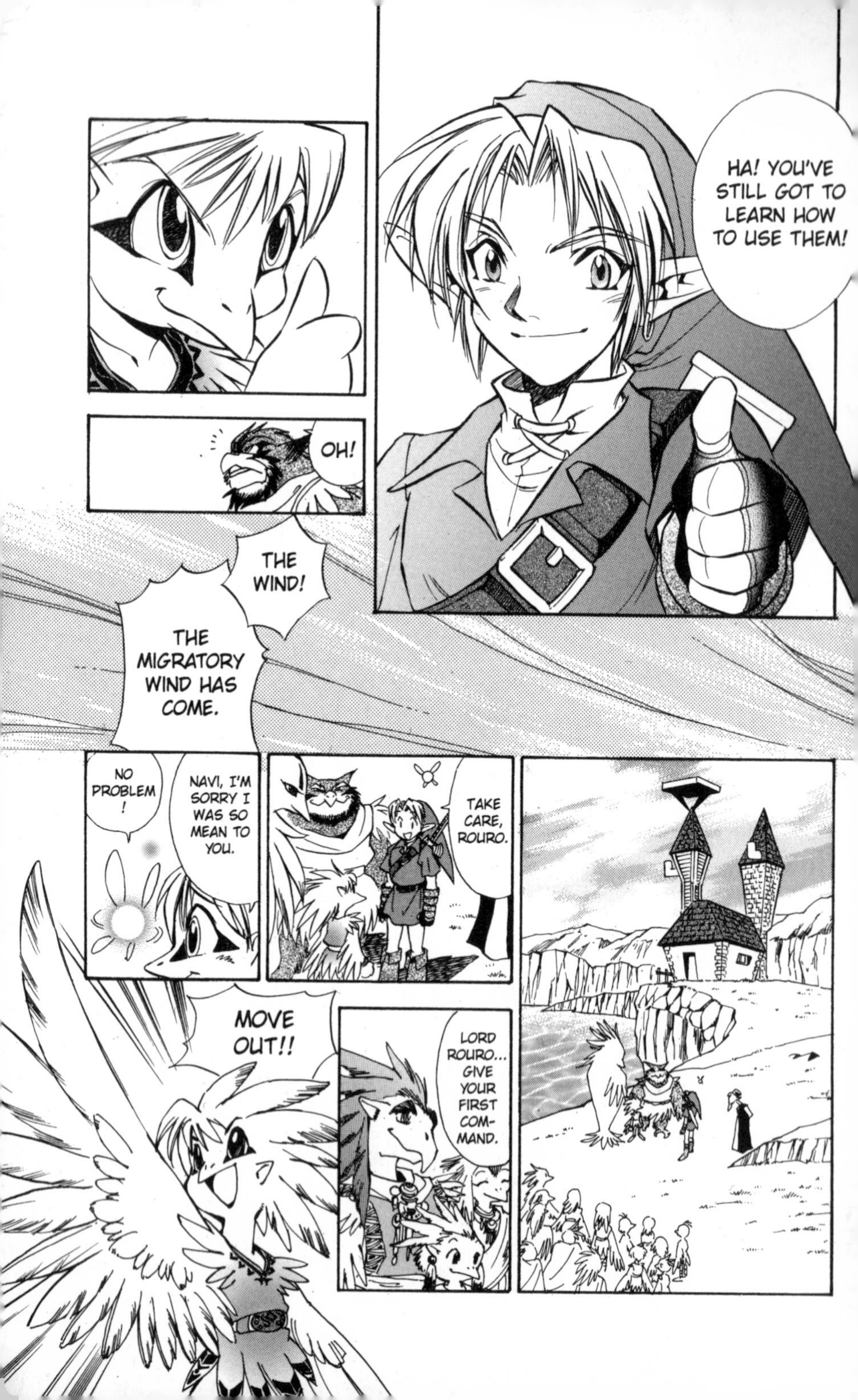
HA! YOU'VE STILL GOT TO LEARN HOW TO USE THEM!
OH!
THE WIND!
THE MIGRATORY WIND HAS COME.
TAKE CARE, ROURO.
NAVI, I'M SORRY I WAS SO MEAN TO YOU.
NO PROBLEM!
LORD ROURO... GIVE YOUR FIRST COMMAND.
MOVE OUT!!

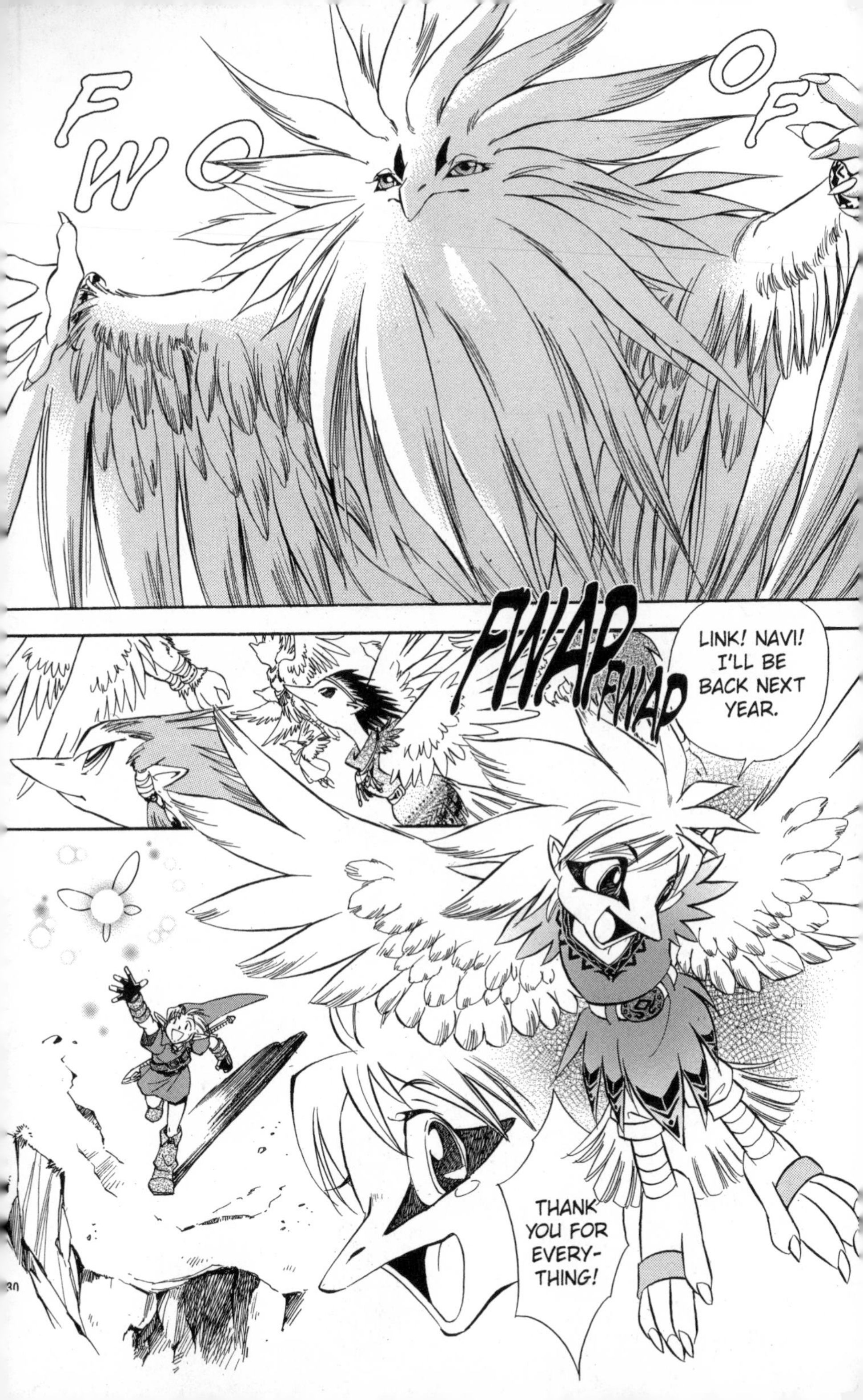
FWOOF
FWAP FWAP
LINK! NAVI! I'LL BE BACK NEXT YEAR.
THANK YOU FOR EVERY-THING!

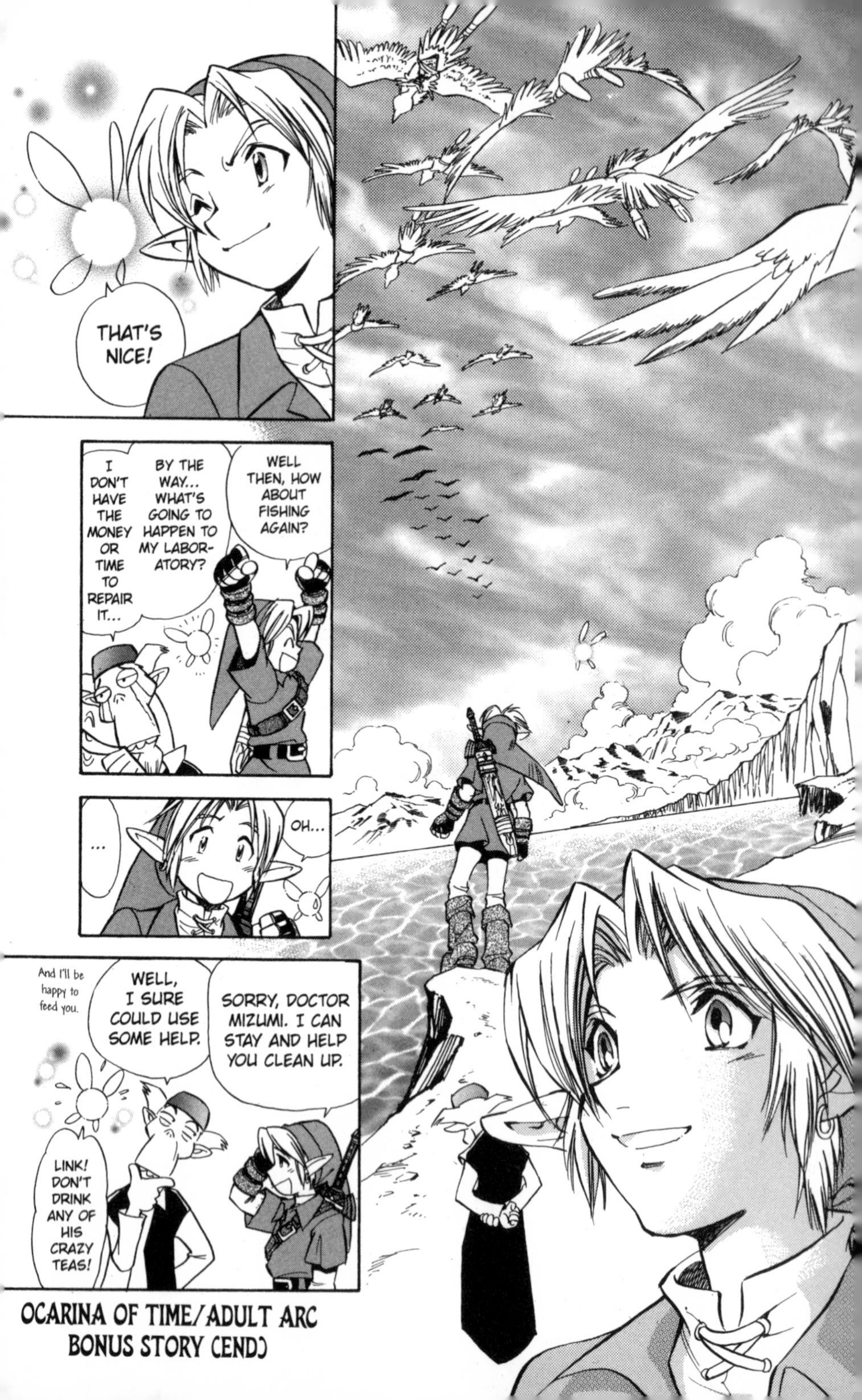
THAT'S NICE!
WELL THEN, HOW ABOUT FISHING AGAIN?
BY THE WAY... WHAT'S GOING TO HAPPEN TO MY LABOR-ATORY?
I DON'T HAVE THE MONEY OR TIME TO REPAIR IT...
OH...
...
SORRY, DOCTOR MIZUMI. I CAN STAY AND HELP YOU CLEAN UP.
WELL, I SURE COULD USE SOME HELP.
And I'll be happy to feed you.
LINK! DON'T DRINK ANY OF HIS CRAZY TEAS!

OCARINA OF TIME/ADULT ARC
BONUS STORY (END)

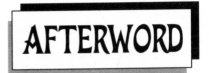

AFTERWORD

THIS WAS LIKE PLAYING A VIDEO GAME FOR THE FIRST TIME.

IT'S NOT LIKE WE'D NEVER PLAYED VIDEO GAMES, BUT NEITHER OF US WAS VERY GOOD AT THEM. EVEN THOUGH WE BOTH PLAYED ONCE IN A WHILE, WE NEVER FELT ANY DRIVE TO PLAY MORE OFTEN. THEN ONE DAY IN 1998 A TV COMMERCIAL CHANGED OUR LIVES. IT WAS FOR *THE LEGEND OF ZELDA: OCARINA OF TIME*, AND IT SHOWED A YOUNG BOY BRANDISHING A SWORD FROM ATOP A HORSE THAT WAS REARING UP AGAINST A BACKGROUND OF FLAMES. AT THAT MOMENT, MY INTUITION (SO POOR AT VIDEO GAMES) SPOKE TO ME AND, AT THE SAME TIME, SO DID MY PARTNER'S. SOMEHOW WE KNEW THE CHARACTER IN THAT BRIEF TELEVISION COMMERCIAL HAD SOMETHING TO DO WITH US!!

BEFORE WE COULD GET OUT TO BUY A NINTENDO 64 FOR OUR STUDIO, WE RECEIVED A CALL FROM CHIEF EDITOR NAKAHARA (DEPUTY EDITOR AT THE TIME) OF *SHOGAKU ROKUNENSEI* MAGAZINE. HE WONDERED IF WE WOULD LIKE TO WORK ON A SERIALIZED MANGA FOR *OCARINA OF TIME*. WHAT INCREDIBLY GOOD TIMING! WE JUST LOOKED AT EACH OTHER AND BROKE OUT LAUGHING.

ACCEPTING THAT IT WAS FATE, WE STARTED WORK. AT FIRST WE THOUGHT THE MANGA MIGHT BE BEST SERVED BY SIMPLY BREAKING THE VIDEO GAME STORY INTO PANELS AND TURNING THOSE INTO EXCITING SCENES, BUT THAT DIDN'T GO WELL AT ALL. WE BEGAN TO REALIZE THAT THIS JOB WAS MORE COMPLICATED THAN JUST RETELLING THE SAME STORY. IT NEEDED MORE.

～ OCARINA OF TIME ～

FIRST, WE HAD TO PLAY THE GAME, THE WHOLE GAME, BEFORE WE COULD EVEN START. THAT WAS PRETTY HARD FOR US, BUT WHEN WE FINALLY FINISHED THE GAME WE LOOKED AT EACH OTHER AND SAID, "VIDEO GAMES ARE AWESOME!!"

FOR THE FIRST TIME WE UNDERSTOOD COMPLETELY HOW VIDEO GAMES CAN BE JUST AS FUN AND JUST AS INTERESTING AS MANGA. BOTH OF THEM TELL A STORY, BUT VIDEO GAMES TELL THAT STORY IN A COMPLETELY DIFFERENT WAY THAN MANGA DO. PLUS YOU GET COMPLETELY CAUGHT UP IN THE GAME!

THAT WAS IMPORTANT. PRECISELY BECAUSE WE WERE SO DEEPLY INVOLVED, WE WERE ABLE TO RELAX, STOP THINKING LIKE MANGA AUTHORS, AND JUST ENJOY THE STORY. MORE THAN ANYTHING ELSE, THE WORLD OF THE GAME WAS SO BEAUTIFUL. IT RADIATED LIFE AND WARMTH...A KIND OF HEAT...AND HUMAN EMOTION THAT WE'D NEVER FOUND IN A COLD DIGITAL WORLD BEFORE.

WE THOUGHT ABOUT THE FACT THAT SO MANY PEOPLE WORKED FOR LITERALLY YEARS TO MAKE THE GAME, BUT HERE WE WERE WORKING ON THE MANGA, JUST THE TWO OF US. SUDDENLY IT SEEMED LIKE TOO BIG A JOB. WE GOT A LITTLE FREAKED OUT.

BUT DISCOVERING THE TRUE CHARACTER OF LINK MADE US FEEL BETTER, LIKE A COOL BREEZE ON A SUMMER DAY.

LINK ISN'T STRIKINGLY GOOD-LOOKING. HE'S JUST MILDLY HANDSOME AND, FOR SOME REASON, THAT SEEMED APPEALING. AND IT'D BEEN A LONG TIME SINCE SUCH A NICE HERO APPEARED IN THE MANGA WORLD. (IT SEEMS LIKE THERE SHOULD BE MORE OF THEM, BUT THERE AREN'T). AT FIRST WE THOUGHT IT WOULD BE EASY TO CRAFT SUCH A HERO (SO WE HAD NO EXCUSE FOR FAILURE), BUT IT TURNED OUT TO BE QUITE DIFFICULT.

IN THE PAST, ALL THE HEROES WE CREATED WERE ANTI-HEROES (WHICH REFLECTED OUR VIEW OF THE WORLD). IF WE MADE HEROES TOO NICE OR TOO GOOD, WE THOUGHT THEY'D SEEM FALSE AND UNBELIEVABLE. BUT THE MORE TIME WE SPENT IN THE WORLD OF *ZELDA*, THE MORE WE REALIZED THAT IT HAD ITS OWN KIND OF REALITY.

I WAS USED TO WRITING MYSTERIOUS, CONFLICTED CHARACTERS LIKE SHEIK, BUT FOR THE FIRST TIME I UNDERSTOOD IN THE BOTTOM OF MY HEART THAT GOOD GUYS COULD BE COOL, TOO. LINK WAS COOL.

AND MY PARTNER ALWAYS THOUGHT THAT ATTRACTIVE VISUALS COULD ONLY COME FROM TOUGH, EDGY SETTINGS, BUT *OCARINA OF TIME* HAS A DIFFERENT KIND OF ATTRACTION. THE IMAGES FROM THE VIDEO GAME BREATHE WITH LIFE—INCREDIBLY SOFT, PURE, NOBLE AND WELL THOUGHT OUT. THE POLYGONS SOMEHOW REMINDED US OF THE STOP-MOTION ANIME WE USED TO LOVE (BUT WHICH NEVER FELT PARTICULARLY "REAL") AND PERFECTLY PORTRAYED A SENSE OF SPACE, GESTURES, AND TIMING. IN GENERAL WE PREFER GAMES THAT ARE NOT TOO INTENSELY CHEESY OR MELODRAMATIC.

WHEN WE HAD OUR FIRST MEETINGS WITH SHIGERU MIYAMOTO AND THE OTHERS DOING THE HARD WORK ON THE *ZELDA* GAMES, WE WERE EXCITED, NERVOUS, HAPPY, AND SCARED ALL AT THE SAME TIME. IT WAS AN INCREDIBLE HONOR THAT THEY WOULD ENTRUST ONE OF THEIR IMPORTANT WORLDS TO OUR HANDS.

THE LEGEND OF ZELDA

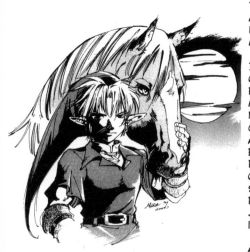

WE ALSO HAVE TO SEND UNENDING THANKS TO OUR CHIEF EDITOR, WHO INTRODUCED US TO THIS WORLD AND LET US BRING OUR OWN ARTISTIC VISION TO THE PROJECT, AND TO EVERYONE ELSE AT *SHOGAKU ROKUNENSEI* MAGAZINE! THANK YOU VERY MUCH!

IN ELEMENTARY SCHOOL WE BOTH READ A LOT OF MANGA MAGAZINES. AND WE AGREE THAT BACK THEN IT FELT LIKE ONE YEAR WAS A MUCH LONGER SPAN OF TIME THAN IT SEEMS NOW. THAT'S WHY WE REFUSED TO CUT ANY CORNERS, TREATED THIS WORK WITH LOVE, AND PUT ALL OUR CARE AND EFFORT INTO BRINGING IT TO LIFE. WE HOPE THAT YOU READERS, WHO ARE EVEN NOW ON THE CUSP OF ADOLESCENCE, WHEN THE DOORS OF SENSIBILITY ARE WIDE OPEN, WILL FEEL THE REALITY OF *LEGEND OF ZELDA* AND, IF EVEN JUST A LITTLE, FIND SOME OF LINK'S PURITY IN YOURSELVES.

AKIRA HIMEKAWA

A MESSAGE FROM THE AUTHOR
FOR THE LEGENDARY EDITION

Ten volumes of *The Legend of Zelda* manga series, which started in 1999, will now be collected into five deluxe volumes. It's so incredible to see them be "reincarnated" like this. It's as if all of Link's incarnations are returning to Hyrule again, just like the Hero of Time in *Ocarina of Time*. It's just as exciting to see them again now as it was back then, and they haven't lost one bit of their luster. Those of you who were in elementary school at the time are now all grown up as well. Now it's time to relive those memories and head out on an adventure once again!

AKIRA HIMEKAWA

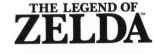

THE LEGEND OF ZELDA: LEGENDARY EDITION -OCARINA OF TIME-

VIZ MEDIA EDITION

STORY AND ART BY AKIRA HIMEKAWA

TRANSLATION John Werry, Honyaku Center, Inc.
ENGLISH ADAPTATION Steven "Stan!" Brown
LETTERING John Hunt
ORIGINAL SERIES DESIGN Izumi Hirayama
ORIGINAL SERIES EDITOR Mike Montesa
LEGENDARY EDITION DESIGN Shawn Carrico
LEGENDARY EDITION EDITOR Joel Enos

The Legend of Zelda: Ocarina of Time - Legendary Edition - TM & © 2016 Nintendo. All Rights Reserved.

ZELDA NO DENSETSU TOKI NO OCARINA [KANZENBAN] by Akira HIMEKAWA
© 2016 Akira HIMEKAWA
All rights reserved.
Original Japanese edition published by SHOGAKUKAN.
English translation rights in the United States of America, Canada, the United Kingdom, Ireland, Australia and New Zealand arranged with SHOGAKUKAN.

ORIGINAL DESIGN Kazutada YOKOYAMA

Printed in the U.S.A.

D1057626

www.viz.com

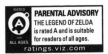